Adaptive Object-Oriented Software

The
Demeter Method

WITH PROPAGATION PATTERNS

The PWS Series in Computer Science: Selected Titles

Abernethy and Allen	*Experiments in Computing: Laboratories for Introductory Computer Science in Think Pascal*
Abernethy and Allen	*Experiments in Computing: Laboratories for Introductory Computer Science in Turbo Pascal*
Abernethy and Allen	*Exploring the Science of Computing*
Bailey and Lundgaard	*Program Design with Pseudocode, Third Edition*
Bent and Sethares	*BASIC: An Introduction to Computer Programming, Fourth Edition*
Bent and Sethares	*Microsoft BASIC: Programming the IBM PC, Third Edition*
Bent and Sethares	*QBASIC*
Bent and Sethares	*QuickBASIC: An Introduction to Computer Science Programming with the IBM PC*
Clements	*68000 Family Assembly Language*
Clements	*Principles of Computer Hardware, Second Edition*
Coburn	*Visual BASIC Made Easy*
Cosnard and Trystram	*Parallel Algorithms and Architecture*
Decker and Hirshfeld	*Pascal's Triangle: Reading, Writing, and Reasoning About Programs*
Decker and Hirshfeld	*The Analytical Engine: An Introduction to Computer Science Using HyperCard 2.1, Second Edition*
Decker and Hirshfeld	*The Analytical Engine: An Introduction to Computer Science Using ToolBook*
Decker and Hirshfeld	*The Object Concept: An Introduction to Computer Programming Using C++*
Decker and Hirshfeld	*Working Classes: Data Structures and Algorithms Using C++*
Dershem and Jipping	*Programming Languages: Structures and Models, Second Edition*
Drozdek	*Data Structures and Algorithms in C++*
Drozdek and Simon	*Data Structures in C*
Eggen and Eggen	*An Introduction to Computer Science Using C*
Firebaugh	*Artificial Intelligence: A Knowledge-Based Approach*
Flynn and McHoes	*Understanding Operating Systems*
Giarratano and Riley	*Expert Systems: Principles and Programming, Second Edition*
Hennefeld	*Using Turbo Pascal 6.0-7.0, Third Edition*
Hochbaum	*Approximation Algorithms for NP-hard Problems*
House	*Beginning with C*
Jamison, Russell, and Snover	*Laboratories for a Second Course in Computer Science: ANSI Pascal*
Jamison, Russell, and Snover	*Laboratories for a Second Course in Computer Science: Turbo Pascal*
Lieberherr	*Adaptive Object-Oriented Programming: The Demeter Method with Propagation Patterns*
Louden	*Programming Languages: Principles and Practice*
Pavlidis	*Interactive Computer Graphics in X*
Popkin	*Comprehensive Structured COBOL, Fourth Edition*
Rood	*Logic and Structured Design for Computer Programmers, Second Edition*
Runnion	*Structured Programming in Assembly Language for the IBM PC and PS/2, Second Edition*
Saad	*Iterative Methods for Sparse Linear Systems*
Shay	*Understanding Data Communications and Networks*
Sipser	*Introduction to the Theory of Computation, Preliminary Edition*
Stubbs and Webre	*Data Structures with Abstract Data Types and Ada*
Stubbs and Webre	*Data Structures with Abstract Data Types and Pascal, Second Edition*
Suhy	*CICS using COBOL: A Structured Approach*
Wang	*An Introduction to ANSI C on UNIX*
Wang	*An Introduction to Berkeley UNIX*
Wang	*C++ with Object-Oriented Programming*
Whale	*Data Structures and Abstraction Using C*
Zirkel and Berlinger	*Understanding FORTRAN 77 & 90*

Adaptive Object-Oriented Software

The Demeter Method

WITH PROPAGATION PATTERNS

KARL J. LIEBERHERR
Northeastern University

PWS Publishing Company

I ⓣ P   **An International Thomson Publishing Company**

Boston • Albany • Belmont • Bonn • Cincinnati • Detroit • London • Madrid
Melbourne • Mexico City • New York • Paris • Singapore • Tokyo • Washington

PWS PUBLISHING COMPANY
20 Park Plaza Boston, MA 02116-4324

Copyright © 1996 by Karl J. Lieberherr. *All rights reserved* by PWS Publishing Company, a division of International Thomson Publishing Inc. No part of this book may be reproduced, stored in a retrieval system, or transcribed, in any form or by any means—electronic, mechanical, photocopying, recording, or otherwise—without the prior written permission of PWS Publishing Company.

International Thomson Publishing
The trademark ITP is used under license.

For more information, contact:

PWS Publishing Co.
20 Park Plaza
Boston, MA 02116

International Thomson Publishing Europe
Berkshire House 168–173
High Holborn
London WC1V 7AA   England

International Thomson Publishing Asia
221 Henderson Road
#05–10 Henderson Building
Singapore 0315

International Thomson Publishing Japan
Hirakawacho Kyowa Building, 31
2-2-1 Hirakawacho
Chiyoda-ku, Tokyo 102
Japan

International Thomson Editores
Campos Eliseos 385, Piso 7
Col. Polanco
11560 Mexico D.F., Mexico

International Thomson Publishing GmbH
Königswinterer Strasse 418
53227 Bonn, Germany

Thomas Nelson Australia
102 Dodds Street
South Melbourne, 3205
Victoria, Australia

Nelson Canada
1120 Birchmount Road
Scarborough, Ontario
Canada M1K 5G4

Library of Congress Cataloging-in-Publication Data
Lieberherr, Karl J.
   Adaptive object-oriented programming: the Demeter Method with propagation patterns / Karl J. Lieberherr.
       p. cm.
   Includes bibliographical references and index.
   ISBN 0-534-94602-X
   1. Object-oriented programming (Computer science)
I. Title.
QA76.64.L49   1995   95-21469
005.1'2—dc20   CIP

Sponsoring Editor: Michael J. Sugarman
Developmental Editor: Mary Thomas Stone
Editorial Assistant: Tanja Brull
Production Editor: Abigail M. Heim
Marketing Manager: Nathan Wilbur
Manufacturing Coordinator: Wendy Kilborn
Text Printer and Binder: Quebecor/Martinsburg
Cover Design: Monique Calello
Cover Photo: P. Curton, © The IMAGEBank
Cover Printer: New England Book Components, Inc.

Printed and bound in the United States of America.
95 96 97 98 99—10 9 8 7 6 5 4 3 2 1

to
Ruth, Andrea, and Eva

Contents

Foreword by Gregor Kiczales and John Lamping		xxiii
Preface		xxv

1 Introduction   1
- 1.1 EVOLUTIONARY LIFE CYCLE WITH ADAPTIVE SOFTWARE 1
  - 1.1.1 How is Adaptiveness Achieved? 2
  - 1.1.2 Applications of Adaptiveness 2
  - 1.1.3 Adaptiveness with the Demeter Method 2
  - 1.1.4 Demeter Life-Cycle 3
  - 1.1.5 Symmetry Between Adaptive Programs and Customizers 5
  - 1.1.6 Symmetry Between Object Descriptions and Customizers 5
- 1.2 DISADVANTAGES OF OBJECT-ORIENTED SOFTWARE 6
- 1.3 ADAPTIVE PROGRAMMING 7
- 1.4 PROPAGATION PATTERNS 10
- 1.5 CUSTOMIZATION 12
- 1.6 SUMMARY 16
- 1.7 EXERCISES 16
- 1.8 BIBLIOGRAPHIC REMARKS 17

2 Introduction to Object-Oriented Software   18
- 2.1 CONCEPTS 24
  - 2.1.1 Abstractions 26
  - 2.1.2 Classes, Methods, and Delayed Binding 26
  - 2.1.3 Overloading and Delayed Binding 30
  - 2.1.4 Reduced Dependencies 30
  - 2.1.5 Sharing 30
  - 2.1.6 Making Instances 33
- 2.2 EASE OF EVOLUTION 33
- 2.3 TERMINOLOGY 34
- 2.4 CONVENTIONS 35
  - 2.4.1 Symbol Usage 36
- 2.5 EXERCISES 36
- 2.6 BIBLIOGRAPHIC REMARKS 38

3 From C++ to Demeter — 40
- 3.1 C++ PROGRAM — 42
- 3.2 ADAPTIVE PROGRAM — 55
- 3.3 EVOLUTION — 60
  - 3.3.1 Changing Object Structure — 60
  - 3.3.2 Evolving the Functionality — 63
- 3.4 WHAT IS THE PRICE? — 68
- 3.5 APPENDIX: FROM C TO C++ — 70
- 3.6 SUMMARY — 75
- 3.7 EXERCISES — 75
- 3.8 BIBLIOGRAPHIC REMARKS — 76

4 Thinking Adaptively — 77
- 4.1 KEY IDEAS — 80
  - 4.1.1 Inventor's Paradox — 80
  - 4.1.2 Stepwise Refinement — 81
  - 4.1.3 Representation/Interface Independence — 81
- 4.2 MODELING COMPLEX SYSTEMS — 83
- 4.3 JUSTIFICATION — 86
- 4.4 CUSTOMIZATION — 87
- 4.5 THE ITINERARY PROBLEM — 88
  - 4.5.1 Customizing the Adaptive Program — 90
  - 4.5.2 Transporting Objects — 95
- 4.6 POSITIONING IN THE HISTORY OF SOFTWARE DEVELOPMENT — 96
- 4.7 THE TOOLS — 99
- 4.8 EXPERIENCES WITH ADAPTIVE SOFTWARE — 101
- 4.9 SUMMARY — 103
- 4.10 BIBLIOGRAPHIC REMARKS — 104

5 Adaptive Software by Example — 112
- 5.1 CHANGING REQUIREMENTS — 112
- 5.2 CUSTOMIZING WITH CLASS DICTIONARIES — 116
- 5.3 OBJECT TRAVERSAL AND TRANSPORTATION — 129
- 5.4 SUMMARY — 131
- 5.5 EXERCISES — 132
- 5.6 BIBLIOGRAPHIC REMARKS — 134
- 5.7 SOLUTIONS — 134

6 Class Dictionary Graphs and Objects — 135
- 6.1 INTRODUCTORY EXAMPLE — 136
- 6.2 CLASS DICTIONARY GRAPH RULES — 144
  - 6.2.1 Convenient Extensions — 146
- 6.3 OBJECTS — 149
  - 6.3.1 Textual Representation — 150
  - 6.3.2 Size — 152

6.4	TRANSLATION TO C++	152
6.5	PARAMETERIZED CLASSES	156
6.6	CLASS DICTIONARY GRAPH DESIGN	157
	6.6.1 Why Alternation Classes are Abstract	157
	6.6.2 Taxonomy and Class Dictionary Graphs	157
	6.6.3 Construction versus Alternation Edges	161
6.7	SUMMARY	163
6.8	EXERCISES	163
6.9	BIBLIOGRAPHIC REMARKS	166
6.10	SOLUTIONS	167

7 Propagation Directives — 169

7.1	SIMPLE PROPAGATION DIRECTIVES	171
	7.1.1 Edge Patterns	178
7.2	SYNTAX SUMMARY FOR PROPAGATION DIRECTIVES	179
7.3	APPLYING PROPAGATION DIRECTIVES	182
7.4	AVOIDING INFORMATION LOSS	182
7.5	FINDING PROPAGATION DIRECTIVES	185
	7.5.1 Evolution of Propagation Directives	187
7.6	TESTING OF PROPAGATION DIRECTIVES	188
7.7	OPERATIONS ON PROPAGATION DIRECTIVES	188
	7.7.1 Join Operator	188
	7.7.2 Merge Operator	189
	7.7.3 Restrict Operator	189
	7.7.4 Propagation Graph Calculus	190
	7.7.5 Propagation Directive Expressions	191
	7.7.6 Customization Space	193
7.8	SUMMARY	193
7.9	EXERCISES	193
7.10	BIBLIOGRAPHIC REMARKS	199
7.11	SOLUTIONS	200

8 Propagation Patterns — 202

8.1	CONNECTION TO LAW OF DEMETER	202
8.2	OBJECT-ORIENTED IMPLEMENTATION	207
8.3	SYNTAX SUMMARY FOR PROPAGATION PATTERNS	211
8.4	EXAMPLES	212
	8.4.1 Graph Algorithms	212
	8.4.2 Chess Board	219
	8.4.3 Painting a Car	220
	8.4.4 Meal	223
	8.4.5 Compiler	225
8.5	COMPONENTS: SETS OF PROPAGATION PATTERNS	225
8.6	EDGE WRAPPERS AND VERTEX WRAPPERS	229
8.7	PROGRAMMING WITH PROPAGATION PATTERNS	234

		8.7.1	Evolution Histories 234

- 8.7.1 Evolution Histories 234
- 8.7.2 Three-Stage Development 237
- 8.7.3 Propagation and Alternation 237
- 8.7.4 Wrappers Simulating Inheritance 241
- 8.7.5 Readers and Writers 243
- 8.8 SUMMARY 245
- 8.9 EXERCISES 246
- 8.10 BIBLIOGRAPHIC REMARKS 253
- 8.11 SOLUTIONS 254

9 Propagation Pattern Interpretation — 255

- 9.1 HOW TO RUN A PROPAGATION PATTERN 256
  - 9.1.1 Discussion of the Rules 259
- 9.2 CUSTOMIZER RESTRICTIONS 260
  - 9.2.1 Compatibility Restriction 261
  - 9.2.2 Propagation Restriction 261
  - 9.2.3 Information Loss Restriction 262
  - 9.2.4 Delayed Binding Restriction 265
  - 9.2.5 Inheritance Restriction 269
- 9.3 PROPAGATION PATTERN PROPERTIES 271
  - 9.3.1 Alternation Property 272
  - 9.3.2 Propagation Directive Satisfaction 272
  - 9.3.3 Propagation Graph Properties 276
  - 9.3.4 Consistent Ordering 276
  - 9.3.5 Robustness Under Class Dictionary Transformations 277
  - 9.3.6 Access Independence 279
  - 9.3.7 Method Selection Rule 279
  - 9.3.8 Split Alternation Class 280
  - 9.3.9 Symmetry 281
  - 9.3.10 No Wrapper Shadowing 282
  - 9.3.11 Customizer Analysis 282
- 9.4 OBJECT-ORIENTED IMPLEMENTATION 285
  - 9.4.1 Exiting Alternation Edges 286
  - 9.4.2 Wrapper Pushing 291
  - 9.4.3 Propagation Patterns with Return Types 293
- 9.5 SUMMARY 296
  - 9.5.1 The Flat Demeter Method 297
- 9.6 EXERCISES 298
- 9.7 BIBLIOGRAPHIC REMARKS 308
- 9.8 SOLUTIONS 308

10 Transportation Patterns — 309
- 10.1 SPECIFYING OBJECT TRANSPORTATION — 309
- 10.2 TRANSPORTATION CUSTOMIZER RESTRICTIONS — 312
  - 10.2.1 Type-Correctness — 314
  - 10.2.2 Traversal Restrictions — 315
  - 10.2.3 Transportation Restrictions — 315
- 10.3 TRANSPORTATION PATTERN EXAMPLES — 318
  - 10.3.1 Triples Example — 320
  - 10.3.2 Avoiding Conditional Statements — 326
  - 10.3.3 DFT Example — 327
- 10.4 CODE GENERATION — 329
  - 10.4.1 Code Generation with Two Transportation Patterns — 330
  - 10.4.2 Combining Two Propagation Patterns — 343
- 10.5 SUMMARY — 344
- 10.6 EXERCISES — 345
- 10.7 BIBLIOGRAPHIC REMARKS — 356
- 10.8 SOLUTIONS — 356

11 Class Dictionaries — 358
- 11.1 PARSING — 363
- 11.2 LL(1) CONDITIONS AND LEFT-RECURSION — 369
  - 11.2.1 Left-Recursion — 371
- 11.3 SUMMARY — 372
- 11.4 EXERCISES — 374
- 11.5 BIBLIOGRAPHIC REMARKS — 379
- 11.6 SOLUTIONS — 381

12 Style Rules for Class Dictionaries — 382
- 12.1 LAW OF DEMETER FOR CLASSES — 382
- 12.2 CLASS DICTIONARY GRAPH OPTIMIZATION — 386
  - 12.2.1 Minimizing Construction Edges — 387
  - 12.2.2 Minimizing Alternation Edges — 388
- 12.3 PARAMETERIZATION — 390
- 12.4 REGULARITY — 393
  - 12.4.1 Regular Structures — 393
- 12.5 PREFER ALTERNATION — 394
- 12.6 NORMALIZATION — 396
- 12.7 COGNITIVE ASPECTS OF NOTATIONS — 397
- 12.8 EXTENDED EXAMPLES — 398
  - 12.8.1 VLSI Architecture Design — 398
  - 12.8.2 Business Applications — 400
- 12.9 SUMMARY — 401
- 12.10 EXERCISES — 402
- 12.11 BIBLIOGRAPHIC REMARKS — 402

13 Case Study: A Class Structure Comparison Tool — 403
- 13.1 THE DEMETER METHOD 403
  - 13.1.1 The Demeter Method in a Nutshell 404
  - 13.1.2 Design Checklist 404
  - 13.1.3 Analysis/Design/Implementation 407
- 13.2 GROWING ADAPTIVE SOFTWARE 407
- 13.3 PROBLEM FORMULATION 410
  - 13.3.1 Class Dictionary Graph Extension 410
  - 13.3.2 Precise Problem Statement 414
- 13.4 PROBLEM SOLUTION 414
  - 13.4.1 Finding the Class Dictionary 416
  - 13.4.2 Component superclasses 417
  - 13.4.3 Component partclusters 419
  - 13.4.4 Component associated 422
- 13.5 SUMMARY 425
- 13.6 EXERCISES 425
- 13.7 BIBLIOGRAPHIC REMARKS 428

14 Instructional Objectives — 429

15 Core Concepts and Implementation — 453
- 15.1 INTRODUCTION 454
  - 15.1.1 Background 454
  - 15.1.2 Our Results 455
  - 15.1.3 Example 455
  - 15.1.4 Compatibility, Consistency, and Subclass Invariance . 461
- 15.2 THE SEMANTICS OF ADAPTIVE PROGRAMS 466
  - 15.2.1 Graphs 466
  - 15.2.2 Paths 467
  - 15.2.3 Class Graphs 468
  - 15.2.4 Object Graphs 469
  - 15.2.5 Traversal Specifications 469
  - 15.2.6 Wrappers 471
  - 15.2.7 Adaptive Programs 472
  - 15.2.8 The Target Language 473
- 15.3 IMPLEMENTATION OF ADAPTIVE PROGRAMS 474
- 15.4 COMPOSITIONAL CONSISTENCY 477
- 15.5 RELATED WORK 480
- 15.6 SUMMARY 482
- 15.7 EXERCISES 486
- 15.8 BIBLIOGRAPHIC REMARKS 496

16 Theory of Class Dictionaries — 497

- 16.1 CLASS DICTIONARY GRAPHS 497
  - 16.1.1 Semi-Class Dictionary Graphs 498
  - 16.1.2 Class Dictionary Graph Slices 500
  - 16.1.3 Class Dictionary Graphs 501
  - 16.1.4 Object Graphs 502
  - 16.1.5 Inductive Class Dictionary Graphs 507
- 16.2 CLASS DICTIONARIES 508
  - 16.2.1 Definitions 509
  - 16.2.2 Flat Class Dictionaries 512
  - 16.2.3 Languages 514
- 16.3 LL(1) RULES 517
- 16.4 IMPLICATIONS OF LL(1) RULES 521
  - 16.4.1 Printing 521
  - 16.4.2 Parsing 523
  - 16.4.3 LL(1) Rules and Ambiguous Context-Free Grammars 527
- 16.5 DEMETER DATA MODEL SUMMARY 527
- 16.6 SELF APPLICATION 527
  - 16.6.1 Self-Describing Class Dictionary Graphs 529
  - 16.6.2 Parameterized Class Dictionaries 529
  - 16.6.3 Object Graphs 531
  - 16.6.4 Mapping to C++ 532
- 16.7 KNOWLEDGE PATHS AND OBJECT PATHS 535
- 16.8 SUMMARY 540
- 16.9 EXERCISES 540
- 16.10 BIBLIOGRAPHIC REMARKS 541

17 Selfstudy/Teacher's Guide — 542

- 17.1 INTRODUCTION 542
- 17.2 EXPANDED SYLLABUS 542
- 17.3 ASSIGNMENT 1 545
  - 17.3.1 Background Tasks 545
  - 17.3.2 Part 1: C++ Program Completion 545
  - 17.3.3 Part 2: Laboratory Guide 547
- 17.4 ASSIGNMENT 2 547
  - 17.4.1 Background Tasks 547
  - 17.4.2 Objectives 547
  - 17.4.3 Part 1: Writing a Pocket Calculator in C++ 547
  - 17.4.4 Part 2: Checking Your Solution with Demeter 549
  - 17.4.5 Part 3: Learning C++ 550
  - 17.4.6 Part 4: Develop Your Own Class Dictionary Graph 551
- 17.5 ASSIGNMENT 3 551
  - 17.5.1 Background Tasks 551
  - 17.5.2 Part 1: Trip Class Dictionary 552
  - 17.5.3 Part 2: Inventing and Debugging Class Dictionaries 552

		17.5.4	Part 3: Time Consuming 553

      17.5.4 Part 3: Time Consuming 553
      17.5.5 Part 4: Redoing the Last Part with Demeter 554
17.6 ASSIGNMENT 4 554
      17.6.1 Background Tasks 555
      17.6.2 Part 1: Writing a Compiler 555
      17.6.3 Part 2: Compute the Size of an Expression 557
      17.6.4 Part 3: Compute the Size of a Class Dictionary 557
17.7 ASSIGNMENT 5 558
      17.7.1 Background Tasks 559
      17.7.2 Part 1: Write Your Own Propagation Pattern 559
      17.7.3 Part 2: Evolution of a Programming Tool 559
17.8 LEARNING C++ WITH DEMETER 563
      17.8.1 Class Library Generator 563
      17.8.2 Member Function Skeleton Generator 563
      17.8.3 Simulating the Demeter Library 564

18 Glossary   565
18.1 DEFINITIONS 565
18.2 QUICK REFERENCE GUIDE WITH SYNTAX SUMMARY 578
18.3 SYNTAX DEFINITIONS 585
      18.3.1 Class Dictionary Syntax 585
18.4 BIBLIOGRAPHIC REMARKS 588

A Electronic Access   589

Bibliography   591

Index   606

List of Figures

0.1	Tip of an iceberg	xxvi
1.1	Implementation of adaptive programming	4
1.2	Customizer reuse	5
1.3	Adaptive program reuse	6
1.4	Duplication of class structure in object-oriented programming	7
1.5	An infinite family of programs denoted by an adaptive program	8
1.6	Informal description of computeSalary adaptive program	9
1.7	Propagation pattern for the computeSalary adaptive program	11
1.8	Class dictionary graph representing conglomerates of companies	12
1.9	Propagation graph for a customization of the computeSalary adaptive program	14
1.10	Another representation for conglomerates of companies	15
1.11	Propagation graph with code for second customization	15
2.1	Graphical class definition	20
2.2	Textual class definition	20
2.3	Class settlement and subclasses	21
2.4	Graphical alternation class definition	22
2.5	Textual alternation class definition	22
2.6	Class dictionary graph	27
2.7	Symbol use	36
3.1	Conglomerate class dictionary: A view of the C++ program	43
3.2	Traversal code for salary addition	45
3.3	Propagation graph	57
3.4	English description of conglomerate	59
3.5	Alternative class dictionary	61
3.6	Alternative class dictionary, textual form	62
3.7	Propagation graph for alternative class dictionary	63
3.8	Propagation graph for increasing salary of officers	65
3.9	Increase salary of top-level officers	66
4.1	Generic data model	79
4.2	Adaptive Software	82
4.3	Programming with hooks	83

4.4	Adaptability of object-oriented program	84
4.5	Adaptability of object-oriented program	85
4.6	Propagation pattern print_itinerary	89
4.7	Program customizer Trip 1	90
4.8	Program customizer Trip 2	91
4.9	Propagation graph Trip 1	91
4.10	Propagation graph Trip 2	92
4.11	Adaptive versus object-oriented	93
4.12	A textual form of trip class dictionary	94
4.13	Corresponding trip description	94
4.14	Propagation pattern with object transportation	95
4.15	Class dictionary graph, propagation graph, and C++ program	96
4.16	Comparison of programming paradigms	97
4.17	Delayed-binding viewpoint	98
4.18	Demeter	102
5.1	Simple container: graphical representation	113
5.2	Simple container: textual representation	113
5.3	One intermediate class	114
5.4	Propagation directive	114
5.5	Propagation pattern	116
5.6	Apple basket object	117
5.7	Apple basket class dictionary	118
5.8	Apple basket	118
5.9	Class dictionary graph for apple/orange basket	121
5.10	Textual form of class dictionary for apple/orange basket	121
5.11	Additional C++ code	122
5.12	Optimized fruit basket class dictionary	122
5.13	Optimized class dictionary in textual form	123
5.14	Generated code	124
5.15	Class definitions	125
5.16	Baskets containing several things	125
5.17	Thing basket	126
5.18	Updated propagation pattern	127
5.19	Generated code for modified program	128
5.20	Nested baskets	129
5.21	Nested baskets, textual form	130
6.1	Graphical representation of construction class Meal	138
6.2	Textual representation of construction class Meal	138
6.3	Graphical representation of construction class ShrimpCocktail	139
6.4	Textual representation of construction class ShrimpCocktail	139
6.5	Graphical representation of an alternation class without common parts	140
6.6	Textual representation of an alternation class without common parts	140
6.7	Graphical representation of alternation class with common parts	141

LIST OF FIGURES

6.8	Textual representation of alternation class with common parts	141
6.9	Graphical representation of repetition class, zero or more	141
6.10	Textual representation of repetition class, zero or more	141
6.11	Graphical representation of repetition class, one or more	142
6.12	Textual representation of repetition class, one or more	142
6.13	Class dictionary graph for lists	145
6.14	Connections	148
6.15	Definition of associated	149
6.16	Class dictionary graph for expressions	153
6.17	Part-centered versus specialization-centered designs	161
6.18	Edge choice	162
7.1	Class dictionary graph without inheritance edges, textual	171
7.2	Class dictionary graph without inheritance edges, graphical	172
7.3	Class dictionary graph with inheritance edges, textual	173
7.4	Class dictionary graph with inheritance edges, graphical	174
7.5	Semi-class dictionary graph that is not a class dictionary graph	175
7.6	Syntax summary for propagation directives	180
7.7	Syntax summary for join and merge	180
7.8	Customizer 1: Class dictionary graph **Company1**	186
7.9	Propagation graph calculus	191
8.1	Programming by hooks	203
8.2	Violations of the Law of Demeter	204
8.3	Class dictionary graph to discuss Law of Demeter	205
8.4	Before the Law of Demeter	205
8.5	After the Law of Demeter	206
8.6	Class dictionary graph using all features	209
8.7	Graph example	212
8.8	Graph class dictionary graph	213
8.9	Depth-first traversal	214
8.10	Propagation graph dft (extension at Adjacency)	214
8.11	Propagation graph uncond_dft	215
8.12	Propagation graph find	215
8.13	Propagation graph for extended graph data model	218
8.14	Extended graph data model	218
8.15	Chess board class dictionary graph	219
8.16	Count pawns	219
8.17	Annotated propagation graph	220
8.18	Car	221
8.19	Painting a car	222
8.20	Painting a car, except doors	222
8.21	Painting car doors only	222
8.22	Simple counting of X-objects	223
8.23	Meal example	224

8.24	Expressions	226
8.25	Compiler	226
8.26	Equivalent wrappers	231
8.27	Code for test1 in edge wrapper example	232
8.28	Code for test2 in edge wrapper example	233
8.29	Simplifying the cycle checking problem	235
8.30	Evolution history	236
8.31	Classification hierarchy	241
8.32	Simulating method inheritance	242
8.33	Classification with construction edges	243
9.1	Interpreter TRAVERSE to run a propagation pattern	257
9.2	Refrigerator propagation pattern	262
9.3	Propagation directive information loss	263
9.4	Customizer with information loss	263
9.5	Propagation graph	264
9.6	Delayed binding restriction violated	266
9.7	Propagation graph	267
9.8	Bad customizer	267
9.9	Class dictionary graph Dish	268
9.10	A propagation pattern	268
9.11	Propagation graph for eat/Dish	269
9.12	A propagation pattern	270
9.13	Overlap of restrictions	270
9.14	Ordering of wrapper calls	277
9.15	Class dictionary graph	280
9.16	Class dictionary graph	281
9.17	Knowledge paths for object path	284
9.18	Patchwork class dictionary, textual	286
9.19	Patchwork class dictionary, graphical	287
9.20	Propagation graph	288
9.21	Traversal code	289
9.22	Coping with unintended inheritance	290
9.23	Car dealer semi-class dictionary graph with traversal code	291
9.24	Propagation graph for car dealer semi-class dictionary graph	292
9.25	Wrapper pushing	292
10.1	Redundant propagation patterns	310
10.2	Nonredundant propagation pattern	310
10.3	Town without a dog catcher	316
10.4	Town with a dog catcher	317
10.5	Town of SelfEmployed	317
10.6	Transportation restrictions: Disallowed edges	319
10.7	Propagation directive	321
10.8	Propagation pattern triples	322

10.9	Customizer 1: Class dictionary graph Company1	323
10.10	Bringing the actors on stage	323
10.11	After customization of triples with class dictionary graph Company1	325
10.12	Customizer 2: Class dictionary graph Company2 with repetition vertices	325
10.13	Work flow management	331
10.14	Transporting resources	332
10.15	Code for resource transportation	333
10.16	Code generation with transportation	334
10.17	Summary: Case 1	334
10.18	Base/Derived-wrappers	336
10.19	Summary: Case 2	338
10.20	Summary: Case 3	340
10.21	Summary: Case 4	342
10.22	Transportation pattern terminology	345
11.1	Meal language	360
11.2	Two grammars defining the same language	363
11.3	Syntax graph construction	365
11.4	Syntax graph repetition	366
11.5	Syntax graph repetition (nonempty)	366
11.6	Syntax graph alternation	366
11.7	Venn diagram for class dictionaries	372
11.8	LL(1), left-recursive, noninductive	373
11.9	LL(1), nonleft-recursive, inductive	373
12.1	Illustration of class dictionary graph slices	383
12.2	Car and motor	384
12.3	Three dimensions of class dictionary design	385
12.4	a has smaller size than b	386
12.5	Class dictionary to be minimized	387
12.6	Optimized class dictionary	388
12.7	Class dictionary that satisfies tree property	390
12.8	Single inheritance class dictionary	390
13.1	Castle building analogy	408
13.2	Experimental heating system: class dictionary graph Furnace	411
13.3	Example of object-equivalence: $\Gamma_1 \equiv \Gamma_2$	412
13.4	Example of weak-extension: $\Gamma_1 \preceq \Gamma_2$	413
13.5	Example of extension: $\Gamma_1 \leq \Gamma_2$	413
14.1	Class dictionary	432
14.2	C++ translation	434
14.3	Object-equivalence	435
14.4	Class dictionary and object graph	437
14.5	Object construction	438
14.6	Class dictionary	438

14.7	Objects and sentences	440
14.8	First sets	441
14.9	Syntax analysis	442
14.10	Follow sets	443
14.11	Common normal form	444
14.12	Growth plan	446
15.1	Class graph	455
15.2	C++ program	456
15.3	Adaptive program	456
15.4	A regular expression	457
15.5	Exp-object	459
15.6	Propagation graph	460
15.7	Traversal skeleton	460
15.8	Generated C++ program	461
15.9	Another class graph	462
15.10	Adapted C++ program	462
15.11	Inconsistency	464
15.12	Violation of subclass invariance	465
15.13	Find refrigerators owned by families	466
15.14	Shortcut 1	477
15.15	Shortcut 2	477
15.16	Shortcut 3	478
16.1	A semi-class dictionary graph	498
16.2	Forbidden graph	499
16.3	A semi-class dictionary graph that cannot define objects	500
16.4	A class dictionary graph slice	501
16.5	A class dictionary graph slice	502
16.6	The relations between concepts	503
16.7	An object of vertex **Graduate**	504
16.8	Illegal object	506
16.9	Illustration of class dictionary graph slices	507
16.10	Class dictionary graph **Graduate_school**	509
16.11	Class dictionary **Graduate_school**	510
16.12	Order all vertices from which vertex **A** is alternation-reachable	513
16.13	Flat class dictionary **Graduate_school**	515
16.14	**Faculty-tree** object	516
16.15	g_print	517
16.16	Two $AorB\_CorD$-objects	521
16.17	$g\_print(D)$ and $g\_parse(D)$ with D satisfying the LL(1) rules	524
16.18	g_parse	525
16.19	Notations	532
16.20	**Fruit_List**	533
16.21	Weaker path concept	536

16.22 Path instantiations 538
16.23 Class dictionary graph 2_graph for cycle checking on graphs with two kinds of edges 539

A.1 Access to software, documentation, and course material 589
A.2 E-mail information 590

List of Tables

2.1	Objects and operations	33
6.1	Identifying symbols for classes	142
6.2	Identifying symbols for edges	143
7.1	Earlier examples of propagation graphs	183
15.1	Terminology	483
16.1	The grammar interpretation of a flat class dictionary	515
16.2	Demeter data model summary	528
16.3	The comparison	528

Foreword

Gregor Kiczales and John Lamping

As we write this foreword, it is Earth Day, a day to think about the interrelatedness of life on Earth. It is a day to contemplate that while each living thing is an individual organism, all the organisms in an ecosystem are connected by a complex web of interaction, upon which they all depend for their continuing existence. One lesson of ecological studies is that while it is comparatively easy to identify, isolate, and categorize individual organisms, the relationships among them are much more difficult to identify and don't fall into nicely separated categories.

Object-oriented programs are much simpler than natural ecosystems—even though a programmer trying to chase down a recalcitrant bug might be inclined to disagree—but they have a similar structure. Like ecosystems, they are composed of individuals, objects in this case. Also like ecosystems, the behavior of the system arises out of the interrelationships and interactions of those individuals.

Object-oriented design recognizes this interdependence, and uses notations like class graphs to help describe the relationships among the objects. Because these relationships are so important, their design is one of the first steps in a typical object-oriented design. The detailed design of the individual objects or classes only happens after a system design is in place.

But because the interrelationships among objects are complex, it is almost impossible to design them exactly right the first time, as anyone who has built a reasonably large object-oriented program knows from hard-won experience. The design process is iterative, with the interactions among objects being redesigned as problems are uncovered during design or coding of individual objects or classes. And the design process is only the beginning of changes to the interactions. Other changes will become necessary during maintenance as the system evolves to meet changing requirements, and still more changes will be necessary if parts of the system are reused for other applications.

Traditional object-oriented programming has been a great success, partly because of the kinds of flexibility that object encapsulation provides. But it doesn't provide comparable support for flexibility in object interrelationships. For example, object-oriented languages require coding in the smallest details of the relationships among objects, such as navigation paths among interacting objects. Often a great deal of code needs to be edited in the face of even a small change to the conceptual interdependence structure. There are similar challenges for flexibility in what class should be used for newly created objects, and in allowing different parts of an evolving program to have different viewpoints on the same object.

Adaptive object-oriented programming allows programs to be written in a way that makes them less brittle in the face of such changes. Adaptive object-oriented programming works by having the programmer program at a higher, schematic level that abstracts away from details like navigation paths. These schematic patterns can be instantiated to a particular class graph to get an executable program. In this way it is a kind of metaprogramming. In many cases, programs can be adapted to new situations simply by changing the instantiation of the schematic patterns, without having to change the high-level program. By thinking in such terms of higher-level of abstraction, the programmer can write code that is both simpler and more tolerant of changes.

This book presents a complete, well-designed methodology for adaptive programming in C++ and tools for supporting the methodology. And because the methodology is programming-language independent, any programmer interested in writing cleaner, more flexible OBJECT-ORIENTED code should read this book.

We hope the work presented in this book will become one of the building blocks for a new trend in object-oriented programming, moving beyond object encapsulation to provide new abstraction tools for the interaction among objects.

Gregor Kiczales

John Lamping

Xerox PARC
Palo Alto, California

Preface

The Purpose of the Book

This book introduces a software development method, called the Demeter[1] Method, for developing adaptive object-oriented software. The reader will learn the Demeter Method for evolutionary software development by specifying class dictionaries for defining the structure of objects and by specifying propagation patterns for implementing the behavior of the objects. The reader will learn how class dictionaries and propagation patterns are translated to C++. Translation to other languages that support the object-oriented paradigm is very similar. The behavior of objects may be implemented with only partial knowledge of the object structure.

The Demeter Method is not yet another object-oriented method; it enhances and complements other object-oriented methods, such as Booch, Jacobson, Rumbaugh, and Wirfs-Brock, by lifting object-oriented software development to a higher level of abstraction by considering entire families of object-oriented designs and programs. This generalization of object-oriented software development amplifies the advantages of object-oriented technology and eliminates some of its disadvantages, such as the many tiny methods that hinder program understanding and reusability.

One important insight of the Demeter Method is that for a significant fraction of programming tasks, solving a more general problem is easier than solving a specialized problem. This is why we work with families of programs and designs; it often happens that the families can be described much more succinctly than the individual programs.

Let's take a look at nature to better understand how adaptive object-oriented software (adaptive software from now on) works. You find the essential information about an organism in its genes. We can view the genes as a process model of the organism, which will later be complemented by an environment or structural model that customizes the behavior of the organism. However, the process model puts certain constraints on the applicable environments. A palm tree will not thrive in Alaska.

From the analogy to nature, we obtain the idea of focusing on the essence in process models, and we develop our software in terms of process and corresponding structural models. The process models (which are not only software development processes, but any kind

---

[1]Pronunciation: di mē'tr. The stress is on ē, which is pronounced like the *e* in *equal*.
Demeter is a registered trademark of Demeter-Bund e.V. for agricultural products and a trademark of Northeastern University for software. Demeter is the ancient greek goddess of farming and gardening, identified by the Romans with Ceres. The metaphor of gardening and growing software is occasionally used in the Demeter Method.

of processes) focus on the essence of a given task, and they define constraints on applicable structural models.

Why is it easier, for many programming tasks, to solve a more general problem? The essence of a process model is often more easily specified in terms of a partial structural model (for example, a partial data structure) than of a detailed structural model (for example, a complete data structure). The process models expressed as adaptive software therefore describe entire families of programs.

The Demeter Method provides an approach to object-oriented software development that is, by experience, easier to use than traditional object-oriented software development methods.

The purpose of the book is to make the concepts of adaptive software available in a form that is useful to software developers who currently use object-oriented languages. The book is the entry point to a wealth of other information on an adaptive software (see Fig. 0.1). Ways to access the rest of the information are discussed in Appendix A (page 589).

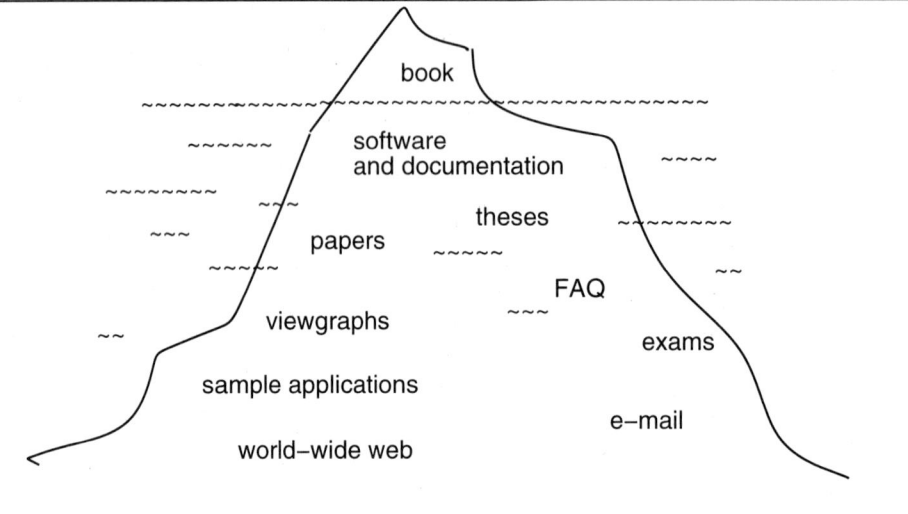

Figure 0.1: Tip of an iceberg

The Purpose of Adaptive Software

Adaptive software is an extension of object-oriented software where relationships between functions and data are left flexible, that is, where functions and data are loosely coupled through navigation specifications. Adaptive means that the software heuristically changes itself to handle an interesting class of requirements changes related to changing the object structure.

Adaptive software is a natural evolution of object-oriented software since every object-oriented program is essentially an adaptive program. In many cases however, the adaptiveness of the object-oriented program can be significantly improved. Although object-oriented programs are easier to reuse than programs that are not written in an object-oriented style, object-oriented programs are still very rigid and hard to evolve. Our experience shows that for most application domains, object-oriented programs can be made significantly more general and extensible by expressing them as adaptive programs. An adaptive program allows us to express the "intention" of a program without being side-tracked by the details of the object structure.

Adaptive software has several benefits:

- *Shorter programs and a higher level of abstraction*

  Adaptive software allows shorter programs by focusing only on the interesting parts and by having the tedious work done automatically. Programs get shorter by several factors. The higher the level of a programming tool, the clearer and simpler are the programs.

- *Reusable software libraries*

  Adaptive software is easier to extend than standard object-oriented software and allows for unplanned reuse. The "elastic" class structures used during adaptive software development facilitate reuse.

  Adaptive software allows the building of application-oriented, domain-specific reusable libraries, which can be used in similar projects with no extra cost for the reusability property (beyond the cost of object-oriented software). Adaptive software provides the unique capability of parameterizing software with minimal assumptions on how the software will be used. Producing adaptive software incurs no extra cost since the software is much shorter when written in adaptive form. Adaptiveness enhances reusability and the adaptiveness/reusability property pays off in the first project.

- *Ability to plan for changes, allow for learning*

  An important advantage of adaptive software is that it allows for initial error and subsequent adjustment. Many problems are complex, and often it is not clear how best to structure the classes at the beginning. With adaptive software, we can easily make a first approach to the class structure and write the behavior with minimal dependency on that first approach, so that changing to a better class structure is much easier.

- *Ability to build on familiar object technology*

  Adaptive software builds on the advantages of object-oriented technology. Object-oriented programs can often be gradually transformed into shorter, more flexible adaptive programs. Adaptive software can take advantage of any feature that the underlying object-oriented base language offers; therefore adaptive software does not limit the creativity of the object-oriented programmer in any way.

- *Risk avoidance*

  Adaptive software has no disadvantages with respect to object-oriented software. Adaptive software is usually significantly more expressive than object-oriented software, and the best adaptive software can be no worse than the best object-oriented software that can be written for a given application. Adaptive software can always be expanded into ordinary object-oriented software.

Adaptive software can be learned in a few hours by someone who knows an object-oriented language and object-oriented design.

- *Minimal reliance on an object-oriented programming language such as C++ or Smalltalk*

  Adaptive software provides a tool that allows development of the important parts of software above the object-oriented programming level.

Object-oriented programming is a promising technology that has been developed over the last twenty years. One important advantage of object-oriented programming is that it reduces the semantic gap between a program and the world it models because the world consists of physical and abstract objects that are represented naturally by software objects in an object-oriented program.

However, object-oriented design and programming has several disadvantages, the most significant of which is that it binds functions and data too tightly. A loose binding between functions and data allows very generic software where data structure information in the functions or procedures is only used to constrain the applicable data structures. Before a program can be run, we select one of the applicable data structures, which in turn usually determines the structure of the input objects. The goal when writing the functions is to minimize the assumptions we make about the data structures. This technique could be called data-structure-shy programming, and it leads to generic software that can be flexibly customized later. One data-structure-shy program potentially describes an infinite collection of object-oriented programs.

Scope

This book has two functions:

- It serves as an introduction to advanced object-oriented design and programmming for the professional and student. We serve the following audiences:

  - *Those interested in object-oriented design and programming.*

    This book provides a programming-language independent introduction to advanced object-oriented design and programming. Since our design notation is executable after behavioral and structural information is merged, we need to use a programming notation to explain the execution of the designs. We have chosen C++ as our programming language and therefore the reader should know a subset of C++ (summarized in an appendix). We attempt to use a subset of C++, which is available with different syntax in programming languages such as Smalltalk, CLOS, and Objective-C.

  - *Those interested in C++.*

    This book introduces a useful design and programming method and shows the reader how to apply it to C++.

PREFACE   xxix

   – *Those interested in conceptual object-oriented database design.*

     A high-level conceptual modeling language is taught that can be applied to the reader's favorite object base.

- It provides a detailed introduction to developing adaptive software for the professional and the student. We serve the following audiences:

   – *Those interested in analysis and design methods.*

     The Demeter Method for developing adaptive software is introduced.

   – *Those interested in programming languages.*

     A new programming language is taught that allows the reader to describe object-oriented programs at a higher-level of abstraction than in current object-oriented languages.

   – *Those interested in knowledge representation and computer science education.*

     The reader learns about a new graphical notation for presenting and manipulating algorithmic knowledge.

The adaptive software concepts serve as a foundation to deliver any kind of algorithmic knowledge at a high level of abstraction. Adaptive software is a new kind of algorithmic knowledge representation language applicable to many different areas.

We have been using earlier versions of this book in undergraduate and graduate courses at Northeastern University since September 1986. The book is ideal for a course on advanced object-oriented design and object-oriented programming and it is a useful supplement for any advanced undergraduate or graduate course in which students write C++ programs. The only prerequisites are a knowledge of a small subset of C++ (or the ability to learn C++ and some object-oriented design from some C++ book, for example, [Wan94, Lip89, Poh91, DS89]), and a basic knowledge of discrete mathematics as covered, for example, in [WL88].

This book can be used in two ways:

- as the primary source for learning/teaching advanced object-oriented software development and for in-house courses on object-oriented analysis, design and programming (e.g., it has been used at IBM, Mettler-Toledo, Data General, Ciba Geigy, Citibank, Goodyear);

- as a supplement: In the *Principles of Programming Languages* and *Analysis of Programming Languages* courses we are using this book for writing interpreters for several sublanguages of real programming languages, including several subsets of Lisp and a subset of Prolog. This approach is promoted by [FHW92]. We are using this book for several projects, including scanner generation, generation of parsers with error recovery, compilers, graphical user interfaces with Tcl/Tk, an adaptive scripting tool (called Isthmus), and for implementing and maintaining the Demeter Tools/C++.

The Organization of the Book

The book is organized so that it is independent of a specific implementation of adaptive software. The book focuses on the concepts important to adaptive software development and the Demeter Method and is not a user's guide for the Demeter Software. The Demeter software, documentation, and related course material are available on the World-Wide Web as shown by the uniform resource locators (URLs) in Fig. A.1 (page 589). Further information about electronic access is in Appendix A (page 589).

The book starts with an introduction to adaptive software specifically for C++ programmers. Adaptive software is viewed as a notation to describe C++ programs by eliminating much of the redundancy C++ programs contain.

The book introduces many nonstandard terms (such as propagation pattern, propagation directive, class dictionary graph, class dictionary, and class-valued variable) for explaining adaptive software. Such terms are not standard because adaptive software is new and has not been discussed previously in book form. We introduce the terms in stages and use them in more and more complex contexts. In Chapter 5 we gradually introduce the various features of class dictionary graphs and propagation patterns. In later chapters, the concepts are introduced in more detail.

The book uses two approaches to explaining adaptive and object-oriented software development. The first approach, which is the usual informal style used in software development books, is used in Chapters 1 through 13. The second, more formal approach, which is not required for using adaptive software, is used in Chapters 15 and 16. The two approaches are linked together through approximately one hundred instructional objectives described in Chapter 14.

When a concept or method is explained informally, a related instructional objective is mentioned. An instructional objective defines a learning unit that the reader should master and that can be used to prepare exams to test the material learned. An instructional objective is referenced in a footnote with its page number (and the number of the instructional objective in parentheses). The reader may follow the link to the instructional objectives chapter (Chapter 14), which is essentially a road map to the adaptive software knowledge. The instructional objectives have prerequisites that can be followed to find the context of a given instructional objective.

Most instructional objectives refer to formal definitions; these may be useful to some of the advanced users of adaptive software. The formal definitions present the material in yet another way by trying to optimally cluster the mathematical definitions.

This book contains a glossary, an index, and a self-study guide (Chapter 17) with suggestions for using the book, the tools, and the documentation together.

Usage Scenarios

The organization of the book is useful for

1. beginning C++ developers, who want to write adaptive software quickly:

    Chapters 1, 2, 3, 5, 6, 7.1 to 7.5, 8, 9.1, 10, 11.1.

    For a deeper understanding, complete all of Chapters 7, 9, 11, and read Chapters 12, 13, and 16. Chapter 3 summarizes the subset of C++ that is used.

2. intermediate C++ developers, who want to write adaptive software quickly:

   Same as above for #1, but Chapter 2 may be skipped.

3. those who have read about Demeter before in magazines, conference proceedings, or journals, and who want a quick but thorough review: Start with Chapter 15, skipping some of the formal semantics on first reading, and continue with Chapters 6, etc., as in #1.

4. intermediate software developers using some object-oriented language (not necessarily C++). Same as #1, but skip Chapters 2 and 3, except Section 3.5, which discusses the subset of object-oriented concepts, which are relevant and which you need to learn to read in C++ syntax instead of in the syntax of your object-oriented language.

5. instructors, who will benefit from reading Chapter 15 to get a thorough understanding of the core concepts. This chapter is self-contained. To write a course syllabus, it is helpful to select some of the instructional objectives in Chapter 14 and complement them with your own. Chapter 17 proposes one way of coordinating the learning of the concepts with tool use and it contains ideas for homework. At the end of most chapters are chapter-specific exercises.

Chapter 4 (Thinking Adaptively) is a motivational chapter which explains why adaptive software is useful and how it fits into other key ideas of computer science as well as informally explaining the key concepts. Assignments 1-5 in Chapter 17 can be done if the reader has the Demeter Tools/C++ installed.

The order of the chapters should be followed, except that Chapters 4 and 15 can be read independently. Also, Chapter 11 may be read immediately after Chapter 6.

The History of the Demeter Project

During a visiting professorship at the Swiss Federal Institute of Technology in Zurich in the 1982-1983 winter semester (on leave from Princeton University), I was teaching a course on the theory of VLSI design. It was during preparation of this course that I learned about Niklaus Wirth's new hardware description language, called Hades [Wir82]. Svend Knudsen, a doctoral student of Niklaus Wirth, and I became very interested in Hades and we started to use it to describe chip architectures. This was the starting point of Zeus [Lie85], a hardware description language that improved on Hades.

I moved to GTE Laboratories where Zeus was implemented. In 1984, after suggestions from Gerald Jones, Andrew Goldberg and I first developed a metaprogramming tool [GL85b] on top of Pascal to simplify the implementation of Zeus; this metaprogramming tool was the starting point of the Demeter System, and it was used for several design automation projects other than the Zeus implementation. (Demeter is a sister of Zeus.)

GTE Laboratories gave me permission to continue the Demeter work at Northeastern, where the project is carried out by numerous dedicated graduate and undergraduate students who are supported by the College of Computer Science, the National Science Foundation, ARPA, and several companies, including IBM, Ciba-Geigy, and Citibank.

Executive Summary

This book introduces the Demeter Method for developing adaptive object-oriented software. What is an adaptive program? We give several intuitive explanations in common terminology.

- An adaptive program is similar to a genre. According to the *Random House Dictionary*, a genre is a category of artistic endeavor having a particular form, content, or technique. An adaptive program describes a category of object-oriented programs that all have a particular form, but the details of the programs are left open. Even the input objects to the programs are left flexible. The artistic metaphor of a genre carries further: an adaptive program describes how to "bring the actors on the stage" without hardcoding the class structure. Bringing the actors on the stage means assembling the right objects so that an operation can be called that takes those objects as arguments.

- An adaptive program, like a multipurpose mechanism, is useful in a set of related contexts. In some contexts an adaptive program does exactly what is required and in other contexts it approximates what is required.

- An adaptive program is a family of analogous object-oriented programs. A member of the family is called an instance of the adaptive program. An instance is selected by customizing the adaptive program with a specific class structure.

- An adaptive program is like the genes of a fruit-bearing tree. A specific tree is an instance of the genes in the same way that an object-oriented program is an instance of an adaptive program. The genes produce similar looking trees, depending on the environment. In some environments we will get big trees with sweet fruit and in others only small trees with sour fruit. By analogy, all instances of an adaptive program have a similar look. They are all built according to the same pattern, but some work better than others.

- An adaptive program sketches the solution strategy for a class of problems. It is well known that solving a more general problem is often *simpler* than solving a specific one. The solution of the more general problem is reusable in many situations.

The book explains how to grow adaptive software in a programming-language independent way. Since an object-oriented program is a special case of an adaptive program the book provides a very effective introduction to object-oriented software development. The adaptive software paradigm proposes a useful way of structuring object-oriented software.

Coverage of Computer Science Subject Areas

"Computing as a Discipline" [DCG+89] presents nine subject areas comprising the discipline of computing. Accreditation boards are using the classifications in "Computing as a Discipline" to evaluate computer science programs. This book includes some of the material in six of the nine areas.

1. *Algorithms and data structures*

   Readers learn to write algorithms without encoding the details of the data structures in the algorithms. This makes the algorithms more general and more reusable.

2. *Artificial intelligence and robotics*

   Readers learn to express algorithmic knowledge at a high level of abstraction through propagation patterns. Structural knowledge representation is introduced through class dictionaries. Readers learn about analogical reasoning by transforming a program from one data structure to another.

3. *Database and information retrieval*

   Readers learn to design schemas for object-oriented databases. They also learn a novel query notation: propagation patterns.

4. *Human-to-computer communication*

   Readers learn a new visualization of programs based on collaborating objects and classes.

5. *Programming languages*

   Readers learn to use a family of programming languages that live on top of object-oriented languages. Implementation of these languages is discussed through both operational and translational semantics.

   Class dictionaries and propagation patterns are a new programming language and at the same time a new specification and design language.

6. *Software methodology and engineering*

   Readers learn principles of development of *flexible* software systems.

   Readers learn the adaptive programming principle: A program should be designed so that the interfaces of objects can be changed within certain constraints without affecting the program *at all*.

"Computing as a Discipline" describes three important processes used in the computing discipline: Theory, Abstraction, and Design. This book covers aspects of all three processes:

- Theory

  Readers learn definitions of class dictionaries and propagation patterns and a few theorems and proofs. They become experts at proving very simple "theorems" of the form: This object O is a legal object with respect to a given set of classes.

- Abstraction

  Readers learn to abstract class dictionaries from objects. They learn to abstract adaptive programs from object-oriented programs. They learn to abstract parameterized classes from classes.

- Design

    Readers learn about requirements in the form of use-cases. Readers learn about specification, design, implementation, and testing of adaptive software.

    A large part of the book explains how adaptive software works. Since adaptive software uses an excutable specification language for object-oriented programs, specification, design, and implementation are closer together than in other approaches to software development.

Finally, "Computing as a Discipline" identifies twelve recurring concepts fundamental to computing. The following concepts are covered extensively in this book:

- Binding

    Adaptive software uses a sophisticated mechanism to bind methods to classes.

- Conceptual and formal models

    Readers learn to design their own models and to debug them first with respect to structure and then with respect to functionality. Debugging of the structure is accomplished through parsing. Debugging of the functionality is achieved through "evolution histories" which allow debugging in layers.

- Evolution

    Ease of evolution is one of the key properties of adaptive software. Readers learn how to evolve their C++ programs by controlling the evolution through class dictionaries and propagation patterns.

- Levels of abstraction

    Readers learn to effectively deal with multiple levels of abstraction, most importantly learning the distinction between groups of objects and groups of classes. Readers are challenged by abstraction level collapsing, such as when a group of classes is suddenly viewed as a group of objects (which happens, for example, when readers learn about self-describing class dictionaries and how to write programs for them). Parameterized classes are also used extensively, adding a third layer of abstraction.

    When readers write propagation patterns they operate at multiple levels of abstraction: the object, class, and parameterized class level for the structural information, and the adaptive and object-oriented level for the behavioral information. Also, when readers write a propagation pattern, they often think about how the corresponding C++ program looks.

- Reuse

    Ease of reuse is one of the driving forces behind adaptive software. Readers learn how to write software with fewer built-in assumptions, which makes the software easier to reuse in new environments. The Law of Demeter plays an important role.

Acknowledgments

This book would not exist in its current form without the Demeter Research Group, a group of highly talented computer science professionals from around the world who are or have been doctoral students in the College of Computer Science at Northeastern University.

The individual contributions of the Demeter Research Group members are acknowledged by the papers we have written and continue to write (see the bibliographic remarks at the end of each chapter and in the bibliography). Those papers are the basis of separately published theses. Previous and current team members come from six different countries and three different continents and include, in alphabetical order (the number in parentheses is the year of Ph.D. graduation): Paul Bergstein (1994), Ian Holland (1993), Walter Hürsch (1995), Linda Keszenheimer, Yang Liu, Cristina Lopes, Salil Pradhan, Arthur Riel, Ignacio Silva-Lepe (1994), Cun Xiao (1994).

Financial support by the National Science Foundation (Richard DeMillo, K.C. Tai, Bruce Barnes, Helen Gill) and ARPA (John Salasin) and the following companies is very much appreciated: IBM (Brent Hailpern, Mark Wegman, Clarence Clark, Ashok Malhotra, Harold Ossher), Mettler-Toledo (Rolf W. Arndt and Linus Meier), Citibank (Jeff Chittenden, Jim Caldarella), Mitsubishi (Les Belady) and SAIC (George Brown).

I would like to thank Dean Cynthia Brown and Dean Larry Finkelstein for their support of my project through its entire development. This support has come in several forms: support of my graduate students, moral support, state-of-the-art equipment, and allowing me to teach courses where adaptive software can be used, for which many thanks are also due to Agnes Chan, Richard Rasala, and Mitchell Wand. Rémy Evard, the director of Technology at Northeastern University's College of Computer Science, and his systems group, deserve special thanks for providing a well-maintained network which was essential for the development of the Demeter Tools and for writing the book.

This book has benefited from many stimulating discussions with Mitchell Wand. Mitch helped with a thorough review of our papers and proposals and the thesis work of my doctoral students. Ken Baclawski has helped in several discussions on adaptive software and served on the Ph.D. committees of several of my students. Since the fall of 1993, Jens Palsberg has actively contributed to the development of adaptive software by writing an influential paper and by serving on the Ph.D. committees of Paul Bergstein, Walter Hürsch, Ignacio Silva-Lepe, and Cun Xiao. Boaz Patt-Shamir has made several contributions to the type theory for adaptive software.

It was a pleasure to work with my publisher, PWS Publishing Company. They gave me the feeling throughout that my book is important to them. Mike Sugarman, my editor at PWS, deserves special thanks for being very enthusiastic about this project from the first day and for guiding me through the process of review, revision, and production. Mike was a constant source of encouragement and he provided resources to improve the software and to demonstrate it at OOPSLA even before the review cycle was complete. I appreciate the work of Mary Thomas Stone for sending out numerous review copies, for collecting the reviews, for organizing and summarizing them, for organizing the Demeter focus group and for compiling the Demeter address list.

I would like to thank Abby Heim for organizing and guiding the production of the book. Her constant availability was very important in working out all the details. The copyediting phase has eliminated many inelegant phrases from my writing. Many thanks to Adrienne Rebello, the copyeditor.

Many thanks to Nathan Wilbur for his support and his marketing efforts and to Leslie Bondaryk for her suggestions regarding the software, specifically for her suggestion to produce a Laboratory Guide. This guide has been praised by many users of the Demeter Tools/C++.

Thanks to the following PWS reviewers, who have given detailed feedback on earlier versions of the manuscript:

Dr. Sergio Antoy, *Portland State University*;
Dr. Bard Bloom, *Cornell University*;
Dr. H. E. Dunsmore, *Purdue University*;
Dr. Terry Glagowski, *Washington State University*;
Dr. Douglas B. Guptill, *Technical University of Nova Scotia*;
Dr. Joan Lukas, *University of Massachusetts-Boston*;
Dr. Nenad Marovac, *San Diego State University*;
Dr. Satoshi Matsuoka, *University of Tokyo*;
Dr. David C. Rine, *George Mason University*;
Dr. Wilhelm Rossak, *New Jersey Institute of Technology*;
Dr. Spencer Rugaber, *Georgia Institute of Technology*;
Dr. Justin R. Smith, *Drexel University*;
Dr. Dwight Spencer, *Oregon Graduate Institute*;
Dr. Peter Wegner, *Brown University*;
Dr. Laurie H. Werth, *University of Texas-Austin*;
Dr. Ka-Wing Wong, *Eastern Kentucky University*.

The reviewers feedback was very helpful in revising the book and was essential to improve the presentation.

Special thanks to Joan Lukas, Satoshi Matsuoka, and Peter Wegner for participating in The Demeter Focus Group and their valuable input. Peter Wegner has given me input over many years.

A very inspiring force in the development of adaptive software has been the many students who took my courses at Northeastern and at conferences. They are too numerous to mention individually. Arthur Riel was a very important team member in the early days of Demeter. Greg Sullivan has contributed to the project through his regular participation during his initial years at Northeastern. Cole Harrison applied adaptiveness to object-oriented query languages in his Master's thesis. Martin Spit from the University of Twente in The Netherlands gave very detailed feedback on the book while he wrote his Master's thesis on the Demeter Method from a method modeling point of view. Joseph Coco, Bob Familiar, John Janeri, and Wayne Vetrone, have given me detailed feedback on the book.

I would like to thank Cun Xiao, Ke Wang, and Yang Liu for drawing many of the pictures in the book. Many thanks to Salil Pradhan for helping with the index, with finetuning the typesetting, and with production.

I would like to thank my wife, Ruth, for her support during the writing of this book. It was also Ruth who told me about the old Greek stories from which I chose the name *Demeter*.

Many thanks to George McQuilken, president of Demeter International Inc., for his continued support.

Richard Rasala and Robert Futrelle gave me detailed feedback on an early version of the book a few years ago. Several of the chapters they edited have survived into this final version.

Finally, my thanks to Leslie Lamport for producing Latex with which this book was produced.

Credits

All or parts of the following papers are reprinted with permission.

- Portions reprinted, with permission, from *Communications of the ACM* [LSLX94]. ©1994 ACM. Used primarily in Chapter 1.

- Paper reprinted, with permission, from *ACM Transactions on Programming Languages and Systems* [PXL95]. ©1994 ACM. Used in Chapter 15.

- Portions reprinted, with permission, from IEEE Transactions on Software Engineering [LX93c]. ©1994 IEEE. Used in Chapters 7, 8, and 16.

- Portions reprinted, with permission, from *IEEE Transactions on Knowledge and Data Engineering* [LX93a]. ©1994 IEEE. Used primarily in Chapters 12, and 16.

- Portions reprinted, with permission, from *International Journal of Foundations of Computer Science* [LX94]. ©1994 World Scientific Publishing Company. Used primarily in Chapter 16.

- Portions reprinted, with permission, from *Formal Aspects of Computing* [LHX94]. ©1994 British Computer Society. Used primarily in Chapter 13.

- Portions reprinted, with permission, from *Lisp and Symbolic Computation* [Lie88]. ©1988 Kluwer Academic Publishers. Used primarily in Chapter 12.

- Portions reprinted, with permission, from *Journal of Software Engineering* [LBSL91]. ©1991 IEE. Used primarily in Chapters 12 and 13.

- Portions reprinted, with permission, from *Proceedings of International Conference on Data Engineering* [LZHL94]. ©1994 IEEE. Used primarily in Chapter 4.

- Portions reprinted, with permission, from *Proceedings of International Conference on Software Engineering* [LR88a]. ©1988 IEEE. Used primarily in Chapter 6.

- Portions reprinted, with permission, from *Proceedings of International Workshop on CASE* [LHSLX92]. ©1992 IEEE. Used primarily in Chapter 4.

- Portions reprinted, with permission, from *Proceedings of Object-Oriented Programming Systems, Languages and Applications Conference* [LHR88]. ©1988 ACM. Used primarily in Chapter 8.

- Portions reprinted, with permission, from *Proceedings of Object-Oriented Programming Systems, Languages and Applications Conference* [LR89]. ©1989 ACM. Used primarily in Chapter 14.

- Portions reprinted, with permission, from *Proceedings of European Conference on Object-Oriented Programming* [BL91]. ©1991 Springer Verlag. Used primarily in Chapter 5.

- Portions reprinted, with permission, from *Proceedings of International Symposium on Object Technologies for Advanced Software* [LX93b]. ©1993 Springer Verlag. Used primarily in Chapter 10.

- Portions reprinted, with permission, from *Proceedings of Information Processing '92, 12th World Computer Congress* [Lie92]. ©1992 Elsevier Science B.V. Used in Chapter 8.

- Portions reprinted, with permission, from *Journal of Object-Oriented Programming* [LR88b]. ©1988 SIGS Publications Inc. Used primarily in Chapter 6.

Karl J. Lieberherr

Adaptive Object-Oriented Software

The

Demeter Method

WITH PROPAGATION PATTERNS

Chapter 1

Introduction

This chapter provides an introduction to adaptive software in a top-down fashion, going from an abstract adaptive program to a concrete payroll example in C++. If your learning style is more towards going from the concrete to the abstract, please jump safely ahead to Chapter 3, From C++ to Demeter, provided you already know some C++. That chapter shows you the transition from a C++ program to an adaptive program. A third entry point to the book is through Chapter 5, Adaptive Software by Example, which also uses a simple-to-general approach starting with very small examples. There is yet a fourth entry point into the book, which is recommended for advanced readers only: the self-contained Chapter 15, Core Concepts and Implementation, which gives you the essence of adaptive software and a provably correct implementation in forty pages.

1.1 EVOLUTIONARY LIFE CYCLE WITH ADAPTIVE SOFTWARE

When developing innovative and complex software systems, traditional software engineering approaches such as the waterfall model are no longer suitable. Evolutionary software development, as described by the spiral model, is used more and more as an important method to develop innovative software. Evolutionary software development uses an incremental or evolutionary life-cycle model instead of the traditional sequential life-cycle models.

Adaptive software is an improved form of object-oriented software that has been developed to support evolutionary development. It is in the nature of evolutionary development that there will be many software changes. Therefore, software should be written so that the impact of changes is limited. Adaptiveness leads to the desired reduction of change impact and may be combined with other proven techniques for object-oriented software development.

Adaptive object-oriented software is software that adapts automatically to changing contexts. Contexts may be behavior, implementation class structures, synchronization structures, object migration structures, etc.

1.1.1 How is Adaptiveness Achieved?

Adaptiveness is achieved by expressing programs as loosely coupled, cooperating fragments, each one describing only the concerns of one context. The loose coupling is achieved with novel means such as succinct object navigation specifications. The loose coupling of the fragments leads to adaptiveness since many changes in one fragment preserve the intent of the other cooperating fragments, which then adjust automatically to the changed fragment.

1.1.2 Applications of Adaptiveness

Adaptive software has other applications beyond applications to evolutionary software development.

- Object-oriented databases

  One of the applications of adaptive programming is relaxing the need for the programmer to know the class structure in detail. This point of partial or high-level knowledge of the class structure as opposed to its changeability has been explored by the database community. Adaptiveness makes a new contribution to the area of structure-shy query languages for object-oriented databases.

- Programming languages

  Most programming languages offer some kind of data structure notation. Adaptiveness may be added to those programming languages by introducing partial data structures that loosely constrain the set of data structures with which a program can work. The traditional approach views a data structure as an integral part of a program whereas adaptive programming views the data structure as something changeable.

1.1.3 Adaptiveness with the Demeter Method

In the Demeter Method we focus on adaptive programs that are a powerful variant of object-oriented programs. The variant consists of making the programs structure-shy by using only minimal information about the implementation-specific class structure when writing the behavior. The advantage of the structure-shy programs is that they express their intent at a high level of abstraction. Therefore, both readers and writers of those programs have the advantage that they don't have to learn a complex class structure. It is sufficient to have partial knowledge of the class structure. The high level of abstraction also makes the programs shorter and easier to maintain. Adaptive programs are written using two loosely coupled fragments: behavior and implementation class structures.

Adaptive software works with partial knowledge about class structures that directly supports an iterative software life-cycle. When a complex project starts, the optimal class structure is not known and will be determined iteratively during the project. Changes to the class structure can be done much more easily with adaptive software than with object-oriented software. Class libraries can be specified in a flexible way by defining the behavior as loosely coupled to the structure. Adaptive programs can be written to run with different class libraries provided the resources needed by the adaptive program are supplied by the class library.

1.1.4 Demeter Life-Cycle

The two basic components of a life-cycle model are the set of development phases (described by activities and deliverables) and the execution order in which the activities are performed to produce the deliverables. The Demeter life-cycle model is an adaptation of the spiral model to adaptive software. The four major activities of the spiral model are planning, risk analysis, engineering, and customer evaluations. The engineering activity develops the next-level product and consists of software design, coding, and testing. The engineering activity gets as input the use cases and application objects that have been identified in the planning phase and the output of the risk analysis to decide what to implement next.

The design phase translates the requirements for the software into a set of representations. The first representation is a set of customizers that describe class structure, architecture, and object languages. The second representation is a set of adaptive programs (without wrappers), that approximate the intended behavior. The third representation is a set of evolution histories that say in which order the customizers and adaptive programs are developed. Both adaptive programs and evolution histories are described using succinct subgraph specifications.

There are design rules for customizers that allow us to evaluate the quality of customizers. Customizers are checked for rules whose violation would cause the programs produced from them to misbehave. Customizers can be optimized after design rule checking.

There are design rules for adaptive programs which allow to measure the quality of adaptive programs. One such design rule is the Law of Demeter which says that when writing a wrapper, we should use only a very limited set of classes. Adaptive programs are written in terms of partial class structures and many of the patterns about class-structure design developed by the patterns community can be applied when developing adaptive programs.

The coding phase consists of developing all the wrappers and calling the Demeter compiler to translate the adaptive programs and the customizers into executable object-oriented programs.

The testing phase checks whether all use cases have been implemented properly. Test inputs are often specified using the object languages defined by the customizers.

The Demeter life-cycle model is built on the foundation of delaying the binding of methods to classes beyond program writing time. This is achieved through succinct subgraph specifications. No other life-cycle model uses this approach, which leads to loosely coupled software. However, the Demeter life-cycle model is open and the good ideas from other life-cycle models can be reused. For example, use cases from the Jacobson Use-Case method are reused. Adaptive software promotes a new kind of nonblack-box reuse where the important information about the organization of software is revealed to improve reusability. Nonblack-box reuse is also promoted by Gregor Kiczales' group at Xerox PARC.

Adaptive programming, as used in the Demeter Method/C++, builds on the programming language C++ although the adaptive programming approach is programming-language independent. However, we need a language to make the concepts concrete and for various reasons we have chosen C++. Tools have been developed already that support the Demeter Method for C++, Borland Pascal, and Lisp with an object-oriented extension.

Adaptive programs are improved object-oriented programs that allow us to take full advantage of object-oriented technology. The advantages of adaptiveness play a stronger role, the larger the class structures and the longer the software will live. Adaptive software has an efficient implementation, incurring no run-time costs over object-oriented software. Compilation of adaptive software into C++ is also fast.

Maintainability is a key consideration because most costs associated with software products are incurred after the software has been put to use. Adaptive software improves maintainability because it is written at a higher level of abstraction.

The Demeter Tools/C++ provide one possible implementation of adaptive software (see Fig. 1.1).

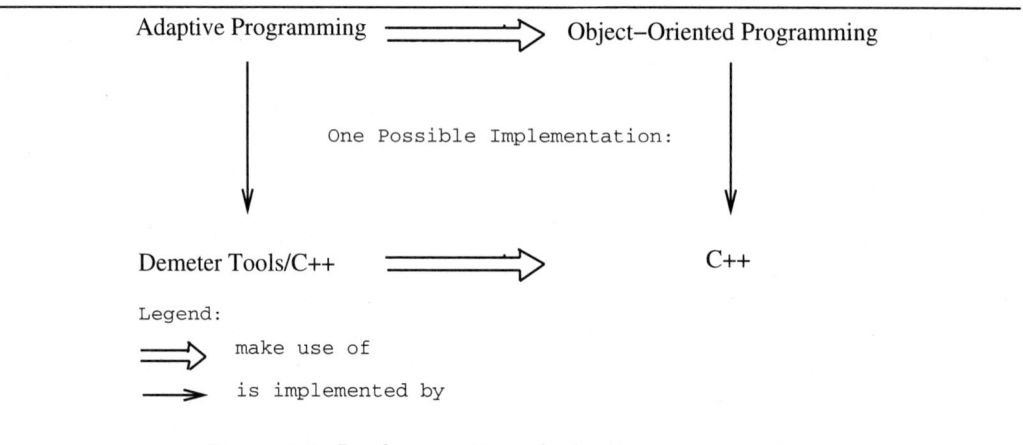

Figure 1.1: Implementation of adaptive programming

The process of developing simple adaptive software with the Demeter Tools/C++ consists of the following steps:

1. Write the customizer that specifies the class library and object language.

2. Run the design check tool to check consistency of the customizer.

3. Write the adaptive program that specifies the intended behavior of the application.

4. Run the design check tool to check that the adaptive program is consistent and that the adaptive program is compatible with the customizer.

5. Generate the C++ code by executing the Demeter compiler. Compile the C++ code.

    `compile(ADAPTIVE PROGRAMS, CUSTOMIZER) -> executable C++ program`

6. Run the executable by using as input object descriptions that are legal with respect to the customizer.

1.1.5 Symmetry Between Adaptive Programs and Customizers

Adaptive software development is based on first selecting the needed resources from a class library, then the adaptations to those resources. The resource selection is expressed by navigation specifications and the adaptations by wrappers.

Adaptive programs consist of navigation specifications that describe how objects are traversed augmented by wrappers that specify executable programs (C++ member function statements) executed before or after traversal of an object. Adaptive programs often also contain transportation specifications that transport objects to other objects to get a job done collectively.

There is a symmetrical relationship between customizers and adaptive programs. A customizer is written once to be used with several adaptive programs that are consistent with the customizer. This customizer reuse happens, for example, inside one application when the functionality is expressed in terms of several adaptive programs that will be customized together (see Fig. 1.2).

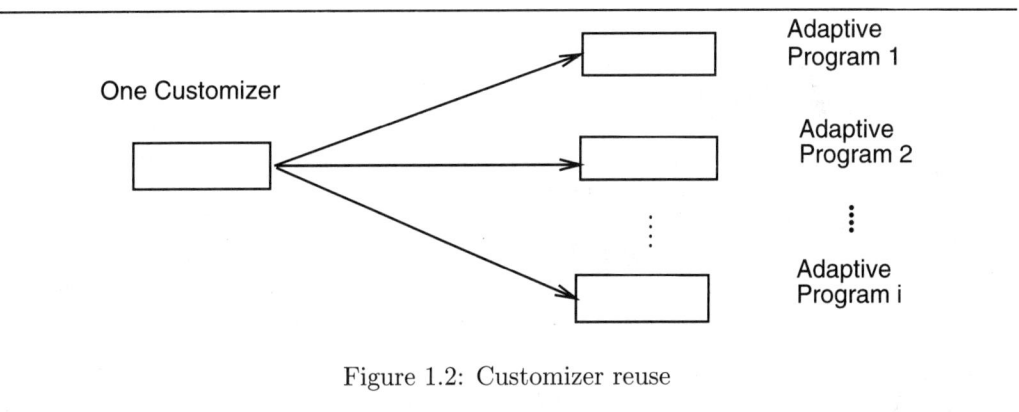

Figure 1.2: Customizer reuse

An adaptive program can be customized with many different customizers that are consistent with the adaptive program (see Fig. 1.3). This adaptive program reuse happens, for example, during maintenance when the object structure changes.

1.1.6 Symmetry Between Object Descriptions and Customizers

Defining objects using statements of an object-oriented programming language can be a tedious task. The reason is that the object structure is encoded in great detail into the statements. Therefore, adaptive software uses so-called sentences to describe families of objects. By a sentence we mean a sequence of tokens in the sense of language and grammar theory (see Chapter 11). A specific object can be selected from the family by using a customizer.

There is a symmetrical relationship between customizers and sentences. A customizer can be used with several sentences to select objects from the families described by the sentences. And one sentence can be used with several different customizers to select different objects.

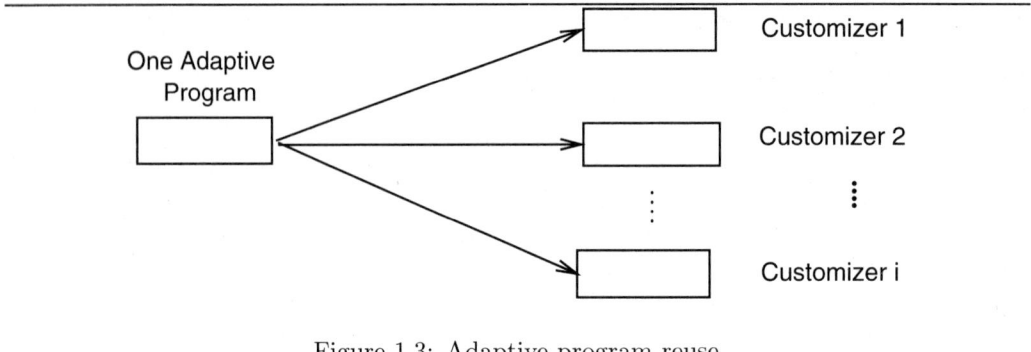

Figure 1.3: Adaptive program reuse

1.2 DISADVANTAGES OF OBJECT-ORIENTED SOFTWARE

Object-oriented programs are easier to extend than programs that are not written in an object-oriented style, but object-oriented programs are still very rigid and hard to adapt and maintain. A key feature of most popular approaches to object-oriented programming is that methods are attached to classes—C++, Smalltalk, Eiffel, Beta—or to groups of classes—CLOS. This feature is both a blessing and a curse. On the brighter side, attaching methods to classes is at the core of objects being able to receive messages, different classes of objects responding differently to a given message, and the ability to define standard protocols. On the darker side, by explicitly attaching every single method to a specific class, the details of the class structure are encoded into the program unnecessarily. This leads to programs that are hard to evolve and maintain. In other words, today's object-oriented programs often contain more redundant application-specific information than is necessary, thus limiting their reusability.

Does this mean that we either have to take the curse in order to enjoy the blessing or give up the blessing altogether? Analyzing the problem we realize that all is not lost. We need to be able to specify only those elements that are essential to an object-oriented program and then specify them in a way that allows them to adapt to new environments.

What do we mean by specifying only those elements—classes and methods—that are essential to an object-oriented program? There is a general impression that object-oriented programs are structured differently from conventional programs. For many tasks very brief methods are written that simply "pass through" a message to another method. We regard "traversal, pass through" methods as nonessential. But more importantly, we intend to focus on classes and methods that are essential not only to a particular application but also potentially to a family of related applications.

What is wrong with object-oriented programs? Object-oriented programmers have to write the details of the class structure repeatedly into their methods. This leads to programs with high entropy that are polluted by accidental details about the class structure. Figure 1.4 shows a class structure (the full square) and four behaviors which have been written for various parts of the class structure. The first behavior (f1) uses the right two thirds, the second behavior (f2) the left two thirds, the third behavior (f3) uses the bottom two thirds and the fourth behavior (f4) uses the top two thirds. The part of the class structure that is in the center is encoded four times into the methods that implement the four behaviors! Should there be a change to the class structure in the center area, we would have to update the four behaviors!

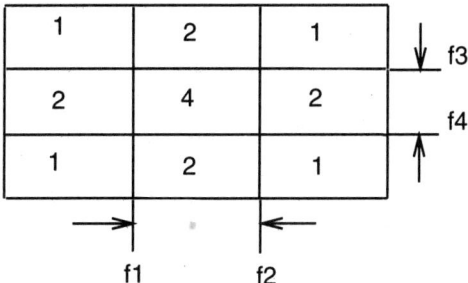

Figure 1.4: Duplication of class structure in object-oriented programming

In this book we introduce **adaptive object-oriented programming** as an extension to conventional object-oriented programming. Adaptive object-oriented programming facilitates expressing the elements—classes and methods—that are essential to an application by avoiding a commitment on the particular class structure of the application. Adaptive object-oriented programs specify essential classes and methods by constraining the configuration of a class structure that attempts to customize the adaptive program, without spelling out all the details of such a class structure. This way, adaptive object-oriented programmers are encouraged to think about families of programs by finding appropriate generalizations.

The remainder of this chapter is organized as follows. Section 1.3 introduces adaptive programs, describing their structure. Adaptive programs[1] are specified using **propagation patterns**, which express program constraints. Propagation patterns are introduced in Section 1.4. An adaptive program denotes an entire family of programs, as many programs as there are class structures that satisfy its constraints. A class structure that satisfies the constraints of an adaptive program is said to customize the program, and is specified as a **class dictionary graph**. Class dictionary graphs and customization of adaptive programs are introduced in Section 1.5.

1.3 ADAPTIVE PROGRAMMING

Conventional object-oriented programs consist of a structural definition in which a class structure is detailed, and a behavioral definition where methods attached to the classes in the class structure are implemented. Likewise, adaptive programs are defined structurally

---

[1] In the remainder of this book we refer to adaptive object-oriented programs simply as adaptive programs.

and behaviorally. What makes an adaptive program different is that class structures are described only partially, by giving a number of constraints that must be satisfied by a customizing class structure. In addition, behavior is not implemented exhaustively. That is, methods in an adaptive program are specified only when they are needed, when they implement an essential piece of behavior. Constraint-based partial specifications can be satisfied by a vast number of class structures which, when annotated with essential methods and automatically generated methods, denote a potentially infinite family of conventional object-oriented programs. This situation is illustrated in Fig. 1.5.

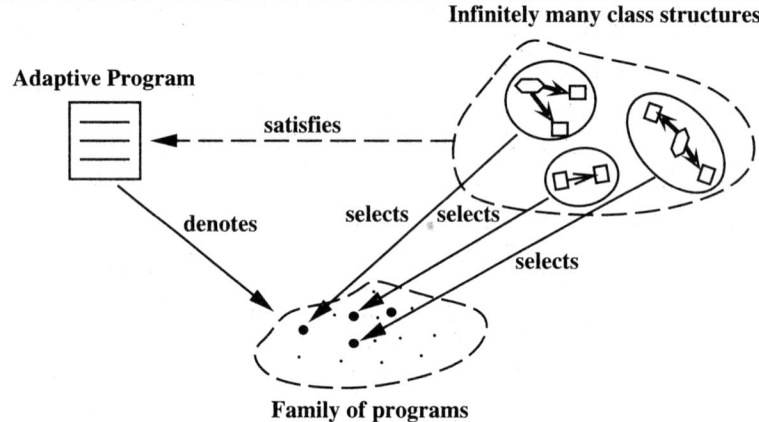

Figure 1.5: An infinite family of programs denoted by an adaptive program

Let us further illustrate the process of writing an adaptive program with an example. We are interested in computing the salaries of the top-level officers in a conglomerate of companies.

Statement of the computeSalary *problem.*

Given a conglomerate object that references the salaries of all officers in the conglomerate, sum up the total salary of only the top-level officers, i.e., the officers that work directly for the head company of the conglomerate and not for any of its subsidiaries.

In fact, the process of writing an adaptive program can be seen as a process of making assumptions. These assumptions are expressed as constraints in the class structures that customize an adaptive program. Such constraints specify groups of collaborating classes in the customizing class structures.

What is important about the computeSalary problem? We assume there is a **Conglomerate** object that contains somewhere inside of it an **Officer** object, which contains a **Salary** object. These assumptions imply that for any class structure to successfully customize the computeSalary adaptive program, it must define a **Company** class that contains a nested **Officer** class, which contains in turn a **Salary** class. In addition, we require that the compute-Salary program must not consider officers in subsidiary companies of the conglomerate. This turns into an assumption that the adaptive program must somehow bypass the relationship subsidiaries of any company in the conglomerate. Thus, the structural section of an adaptive program should specify a number of constraints, expressed using class-valued and relation-valued variables. **Class-valued** variables itemize assumptions on the existence of classes in a customizing class structure. **Relation-valued** variables further restrict customizing class structures by excluding or forcibly including relationships among classes.

Behaviorally, the computeSalary program requires only one essential element, a method that accumulates the salary values for the Conglomerate class. Nevertheless, every other method that constitutes a denoted object-oriented program should share a common signature. In particular, we would like an accumulator totalSalary to be handed to the specified method for update and to be accessible at the completion of the program. This can be done by using a modifiable argument, defined by each method in the program. Thus, the behavioral section of an adaptive program should define a common signature for its methods, and the code fragments that implement the required essential methods, attached to the appropriate class-valued variables.

The table in Fig. 1.6 describes informally the structure of the computeSalary adaptive program. Getting this adaptive program up and running involves the following steps. First, formally specify the program using a new notation that extends existing object-oriented languages; Section 1.4 introduces specification of adaptive programs using the **propagation pattern** notation. See Fig. 1.7. Second, customize the adaptive program with a particular class structure that satisfies the program's constraints; customization is discussed in Section 1.5. We give two different customizers: Fig. 1.8, which selects the C++ program in Fig. 1.9, and Fig. 1.10, which selects the C++ program in Fig. 1.11.

Structural Constraints Section		
Variables		*Constraints*
Type	*Value*	Find all Salary-objects which are contained in Officer objects which are contained in Conglomerate objects but not reachable through the subsidiaries relation.
Class	Conglomerate	
Class	Salary	
Relation	subsidiaries	
Behavioral Section		
Signature	void computeSalary(int& totalSalary)	
Methods	*Attached to*	*Code fragment*
Methods	Salary	totalSalary = totalSalary + *(this->get_value());

Figure 1.6: Informal description of computeSalary adaptive program

Adaptive programming, as would be expected, is realized by delayed binding. We read in the Encyclopedia of Computer Science: "Broadly speaking, the history of software development is the history of ever-later binding time ..." Indeed, in the early days, machine language programmers used to bind variables to memory locations, while assembly language programmers left this task to the assembler. Later on, Pascal programmers bound function calls to code; now C++ programmers have the choice to delay this decision until run-time. Adaptive programming introduces a subsequent degree of delayed binding. While conventional object-oriented programmers bind methods explicitly to classes, adaptive programmers delay binding of methods until a class structure customizer is provided.

1.4 PROPAGATION PATTERNS

An adaptive program is specified using a collection of propagation patterns, each of which specifies a set of related constraints in the adaptive program. Adaptive programs, as we have pointed out, are customized by class structures. Although we cannot assume the composition of a specific customizing class structure,[2] it seems reasonable to assume that it conforms to some given representation. Propagation patterns take advantage of this, assuming that customizing class structures are represented as graphs; specifically, as **class dictionary graphs**.[3] Assumptions, such as a class Conglomerate that contains a nested Salary class, are represented in a propagation pattern as constraints of the form: the traversal from vertex Conglomerate to vertex Salary must be possible in any class dictionary graph that customizes this propagation pattern.

Given a customizing class dictionary graph, a propagation pattern produces an object-oriented program in the family denoted by the adaptive program it specifies. The object-oriented program is produced in two steps. First we generate a subgraph of the class dictionary graph, denoting the set of collaborating classes specified by the structural constraints in the adaptive program. Then, a method is attached to each vertex in the generated subgraph, sharing the signature given by the adaptive program in its behavioral section. Finally, each method specification in the behavioral section—class and code fragment—is used to either fill in or annotate some generated method.

Consider again the adaptive program for computing salaries of officers outlined in the previous section, and summarized in Fig. 1.6. The propagation pattern in Fig. 1.7 specifies this adaptive program, using the following elements.

1. An operation clause. The signature void computeSalary(int& totalSalary), shared by every method that implements the compute salary adaptive program, is specified with the keyword *operation*.

2. A traversal clause. The class-valued variables in the clauses *from* Conglomerate, *via* Officer, *to* Salary specify vertices delimiting a traversal in a customizing class dictionary graph. The relation-valued variable, which in the clause *bypassing* -> *, subsidiaries, * represents an edge in a customizing class dictionary graph, further constrains the traversal to only those paths that do not include the edge. Given a customizing class dictionary graph, the traversal specified by this clause induces a set of vertices representing classes which include the classes in the customizing class dictionary graph that match the class-valued variables in this traversal clause, and any class contained in any path denoted by this traversal clause. Each class in such an

---

[2]That is, how many classes of what kind it has and with how many parts.
[3]Class dictionary graphs are introduced in Section 1.5.

```
*operation* void computeSalary(int& totalSalary)
  *traverse*            // structural constraints section
    *from* Conglomerate
      *bypassing* -> *,subsidiaries,*
      *via* Officer
    *to* Salary
  *wrapper* Salary      // behavioral section
    *prefix*
      (@ totalSalary = totalSalary + *(this->get_value()); @)
```

Figure 1.7: Propagation pattern for the computeSalary adaptive program

induced set of classes gets a method generated automatically, all of which define one object-oriented program in the family denoted by the adaptive program computeSalary.

3. A code fragment clause. The class-valued variable in *wrapper* Salary, indicates that the code totalSalary = totalSalary + *(this->get_value()); fills in the body of the method generated automatically for class Salary. (@ and @) are used to delimit C++ statements.

In general, a propagation pattern consists of an operation clause, a traversal clause, and a set of code fragment clauses. A traversal clause is defined as a set of propagation directives, each of which is a 4-tuple composed of the following elements.

1. A nonempty set of source vertices from which a traversal starts, indicated by the keyword *from*.

2. A possibly empty set of target vertices where a traversal ends, indicated by the keyword *to*.

3. A possibly empty set of through edges, out of which each path denoted by a traversal is required to include at least one. Through edges are indicated by the keyword *through*.

4. A possibly empty set of bypassing edges, none of which may be included in any path denoted by a traversal. Bypassing edges are indicated by the keyword *bypassing*. Through and bypassing edges are specified with relation variables.

A *wrapper* code fragment is associated with a class-valued variable or with a relation-valued variable and can be either *prefix*, or *suffix*. Wrapper code fragments are prefixed or appended to the code that is generated automatically to properly implement traversals, depending on whether the code fragments are *prefix* or *suffix*, respectively.

1.5 CUSTOMIZATION

Adaptive programs, specified using the propagation pattern notation, exist at a higher level of abstraction than conventional object-oriented programs, much in the same way that parameterized classes exist at a more abstract level than nonparameterized or, for that matter, instantiated classes. To select a particular object-oriented program for execution from the family denoted by an adaptive program, the adaptive program must be customized or instantiated, the same way a parameterized class is instantiated. As we have indicated, propagation patterns expect customizing class structures to be represented as class dictionary graphs.

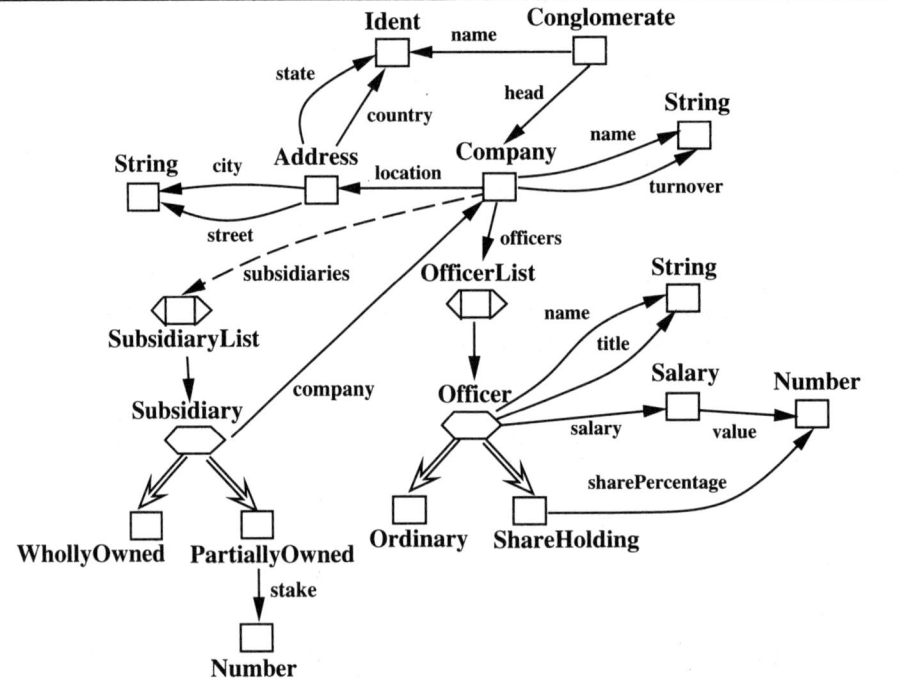

Figure 1.8: Class dictionary graph representing conglomerates of companies

Class dictionary graphs represent class structures at a programming-language independent level using vertices to represent classes, and edges to represent relationships between classes. An example of a class dictionary graph is illustrated in Fig. 1.8.[4] There are three kinds of vertices in a class dictionary graph: construction, alternation, and repetition vertices. The vertex labeled **Conglomerate** is a construction vertex. A **construction** vertex, represented as a rectangle (□), is an abstraction of a class definition in a typical statically typed programming language (e.g., C++).

---

[4]When you run this example with the Demeter Tools/C++, replace String by DemString, Ident by DemIdent, and Number by DemNumber.

1.5. CUSTOMIZATION

The vertex labeled Officer is an alternation vertex. **Alternation** vertices define union classes, and are represented as ◇. When modeling an application domain it is natural to take the union of sets of objects defined by construction classes. Alternation vertices are implemented as abstract classes and their alternatives as subclasses through inheritance. In our example, the vertices labeled Ordinary and ShareHolding are the alternatives of Officer and define classes that inherit from class Officer. The alternative relationship is indicated using **alternation edges** ($\Longrightarrow$), outgoing from an alternation vertex into either a construction or another alternation vertex.

Construction and alternation vertices can have outgoing **construction edges** ($\longrightarrow$), which represent parts. Part is a high-level concept that might be implemented as a method, not necessarily as an instance variable. Construction edges outgoing from alternation vertices indicate common parts, inherited by each alternative of the alternation.

Finally, the vertex labeled SubsidiaryList is a repetition vertex. Repetition vertices represent container classes that have as their instances collections of objects from a given repeated class. Two important advantages of using repetition vertices are that the designer need not be concerned with a class belonging to a collection when designing such a class, and that all the functionality common to container classes, such as iteration, appending, and element count, can be abstracted into a single class.

Let the class dictionary graph in Fig. 1.8 be a customizer for the propagation pattern in Fig. 1.7, which specifies the computeSalary adaptive program. First, we verify that the class dictionary graph satisfies the constraints in the adaptive program. The class dictionary graph does define classes Conglomerate and Salary in such a way that the traversal specified by the propagation pattern is possible. The class dictionary graph in Fig. 1.8 is quite complex compared to the simple propagation pattern in Fig. 1.7. It is very typical that the class dictionary graph contains a lot of noise, which is important for other tasks but irrelevant for the current task.

When a propagation pattern is customized with a class dictionary graph, its traversal specifications induce a set of paths as follows. Every path from each *from* to each *to* vertex in the class dictionary graph is taken. In our example, some of those paths are:

1. Conglomerate $\xrightarrow{head}$ Company $\xrightarrow{officers}$ OfficerList $\longrightarrow$ Officer $\xrightarrow{salary}$ Salary

2. Conglomerate $\xrightarrow{head}$ Company $\xrightarrow{subsidiaries}$ SubsidiaryList $\longrightarrow$ Subsidiary $\xrightarrow{company}$ Company $\xrightarrow{officers}$ OfficerList $\longrightarrow$ Officer $\xrightarrow{salary}$ Salary

The set of paths is restricted to those paths that contain at least one *through* edge and that do not contain any *bypassing* edge. In our example, the path Conglomerate $\xrightarrow{head}$ Company $\xrightarrow{subsidiaries}$ SubsidiaryList $\longrightarrow$ Subsidiary $\xrightarrow{company}$ Company $\xrightarrow{officers}$ OfficerList $\longrightarrow$ Officer $\xrightarrow{salary}$ Salary would be eliminated, since it contains the edge $\xrightarrow{subsidiaries}$, which must not be included. The resulting set of paths defines a subgraph of the customizing class dictionary graph referred to as the **propagation graph** of the customization. The propagation graph induced by the propagation pattern in our example is shown in Fig. 1.9.

This propagation graph also shows the code that defines the object-oriented program selected by the customizing class dictionary graph of Fig. 1.8. Once the propagation graph for a customization is computed, the code attached to it is generated as follows. For each

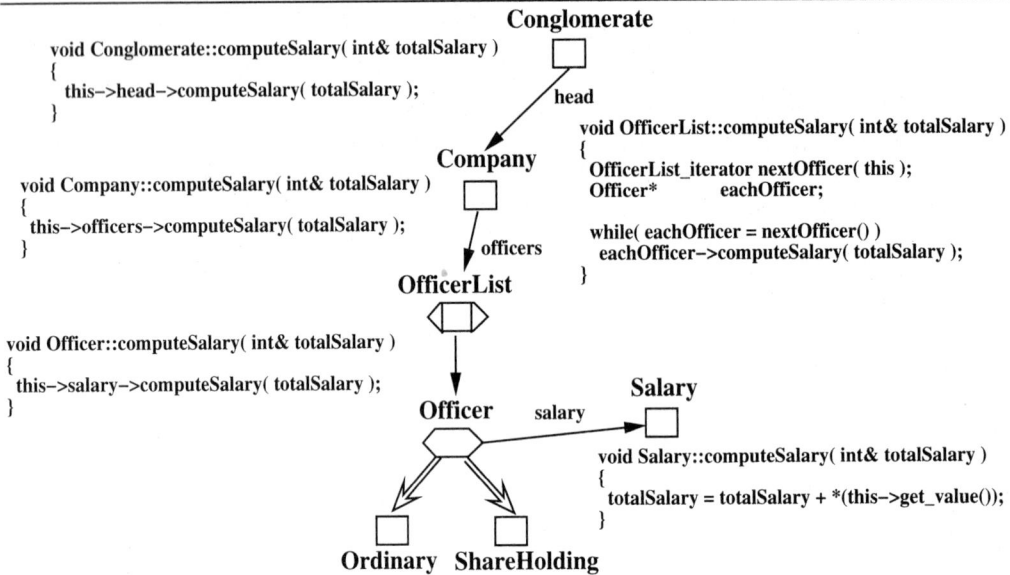

Figure 1.9: Propagation graph for a customization of the computeSalary adaptive program

vertex in the propagation graph, a method is created with the signature given by the operation specification in the propagation pattern. The body for this method contains as many calls as the given vertex has outgoing construction edges in the propagation graph.[5] Each call is made to the method with the same signature attached to the vertex target of the corresponding construction edge. Finally, each wrapper code fragment in the propagation pattern is prefixed or appended to the generated code for the vertex or edge it specifies. When a wrapper is associated to a class-valued variable, the code fragment is prefixed or appended to the entire method generated for the class the variable stands for. Relation-valued variables, implemented as edges, get code generated in the form of a message send to the target of the edge. Wrappers associated with relation-valued variables prefix or append their code to this message-send code.

To further illustrate the adaptiveness of the propagation pattern in Fig. 1.7, consider the class dictionary graph in Fig. 1.10, a second customizer for the propagation pattern. In this customizer, conglomerates have lists of companies with simpler subsidiaries and officers. Again, we verify that this customizer satisfies the constraints posed by the parameters for the adaptive program specified by the propagation pattern. There is a vertex **Conglomerate** from which a traversal is possible to a vertex **Salary**. Hence, this second customizer induces the propagation graph of Fig. 1.11, which is also annotated by the code generated for each vertex.

So far we have discussed customization of adaptive programs using class dictionary graphs. Another possibility is to use sample objects to automatically generate a customiz-

---

[5]Notice, in the propagation graph, as opposed to the class dictionary graph.

1.5. CUSTOMIZATION

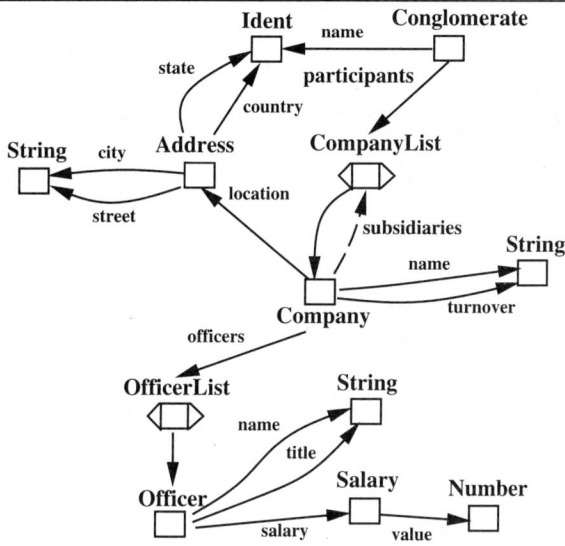

Figure 1.10: Another representation for conglomerates of companies

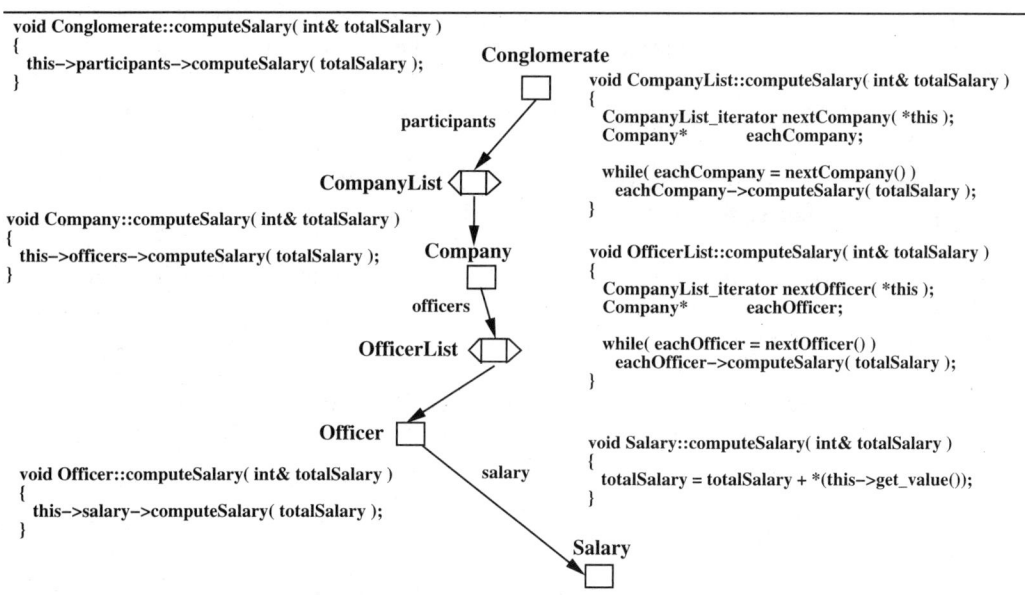

Figure 1.11: Propagation graph with code for second customization

ing class dictionary graph. A technique can be used to generate class dictionary graphs automatically from object samples. This method first generates some class dictionary graph that describes at least those objects given as samples. In a second stage, the method optimizes the generated class dictionary graph by eliminating redundant parts and reducing the amount of multiple inheritance, while preserving the set of objects described by the class dictionary graph.

1.6 SUMMARY

Propagation patterns are motivated by the key idea behind the Law of Demeter. The Law of Demeter essentially says that when writing a method, one should not hardwire the details of the class structure into that method. Propagation patterns take this idea one step further by keeping class structure details out of entire programs as much as possible.

Adaptive programming, realized by the use of propagation patterns, extends the object-oriented paradigm by lifting programming to a higher level of abstraction. In their simplest form, which also turns out to be the worst in terms of adaptiveness, adaptive programs are nothing more than conventional object-oriented programs, where no traversal is used and where every class gets a method explicitly. But, for a large number of applications, represented by related customizers, nothing has to be done to an adaptive program to select the conventional object-oriented program corresponding to any of the customizers. Moreover, when changes to an adaptive program are indeed necessary, they are considerably easier to incorporate given the ability that adaptive programs offer to specify only those elements that are essential and to specify them in a way that allows them to adapt to new environments. This means that the flexibility of object-oriented programs can be significantly improved by expressing them as adaptive programs, which specify them by minimizing their dependency on their class structures.

The following advantages stem from the use of adaptive programs.

- Adaptive programs focus on the essence of a problem to be solved and are therefore simpler and shorter than conventional object-oriented programs.

- Adaptive programs promote reuse. Many behaviors require the same customization and thus customizers are effectively reused. More importantly, every time an adaptive program is customized reuse is taking place.

- There is no run-time performance penalty over object-oriented programs. By using appropriate inlining techniques, traversal methods can be optimized, eliminating apparent performance penalties.

1.7 EXERCISES

Exercise 1.1 (Suitable only if you have previous experience with object-oriented software.) Exercise suggested by Joan Lukas.

Reflect on your experiences with object-oriented programming to see where the disadvantages of object-oriented programming are manifest in your earlier work.

1.8 BIBLIOGRAPHIC REMARKS

- Parts of this chapter are taken from [LSLX94].

- The discussion of adaptive software as collaborating, loosely coupled views has benefitted from discussions with Gregor Kiczales and John Lamping at ECOOP '94 in Bologna, Italy.

- The spiral model [Boe88] supports evolutionary software development.

Chapter 2

Introduction to Object-Oriented Software

In the previous chapter we introduced some basic ideas behind adaptive software. We learned that adaptive software is a generalization of object-oriented software. Adaptive software intends to enhance the advantages of object-oriented software and to eliminate some of its disadvantages. In this chapter we give an introduction to object-oriented software. Readers already familiar with object-oriented concepts may skip to the next chapter.

Let's assume that we have to provide a program that produces a list of cities in Switzerland that have certain properties. Which data do we need? Which operations does the program have to perform?

We will need data structures to represent the structure of the cities. The data structures are encapsulated with functions that provide access to the data. The data is accessible only through the functions, that is, the functions provide an interface to the data. The idea behind encapsulation is that the low-level data structures are hidden and allowed to change more easily without requiring a big maintenance effort. For example, when the internal data type of an encapsulated data structure changes, and the interface stays the same, there is no need to update other parts of the software. Another advantage of encapsulated data structure is that data consistency can be enforced.

We can choose between four different methods for constructing a program.

1. Write the interface of encapsulated data structures first. Then write procedures that refer to the interface of encapsulated data structures

    (a) using detailed information in interfaces of encapsulated data structures

    (b) using minimal information in interfaces of encapsulated data structures.

2. Write procedures first, and in parallel derive

    (a) detailed encapsulated data structures

    (b) constraints on encapsulated data structures with which the procedures work and encapsulated data structures that satisfy the constraints.

1a is used in data-centered software development methods, including in object-oriented methods. 2a is also used in object-oriented methods.

1b and 2b are used in the adaptive software approach described in this book. Adaptive software can be viewed as a higher-level description of object-oriented software. One adaptive program describes a collection of object-oriented programs from which we can select one by giving a specific encapsulated data structures. 1b and 2b are closely related. In 1b we start out with a detailed encapsulated data structure but when we write the program we use only the important information from the data structure that is relevant to the program. Data structure information not relevant to this program, but to some other program, will be ignored. In 2b we formulate the functionality referring only to data structure information that is relevant for the functionality. In the following introductory example we use method 1a. In Chapter 4 and in later chapters, method 2b is used. Adaptive software is usually developed following method 1b.

How can we characterize the object-oriented organization of programs? Using the data to organize the programs is not sufficient to write programs in an object-oriented style. In the object-oriented approach, a program is viewed as a model of reality. Reality consists of physical and mental objects that are mapped directly into programs that are written in the object-oriented style.

Different objects can react differently to the same influence. For example, if we push a stick that has been placed vertically, it will fall. If we give the same push to a thirty foot high tree it will not move. The objects decide how to react to actions or requests. Program objects that are used in object-oriented programming have the same property.

Object-oriented and adaptive programming are important software technologies. They do not replace careful thinking during the design and programming process, but they lead, if used properly, to a significant simplification of the development and maintenance of programs.

An object is either a physical object (e.g., a village) or an abstract object (e.g., a mathematical expression (* 3 5)). In most programming languages that support object-oriented programming, objects are organized into classes. A class defines the structure of the objects that belong to the class.

The following class **Village** describes villages for a tourist office application.

```
CLASS Village HAS PARTS
  name : Text
  inhabitantData : List(Inhabitant)
  numberOfMuseums : DemNumber
  OPTIONAL
    swimmingPools : List(SwimmingPool);
  OPTIONAL
    neighbors : List(Settlement);
END CLASS Village.
```

A village has five parts for the purpose of this application. These parts are called: **name**, **inhabitantData**, **numberOfMuseums**, **swimmingPools** and **neighbors**. The first three parts are compulsory and the last two optional: they do not have to be given in every object of the class.

The parts themselves are defined by classes. For example, the name of a village is given as an object of class Text. The data about the inhabitants is given as an object belonging to class List(Inhabitant). The objects of the class List(Inhabitant) have objects of class Inhabitant as their parts.

Instead of using the verbose notation shown in Fig. 2.3, we use either the graphical notation in Fig. 2.1 or the more succinct notation in Fig. 2.2. Both figures show the notation used by the Demeter Method.[1]

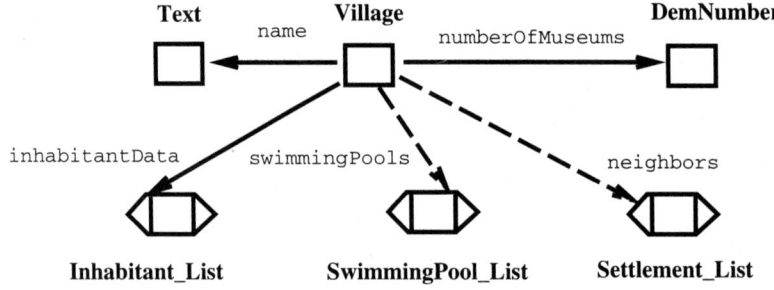

Figure 2.1: Graphical class definition

```
Village =
  <name> Text
  <inhabitantData> List(Inhabitant)
  <numberOfMuseums> DemNumber
  [<swimmingPools> List(SwimmingPool)]
  [<neighbors> List(Settlement)].
```

Figure 2.2: Textual class definition

A class can be used as a cookie cutter to cut an object. For example, we can use the class Village to construct the village called Ebnat. We have to provide the information for

---

[1] Class dictionary graph graphical representation, page 431 (6). This is a reference to an instructional objective in Chapter 14, the "nerve center" of the book. See also the explanation on page xxx.

the required parts of a village: the name, the data about the inhabitants, and the number of museums.

Classes are organized hierarchically in object-oriented and adaptive programming. For example, the class **Village** and the class **Town** have a common ancestor class that we call **Settlement**. Villages and towns have many commonalities that are defined for class **Settlement**. Fig. 2.3 shows class **Settlement** and its subclasses.

```
CLASS Settlement IS EITHER
    Village OR Town
  COMMON PARTS
    name : Text
    inhabitantData : List(Inhabitant)
    numberOfMuseums : DemNumber
    OPTIONAL
      swimmingPools : List(SwimmingPool);
    OPTIONAL
      neighbors : List(Settlement);
END CLASS Settlement.

CLASS Village HAS PARTS
END CLASS Village.

CLASS Town HAS PARTS
  universityData : List(University)
END CLASS Town.
```

Figure 2.3: Class settlement and subclasses

Class **Town** has all the parts of class **Settlement** and additionally a part called universityData. Class **Village** has only the parts of class **Settlement**. We still need to express functionality specific to villages.

In this context object-oriented programming uses the concept of inheritance. We say that the class **Town** and the class **Village** inherit from class **Settlement**. A descendant class inherits the parts of the ancestor class. The values of the parts may be different for each object. The descendant classes also inherit all the operations of the ancestor class.

Instead of using the verbose notation shown in Fig. 2.3, we use either the graphical notation in Fig. 2.4 or the more succinct notation in Fig. 2.5.

So far we have dealt with the structure of objects; that is, we considered their composition from parts. Now we focus on the functionality of objects. Objects can react to requests. A request consists of a name that describes a command and a list of arguments. An example of a request is (we may send such a request to a **Town**-object):

```
determine_neighbors_larger_than(7000)
```

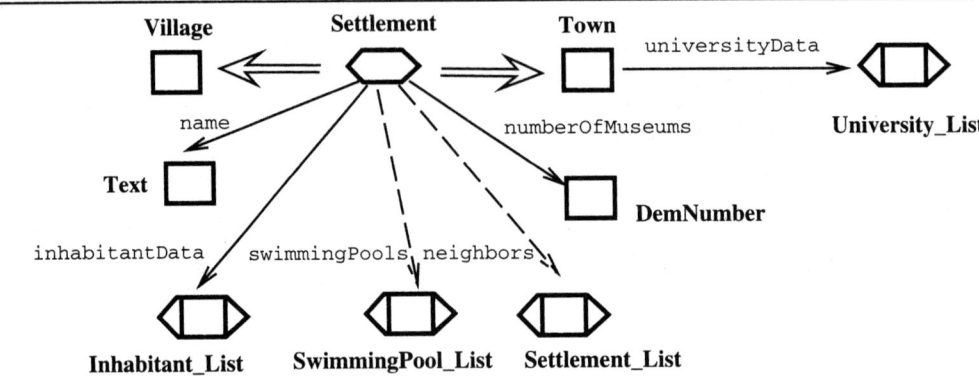

Figure 2.4: Graphical alternation class definition

```
Settlement :
    Village | Town
  *common*
    <name> Text
    <inhabitantData> List(Inhabitant)
    <numberOfMuseums> DemNumber
    [<swimmingPools> List(SwimmingPool)]
    [<neighbors> List(Settlement)].

Village = .

Town =
  <universityData> List(University).
```

Figure 2.5: Textual alternation class definition

A request has a signature that defines all similar requests. A signature consists of a function name, arguments with argument types and a return type. The signature of the above request is

```
List(Settlement)   // return type
  determine_neighbors_larger_than(int NumberOfStudents)
```

To implement a signature, we need a set of collaborating classes. For the above signature, we need only class **Settlement**. The request determine_neighbors_larger_than(7000) can be sent to a settlement (e.g., Lexington), which is stored in the variable **TownVariable**. More precisely, **TownVariable** is a pointer variable that points to a storage location containing the **Town**-object.

```
TownVariable ->
  determine_neighbors_larger_than(7000)
```

This invocation (written in C++ syntax) returns a list of settlements that are neighbors of town Lexington and have more than 7000 inhabitants.

Objects are stored in the storage device of a computer. The parts of an object are often not objects themselves, but pointers to other objects. Conversely, this means that an object can be a part of several objects. For example, the objects Concord and Winchester contain in their list of neighbors a pointer to the town Lexington. This means that Lexington is a part of two different objects.

Pointers to objects are not only stored in parts of objects, but also in so-called variables that are needed for the computations. We have already seen an example: the variable **TownVariable**. A variable can be viewed as a container that can store pointers to objects of some class. For example, **SettlementVariable** is a variable that can store either a pointer to a village or a town.

The invocation

```
SettlementVariable ->
  determine_neighbors_larger_than(7000)
```

returns a list of settlements that are neighbors of the object to which **SettlementVariable** points and that count over 7000 inhabitants. How the list is computed is independent of whether a town or village is in the variable. We see here a big advantage of inheritance. Functionality, which is useful for both towns and villages, has to be defined only once for settlements.

Now we consider an example where the computation is different for towns and villages. We implement for class **Settlement** the operation with signature

```
Boolean Settlement::has_university_with_more_than (int NumberOfStudents)
```

This operation computes whether a settlement has a university with a certain number of students. To implement this functionality, we need the collaboration of three classes: besides **Settlement**, we also need **Village** and **Town**. For a village the computation is simple: we always give the answer no since in our model (see the definitions of classes **Village** and **Town** in Fig. 2.5) a village cannot have a university.

```
Boolean Village::has_university_with_more_than (int NumberOfStudents)
  {return False;}
```

For a town, the computation needs to request a service from **universityData** to determine whether the town has a university with more than **NumberOfStudents**.

```
Boolean Town::has_university_with_more_than (int NumberOfStudents)
  {return universityData ->
    more_than(NumberOfStudents);}
```

Now we consider the invocation

```
SettlementVariable ->
  has_university_with_more_than(10000)
```

This invocation first determines whether **SettlementVariable** contains a pointer to a town or a village and depending on the answer, the code of the town or the village class is activated.

Here we see an important property of object-oriented programs: delayed operation selection. A request of a service can activate one of several operations. The operation selected depends on the value of the variable at run-time.

2.1 CONCEPTS

Object-oriented programming was made popular initially by the programming language *Smalltalk* [GR83], developed at Xerox PARC, but the important concepts of object-oriented programming were, however, already present in the programming language *Simula 67*. There are three major ideas in object-oriented programming.

1. *Modularity, Information hiding*: Objects define programs. Each object is in relation with other objects and has behavior associated with it. The relations with other objects are often conveniently stored as local values. In some object-oriented systems, objects are defined in terms of classes. A class defines the information that is stored in the objects of that class as well as the operations, implemented as methods, that define behavior. Many object-oriented systems allow **information hiding**; that is, the detailed low-level definitions may be hidden from the user of an object and are only accessible to the implementor.

    The software is organized around objects rather than operations. This usually leads to a more stable software architecture since the object structure is usually more stable than the functionality.

2. *Method resolution, delayed method selection*: Behavior is invoked by requesting a service from an object. The request will activate one or several methods. **Dynamic method selection** determines which method to activate at run-time, depending on the object arguments that were given to the operation or depending on the object to which the request was sent.

3. *Sharing*: An object can utilize behavior that appears in other already defined objects. There are two approaches to **sharing**: The class hierarchy approach and the prototype approach. In the class hierarchy approach, object classes are organized in a hierarchy to avoid duplication of information. Descriptions of objects may be inherited from more general classes. Inheritance also opens the way to numerous method combining techniques. In the prototype approach, an object can share information with a prototype. Any object can serve as a prototype. To create an object that shares information with a prototype, you construct an extension object containing a list of prototypes and personal information idiosyncratic to the object. The notion of sharing is critically associated with object-oriented programming.

Although these three notions seem straight-forward, their combination creates a programming style that revolutionizes software development. **Dynamic method selection** as well as **sharing** help to reduce the size of object-oriented programs.

The object-oriented programming style can be used in any programming language, even in assembly language. Many languages support object-oriented programming directly.

For most of the object-oriented programming in this book we use the class hierarchy approach since it is the most appropriate for our applications. However the prototype approach is superior in some cases, for example, for applications where the sharing relationships are dynamically changing. An example of such an application is knowledge engineering with learning. The learning is implemented by changing sharing relationships as well as adjusting weight parameters.

This book promotes primarily the adaptive programming style with the object-oriented programming style as a special case. Other approaches to programming are also important.

Functional programming

This style is supported by languages such as Scheme (a dialect of Lisp) and to some degree by Common Lisp. In pure functional programming, functions are without side effects, and they are treated as *first class objects*. This means that they can be computed and passed around like numerical values. For example, a function can be assigned to a variable or a function call may return a function, etc. Examples of functional languages are Hope, FP, Haskell.

Constraint-based programming

This style is supported by languages such as Prolog or by algebraic specification languages. Constraint-based programming promotes the point of view that a programmer should specify only the constraints that the solution must satisfy. This relieves the programmer from giving a detailed algorithm to find a solution. In this book we will study constraint-based programming by discussing interpreters for subsets of Prolog.

Grammar-based programming

This style is supported by adaptive programming. Grammar-based programming promotes the point of view that data structures are grammars. In grammar-based programming, grammars are used not only to define languages and corresponding parsers, but also for defining all data structures. In this book we will make heavy use of the grammar-based approach.

The constraint-based and grammar-based styles are naturally combinable with the object-oriented style. The theory of functional programming is used to better understand object-oriented programming.

2.1.1 Abstractions

The way people deal with complexity is by abstraction. The goal of abstraction is to factor out recurring patterns for later use. Abstraction hides details. Three abstractions that are almost second nature to the way we think are

- an-instance-of abstraction
- a-subclass-of abstraction
- a-part-of abstraction (association)

We recognize certain properties as being true of all elephants, for instance. Therefore we need not postulate those properties separately of each individual elephant. In our terminology, each elephant is **an-instance-of** the class ELEPHANT, and therefore has four legs, a tail, a trunk, etc. ELEPHANT is **a-subclass-of** ANIMAL and we can therefore modularize our knowledge further. Those things that are true of all animals we need not repeat specifically for lions, cats, dogs, etc. Finally, the left leg of an elephant is **a-part-of** the elephant as a whole, so if the elephant moves to the other side of a river, we can assume that his leg does also; we need not record separate position information, except relative position information, for each piece of the elephant. In each case the abstractions have allowed us to modularize and organize our knowledge, considerably simplifying the knowledge representation.

Part-of abstractions are subdivided into associations (any kind of binary relationship between two classes) and physical part-of relationships. For example, the owner of an elephant is not a physical part of the elephant. However the leg is a physical part.

2.1.2 Classes, Methods, and Delayed Binding

We introduce object-oriented programming with a simple example that demonstrates the main ideas. We demonstrate the concepts in a language-independent way using our own notation.

Consider the following simple task: Given a box containing several objects, each one having a weight, we need a program that returns the total weight of all the objects in the box plus the weight of the box. When we write the operation for adding the weights, we do not know what kind of objects may be in the box. In other words, we would like to write the operation for adding the weights in a generic way that is independent of the classes of the objects in the box. For every object in the box we need a mechanism to compute the weight of the object. We do this by invoking a weight operation that takes an object as an argument. This operation first determines the class of the object and, depending on the class, it then calls the appropriate function to compute the weight. Such an operation is called a **generic** or **virtual** operation. The weight computation may be individualized for each class. Suppose our box contains a pencil and a sponge. Therefore we consider the classes in Fig. 2.6 which shows an example of a class dictionary graph.

2.1. CONCEPTS

```
CLASS Object IS EITHER
   Pencil Or Sponge
END CLASS Object.

CLASS Pencil HAS PARTS
   weight : Weight
END CLASS Pencil.

CLASS Sponge HAS PARTS
   waterWeight, spongeMaterialWeight : Weight
END CLASS Sponge.

CLASS Weight HAS PARTS
   val : DemNumber
END CLASS Weight.
```

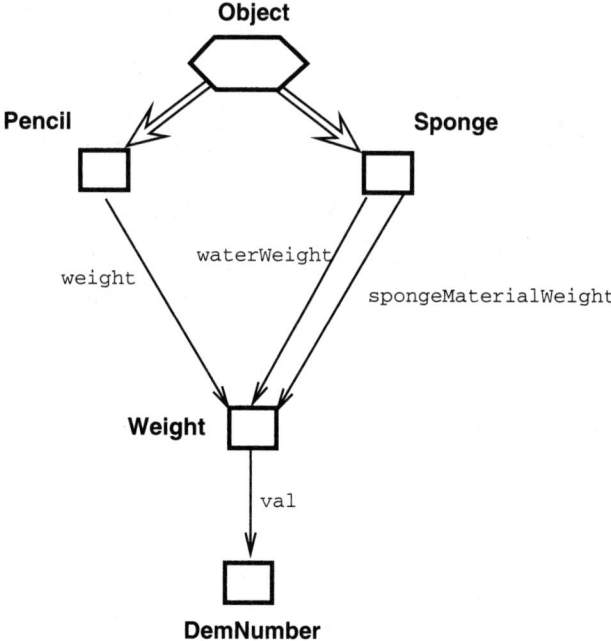

Figure 2.6: Class dictionary graph

A class defines a type but not necessarily vice versa. The type concept is more general than the class concept. We say that a variable is of class C if it can contain only objects of class C. When a variable is of type T, where T is a type defined in some programming language, the variable may contain only T values that are legal with respect to the programming language. But those values might not behave like objects of a class. We maintain this distinction between types and classes since we want to work with programming languages that support both object-oriented and traditional programming.

To make programming easier, we use two kinds of classes: **concrete** classes, such as Village and **abstract** classes, such as Settlement. An abstract class must have subclasses but cannot directly create instances, whereas a concrete class must have instances but cannot have subclasses. For example, concrete class Town is a subclass of abstract class Settlement and Lexington is an instance of concrete class Town.

To talk about objects, we use the following synonymous statements interchangeably for any class C:

- An object belongs to class C
- An object is a member of class C

Those statements can also be used for abstract classes. An object belongs to class C if it is an instance of a concrete subclass of class C. The statement: "An object is an instance of class C" can be used only when C is a concrete class.

We store the weight of the pencil inside of each object belonging to class Pencil. Therefore, computing the weight of a pencil is easy: we return the value of the **part variable** weight. As a synonym to part variable we use **data member** or **instance variable** or slot.

A class can have any number of part variables. They serve to store the local state of an object. Each part variable has a type (which might be a class) that describes the set of values or objects the part variable can contain. This type information is used for improving both the reliability and efficiency of the program. The type of a variable is first checked before executing a program (static type checking) and, if necessary, during execution (dynamic type checking).

A class can be considered as the direct product of the types of the part variables (ignoring the methods). Each component of the direct product is named. In this context, an object of a class is an element of the direct product given in the class definition. For example, the class Sponge can be viewed as the direct product Weight × Weight. The first component is called waterWeight and the second spongeMaterialWeight and an object is a pair, for example (waterWeight = 20, spongeMaterialWeight = 5).

We use the following notation for attaching a method to the classes Pencil and Weight. The weight is returned in a reference argument, assumed to be initialized with 0.

```
void Pencil::add_weight(int& w)
  {weight -> add_weight(w);}
void Weight::add_weight(int& w)
  {w = val + w;}
```

The class Sponge describes all sponges. In each instance of the class Sponge we store separately the weight of the water in the sponge and the weight of the sponge material itself. To compute the weight of the sponge, we have to add these two weights. Formally, we write:

2.1. CONCEPTS

```
void Sponge::add_weight(int& w)
  { waterWeight -> add_weight(w);
    spongeMaterialWeight -> add_weight(w); }
```

In a compiled language such as C++, it is also necessary to define an operation for class Object.

```
void Object::add_weight(int& w) = 0 //pure virtual
```

The = 0 means that the implementation must be defined in subclasses, here in Pencil and Sponge. The operation is said to be pure virtual or deferred.

Any of the weight methods we have defined can be called by the operation invocation (function call) x -> add_weight (...), where the value of variable x is either an object of the Pencil class, the Sponge class, or the Weight class. x may be declared as a variable of class Object. In this case, the function call will select either the code in class Pencil or in class Sponge, depending on whether a Pencil-object or a Sponge-object is in x. add_weight is called a virtual function in C++.

Next we define the class that represents all boxes. The local state of a box is a list of all objects contained in the box, the box name, and the box weight.

```
Box =
  <boxName> DemIdent
  <boxWeight> Weight
  <objects> List(Object).
```

Now it is easy to define an operation that returns the sum of the weights of the pencils and sponges contained in a box plus the weight of the box. We consider each object in the list that is the value of the part objects, and we add up the weights.

```
void Box::add_weight(int& w)
  { boxWeight -> add_weight(w);
    objects -> add_weight(w); }

void List(Object)::add_weight(int& w)
  { for each object in this
      object -> add_weight(w);}
```

This implementation for class List(Object) is independent of sponges and pencils: It works for any box that contains objects for which an add_weight operation is defined. This contrasts with procedural code where there would be a switch or case statement that checks whether we have a pencil or a sponge. We have already achieved our goal of writing a generic operation for adding up the weights of the objects in a box.

Notice how regular the preceding code is: we call the operation add_weight for the parts of every object. Later we will exploit this observation by generating most of this code automatically.[2] To achieve this code regularity, however, we had to give up our habit of using operations which return a result! Instead we use an operation with a reference argument. To make progress, we have to *give up some old habits*.

---
[2]Propagation pattern partial evaluation, page 448 (64).

2.1.3 Overloading and Delayed Binding

Most programming languages provide overloading of operators and some languages even allow the user to overload operators. Consider the following Pascal expressions: (1.0 + a) and (1 + b) where a and b are of type integer. The two addition operations will activate different code: The first will activate a routine for adding real numbers and the second will activate a routine for adding integers. In other words, the types of the arguments of the addition operator will determine which routines to call.

In object-oriented languages such as C++, most functions may be overloaded. For example, we may have two functions named f for the same class A.

```
void A::f(int& s){ ... }
int A::f(){ ... }
```

As in the Pascal case, the compiler will determine from the context of the arguments, which f is intended. For example, a call a -> f(i) must be a call of the first f and int b = f() must be a call of the second f.

Overloading of functions is a different concept from virtual functions that delay the binding of calls to code. In overloading, the types are used to disambiguate at compile-time. But with virtual functions, the type of the object contained in a variable at run-time will disambiguate. In both the overloading and virtual function cases, types are used to disambiguate at compile-time or run-time, respectively.

2.1.4 Reduced Dependencies

The weight addition example demonstrates another important property of object-oriented programming : modularity. Each class defines the local state of its objects and the methods that operate on this data. This is a well proven technique that is also available in languages that do not directly support object-oriented programming (e.g., modules in Modula-2 or packages in Ada).

Modularity combined with delayed method selection yields a flexible mechanism for decoupling software. Consider two programmers who implement the above weight addition program. One programmer is responsible for writing the code for class List(Object) and the other for all the other classes. The two programmers do not have to agree on a list of subclasses of Object that will be supported. In a straight-forward Pascal program for the weight addition problem it would be necessary to communicate the list of subclasses, since the programmer of the List(Object)-code would have to include the class information in a case statement. Object-oriented programming makes it easier to make software pieces more independent.

The object-oriented approach also makes it easier to update software. If we add another class of box objects, we do not have to modify the existing software. We just have to *add* a class definition and a weight method.

2.1.5 Sharing

Next we want to demonstrate the sharing aspects of object-oriented programming. We assume that most objects in a box are unstructured and have an explicit part variable for storing the weight. It would be inconvenient to have to define the weight part as well as

2.1. CONCEPTS

a method for accessing it for each such object. Therefore we introduce a new class called UnstructuredObject which has a part weight.

```
UnstructuredObject : // subclasses
  *common* <weight> Weight.
```

We attach a method to this class that returns the value of the part weight.

```
void UnstructuredObject::add_weight(int& w)
  { weight -> add_weight(w);}
```

We **inherit** from this class in all object classes that are considered to be unstructured objects. All the functionality that is defined for the UnstructuredObject class is also available in the classes in which we inherit from UnstructuredObject. Specifically, in every class that inherits from the class UnstructuredObject there will be a part called weight. Furthermore, every class that inherits from the unstructured object class will know how to compute the weight of an object of the class.

We redefine the Pencil class using inheritance

```
Pencil = .
UnstructuredObject : Pencil.
  *common* <weight> Weight.
```

The first line means that Pencil has no immediate parts anymore. The second and third lines mean that Pencil now inherits from class UnstructuredObject.

This notation is different from conventional object-oriented notation. Inheritance relationships are usually expressed in the other direction, such as

```
CLASS Pencil HAS PARTS
  INHERITS FROM CLASS UnstructuredObject;
END CLASS Pencil.
```

In other words, the normal notation lists the immediate superclasses for each class while we list the subclasses for each superclass. Both notations convey the same information but there are several advantages to our notation, such as the capability to define application-specific object languages (see Chapter 11). However, our notation does require that a superclass be modified when a subclass is added.

We call class Pencil a subclass of class UnstructuredObject. Every object of the Pencil class will have its own part weight.

This is an appropriate point to introduce the concept of instantiation and to compare it with the membership concept. An object is an instance of a class C if it has been created with the instantiation function of the system using C as an argument. Such a function is typically called **new** or **make-instance**. For an example of the use of new, see page 33. Some object-oriented languages use factory objects or constructor functions for creating an object. If an object is an instance of class C it belongs to class C but the opposite is not necessarily true. For example, an instance of class Pencil belongs to class UnstructuredObject, but it is not an instance of class UnstructuredObject. This class is viewed as an *abstract class*;

that is, a class that cannot be instantiated. No object can be an instance of such a class; it can only belong to that class.

The concept of inheritance allows an object to belong to several classes. For example, an instance of class **Pencil** belongs to both the class **Pencil** and the class **UnstructuredObject**. If we inherit a method m from some class but we don't want that method in the specific subclass, it is possible to override the inherited method by defining a method with name m attached to the subclass.

There are situations where we would like to inherit from several classes. Let's assume that all the objects in a box also belong to a class called **Contained**. This class has a part called contained_in that allows us to store the containing object. The purpose of the contained_in variable is to point back to the box. If we have several objects distributed in several boxes, we can use the contained_in variable for finding out in which box the object resides. We assume that an object can be in at most one box.

Class **Contained** is defined by

```
Contained : //subclasses
  *common* [<contained_in> Universal]. // anytype
```

From now on we assume that for each part an **accessing** method and a **setting** method are automatically defined. For a part x the accessing method is also called get_x and the setting method is called set_x. The setting method takes a second argument that defines how the part is set. We inherit now from two classes in the definition of the **Pencil** class.

```
Pencil = .
UnstructuredObject : Pencil.
  *common* <weight> Weight.
Contained : Pencil
  *common* [<contained_in> Universal].
```

In ordinary object-oriented notation this would be written as

```
CLASS Pencil HAS PARTS
  INHERITS FROM CLASSES
    UnstructuredObject, Contained;
END CLASS Pencil.
```

The contained_in variable will be set with the following code:

```
void Box::define_contained_in()
  { objects -> define_contained_in(this);}
void List(Object)::define_contained_in(Box* b)
  { for each object in this // not legal C++ code (pseudo code)
      object ->  set_contained_in(b);}
```

This example shows the concept of multiple inheritance, which is available in most object-oriented programming languages.

The define_contained_in method uses the variable this (some programming languages use self instead of this). this is defined inside a method definition and its value is the object for which the method is called.

Operator	DemIdent	DemNumber	Compound
eval	code for identifiers	code for numbers	code for compound expressions

Table 2.1: Objects and operations

2.1.6 Making Instances

Finally, we need a mechanism to build a box with some objects in it. We assume that we have a generic operation **new** for creating an instance of a class. The first argument to **new** is a class name that specifies for which class to create an object. The remaining arguments specify how to initialize the parts of the instance.

To set up a box containing two pencils with weight 10 and 12, a sponge with water weight 20, and sponge material weight 5 we use the following assignment:

```
box_instance =
  new Box("secret-box",                   // boxName
          new Weight(new DemNumber(5)),   // boxWeight
          new List(Object) (              // objects
            new Pencil(new Weight(new DemNumber(10))),
            new Pencil(new Weight(new DemNumber(12))),
            new Sponge
               //waterWeight
                    (new Weight(new DemNumber(20))),
               //spongeMaterialWeight
                    new Weight(new DemNumber(5))))
```

This assignment sets the value of the variable box_instance to a specific instance of the Box class.

The notation we have used in these examples attempts to stay as close as possible to either the C++ notation or the notations used in the Demeter Method. But the concepts presented are intended to be programming-language independent.

2.2 EASE OF EVOLUTION

As an example, consider the evaluation of simple prefix expressions. For this example, a prefix expression is either an identifier (e.g., speed), a number (e.g., 3), or a compound prefix expression (e.g., (* 7 9)). A compound prefix expression consists of two prefix expressions, preceded by an operator that can be either multiplication or addition. In this simple example we can identify five object classes: the class of identifiers (DemIdent), the class of numbers (DemNumber), the class of compound prefix expressions (Compound), the class consisting only of the multiplication symbol (MulSym), and the class consisting only of the addition symbol (AddSym). The operation that we want to perform is evaluation (abbreviated eval). Let's consider Table 2.1, "Objects and operations," which shows a table of three object classes and one operation. In procedural programming we would write a one-argument function for evaluation that would look like

```
int eval(Exp* expression)
  {switch (expression -> kind())
    case DemIdent: ...
    case DemNumber: ...
    case Compound:   ... }
```

This function contains a conditional statement to distinguish between the three possible types of the argument. In other words, in procedural programming the objects versus operations table is encoded into one function. This contrasts with object-oriented programming where the objects and operations table is encoded into several functions. With the **DemNumber** class, for example, we will define a method **eval**, which defines how a number is evaluated. A key difference between procedural and object-oriented programming is that in object-oriented programming the code is broken into smaller pieces. In the above example we get three small pieces of code in the object-oriented version and one bigger piece in the procedural approach.

The delayed method selection mechanism of object-oriented programming allows the implementation of generic operations. Consider the problem of evaluating a compound prefix expression. We want to write this evaluation method in a generic way so that it will work for expressions independent of the operator involved. Therefore we store the evaluation instructions with the operator. The evaluation method for the class of compound prefix expressions will then simply request the operator to evaluate. If we want to add more operators later on (e.g., division) we only have to provide an additional method for the division operator. In procedural programming we would have to perform procedure surgery to add an additional operator.

2.3 TERMINOLOGY

Since the area of object-oriented programming draws on three fields (Programming Languages, Artificial Intelligence, and Databases), a large number of synonyms are used. Here we give some of the (approximate) synonyms and some of their sources. OMG stands for Object Management Group. We adopt some of their terminology.

- Collections of persistent data: knowledge base, database, object base.

- Collections of classes: schema (database), concept map (AI), concept hierarchy (AI), class dictionary, class hierarchy.

- For collections of related objects: class (Simula, Smalltalk, C++, CLOS, Eiffel), structure (C++)), flavor (Flavors), concept (AI), entity set.

- For naming the parts: instance variable (Smalltalk, Flavors), slot (CLOS, frame-based systems), feature (Eiffel), data member (C++), role (KL-ONE), part (Demeter), attribute (OMG), local state variable.

- For functionality pieces: method (Smalltalk, Flavors, CLOS, OMG), member function or friend function (C++), routine (Eiffel), operation (OMG).

- For functionality groups: message (Smalltalk, Eiffel), virtual function (C++), generic function (CLOS, New Flavors).

- For making instances: instantiation function (Flavors, CLOS), constructor function (C++), factory class message (Objective-C), class message (Smalltalk).

- For guaranteeing the existence of functionality at lower levels (in statically typed systems): deferred routine (Eiffel), pure virtual member function (C++).

- Class variable (Smalltalk, Objective-C), shared slot (CLOS), static data member (C++).

- Entity, object, class instance.

- Is-a link (semantic networks), inheritance link.

- Class A is a derived class of base class B (C++), class A is a subclass class of class B (Smalltalk), class A inherits from class B (Flavors).

2.4 CONVENTIONS

Adaptive software is based on the concepts of propagation patterns and sentences that are both customized by class dictionaries. A terminology and a set of symbols are needed to explain the concepts of propagation patterns, class dictionaries, and sentences. The terminology is summarized in the glossary chapter.

We use the following conventions throughout the book:

- Verbatim and sanserif fonts are used to represent programming and design notations.

  For example, a class definition is given by

  `Company = <divisions> List(Division).`

  If we refer to the above class in the text, we use sanserif font: "A Company-object consists of one part ... " which looks similar to verbatim font.

- Italics font is used for emphasis and for mathematical symbols.

  For example: "A **propagation directive** consists of a triple (F;c;T), where F and T are class-valued variables ..." Here, F, c, and T are in italics since they are mathematical symbols for sets.

- Boldface font is used for newly defined terms.

  For example: "A **propagation directive** consists of ..."

The comment character in design and programming notations as well as in sentences is `//` (borrowed from C++). The comment starts with `//` and goes to the end of the line.

2.4.1 Symbol Usage

In naming design objects such as class dictionaries and propagation patterns, we try to use symbols consistently as shown in Fig. 2.7. Consistent symbol use allows you to recognize an object by its symbol only. The primary columns indicate which symbols are used in the Demeter theory. They are typically greek symbols. The book primarily uses symbols in the secondary columns since we don't want to burden you with Greek symbols. The first letter in the two single columns indicates the main designation (e.g., a class dictionary graph's main designation is G).

Demeter Terminology		
Object	Primary	Secondary
Class dictionary	$\Delta;\Theta$	D, E
Class dictionary graph	$\Gamma;\Psi$	G, H
Semi-class dictionary graph	$\Sigma;\Upsilon$	S, T
Class dictionary graph slice	$\Pi;\Xi$	P, Q
Graph vertices	v, w, u, x, y	as primary
Graph edges	e, d	as primary
Set of labels	Λ	
Particular labels	l, k	as primary
Propagation pattern	pp,p,q	as primary
Propagation directive	d,e	as primary
Object graph	$\Omega;\Phi$	O, N, I
Object identifiers	i, j	as primary
Object graph vertices	o, p, m, n	as primary

Figure 2.7: Symbol use

2.5 EXERCISES

You are encouraged to follow the exercises in the self-study guide in Chapter 17.

Exercise 2.1 Consider the following specification: Given an A-object, print all C-objects that are contained in the A-object, and for each such C-object, print all E-objects contained in the C-object (and A-object).

A B-object is contained in an A-object if the B-object can be reached from the root of the A-object following zero or more part-of relationships.

Do the following:

- For each of the following programs (Program 1 and Program 2), give an example of an input for which they fail to meet the specification above.

2.5. EXERCISES

- Then correct each program by making minimal changes.

- Can you identify a generic reason for the failure of program 2? Can you give a property which the specification must satisfy with respect to the class structure so that this kind of failure cannot happen?

The programming language which we use here supports dynamic binding, overloading and inheritance. Functions attached to superclasses are assumed to be dynamically bound.

The methods f below are supposed to implement the above specification. A::f means that method f is attached to class A. a->f() is a call of function f for variable a.

Note: Program 1 is harder to repair than program 2. You might want to do first program 2.

- Program 1:

  Class structure:

  ```
  A   HAS PART <b : B> .
  B   HAS PARTS <c : C>  <e : E>.
  C   HAS PART <c1 : C1>.
  C1  HAS SUBCLASSES D AND A.
  E   HAS NO PARTS.
  D   HAS NO PARTS.
  ```

  Methods:

  ```
  void A::f( )
  { get_b()->f( ); }

  void B::f( )
  { get_c()->f( );
    get_e()->f( ); }

  void C::f( )
  { print(); get_c1()->f( ); }

  void C1::f( )
  { }

  void E::f( )
  { print(); }
  ```

- Program 2:

  Class structure:

```
A   HAS PART <b2 : B2>.
B2 HAS PART <x : X>.
X HAS SUBCLASSES C AND F.
F HAS SUBCLASS E.
C HAS PART <e : E>.
E HAS NO PARTS.
```

Methods:

```
void A::f( )
{ get_b2()->f( ); }

void B2::f( )
{ get_x()->f( ); }

void X::f( )
{ }

void C::f( )
{ print(); get_e()->f( );}

void E::f( )
{ print(); }
```

This question shows some of the pitfalls awaiting object-oriented programmers: Both programs are the "obvious" solution to the above specification, but unfortunately, they are both wrong.

2.6 BIBLIOGRAPHIC REMARKS

- Object-oriented programming: Object-oriented programming is promoted and supported by Simula-67 [DMN70], Smalltalk-80 [GR83], Flavors [Moo86], Objective-C [Cox86], C++ [Str86], CLOS [BMG+88], Eiffel [Mey88], and many other languages. The implementation of the Demeter Tools/C++ is written in its own technology, primarily with propagation patterns, and generates C++ code [LHSLX92]. An earlier prototype implementation used Flavors and an extension of Lisp [Lie88, LR88b].

  Here is a list of programming languages that support the object-oriented paradigm. The list is far from exhaustive.

  class hierarchy approach
  Smalltalk [GR83], Flavors [Moo86], Objective-C [Cox86], Loops, C++ [Str94], OBJVLISP [BC86], CLOS [BDG+88].

  prototype approach
  Self [US87], Actors [HB77, Agh86], T [Rees (1985)].

2.6. BIBLIOGRAPHIC REMARKS

combined class hierarchy and prototype approach
    NewtonScript by Apple Computer [Evi94], Exemplars [LTP86, LaL89].

Some of the important approaches to object-oriented programming are discussed in [Weg87].

- Metaphors: The "growing" metaphor was used by [Mil71],[Bro87]. The GARDEN system developed at Brown by Reiss [Rei87] also uses the gardening metaphor.

Chapter 3

From C++ to Demeter

In this introduction we give an example that demonstrates some of the advantages of adaptive object-oriented software over C++ software. This chapter is hands-on and both design and programming oriented to show you how adaptive software is *softer* than ordinary software. The general principles behind adaptive software are explained in Chapter 4.

We are going to introduce a notation to describe C++ programs. This notation is an extension of C++ with a small language to describe object-oriented designs. The design notation has two components: a behavioral component and a structural component. The behavioral design notation describes only incomplete C++ programs since it is a design notation. The same is true for the structural design notation: it describes only incomplete C++ programs. A very nice property of our design notation is that a behavioral design can be completed with a structural design to form an executable C++ program.

A behavioral design outlines how the object-oriented program should be built when a completing structural design is presented. Of course, the behavioral design has to make some assumption about the completing structural design, but usually infinitely many structural designs can complete a behavioral design. The completion mechanism will be demonstrated with several examples in this chapter.

To introduce adaptive software quickly, we rely on your knowledge of C++. We assume that you have the following knowledge about a small subset of C++:

- Class definitions with public and private members (both data and function).

    A class definition has the form (// is the comment character)

    ```
    class ClassName : public SuperClass {
      private:
        // members
      public:
        // members
    }
    ```

    The superclass part exists only if there is a superclass.

Data members are used to describe the local state of objects. They should all be private to encapsulate the data. A data member has either the form

`ClassName* dataMemberName;`

or

`CType dataMemberName;`

CType is any C type that is not a class, like long, int, float, etc.

Since all data members are private, usually member functions manipulate the data members.

- Member function declarations, sometimes called signatures, have the form

`ClassName* functionName(A* a1, A*& a2, Ctype i1, Ctype& i2 ...)`

`CType functionName(A* a1, A*& a2, Ctype i1, Ctype& i2, ...)`

where A is some class name. A* a1 declares a pointer argument and A*& a1 declares a reference parameter that is a pointer. The actual parameter must be some l-value that may be assigned a new pointer during execution of the function. Ctype& declares a reference parameter of some C type.

- Constructors

They are a special kind of member function. The name of the function is the same as the class name. The syntax of a constructor signature is

`ClassName(Argument* arg, Ctype i, ...);`

Constructors are used to allocate objects in the free store with

`new ClassName(actualArgument1, ...)`

- Function calls, polymorphism

Often objects are put on the free store and allocated with new. In this case, functions are called with the syntax

`variableName -> functionName(actualArgument1, ...);`

If the function is a virtual function, the decision regarding which function to call will be made at run-time, depending on what kind of object is contained in the variable.

3.1 C++ PROGRAM

We first write a C++ program for the following simple problem before we develop an adaptive program for the same problem. We are given a conglomerate of companies and we have to compute the total salary paid by the entire conglomerate. The goal of this chapter is only to demonstrate how adaptive object-oriented programming improves object-oriented programming. The C++ programs and the corresponding adaptive programs are shown without explaining them in full detail.

When we write an object-oriented program, we rarely start from scratch. Often we use common classes like List, Ident, String from a class library. In the following we give a fairly complete C++ program, which only references an external class library for input-output.

To implement the salary addition, we define a class Conglomerate that defines the structure of conglomerate objects. A specific conglomerate of companies will be an object of class Conglomerate. Any number of conglomerates can be created at run-time from class Conglomerate. The Conglomerate class needs an important helper class for keeping track of the salaries: class Salary. A Conglomerate object will contain many Salary-objects representing the salaries paid by the conglomerate. Adding together all salaries should be a very simple task: We have to find all the Salary-objects contained in a given Conglomerate-object and add them together.

First we need to organize the classes. Suppose we use the list of classes that are itemized at the beginning of file totalSalary.h below. As a first guess, let's structure the classes as shown in the remaining part of totalSalary.h. We decided to represent lists as recursive structures like in Lisp and similar languages. Later in the chapter we will use an iterative structure instead. The iterative structure is usually preferred by C++ programmers; it uses fewer classes.

The structure is summarized in Fig. 3.1 using adaptive software terminology.[1] We call such a figure a class dictionary, and its purpose is to describe object structure. The figure uses two kinds of classes: construction classes (drawn as □) which are used to instantiate objects with a fixed number of parts, and alternation classes (drawn as ⬡) which are abstract classes. The figure uses two kinds of edges: alternation edges (drawn as $\Longrightarrow$) represent kind-of relations, and construction edges (drawn as $\longrightarrow$ and with labels) represent has-a relations. Construction edges represent references to other objects and those references can have many different interpretations. It could mean a physical part-of reference, also called an aggregation relationship.

For example, the alternation edge Officer$\Longrightarrow$ShareHolding_Officer means that class Officer is a super class of class ShareHolding_Officer; the construction edge Conglomerate$\overset{head}{\longrightarrow}$Company means that class Conglomerate has a data member called head of type Company.

Figure 3.1 defines classes whose objects have the following properties. A Conglomerate-object has a name and consists of a Company-object. A Company-object optionally contains a list of Subsidiary-objects and it contains a list of Officer-objects and has a name, a location, and a turnover. A Subsidiary-object is either an instance of WhollyOwned or an instance of PartiallyOwned and contains a Company-object. An Officer-object is either an instance of ShareHolding_Officer or of Ordinary_Officer.

---

[1]Class dictionary graph graphical representation, page 431 (6). This is a reference to an instructional objective in Chapter 14, the "nerve center" of the book. See also the explanation on page xxx.

3.1. C++ PROGRAM

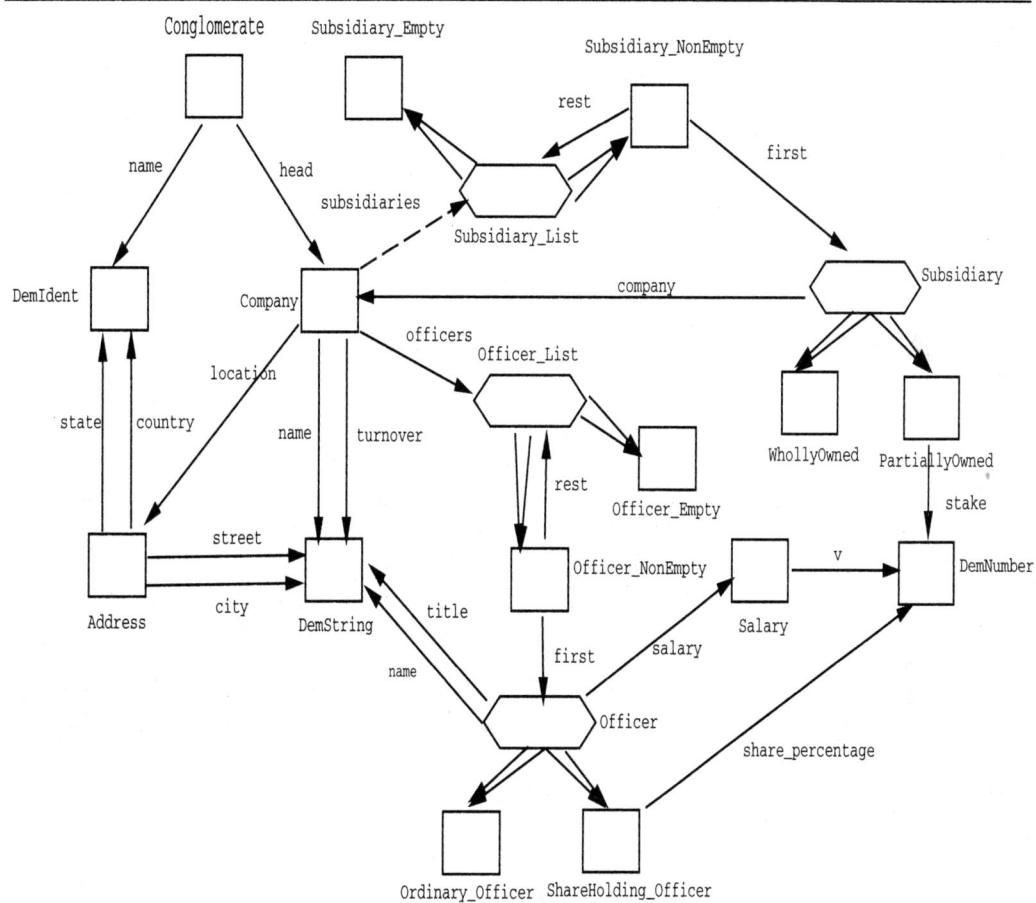

Figure 3.1: Conglomerate class dictionary: A view of the C++ program

If we write the salary computation program directly in C++, a natural solution is to first write member functions, all called say add_salary_, for the following classes to specify a traversal: Conglomerate, Subsidiary, Company, Officer, Salary, Officer_List, Subsidiary_List, Officer_NonEmpty, Subsidiary_NonEmpty.

We need to write traversal code to find all Salary-objects contained in the Conglomerate-object. If one chooses to call a behavior at the bottom of a composite Conglomerate-object, many objects in the Conglomerate-object must have a behavior that passes-the-call down one level. This sequence of behaviors is absolutely dependent on the existing class structure, and any changes to the class structure require that this sequence be examined, and possibly modified.

As we show in this chapter, adaptive software can express such passes-the-call behaviors without listing all the participating classes. Instead, the behaviors are written in compact traversal specification with necessary code fragments added. As a class structure is given, all the pass-the-call behaviors are generated *automatically* for all classes for which they are required, and the code for the desired behavior is inserted in the bottom class and in important classes in between. In other words, methods are being attached to classes during adaptive software interpretation in a context of a class structure. The important observation is that object behaviors coded as adaptive software are *not* specifically attached, at coding time, to any class. Since the pass-the-call behaviors are generated automatically, they are somewhat insensitive to changes in the class structure.

With this preview of what adaptive software is, let's return to the concrete C++ program. The traversal code that a person would write is shown in Fig. 3.2. The member function of Conglomerate invokes the member function of Company through data member head. The member function of Company invokes the member function of Officer_List through data member officers. It also checks if the company has subsidiaries and if it does, it invokes the member function of Subsidiary_List through data member subsidiaries. The member function of Subsidiary_List is empty. The member function of Subsidiary_NonEmpty invokes the member function of Subsidiary through data member first and the member function of Subsidiary_List through data member rest. The member function of Subsidiary invokes the member function of Company through data member company. WhollyOwned and PartiallyOwned will inherit their behavior from class Subsidiary. The traversal code continues in this form until we reach class Salary.

Note that Address-objects need not be traversed since they don't contain Salary-objects. The traversal program in Fig. 3.2 visits all the Salary-objects contained in a Conglomerate-object and therefore almost solves the problem.

Some C++ programmers would write the above traversal code slightly differently, as shown in the traversal part of file totalSalary.C on page 51. But the code is essentially the same and has the same efficiency.

The complete C++ solution to the Salary addition problem is given in two parts. Part 1 is an interface file (totalSalary.h) that defines the interface of classes such as Conglomerate and Salary. Part 2 actually implements the functions that have been announced by the interface. The implementation file is called totalSalary.C. An alternative way to organize the program would be to use two files for each class. We first show the interface file, sometimes called a header file.

3.1. C++ PROGRAM

```
long Conglomerate::add_salary( )
{ long return_val ;
  this->add_salary_( return_val );
  return return_val; }

void Conglomerate::add_salary_( long& return_val )
{ head->add_salary_( return_val ); }

void Subsidiary::add_salary_( long& return_val )
{ company->add_salary_( return_val ); }

void Company::add_salary_( long& return_val )
{ officers->add_salary_( return_val );
  if ( subsidiaries != NULL )
  { subsidiaries->add_salary_( return_val ); } }

void Officer::add_salary_( long& return_val )
{ salary->add_salary_( return_val ); }

void Salary::add_salary_( long& return_val ) { }

void Officer_List::add_salary_( long& return_val ) { }

void Subsidiary_List::add_salary_( long& return_val ) { }

void Officer_NonEmpty::add_salary_( long& return_val )
{ first->add_salary_( return_val );
  rest->add_salary_( return_val ); }

void Subsidiary_NonEmpty::add_salary_( long& return_val )
{ first->add_salary_( return_val );
  rest->add_salary_( return_val ); }
```

Figure 3.2: Traversal code for salary addition

```
// File totalSalary.h
// This is the header file for totalSalary.C

//   Class Declarations.
class Conglomerate;
class Subsidiary;
class WhollyOwned;
class PartiallyOwned;
class Company;
class Address;
class Officer;
class Salary;
class Shareholding_Officer;
class Ordinary_Officer;
class Officer_List;
class Subsidiary_List;
class Officer_Empty;
class Officer_NonEmpty;
class Subsidiary_Empty;
class Subsidiary_NonEmpty;
class DemString;
class DemIdent;
class DemNumber;
```

The following class definitions specify the relationships between the classes. For example, class **Subsidiary** inherits from class **PartiallyOwned**. And class **Company** and **Subsidiary_List** are in direct relationship through the binary relation **subsidiaries**.

```
// File totalSalary.h continued
// Class definitions
class DemString {
public:
  // Constructor
  DemString(char *s);
private:
  char *val; };

class DemIdent {
public:
  // Constructor
  DemIdent(char *s);
private:
  char *val; };
```

3.1. C++ PROGRAM

```cpp
class DemNumber {
public:
  // Constructor
  DemNumber(long n) { val = n; }
  // Member function
  long evaluate(void) { return val; }
private:
  long val; };

class Conglomerate {
public:
  // Constructor
  Conglomerate(DemIdent *n, Company *c) { name = n; head = c; }
  // Member function add_salary()
  long add_salary(void);
private:
  DemIdent *name;
  Company *head; };


class Subsidiary {
public:
  // Member functions
  virtual long add_salary(void);
  void set_company(Company* c) {company = c;}
private:
  // common parts of class Subsidiary
  Company *company; };

class WhollyOwned : public Subsidiary {
public:
  WhollyOwned(Company* c)
    {this -> set_company(c);} };

class PartiallyOwned : public Subsidiary {
public:
  // Constructor
  PartiallyOwned(Company* c, DemNumber *n)
    { this -> set_company(c); stake = n; }
private:
  DemNumber *stake; };

class Company {
public:
  // Constructor
```

```cpp
  Company(DemString *s1, Address *a,
          DemString *s2, Officer_List *ol,
          Subsidiary_List *sl)
  { name = s1; location = a; turnover = s2;
    officers = ol; subsidiaries = sl;
  }
  // Member function add_salary()
  long add_salary(void);
private:
  DemString *name;
  Address *location;
  DemString *turnover;
  Officer_List *officers;
  Subsidiary_List *subsidiaries; };

class Address {
public:
  // Constructor
  Address(DemString *s1, DemString *s2,
          DemIdent *i1, DemIdent *i2)
  { street = s1; city = s2; state = i1; country = i2; }
private:
  DemString *street;
  DemString *city;
  DemIdent *state;
  DemIdent *country; };

class Officer {
public:
  // Member functions
  virtual long add_salary(void);
  void set_name(DemString* n) {name = n;}
  void set_title(DemString* t) {title = t;}
  void set_salary(Salary* s) {salary = s;}
private:
  // common parts of class Officer
  DemString *name;
  DemString *title;
  Salary *salary; };

class Shareholding_Officer : public Officer {
public:
  // Constructor
  Shareholding_Officer(DemNumber* num, DemString* n,
    DemString* t, Salary* s)
```

3.1. C++ PROGRAM

```cpp
    { share_percentage = num;
      this->set_name(n); this->set_title(t);
      this->set_salary(s);}
private:
  DemNumber *share_percentage; };

class Ordinary_Officer : public Officer {
public:
  // Member function
  Ordinary_Officer(DemString* n, DemString* t, Salary* s)
    { this->set_name(n); this->set_title(t);
      this->set_salary(s);} };

class Salary {
public:
  // Constructor
  Salary(DemNumber *n) { v = n; }
  // Member function add_salary()
  long add_salary(void);
private:
  DemNumber *v; };

class Officer_List {
public:
  // Virtual function add_salary()
  virtual long add_salary(void) = 0; };

class Officer_Empty : public Officer_List {
public:
  // Member function add_salary()
  long add_salary(void); };

class Officer_NonEmpty : public Officer_List {
public:
  // Constructor
  Officer_NonEmpty(Officer *f, Officer_List *r)
    { first = f; rest = r; }
  // Member function
  long add_salary(void);
private:
  Officer *first;
  Officer_List *rest; };

class Subsidiary_List {
public:
```

```cpp
  // Virtual function add_salary()
  virtual long add_salary(void) = 0; };

class Subsidiary_Empty : public Subsidiary_List {
public:
  // Member function
  long add_salary(void); };

class Subsidiary_NonEmpty : public Subsidiary_List {
public:
  // Constructor
  Subsidiary_NonEmpty(Subsidiary *f, Subsidiary_List *r)
    { first = f; rest = r;}
  // Member function add_salary()
  long add_salary(void);
private:
  Subsidiary *first;
  Subsidiary_List *rest; };
```

The implementation file totalSalary.C follows next.

```cpp
// File totalSalary.C
// This program computes the total
// salaries in a conglomerate.

  #include <iostream.h>
  #include <string.h>
  #include "Salary.h"




// define remaining constructors

DemString::DemString( char* val_in )
{ // Copy the string to val of DemString object.
   if( val_in )
     {
        this->val = new char[strlen( val_in ) + 1];
        strcpy( this->val,val_in );
     }
   else
      this->val = NULL; }

DemIdent::DemIdent( char* val_in )
```

3.1. C++ PROGRAM

```cpp
{ // Copy the string to val of DemIdent object.
  if( val_in )
    {
      this->val = new char[strlen( val_in ) + 1];
      strcpy( this->val,val_in );
    }
  else
    this->val = NULL; }
```

Next is the traversal part of the C++ program.

```cpp
// File totalSalary.C continued
long Conglomerate::add_salary(void)
{ long total;
  // Compute the total salary for Conglomerate
  // class by adding all salaries in
  // the head company.
  total = head->add_salary();
  return total; }

long Subsidiary::add_salary(void)
{ long total;
  // Compute the total salary for Subsidiary
  // by adding all salaries of all the
  // subsidiary companies.
  total = company->add_salary();
  return total; }

long Company::add_salary(void)
{ long total;
  // Compute the total salary for Company
  // by adding the sum of salaries of
  // all the officers and subsidiaries.
  if (subsidiaries != NULL)
    total = officers->add_salary() +
            subsidiaries->add_salary();
  else
    total = officers->add_salary();
  return total; }

long Officer::add_salary(void)
{ long total;
  // Compute salary of officer.
  total = salary->add_salary();
  return total; }
```

```
long Salary::add_salary(void)
{ long total;
  // Return salary.
  total = v->evaluate(); }
  return total; }

long Officer_Empty::add_salary(void)
{ // Total salaries of Officer_Empty is 0.
  return 0; }

long Officer_NonEmpty::add_salary(void)
{ long total;
  // Compute salary of all the officers.
  total = first->add_salary() + rest->add_salary();
  return total; }

long Subsidiary_Empty::add_salary(void)
{ return 0; }

long Subsidiary_NonEmpty::add_salary(void)
{ long total;
  // Compute salary of subsidiaries.
  total = first->add_salary() + rest->add_salary();
  return total; }
```

Next comes the object construction part of the C++ program. An English description of the same information is in Fig. 3.4.

```
// File totalSalary.C continued
//   Main Function
main ()
{
  DemIdent* iDemIdent1 = new DemIdent( "TransGlobal" );
  DemString* iDemString2 = new DemString( "TransGlobal Illumination" );
  DemString* iDemString3 = new DemString( "23 Rue du Lac" );
  DemString* iDemString4 = new DemString( "Geneva" );
  DemIdent* iDemIdent5 = new DemIdent( "GE" );
  DemIdent* iDemIdent6 = new DemIdent( "Switzerland" );
  Address* iAddress7 =
    new Address( iDemString3,iDemString4,iDemIdent5,iDemIdent6 );
  DemString* iDemString8 = new DemString( "4bn" );
  DemNumber* iDemNumber9 = new DemNumber( 60 );
  DemString* iDemString11 = new DemString( "Karl Soller" );
  DemString* iDemString12 =
```

3.1. C++ PROGRAM

```
    new DemString( "Chief Executive Officer and President" );
DemNumber* iDemNumber13 = new DemNumber( 200000 );
Salary* iSalary14 = new Salary( iDemNumber13 );
Shareholding_Officer* iShareholding_Officer10 =
  new Shareholding_Officer(
    iDemNumber9,
    iDemString11,
    iDemString12,
    iSalary14);
DemNumber* iDemNumber15 = new DemNumber( 30 );
DemString* iDemString17 = new DemString( "Jim Miller" );
DemString* iDemString18 = new DemString( "Chief Financial Officer" );
DemNumber* iDemNumber19 = new DemNumber( 150000 );
Salary* iSalary20 = new Salary( iDemNumber19 );
Shareholding_Officer* iShareholding_Officer16 =
  new Shareholding_Officer(
    iDemNumber15,
    iDemString17,
    iDemString18,
    iSalary20);
DemString* iDemString22 = new DemString( "Guy Jenny" );
DemString* iDemString23 = new DemString( "Secretary" );
DemNumber* iDemNumber24 = new DemNumber( 100000 );
Salary* iSalary25 = new Salary( iDemNumber24 );
Ordinary_Officer* iOrdinary_Officer21 =
  new Ordinary_Officer(
    iDemString22,
    iDemString23,
    iSalary25);
Officer_Empty* iOfficer_Empty26 = new Officer_Empty(  );
Officer_NonEmpty* iOfficer_NonEmpty27 =
  new Officer_NonEmpty( iOrdinary_Officer21,iOfficer_Empty26 );
Officer_NonEmpty* iOfficer_NonEmpty28 =
  new Officer_NonEmpty( iShareholding_Officer16,iOfficer_NonEmpty27 );
Officer_NonEmpty* iOfficer_NonEmpty29 =
  new Officer_NonEmpty( iShareholding_Officer10,iOfficer_NonEmpty28 );
DemString* iDemString31 = new DemString( "TransGlobal Adventures" );
DemString* iDemString32 = new DemString( "12 Borisinsky Way" );
DemString* iDemString33 = new DemString( "Moscow" );
DemIdent* iDemIdent34 = new DemIdent( "Russia" );
DemIdent* iDemIdent35 = new DemIdent( "USSR" );
Address* iAddress36 =
  new Address( iDemString32,iDemString33,iDemIdent34,iDemIdent35 );
DemString* iDemString37 = new DemString( "2bn" );
DemNumber* iDemNumber38 = new DemNumber( 80 );
```

```
DemString* iDemString40 = new DemString( "Boris Kasparov" );
DemString* iDemString41 = new DemString( "Chief Executive Officer" );
DemNumber* iDemNumber42 = new DemNumber( 200000 );
Salary* iSalary43 = new Salary( iDemNumber42 );
Shareholding_Officer* iShareholding_Officer39 =
  new Shareholding_Officer(
    iDemNumber38,
    iDemString40,
    iDemString41,
    iSalary43);
DemNumber* iDemNumber44 = new DemNumber( 5 );
DemString* iDemString46 = new DemString( "Ivan Spassky" );
DemString* iDemString47 = new DemString( "President" );
DemNumber* iDemNumber48 = new DemNumber( 150000 );
Salary* iSalary49 = new Salary( iDemNumber48 );
Shareholding_Officer* iShareholding_Officer45 =
  new Shareholding_Officer(
    iDemNumber44,
    iDemString46,
    iDemString47,
    iSalary49);
DemString* iDemString51 = new DemString( "Georg Giezendanner" );
DemString* iDemString52 = new DemString( "Secretary" );
DemNumber* iDemNumber53 = new DemNumber( 100000 );
Salary* iSalary54 = new Salary( iDemNumber53 );
Ordinary_Officer* iOrdinary_Officer50 =
  new Ordinary_Officer(
    iDemString51, iDemString52, iSalary54);
Officer_Empty* iOfficer_Empty55 = new Officer_Empty( );
Officer_NonEmpty* iOfficer_NonEmpty56 =
  new Officer_NonEmpty( iOrdinary_Officer50,iOfficer_Empty55 );
Officer_NonEmpty* iOfficer_NonEmpty57 =
  new Officer_NonEmpty( iShareholding_Officer45,iOfficer_NonEmpty56 );
Officer_NonEmpty* iOfficer_NonEmpty58 =
  new Officer_NonEmpty( iShareholding_Officer39,iOfficer_NonEmpty57 );
Company* iCompany59 =
  new Company( iDemString31,iAddress36,iDemString37,
    iOfficer_NonEmpty58,NULL );
WhollyOwned* iWhollyOwned30 = new WhollyOwned(iCompany59);
Subsidiary_Empty* iSubsidiary_Empty60 = new Subsidiary_Empty( );
Subsidiary_NonEmpty* iSubsidiary_NonEmpty61 =
  new Subsidiary_NonEmpty( iWhollyOwned30,iSubsidiary_Empty60 );
Company* iCompany62 =
  new Company( iDemString2,iAddress7,iDemString8,
    iOfficer_NonEmpty29,iSubsidiary_NonEmpty61 );
```

```
    Conglomerate* iConglomerate63 =
      new Conglomerate( iDemIdent1,iCompany62 );

    cout << "Total salary = " << iConglomerate63->add_salary() << endl;
}
```

3.2 ADAPTIVE PROGRAM

Why is the C++ solution so long? There are several reasons, but here we focus only on the most important one. The C++ program contains significant redundancy which makes this program inherently rigid and not reusable. This issue shows up in most object-oriented programs making them rigid and not reusable. (But they are better than nonobject-oriented programs regarding reusability!)

Let's do the following *Gedankenexperiment*. Suppose you are given only the implementation file totalSalary.C. What can you learn about the interface file? Well, the implementation file tells a lot about how conglomerates are organized. From the add_salary implementation we learn that there is a head company that has subsidiary companies and that a company has officers who are paid a salary. We don't learn the full story about the conglomerates from the add_salary implementation, but we learn a lot. When we look at the part of the implementation file that builds a conglomerate object through constructor calls, we learn even more about the structure of conglomerate objects.

Adaptive software eliminates the redundancy present in the C++ program by telling the story about the structure and appearance of Conglomerate-objects only once in the class dictionary in Fig. 3.1, which we explained on page 42. The corresponding textual form of the class dictionary follows, sprinkled with some comments that explain the notation.[2] The complete notation is explained in detail in Chapters 6 and 11.

```
Conglomerate   =                        // construction class
        "Conglomerate" ":"              // for external representation
   <name> DemIdent                      // data member "name" of class DemIdent
        "Head Office" ":"
   <head> Company .                     // data member "head" of class Company
Subsidiary :                            // Alternation class
   WholyOwned |                         // subclass
   PartiallyOwned                       // subclass
      *common* <company> Company .      // data member of Subsidiary
WholyOwned  =                           // construction class
        "Wholy" "owned" .
PartiallyOwned =                        // construction class
        "Partially" "owned" "stake" "="
   <stake> DemNumber .
Company   =
   <name> DemString
```

---

[2] Class dictionary textual representation, page 437 (31).

```
            "Registered" "Office"
    <location> Address
            "Turnover" ":"
    <turnover> DemString
            "Officers" ":"
    <officers> Officer_List
    [ "Subsidiaries" "{" <subsidiaries> Subsidiary_List "}" ] .
                                // optional part
Address =
            "Street" "-"
    <street> DemString
            "City" "-"
    <city> DemString
            "State" "-"
    <state> DemIdent
            "Country" "-"
    <country> DemIdent "." .
Officer :                       // alternation class
    Shareholding_Officer | Ordinary_Officer
      *common*                  // data members of Officer
                "Name" "-"
        <name> DemString
                "Title" "-"
        <title> DemString
                "Salary" "-"
        <salary> Salary "." .
Salary = <v> DemNumber .
Shareholding_Officer =
            "Shareholder"
    <share_percentage> DemNumber
            "percent control" .
Ordinary_Officer =
            "Ordinary" .
Officer_List    : Officer_Empty | Officer_NonEmpty .
Subsidiary_List : Subsidiary_Empty | Subsidiary_NonEmpty .
Officer_Empty       = .
Officer_NonEmpty    = <first> Officer <rest> Officer_List .
Subsidiary_Empty    = .
Subsidiary_NonEmpty = <first> Subsidiary <rest> Subsidiary_List .
```

A corresponding graphical form is in Fig. 3.1.

The functionality is now formulated without mentioning the details of the class structure again. We first focus on the traversal and write a specification with which we can generate the traversal code.

3.2. ADAPTIVE PROGRAM

In Demeter notation, we write the following propagation pattern:[3]

```
*operation* long add_salary()
  // find all Salary-objects in
  // Conglomerate-object
  *traverse*
    *from* Conglomerate *to* Salary
```

The important part of this propagation pattern is the traversal specification (also called a propagation directive):

```
*from* Conglomerate *to* Salary
```

This line generates exactly the traversal code that we saw earlier in Fig. 3.2. Before going into the details of writing code for adding the salaries, let us show how this traversal specification is translated into the C++ program skeleton in Fig. 3.2.

First we interpret the traversal directive as specifying the set of paths from Conglomerate to Salary.[4] Figure 3.3 shows the union of all the paths from Conglomerate to Salary. This

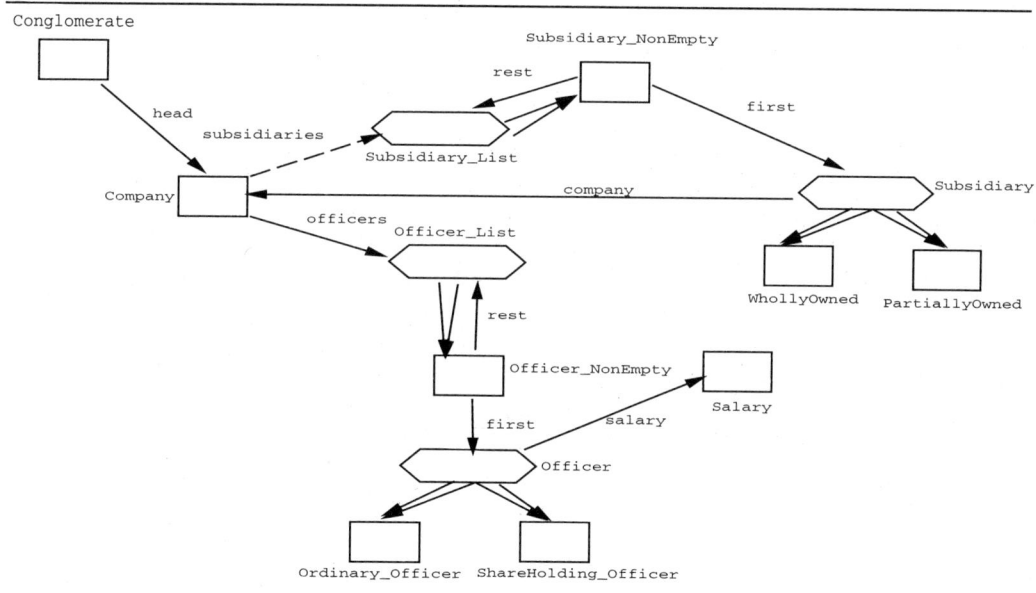

Figure 3.3: Propagation graph

graph is called a **propagation graph**. The rules of translating the propagation graph into a C++ program skeleton are (simplified to the current example):[5]

---

[3]Legal propagation patterns, page 447 (61).
[4]Propagation operator, page 446 (59).
[5]Propagation pattern partial evaluation, page 448 (64).

- All the classes in the graph get a member function with the signature specified on the first line of the propagation pattern.

- If a class has an outgoing construction edge in the propagation graph, the member function of the class will contain a member function invocation through the corresponding data member.

- Functions attached to alternation classes are declared to be virtual.

Based on these rules, the propagation graph in Fig. 3.3 is translated into the program skeleton in Fig. 3.2, except for the arguments in the skeleton.

To add the salaries, we need to add a little bit of code. This is accomplished by writing a wrapper for the Salary-class that updates a predefined variable return_val. The complete propagation pattern follows:[6]

```
*operation* long add_salary() *init* (@ 0 @)
  // find all Salary-objects in
  // Conglomerate-object
  *traverse*
    *from* Conglomerate *to* Salary

  // when a Salary-object is found,
  // add it to the total salary
  *wrapper* Salary
    *prefix* (@ return_val += *v; @)
```

The wrapper adds a line to class Salary. Code between (@ and @) is C++ code. The *init* (@ 0 @) initializes the variable return_val.

```
long Conglomerate::add_salary(  )
{ long return_val
       = 0 ;           // <============== NEW from *init* (@ 0 @)
  this->add_salary_( return_val );
  return return_val; }

void Salary::add_salary_( long& return_val )
{
  return_val += *v;    // <============== NEW from wrapper Salary
}
```

Please check the structure of the generated C++ code. First, it is code that resembles the object structure closely. Second it is code that a human would write.

We call the propagation pattern with

```
cout << "TotalSalary = " << iConglomerate->add_salary() << endl ;
```

```
Conglomerate : TransGlobal
        Head Office : "TransGlobal Illumination"
        Registered Office
                Street - "23 Rue du Lac" City - "Geneva"
                State - GE Country - Switzerland.
        Turnover : "4bn"
        Officers :
                Shareholder 60 percent control
                Name - "Karl Soller"
                Title - "Chief Executive Officer and President"
                Salary - 200000.

                Shareholder 30 percent control
                Name - "Jim Miller"
                Title - "Chief Financial Officer" Salary - 150000.

                Ordinary
                Name - "Guy Jenny"
                Title - "Secretary" Salary - 100000.
        Subsidiaries {
                Wholly owned "TransGlobal Adventures"
                Registered Office
                        Street - "12 Borisinsky Way"
                        City - "Moscow" State - Russia
                        Country - USSR.
                Turnover : "2bn"
                Officers :
                        Shareholder 80 percent control
                        Name - "Boris Kasparov"
                        Title - "Chief Executive Officer"
                        Salary - 200000.

                        Shareholder 5 percent control
                        Name - "Ivan Spassky"
                        Title - "President" Salary - 150000.

                        Ordinary
                        Name - "Georg Giezendanner"
                        Title - "Secretary" Salary - 100000.
                        }
```

Figure 3.4: English description of conglomerate

The specific conglomerate in iConglomerate is defined by an English description in Fig. 3.4.

The English description in Fig. 3.4 is much easier to follow than the corresponding C++ code that defines the same object. The C++ code is at the end of file totalSalary.C shown earlier. This example illustrates that C++ is not suitable as an object-oriented design notation. We need a high-level design notation that abstracts from low-level details, and we achieve this with propagation patterns. The propagation pattern we have seen above is very *soft* software. It is not married at all to the current class dictionary and can be used with many other class dictionaries. With adaptive software we achieve two goals in one step. Software becomes easier to produce since we have to write significantly less *and* software becomes more flexible.

3.3 EVOLUTION

One goal of adaptive software is to make software soft. We divide the discussion of evolution in a structural evolution part and in a behavioral evolution part. We compare the evolution of both a C++ and a corresponding adaptive program.

3.3.1 Changing Object Structure

Classes are like stereotypes. Stereotypical thinking is very useful as long as we constantly evolve the stereotypes. If we stop to evolve the stereotypes, we become discriminatory and we start to put objects in the wrong classes. We evolve classes based on objects we have observed.

Object-oriented programming languages support a discriminatory style of programming since programmers are unwilling to modify class definitions that are replicated in many program parts. A change in a class definition might imply numerous changes in the program. Adaptive object-oriented programming with propagation patterns and class dictionaries supports a nondiscriminatory programming style since class descriptions are kept separate from the programs and are only minimally duplicated in the programs. A change in a class definition involves usually a small number of updates in the programs.

For example, for the class dictionary in Fig. 3.5 no update is needed to the program! The new class dictionary uses repetition classes for representing lists of officers and lists of subsidiaries.[7] A repetition object describes a collection of other objects. A repetition class is represented by the symbol ◁▷. More importantly, the structure of Company-objects has been changed. Officers are now employees and in addition to officers, the companies now have regular employees and pay salaries to them. An employee may be shareholding.

At the level of C++, the code will look very different when the class dictionary in Fig. 3.5 (the textual form is in Fig. 3.6) is used to customize the propagation pattern. The propagation graph is shown in Fig. 3.7. It contains several new classes for which new C++ code has to be produced.

The code of class Company now has additional traversal code for the employees data member.

```
void Company::add_salary_( long& return_val )
```

---

[6]Legal propagation patterns, page 447 (61).
[7]Class dictionary textual representation, page 437 (31).

3.3. EVOLUTION

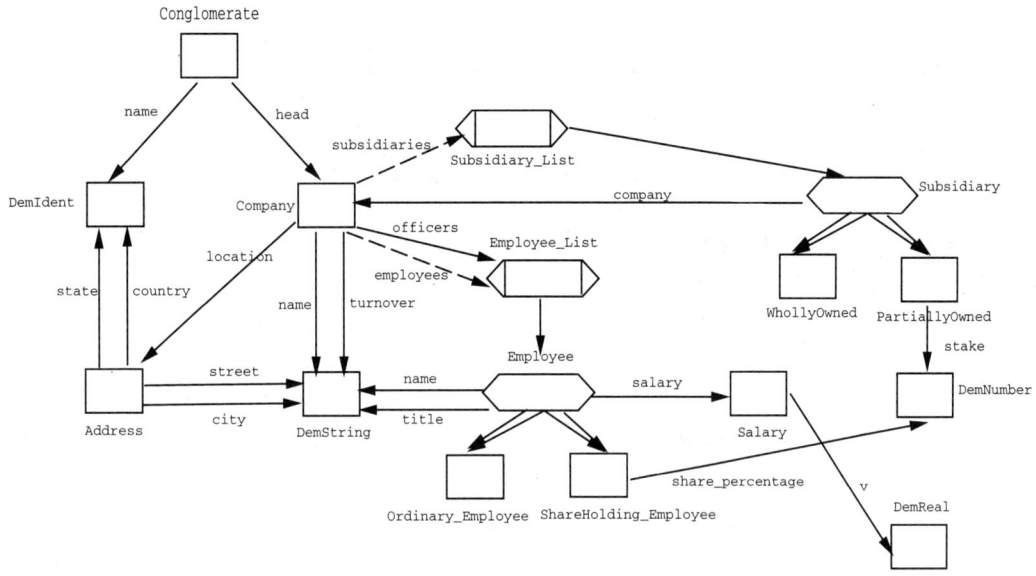

Figure 3.5: Alternative class dictionary

```
{
  // outgoing calls
  this->get_officers()->add_salary_( return_val );
  if ( this->get_employees() != NULL )
  {
    this->get_employees()->add_salary_( return_val );
  }
  if ( this->get_subsidiaries() != NULL )
  {
    this->get_subsidiaries()->add_salary_( return_val );
  }
}
```

The traversal code for class Employee_List uses an iterator class (not shown) to visit all elements of the list.

```
void Employee_List::add_salary_( long& return_val )
{
  // outgoing calls
  Employee_list_iterator      next_Employee(*this);
  Employee*            each_Employee;

  while ( each_Employee = next_Employee() )
```

```
Conglomerate = "Conglomerate" ":" <name>  DemIdent
               "Head Office" ":" <head> Company .

Subsidiary : WhollyOwned | PartiallyOwned
              *common* <company> Company.

WhollyOwned = "Wholly" "owned".
PartiallyOwned = "Partially"  "owned" "stake" "=" <stake> DemNumber.

Company = <name> DemString
        "Registered" "Office" <location> Address
        "Turnover" ":" <turnover> DemString
        "Officers" ":" <officers> List(Employee)
        ["Other" "Employees" ":" <employees> List(Employee)]
          // List(Employee) is an instantiation
          // of parameterized class List defined below
        ["Subsidiaries"   "{" <subsidiaries> List(Subsidiary) "}" ].

Address = "Street" "-" <street > DemString
          "City" "-" <city> DemString
          "State" "-" <state> DemIdent
          "Country" "-" <country> DemIdent ".".

Employee : Shareholding_Employee | Ordinary_Employee *common*
              "Name" "-" <name> DemString
              "Title" "-" <title>  DemString
              "Salary" "-" <salary> Salary "." .

Salary = <v> DemReal.

Shareholding_Employee = "Shareholder" <share_percentage> DemNumber
              "percent control".

Ordinary_Employee  = "Ordinary".
List(S) ~ { S }. // parameterized repetition class
```

Figure 3.6: Alternative class dictionary, textual form

3.3. EVOLUTION

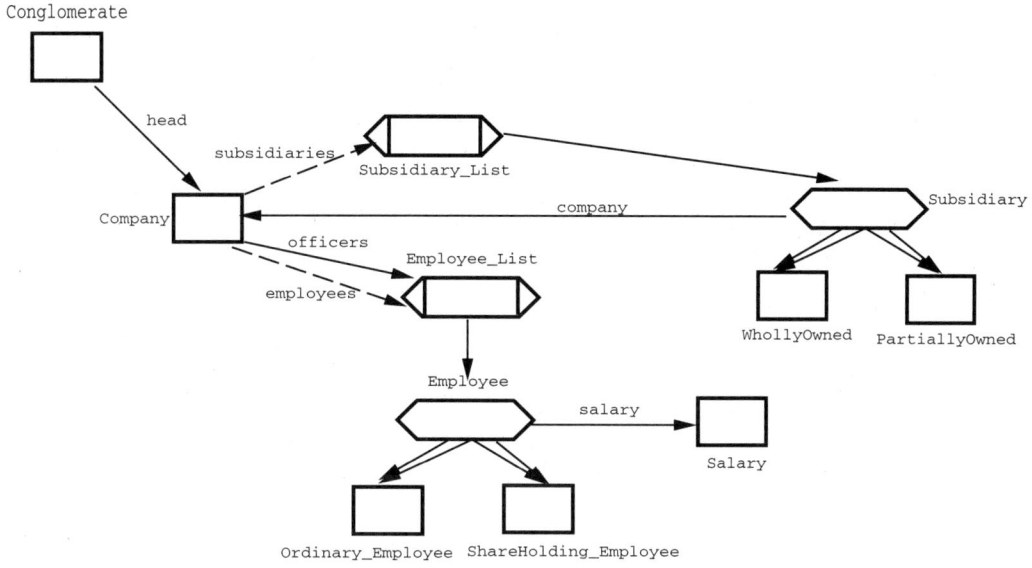

Figure 3.7: Propagation graph for alternative class dictionary

```
    {
      each_Employee->add_salary_( return_val );
    }
}
```

The C++ program needs many more changes. The reason the adaptive program needs no update is that there is still a relationship between **Conglomerate** and **Salary** in the class dictionary.[8] And the task is still to find all the **Salary**-objects in a **Conglomerate**-object.

3.3.2 Evolving the Functionality

Changing the object structure was easy, and it was equally as easy to update the C++ programs working on the objects. We noticed that when the C++ programs were described by an adaptive program, no change to the program was needed at all. We now go back to the original class dictionary in Fig. 3.1.

Updating Objects

Next we add functionality to the application. Suppose we want to increase the salary of all officers of the head company by **percent** percent. Because a salary can now be a real number, we update the data member type of v in class **Salary** to **DemReal**.

To update the salaries, the C++ programmer would have to write traversal code for the following classes:

---

[8]Legal propagation pattern customization, page 447 (62).

```
        Conglomerate
        Company
        Officer
        Salary
        Shareholding_Officer
        Ordinary_Officer
        Officer_List
        Officer_NonEmpty
```

The detailed traversal code the C++ programmer would produce is[9]

```
void Conglomerate::increase_salary( int percent )
{ this->get_head()->increase_salary( percent ); }

void Company::increase_salary( int percent )
{ this->get_officers()->increase_salary( percent ); }

void Officer::increase_salary( int percent )
{ this->get_salary()->increase_salary( percent ); }

void Salary::increase_salary( int percent )
{ }

void Officer_List::increase_salary( int percent )
{ }

void Officer_NonEmpty::increase_salary( int percent )
{ this->get_first()->increase_salary( percent );
  this->get_rest()->increase_salary( percent ); }
```

The traversal code is almost the correct solution. We need to add a little bit of code to the member functions of class **Conglomerate** and class **Salary**.

```
void Conglomerate::increase_salary( int percent )
{ this->get_head()->increase_salary( percent );
  // suffix wrappers
  cout << " after " <<  this;                         // <=== new
}
```

The last line in the **Conglomerate** member function serves to print out the conglomerate object after it was modified.

For class **Salary** we use a prefix wrapper, introduced with *prefix*, and a suffix wrapper, introduced with *suffix*. *prefix* is like an editing instruction that puts the code at the beginning of the member function. *suffix* is like an editing instruction that puts the code at the end of the member function.

---

[9] Propagation pattern partial evaluation, page 448 (64).

3.3. EVOLUTION

```
void Salary::increase_salary( int percent )
{ // prefix wrappers
    this ->                                               // <=== new
      set_v(new DemReal(*v * (1 + (percent/100.0))));     // <=== new
  // suffix wrappers
    cout << " new salary " << this <<                     // <=== new
      " percentage " << (1 + (percent/100.0));            // <=== new
}
```

The bad news about the C++ program we just wrote is that it contains a lot of information about the class dictionary. Should the class dictionary change we will have to work hard to maintain the C++ program.

The adaptive programmer has it comparatively easier. She identifies the classes that are involved in the traversal; the propagation graph that describes the traversal to be done for objects of class **Conglomerate** defined by the class dictionary in Fig. 3.1 is in Fig. 3.8.

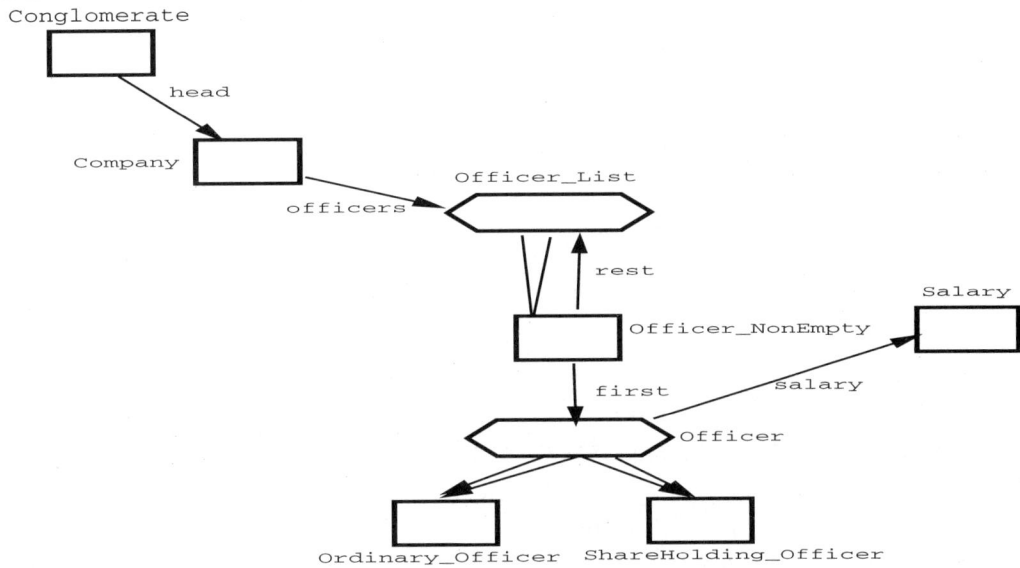

Figure 3.8: Propagation graph for increasing salary of officers

Instead of writing the traversal code manually, we write a propagation directive:

```
*from* Conglomerate
  *bypassing* -> *,subsidiaries,*
*to* Salary
```

that defines the above propagation graph and the corresponding traversal code.[10] With *bypassing*, we can influence the size of the propagation graph. The bypassing clause means

---
[10]Legal propagation patterns, page 447 (61).

that the construction edge starting from any class (denoted by *), with label **subsidiaries**, and terminating at any class (denoted by *), is bypassed. In the specific class dictionary that we are using, only the construction edge from Company to Subsidiary_List with label subsidiaries

```
-> Company, subsidiaries, Subsidiary_List
```

is matching and therefore bypassed. Instead of manually editing the C++ traversal code, we add editing instructions in the form of wrappers to the propagation pattern. The complete propagation pattern is in Fig. 3.9. This propagation pattern was developed with the cus-

```
*operation* void increase_salary(int percent)
  *traverse*
    *from* Conglomerate
      *bypassing* -> *,subsidiaries,*
    *to* Salary

  *wrapper* Salary
    *prefix* (@ this ->
      set_v(new DemReal(*v * (1 + (percent/100.0)))); @)
    *suffix* (@ cout << " new salary " << this <<
      " percentage " << (1 + (percent/100.0)); @)
  *wrapper* Conglomerate
    *suffix* // to check the result
      (@ cout << " after " <<  this; @)
```

Figure 3.9: Increase salary of top-level officers

tomizer in Fig. 3.1 in mind.[11] But how does it behave with the class dictionary in Fig. 3.5 that also allows employees, not only officers in the companies? The salary increase program is supposed to increase only the salary of the top-level officers and not of all employees. Therefore, for the class dictionary in Fig. 3.5, we need to make sure that only the officers are considered. The propagation directive

```
*from* Conglomerate
  *bypassing* -> *,subsidiaries,*
  *through* -> *,officers,*
*to* Salary
```

selects the appropriate propagation graph. At the C++ level, the impact of the *through* clause is to eliminate statements. For example, in class **Company** there will be no code that calls the function for data member **officers**. Similar to the *bypassing* clause, the *through*

---

[11] Legal propagation pattern customization, page 447 (62).

3.3. EVOLUTION

clause allows us to reduce the size of the propagation graph. The *bypassing* clause takes an explicit attitude by explicitly excluding certain edges. The *through* clause takes an implicit attitude by implicitly excluding certain edges through forcing other edges.

It is interesting to notice that to make the C++ program *smaller*, we *add* constraints to the adaptive program. This is unexpected until we realize that adaptive programs are constraints that constrain object-oriented programs. The more constraints we add, the smaller the object-oriented program becomes. Could it be that we might have to add so many constraints that the adaptive program gets larger than the object-oriented program? Fortunately, adaptive object-oriented programs can always be written in such a way that they are better or equally as good as object-oriented programs. We can always write an adaptive program in the following form:

```
*operation* // signature
  // no traversal specification
*wrapper* A ...
*wrapper* B ...
...
*wrapper* C ...
```

In this form, an adaptive program is like an object-oriented program.

Let's do one last evolution step to our salary increase program. This step we will perform only at the adaptive level since we can easily visualize the mapping to the C++ level. The functionality we add, in addition to increasing the salaries, will compute the maximum of all the salaries after the increase. We prepare for this enhancement by adding a reference argument to the signature. The variable is updated during the traversal and printed out at the end.

The updated propagation pattern for the class dictionary in Fig. 3.5 is shown below.

```
*operation* void increase_salary        // name of functionality
  (                                     // arguments
    int percent,
    long& max_salary       // <===== new: extra argument
  )
  *traverse*                            // describes C++ skeleton
    *from* Conglomerate
      *bypassing* -> *,subsidiaries,*
      *through* -> *,officers,*
    *to* Salary

  *wrapper* Salary                      // for Salary member function
    *prefix*                            // add at beginning
      (@ this -> set_v(new DemReal(*v * (1 + (percent/100.0)))); @)
    *suffix*
      (@ cout << " new salary " << this <<     // add at end
      " percentage " << (1 + (percent/100.0)); @)
  *wrapper* Conglomerate                // for Conglomerate member function
```

```
        *suffix*  // to check result          // add at end: after traversal!
            (@ cout << " after " << this; @)

// further updates for computing maximum salary
     *wrapper* Salary        // also for Salary member function
         *prefix*            // add at beginning
             (@ if (*v > max_salary) {   // <===== new: test
                 max_salary = *v;         // <===== new: update
             @)
         *suffix*            // add at end; completes syntax of prefix part
             (@ } else                                // <===== new: debug
                 cout << endl << " no new maximum ";  // <===== new: debug
             @)

     *wrapper* Conglomerate     // also for Conglomerate member function
         *suffix*               // add at end: after traversal
             (@
                 cout << endl <<
                     " maximum salary " << max_salary;  // <===== new: print
             @)
```

Six lines have been added to the propagation pattern we had before. How many lines need to be added to the C++ program? The last five of the six lines are also added to the C++ program. The first line, however, is added many times to the C++ program, depending on how many classes are in the propagation graph. This example nicely demonstrates the localization of signature information in propagation patterns that significantly simplifies signature changes.

The reader may judge from the conglomerate example which notation is easier to use: a first generation object-oriented language such as C++ or a second generation object-oriented language using propagation patterns and class dictionaries on top of C++.

3.4 WHAT IS THE PRICE?

Adaptive object-oriented software has inherent advantages over object-oriented software. But what does one have to know to successfully write and maintain adaptive object-oriented software?

You have to know about class dictionaries and propagation patterns and how they relate to object-oriented programs. Equipped with this knowledge it is easy for an object-oriented programmer to write adaptive programs. It takes only about fifteen hours of reading time to learn the necessary skills plus the time to do five homeworks on the computer.

Adaptive software is developed according to the following method.

The Demeter Method in a Nutshell

- Start with requirements, written in the form of use cases. A use case is an English description of how the desired system should react in a specific situation. Derive a class dictionary, a general graph structure to describe the structure of objects. The class

3.4. WHAT IS THE PRICE?

dictionary has secondary importance, since, after the project is complete, the class dictionary is replaceable by many other class dictionaries without requiring changes (or only minimal changes) to the rest of the software.

- For each use case, focus on subgraphs of collaborating classes that implement the use case. Focus on how the collaborating classes cluster objects together. Express the collaborations as propagation patterns with minimal dependency on the class dictionary. The propagation patterns give an implicit specification of the group of collaborating classes, focusing on the classes and relationships that are really important for the current use case.

- Enhance the propagation patterns by adding specific functionality through wrappers at vertices and at edges of the class dictionary. The wrappers use the object clusters. Derive test inputs from use cases and check whether all use cases are satisfied.

Use cases are helpful to trace requirements throughout the software development process. Use cases are translated into class dictionaries to have a precise vocabulary to talk about the classes. There are three kinds of classes and four kinds of relationships between classes in class dictionaries. You have to learn a few design rules about class dictionaries.

Use cases are also translated into propagation patterns to provide the functionality of the objects. To work with propagation patterns, you have to learn about propagation directives. Propagation directives are succinct specifications of object-oriented programs both for traversing objects as well as for transporting objects. Most propagation patterns contain a propagation directive but there are also propagation patterns without a propagation directive. Propagation patterns without a propagation directive are like ordinary object-oriented programs. Propagation patterns with a propagation directive define an entire family of C++ programs.

Besides propagation directives, propagation patterns contain other important ingredients: wrappers. Wrappers are like editing instructions to add to an object-oriented program. The reason we need the wrappers is that the traversal code defined by propagation directives is not sufficient to express the desired functionality. With wrappers we can use any kind of C++ statements to express the details of the processing.

What is important here is that C++ statements are used late in the development process. First, analysis and design are done in terms of class dictionaries and propagation directives. Those concepts are very high level and visual feedback is available to check for correctness. The detailed processing is expressed in terms of wrappers once the class dictionaries and the propagation directives are in good shape.

To summarize, to develop adaptive software you need to know about class dictionaries and propagation patterns. Class dictionaries consist of partial class definitions sufficient to define the structure of application objects. Propagation patterns may contain propagation directives to define entire families of object-oriented programs. Propagation patterns also contain wrappers that may contain any C++ statements.

Learning to write adaptive software requires that you acquire some new concepts. An adequate set of concepts you need to write useful adaptive programs successfully are:

- Structural specification: class dictionary G

  Defines a set of classes and their relationships and standard functionality.

- Objects defined by G

  G requires that objects created from its classes have specific parts.

- Flattened class dictionary $F = flatten(G)$

  The *flatten* function distributes common parts of abstract classes to concrete subclasses.[12] The *flatten* function is useful since it allows us to bring a class dictionary to a normal form for manipulating it, usually selecting a subgraph. After the manipulation, the flattening may be undone for the selected subgraph. Flat class dictionaries are usually not written by the user but are produced from nonflat class dictionaries by tools. Flat class dictionaries are a useful intermediate form. Notice that the flattening operation is well defined since there can be no cycles of alternation edges in a class dictionary.

  In the examples in this chapter we omitted the flattening and unflattening steps.

- Propagation directive d for F

  A propagation directive specifies a subgraph of F by selecting only some of the paths in F.

- Propagation graph $pg = propagate(d, F)$

  A propagation graph is essentially the union of paths in F that satisfy propagation directive d. An important use of propagation graphs is to specify object traversals.

- Behavioral specification: propagation pattern $pp = (signature, d, wrappers)$

  A propagation pattern consists of a signature, an optional propagation directive, and a set of wrappers. The wrappers are enhancements to the traversal code specified by propagation directive d. The signature gives the argument names and types of the behavior.

- Code generation for pp in F

  The code generation for $pp = (signature, d, wrappers)$ produces essentially a member function for every class in the propagation graph determined by d and F. The construction edges in the propagation graph determine the traversal function calls that are made by the member functions. The wrappers are wrapped around the traversal code.

3.5 APPENDIX: FROM C TO C++

Basic knowledge of C++ is a prerequisite for the readers of this book. In this appendix we summarize the subset of C++ that is needed for writing challenging adaptive programs. The subset is described from the point of view of adaptive software.

Since we cover only a subset of C++ here, it is important to repeat that adaptive software is an add-on tool to object-oriented software. When writing adaptive software, we can use the full power of C++ for the following reasons:

---

[12]Class dictionary flattening, page 439 (33).

3.5. APPENDIX: FROM C TO C++

- In wrappers any C++ statement may be used.
- Often we use external class libraries when developing adaptive software. Those class libraries may be produced by Demeter, or they may be written by the adaptive software developer, or bought from a third party.

The subset of C++ that we use tends to cover features that are available in similar form in most programming languages covering the object-oriented paradigm.

We take a uniform approach and put all objects on the heap, with a few exceptions. The advantage is that member functions are called uniformly with the same syntax. Objects are allocated uniformly with the **new** operator.

- Declaring variables

  All variables for storing objects defined by a class dictionary are declared as pointer variables.

  ```
  Fruit = ...
  ```

  ```
  Fruit* my_fruit;
  ```

  There is an exception: variables for storing iterator objects for repetition classes are declared as regular objects.

- Members

  Each class has members of two kinds:

  - data members: define the local state of objects
  - function members: define the functionality.

  There are three visibility categories for members:

  - public
  - private
  - protected.

  We make all data members private and provide public access and writing functions. Data members are defined by the class dictionary and the C++ code for accessing and writing is generated.

- Member functions

  The protection of member functions is user controlled. The default is public. The header file of a member function is generated from implementation.

  Attaching a public member function **cost** to class **Apple** uses the following syntax:

  ```
  int Apple::cost(...)
    {...}
  ```

If Apple is an alternation class, then cost will be a virtual function by default. If Apple is a construction or repetition class, cost is a normal member function.

A public member function can be called everywhere (but we will follow the Law of Demeter to avoid maintenance problems).

Arguments to member functions typically have one of the forms used in the following argument list:

```
(A* a1, A*& a2, Ctype i1, Ctype& i2, ...)
```

where A is some class name. A* a1 declares a pointer argument and A*& a1 declares a reference parameter that is a pointer. The actual parameter must be some l-value that may be assigned a new pointer during execution of the function. Ctype& declares a reference parameter of some C type.

- Meaning of function calls

  Member functions are called with the -> operator.

  First we consider calling functions of construction or repetition classes. Consider the example:

  ```
  // Contents = ... or Contents ~ ...
  Contents* iContents; iContents = ...;
  iContents -> weight(...);
  ```

  The last line is a call of function weight for the object in variable iContents that must be an instance of class Contents. This is like a regular C function call

  ```
  weight1(iContents, ...)
  ```

  The meaning of -> for calling functions of alternation classes is different. The default is that functions of alternation classes are virtual and we assume this default in the following discussion. Consider the following example for discussing the meaning of calling virtual functions.

  ```
  // Telephone : Cordless | Standard ...
  // Cordless = .
  // Standard = .
  Telephone* iTelephone; iTelephone = ...;
  iTelephone -> ringing(...);
  ```

  The last line is a call of function ringing for the object in variable iTelephone. The object in variable iTelephone can be an instance of any construction class that is alternation-reachable from Telephone. A class is **alternation-reachable** from an alternation class if it can be reached following alternation edges only.

  The call

3.5. APPENDIX: FROM C TO C++

```
iTelephone -> ringing(...)
```

does not tell us which code will be called at run-time. We know only that it will be code that is accessible from construction classes alternation-reachable from **Telephone**. Consider the case

```
// Telephone : Cordless ...
Telephone* iTelephone;
iTelephone = new Cordless(...);
iTelephone -> ringing(...)
```

Here the last line will activate the ringing function of **Cordless** (if there is one) or the ringing function of an alternation predecessor of **Cordless**.

- this

  Member functions have a hidden argument and **this** allows us to talk about it explicitly. Consider the member function

  ```
  void Telephone::ringing(...)
    { ... this ...}
  ```

  and the call

  ```
  iTelephone->ringing(...);
  ```

  When **Telephone::ringing** is called by the above call, **this** will contain the object in iTelephone.

- Simulating super

  C++ allows us to use the scope resolution operator to call a function of a super class directly. An example is

  ```
  // Telephone : Cordless ...
  // Cordless is a subclass of Telephone
  void Cordless::print()
    { ... Telephone::print(); ...}
  ```

- Overloading of functions and operators <<, >>, () etc.

  The same class may have several functions with the same name, provided the argument types are distinct. The same holds true for operators. For example, the input/output classes provided with C++ compilers use overloaded shift operators for input and output. **cout** is an object of class **ostream** and we can use the "put to" operator, called <<, for output. Each time the << is used with **cout**, printing continues from the position where it previously left off. For example,

```
cout << "x= " << iD->f() << endl;
```

first prints a comment, then the object that f returns, followed by an end-of-line.

The class **istream** uses the overloaded operator >> for input. For example,

```
cin >> d >> z
```

reads from the standard input (usually the keyboard), a value for d and then for z. White space is ignored.

To iterate through a repetition object, we use the overloaded function call operator ().

```
// Fruit_List ~ Fruit { Fruit }.
void   Fruit_List::add_cost(float &size )
{
    Fruit_list_iterator     next_arg(*this);
    Fruit*                  each_arg;

    while ( each_arg = next_arg() ) // <=== calls ()
                                    // to get next list element
        each_arg->add_cost(size );
}
```

- Constructors

  For construction and repetition classes, constructors are created. They are used to create objects.

  For a construction class

  ```
  Motor = <horsepower> Number <shaft> DriveShaft.
  ```

  a constructor

  ```
  Motor::Motor(Number* x = NULL, DriveShaft* y = NULL)
  ```

  is created. It has default arguments for x and y.

  Motor() is equivalent to Motor(NULL,NULL),
  Motor(x1) is equivalent to Motor(x1,NULL).

- Comment character

  The comment character in C++ is //. The C comment characters may also be used.

3.6 SUMMARY

In this chapter we viewed adaptive software as a convenient way to describe C++ software. Adaptive software is to C++ software what stenography is to the English language. But adaptive software is succinct stenography since one adaptive program describes an entire family of C++ programs.

We studied the evolution of a C++ program. We first wrote a program to compute the total salary paid by a conglomerate of companies. Then we decided that the structure of the conglomerate objects needs to be changed and we rewrote the C++ program. We then added more functionality to the program and made it work for both class structures we considered.

We noticed that the changes we did to the software were very time consuming when done directly at the C++ level. When the C++ programs were described by adaptive programs, the changes were significantly easier.

In this chapter we showed the most important components of adaptive software and how they relate to C++. Two important features of adaptive software that we did not mention are: *transportation patterns* and *edge wrappers*. Transportation patterns are used to transport objects around so that at the right time the appropriate objects are simultaneously available to do a particular task. Solving a task through objects is like solving a task with people: It is important that the right people get together at the right time. With transportation patterns we can achieve the grouping of objects without knowing the detailed interfaces of the objects.

This chapter has used a small subset of C++ to introduce adaptive software to the C++ programmer. It is very important to remember that adaptive software is a technique that can be used with any object-oriented programming language. An earlier version of adaptive software was developed with an extension of Lisp, now known as CLOS.

3.7 EXERCISES

Exercise 3.1 Directly implement the C++ programs dicussed in this chapter and compile and run them on your computer system. Go through all the evolution steps.

Measure the time it takes to do the exercise. If you spend more than five hours, switch to the next exercise.

Exercise 3.2 Do the previous exercise but describe the C++ programs through adaptive programs. Use the Demeter Tools/C++ to turn the adaptive programs into C++ programs.

Measure the time it takes to do the exercise. Compare with the time measurement for the previous exercise.

Further exercises are in the self-study guide (Chapter 17).

Exercise 3.3 How would you implement repetition classes in Demeter?
Hint:
Use parameterized classes as follows to avoid code replication and slow compilation.

```
template<class T>
  class Repetition {
```

```
  private:
    ...
  public:
    Repetition();
    void append(T*);
    T* n_th(int);
  };

template<class T>
  class List : Repetition<void*> {
  public:
    List() : Repetition<void*> {}
    void append(T* p) {Repetition<void*>::append(p);}
    T* n_th(int a){(T*) Repetition<void*>::n_th(a);}
  };
```

To define

List(A)
List(B)

you can now use:

List<A>*
List(B>*

3.8 BIBLIOGRAPHIC REMARKS

The conglomerate example is due to Ian Holland and was used in numerous demonstrations of the Demeter Tools/C++ and in [LSLX94].

The reference manual for C++ is [ES90].

Chapter 4

Thinking Adaptively

What system developers need to realize is that developing an information system is not a one-time effort. Information systems resemble the complexity of living systems as they **keep on evolving**. Among the important features required of a system to ensure a fruitful life for it are: Adaptability, Flexibility, Scalability, Maintainability, Reliability.

Lloyd Osborn (Manager, Boeing Defense & Space Group) in [Osb93].

In this chapter we present the key ideas behind adaptive software, we show adaptive software development by example, and we report on experiences.

First we address the question: What is adaptive software? A program is called **adaptive** if it changes its behavior[1] according to its context.

This is a high-level definition that has to be taken with a grain of salt. Different kinds of adaptiveness can be achieved depending on what we view as context. In this book we focus on data structures, class structures, or data models as context. Instead of viewing a data structure as an integral part of an algorithm (as is done traditionally), we view it as context that can be changed significantly without modifying the program. A number of other artifacts can be viewed as context to a program. For example, we could view the inputs to a program as being context. Then every program becomes adaptive. Other, more interesting contexts would be

- Run-time environment

  Depending on the other processes with which the program runs, the program will optimize a parameter to achieve better performance.

- Concurrency properties

  Instead of viewing the concurrency-related part of a program as being hardwired to the program, we view it as context that can be changed. The same program can then work with many concurrency schemes.

---

[1] We use behavior and function as synonyms although others make a distinction. We could distinguish between two different models for a piece of software: behavior (how it works), function (the role it plays; what the software does in its environment). Function is viewed as an interpretation of the behavior.

- Distribution properties

    Instead of hardwiring object migration into the program, we view it as context. The same program can then be used together with different object migration strategies.

- Software architecture

    Instead of hardwiring the connection between software components into the program, we view it as context that can be changed. The same program can then work with a class of software architectures.

- Computational resources (printers, displays, name servers, etc.)

    Instead of hardwiring information about computational resources into a program, we view it as context. The same program can then work with a family of computational resources.

- Exceptions, failures

    Instead of hardwiring exceptions into a program, we view them as context. The same program can then work with a family of failure-handling schemes.

How can we achieve adaptiveness? A generic mechanism to achieve adaptiveness is to use loosely coupled collaborating views. For simplicity, we use two sets of complementary, collaborating views $V1$ and $V2$, which are loosely coupled in the following way:

> An element $v1$ of $V1$ is formulated in terms of partial information about elements of $V2$. More explicitly, view $v1$ is formulated in terms of constraints that specify the set of views in $V2$ that are compatible with $v1$.

View $v1$ is called adaptive since it adapts automatically to elements in $V2$ that are compatible with $v1$.

Let's consider an example. As $V2$ we take class graphs that describe object structures. Elements of $V1$ are programs that specify a group G of collaborating classes for each class graph in a subset of $V2$. Group G is used to formulate the desired functionality. The groups of collaborating classes are specified implicitly without enumerating them explicitly. In this example, instead of writing an algorithm for a specific data structure, you write an algorithm for constraints that specify the data structures with which the algorithm works. In other words, you write an algorithm for a generic data structure defined by constraints.

Adaptive software described in this book is specified by complementary, collaborating views, each one addressing a different concern of the application. The main goal of adaptive programming is to separate concerns by minimizing dependencies between the complementary views, so that a large class of modifications in one view has a minimum impact on the other views. The complementary views approach has the advantage that programs become more flexible, understandable, and shorter, without loss of run-time efficiency.

In this book we focus on treating class structures as context. An adaptive program, instead of being written for a specific data model, is written for a generic data model restricted by a set of structural constraints (see Fig. 4.1). This implies that adaptive software has the following property: **Adaptive software** is generic software that defines a family of programs with a large variability in architecture. By the architecture of a program

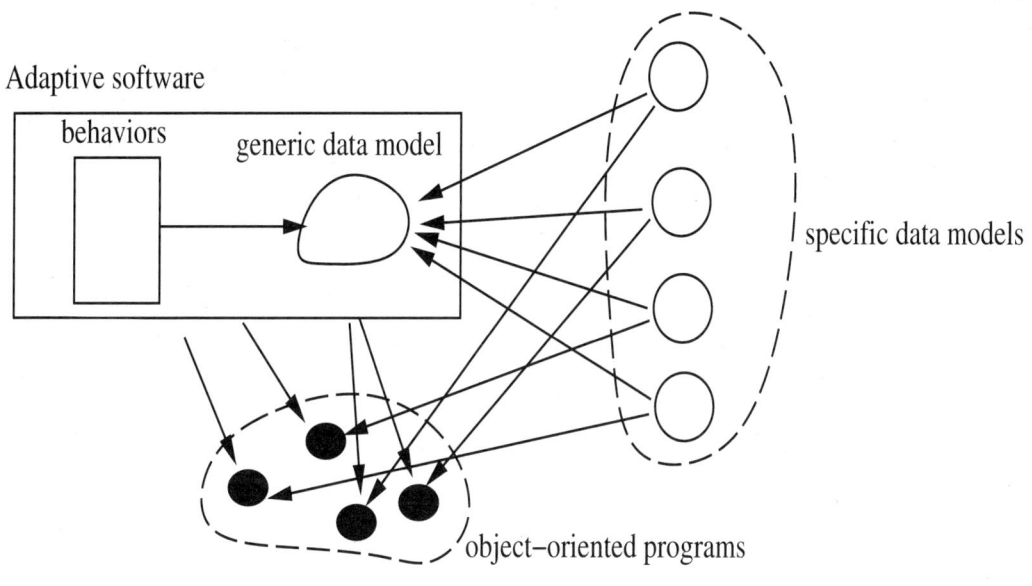

Figure 4.1: Generic data model

we mean the interfaces contained in the program, including the connections between the interfaces.

Adaptive software can be realized in different ways and a useful realization is described in this book. A key ingredient to the realization of adaptive software is the concept of a succinct graph specification. A graph consists of vertices and edges between the vertices. During software development it is often necessary to describe subgraphs of larger graphs. For example, the larger graph maybe a datamodel and the subgraph a subdatamodel relevant to implementing a certain task. A subgraph specification for a graph G is called **succinct** if it is smaller than the size of G. The size of a graph is the number of vertices and edges it contains. An example of a succinct graph specification is: "take all vertices and edges that are on paths from vertex A to vertex Z." For a big graph with 1000 vertices and 2000 edges and many paths between vertices A and Z, the above specification might describe a subgraph with 500 vertices and 800 edges. Such a graph is clearly much larger than the above specification and therefore we call the above specification succinct.

This paragraph summarizes the realization of adaptive software in this book.[2] This summary is abstract and may be skipped on first reading. Adaptive software is realized in terms of succinct graph specifications that constrain the structural architectures in which the adaptive software works. More explicitly, adaptive software is realized as follows. Adaptive software is generic software that needs to be instantiated by architectures. Adaptive software consists of three parts: succinct subgraph specifications $\mathcal{C}$, initial behavior specifi-

---

[2]Propagation pattern partial evaluation, page 448 (64). This is a reference to an instructional objective in Chapter 14, the "nerve center" of the book. See also the explanation on page xxx.

cations expressed in terms of $\mathcal{C}$, and behavior enhancements expressed in terms of $\mathcal{C}$. The succinct subgraph specifications express the permissible architectures. The initial behavior specifications express simple behavior in terms of the subgraph specifications, and the behavior enhancements express (in terms of the subgraph specifications) how the simple behavior is enhanced to get the desired behavior.

4.1 KEY IDEAS

We relate adaptive software to important problem-solving principles: inventor's paradox, stepwise refinement, and representation independence.

4.1.1 Inventor's Paradox

The "paradox of the inventor," posed by mathematician George Polya [Pol49], is one of the cornerstones of adaptive software. Polya observed that it is often easier to solve a more general problem than the one at hand and then to use the solution of the general problem to solve the specific problem. The hard work consists of finding the appropriate generalization. Polya uses the following example to demonstrate the technique. Given a line and a regular octahedron, find a plane that contains the line and that cuts the volume of the octahedron in half. What is important about the regular octahedron to provide for an easy solution? The fact that it is a symmetric body is important. Given any symmetric body, the solution consists of choosing the plane that contains the given line and the center of symmetry. The general solution is easily applied to solve the specific octahedron problem.

What is the paradox? Why is it called inventor's paradox? It is a paradox because we would expect that solving a more general problem is harder than solving a specific problem. It is called inventor's paradox because an invention needs to be done: we have to invent the proper generalization of the given problem.

Applying Polya's paradox of the inventor to object-oriented program design results in more adaptive programs being written, programs that adjust gracefully to specializations of the generalization for which they were designed.

In this book we introduce **adaptive object-oriented programming** as an extension to conventional object-oriented programming. We adopt the convention that adaptive object-oriented programs are just called **adaptive programs**. Adaptive programming facilitates expressing the algorithms that are essential to an application without committing to any particular data structure. Adaptive object-oriented programs specify essential data structure elements that constrain the configuration of any data structure that attempts to customize the adaptive program. This way, programmers are encouraged to think about families of programs by finding appropriate data structure generalizations, in the spirit of Polya.

In adaptive programming, the inventor's paradox has the following interpretation. The invention consists of inventing a generalized data structure for a specific data structure. The paradox is that it is easier to write programs for the generalized data structure than for the specific data structure.

Soon we will apply the inventor's paradox to writing an application for a travel agency. Instead of writing the application for a specific travel agency, we will write it for an entire family of travel agencies, and the surprising news is that the generalization simplifies the programming task.

4.1.2 Stepwise Refinement

> The development of an algorithm is very often a complex process where the final solution is achieved by stepwise refinement. In every step certain details get specified which have been left open in the previous step.
>
> Niklaus Wirth, circa 1970.

The idea of stepwise refinement is another cornerstone of adaptive software. Adaptive software lets us write algorithms without knowing the detailed data structures and even without knowing the interfaces of the data structures. It is only after a refinement step, called customization, where the data structures get fully specified.

Adaptive software uses a two-step refinement method. First get the important parts of your application right and then worry about the accidental details of your data structures.

Readers might object that delaying commitments to data structures is a well-known approach to software development. What is the essential difference of adaptive software to the other approaches? Adaptive software is written in two parts: the data part and the functional part, which are loosely coupled through constraints. This allows the same functional part to work with different data parts and the same data part can be matched with different functional parts. The adaptation occurs by a simple form of analogical reasoning that is rooted in a path calculus for class structures (see Chapter 7, Propagation Directives).

4.1.3 Representation/Interface Independence

The idea of making software independent of the details of data structures is another cornerstone of adaptive software. It is traditional in object-oriented software development to hide representation and implementation information. This comes out of early work of Parnas [PCW86]. Although we agree with the spirit of the information hiding principle, we feel that it is too restrictive. It is good to hide low-level representation information but it is not appropriate to hide essential logical information about object structure. It is good to make assumptions about the internal structure of objects! I have to repeat this twice since so many books and papers say the opposite. It is good to make assumptions about the internal structure of objects!

Sethi [Set89] summarizes information hiding with the informal **representation independence principle**.

> A program should be designed so that the representation of an object can be changed without affecting the rest of the program.

We propose a stronger principle, the **adaptive programming principle**.

> A program should be designed so that the interfaces of objects can be changed within certain constraints without affecting the program *at all*.

The interface of an object is the set of functions that can be called for the object to manipulate its data. The adaptive programming principle implies that the program must be written parameterized by interface information. Indeed, an adaptive program is parameterized by constraints that say what kind of interface information is expected by the program. Therefore, an adaptive program does not completely hide all interface information of its local objects, but it exposes some essential properties of local objects.

By giving up strict information hiding, we surprisingly get better representation independence. The reason is that adaptive software keeps only a loose coupling between functions and data expressed by parameterization constraints. The same program works for an entire family of representations that satisfy the constraints (see Fig. 4.2).

Adaptive programs are data structure-shy programs that are written in terms of hooks into a data structure (see Fig. 4.3). A hook means an important data structure element. The adaptive program is written in terms of paths between important data structure elements.

Data-structure-shy software opposes any attempt to encode too many data structure details into it. This opposition is enforced by a dependency metric that measures the dependency of a program on a specific data structure. The hooks may refer to data types or relations. Between the hooks there may be a lot of additional information that is ignored by the adaptive program although the information will be considered when the adaptive program is used in a specific context.

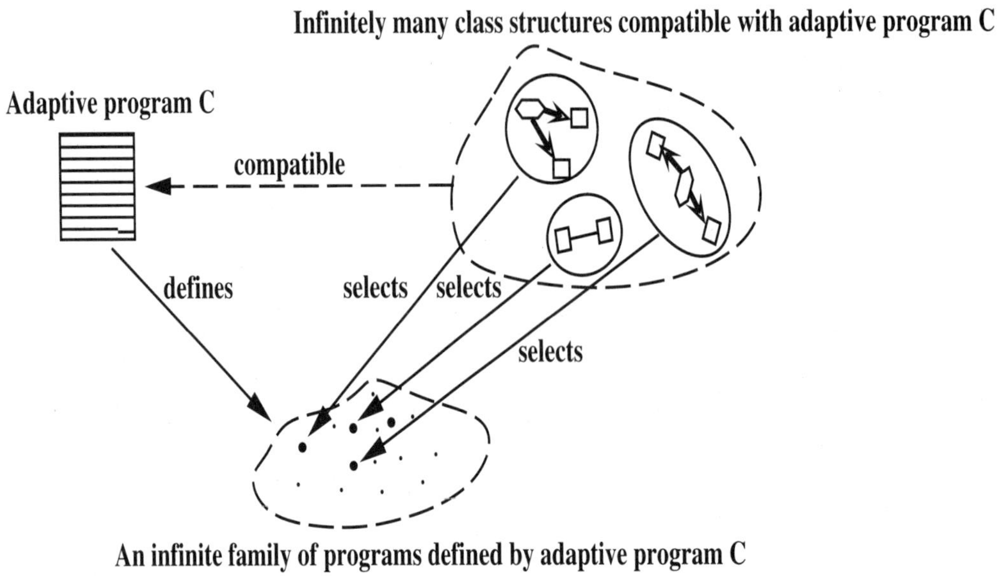

Figure 4.2: Adaptive Software

The need to program in a data structure-shy way has been recognized by others. In [GTC+90], we read

> ... the class hierarchy may become a rigid constraining structure that hampers innovation and evolution.

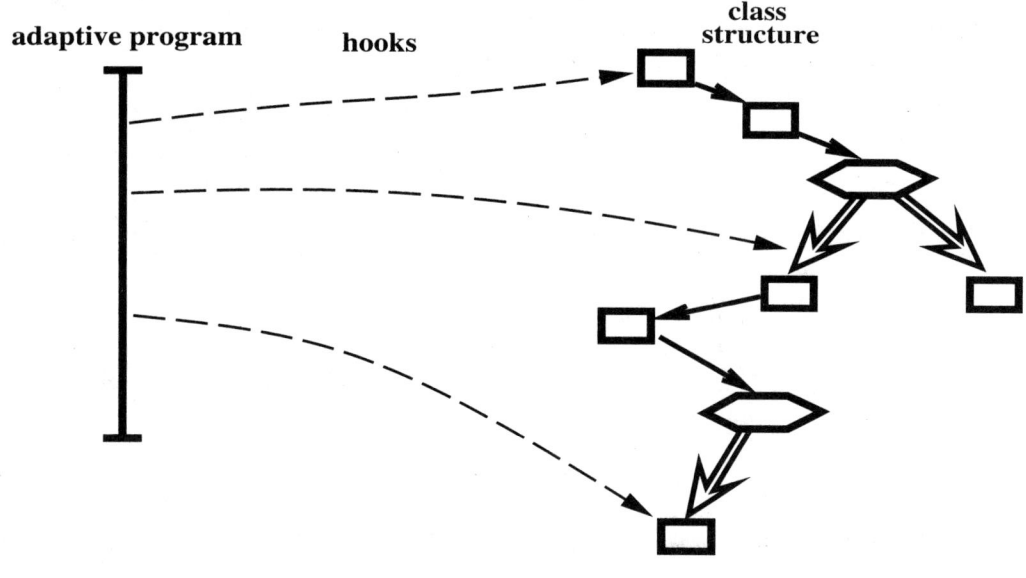

Figure 4.3: Programming with hooks

This suggests that class hierarchy information should be abstracted out and the programs should be written relatively independent of the hierarchy.

4.2 MODELING COMPLEX SYSTEMS

We first present adaptive software as a new modeling technique for complex systems and then relate adaptive and object-oriented software. The explanation in terms of modeling has the advantage that it allows us to define adaptive programming without reference to object-oriented programming.

According to the *Encyclopedia of Computer Science and Engineering* [Ral83], a complete model frequently includes both a structural model and a process model. The structural model describes the organization of the system and the process model describes the operation or behavior of the system. With this context, we can give a concise informal definition of adaptive programs.

> An adaptive program is a generic process model parameterized by graph constraints which define compatible structural models as parameters of the process model.

The graph constraints indicate what kind of paths need to exist in the structural models that are graphs. The compatible structural models are also called customizers. A traditional model is the result of applying a customizer to an adaptive program. The innovative feature of adaptive programs is that they use graph constraints to specify possible customizers. An example of a graph constraint is that certain paths exist using or avoiding certain edges.

Adaptive models have several advantages over traditional models.

- Adaptive models focus on the essence of the system being modeled and are therefore simpler and shorter than traditional models. Adaptive models are not distorted by an accidental structure that is currently in use, but which makes the model unnecessarily complex.

- Many behaviors require the same customization. Therefore customizers are effectively reused.

- Graph constraints allow for easy internal changes to the model before customization, that is, adaptive models can be reused easily in unplanned ways. They are not only adaptive but also adaptable should the adaptiveness not be sufficient. This means that when we apply an adaptive program to a customizing class structure and we don't get the desired behavior, the adjustment necessary at the adaptive level is usually smaller than the adjustment at the object-oriented language level. We distinguish between adaptable and adaptive programs. An adaptable program is one that is easy to change manually to a new context and an adaptive program adjusts automatically to a new context.

- Graph constraints allow for implicit parameterization of models without giving explicit parameters. Adaptive models can be refined easily before they are customized.

The above list discusses the advantages of an adaptive model with respect to traditional modeling. With the current interest in object-oriented modeling, it is useful to discuss the relationship between adaptive and object-oriented modeling.

Object-oriented modeling is a special case of adaptive modeling in that object-oriented modeling uses very strong graph constraints that determine only a small number of customizers. Here we view an object-oriented model as consisting only of the methods. The same set of methods works with several class structures that differ by the number of inheritance relationships between the class structures.

For example, the two methods

```
void A::t() {c -> t();}
void B::t() {print ("hello");}
```

work with the class structure in Fig. 4.4. Class A has one part (data member, instance

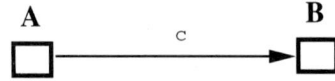

Figure 4.4: Adaptability of object-oriented program

variable) named c of class B.

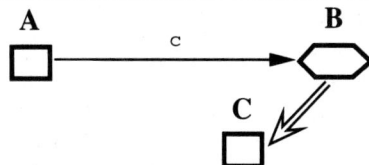

Figure 4.5: Adaptability of object-oriented program

And the same two methods also work with the class structure in Fig. 4.5. Class A has one part (instance variable) named c of class B. Class C inherits from class B and class C has no additional parts.

Advantages of adaptive over object-oriented modeling are

- An adaptive model describes a large family of object-oriented models and is therefore at a higher level of abstraction. An object-oriented model assigns methods to classes at program-write-time whereas an adaptive program delays many of those bindings past write-time.

- An adaptive model together with the customizer is usually shorter than the corresponding object-oriented model (i.e., the result of the application of the customizer to the adaptive model). The reason is that the same parts of the customizer are usually applied many times.

- Adaptive models can be specialized more flexibly than object-oriented models since they have many specialization points that are not controlled by explicit parameters. Prefix and suffix wrappers play an important role.

- There is no run-time performance penalty over object-oriented models due to inlining compiler technology.

There are only a few disadvantages of adaptive over object-oriented modeling:

- Writers of adaptive models need to learn a small extension to object-oriented languages (the propagation pattern and class dictionary notation). They need to learn a new debugging technique (see Chapter 13).

- There are no other disadvantages of adaptive models that do not also apply to object-oriented models. The reason is that adaptive software is simply a concise representation of object-oriented software. The conciseness does not introduce new problems but improves generality of the software and solves (via propagation) the small-methods problem of object-oriented software. The small-methods problem says that large object-oriented applications tend to contain a significant number of methods only two or three lines long.

To explain the difference between adaptive and object-oriented models further, we show the following relationships.

Every object-oriented program is an adaptive program (no graph constraints are used to specify customizers, and all methods are programmed). Only a few of the object-oriented programs are "good" adaptive programs. By a "good" adaptive program we mean a program that makes minimal assumptions on its class structures. Every adaptive program corresponds, through customization, to a family of object-oriented programs.

We have compared adaptive software development with object-oriented software development. We briefly compare object-oriented software development with traditional software development. Despite hype to the contrary, object-oriented development incurs extra cost over procedural development.

- Design time

  We need to design a class hierarchy using information about the domain. In our experience, this is a significant cost factor since often designers try to find an optimal class hierarchy. The reason why they want an optimal class hierarchy is that it should change only minimally over the life-cycle of the software. Unfortunately, this is an illusion and a lot of time is wasted since class hierarchies will always change. Adaptive software reduces the need for an optimal class hierarchy since changes in the class hierarchy can be absorbed easily by adaptive software.

- Maintenance time

  In an object-oriented program it is more difficult to find the exact line of code providing some function because of virtual functions and the prevalence of many small methods. To understand a program, we have to wade through many small methods that do simple things. Adaptive software eliminates the small methods problem and therefore helps with program understanding at maintenance time.

4.3 JUSTIFICATION

Any new software development method needs good reasons for its existence since many methods are already available and practitioners have difficulty in choosing one. Here are some of the reasons why adaptive software is worthwhile. Adaptive software is easier to maintain than object-oriented software since it is written with fewer assumptions on class structures. Adaptive software is usually considerably shorter than the corresponding object-oriented software and therefore, it requires less typing than object-oriented software. Adaptive software has a higher probability of being reusable than corresponding object-oriented software. The reason is that one adaptive program defines an infinite collection of object-oriented programs. Adaptive software is generic software that does not have to be parameterized explicitly. The software can be flexibly extended in unforeseen ways by adding arguments and by wrapping code around already existing code.

In a commercial software development environment, it is important that software is designed to be reusable from the beginning. Often no time is left to make the software reusable later. And with object-oriented programs, it is often unclear how to make a class reusable—much effort is wasted on useless generalization. Adaptive software makes a contribution in this area since adaptive programs are never harder to write than object-oriented programs, but are usually more reusable (an adaptive program defines a big family of object-oriented programs). Furthermore the best adaptive programs are much more expressive than the corresponding object-oriented programs and, in the worst case, an adaptive program is an object-oriented program. Adaptive software may be used whenever object-oriented software is used since it can only improve the flexibility of the software. Adaptive software can always be made at least as good as the best object-oriented software that can be written for a given application.

An advantage of adaptive software is that it allows for initial error and subsequent adjustment. Many problems are complex, and initially it is not clear how to best structure the classes. Often we know the best class structure only after the project is completed. Not knowing how to start can easily lead to procrastination. With adaptive software, we can easily make a first guess at the class structure and then write the functionality with minimal dependency on the class structure. Changing to a better class structure is then much easier.

Adaptive software is a good tool to teach advanced object-oriented software development. Adaptive software provides for a better understanding and better use of object-oriented software. The object-oriented concepts are learned or reinforced as a side effect when the adaptive concepts are learned.

4.4 CUSTOMIZATION

Adaptive programs are written in terms of partial class structures and they need to be customized into object-oriented programs. An adaptive program can be used with any complete class structure that is compatible with the given partial class structure. The customization of an adaptive program can be achieved in at least three ways:

- A few sample objects can be selected that describe by example on what kind of objects the program is supposed to operate.

- A graph similar to an entity relationship diagram can be used to complete a given partial class structure (see Fig. 4.2).

- A grammar similar to a BNF (Backus-Naur-Form) grammar can be used to complete a given partial class structure and to specify an application-specific language simultaneously.

An object-oriented program is typically built by customizing several adaptive programs into the same class structure, as we have shown with the conglomerate example. This usually requires renaming to avoid name conflicts.

Adaptive software uses a graphical approach to develop object-oriented software. When developing adaptive software we can proceed in two ways.

- Structure first

    First develop a class structure, check it for design-rule violations, and check it for completeness with respect to the structure of the objects it has to represent. Then for each subtask to be implemented, choose groups of collaborating classes that are described using minimal knowledge about the class structure in a propagation pattern. The resulting propagation patterns are customized with the class structure.

- Functionality first

For each subtask to be implemented, choose a partial class structure that contains the important classes for the subtask. The functionality is then implemented generically for this partial class structure. Later, the program is customized to an object-oriented program by using a compatible class structure that has been checked for completeness and design-rule violations.

In both approaches, much of software development consists of graph manipulation.

Adaptive software introduces a new way to parameterize object-oriented software that goes beyond parameterized classes or templates. An adaptive program describes an object-oriented program parameterized by classes and their relationships. A parameter has a type that is a predicate on a graph. It is interesting that the parameters influence the input and output language and the detailed structure of the classes and object-oriented programs. In other words, an adaptive program is written *without* knowing the input language or the detailed structure of the resulting object-oriented program!

4.5 THE ITINERARY PROBLEM

We turn now to a concrete example. Suppose we are developing a trip itinerary program to be used by travel agencies. Consider a trip object that describes the structure of a multi-day trip. The task is to print the itinerary, that is, the list of all locations visited during the trip. Since we don't know the travel agency to which we will sell the program yet, we are forced to apply the "paradox of the inventor." (Normally, adaptive software development starts with a concrete class structure from which the designer/programmer tries to use minimal information.)

What is important about the trip object to provide for an easy solution? The fact that it contains location objects; the information that it is a multiday trip object can be ignored.

Specifically, we want to implement the following algorithm:

1. Print the departure time at the beginning of the itinerary.

2. For each location visited on the itinerary:
   —Print the name of the location.

3. Print the arrival time at the end of the itinerary.

To formulate the adaptive program for the itinerary problem, we use two class-valued variables called **Trip** and **Location**. Those variables will be assigned a specific class when the adaptive program is customized. We then formulate the following minimal assumption on the class structure:

- **Trip**: We assume that objects of class **Trip** contain **Location**-objects that describe the itinerary. We assume that a **Trip**-object has a departure and arrival time.

We will print the departure time at the beginning of the itinerary and the arrival time at the end of the itinerary.

Next we formulate a propagation pattern that describes a family of implementations of one signature for a varying group of classes. An adaptive program is a collection of propagation patterns. A propagation pattern is expressed in terms of class-valued and relation-valued variables. Class-valued variables will be mapped into classes when the propagation

4.5. THE ITINERARY PROBLEM

pattern is used in the context of a concrete class dictionary graph. Relation-valued variables will be replaced by class-relationship names when the propagation pattern is customized. Both class-valued and relation-valued variables may be renamed before the propagation pattern is customized to an object-oriented program. A propagation pattern consists of a propagation directive and a list of annotations, called wrappers (see Fig. 4.6).

Next, the propagation pattern is explained in more detail. Our goal is to implement the print_itinerary task and therefore we write an operation with the signature void print_itinerary(). To accomplish the task, we need the collaboration of a group of classes. Since we don't know yet for which travel agency we are writing the program, we cannot itemize the group of collaborators; we can give only a generic specification. We want all the classes from Trip to Location to help us. This information is expressed in the propagation directive *from* Trip *to* Location. Besides describing the collaborating classes, a propagation directive has a second very important function: it describes traversal code. The directive in the example says how to traverse Trip-objects: Traverse all Location-objects.

For this simple example, the traversal code does most of the work needed to solve the itinerary printing problem. But we need a mechanism to enhance the traversal code so that exactly the posed problem is solved. Traversal code enhancements are done with wrappers. A wrapper is attached to a class-valued variable and must contain either a prefix code fragment or a suffix code fragment or both. Prefix code is placed before the traversal code and suffix code is put after the traversal code. The C++ code itself is placed between the symbols (@ and @).[3]

```
// functionality to be implemented
*operation* void print_itinerary()
  // define group of collaborating classes and
  // corresponding traversal code
  *traverse*
    *from* Trip *to* Location
  // annotate the traversal code
  *wrapper* Trip
    *prefix* (@ departure -> g_print(); @)
    *suffix* (@ arrival -> g_print(); @)
  *wrapper* Location
    *prefix* (@ this -> g_print(); @)
```

Figure 4.6: Propagation pattern print_itinerary

The propagation pattern in Fig. 4.6 is formulated in terms of two class-valued variables, called Trip and Location, and two relation-valued variables called departure and arrival.

The advantage of this notation is that there is not an entire new programming language

---

[3]Legal propagation patterns, page 447 (61).

to learn but only the relatively small propagation language. All the facilities of C++ to express member functions can be used freely.

4.5.1 Customizing the Adaptive Program

How can the propagation pattern be run?[4] We need to select a program from the family of programs we have written in Fig. 4.6. For this purpose, we need to find a class structure that satisfies the constraints: There exists a path from class Trip to class Location and a departure and arrival attribute at class Trip. The path concept is used informally here and will be explained later. There are infinitely many such class structures since the propagation pattern is expressed with minimal knowledge of the class structure to keep the software robust under changes.

Two compatible class structures are shown in Figs. 4.7 and 4.8. The first customizer is for a travel agency that uses very simple trip objects. The second customizer expresses multiday trip objects. Both customizers use two kinds of classes: construction classes (drawn as □) that are used to instantiate objects with a fixed number of parts, and repetition classes (drawn as ⬡) that are used to instantiate objects with a variable number of parts.[5] Edges leaving construction vertices are called construction edges (drawn as ⟶) and are labeled to name the parts. Edges leaving repetition vertices are called repetition edges. Optional parts are shown with a dashed line (drawn as ┈▶).

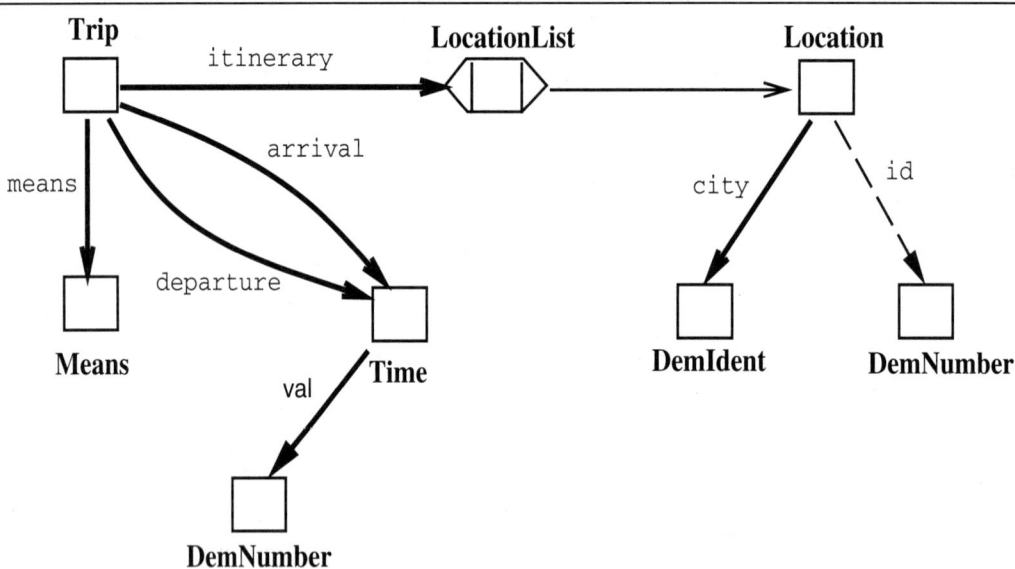

Figure 4.7: Program customizer Trip 1

---

[4]Legal propagation pattern customization, page 447 (62).
[5]Class dictionary graph graphical representation, page 431 (6).

4.5. THE ITINERARY PROBLEM

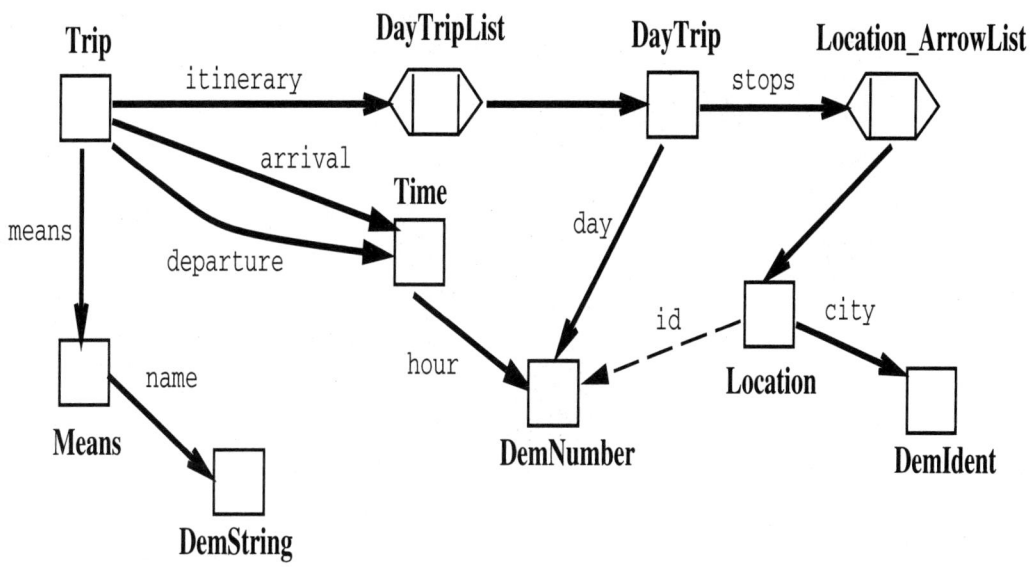

Figure 4.8: Program customizer Trip 2

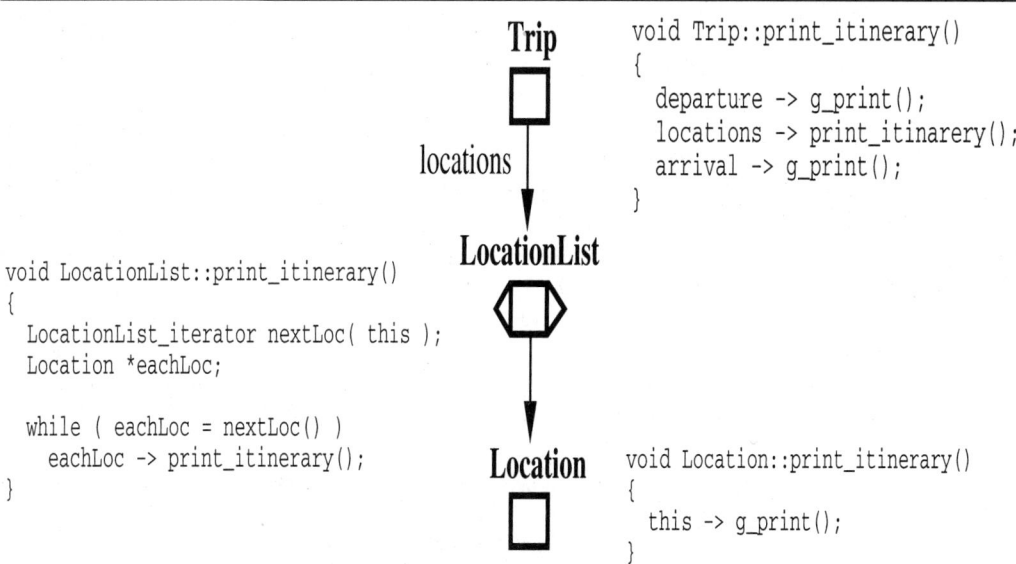

Figure 4.9: Propagation graph Trip 1

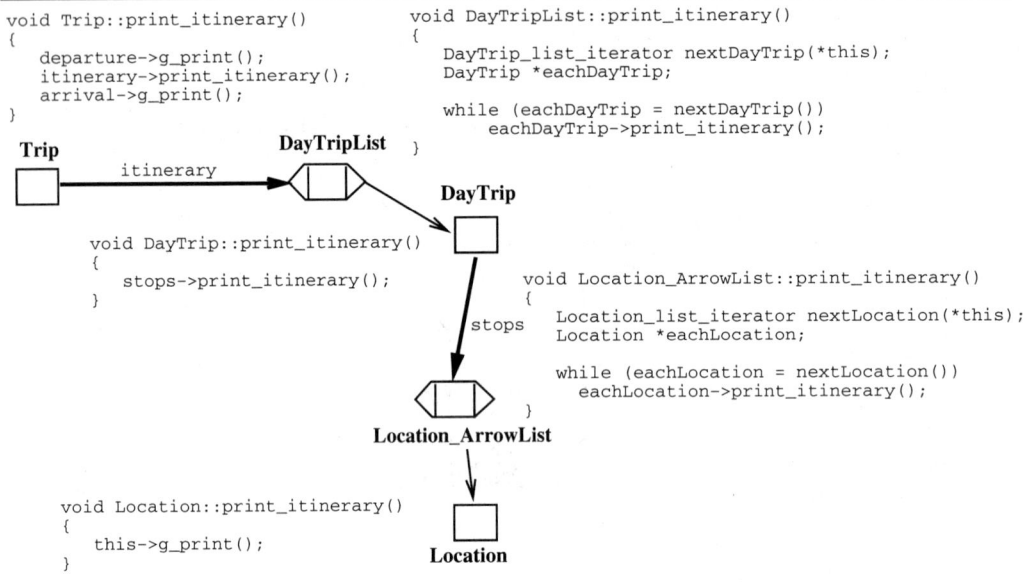

Figure 4.10: Propagation graph Trip 2

Each of the two customizers specifies an object-oriented program that is shown in Figs. 4.9 and 4.10. We can view the initial propagation pattern in Fig. 4.6 as a common abstraction of the two object-oriented programs obtained by the customizations. The two customizations demonstrate the adaptiveness of the adaptive program in Fig. 4.6.

How is the object-oriented program constructed from the adaptive program when a customizer is given? This is the task of the propagation pattern compiler whose operation is briefly summarized here. First all the paths specified by the propagation directive *from* Trip *to* Location are computed. The union of the paths forms a subgraph, called a propagation graph. Examples of propagation graphs are shown in Figs. 4.9 and 4.10 if you ignore the C++ code. The propagation graph is a class structure that we are going to interpret as a set of methods, not a set of classes. The propagation graph is mapped into a program by translating each vertex into a method as follows. An outgoing construction edge results in a call to the corresponding part; an outgoing repetition edge results in the iteration code through the collection. Then the wrapper code is added.

A look at the C++ code in Fig. 4.10 shows little resemblance to the adaptive program in Fig. 4.6. The code fragments used in the adaptive program appear in the C++ program at the appropriate places. The signature that is written once in the adaptive program appears several times in the C++ program. The adaptive program saved us a lot of typing.

There is a second translation, called *generate*, which must take place before the object-oriented program can be run. The customizing class dictionary graph is translated into an application-specific class library that contains generic functionality for manipulating objects, such as copying, printing, comparing, accessing, constructing, etc. The class library

4.5. THE ITINERARY PROBLEM

produced by *generate* and the member functions computed by *propagate* are combined with a call of the correct member function to form an executable C++ program.

What is the difference between an object-oriented program and an adaptive program? We use the picture in Fig. 4.11 to describe the difference. Fig. 4.11 refers to the propagation pattern in 4.6 and to the C++ program in Fig. 4.10 (Trip 2). In the adaptive program

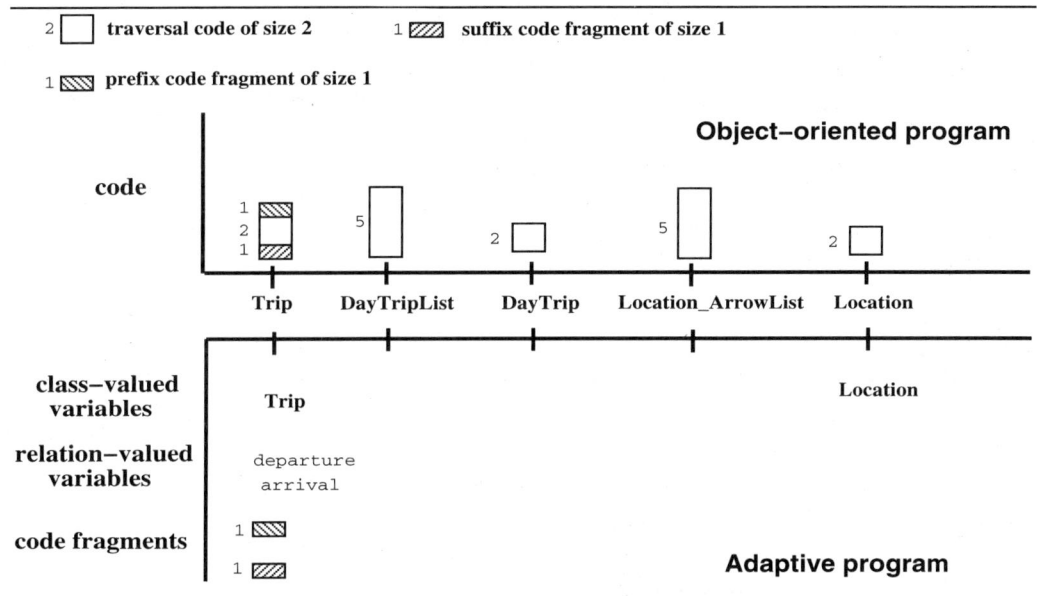

Figure 4.11: Adaptive versus object-oriented

we can focus only on the essential information. The adaptive program is formulated only in terms of interesting classes and the traversal code is completely ignored. This example demonstrates that the Pareto-principle also applies here: for a given task, 80% of the work is done by 20% of the interesting classes. Propagation patterns allow us to focus on those interesting classes.

We have discussed how to customize an adaptive program with a class structure. But this is only one possibility. We can expect that when we put more information into a customizer, we get a customization with more functionality. What kind of information can we use for customization? We could use cardinality constraints (e.g., a list must have between three and four elements), or sharing constraints (e.g., two objects specified by paths in the class structure must be identical), or external representation information (e.g., the object must be printed with certain syntactic elements).

Let's look at an example of a class structure with external representation information, that is, a grammar (see Fig. 4.12). We use a familiar textual representation for grammars that is an extension of Wirth's EBNF notation [Wir77]. With such a customization we can now conveniently tell stories about trip objects in an English-like notation. An example is given in Fig. 4.13. We use // as the comment character.

```
Trip     = "TRIP"
           "by"         <means>      Means
           "departure"  <departure>  Time
           "arrival"    <arrival>    Time
           "ITINERARY"  <itinerary>  DayTripList.
DayTrip  = "day"        <day>        DemNumber
           "stops"      <stops>      Location_ArrowList.
Location = <city> DemIdent ["(" <id> DemNumber ")"].
Time     = "time" <hour> DemNumber.
Means    = "direct train" <name> DemString.
Location_ArrowList ~ Location{ "-->" Location}.
DayTripList ~ DayTrip { DayTrip}.
```

Figure 4.12: A textual form of trip class dictionary

```
TRIP by
  // Means-object
  direct train "Glacier Express"
departure
  // Time-object
  time 10
arrival
  // Time-object
  time 17
ITINERARY
// DayTripList-object
            day 1 stops
// LocationList-object
SaintMoritz ( 10 ) --> Thusis ( 11 ) -->
Chur ( 12 ) --> Andermatt ( 13 )

            day 2 stops
// LocationList-object
Andermatt ( 13 ) --> Brig ( 14 ) --> Zermatt ( 15 )
```

Figure 4.13: Corresponding trip description

4.5.2 Transporting Objects

So far we have seen how to express object traversals in a data structure-shy way. Next we look at an example of how to transport objects in the same style. Object-transportation is fundamental to object-oriented programming in that objects need to be transported around in object structures. When we call a function, we often need several objects to be present simultaneously to be used as arguments to the function. How can we assemble the objects together? We could do it the old-fashioned way and explicitly transport an object along a chain of, say, five objects that are objects of classes A,B,C,D, and E. This requires us to write simple methods for those classes A,B,C,D, and E. The methods have an argument for the object that is transported. Unfortunately, this technique encodes the object structure into the program. A better approach is to express the transportation information at a higher level of abstraction with transportation patterns.

A transportation pattern consists of a carry clause that defines parameters for object transportation, a transportation scope definition in the form of a propagation directive followed by wrappers that refer to the parameters. Statements to initialize and update transported objects may also occur inside a transportation pattern. A transportation pattern describes a family of algorithms to select and transport objects. The selection of subobjects and the transporting of objects is expressed with minimal knowledge of the class structure to keep the software robust under changes.

Consider an example of a transportation pattern in Fig. 4.14. The carry clause transports two objects, called i and s along the path from **Person** to **Unemployed** and at **Person** the objects are assigned.[6] The adaptive program is written in terms of the class-valued

---

```
*operation* void income_ssn_unemployed()
  *traverse*
    *from* Town *to* Unemployed
//transportation pattern
  *carry* *in* Income* i = (@ income; @),
          *in* DemNumber* s = (@ ssn; @)
  *along*
    *from* Person *to* Unemployed
  *wrapper* Unemployed
    *prefix*
      (@ i -> g_print(); s -> g_print(); @)
```

Figure 4.14: Propagation pattern with object transportation

---

variables: **Town, Person, Unemployed, Income, DemNumber** and the relation-valued variables **income** and **ssn**. At run-time, an **Income**-object and a **DemNumber**-object will be transported to an **Unemployed**-object.

---

[6] Legal transportation patterns, page 448 (66).

A customizer for the propagation pattern in Fig. 4.14 is shown in Fig. 4.15a and the resulting propagation graph and object-oriented program is in Fig. 4.15b.[7] The customizer uses an alternation class called **EmploymentStatus** (drawn as ◇). An alternation class is the dual of a construction class. Although a construction class, such as **Trip**, must have instances but cannot have subclasses, an alternation class, such as **EmploymentStatus** cannot have instances, but must have subclasses.[8] The subclasses of an alternation class are shown through alternation edges (drawn as ⟹). For example, **Employed** is a subclass of **EmploymentStatus** and therefore there is an alternation edge from **EmploymentStatus** to **Employed**. Methods attached to alternation classes are all considered virtual (although sometimes an optimization could be done by making some of the functions nonvirtual). The transportation

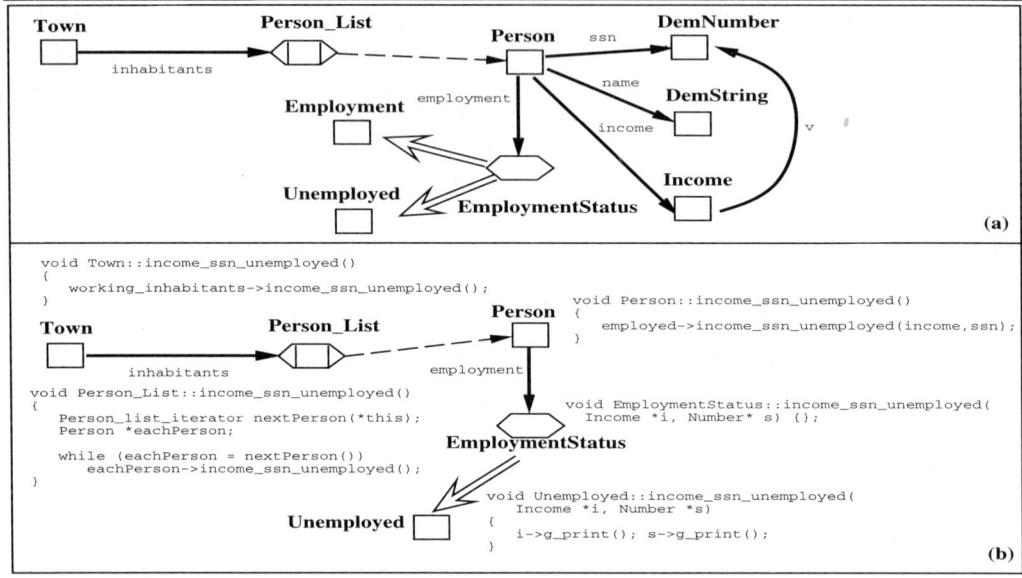

Figure 4.15: Class dictionary graph, propagation graph, and C++ program

is implemented by two extra arguments that are used from **Person** to **Unemployed**.[9]

4.6 POSITIONING IN THE HISTORY OF SOFTWARE DEVELOPMENT

We sketch the history of software development from procedural to object-oriented to adaptive. Adaptive programming is an improvement over object-oriented programming in the same way that object-oriented programming is over procedural programming (see Fig. 4.16). Object-oriented programming introduces the binding of functions to data structures and

---

[7] Legal transportation pattern customization, page 448 (67).
[8] Class dictionary graph graphical representation, page 431 (6).
[9] Transportation pattern partial evaluation, page 449 (69).

4.6. POSITIONING IN THE HISTORY OF SOFTWARE DEVELOPMENT

adaptive object-oriented programming introduces the binding of functions to constraint-induced partial data structures. Both bindings are done at write-time. Object-oriented programming introduces inheritance to express programs at a higher level of abstraction and adaptive programming uses partial data structures to lift the level of abstraction. Object-oriented programming employs inheritance to delay the binding of calls to code from compile-time to run-time and adaptive programming uses partial data structures to delay the binding of methods to classes from write-time to compile-time. Adaptive programming is therefore a natural step in the evolution of software development methods.

Paradigm	*Write-time association*	*Resulting delayed binding*	*Due to*
Procedural	*Function calls $\rightarrow$ code*		
Object-oriented	*Functions $\rightarrow$ Data structures*	*Function calls $\xrightarrow{run-time}$ code*	Inheritance
Adaptive	*Functions $\rightarrow$ Partial data structures*	*Functions $\xrightarrow{compile-time}$ data structures*	Partial data structures

Figure 4.16: Comparison of programming paradigms

In Fig. 4.17 the history of software development from the delayed binding point of view is shown in more detail. The figure shows the progression from procedural to object-oriented to adaptive software development. In procedural software development the following concepts are used: data structures, functions, variables, data, and calls. They are mapped as follows:

```
procedural:

write-time:
  variables -> data structures

compile-time:
  functions -> addresses
  variables -> addresses
  calls -> addresses

run-time:
  data -> addresses
```

In object-oriented software development, functions are mapped to data structures. This leads to encapsulation of data and functionality, which avoids a lot of parameter passing. Furthermore, object-oriented software development extends data structures with inheritance that allows delaying the binding of calls to addresses to run-time.

```
object-oriented:
```

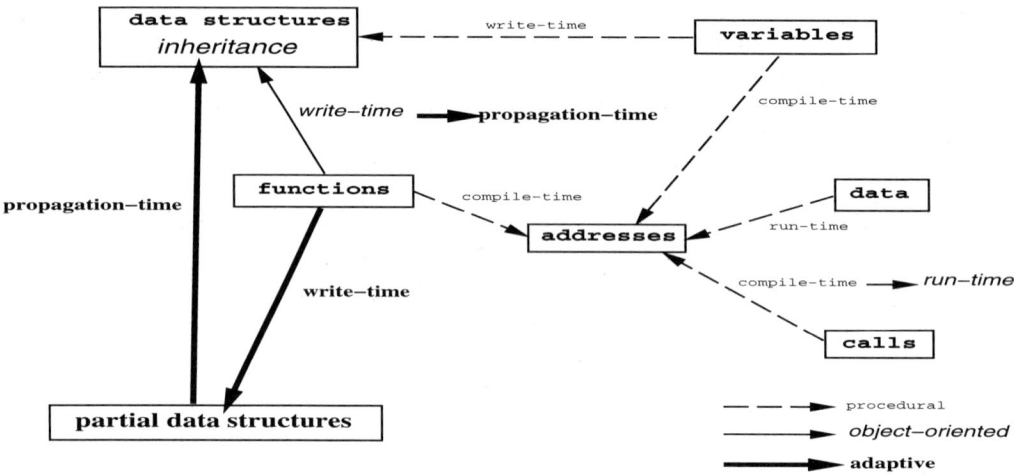

Figure 4.17: Delayed-binding viewpoint

```
write-time:
  variables -> data structures
  functions -> data structures

compile-time:
  functions -> addresses
  variables -> addresses

run-time:
  data -> addresses
  calls -> addresses
```

Adaptive software development delays the binding of functions to data structures beyond write-time. The new binding time is called propagate-time. The binding is delayed by introducing partial data structures that are mapped to complete data structures at customization-time.

```
adaptive:

write-time:
  variables -> partial data structures
```

4.7. THE TOOLS

```
    functions -> partial data structures

propagate-time:
    partial data structures -> data structures
    variables -> data structures
    functions -> data structures

compile-time:
    functions -> addresses
    variables -> addresses

run-time:
    data -> addresses
    calls -> addresses
```

From the delayed binding point of view, we can summarize the history of software development as follows:

- Object-oriented

    Introduces the binding of functions to data structures. Introduces inheritance as a new mechanism to describe data structures. Inheritance allows us more flexibility in specifying the structure of objects. If a superclass gets an additional part, all instances of subclasses of the superclass also have that part. Inheritance allows delaying the binding of calls to code to run-time (polymorphism). In some languages, polymorphism and inheritance are independent.

- Adaptive

    Introduces the binding of functions and variables to partial data structures. Partial data structures are used to describe data structures generically. Partial data structures allow a programmer to delay the binding of functions to data structures beyond write-time.

The object-oriented approach and the adaptive approach are analogous in the way they extend the previous approach. The adaptive approach is a natural evolution of the object-oriented approach.

4.7 THE TOOLS

To increase the robustness of this book under changing technology, we focus on key concepts and techniques to develop adaptive object-oriented software. The book is written without referring to the current implementation of adaptive technology in the Demeter Tools/C++, except in this section where we describe the existing Demeter Tools/C++. The documentation available with the software provides detailed glue between the concepts and the current implementation. Ways to access the tools and related information are discussed in Appendix A (page 589).

The Demeter Tools/C++ are a set of tools that support the Demeter Method with C++ as implementation language. The Demeter Method taught in this book is, to a large extent, programming-language independent and can be used with several programming languages. Future versions of the Demeter Tools plan to include other programming languages, such as Smalltalk and Ada, resulting in Demeter Tools/Smalltalk and Demeter Tools/Ada.

The Demeter Tools/C++ support the engineering of adaptive object-oriented software using C++. The tools are an add-on product that can be used with standard C++ compilers and development environments to support analysis, design, and implementation of C++ applications. The tools allow you to manipulate C++ code effectively by using a specification language that is above the object-oriented level. The specification language and its implementation have been carefully researched and formally specified, as described in numerous scholarly publications. The specification language is an easy to learn superset of C++.

The Demeter Tools/C++ interface readily with other programming tools such as external C libraries, for example, with Motif (Open Software Foundation) and Tcl/Tk (University of California at Berkeley), and external C++ class libraries, such as NIHCL (US Government).

Programming with the Demeter Tools typically starts with a structural specification (called a class dictionary) followed by a behavioral specification (called propagation patterns). The class dictionary, although we start with it, plays a secondary role during software development since we use it only as a guidance to develop the propagation patterns. We try to put only minimal information about the class dictionary into the propagation patterns.

An adaptive program for the Demeter Tools/C++ consists of three parts: the class dictionary in a file ending in .cd, the propagation patterns in files ending in .pp and a main program in file main.C. The main program calls the functionality defined in the propagation patterns. The Demeter Tools/C++ take those three parts and produce an executable program using a C++ compiler.

Beginning users need to know only one command to get an executable program from their adaptive software. Advanced users need to use three commands to process their adaptive software and they must learn how to set parameters in an Imakefile to customize the compilation of adaptive software. The three commands are: **gen-imake**, **gen-make**, and **make**. **gen-imake** creates a sample Imakefile for the user to customize if desired; **gen-make** creates the corresponding Makefile which knows about all the dependencies in the adaptive application software, and **make** will call the right tools appropriately as the adaptive software is developed and maintained.

The Demeter Tools/C++ provide the following functionality:

- A compiler and design-rule checker for class dictionaries. Proposes changes to the class dictionary. The output is C++ source code which provides generic functionality for manipulating the objects defined by the class dictionary (i.e., reading, writing, comparing, accessing, checking, etc.).

- A compiler and design rule checker for propagation patterns. Checks the consistency between class dictionaries and propagation patterns. The output is C++ source code.

- A consistency checker for checking the consistency between a class dictionary and concise textual representations of objects. Used for high-level debugging of class dictionaries.

- A graphical tool for developing class dictionaries.

- A report generator that documents the groups of collaborating classes for each propagation pattern.

- A run-time library that implements a couple of classes that are needed in any application.

- Utility tools for documenting class dictionaries.

4.8 EXPERIENCES WITH ADAPTIVE SOFTWARE

We first talk about teaching experience and then about software experiences.

- Teaching

  We have taught the Demeter Method for several years and developed a way to teach it in fifteen hours of instruction plus five exercises for professionals who know C. The Demeter Method is easy to learn: to write adaptive programs, you have to learn about propagation patterns, class dictionaries, and objects. To understand propagation patterns, you need to know about propagation directives and their relationship to traversals, about transportation directives, and about a programming language for writing the code fragments to enhance the traversal and transportation code.

- Software

  Adaptive software is a strong user of itself. The Demeter System/C++ is implemented in terms of class dictionaries and propagation patterns, and we find that the maintenance of the system is considerably simplified due to adaptiveness.

  Adaptive software has been used in several industrial projects. At Citibank, a simulator for a part of their object-oriented business model was written and maintained while the class structure underwent frequent changes. The simulator was written with propagation patterns and therefore with minimal assumptions on the class structure. Therefore, the simulator was much easier to maintain.

  The following quote from a heavy user of adaptive software indicates that adaptive software is easier to manipulate than object-oriented software. "Sometimes ... I come to the conclusion that I would have preferred another structure of classes after all. Well, I am more or less convinced that without propagation patterns I'd never take the pain to actually change the whole system unless absolutely necessary. With propagation patterns however the effort for such an undertaking is comparatively small."

- Without tool use

  The techniques described in this book have also been applied successfully to software development without using the Demeter Tools/C++.

The Law of Demeter, which is one of the corner stones of adaptive software, is used as a style rule at several companies.

Class dictionaries are used during the analysis and design phase, to express both class hierarchies and object hierarchies. One engineer used the Demeter graphical notation to describe object hierarchies, starting with the full class dictionary and then trimmed alternations to a single choice to show a run-time object. The engineers on the team found this to be easy to understand.

The simple diagramming language for class dictionaries, three vertex shapes and two line styles, is easy to use. One project leader writes: "Working with a group of engineers who were mostly new to C++ and object-oriented development, I found the Demeter diagrams to be very useful in communicating the software architecture and object relationships."

Propagation patterns and object traversals were used during the design phase. One project leader writes (a 50000 lines C++ project using Visual C++ and the Microsoft foundation classes, 9 engineers): "To ensure that the Law of Demeter was applied when implementing a feature, the Law of Demeter was expressed as a coding standard that was strictly enforced via code reviews. All functionality that stretched from the user interface layer of the product through the document layer and down into the mail transport were expressed as object traversals."

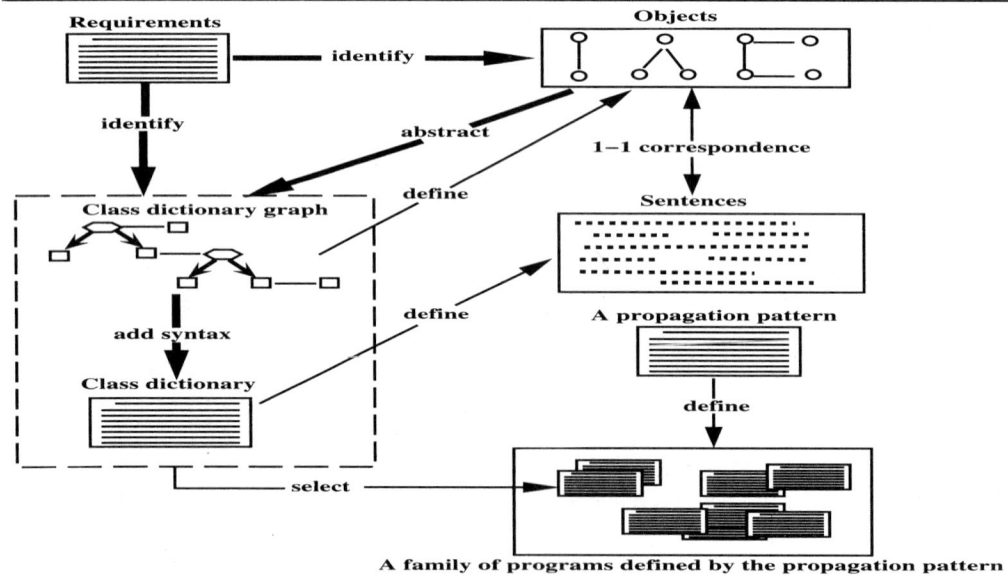

Figure 4.18: Demeter

4.9 SUMMARY

The concepts of adaptive software and their relationships are summarized in Fig. 4.18. This chapter presented a new approach to develop software, namely the the Demeter Method.

Somewhat provocatively, the Demeter Method almost goes back to the good old times when functions and data were separated. Adaptive software plays with a loose coupling between functionality and class structure.

What is new? An adaptive program differs from an object-oriented program in at least the following ways.

Delayed Binding of Methods

From the article "Binding" in the *Encyclopedia of Computer Science*:

> Broadly speaking, the history of software development is the history of ever-later binding time :::.

In an object-oriented program, we code object behavior as operations attached to specific classes. If we desire to call a behavior at the bottom of a composite object, many objects in that hierarchy must have a behavior that passes-the-call down one level. This sequence of behaviors is absolutely dependent on the existing class structure, and any changes to the class structure require that this sequence be examined, and possibly modified.

Propagation patterns can express such passes-the-call behaviors without listing all the participating classes. Instead, the behaviors are written in compact traversal clauses with necessary code fragments added. As a class structure is given, all the pass-the-call behaviors are generated *automatically* for all classes for which they are required, and the code for the desired behavior is inserted in the bottom class and in important classes in between. In other words, methods are being attached to classes during propagation pattern interpretation in the context of a class structure.

The important observation is that object behaviors coded as propagation patterns are *not* specifically attached to any class at coding time.

Adaptiveness and Succinctness

Propagation pattern programs are data-structure-shy programs that repel data structure details. Object behaviors coded as propagation patterns can be reused also, sometimes without modification in a different context (i.e., for a different application with different classes and a different class structure). Therefore, propagation patterns are adaptive programs.

An important question is whether adaptive software is useful for large applications; that is, does adaptive software scale well? The answer is a definite yes since the larger the class structures and the more relations there are, the more opportunities there are to propagate. Adaptive software is useful in any application that has a nontrivial data model, and there is no loss of execution efficiency compared to object-oriented software. Object-oriented software often uses the inlining technique during compilation. Inlining will not generate a function call for small functions; the code of the function is copied directly into the compiled code without creating a function call.

4.10 BIBLIOGRAPHIC REMARKS

- Niklaus Wirth

  Several ideas that have been promoted by Niklaus Wirth and which I learned during my studies at ETH have influenced this book.

  - Stepwise refinement: The idea of stepwise refinement [Wir71a, Wir74a] is one of the foundations on which adaptive software is built. It is only after a refinement step, called customization, that the data structures and input languages get fully specified.
  - LL(1) languages: Niklaus Wirth has consistently designed languages that are easy to learn and read. This was achieved by making the languages parsable by recursive descent parsers with one symbol look-ahead [Wir76]. We use program customizers, called class dictionaries, that also must all have the LL(1) property. LL(1) languages will be used in Chapter 11.
  - EBNF: Niklaus Wirth proposed a standard way to describe languages [Wir77]. We have extended this notation to make it simultaneously a suitable notation for program customizers used during stepwise refinement.
  - Lean languages: Niklaus Wirth has resisted attempts to make his notations baroque [Wir71b, Wir74b, Wir82, Wir84, Wir88, WG89]. The notations used in the Demeter System have followed his example. For example, the class dictionary notation used for object-oriented design is considerably simpler than other object-oriented design notations.

- Contracts

  Many mechanisms have been invented to make software more flexible, for example, implementational reflection [Rao91] and contracts [HHG90, Hol92]. Rao [Rao91] defines implementational reflection as reflection involving inspection or manipulation of the implementational structures of other systems used by a program. He argues that implementation architectures be made explicit and open, allowing customization. Propagation patterns follow this approach.

  A contract describes the collaboration of a group of objects. Adaptive software is a generalization of contracts by making many participants implicit, increasing the reusability of the contracts. Some aspects of contracts still have not been integrated into adaptive software, like run-time switching between contracts.

- Small methods

  Several studies (for example, [WH91, WMH93, WH92]) have shown that methods tend to be very small, most of them serving as a simple bridge to other methods. This is a natural consequence of encapsulation, and is encouraged by style guidelines for good programming, such as the Law of Demeter. Another problem is that all these little methods are explicitly attached to classes in the programming phase, introducing an implicit commitment to maintain each method's code dependencies on its own class and on the classes to which the code refers. These characteristics have two undesirable

4.10. BIBLIOGRAPHIC REMARKS

consequences: one, understanding each class's functionality is easy, but understanding programs as a whole can be very hard; two, with class structures changing frequently, the effort to maintain the code can be substantial. The Pareto-principle also applies in object-oriented programming: for a given task, 80% of the work is done by 20% of the interesting classes. Propagation patterns allow us to focus on those interesting classes.

- Use cases

Ivar Jacobson writes in [Jac92]: "Use cases are a way to make complex systems understandable without, as a first step, trying to structure the system into ... objects ... Such structuring creates very technical descriptions which tend to shift the focus from the problem of understanding the requirement to dealing with implementation-like descriptions." We use Jacobson's vision when we work with propagation patterns: they can describe specific uses or views of an object system without, as a first step, defining the detailed structure of objects.

- Views

In [AB92], Aksit and Bergmans write: "Many object-oriented methods ... expound the importance of domain knowledge while preparing the user's requirement specifications. Integrating the domain knowledge with these specifications, however, can create an excessive number of objects, although only a few of these objects may be relevant to the problem ..." Propagation patterns address the issue on focusing on the interesting objects. The class-valued variables and relation-valued variables focus on what is important to the problem and the unimportant classes are either ignored or code is produced automatically for them. A propagation pattern is a view of an integrated (and properly extended) domain model.

- Law of Demeter

Markku Sakkinen writes in [Sak88a]: "The methods of a class should not depend in any way on the structure of any class, except the immediate top-level structure of their own class." With propagation patterns we can now go further and require that in addition to Sakkinen's view of the Law of Demeter, methods depend only on the really interesting classes.

- Navigation

Rumbaugh [Rum88] has proposed an operation propagation mechanism. The most significant difference is that his is run-time-based and not using succinct subgraph specifications while our mechanism is compile-time based and geared towards a new method for developing object-oriented software.

- Unplanned software reuse

A key question behind writing generic software is: what is the level of instantiation-look-ahead that is needed for writing a generic algorithm. If the generic algorithm needs to account for each possible use, then it will be difficult to write and reuse. It is our experience that propagation patterns have a small instantiation-look-ahead. For example, writing generic algorithms in contract form [HHG90, Hol92] requires more planning on how the contract will be used.

- Programming by example

  Propagation patterns are self-contained specifications that define requirements for class dictionary graphs that can be used with them. A propagation pattern is usually developed and tested for an example class dictionary graph, although a propagation pattern works for many more class dictionary graphs. Therefore, propagation pattern programming is an advanced form of programming by example.

  Programming by example was an active topic in the early 1970s [BK76]. Programs were derived from examples of inputs and corresponding outputs. In our case, we write a program for a sample data structure and we automatically generalize this program to other data structures.

- Grammar-based programming

  The idea of data-structure-shy programming with partial data structures relates to other areas of computer science outside of object-oriented programming. In the area of syntax directed semantics, the meaning of a sentence is defined as a function of the structure of the sentence. This is an old and good idea going back to the last century, but all current implementations seem to encode the details of the structure into the meaning function. This leads to software that is hard to maintain under changing structures, and those structures do change frequently. There is a lot of research that should be reevaluated from the point of view of data-structure-shy programming, for example, attribute grammars [RTD83], logic programming [BGV90], and natural semantics [BDD$^+$88]. Recent work at Carnegie Mellon University [GCN92, SKG88] investigates grammar transformations and semiautomatic updating of programs written for the grammars. If the programs would be written in a data-structure-shy (or grammar-shy) way, the program transformations are simplified. For example, for many grammar transformations, the program does not require an update at all.

- Paradox of the inventor

  See [Pol49].

- Frameworks

  What is a framework? Johnson writes in [Joh92]:

  > "A framework is a reusable design of a program or a part of a program expressed as a set of classes [Deu89, JF88]. ... Frameworks are designed by experts in a particular domain and then used by non-experts."

  In other words, a framework is a class library plus documentation on how to use it and on how it is designed.

  Let's define

```
adaptive framework =
  library of
    propagation patterns (pps) and
    class dictionaries (cds) +
  documentation (purpose, use, design)
```

The class dictionaries serve as sample customizers to better show typical uses of the adaptive framework.

To compare informally frameworks with their adaptive counterparts, we could use the following equations:

```
framework = customization of adaptive framework
adaptive framework = family of frameworks

framework:class library =
  adaptive framework:library of pps/cds
adaptive framework:framework = class:instance
adaptive framework:framework = genre:play
adaptive framework:framework = species:animal
```

- Decontextualized components

  In [WB94] Wile and Balzer discuss decontextualized components. In a decontextualized component, an architecture description language provides the usage context. Compilation decisions are delayed until the context information is available. Decontextualized components make fewer commitments to data and control decisions than ordinary components. Wile and Balzer also want to make software more flexible and adaptable. They don't use the succinct subgraph specifications used in adaptive software.

- Methods as assertions

  Other attempts have been made to generalize object-oriented programming. In [LA94] the methods-as-assertions view is discussed. This view generalizes object-oriented programming and helps the programmer to flexibly express when a certain piece of code will correctly implement an operation. The methods-as-assertions view is consistent with the adaptive view but the two are complementary and they could be integrated.

- Intentional programming

  Microsoft started a proprietary project on intentional programming at about the same time our adaptive programming work started (1988).

  According to Charles Simonyi from Microsoft (he hired and led the teams that developed Microsoft Word, Excel, and other applications whose business has grown to over $2 billion per year), intentional programming addresses each of the following (from: "Software 2000: A View of the Future," edited by Brian Randell, Gill Ringland, and Bill Wulf, sponsored by Esprit and ICL):

– implementation detail is separated from computational intent (hence the name intentional programming); so we have the benefits of program generators but without their costs.

– domain-specific knowledge can be added routinely using program transformations.

– trade-offs are simply eliminated by providing great abstraction capabilities (to express the commonality) and similarly powerful specialization capabilities (to express the specific needs without run-time costs.) The latter is achieved using partial evaluation.

Intentional programming, because of its proprietary nature, cannot be compared fully to adaptive programming. The three points above, however, apply to adaptive software as well. Adaptive programming separates computational intent from object structure. Adaptive software also adds domain specific knowledge about object structure after the program is written. Adaptive software also uses partial evaluation.

There seems to be one important difference between intentional and adaptive programming: adaptive programming relies on succinct specifications of subgraphs.

- Requirement for design notations

    At a CASE workshop at Index Technology in Cambridge in the late 1980s, Peter Deutsch recommended the following requirement for any design notation: "assignment of responsibilities to objects without making a commitment about their structure." Adaptive software satisfies this requirement.

- Structure-shy queries

    There is a growing field of research in databases related to structure-shy queries. Those are queries that are relatively independent of the schema of the databases. Abbreviated path expressions are a technique that is often used. For a detailed comparison see [Har94].

- Open implementations

    The work on open implementations of Gregor Kiczales and his group at Xerox PARC has several connections to adaptive software. In [Kic92], Kiczales writes: "The idea is that reusable code should be like a sponge: It provides basic functionality (the base-level interface), basic structure (the default implementation) but also allows the user to pour in important customizations from above to firm it up." An adaptive program can also be compared to a sponge that can be brought into various forms through customizations.

    Open implementations support a dual interface: a traditional interface and an adjustment interface. So do adaptive programs: a traditional interface and a customization interface. The customization interface is defined by constraints that define the legal customizers.

    Adaptive programs expose important parts of the implementation and pursue a similar goal to that of open implementations. The class-valued and relation-valued variables in an adaptive program expose parts of the implementation. Those variables are used to control the customization of the adaptive program.

Open implementations of the Xerox PARC kind have grown out of the reflection and meta-level architectures community [KRB91]. The distinguishing feature of adaptive programs as compared to open implementations is the use of succinct subgraph specifications.

Some of the papers by the Xerox PARC group on open implementations are [Kic92, KL92, Kic93].

- Software Architecture [AG92, GSOS92]

Architecture description languages (ADLs) are between requirement definition languages and programming languages. ADLs have a similar motivation to that of languages for the expression of the output of the analysis and design phase of object-oriented systems.

ADLs have two intended advantages:

- to facilitate evolution and maintenance by improving maintenance and development productivity, and
- to improve interoperability between independently developed software components.

ADLs work with components and interconnections between them. Useful combinations of component and connector types are called architectural styles. The architecture of a system may be viewed as a high-level description of a system's organization. Many systems conform to the same architecture; an architecture defines an entire family of systems.

There are many analogies between an architectural description and an adaptive program. Indeed, an adaptive program qualifies as a high-level architectural description where many connectors are left implicit. An adaptive program describes a fluid behavioral architecture that is customized by a structural architecture. An adaptive program describes a family of object systems that can be obtained from the adaptive program by two processes: refinement and customization. Refinement adds more wrappers and refines propagation directives [LZHL94]. Customization selects a class structure to freeze the behavioral architecture into a structural architecture.

- Controlling impact of change versus reuse capability

In their paper on object definition techniques and prototyping, Wileden, Clarke, and Wolf write [WCW90]:

> On the one hand, the desire to make an object easy to reuse ... seems to argue for having an information-rich interface—that is an interface that ... is revealing the objects' structure.

> On the other hand, the desire to limit the impact of change seems to argue for an information-poor interface so that the details of the object can change without necessarily affecting all clients of the object.

The interface they refer to is a signature interface with parameters and their types. The tension between information-rich and information-poor interfaces is very real. It is at the same time a tension between reuse and information hiding. How can we best balance information-richness and information-poverty in interfaces?

Objects are usually multifunctional and for each function only some parts of the object are important. Therefore, only the classes of the relevant parts should be put into the "customization" interface of that function. This approach allows us, surprisingly, to change the details of objects while automatically preserving an analogous functionality.

The customization interface describing the important classes for a given function has different properties from the signature interface. When the customization interface is richer than it should be, we have *less* reuse (different from signature interface) and changes will have more impact (same as for signature interface).

Through the customization interface we can control reusability (adaptiveness) and the impact of changes.

- Disadvantage of object-oriented software

  In [GS93], Garlan and Shaw write:

  > Object-oriented systems have disadvantages the most significant of which is that in order for one object to interact with another it must know the identity of that other object. The significance of this is that whenever the identity of an object changes, it is necessary to modify all other objects that explicitly invoke it.

  This disadvantage does not hold for adaptive object-oriented systems. Interaction can be specified by elastic relationships, like *from* A *to* B, where the identity of B-objects is only known to A-objects after customization with a class dictionary. But at the adaptive program level, A and B can be in a variety of different relationships.

- Subject-oriented programming

  Subject-oriented programming supports the packaging of object-oriented systems into subjects [HO93]. Each subject models its domain in its own subjective way as a possibly incomplete object-oriented program. Each subject has its own class hierarchy that contains only the relevant details. Subjects may be composed by a composition designer.

  Subject-oriented programming and adaptive programming package object-oriented software in a similar way. Adaptive programming can benefit from the work on composition of subjects and subjective programming can benefit from the succinct subgraph specifications used in adaptive programs. They allow the expression of more flexible subjects.

- Hot-spot-driven approach

  In [Pre94], Wolfgang Pree promotes the idea of hot-spot-driven design. A hot spot is an aspect of an application domain that needs to be kept flexible. Metapatterns are used to implement the hot spots and to gain flexibility.

Adaptive programming complements the idea of hot-spot-driven design. In adaptive programming, the object structure is viewed as a hot spot both for defining behavior and for object creation. Propagation patterns deal with flexible behavior from the point of view of the hot spot of class structure. Parsing deals with flexible object creation from the point of view of the hot spot of class structure.

Chapter 5

Adaptive Software by Example

In this chapter the important features of adaptive programs, namely propagation patterns and class dictionaries, are introduced by simple examples that become increasingly more complex. This chapter intentionally gives definitions by examples without introducing the concepts in full before they are used. Later chapters explain class dictionaries and propagation patterns in detail.

Besides introducing the concepts by examples, this chapter serves a second purpose: it shows how adaptive programs behave under evolution of the class structure. We will use essentially one adaptive program in the context of several class dictionaries. Software evolution and maintenance are very costly activities and we show how adaptiveness simplifies software maintenance.

In this chapter we use adaptive programs to query objects. We must stress that adaptive software is not only useful for querying objects, but for modifying them as well. Adaptive software is useful for any programming task that requires more than a couple of classes.

5.1 CHANGING REQUIREMENTS

Assume that a customer asks us to write a program to compute the weight of a container. When we ask what kind of containers they have and how their containers are structured, we get a rather confusing answer. They say that their containers contain items that have weights. The structure of the containers varies and they will know the details in an hour, but by then the program should almost be ready. This situation is quite typical; often customers keep changing their requirements, but they want to have the programs immediately.

So we are left with the task of writing a program that computes the weight of containers without knowing their structure. This task looks hard initially, but after some analysis it turns out to be the right way to approach the problem anyway. Consider an airplane, and consider that we know the weights of all its parts. The airplane is represented by some data structure that contains weight fields and all we have to do is add together the numbers in all those weight fields.

How can we find all the weight fields, or weight objects? We traverse the airplane data structure and visit all the parts that contain weight information. When we get to weight

5.1. CHANGING REQUIREMENTS

information, we add it to a variable that reflects the weight of the section of the airplane we have already traversed.

Now go back to the generic container problem and apply the airplane idea to it. Since the data structure that we use to represent the container is not important, we may as well use a simple data structure first and use a more complex one later. So we start with the very simple data structure that describes a container having a weight field (see Fig. 5.1).

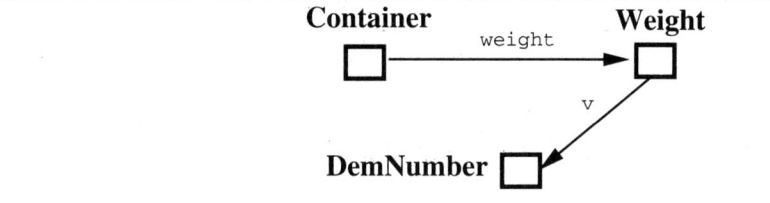

Figure 5.1: Simple container: graphical representation

```
Container = <weight> Weight.
Weight = <v> DemNumber.
```

Figure 5.2: Simple container: textual representation

We use a programming-language independent data structure notation, called the class dictionary notation which has a textual as well as a graphical representation. In Fig. 5.1, we graphically define two construction classes, one called **Weight** and the other called **Container**. Fig. 5.2 shows the corresponding textual representation. When we use the word class in this chapter, think of a Pascal record type or a C struct. **Container** has a weight part and **Weight** has a **DemNumber** part. **DemNumber** is assumed to be a predefined class, called a terminal class, for which the basic number operations, for example, addition, subtraction, etc., are defined. Later we will learn other terminal classes, such as **DemReal** and **DemString**. The prefix **Dem** is an abbreviation of Demeter and is used to avoid name conflicts with classes you might use from another class library.

Next we write a program for the data structures in Fig. 5.1 with the attitude that the data structure is very volatile and subject to frequent changes. Therefore, we solve the problem using only minimal information about the data structure. For example, we don't want to hard-code the information that a container has a part called **weight**. This kind of programming style is naturally called data structure-shy since the program is using as little information as possible about the data structure.

A useful way to think about the problem is to think in terms of collaborating classes for solving the weight addition problem. We need all the classes from **Container** to **Weight** to solve the problem. There could be a number of intermediate classes between **Container** and Weight. For example, in Fig. 5.3, Item is an intermediate class between Container and

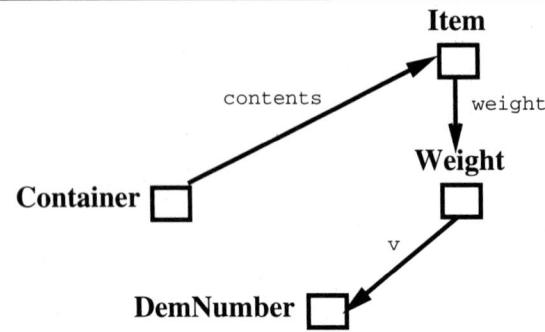

Figure 5.3: One intermediate class

Weight.

We need to find a generic way to define the group of collaborating classes.[1] What about the specification in Fig. 5.4 that we call a propagation directive? It serves our purpose very

```
*from* Container *to* Weight
```

Figure 5.4: Propagation directive

well since it constrains the group of collaborating classes with minimal knowledge of the class structure. For the previous example in Fig. 5.3, the specification in Fig. 5.4 will include the class Item that is between Container and Weight. We call such a specification a propagation directive. It is a concise description of a group of collaborating classes. A propagation directive defines a group of collaborating classes using a *from* ... *to* directive.

Propagation directives play a very important role in object-oriented design. They allow us to describe object-oriented software in a highly flexible form. For example, we can describe software without knowing what the detailed input objects will be.

To use an analogy from the automobile industry, with propagation directives we can build standard cars whose architecture can be changed after they are built. For example, a standard car can be customized to a sedan or a bus.

For any given container data structure, the propagation directive will select a subdata structure that describes the group of collaborating classes. We call such a subdata structure a propagation graph. In the examples in Fig. 5.1 and Fig. 5.3, all classes except DemNumber are included in the propagation graph by the propagation directive in Fig. 5.4.

---

[1]Propagation directive abstraction, page 447 (60).

So the propagation graph (subdata structure) defines a group of collaborating classes, but it has an additional, very useful interpretation: it defines an algorithm to traverse a given data structure instance, in our example a Container-object. In the example in Fig. 5.3, the algorithm would visit objects in the following order: Container, Item, Weight.

The traversal does most of the work for computing the weight. All we need to do is add additional code to the traversal code. Consider class Weight: its traversal code has an empty body. We want to add code that adds the current weight to a variable called return_val.

```
*wrapper* Weight
  *prefix*
    (@ return_val = return_val + *v; @)
```

This wrapper adds code to class Weight by wrapping the C++ code between "(@" and "@)" around the empty body of class Weight.

A wrapper can be viewed as an editing instruction for an object-oriented program. A prefix wrapper, such as the one above, adds code that needs to be executed before the traversal code. When a wrapper is specified without the *prefix* keyword, it is a prefix wrapper by default. The above wrapper can be written in shorter form as

```
*wrapper* Weight
  (@ return_val = return_val + *v; @)
```

In the rest of the chapter we will use this short form.

Why do we choose to make the Weight wrapper a prefix wrapper? We could also have made it a suffix wrapper, using the keyword *suffix*, which would append the code at the end of the traversal code. In this case it does not matter since the traversal code is empty for class Weight. We can choose a prefix or a suffix wrapper.

The code between "(@" and "@)" is C++ code, which needs a little explanation because of the star appearing before v. Variable v refers to the DemNumber-object that is contained in Weight. The type of v is a pointer type to DemNumber, in C++ notation the type is DemNumber*. As a general rule, parts are implemented by pointer types unless a special notation is used in the class dictionary. This is a general and useful approach in object-oriented programming.

Since v is a pointer to a DemNumber-object, *v is a DemNumber-object; that is, * is the dereferencing operator of C++. For class DemNumber we assume (not shown) that a constructor has been defined that creates a DemNumber-object from an int value. The conversion rules of C++ then call implicitly the constructor as a conversion function during the evaluation of return_val + *v. Readers not familiar with C++ can find a transition from C to C++ for the purpose of writing adaptive software in Chapter 3, Section 3.5.[2]

Finally we need to agree on a signature for the weight addition function that will be attached to all the collaborating classes.

```
*operation* int add_weight()    // signature
   *init* (@ 0 @)               // initialization
```

---

[2] It is important to notice that the adaptive software concept is independent of C++ and it can be used with many other object-oriented programming languages such as Smalltalk or CLOS.

The function has an implicit variable, called return_val, which will be returned when the function returns. The return_val variable can be initialized by giving an expression after the *init* keyword. In this example, we initialize to 0 since we solve a counting problem.

We now have all the pieces of the program which is given in complete form in Fig. 5.5. Such a program is called a propagation pattern. It makes few assumptions about the class

---

```
*operation* int add_weight()
    *init*
      (@ 0 @) // C++ code fragment
  *traverse*
    *from* Container *to* Weight
  *wrapper* Weight
      (@ return_val = return_val + *v; @) // C++ code fragment
```

Figure 5.5: Propagation pattern

---

structure with which it can be used. That is the main point we want to make here. We view Container and Weight to be class-valued variables that will be mapped onto ordinary classes later. The algorithm is formulated in terms of the class-valued variables. We make only two assumptions about the Container and Weight class: one, that a relationship between the two exists that allows traversal from Container to Weight and two, that Weight has a part called v for which the addition operator is defined. The relationship could be a one-to-one relationship or a one-to-many relationship; we keep the algorithm independent of such details.

We further explain the propagation pattern in Fig. 5.5. To implement the add_weight operation, we need the collaboration of a group of classes all having an operation with the given signature. Since we do not know the group of collaborating classes, we cannot itemize them, but we can outline them. We need all the classes that are involved in the relationship between Container and Weight. The specification *from* Container *to* Weight succinctly defines the group of collaborators. They have the important task traversing a Container-object and finding all the Weight-objects contained in it. But the traversal itself docs not accomplish any addition. Therefore, we need an editing mechanism that allows us to personalize the traversal code. The editing is accomplished by wrappers that add additional code. A wrapper may contain two kinds of code fragments between (@ and @), at least one of which has to be present. The first kind is a prefix code fragment and the second kind is a suffix code fragment. The prefix and suffix code fragments are wrapped around the traversal code. In the example above we used only a prefix code fragment.

5.2 CUSTOMIZING WITH CLASS DICTIONARIES

The program in Fig. 5.5 describes a potentially infinite number of programs for computing weights of containers and we would like to select a few additional example programs. A selection is accomplished by writing a class structure called a class dictionary, that satisfies

5.2. CUSTOMIZING WITH CLASS DICTIONARIES

the assumptions. We need a class dictionary containing a path from **Container** to **Weight**. This selection can also be viewed as a customization of the original generic program. We next customize the program in Fig. 5.5 so that it will work on **Basket**-objects.

First, the program should run on baskets that contain exactly two apples. Later we will generalize to baskets with several kinds of fruit.

Fig. 5.6 contains a description of a basket, called **AppleBasket**, containing two apples. The format of this notation is

```
ClassName0(
  <part1> ClassName1(
    <part2> ClassName2 token))
```

The object **AppleBasket** has one part, called **contents**, that contains an object of some class called **TwoFruit**. The **TwoFruit**-object itself contains an **Apple**-object whose weight is 9 and an **Apple**-object whose weight is 12.

```
Basket(
  <contents> TwoFruit(
    <fruit1> Apple(
      <weight> Weight(
        <v> DemNumber "9"))
    <fruit2> Apple(
      <weight> Weight(
        <v> DemNumber "12")))
```

Figure 5.6: Apple basket object

The object description uses one line per object part. Each such line contains a class name and in this example each line, except the first, also contains a part name.

We abstract the following class definitions from this object, which we summarize with a class dictionary graph shown in Fig. 5.7.[3] The vertices drawn as □ stand for instantiable classes and they are called **construction vertices**. The single-shafted edges (⟶) stand for part-of relationships. Those edges are called construction edges. The label of the edge is a part-name.[4] For big class dictionaries, like for big object graphs, the graphical representation becomes clumsy. Therefore we also use a textual notation that lists the successors of every vertex in a linear format. The equivalent textual representation for the class dictionary in Fig. 5.7 is given in Fig. 5.8.[5]

There is a simple technique to derive the textual notation from the graphical notation: We traverse each vertex of the graph and for each vertex we write down all its successors.

---
[3] Class dictionary graph learning, page 432 (14).
[4] Class dictionary graph graphical representation, page 431 (6).
[5] Legal class dictionary graph, page 431 (9).

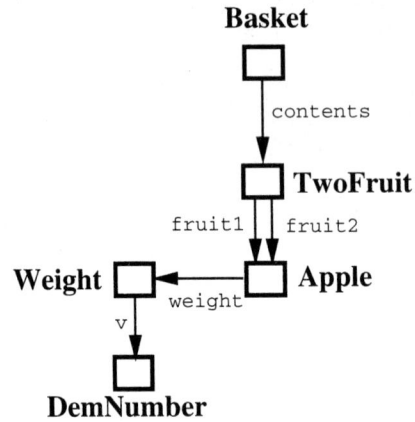

Figure 5.7: Apple basket class dictionary

```
Basket = <contents> TwoFruit.
TwoFruit = <fruit1> Apple <fruit2> Apple.
Apple = <weight> Weight.
Weight = <v> DemNumber.
```

Figure 5.8: Apple basket

5.2. CUSTOMIZING WITH CLASS DICTIONARIES

The edge labels precede the corresponding successor. There is a minimal amount of concrete syntax to learn: "=" is used to define construction classes. "<" and ">" are used to surround part names.[6] A "." is used to terminate each class definition.

A program to compute the weight of the apples in a basket needs the collaboration of all classes. All classes need an operation with signature int add_weight() . We note that the classes to which we want to propagate the signature lie on a path from Basket to Weight. For each class, the add_weight operation should call add_weight for all the subparts.

The propagation pattern in Fig. 5.5, with the renaming Container => Basket, propagates the signature void add_weight(int& t) to all the classes and for each class the operation is called on all the part classes. However, there is one exception: for class Weight the propagation pattern gives the implementation. We use "(@" and "@)" to mark C++ code. The operation add_weight, if called for the AppleBasket object in Fig. 5.6, will return 21.

The code defined by this customization explains the meaning of the propagation pattern in more detail.[7] The C++ code uses the auxiliary function add_weight_. The reason why function names like add_weight_ rather than add_weight are used for the generated functions is to hide the auxiliary functions.

```
  int Basket::add_weight() {
    int return_val = 0; this->add_weight_(return_val);
    return return_val;}
//Weight
void Weight::add_weight_(int& return_val)
{return_val = return_val + *v;}

// Basket = <contents> TwoFruit .
void  Basket::add_weight_(int& return_val )
{
   this->contents->add_weight_(return_val );
}

// TwoFruit = <fruit1> Apple <fruit2> Apple .
void  TwoFruit::add_weight_(int& return_val )
{
   this->fruit1->add_weight_(return_val );
   this->fruit2->add_weight_(return_val );
}

// Apple = <weight> Weight .
void  Apple::add_weight_(int& return_val )
{
   this->weight->add_weight_(return_val );
}
```

---

[6]Class dictionary graph textual representation, page 431 (7).
[7]Propagation pattern partial evaluation, page 448 (64).

The generated C++ code contains many more details than the original adaptive program. The knowledge about the details comes from the class dictionary we used for customization. Your favorite C++ book will help you understand the C++ code, but here is a pointer. A reference argument is used to pass around the variable return_val to collect all the weight information. The type `int&` denotes a reference argument (a variable parameter in Pascal).

Next we want to run the propagation pattern in Fig. 5.5 on more **Basket**-objects. We add a second example to the previous basket in Fig. 5.6. We also want to deal with baskets of the following kind:

```
Basket(
  <contents> TwoFruit(
    <fruit1> Orange(
      <weight> Weight(
        <v> DemNumber "10"))
    <fruit2> Orange(
      <weight> Weight(
        <v> DemNumber "10"))))
```

With this additional object, called **OrangeBasket**, the previous class dictionary is no longer satisfactory.[8] We modify the class dictionary as follows to express that a fruit can be either an apple or an orange: we introduce an abstract class **Fruit**. The graphical representation of the new class dictionary is shown in Fig. 5.9. The vertex drawn as ⬡ stands for the abstract **Fruit** class. The class is abstract since it cannot instantiate objects. Such classes are called **alternation classes** and are graphically represented by hexagonal vertices. The double-shafted arrows($\Longrightarrow$) stand for kind-of relationships and are called **alternation edges**. An alternation edge must start at an alternation vertex, that is, at a hexagonal vertex.[9] The corresponding textual representation of the class dictionary in Fig. 5.9 is in Fig. 5.10.

We learn that alternation classes are introduced by `":"` and the alternatives of an alternation class definition are separated by `"|"`.[10]

Luckily, we do not have to change the propagation pattern in Fig. 5.5 to compute the weight of the fruit in the basket (we still use, of course, the renaming: **Container => Basket**). However, the expanded program now looks different in that it contains the two additional operations shown in Fig. 5.11. We adopt the general rule that operations attached to abstract classes are virtual, that is, the operation for class **Fruit** is virtual. Your C++ book contains an explanation of virtual functions. Essentially, virtual means the function is late bound. In the context of this example virtual means that if, for example, fruit1 contains an **Apple**-object, the code of class **Apple** will be called, and if it contains an **Orange**-object, the code of class **Orange** is called.[11]

The operation add_weight will add 20 to argument return_val if it is requested for basket **OrangeBasket**. But the expanded program is not elegant. We have the function add_weight

---

[8]Incremental class dictionary graph learning, page 433 (15).
[9]Class dictionary graph graphical representation, page 431(6).
[10]Class dictionary graph textual representationpage 431 (7).
[11]Propagation operator, page 446 (59).

5.2. CUSTOMIZING WITH CLASS DICTIONARIES

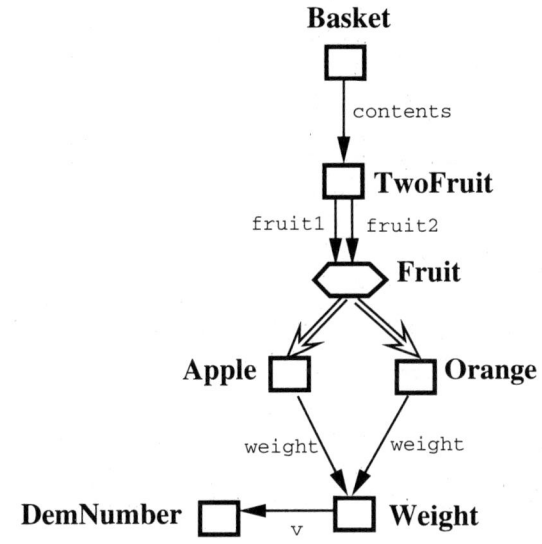

Figure 5.9: Class dictionary graph for apple/orange basket

```
Basket = <contents> TwoFruit.
TwoFruit = <fruit1> Fruit <fruit2> Fruit.
Fruit : Apple | Orange.
Apple = <weight> Weight.
Orange = <weight> Weight.
Weight = <v> DemNumber.
```

Figure 5.10: Textual form of class dictionary for apple/orange basket

```
// Fruit : Apple | Orange .
void  Fruit::add_weight(int & return_val ) // virtual
{
}

// Orange = <weight> DemNumber .
void  Orange::add_weight(int & return_val )
{
   weight->add_weight(return_val);
}
```

Figure 5.11: Additional C++ code

for DemNumber called twice, once from the Apple class and once from the Orange class. The weights are common to Fruit and therefore the weight computation should be implemented at class Fruit. Therefore, we now improve the class dictionary.[12] The graphical form is shown in Fig. 5.12 and the textual form is in Fig. 5.13.

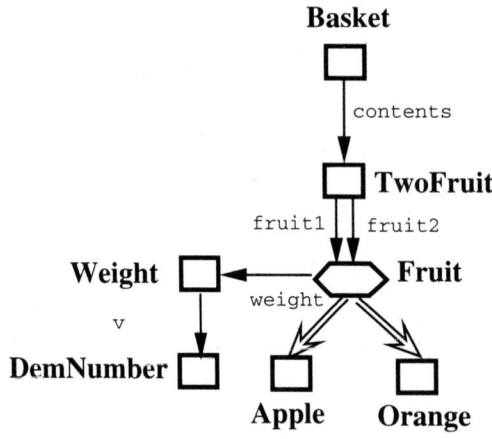

Figure 5.12: Optimized fruit basket class dictionary

We observe that an alternation vertex may have outgoing construction edges. In the textual representation, construction edge successors follow the alternation edge successors and they are separated by the keyword *common*.[13]

---

[12]Common normal form, page 444 (47).
[13]Class dictionary graph textual representation, page 431 (7).

5.2. CUSTOMIZING WITH CLASS DICTIONARIES

```
Basket = <contents> TwoFruit.
TwoFruit = <fruit1> Fruit <fruit2> Fruit.
Fruit : Apple | Orange *common* <weight> Weight.
Apple = .
Orange = .
Weight = <v> DemNumber.
```

Figure 5.13: Optimized class dictionary in textual form

The propagation pattern stays the same, but the expanded program is now more elegant and is shown in Fig. 5.14. The change is in the last three functions. (This code can be optimized for this simple example: delete the two functions for classes **Apple** and **Orange**!)

So far we have hidden the C++ code for the class definitions.[14] Fig. 5.15 shows some of the class definitions needed for the class dictionary in Fig. 5.12. The translation process is straight-forward. Every class (vertex) in the class dictionary is translated into a C++ class. The relationships between the classes are translated as follows: construction edges are translated into data members and alternation edges into inheritance relationships, but in the other direction. The line **class Apple :public Fruit** says that class **Apple** inherits from class **Fruit**, and the alternation edge goes from **Fruit** to **Apple**.

Next we want to work with baskets that can contain any number of fruit, not just two. Instead of naming them explicitly, we want to refer to them by their position in a list. We use the examples in Fig. 5.16 to define baskets that may contain several objects. The opening curly bracket "{" indicates that we start to enumerate objects and the closing curly bracket "}" terminates the enumeration. The enumerated elements are separated by a comma.

From the two basket examples in Fig. 5.16, we derive the class definitions shown in Fig. 5.17 in graphical form. In this example we learn about the third and last (after construction and alternation) kind of class used in class dictionaries, namely repetition classes, which represent collections of objects, such as lists, arrays, doubly linked lists, sets, etc. Repetition classes are represented graphically as ⟁ such as class **SeveralThings** in Fig. 5.17. A repetition class has an outgoing edge that indicates the class whose objects are repeated. For example, class **SeveralThings** has an outgoing repetition edge (drawn as ⟶) to class **Thing**. This means that a **SeveralThings**-object consists of a list of at least one **Thing**-object.

The textual form corresponding to Fig. 5.17 is shown below.[15]

```
Basket = <contents> SeveralThings.
SeveralThings ~ Thing {Thing}.
Thing : Apple | Orange *common* <weight> DemNumber.
```

---

[14]Class dictionary graph translation, page 433 (18).
[15]Class dictionary graph textual representation, page 431 (7).

```
// Basket = <contents>TwoFruit .
int Basket::add_weight() {
   int return_val = 0; this->add_weight_(return_val);
   return return_val;}

// Weight = <v> DemNumber.
void Weight::add_weight_(int& return_val)
 {return_val = return_val + *v;}

// Basket = <contents>TwoFruit .
void  Basket::add_weight_(int &return_val )
{
   contents->add_weight_(return_val );
}

// TwoFruit = <fruit1> Fruit <fruit2> Fruit .
void  TwoFruit::add_weight_(int &return_val )
{
   fruit1->add_weight_(return_val );
   fruit2->add_weight_(return_val );
}

// Fruit : Apple | Orange *common* <weight> Weight .
void  Fruit::add_weight_(int &return_val )
{
   weight->add_weight_(return_val );
}

// Apple = .
void  Apple::add_weight_(int &return_val )
{
   this->Fruit::add_weight_(return_val );
}

// Orange = .
void  Orange::add_weight_(int &return_val )
{
   this->Fruit::add_weight_(return_val );
}
```

Figure 5.14: Generated code

5.2. CUSTOMIZING WITH CLASS DICTIONARIES

```
class Basket {
  private:
    TwoFruit* contents;
  public:
    void add_weight_(int& s);
    int add_weight();
    Basket(TwoFruit* = 0);
}
class Fruit {
  private:
    Weight* weight;
  public:
    // virtual because Fruit is abstract class
    virtual void add_weight_(int& s);
}

class Apple :public Fruit {
  public:
    void add_weight_(int& s);
    Apple();
}
```

Figure 5.15: Class definitions

```
1. Basket(
     <contents> SeveralThings{
       Orange(
         <weight>  DemNumber "9"),
       Apple(
         <weight> DemNumber "12")})
2. Basket(
     <contents> SeveralThings{
       Orange(
         <weight>  DemNumber "5")})
```

Figure 5.16: Baskets containing several things

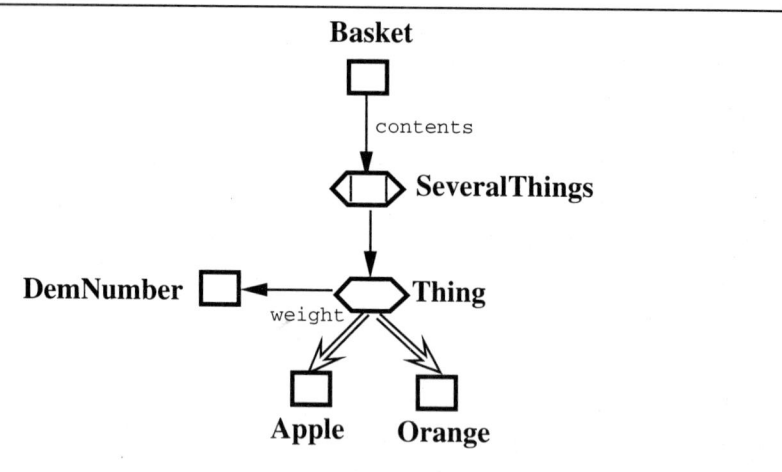

Figure 5.17: Thing basket

```
Apple = .
Orange = .
```

We observe that repetition classes are introduced by the "~" symbol. The repeated part is written twice, once between "{" and "}".

Note the change in the weight structure. A weight is now directly represented by a number object. Therefore, the propagation pattern in Fig. 5.5 needs to be changed. We rename Weight to Thing and write a code fragment for Thing.

The previous class dictionary that has a class Weight is better than this class dictionary that does not have a Weight class. It is good practice to wrap the terminal classes such as DemNumber with a properly named construction class.

The updated propagation pattern is shown in Fig. 5.18.

Why was the change made in the way the weight is represented? First, we want to point out that the initial solution was better and second, we want to indicate that the update needed at the propagation pattern level is smaller than the update needed at the C++ level. The initial solution was better, since it is good practice to buffer each terminal class, such as DemNumber, by a construction class that indicates the purpose of the number in the given context.

Fortunately, the propagation pattern stays almost the same. Instead of propagating to Weight, we propagate to Thing. We cannot propagate into DemNumber since it is a predefined, precompiled class and propagating into it would mean that we add more functionality to the class.

The code at the object-oriented level (in C++) is now very different. The generated code is given in Fig. 5.19. Again, we refer you to your favorite C++ book to understand the details. The code in the repetition class deserves some explanation. The loop is implemented through an iterator class. We assume that a class Thing_list_iterator is defined elsewhere, which has an operation to get the next element from the list. The declaration,

5.2. CUSTOMIZING WITH CLASS DICTIONARIES

```
*operation* int add_weight() *init* (@ 0 @)
  *traverse*
    *from* Basket *to* Thing
  *wrapper* Thing
      (@ return_val = return_val + *weight; @)
```

Figure 5.18: Updated propagation pattern

```
Thing_list_iterator    next_arg(*this);
```

defines an object, called next_arg of class Thing_list_iterator. In C++ an operator can be overloaded to have a new meaning. Class Thing_list_iterator has the function call operator () overloaded. Its meaning is to get the next element from the list.

The line

```
while ( each_arg = next_arg() )
```

calls the overloaded function call operator to retrieve a list element and to store it in variable each_arg. (C and C++ allow assignments in boolean expressions that look unusual to a Pascal/Modula-2 programmer.)

It is important to stress here how easy it was to get the C++ code we need. With propagation patterns we have a tool with which we can control large quantities of C++ code with just small changes.

The previous class dictionary in Fig. 5.17 allows only fruit to appear in baskets. Next we want to consider baskets that may contain other baskets. Here is an example, called NestedBasket:

```
Basket(
  <contents> SeveralThings{
    Orange(
      <weight> Weight
        (<v> DemNumber "10"))
    Basket(
      <contents> SeveralThings{
      Apple(
        <weight> Weight
          (<v> DemNumber "10"))})})
```

From the object NestedBasket we derive the class dictionary graph in Fig. 5.20. The corresponding textual form is shown in Fig. 5.21. The nesting at the object level is represented as a cycle in the class dictionary. There is a cycle from Basket to SeveralThings to Thing and back to Basket. A class dictionary that contains such cycles is called inductive. Inductive class dictionaries are very common in object-oriented applications. An inductive

```
int Basket::add_weight() {
   int return_val = 0; this->add_weight_(return_val);
   return return_val;}

// Thing : Apple | Orange *common* <weight> DemNumber .
void Thing::add_weight_(int& return_val)
   {return_val = return_val + *weight;}

// Basket = <contents> SeveralThings .

void  Basket::add_weight_(int &return_val )
{
   contents->add_weight_(return_val );
}

// SeveralThings ~ Thing {Thing }.
void  SeveralThings::add_weight_(int &return_val )
{
   Thing_list_iterator     next_arg(*this);
   Thing*                  each_arg;
   while ( each_arg = next_arg() )
       each_arg->add_weight_(return_val );
}
```

Figure 5.19: Generated code for modified program

5.3. OBJECT TRAVERSAL AND TRANSPORTATION

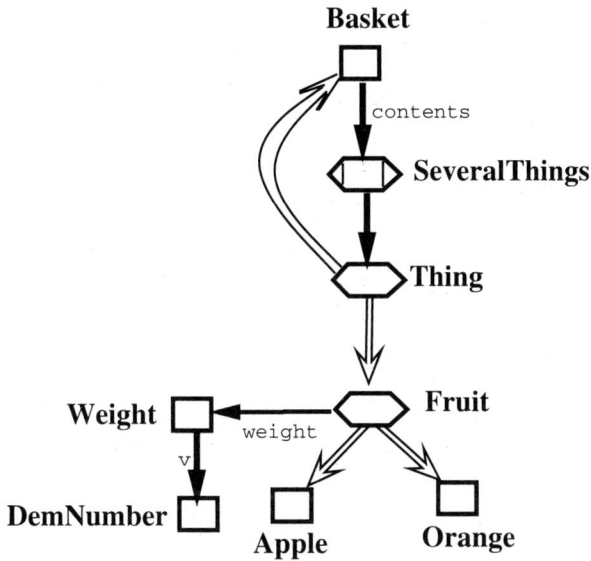

Figure 5.20: Nested baskets

class dictionary has the property that every cycle is well behaved in a sense that is made precise later (see the chapter on style rules for class dictionaries, Chapter 12). Intuitively, a cycle is well behaved if there is an edge exiting the cycle.

The propagation pattern from Fig. 5.5 does not need updating, except the already familiar renaming of Container to Basket; the same program will work for the class dictionary for nested fruit baskets. This shows the power of propagation patterns as well as the power of delayed binding of calls to code. When the function add_weights is called for an element of SeveralThings, the class of the element will determine whether the function for Basket or Fruit will be called. All the functions of classes that describe alternatives, such as Thing and Fruit are virtual functions.

5.3 OBJECT TRAVERSAL AND TRANSPORTATION

Next we consider a more interesting propagation pattern. Let's assume that we need to find all Apple-objects contained in a Basket-object of a given Household-object. We do not care about the apples that are not in a basket. The following propagation pattern solves the problem.

```
*operation* void apples_in_basket()
  *traverse*
    *from* Household *via* Basket *to* Apple
  *wrapper* Apple
     (@ this -> g_print(); @)
```

```
Basket = <contents> SeveralThings.
SeveralThings ~ Thing {Thing}.
Thing : Basket | Fruit.
Fruit : Apple | Orange *common* <weight> Weight.
Apple = .
Orange = .
Weight = <v> DemNumber.
```

Figure 5.21: Nested baskets, textual form

The via clause in the propagation directive forces the traversal through class **Basket** as desired. Instead of using

```
*from* Household *via* Basket *to* Apple
```

we can use equivalently a **through** clause (assuming **Basket** is a construction class)

```
*from* Household
  *through* -> Basket,*,*
*to* Apple
```

The **through** clause forces paths through relationships. Here we force the paths through at least one construction relationship that starts at **Basket**. The expression -> Basket,*,* is an edge pattern that describes the set of construction edges starting at class **Basket**. Edge patterns are used to make the software more flexible by minimizing dependency on the class dictionary.

Next we only want to print apples that are not in a refrigerator. This is achieved by the following propagation pattern:

```
*operation* void not_in_refrigerator()
  *traverse*
    *from* Household
      *bypassing* -> Refrigerator,*,*
    *to* Apple
  *wrapper* Apple
    (@ this -> g_print(); @)
```

The **bypassing** clause makes paths avoid certain relationships. Here any construction relationship that starts at **Refrigerator** will be bypassed. Again an edge pattern is used to minimize dependency on the class dictionary.

To illustrate wrappers with prefix and suffix code fragments, we want to print the total number of apples in every refrigerator contained in a household.

5.4. SUMMARY

```
*operation* void count_apples_in_refrigerator()
  *wrapper* Household
      (@ int s = 0; this -> count(s); @)

*operation* void count(int& s)
  *traverse*
    *from* Household
    *via* Refrigerator
    *to* Apple
  *wrapper* Refrigerator
    *prefix*
      (@ int in_frig = s; @)
    *suffix*
      (@ in_frig = in_frig - s;
         cout << "Apples in refrigerator ="
              << in_frig; @)
  *wrapper* Apple
    (@ s = s + 1; @)
```

The default traversal code for Refrigerator is wrapped with the prefix and suffix wrapper. The suffix wrapper uses the shift operator << to produce output. cout is the output stream. Further details on the stream classes are in your C++ book.

Transporting objects to the right locations is an important subtask in object-oriented programming. To illustrate how we can transport objects independently of detailed class structure knowledge, we consider the following problem that we solve through a transportation directive.

For every apple in a household, print the apple information and the address of the household containing the apple.

```
HouseholdApple = *from* Household *to* Apple

*operation* apple_address()
  *traverse* HouseholdApple
  *carry* *in* Address* a *along* HouseholdApple
    *at* Household (@ a = address @)
  *wrapper* Apple
    (@ cout << this << a; @)
```

The carry statement introduces the transportation directive and defines a local variable called a that is loaded with an address of a Household-object at class Household and that is used at class Apple.

5.4 SUMMARY

We have shown how adaptive programs are used and how they can be customized by class dictionaries. First we showed different ways of customizing a propagation directive with increasingly more complex class dictionaries. Then we turned to more complex propagation patterns, showing several ways to control paths and to annotate object traversals. Two important properties of propagation patterns have been demonstrated: adaptiveness and extensibility.

We have shown the transition from objects to class dictionaries and to complete C++ programs. We demonstrated the evolution of a C++ program through an adaptive program that is applied to more and more complex objects. This incremental development is typical for object-oriented programming, and adaptive software allows us to automate some of this incremental development through customization. Although we used C++ as the programming language, a similar approach can be used with any other object-oriented programming language.

Two questions that we have left open is how we find the objects and in which order we use them to grow the system in small, easy-to-test steps. We will study those questions in the context of program evolution in the chapter on propagation patterns.

5.5 EXERCISES

Exercise 5.1 Consider the following class dictionary BASKET:

```
Basket = <nested> NestedBasket.
NestedBasket = <contents> SeveralThings.
SeveralThings : None | OneOrMore.
None = .
OneOrMore = <one> Thing <more> SeveralThings .
Thing : NestedBasket | Fruit.
Fruit : Apple | Orange *common* <weight> DemNumber.
Apple = .
Orange = .

Thing_List ~ {Thing}.
```

Find the unknowns below by completing the propagation patterns based on the informal task description at the beginning of each propagation pattern.

This question requires knowledge about propagation patterns returning a value. Such examples have been used in this chapter but a complete treatment is in the chapter on propagation pattern interpretation in the subsection on propagation patterns with return types. In a nutshell, propagation patterns with a return type have a variable return_val available having the same type as the return type. This variable is initialized with an *init* clause.

A final hint: for repetition classes a function append is available that appends its first and only argument to the end of the list.

```
// Add the weight of all Apple-objects.
*operation* int all_apples() *init* (@ UNKNOWN1 @)
  *traverse*
    *from* UNKNOWN2 *to* UNKNOWN3
  *wrapper* UNKNOWN4
    *prefix* (@ UNKNOWN5 += *(this -> UNKNOWN6()); @)
```

5.5. EXERCISES

```
// Add the weight of all Fruit-objects.
*operation* int all_fruit() *init* (@ UNKNOWN7 @)
  *traverse*
    *from* UNKNOWN8 *to* UNKNOWN9
  *wrapper* UNKNOWN10
    *prefix* (@ UNKNOWN11 += *(UNKNOWN12()); @)

// Produce a list of all Thing-objects.
*operation* Thing_List* all_thing() *init* (@ UNKNOWN13 @)
  *traverse*
    *from* Basket *to* UNKNOWN14
  *wrapper* UNKNOWN15
    *prefix* (@ UNKNOWN16 -> UNKNOWN17(this); @)

// Produce a list of all Thing-objects which contain an Apple.
*operation* Thing_List* all_thing_containing_apples(int& apple_count)
  // is called with variable as first argument which has value 0
    *init* (@ new Thing_List() @)
  *traverse*
    *from* Basket *via* Thing *to* Apple
  *wrapper* Apple
    *prefix*
      (@ apple_count ++ ;@)
  *wrapper* Thing
    *prefix* (@ int UNKNOWN18 = apple_count; @)
    *suffix* (@ if (UNKNOWN19) UNKNOWN20 -> UNKNOWN21(this); @)

//Add two to the weight of all Orange-objects.
*operation* void oranges_plus_two()
  *traverse*
    *from* Basket *to* Orange
  *wrapper* Orange
    *prefix* (@
      cout << "weight before change " << this-> get_weight() << endl;
      UNKNOWN22;
      cout << "weight after change " << this-> get_weight() << endl;
    @)
```

Exercise 5.2 Give an object example from which you can abstract the following class dictionary graph.

```
Basket = <contents> SeveralThings.
SeveralThings : None | OneOrMore.
None = .
OneOrMore = <one> Thing <more> SeveralThings.
Thing : Basket | Fruit.
```

```
Fruit : Apple | Orange *common* <weight> DemNumber.
Apple = .
Orange = .
```

5.6 BIBLIOGRAPHIC REMARKS

Incremental and global algorithms for class dictionary graph learning and optimization are in [BL91, LBSL90, LBSL91, Ber94].

The concept of propagation patterns was developed in a series of publications: [LXSL91, LX93c] and applied in [HSX91, LHSLX92, Lie92, LSLX94].

The first, preliminary implementation of propagation patterns in the form of a C++ skeleton generator was done by Christos Stamelos in the winter of 1990. The implementation of propagation patterns was brought to its current form primarily through the efforts of Cun Xiao and the feedback from hundreds of professionals who work in the Boston software industry and who took my courses in which adaptive software is used. Linda Keszenheimer, T. Beutel, and Gregory Bratshpis were early users. Paul Steckler was involved in the early development of propagation patterns.

Propagation patterns were motivated by the Law of Demeter. A strong driving force behind propagation patterns was G. Brown since he involved us in a project with initially vague assumptions on the class structure.

5.7 SOLUTIONS

Solution to Exercise 5.1

```
UNKNOWN1  = 0                       UNKNOWN2  = Basket
UNKNOWN3  = Apple                   UNKNOWN4  = Apple
UNKNOWN5  = return_val              UNKNOWN6  = get_weight
UNKNOWN7  = 0                       UNKNOWN8  = Basket
UNKNOWN9  = Fruit                   UNKNOWN10 = Fruit
UNKNOWN11 = return_val              UNKNOWN12 = this -> get_weight
UNKNOWN13 = new Thing_List()        UNKNOWN14 = Thing
UNKNOWN15 = Thing                   UNKNOWN16 = return_val
UNKNOWN17 = append                  UNKNOWN18 = before
UNKNOWN19 = apple_count > before
UNKNOWN20 = return_val              UNKNOWN21 = append
UNKNOWN22 = this -> set_weight(
            new DemNumber(*(this -> get_weight()) + 2))
```

Chapter 6

Class Dictionary Graphs and Objects

A class dictionary graph serves as a program customizer for propagation patterns that are executable specifications after customization with a class dictionary graph. Propagation patterns are like a sketch of an algorithm that has to be made more explicit with a class dictionary graph. Propagation patterns often do not define the details of input, output, and intermediate objects; those details are provided by a class dictionary graph.

A class dictionary graph consists of a set of class definitions which in turn define the application objects. From the implementation point of view, a class dictionary graph serves as an interface to an object-oriented system. One immediate practical benefit of a class dictionary graph is that it defines software for manipulating the objects that it defines. This software can be provided automatically for the application and therefore does not have to be written by hand.

The term class dictionary is related to the term data dictionary, which is widely used in conjunction with database management systems. Both types of dictionaries contain meta-data: data about data. A class dictionary graph is like a schema for a database. The graphical class dictionary graph notation borrows elements from entity-relationship diagrams that are widely used for data modeling.

How does a class dictionary graph differ from a collection of class definitions written in some object-oriented language such as the class definitions in your C++ book?

- A class dictionary graph serves as a scaffold to define the behavior of the classes.

- A class dictionary graph is an abstraction of the class definitions in some object-oriented language. It focuses only on is-a and has-a relations between classes. Those two kinds of relations are sufficient to define the structure of objects. The level of abstraction of the is-a and has-a relations is useful for several tasks, for example, planning an implementation or querying the objects defined by the class dictionary graph.

- A class dictionary graph, if extended with concrete syntax, also defines a language for describing the objects. We call such an extended class dictionary graph a class dictionary. Sentences of the language defined by a class dictionary are used for high-level debugging of the class dictionary without writing a single line of object-oriented code. Sentences are usually significantly shorter than the corresponding objects and therefore the debugging process is more efficient.

- A class dictionary graph contains sufficient information to define legal objects. Each part of an object has a type. (This also holds true for the class definitions of strongly typed languages, such as C++. However, at compile-time, C++ does not enforce the rule that all objects must be legal in our sense.)

- Class dictionary graphs are more concise and better structured than object-oriented language defined classes. Several kinds of class definitions are used for structuring the classes.

- Class dictionary graphs may contain parameterized class definitions. Parameterized class definitions are not allowed in some object-oriented languages.

- A class dictionary is at a higher level of abstraction than class definitions in many object-oriented languages. In a class dictionary graph, recursive class definitions are free of pointers, and the class definitions are given in a programming-language independent notation.

We use two notations for describing class dictionaries. Both notations define the same information but in different robes. The first notation, called the concise notation, is easier to write and uses less space, but is harder to read without learning it. The second notation, called the graphical notation, is largely self-explanatory. Why should we use two notations? Each has its purpose.

1. The graphical notation is better for the occasional reader and for readers who are used to graphical notations. A disadvantage of the graphical notation is that it requires more space than the concise notation.

2. The concise notation is better for writing big class dictionary graphs, and for people used to concise notations. Editing the concise notation is faster than editing the graphical notation. For editing the concise notation you can use your favorite text editor.

6.1 INTRODUCTORY EXAMPLE

The following is an example of a class dictionary graph defining a meal. We begin by describing a meal in English and then go on to convert the English description into a class dictionary graph.[1] In Chapter 8 we will write a simple program that computes the cost of a given meal.

At some point in defining a class dictionary we must decide what we consider to be atomic objects. In a meal a steak might be considered atomic since we are not interested in breaking the meat down into its basic molecular structure. A shrimp cocktail might be

---

[1]Class dictionary graph recognition, page 430(5).

6.1. INTRODUCTORY EXAMPLE

considered by some to be atomic, but for the purpose of this example we assume that we are ignorant of the notion of a shrimp cocktail and need to break it down further. Atomic objects are presented as classes without any parts. We define our meal structure as follows (this structure can be viewed as a menu describing the choices we have in selecting a meal):

- A meal is an appetizer, an entree, and a dessert. Although a dessert may be considered optional in many households, we consider it a required part of a meal.

- An appetizer is a melon or a shrimp cocktail; that is, there are two appetizer choices.

- A shrimp cocktail is lettuce, one or more shrimp, and possibly cocktail sauce.

- Cocktail sauce is ketchup and horseradish.

- An entree is a steak platter or a baked stuffed shrimp platter.

- A steak platter is a steak and the trimmings.

- A baked stuffed shrimp platter is a stuffed shrimp and the trimmings.

- The trimmings are a potato and two vegetables.

- A vegetable is carrots, peas, or corn.

- A dessert is pie, cake, or jello.

- We assume that the following items are atomic and need no further description: melon, shrimp, lettuce, ketchup, horseradish, steak, stuffed shrimp, potato, carrot, pea, corn, pie, cake, and jello. The decision as to whether an object is atomic is not only domain specific but also specific to the person performing the data abstraction.

Each of the above eleven descriptive phrases falls into one of three categories. Either we are constructing an object in terms of other objects (a construction class), or we state that an object is one of several possible objects (an alternation class), or we are defining an object as being a collection of zero (one) or more of other objects of the same kind (a repetition class).

Examples of these three object descriptions are shown in class dictionary graph notation below.[2]

Construction There are two kinds of construction classes: those without and with optional parts. **Meal** is an example of a construction class without optional parts. An object of class **Meal** has three ordered parts: an object of class **Appetizer** followed by an object of class **Entree** followed by an object of class **Dessert**. The graphical representation of this construction class is in Fig. 6.1 and the textual representation is in Fig.6.2.

Next we show an example of a construction class that has an optional part. An object of class **ShrimpCocktail** has three ordered parts: an object of class **Shrimps** followed by an object of class **Lettuce**, optionally followed by an object of class **CocktailSauce**. The graphical representation of this construction class is in Fig. 6.3 and the textual

---
[2]Class dictionary graph textual representation, page 431 (7).

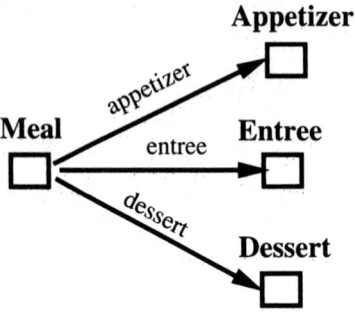

Figure 6.1: Graphical representation of construction class Meal

```
Meal =
  <appetizer> Appetizer
  <entree> Entree
  <dessert> Dessert.
Appetizer = .
Entree = .
Dessert = .
```

Figure 6.2: Textual representation of construction class Meal

6.1. INTRODUCTORY EXAMPLE

representation is in Fig.6.4. In the textual representation, part names are optional. The default value of the part is the name of the part class with all letters changed to lowercase letters. This means that a class used as a part class but without a part name needs to have a least one capital letter in its name. Otherwise there would be no distinction between class and part name.

```
ShrimpCocktail = Shrimps Lettuce [CocktailSauce].
```

is equivalent to

```
ShrimpCocktail =
  <shrimps> Shrimps
  <lettuce> Lettuce
  [<cocktailSauce> CocktailSauce].
```

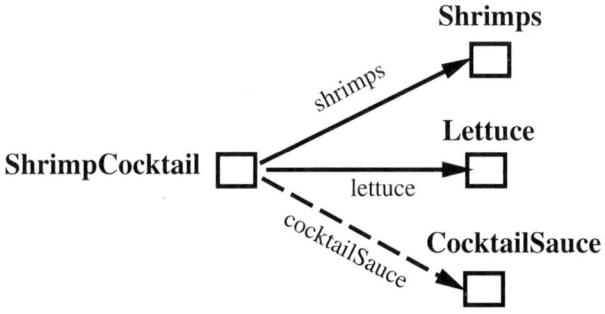

Figure 6.3: Graphical representation of construction class ShrimpCocktail

```
         ShrimpCocktail =
                 Shrimps Lettuce [CocktailSauce].
         Shrimps = .
         Lettuce = .
         CocktailSauce = .
```

Figure 6.4: Textual representation of construction class ShrimpCocktail

Construction classes have two kinds of outgoing edges: construction edges and optional construction edges. In the graphical representation, the construction edges always have a label and the optional construction edges are shown as dashed edges. In the textual representation, the construction edges have an optional label and the optional parts are enclosed by [and].

Alternation There are two kinds of alternation classes: those without common parts and those with common parts. We first consider an example of an alternation class without common parts. In this case the alternatives don't share any common parts. An object of class Fruit is either an object of classes Apple or Orange or Kiwi. The graphical representation of class Fruit is in Fig. 6.5 and the textual representation is in Fig. 6.6.

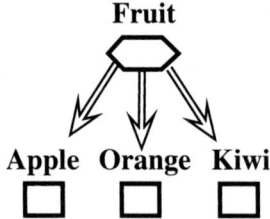

Figure 6.5: Graphical representation of an alternation class without common parts

```
Fruit : Apple | Orange | Kiwi.
Apple = .
Orange = .
Kiwi = .
```

Figure 6.6: Textual representation of an alternation class without common parts

Next we consider an alternation class with common parts. An object of class Roof is either an object of classes Concrete or Shingle. Elements of classes Concrete and Shingle have a part age of class DemNumber.

The graphical representation of class Roof is in Fig. 6.7 and the textual representation is in Fig. 6.8.

Alternation vertices have three kinds of outgoing edges: alternation edges, construction edges, and optional construction edges. Alternation edges are shown as doubly shafted arrows in the graphical representation. In the textual representation, the alternation edges are given first, separated from the construction edges by the keyword *common*. Alternation edges are never labeled.

Repetition There are two kinds of repetition classes: those defining a sequence of zero or more objects and those defining a sequence of one or more objects.

An object of class Banquet has any number of parts: an ordered sequence of zero or more objects of class Meal.

The graphical representation of class Banquet is in Fig. 6.9 and the textual representation is in Fig. 6.10.

6.1. INTRODUCTORY EXAMPLE

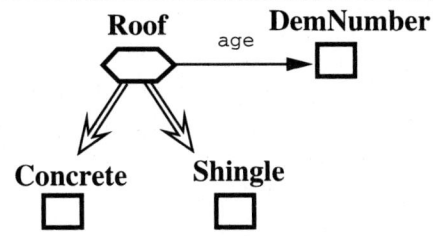

Figure 6.7: Graphical representation of alternation class with common parts

```
Roof : Concrete | Shingle
        *common* <age> DemNumber.
Concrete = .
Shingle = .
```

Figure 6.8: Textual representation of alternation class with common parts

Figure 6.9: Graphical representation of repetition class, zero or more

```
Banquet ~ {Meal}.
Meal = .
```

Figure 6.10: Textual representation of repetition class, zero or more

Symbol	Class Kind	Mnemonic association
= ☐	construction	the equal sign is used for showing composition in terms of parts.
: ⬡	alternation	the colon is often used for introducing a list of alternatives.
~ ⬡	repetition	repeating ocean wave, combination of construction, and alternation.

First symbol is for textual representation, second symbol is for graphical representation.

Table 6.1: Identifying symbols for classes

An object of class AtLeastOneDoor has any number of parts: an ordered sequence of one or more objects of class Door.

The graphical representation of class AtLeastOneDoor is in Fig. 6.11 and the textual representation is in Fig. 6.12.

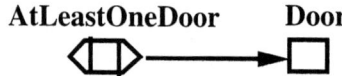

Figure 6.11: Graphical representation of repetition class, one or more

```
AtLeastOneDoor ~ Door { Door }.
Door = .
```

Figure 6.12: Textual representation of repetition class, one or more

Repetition vertices have only one kind of outgoing edge: exactly one repetition edge. Repetition edges are never labeled.

For several reasons we distinguish between the three kinds of descriptions syntactically in the second symbol (see Table 6.1). One reason is that A = B. and A : B. have different meanings. The graphical notation uses three kinds of class symbols (shown in Table 6.1) and five kinds of edge symbols (shown in Table 6.2).

6.1. INTRODUCTORY EXAMPLE

Symbol   Edge Kind

$\xrightarrow{l}$ construction

$\Longrightarrow$ alternation

$\xrightarrow[l]{}$ repetition

⋯▶   optional construction

⋯▶   optional repetition

Table 6.2: Identifying symbols for edges

Many class dictionary graphs make use of descriptive labels in their construction and alternation class definitions. A descriptive label is an identifier that is enclosed in angle brackets and precedes a given class name.

The sole purpose of descriptive labels is to give subobjects mnemonic names that make specifications and programs more readable. Descriptive labels are required if two or more of the same part classes are identified on the right-hand side of a class definition. The following is an example of such a class; it defines A-objects that are comprised of two B-objects.

```
A = <first> B <second> B.
```

We use labels to make the objects more self describing. The following example illustrates this point.

```
GradeReport = Name Percentage.
```

is not self describing. The following is semantically equivalent but makes the class dictionary graph, and any methods written for it, easier to read.

```
GradeReport = <studentName> Name <testScore> Percentage.
```

The description of our meal in the class dictionary graph notation is as follows:

```
Meal = Appetizer Entree Dessert.
Appetizer : Melon | ShrimpCocktail.
ShrimpCocktail = Shrimps Lettuce [CocktailSauce].
CocktailSauce = Ketchup HorseRadish.
Entree : SteakPlatter | BakedStuffedShrimp.
SteakPlatter = Steak Trimmings.
BakedStuffedShrimp = StuffedShrimp Trimmings.
Trimmings = Potato <veggie1> Vegetable <veggie2> Vegetable.
Vegetable : Carrots | Peas | Corn.
Dessert : Pie | Cake | Jello.
```

```
Shrimps ~ Shrimp {Shrimp}.

Shrimp = .
Melon = .
Lettuce = .
Ketchup = .
Steak = .
Potato = .
Carrots = .
Peas = .
Cake = .
Pie = .
Jello = .
Corn = .
StuffedShrimp = .
HorseRadish = .
```

Let us assume we want to create a class dictionary for a banquet or maybe a date between two people. We can define these as follows:

```
Banquet ~ Meal {Meal}.
Date = <person1> Person <person2> Person Meal Movie.
```

The Date class indicates that both persons eat the same meal. We now consider the task of calculating the cost of a banquet or date. To calculate the cost of a banquet we need to add up only the cost of each meal in the banquet, reusing the code already written for the meal. For the cost of a date, we need to write only the methods to find the cost of a movie, again reusing the previous code written for the meal class dictionary. This functionality is easily implemented by propagation patterns, which will be done in Chapter 8.

6.2 CLASS DICTIONARY GRAPH RULES

Class dictionary graphs are mathematical structures that have to satisfy certain rules. Those rules are best explained first for class dictionary graphs containing only construction and alternation vertices and edges. The generalization to repetition vertices and edges and to optional construction edges is straightforward.

To define the rules a class dictionary graph has to satisfy, we define the components of a class dictionary graph. Here we focus only on the absolutely essential components of a class dictionary graph and omit features like repetition classes and optional parts. A class dictionary graph consists of construction vertices VC, alternation vertices VA, $V = VC \cup VA$, labels Λ, construction edges EC, and alternation edges EA.

Construction edges are represented as triples: (Vertex in V, Label in Λ, Vertex in V). Alternation edges are represented as pairs: (Alternation vertex in VA, Vertex in V). Therefore, we describe a class dictionary graph by a tuple $(V, \Lambda; EC, EA)$. In the first part, before the semicolon, we have sets, and after the semicolon we list the relations. We use the following naming convention: V stands for vertices, E stands for edges, C stands for construction, A stands for alternation. V and E have precedence over C and A.

6.2. CLASS DICTIONARY GRAPH RULES

Notice that by this definition, only alternation vertices can have outgoing alternation edges. Edges in a class dictionary graph cannot start from any vertex kind and go to any other vertex kind. The edge/vertex restrictions are summarized below. The table indicates from which vertex kind the edges may originate and to which vertex kind they may go.

```
       VC              VA
----|------------------------
EC  |  from/to        from/to
EA  |    /to          from/to
```

Consider the classes defined in Fig. 6.13. The textual representation of the class dictionary graph is:

```
List : Empty | Nonempty.
Empty = .
Nonempty = <first> Element <rest> List.
Element = .
```

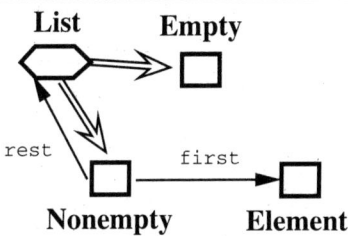

Figure 6.13: Class dictionary graph for lists

This class dictionary graph has the following components:
$V = \{Empty, Nonempty, Element, List\}$,
$VC = \{Empty, Nonempty, Element\}$, //construction vertices
$VA = \{List\}$, //alternation vertex
$EC = \{(Nonempty, rest, List), (Nonempty, first, Element)\}$, //construction edges
$EA = \{(List, Nonempty), (List, Empty)\}$, //alternation edges
$\Lambda = \{first, rest\}$.

A class dictionary graph has to satisfy three rules. The first two rules are essential for allowing a direct translation of a class dictionary graph into a set of compilable class definitions in an object-oriented programming language.

- Unique label rule

    For all vertices v, the labels of construction edges reachable from v by following 0 or more alternation edges in reverse, must be unique.

    This means that the labels of the parts of a vertex, both immediate as well as inherited, must be unique.

    For example, the class dictionary graph

```
Compound =
  <arg> Expression
  <arg> Expression.
Expression = .
```

violates the unique label rule. It can be repaired, for example, by changing the first arg to arg1.

- Cycle-free alternation rule

    No cyclic alternation paths containing one or more edges are allowed in class dictionary graphs.

    An alternation path is a consecutive sequence of alternation edges. A path is cyclic if it starts at some vertex and returns to the same vertex.

    For example, the class dictionary graph

```
Edible : Fruit | Vegetable.
Fruit : Apple | Orange.
Orange : Edible.
Vegetable = .
Apple = .
```

    violates the cycle-free alternation rule.

    In addition to the unique label and cycle-free alternation rules, a class dictionary graph has to satisfy the next rule.

- At-least-one alternative rule

    Every alternation vertex in a class dictionary graph must have at least one outgoing alternation edge.

    The reason for this rule is that a class dictionary graph is used to define objects for every vertex in the class dictionary graph. If there were an alternation vertex v without an outgoing alternation edge, there could be no objects of class v.

6.2.1 Convenient Extensions

Class dictionary graphs with construction and alternation edges provide the important modeling power for describing object structures. Repetition classes can be simulated with construction and repetition classes as Fig. 6.13 shows. But for practical applications it is convenient to have repetition classes directly available. The same applies to optional parts. The optional part in

```
Meal =
  <appetizer> Appetizer
  <entree> Entree
  [<dessert> Dessert].
```

6.2. CLASS DICTIONARY GRAPH RULES

can be simulated by

```
Meal =
  <appetizer> Appetizer
  <entree> Entree
  <dessert> OptDessert.
OptDessert : Dessert | Empty.
Empty = .
```

A class dictionary graph $G = (VC, VA, VR; \Lambda, EC, ECO, EA, ER, ERO)$ consists of construction vertices VC, alternation vertices VA, repetition vertices VR, $V = VC \cup VA \cup VR$, labels Λ, construction edges EC, optional construction edges ECO, alternation edges EA, repetition edges ER, and optional repetition edges ERO. Construction edges, including the optional ones, are represented as triples: (Vertex in $VC \cup VA$, Label in Λ, Vertex in V). Alternation edges are represented as pairs: (Alternation vertex in VA, Vertex in $VC \cup VA$). Repetition edges, including the optional ones, are represented as pairs: (Vertex in VR, Vertex in V).

Notice that by this definition, construction edges can exit only from construction or alternation vertices. Furthermore, an alternation edge cannot terminate in a repetition vertex. The reason is that a repetition class cannot inherit parts from super classes.

Edges in a class dictionary graph cannot start from any vertex kind and go to any other vertex kind. The edge/vertex restrictions are summarized below. VT is explained in the next paragraph.

	VC	VA	VR	VT
EC	from/to	from/to	/to	/to
ECO	from/to	from/to	/to	/to
EA	/to	from/to		
ER	/to	/to	from/to	/to
ERO	/to	/to	from/to	/to

For practical purposes it is convenient to use predefined classes for the most common objects, such as numbers, identifiers, strings, etc. For this purpose we use a fourth class kind, called terminal classes. The terminal classes that we use are: DemNumber, DemReal, DemIdent, DemString, DemText. VT is the set of terminal classes and the table below summarizes the edge/vertex restrictions with the presence of VT. No edge can originate from a terminal class since they are terminal. An alternation edge cannot terminate in a terminal class since it would alter a predefined class.

A graphical version of the previous table is in Fig. 6.14. Terminal classes have a T inside the symbol. The illegal connections are crossed out.

In addition to the previous table there are the following restrictions. A construction or alternation vertex can have zero or more outgoing edges of the EC and ECO kind. A repetition vertex has exactly one outgoing edge, either of the ER or ERO kind. An alternation vertex has at least one outgoing edge of the EA kind.

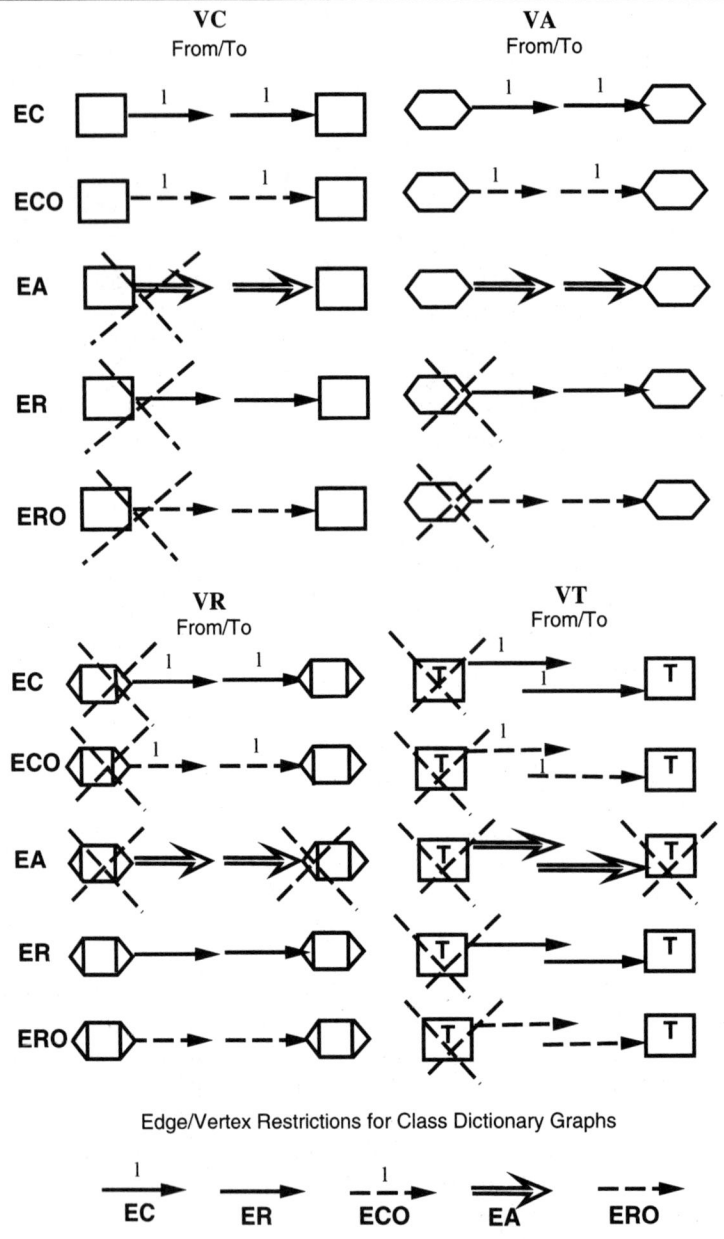

Figure 6.14: Connections

class kind	$\mathcal{A}(S)$
construction class S = ...	unit set { S }
repetition class S ~ ...	unit set { S }
alternation class S : X|Y|Z...	union of $\mathcal{A}(X)$ $\mathcal{A}(Y)$ $\mathcal{A}(Z)$ ...

Figure 6.15: Definition of associated

6.3 OBJECTS

The purpose of a class dictionary graph is to define classes, which in turn define sets of objects.[3]

There is a fixed number of terminal classes that define **terminal objects**. The terminal objects represent a value such as a number, an identifier, or a string. These objects are instances of the classes DemNumber, DemReal, DemIdent, DemString, DemText, respectively.

In addition to the terminal objects, there are **composite** objects that are defined by the class definitions. A special case of the composite objects are the ones without a part. They are called **atomic** objects. The class A = . defines only atomic objects.

To define the set of *legal*[4] objects with respect to a class dictionary graph, we need to define, for any class S, the set $\mathcal{A}(S)$ of construction classes associated with S. The set of classes **associated** with a class is given in Fig. 6.15. It is the set of construction classes that are reachable through alternation edges from class S.

If T is a set of construction classes then a T-object is an object that is an instance of a class in T. A **legal object** with respect to a class dictionary graph is defined inductively as follows. Nothing is a legal object except by virtue of one of the following rules.

1. Every atomic object and every terminal object is a legal object.

2. The following composite objects are legal objects:

   (a) If there is a nonempty class definition

   A = <p1> C1 <p2> C2 ...

   then an A-object is legal if all the p1-parts are $\mathcal{A}(C1)$-objects and if all the p2-parts are $\mathcal{A}(C2)$-objects, etc. An optional part of a construction class may be nil = NULL.

   If A is used as an alternative of an alternation class definition, then the A-objects get all the parts that are defined after *common*: If Ai appears in

   Q : A1 | A2 | ... *common* <m1> M1 <m2> M2 ...

   then Ai-objects have an m1-part that is an $\mathcal{A}(M1)$-object and an m2-part that is an $\mathcal{A}(M2)$-object, etc.

---

[3] Object graph recognition, page 436 (24).
[4] Legal object graph, page 436 (27).

(b) If there is a class definition

    A ~ {B}.

then a legal A-object is an object that has an ordered sequence of legal $\mathcal{A}$(B)-objects as parts.

(c) If there is a class definition

    A ~ B {B}.

then a legal A-object is an object that has a nonempty ordered sequence of legal $\mathcal{A}$(B)-objects as parts.

This definition of legal objects allows objects that share subparts and even circular objects. Instances of the same class may be substituted for each other without changing the legality of an object.

2a can be simplified, if we use the flattening operation.[5] A class dictionary graph G_1 is the **flattened** form of a class dictionary graph G_2, if in G_1 all parts have been pushed down the alternation edges to construction classes. After the flattening, no alternation class has common parts. Flat class dictionary graphs are usually not written by the user but are produced from nonflat class dictionary graphs by tools. Flat class dictionary graphs are a useful intermediate form. Notice that the flattening operation is well defined since there can be no cycles of alternation edges in a class dictionary graph.

Next we introduce a textual notation for objects.

6.3.1 Textual Representation

Objects are fundamental to object oriented programming. Therefore we are using a notation that displays the structure of an object as clearly as possible.[6] An object that does not contain shared subobjects is naturally represented as a tree.

Consider the following class dictionary graph for defining class CocktailSauce:

```
CocktailSauce = <ketchup> Ketchup <horseRadish> HorseRadish.
```

Every object of class CocktailSauce has the following form.

```
CocktailSauce(
  <ketchup> Ketchup()
  <horseRadish> HorseRadish())
```

Consider the following class dictionary for defining nested numerical expressions in prefix form:

---

[5]Class dictionary graph flattening, page 435 (22).
[6]Object graph textual representation, page 436 (26).

6.3. OBJECTS

```
Example = <exps> Expressions.
Expressions ~ { Expression }.
Expression : Variable | Numerical | Compound.
Variable = <name> DemIdent.
Numerical = <value> DemNumber.
Compound =
  <op> Operator
      <argument1> Expression
      <argument2> Expression .
Operator : MulSym | AddSym | SubSym.
MulSym = .
AddSym = .
SubSym = .
```

An example of a textual representation of an object of class **Example** is given by

```
Example (
   < exps > Expressions {
     Compound (
        < op > MulSym ( )
        < argument1 > Compound (
           < op > AddSym ( )
           < argument1 > Compound (
              < op > MulSym ( )
              < argument1 > Numerical (
                 < value > DemNumber "3" )
              < argument2 > Variable (
                 < name > DemIdent "a" ) )
           < argument2 > Numerical (
              < value > DemNumber "5" ) )
        < argument2 > Numerical (
           < value > DemNumber "7" ) ) ,
     Compound (
        < op > SubSym ( )
        < argument1 > Variable (
           < name > DemIdent "a" )
        < argument2 > Numerical (
           < value > DemNumber "88" ) ) } )

// A list of two expressions
( *
  ( +
    ( * 3 a )
    5 )
  7 )
( - a 88 )
```

The tree is laid on its side and has all branches on the same side of the main stem. This notation uses one line for each object or subobject specifying the object's class. An "{" after the class name means that the object is an instance of a repetition class. Therefore such an object has a certain number of unnamed subobjects. They are all listed with the same indentation. A "(" after the class name means that the object is an instance of a construction or terminal class. Therefore such an object has a fixed number of named subobjects. For terminals we show the value of the instance. The last line shows the object in a more familiar form.

An object contains a shared subobject if some subobject is accessible in more than one way. An example of a shared object is the internal representation of a prefix expression in which both arguments share the same expression. A special class of the objects that contain shared subobjects are the circular objects.

An object is called circular if it contains a part that contains itself. An example of a circular object is a compound prefix expression that contains itself in the first argument. Shared and circular objects are important for efficient representation of data structures.

6.3.2 Size

When we analyze the running time of our algorithms or when we discuss the computational complexity of a problem, we need to talk about the size of an object.

The size of an object is the total number of parts of the object. If an object contains shared subobjects, we count each part only once. The size of an object is equal to the number of lines in the drawn object. We count the size of a number, identifier, string, or any other class terminal element as one. For certain applications it makes more sense to count the size of an object of a terminal class as the number of characters it contains.

6.4 TRANSLATION TO C++

To make a class dictionary graph a strong scaffold for expressing behavior, we define a personalized class library for a given class dictionary graph. The functionality of this library is used in adaptive or object-oriented programs that are written for the class dictionary graph.

A class dictionary graph $D = (VC, VA, \Lambda; EC, EA)$ is mapped into C++ as follows. To each element of VC corresponds a C++ class with a constructor, and to each element of VA corresponds an abstract C++ class, that is, a class that has at least one pure virtual function.

Each vertex is translated into a C++ class as follows:[7]

- Data members

  For each outgoing construction edge a private data member is created. The label becomes the name of the data member. The type of the data member is a pointer type of the class corresponding to the target of the construction edge.

  A static data member stores the class name. This is done so that an object knows about the class that it instantiates.

---

[7]Class dictionary graph translation, page 433 (18).

6.4. TRANSLATION TO C++

- Function members

    For construction vertices only; a constructor with as many arguments as there are outgoing construction edges or inherited construction edges. The default value for all arguments is NULL.

    For each data member x, a writing function set_x (with one argument) and a reading function get_x.

- Inheritance

    Each class inherits from its alternation predecessors.

Let's apply the above procedure to the class dictionary graph in Fig. 6.16. The textual representation of the class dictionary graph is

```
Exp : Compound | Simple.
Compound = <op> Op <arg1> Exp <arg2> Exp.
Op : Addsym | Mulsym.
Addsym = .
Mulsym = .
Simple = <numValue> DemNumber.
```

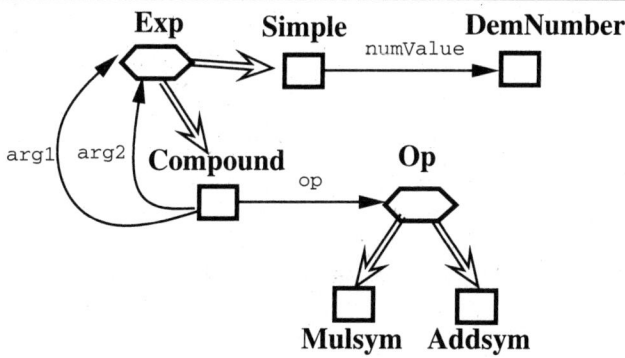

Figure 6.16: Class dictionary graph for expressions

The class library in C++ looks like this:

```
class Exp {
   public:
     #include "Exp.h"
};

class Simple : public Exp {
   private:
   DemNumber *numValue;
```

```cpp
      static char *type;
   public:
     Simple( DemNumber * = NULL );
     DemNumber *get_numValue() { return( numValue ); }
     void set_numValue( DemNumber *new_numValue )
          { numValue = new_numValue; }
     char     *get_type() { return( type ); }
};
```

The implementation of the constructor is not shown; it assigns the arguments to the appropriate data member.

```cpp
class Compound : public Exp {
   private:
     Op *op;
     Exp *arg1;
     Exp *arg2;
     static char *type;
   public:
     Compound( Op * = NULL, Exp * = NULL, Exp * = NULL );
     Op *get_op() { return( op ); }
     void set_op( Op *new_op )
          { op = new_op; }
     Exp *get_arg1() { return( arg1 ); }
     void set_arg1( Exp *new_arg1 )
          { arg1 = new_arg1; }
     Exp *get_arg2() { return( arg2 ); }
     void set_arg2( Exp *new_arg2 )
          { arg2 = new_arg2; }
     char     *get_type() { return( type ); }
};

class Op {
   public:
};

class Addsym : public Op {
   private:
     static char *type;
   public:
     Addsym();
     char     *get_type() { return( type ); }
};

class Mulsym : public Op {
   private:
```

6.4. TRANSLATION TO C++

```cpp
        static char *type;
    public:
        Mulsym();
        char    *get_type() { return( type ); }
};
class DemNumber {
    private:
        int val;
        static char *type;
    public:
        DemNumber( int = 0 );
        char    *get_type() { return( type ); }
        int     get_val() { return( val ); }
        void    set_val( int new_val ) { val = new_val; }
};
```

Now let's solve a simple problem for this class dictionary graph: We write a pocket calculator algorithm in C++ to evaluate the expressions. In a first phase we write a program for simple expressions that are just numbers.[8]

```cpp
// phase 1
int Exp::eval(){} // virtual
int Simple::eval() {
   return numValue->eval();}
int DemNumber::eval() {
   return val;}
```

In a second phase we add to the program of the first phase to get a pocket calculator for additive expressions. We have the privilege of only adding code because of the delayed binding of calls to code. For example, in phase 2, when the apply_op function is called for op, the system will determine what kind of operator we have at run-time and the system will call the right function.

```cpp
// phase 2
int Compound::eval() {
   return op->apply_op(arg1->eval(),
                arg2->eval()); }
int Op::apply_op(int n1,int n2) {} // virtual
int Addsym::apply_op(int n1,int n2) {
   return n1 + n2; }
```

To allow both additive and multiplicative expressions, we need to add a multiplication operator.

---
[8]Growth plan, page 445 (54).

```
// phase 3
int Mulsym::apply_op(int n1,int n2) {
  return n1 * n2; }
```

Now that the program is complete we need to call it from the main program. We create, for example, a Compound-object, called iCompound and then we call function eval with

```
cout << iCompound -> eval();
```

The class library shown above contains more functionality than is needed for this pocket calculator. For example, all the get_val functions are unnecessary.

A class dictionary graph defines universal methods that can be generically provided. This includes methods for copying, computing the size of objects, drawing, comparing, printing, and creating a random object. The implementation of those generic methods is not shown in the class library example.

6.5 PARAMETERIZED CLASSES

Parameterized classes are useful to factor out commonalities in class definitions. For example, if we use the classes

```
College1 =
    <students> Student_NList
    <faculty> Faculty_NList
    <staff> Staff_NList.
Student_NList ~ Student {Student}.
Faculty_NList ~ Faculty {Faculty}.
Staff_NList ~ Staff {Staff}.
```

we can save some typing by using

```
College2 =
    <students> NList(Student)
    <faculty> NList(Faculty)
    <staff> NList(Staff).
NList(S) ~ S {S}.
```

Here NList is a parameterized class that takes one class parameter. The meaning of both college classes is identical. The second formulation allows easier change. For example, if we want to represent the lists differently, we can easily change the definition of the parameterized class to:

```
NList(S) = <first> S <rest> List(S).
List(S) : Empty(S) | NList(S).
Empty(S) = .
```

We use parameterized classes primarily to formulate class dictionaries more elegantly. A class dictionary containing parameterized classes can always be expanded into a class dictionary without parameterized classes by using the mechanism shown above. For example,

NList(Student) is translated to Student_NList. The rule is that the parameterized class call is read backward and the opening parentheses are translated to _. For example, if we have the parameterized class definition A(S1,S2,S3) = ... and a call with A(F,G,H), the class is expanded into H_G_F_A.

I cannot resist the temptation to point out that parameterized classes can easily be misused. For example, we could define a parameterized class A(S):

```
A(S) = <b> B(S) <c> C(S) <s> S.
B(S) = <d> D <s> S <e> E(S).
C(S) = <s> S.
D = .
E(S) = <s> S.
```

Such a description would not be robust under changes to the object structures. It would be better to describe the desired parameterization relatively independent of the class structure.

6.6 CLASS DICTIONARY GRAPH DESIGN

We discuss connections between taxonomy and class dictionary graph design and give guidelines on how to select relationships between classes.

6.6.1 Why Alternation Classes are Abstract

A class has at least two purposes: it is used to create instances and it is used to organize other classes through is-a relationships. In a class dictionary graph, the two purposes cannot be fulfilled simultaneously by the same class. Either a class is a construction class and can be used to create objects but not for is-a relationships, or it is an alternation class and is used to organize other classes through is-a relationships, but not to create objects directly.

Why this separation? There are numerous pros and cons that have been analyzed by Walter Hürsch [Hür94]. The separation has a positive influence on the simplicity of the theory for adaptive software. And the overhead is small should we have to simulate a class that can create objects and have subclasses. Let A be such a class. We define a class A_generalize by

```
A_generalize : A_instantiate.
A_instantiate = .
```

We put the code of class A into class A_generalize and use this class for subclassing, and use class A_instantiate for creating objects. The rule that says that all superclasses must be abstract is called the **abstract superclass rule—DEF**.

6.6.2 Taxonomy and Class Dictionary Graphs

Taxonomy is the science of classification. We discuss class dictionary graph design in the context of two kinds of classifications: specialization-centered and parts-centered.

Often a subconcept is simpler than a super concept; for example, a square is simpler than a rectangle. A square is defined by one real number, but a rectangle needs two. So we are tempted to use the following specialization centered class dictionary graph:

```
Rectangular : Rectangle | Square *common*
  <height> DemNumber
  <width> DemNumber.
Rectangle = .
Square = .
```

However, it is better to follow the guideline for **parts-centered** design:

> If a subclass needs fewer parts than a superclass, rearrange the parts reflecting the different needs.

In the context of our example this rule suggests the following class dictionary graph, since a square needs fewer parts than a rectangle.

```
Rectangular : Rectangle | Square.
Rectangle =
  <height> DemNumber
  <width> DemNumber.
Square = <length> DemNumber.
```

This class dictionary graph allows for rectangles that have height = width but are not classified as squares. This is better than in the previous class dictionary graph where we could have lots of squares with different heights and widths.

To motivate the above design guideline, we derive a class dictionary for rectangles, squares, ellipses, and circles. A first solution is to build a conceptual model such as:

```
Figure: Rectangle | Ellipse.
Rectangle : Square *common*
  <height> DemNumber
  <width> DemNumber.
Ellipse : Circle *common*
  <semiaxis_height> DemNumber
  <semiaxis_width> DemNumber.
Square = .
Circle = .
```

This class dictionary defines only square and circle objects. But let's assume that we would allow alternation classes to be instantiated. We would have the following problems with the above class dictionary graph:

- A square is represented by two numbers, instead of one.

- We can call the functions for changing the height and the width of a square to any value, ignoring the constraint that they need to be equal.

The following class dictionary graph gives a conceptual model with its focus still on specialization, but it no longer assumes that alternation classes are instantiable.

A specialization-centered class dictionary graph follows.

6.6. CLASS DICTIONARY GRAPH DESIGN

```
Figure: Rectangular | Elliptic.
Rectangular : Rectangle | Square *common*
  <height> Measure
  <width> Measure.
Rectangle = .
Square = .
Elliptic : Ellipse | Circle *common*
  <semiaxis_height> Measure
  <semiaxis_width> Measure.
Ellipse = .
Circle = .
Measure = <v> DemNumber.
```

But we still have the two problems mentioned above. However, in this class dictionary graph **Square** is no longer a subclass of **Rectangle**, which will make it easier to improve the solution. The class dictionary graph was obtained from the previous class dictionary graph by following the rule that alternation classes cannot be instantiated. This rule implies the extra classes **Rectangular** and **Elliptic**. These classes allow us to deal with the classes **Rectangle** and **Square** separately. On the other hand, a square is no longer represented as a special kind of rectangle; we only say that a square is a special kind of rectangular object.

Now let's improve the solution and eliminate these two problems. We develop a part-centered class dictionary graph.

```
Figure: Rectangular | Elliptic.
Rectangular : Rectangle | Square.
Rectangle =
  <height> Measure
  <width> Measure.
Square = <length> Measure.
Elliptic : Ellipse | Circle.
Ellipse =
  <semiaxis_height> Measure
  <semiaxis_width> Measure.
Circle = <radius> Measure.
Measure = <v> DemNumber.
```

This class dictionary defines square, circle, rectangle, and ellipse objects. It also provides a conceptual model as did the first one, but the focus is on representing objects with the appropriate parts and not on specializing classes. For example, **Square** is no longer a subclass of **Rectangle**.

Which class dictionary graph is better, the part-centered class dictionary graph or the specialization-centered class dictionary graph? The part-centered class dictionary graph tends to be better (because of the above two problems). Let's compute the area of a **Figure**-object.

For the part-centered class dictionary graph we get the program

```
// compute area of any of the 4 figures
// simulating multiple inheritance with wrappers
// A circle inherits code for two reasons:
//   its area is determined by one side
//   its area is computed using PI
*operation* float area()
  *init* (@ 1.0 @)
  *traverse* *from* Figure *to* Measure
  *wrapper* Measure
    *prefix*
      (@ return_val = return_val * *v;  @)
  // order of the following wrappers is important:
  // first we need to square, then to multiply by PI
  *wrapper* {Circle, Square}
    *suffix*
      (@ return_val = return_val * return_val; @)
  *wrapper* {Circle, Ellipse}
    *suffix*
      (@ float PI = 3.1415; return_val = return_val * PI; @)
```

It is interesting to notice that the preceding propagation pattern also works for the specialization centered class dictionary graph if we delete the wrapper for circle and square. The propagation pattern uses a class set in conjunction with a wrapper. *wrapper* Circle, Square means that the wrapper code will be attached to both classes.

The table in Fig. 6.17 compares part-centered and specialization-centered designs.

In conclusion, many conceptual models for an application domain usually exist. We can distinguish between part-centered and specialization-centered class dictionary graphs and we noticed that part-centered class dictionary graphs are usually better since they have less duplication of parts and their programs can be better checked at compile-time.

We noticed that the transition from a specialization-centered program to the part-centered program is easy. Especially when the program is written with propagation patterns, a changing class structure can be easily absorbed.

We propose the following informal procedure of getting to a part-centered class dictionary graph:

- Start with traditional specialization-centered classification (assume that alternation classes are instantiable).

- Implement the restriction that alternation classes are abstract. Make class-superclass relationships into sibling relationships if different or incompatible parts are needed.

It is interesting to mention that traditional classification hierarchies allow alternation classes to be instantiated. Another example of a specialization-centered classification is

```
RealN : Rational.
Rational : Integer.
Integer : Natural.
```

6.6. CLASS DICTIONARY GRAPH DESIGN

```
Comparison:

part-centered                  specialization-centered

Advantages:
-----------
less duplication               more uniform algorithm

easy to check
at compile time
------------------------------------------------------
Disadvantages:
--------------
less uniform algorithm         run-time check for illegal objects
                               type system allows illegal
                               mutation of objects
```

Figure 6.17: Part-centered versus specialization-centered designs

The corresponding part-centered taxonomy is

```
RealN : Real | Rational | Integer.
Real = <v> float@C.
Rational = <n> DemNumber <d> DemNumber.
Integer = <v> DemNumber.
```

6.6.3 Construction versus Alternation Edges

When you design two closely related classes X and Y you have a choice of three structural relationships between them: construction, alternation, or repetition (see Fig. 6.18).

Which one do you choose?

In all three cases we can say that an X-object contains Y-information. In the construction and repetition case we can access this information by calling a function of a Y-object that is part of an X-object. In the alternation case we can use the Y-information by calling a function of the Y-class.

Here are a few questions that help to decide whether to use a construction/repetition edge over an alternation edge. If the answer to the following questions is positive, use a construction edge or a repetition edge.

Do we need Y-information several times in an X-object?

If we change the Y-information in an X-object, do we get an X-object with the same identity?

```
construction
  Y = ...              Y = ...
  X = <y> Y.           X : alternatives *common* <y> Y.

alternation
  Y : X *common* ...
  X = .

repetition
  Y = ...
  X ~ {Y}.
```

Figure 6.18: Edge choice

If the answer to the following questions is positive, use an alternation edge.

Is an X-object a kind of a Y-object?

Can the set of Y-objects be split into several disjoint sets, one of them being the X-objects?

We provide some examples here.

An expression contains several subexpressions. We use a construction or a repetition edge.

`Compound = Op <arg1> Exp <arg2> Exp.`

`Compound = Op <args> List(Exp).`

We use a construction edge if we want to name the parts and a repetition edge if we want to number the parts.

If we change a tire of a car, we still see it as the same car. Also, if we change the driver of a car, the car keeps its identity. Therefore we use a construction or a repetition edge in the following class definitions:

`Car = <tires> List(Tire) <driver> Driver.`

`ThreeTireCar = <t1> Tire <t2> Tire <t3> Tire <reserve> Tire.`

An apple is a kind of a fruit; therefore we use an alternation edge.

`Fruit : Apple | Orange *common* Weight.`

6.7 SUMMARY

In this section we introduced class dictionary graphs without reference to their cousins, class dictionaries, which are covered in a later chapter.

A class dictionary graph defines a set of objects that is usually infinite. A class dictionary graph is an interface to a set of class definitions written in some programming language. The most important role of a class dictionary graph is as a customizer of adaptive programs.

6.8 EXERCISES

Exercise 6.1 (Class objective)
Consider the following class dictionary graph:

```
Example = <l> L.
L ~ {A} .
A = <x> B.
B : D | E *common* <c> C.
C ~ {DemIdent}.
D = .
E : Description | OrderNumber.
Description = .
OrderNumber = .
```

Give the list of C++ classes defined by this class dictionary graph. For each class indicate what kind of class it is (construction, repetition, or alternation) and whether it is abstract or not, and list all data members, including the inherited ones, and their types.

Exercise 6.2 Write a class dictionary graph for an application of your choice. Describe three objects that are legal with respect to the class dictionary graph (using the object notation) and determine the sizes of the three objects.

Exercise 6.3 Use a class dictionary graph for describing expressions. Give an object that is legal with respect to the class dictionary graph and that:

1. contains shared subobjects but is not circular.

2. is circular.

Exercise 6.4 Write a C++ program from scratch that evaluates expressions and prints them out.

```
Example = <ex> Prefix.
Prefix : Simple | Compound.
Simple = <v> DemNumber.
Compound =  Op <arg1> Prefix <arg2> Prefix .
Op : MulSym | AddSym .
MulSym = .
AddSym = .
```

Required C++ knowledge: Derived classes (for alternation classes), virtual functions (almost always needed with derived classes), ordering of classes, constructors. Hint: use derived classes for the alternatives of an alternation class.

Exercise 6.5 Grow the C++ prefix expression evaluator from the last exercise to a prefix expression evaluator for the following class dictionary graph:

```
Example = <exps> List(Prefix).
Prefix : Simple | Compound.
Simple = <v> DemNumber.
Compound =  Op <args> List(Prefix) .
Op : MulSym | AddSym .
MulSym = .
AddSym = .
List(S) ~ S {S}.
```

Exercise 6.6 Write a C++ program for differentiating (i.e. taking the derivative) of prefix expressions. Use the class dictionary graph of the previous exercise.

Exercise 6.7 You are given a class dictionary graph and several objects and you have to identify missing information in the objects. Find the unknowns below. Class dictionary (for the entire question):

```
A =   <b> B.
B :  C | D | A *common* <w> W.
W ~   {DemIdent} .
C = .
D = .
```

1. Consider the following three legal A-objects a1, a2, a3. Find the unknowns.

    ```
    A-object a1:
          : A (
            < UNKNOWN1 > : C (
              < w > : UNKNOWN2 { } )
            < UNKNOWN3 > : UNKNOWN4 { } )

    A-object a2:
          : A (
            < b > : UNKNOWN5 (
              < b > : UNKNOWN6 (
                < b > : C (
                  < w > : UNKNOWN7 { } )
                < w > : UNKNOWN8 { } )
              < w > : UNKNOWN9 { } )
            < w > : UNKNOWN10 { } )
    ```

6.8. EXERCISES

```
A-object a3:
    : A (
      < b > : A (
          < b > : D (
              < w > : W {
                  : UNKNOWN11 "x" } )
            < UNKNOWN12 > : UNKNOWN13 {
                : UNKNOWN14 "x" ,
                : UNKNOWN15 "y" ,
                : UNKNOWN16 "z" } )
        < w > : W {
            : UNKNOWN17 "z" } ) } )
```

2. For the following A-object,

```
//        : A (
//          < b > : C (
//              < w > : W { } )
//            < w > : W { } ) ,
```

write C++ statements for creating the A-object. Find the unknowns below.

```
UNKNOWN18 c1 =  UNKNOWN19 ;
c1 -> UNKNOWN20(new UNKNOWN21());
UNKNOWN22 a1 = new UNKNOWN23
   (c1);
a1 -> UNKNOWN24(new W());
```

3. Consider the following illegal objects. Find the first error as indicated.

```
A-object i1:
// give three answers in UNKNOWN25
The FIRST error is on line UNKNOWN25:
replace letter UNKNOWN25 by UNKNOWN25
        : A (
          < b > : A (
              < b > : D (
                  < b > : C (
                      < w > : W { } )
                    < w > : W { } )
                < w > : V { } )
            < v > : W { } )
```

```
A-object i2:
The FIRST error is on line UNKNOWN26: UNKNOWN27 is missing.
```

```
        : A (
   < b > : A (
         < b > : D ()
         < w > : W {
               : DemReal "x" ,
               : DemReal "y" ,
               : DemReal "z" } )
   < w > : W {
         : DemReal "z" } ) } )
```

6.9 BIBLIOGRAPHIC REMARKS

The meal example is from [LR88b] and was invented by Arthur Riel.

The comparison of specialization-centered and parts-centered design was motivated by the article "Objectivism: Class considered harmful" on page 128, *Comm. ACM*, Aug. 1992, 128-130, Juergen F. H. Winkler, Technical correspondence.

- Data dictionaries

  A survey on how data dictionaries (related to class dictionaries) are used in database management systems is given in [ALM82], [Wer86].

  The data dictionary approach to program design has been advocated in structured analysis texts, such as [MM85].

  Our basic class dictionary notation (without inheritance or parameterization) was promoted in the early eighties (see e.g. [Pre87, 5.2.2, page 173]). Warnier Diagrams also share many characteristics with our class dictionaries.

- Semantic data modeling

  A survey of semantic database modeling is given in [HK87]. The task of schema integration, which is related to the task of class dictionary integration and evolution, is studied in [BLN86]. View integration is also related to class dictionary integration and is discussed in [NEL86].

- Object bases

  Class dictionary graphs are an important part of the schema of an object base. Work on object-oriented database systems is represented in [MS87], [SZ87], [AB87], [AH87], and [HK87].

- Program transformation systems

  Our development of Demeter has been motivated by work on program transformation systems [PS83],[CI84], [BM84].

  The MENTOR system [DGHK+75], [DGHKL80] is designed for manipulating structured data represented by abstract syntax trees.

  Our approach has the advantage that the grammar-based approach to program transformation and the rule-based approach (used by many program transformation systems) are blended in a natural way. Adaptiveness is not present in the older systems.

The Mjølner project uses a Demeter-like approach [MN88] but does not support adaptiveness.

- Hoare's type definition language

  Hoare proposed the following type definition language back in 1972 in his paper on recursive data structures [Hoa75].

```
TypeDeclaration =
  "type" <typeIdent> Ident "=" Compound.
Compound =
  "(" <generators> BarList(Generator) ")".
TypeExpression : Ident | Compound.
Generator =
  <generatorIdents> CommaList(Ident)
  "(" <types> CommaList(TypeExpression) ")".
BarList(S) ~ S {"|" S}.
CommaList(S) ~ S {"," S}.
```

Examples:

```
TYPE proposition =
  (prop(letter) |
   neg(proposition) |
   conj, disj (proposition, proposition))

TYPE list = (unit(identifier) | cons(list, list)).

TYPE expression =
  (constant(real) |
   variable(identifier) |
   minus(expression) |
   sum, product, quotient
     (expression, expression,
       (unknown | known(expression))).
```

This language contains some core aspects of the Demeter-type definition notation. The Demeter construction classes correspond to Hoare's generators. Hoare considers such a definition as a word algebra. A class is a type that is a subset of a word algebra.

Fig. 6.14 was proposed by John Cosimati.

6.10 SOLUTIONS

Solution to Exercise 6.7

```
UNKNOWN1 = b              UNKNOWN2 = W
UNKNOWN3 = w              UNKNOWN4 = W
UNKNOWN5 = A              UNKNOWN6 = A
UNKNOWN7 = W              UNKNOWN8 = W
UNKNOWN9 = W              UNKNOWN10 = W
UNKNOWN11 = DemIdent      UNKNOWN12 = w
UNKNOWN13 = W             UNKNOWN14 = DemIdent
UNKNOWN15 = DemIdent      UNKNOWN16 = DemIdent
UNKNOWN17 = DemIdent      UNKNOWN18 = C*
UNKNOWN19 = new C()       UNKNOWN20 = set_w
UNKNOWN21 = W             UNKNOWN22 = A*
UNKNOWN23 = A             UNKNOWN24 = set_w
UNKNOWN25 = 3, D, A       UNKNOWN26 = 3
UNKNOWN27 = <w> W()
```

Chapter 7

Propagation Directives

Propagation patterns describe new functionality by flexibly composing existing functionality. The details of the composition are left open and can be customized later in two ways: by adding more functionality and by giving the details of the composition.

Each propagation pattern implements a functionality for a group of collaborating classes. The group of classes is not given explicitly by itemizing elements of the group, but by an implicit specification. This specification focuses on the important classes and relationships that are really relevant to the given functionality.

Implicit specifications of groups of collaborating classes are given by propagation directives, which are the subject of this chapter. A propagation directive is a succinct specification of a group of collaborating classes out of a larger class dictionary graph. The resulting subgraph is called a **propagation graph**. If it is used for the purpose of traversal, it is also called a traversal graph.

A typical example is the specification of the physical part-of structure of a bigger class structure that might contain many more relationships than the physical part-of relationships. For example, a car consists of an engine, transmission, wheels, etc. which are all physical parts of the car, but the driver of the car does not belong to the physical part-of structure.

The need to work with propagation graphs of a class dictionary arises in different situations during object-oriented software development.

- Traversal of objects: We need to traverse an object to retrieve certain subobjects. The extent of the traversal is naturally specified by a propagation directive. This leads to a loose coupling between traversal domain and class structure.

- Transportation of objects: We need to transport an object down to a subobject or up to a containing superobject. The range of the transportation is again specified by a propagation directive. This leads to a loose coupling between transportation domain and class structure.

- Testing of object-oriented software: When testing an object-oriented system, it is best to proceed in phases. First we test a small subsystem consisting of a subset of the classes and then we gradually consider more and more classes. The subsystems are again specified by propagation directives. This leads to a loose coupling between test plan and class structure.

- Controlling universal operations: Objects need to be manipulated by universal operations such as copying, comparing, deleting. Often only parts of an object are relevant to those operations. The relevant parts can be succinctly described by propagation directives. An application of selective object copying would be selective object marshaling for sending objects across a network.

- Clustering classes: Class dictionaries support named binary (construction edges) and generalization (alternation edges) relationships. Other kinds of relationships often appear in clusters and can be succinctly described by propagation directives. An example would be aggregation relationships. We would describe the physical class structure with propagation directives. This leads to a loose coupling between clusters and class structure.

- Opportunistic parameterization: Classes can be reused effectively by parameterizing them with respect to possibly deeply nested part classes. The parameterization range may be succinctly specified using propagation directives. This leads to a loose coupling of genericity and class structure.

- Loose coupling of layers: When building a layered system, each layer should be only loosely coupled to previous layers. If each layer traverses connections of earlier layers using succinct subgraph specifications, we get a loose coupling of the layers. When the earlier layers change, the later layers are not so strongly affected because of the loose coupling between the layers.

Therefore, work with propagation graphs is very important in object-oriented system development. But why are we not using those propagation graphs directly, but work with succinct specifications in the form of propagation directives? The reason is that we want to keep the software flexible. Instead of defining an explicit propagation graph of an explicit graph, we define a pattern that maps the explicit graph to the propagation graph. In other words, we solve a more general problem. An important observation is that the pattern is often shorter than the explicit propagation graph. And furthermore, the pattern will work for many more graphs than the given explicit graph.

We will use a dependency metric to find a good pattern that maps the given graph into the proper propagation graph. The metric measures how dependent the pattern is on the given graph. The goal is to find a pattern that is minimally dependent on the given class structure. The dependency metric plays an important role in helping the programmer find a proper generalization to the current problem she is given. The metric guides the programmer to build only minimal class structure information into the program with two important benefits: more compact software and software that is easier to reuse.

A propagation directive may be applied to many different class dictionaries and for each one the propagation directive defines a propagation graph. Therefore, a propagation directive is expressed not in terms of classes, but in terms of class-valued variables that are later mapped to specific classes when the propagation directive is applied to a class dictionary. A class-valued variable is a placeholder for classes we don't know when we write the adaptive program. For example, in an adaptive program, we may use a class-valued variable called **Container** which is later mapped to classes such as **Basket, Briefcase** or **Suitcase**. In addition, a propagation directive is expressed in terms of relation-valued variables that are mapped to relations between classes. For example, in the adaptive program we refer to a relationship variable called **contains** that may later be mapped to a construction edge label in some class dictionary graph. The name of the construction edge label may be: **containsThings, containsPapers**, or a similar name.

A propagation directive is an elastic class structure. An elastic class structure, when applied to a rigid class structure, will return a substructure of the rigid class structure. The dependency metric measures how elastic an elastic class structure is with respect to a specific class structure. The more dependent the class structure, the less elastic it is. Propagation patterns are written in terms of elastic class structures; they give the adaptiveness property.

7.1 SIMPLE PROPAGATION DIRECTIVES

One application of propagation patterns is the specification of object traversals. At the class level, the object traversal corresponds to a propagation graph that is made up of the union of paths from the source of the traversal. A specific path denotes the sequence of classes whose traversal code is called during a specific time of the traversal.

Consider the class dictionary graph in Figs. 7.1 and 7.2.

```
AppleBasket = <apples> AppleList.
AppleList ~ {Apple}.
Fruit : Apple | Orange *common* Weight.
Weight : Kg | Pound *common* <v> DemNumber.
Kg = .
Pound = .
Apple = .
Orange = .
```

Figure 7.1: Class dictionary graph without inheritance edges, textual

---

Suppose that we want to print a **Kg**-object contained in an **AppleBasket**-object. This means that the classes **AppleBasket, AppleList, Apple, Fruit, Weight**, and **Kg** are all involved in the traversal. For those classes to form a path, it is natural to add an inheritance edge from **Apple** to **Fruit** to the class dictionary and to call the new structure a semi-class dictionary graph. A semi-class dictionary graph is a structure with one additional edge kind: inheritance edges that must terminate at an alternation vertex.

There is an effective way avoid the semi-class dictionary graph concept, if one is willing to work with larger propagation graphs. The trick is to flatten the class dictionary graph before the propagation directive is applied to it.[1] If we want to undo the flattening after the

---

[1] Class dictionary graph flattening, page 435 (22).

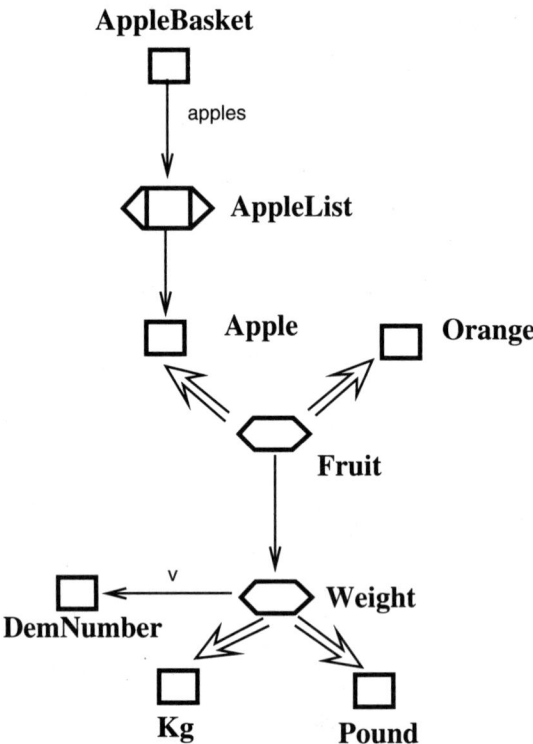

Figure 7.2: Class dictionary graph without inheritance edges, graphical

7.1. SIMPLE PROPAGATION DIRECTIVES

propagation graph has been computed, we naturally arrive at semi-class dictionary graphs. So semi-class dictionary graphs are needed, unless you are willing to work with flattened propagation graphs. In a first attempt to learn adaptive software, it is best to focus on flattened propagation graphs only. Therefore, when we use the term semi-class dictionary graph, you may think of a class dictionary graph, which is the flattened form of the semi-class dictionary graph. Adaptive software for flattened class dictionary graphs is explained in a self-contained way in Chapter 15.

A semi-class dictionary graph is a structure that is more general than the class dictionary graph structure. Every class dictionary graph is a semi-class dictionary graph by definition. So far we have not mentioned the inheritance edges since they were not needed. However, by definition a class dictionary graph has, for every alternation edge, an inheritance edge in the reverse direction. When we show a class dictionary graph we often omit the inheritance edges since we know that every alternation edge has an inheritance edge in the reverse direction, and showing all the inheritance edges would only clutter the pictures. The class dictionary graph in Figs. 7.1 and 7.2 is shown in Figs. 7.3 and 7.4 with the inheritance edges added, in both textual and graphical representation.

```
AppleBasket = <apples> AppleList.
AppleList ~ {Apple}.
Fruit : Apple | Orange *common* Weight.
Weight : Kg | Pound *common* <v> DemNumber.
Kg = .
Pound = .
Apple = (*inherit* Fruit).
Orange = (*inherit* Fruit).
```

Figure 7.3: Class dictionary graph with inheritance edges, textual

---

A semi-class dictionary graph is more general than a class dictionary graph since in a semi-class dictionary graph we might have an inheritance edge without having the corresponding alternation edge. For example, the semi-class dictionary graph in Fig. 7.5 which contains only the path from **AppleBasket** to **Kg** has an inheritance edge from **Apple** to **Fruit** without having the reverse alternation edge. In this example we see another clue why semi-class dictionary graphs are more general than class dictionary graphs. In a class dictionary graph every alternation vertex must have at least one alternative, but in a semi-class dictionary graph such as the one in Fig. 7.5 this property does not hold.

In Figs. 7.5 and 7.4 a path from **AppleBasket** to **Kg** contains the following edges:

construction AppleBasket $\overset{apples}{\longrightarrow}$ AppleList

repetition AppleList $\cdots\blacktriangleright$ Apple

inheritance Apple $\Longrightarrow$ Fruit

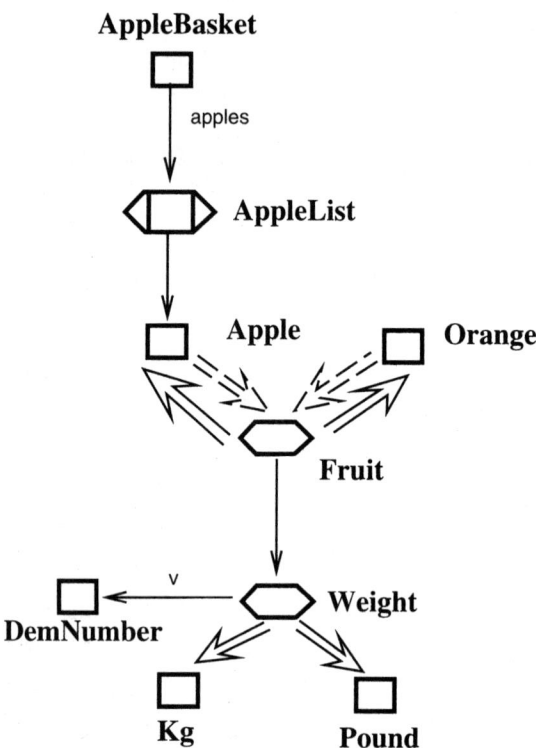

Figure 7.4: Class dictionary graph with inheritance edges, graphical

7.1. SIMPLE PROPAGATION DIRECTIVES

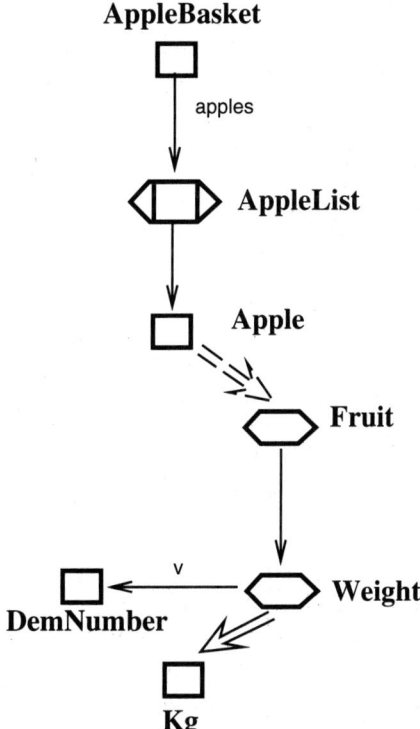

Figure 7.5: Semi-class dictionary graph that is not a class dictionary graph

construction Fruit $\xrightarrow{weight}$ Weight
alternation Weight $\Longrightarrow$ Kg

Inheritance edges are introduced as a convenience to have a natural and intuitive path concept in class dictionary graphs. To define the domain and range of propagation directives and for other applications, we work with semi-class dictionary graphs which, in addition to the construction, alternation, and repetition edges also have inheritance edges. An inheritance edge starts at a construction or alternation vertex and leads to an alternation vertex.

In the same way as class dictionary graphs, semi-class dictionary graphs need to satisfy design rules. Cycles of inheritance edges are forbidden as well as cycles of alternation edges. Also, for each vertex, all its vertex labels need to be unique.

The edge and vertex restrictions for semi-class dictionary graphs are derived from the edge and vertex restrictions for class dictionary graphs and are summarized below.

```
        VC          VA           VR          VT
----|-------------------------------------------------
EC  |   from/to     from/to         /to         /to
ECO |   from/to     from/to         /to         /to
EA  |      /to      from/to
ER  |      /to         /to      from/to         /to
ERO |      /to         /to      from/to         /to
EI  |   from/        from/to
```

Not all paths are meaningful in a semi-class dictionary graph. The intention of the path concept is to mirror object traversal. In other words, the vertices reachable from a given vertex A should all correspond to classes that are needed to build objects of class A.

Consider the path defined by the following edges:

construction AppleBasket $\xrightarrow{apples}$ AppleList

repetition AppleList $\cdots\blacktriangleright$ Apple

inheritance Apple $\cdots\!:\!\!\triangleright$ Fruit

alternation Fruit $\Longrightarrow$ Orange

that leads to class Orange. But Orange-objects may not be contained in AppleBasket-objects and therefore we need to constrain the path concept.[2] The restricted kind of paths are called **knowledge paths** since they express knowledge links between classes or between objects. The only constraint we need is that an inheritance edge can be followed only by another inheritance or a construction edge and that a path may not terminate in a vertex arrived at by following an inheritance edge.

Every knowledge path in a semi-class dictionary graph is a path, but not vice versa. A path consists of any sequence of consecutive construction, alternation, repetition, and inheritance edges. In regular expression notation we would write: $(EC|EA|ER|EI)*$, where $EC, EA, ER,$ and EI are the sets of construction, alternation, repetition, and inheritance

---

[2] Semi-class dictionary graph reachability, page 431 (8).

7.1. SIMPLE PROPAGATION DIRECTIVES

edges, respectively. (The semi-class dictionary graph edge/vertex rules exclude certain paths. For example, it is not possible to have an alternation edge followed by a repetition edge.) A knowledge path must satisfy the regular expression $((EI * EC)|EA|ER)*$ that formalizes the informal description given above.

Several negative examples follow:

- No alternation edge after inheritance edge

  The path

  inheritance Apple ┈┈▷ Fruit
  alternation Fruit $\Longrightarrow$ Orange

  is not a knowledge path since the inheritance edge is followed by an alternation edge.

- Do not stop after inheritance edge

  The path consisting of one edge

  inheritance Apple ┈┈▷ Fruit

  is not a knowledge path since there is no construction edge after the last inheritance edge.

A positive example follows:

- satisfy the regular expression $((EI * EC)|EA|ER)*$

  The path

  inheritance Apple ┈┈▷ Fruit
  construction Fruit $\xrightarrow{weight}$ Weight
  alternation Weight $\Longrightarrow$ Kg

  is a knowledge path from Apple to Weight.

The regular expression $((EI * EC)|EA|ER)*$, which a knowledge path must satisfy, can be used to motivate further the need for both alternation and inheritance edges. Let's assume that we use only one kind of undirected edges instead of alternation and inheritance edges, and let's call the set of edges E. The above regular expression then simplifies to: $((E * EC)|E|ER)* = (E|EC|ER)*$. This means that there would be no restriction that would lead to incorrect results.

However, if we are willing to work with flattened propagation graphs, we don't need to introduce knowledge paths; we just use the ordinary path concept in class dictionary graphs. The reason is that in a flattened propagation graph there can never be a construction edge after traversing an inheritance edge. So the restriction $((EI * EC)|EA|ER)*$ simplifies to $(EC|EA|ER)*$ which is no restriction at all.

We have introduced semi-class dictionary graphs and the knowledge path concept. Both will be needed to define the meaning of propagation directives for general class dictionary graphs. For flat class dictionary graphs, we can use a simpler path concept as explained in Chapter 15. A propagation directive is a triple (F, c, T), where F (*from*) and T (*to*) are sets of class-valued variables and c is a constraint expressed in terms of class-valued variables and relation-valued variables. F stands for "from" and T stands for "to" since F is determined by the "from" vertices and T by the "to" vertices of a propagation directive.

A propagation directive defines a set of knowledge paths in a larger graph. The union of all those knowledge paths is the subgraph we want. This subgraph is called a propagation graph. F will be mapped into a set of vertices from which the knowledge paths start. T will be mapped into a set of vertices at which the knowledge paths end. c is an additional constraint that all knowledge paths have to satisfy such as bypassing and through constraints.

7.1.1 Edge Patterns

The constraints are expressed in terms of edge patterns. An edge pattern, once mapped into a class dictionary graph, defines a single edge or a set of edges if the edge is expressed with the wildcard symbol *. For example, we may define an edge pattern for a construction edge that starts at an unknown vertex, has label m and terminates at an unknown vertex. Such an edge pattern is written as -> *,m,*. An edge pattern may be formulated for construction, alternation, repetition, and inheritance edges (the syntax is given in Fig. 7.6 in the bypassing and through clause). An edge pattern matches an edge in a semi-class dictionary graph if there is an assignment of the class-valued variables, relation-valued variables, and wildcard symbols to classes and relations of the semi-class dictionary graph so that the edge and the pattern coincide.

Two kinds of predicates may be applied to edge patterns: bypassing and through. A knowledge path p of a semi-class dictionary graph S satisfies the bypassing clause e if p does not contain any edge in S that matches e. A knowledge path p of a semi-class dictionary graph S satisfies the through clause e if p contains at least one edge in S that matches e.

For example,

```
*from* A
  *bypassing* -> *,m,*
*to* Z
```

means that we want all knowledge paths from A to Z that do not contain any construction edge with label m.

Bypassing and through clauses may be combined into more complex constraints by the and operator.

For example,

```
*from* A
  *bypassing* -> *,e,* ,
              -> K,m,M
  *through* -> *,x,*
*to* Z
```

means that we want all knowledge paths from A to Z that do not contain any construction edge with label e, nor any construction edge from class K to class M with label m, but that all paths need to contain a construction edge with label x.

We define that an edge pattern is **compatible** with a semi-class dictionary graph S, if the edge pattern matches some edge in S. We define that a constraint c is **compatible** with a semi-class dictionary graph S, if the edge pattern of each bypassing or through clause of c matches some edge in S. A knowledge path p of a semi-class dictionary graph S **satisfies** constraint c if c is compatible with S and if p satisfies all bypassing and through clauses of c.

7.2 SYNTAX SUMMARY FOR PROPAGATION DIRECTIVES

The syntax for propagation directives[3] is summarized in simplified form by example in Fig. 7.6.

Indentation differentiates vertex-oriented constraints from edge-oriented constraints. The propagation must start at a set of classes usually containing only one element. The propagation may go everywhere or it may terminate at a set of classes usually containing only one element.

Propagation directives may be combined with the join and merge operators, which will be discussed in Section 7.7. The syntax of join and merge is summarized in Fig. 7.7. The operators are binary and may be nested to any depth. Join and merge expressions must be well-formed as defined in Section 7.7.

To illustrate the wildcard symbol, the edge pattern

```
-> *, cost, Money
```

means the set of construction edges from some vertex through label **cost** to vertex **Money**. For example, the bypassing clause with an edge pattern

```
*bypassing*
  -> *, cost, Money
```

is equivalent to the bypassing clause

```
*bypassing*
  -> Service, cost, Money ,
     Manufacturing, cost, Money
```

if the class dictionary graph contains the two construction edges.

There may be any number of **via** clauses. They force paths through vertices. Between **via** clauses, or between **from** and **to**, we may have several **bypassing** and **through** clauses.

A propagation directive is defined as triple (F, c, T) composed by the following elements.

- A nonempty set F of source vertices from which the knowledge paths start.

- A set of target vertices T to where the knowledge paths go.

- A constraint c which is itself a triple:

---

[3]Legal propagation patterns, page 447 (61).

```
// exactly one *from*
*from* {A1, A2, ...}
    // zero or more *through*
    *through*  // one or more edge patterns, separated by ","
               // force edges
       -> V,m,W ,   // construction edge with label m
       => V,W   ,   // alternation edge
       :> V,W   ,   // inheritance edge
       ~> V,W       // repetition edge
    // zero or more *bypassing*
    *bypassing*  // one or more edge patterns, separated by ","
                 // avoid edges
       -> V,m,W ,   // construction edge with label m
       => V,W   ,   // alternation edge
       :> V,W   ,   // inheritance edge
       ~> V,W       // repetition edge
// zero or more *via*
// force vertices
*via* {K1, K2, ...}
    ... // more *through* and *bypassing*
*via* {S1, S2, ...}
    ... // more *through* and *bypassing*
//zero or one *to*
*to* {Z1, Z2, ...}
```

Instead of V, W, or m the wildcard symbol (*) may be used.

Figure 7.6: Syntax summary for propagation directives

```
*join* (
  *merge* (
    *from* A *via* B *to* E,   // any *from* ... *to*
    *from* A *via* C *to* E),  // any *from* ... *to*
  *from* E *to* K)             // any *from* ... *to*
```

Figure 7.7: Syntax summary for join and merge

7.2. SYNTAX SUMMARY FOR PROPAGATION DIRECTIVES

- A set of via vertices through which the paths go.
- An optional specification of a set of edges out of which each path in the propagation graph is required to include at least one (through).
- An optional specification of a set of edges that describe knowledge paths that are going to be excluded or bypassed from the propagation graph (bypassing).

via clauses are a shorthand for joins (discussed later in the chapter), for example,

```
*from* {A1, A2} *via* {S1, S2} *to* {Z1, Z2}
```

is a shorthand for

```
*join* (*from* {A1, A2} *to* {S1, S2},
        *from* {S1, S2} *to* {Z1, Z2})
```

The meaning is (as defined shortly) that there must be knowledge paths from A1 to S1 and A1 to S2 and A2 to S1 and A2 to S2. The propagation graph is the union of all those knowledge paths.

It is also possible to use

```
*from* A
*to-stop* Z
```

which is equivalent to

```
*from* A
  *bypassing* -> Z,*,*
  *bypassing* => Z,*
  *bypassing* ~> Z,*
  *bypassing* :> Z,*
*to* Z
```

In other words, the to-stop clause means that there can be no outgoing edges. The to-stop clause is useful in the context of recursive class structures.

In summary, propagation directives define sets of paths. The basic building block is the set of all paths from vertex A to vertex B, written as *from* A *to* B. This often results in too many paths and therefore we need syntax to eliminate paths. We need a mechanism to force edges and vertices. This is accomplished with *through*, for forcing edges, and with *via* or *join*, for forcing vertices. We need a mechanism to avoid edges, which is achieved with *bypassing and *to-stop*. A mechanism to avoid vertices is not needed since we can avoid them by avoiding edges. The complete syntax of propagation directives will be given after we have introduced class dictionaries that allow us to define syntax.

7.3 APPLYING PROPAGATION DIRECTIVES

A propagation directive may be applied to a semi-class dictionary graph to define a propagation graph.[4] This application makes sense only if the propagation directive is compatible with the semi-class dictionary graph. A propagation directive (F, c, T) is compatible with a semi-class dictionary graph S, if the following two conditions hold:

- All names of class-valued variables in F and T appear as class names in S.

- c is compatible with S; that is, the edge pattern of each bypassing or through clause of c matches some edge in S. All names of class-valued variables that are via vertices appear as class names in S.

The propagation graph P defined by a propagation directive (F, c, T) for a compatible semi-class dictionary graph S is the union of all the knowledge paths that satisfy the constraint c.[5] This is the definition of the **propagate** function, which takes as input a propagation directive and a semi-class dictionary graph, and as the result computes the propagation graph: triple $(P, F, T) = propagate((F, c, T), S)$.

We can interpret the arguments of the *propagate* function, the propagation directive pd and the semi-class dictionary graph S a propagation graph in two ways. The first interpretation is high level and the second is low level. The high-level interpretation is intended to capture the programmer's reading of a propagation graph and the low-level interpretation captures the compiler's reading of a propagation graph when generating code.

The high-level interpretation of a propagation directive pd and customizer S, written $H(pd, S)$ is a set of paths in S. The low-level interpretation is a subgraph of S, written $L(pd, S)$. The low-level interpretation provides a summary of the high-level interpretation. Since it is a summary only, things might go wrong in that the summary introduces more paths than intended by the propagation directive. This issue will be discussed shortly as the information loss concept. A synonym that we also use for information loss is inconsistency.

Although the propagate function returns a triple, we allow the function to be nested by defining
$$propagate(p2, (P, F, T)) = propagate(p2, P)$$

Now, $propagate(p2, propagate(p1, S))$ means to apply directive $p1$ to S first, and to apply $p2$ to the resulting propagation graph.

We have already seen several examples of propagation directives, class dictionary graphs, and corresponding propagation graphs (see Fig. 7.1).

7.4 AVOIDING INFORMATION LOSS

An adaptive program may be compared to a seed that can be planted into different environments. Seeds come with planting instructions that tell us when, where, and how the seeds should be planted. Adaptive programs also come with instructions called customizer restrictions, about the contexts in which they may be used.

One important difference between adaptive programs and seeds is that with adaptive programs the planting instructions are enforced by a tool known as the customization

---
[4]Legal propagation pattern customization, page 447 (62).
[5]Propagation operator, page 446 (59).

7.4. AVOIDING INFORMATION LOSS

Example	Propagation directive	Class dictionary graph	Propagation graph
1	Figs. 4.6	4.7	4.9
2	Figs. 4.6	4.8	4.10
3	Figs. 4.14	4.15a	4.15b

Table 7.1: Earlier examples of propagation graphs

checker. If an adaptive program is customized with a customizer that creates no behavior or the wrong, unintended behavior, the customizer checker will inform us. Sample messages to inform us about no behavior look like: "there is no path from A to B," "class A does not appear in graph," "edge e does not appear in graphs," etc. Sample messages to inform us about unintended behavior look like: "there is an inconsistency because of shortcut paths," "there is an inconsistency because of zigzag paths," "there is a violation of the subclass invariance restriction," etc.

As with planting directions for seeds, the customizer restrictions for adaptive programs are very mild and we have a large set of customizers to which an adaptive program may be applied.

The customizer restrictions don't have a negative effect on adaptive software development. Most of the time when an adaptive program is customized none of the restrictions applies. In the rare cases when a restriction applies, the customization checker informs us and we have two choices: we either slightly change the adaptive program or we slightly change the customizer to get the intended behavior. The customization checker is, however, very important to check for those rare situations where we would otherwise get the wrong behavior.

When a propagation pattern is applied to a class dictionary graph, the propagation graph is determined by the union of the knowledge paths. The reason for this encapsulation of a set of knowledge paths into a graph is that one, the propagation graphs can be translated into efficient object-oriented programs and two, the propagation graphs can easily be composed using a graph calculus. To manipulate sets of knowledge paths would be much harder. Unfortunately, the union of the paths into a graph can lose information. The union of paths might create new paths that are not among the original paths. This implies that the meaning of the propagation directive is lost.[6] We also say that the propagation directive is *inconsistent* with the class dictionary graph.

If the propagation directives are formulated without the *merge* operator (see Section 7.7), there is only one kind of information loss (also called inconsistency) known as the **shortcut** violation. A **shortcut** violation happens if the propagation directive requests to go from A to B through some intermediate vertex or edge, but in the selected graph there is a shortcut directly from A to B.

If the propagation directive is formulated by using the *merge* operator, there can be a second kind of information loss or inconsistency known as **zigzag** violation. A **zigzag violation** happens if the propagation directive says to merge two paths and the resulting

---
[6]Legal propagation pattern customization, page 447 (62).

graph contains more paths than the two originally merged paths.

Let's consider the information loss problem with the class dictionary graph "Nested baskets" in Fig. 5.20. To solve the problem "print all the apples in some nested fruit basket," we might use the propagation directive "nested"

```
*from* Basket
  *through* => Thing, Basket
*to* Apple
```

It says that the propagation graph is determined by the union of all paths from **Basket** to **Apple** that pass through the alternation edge from **Thing** to **Basket**. However, the propagation graph also includes the path that does not go through the alternation edge from **Thing** to **Basket**. Therefore we have lost information by taking the union.

We say that the propagation directive "nested" has the shortcut property with respect to class dictionary graph "Nested baskets" since the set of paths from **Basket** to **Apple** in the propagation graph contains a shortcut path disallowed by the propagation directive. The shortcut path goes from **Basket** to **SeveralThings** to **Thing** to **Apple**.

A propagation directive has **information loss** (or is **inconsistent**) with respect to a class dictionary graph if the propagation graph contains a completed knowledge path not allowed by the propagation directive. A completed knowledge path is a knowledge path where every used alternation vertex has an outgoing alternation edge.

If we are willing to work with flattened propagation graphs, we can drop the two adjectives "completed knowledge" from the information loss definition (see Chapter 15).

If information loss exists for a traversal specification, it has to be decomposed into several traversal specifications.

An alternative way to define information loss is to use the high-level interpretation (set of paths) and low-level interpretation (subgraph) of a propagation directive and a customizer. We have information loss if the high-level interpretation and the low-level interpretation differ. More precisely, if the high-level interpretation and the set of paths from a source to a target in the low-level interpretation differ, we have information loss.

A better way to print all the apples in some nested fruit basket is

```
*operation* void print_apples_in_nested_basket()
  *traverse*
  // first find a Thing-object in a basket
  *from* Basket *to* Thing
  *wrapper* Thing
    *prefix*
      (@ this -> find_nested_basket(); @)

*operation* void find_nested_basket()
  *traverse*
  // next find a basket in a basket
  *from* Thing *to* Basket
  *wrapper* Basket
    *prefix*
```

```
        (@ this -> print_apples(); @)

*operation* void print_apples()
  *traverse*
  *from* Basket *to* Apple
    *wrapper* Apple
      *prefix*
        (@ this -> g_print(); @)
```

It is important that three different signatures are used. The program works with many different class dictionary graphs since it uses only three class-valued variables (Basket, Thing, Apple). One might be tempted to use the propagation directives

from Basket *to* Basket

from Basket *to* Apple

but this would not solve the problem since it does not distinguish between top-level and nested baskets.

It is interesting to observe that the information loss property is invariant under flattening of parts. Let's consider the information loss problem with the class dictionary graph in Fig. 5.20. The propagation directive

from Basket *via* Apple *to* Weight

has no information loss for this class dictionary graph. Also when we flatten the weight-part from class Fruit to classes Apple and Orange, there is no information loss.

7.5 FINDING PROPAGATION DIRECTIVES

Propagation directives are used for at least two reasons: to make software shorter and to make it adaptive. Propagation directives may be viewed as a generalization of a pair (S, P): semi-class dictionary graph S and a corresponding propagation graph P. There are many propagation directives that map S into P.[7] In a first step we want to derive a propagation directive that makes minimal assumptions on the information in S. To minimize the assumptions on the existing paths in S, we want to find a propagation directive p_{min} such that p_{min} and S are minimally dependent, which means that we cannot find a smaller propagation directive p' such that p' and p_{min} define the same propagation graph for S.

Consider the class dictionary graph in Fig. 7.8.

The two propagation directives

from Company
to Producer

and

---

[7]Propagation directive abstraction, page 447 (60).

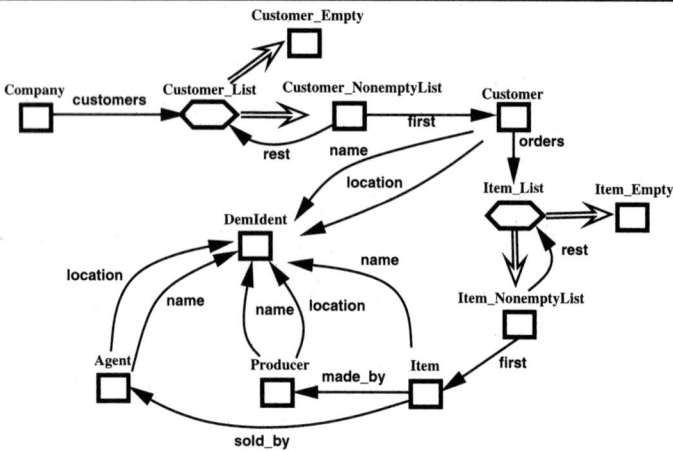

Figure 7.8: Customizer 1: Class dictionary graph Company1

```
*from* Company
  *via* Customer_List
  *via* Customer
  *via* Item_List
  *via* Item
*to* Producer
```

express the same propagation graph. But the first propagation directive is much less dependent on the class dictionary graph. More classes can be added or deleted and the program will still work when the first propagation directive is used.

To formalize the dependency concept used above, we introduce a function $Dep(p, S)$ for a propagation directive p and a semi-class dictionary graph S. $Dep(p, S)$ expresses the succinctness of a propagation directive p with respect to semi-class dictionary graph S. A propagation directive is most succinct if it references a minimal number of class-valued variables or relation-valued variables.

If a propagation directive does not have minimal dependency with respect to a semi-class dictionary graph S then the propagation directive must be motivated by robustness under expected changes to S.

$Dep(p, S)$ says how far away p is from the most succinct propagation directive p_{min} which defines the same propagation graph for S as p.

To formally define dependency, we first introduce a function $metaSize(p)$ for a propagation directive p. It is defined by

$$metaSize(p) = \text{the number of distinct class-valued variables in } p\ +$$
$$\text{the number of distinct relation-valued variables in } p.$$

For an example, consider the following two propagation directives.

$$*\texttt{from}* \texttt{ Company } *\texttt{to}* \texttt{ Money} \tag{7.1}$$

$$*\texttt{from}* \texttt{ Company } *\texttt{through}* \texttt{ -> }*, \texttt{ salary,} * *\texttt{to}* \texttt{ Money} \tag{7.2}$$

The meta size of propagation directive (7.1) is 2, and of (7.2) is 3.

In addition, we need an algorithm that solves the following minimization problem. Given a propagation directive p and a semi-class dictionary graph S, find a propagation directive p_{min} such that $propagate\ (p, S) = propagate\ (p_{min}, S)$ and so that p_{min} has the minimal meta size. (*Propagate* means to compute the propagation graph defined by a propagation directive and a semi-class dictionary graph.) We call the algorithm $PDmin(p, S)$ and it returns a propagation directive that makes minimal assumptions on the existing paths in S.

For example, consider the directive 7.3.

$$*\texttt{from}* \texttt{ Company } *\texttt{via}* \texttt{ Customer } *\texttt{via}* \texttt{ Item } *\texttt{to}* \ \{\texttt{Producer}, \texttt{Agent}\} \tag{7.3}$$

$PDmin$(propagation directive (7.3), Company1) returns the directive:

$$*\texttt{from}* \texttt{ Company } *\texttt{to}* \ \{\texttt{Producer}, \texttt{Agent}\} \tag{7.4}$$

which has meta size 3. We don't give the details of algorithm $PDmin$.

We define the **dependency** for a propagation directive p and a semi-class dictionary graph S to be

$$Dep(p, S) = 1 - metaSize(PDmin(p, S))/metaSize(p).$$

For example, Dep(propagation directive (7.3), Company1) is 2/5. This means that 2 out of 5 class-valued variables are redundant. Nevertheless, propagation directive (7.3) is a good propagation directive since it is more robust under changing class structures. This apparent contradiction will be the topic of the next subsection.

We have $0 \leq Dep(p, S) < 1$. The closer to zero the dependency is, the more succinct the propagation directive.

In an object-oriented program obtained from propagation patterns and a class dictionary, all the classes and their relationships are explicitly mentioned. Instead of being written succinctly as with propagation patterns, each class involved will get a method that tells how the class participates. Therefore, such object-oriented programs have a dependency far away from 0. The consequence is that they are not adaptive and not easy to evolve.

7.5.1 Evolution of Propagation Directives

We want to write propagation directives so that they are robust under changing class dictionary graphs. We don't want to write minimal directives that might give incorrect results if the graph changes.

A propagation directive for a class dictionary graph S has to satisfy two conflicting requirements. On one hand it should succinctly describe the paths that currently exist in S to make the propagation directive more adaptive; on the other hand it should make minimal assumptions about the paths that currently do *not* exist in S. The first requirement says that a propagation directive should use class dictionary graph information (vertices and labels) minimally; the other one says that to plan for future growth we use more than what is needed. An example explains this tradeoff.

For a **Company**-object, we could use propagation directive (7.1) to find all the **Money**-objects that represent salary information if we have a class dictionary graph where **Money** is used only to represent salary information. However, to plan for future growth of the class dictionary graph, it is better to use propagation directive (7.2) or the directive

`*from* Company *via* Salary *to* Money`

To deal with dependencies on paths that don't exist in the current semi-class dictionary graph, we generalize the dependency metric to sets of semi-class dictionary graphs. We need to write a propagation directive in such a way that it properly computes the propagation graph for each class dictionary graph in a set that illustrates possible changes in class structure. We want to find a propagation directive p_{min} such that p_{min} and the set of class dictionary graphs are minimally dependent, which means that we cannot find a smaller propagation directive p' such that p' and p_{min} define the same propagation graph for each class dictionary graph in the set.

To formalize the dependency concept used above, we introduce a function $Dep(p, \Upsilon)$ for a propagation directive p and a set of semi-class dictionary graphs Υ. $Dep(p, \Upsilon)$ expresses the succinctness of a propagation directive p with respect to class dictionary graphs in Υ. A propagation directive is most succinct if it references a minimal number of class-valued variables or relation-valued variables. The generalized function Dep is defined in a similar way as the function that works with one semi-class dictionary graph only.

7.6 TESTING OF PROPAGATION DIRECTIVES

We can also use the dependency function to find semi-class dictionary graphs for testing a propagation directive p. We choose a semi-class dictionary graph S for which $Dep(p, S) = 0$, and among all those we choose one with minimal size. This will result in a semi-class dictionary graph that is minimally complex to justify all the aspects of the propagation directive. For further information on testing propagation directives see the exercise section of Chapter 15.

7.7 OPERATIONS ON PROPAGATION DIRECTIVES

It is useful to define operations for propagation graphs and propagation directives.[8] The operations allow us to express groups of collaborating classes incrementally by building complex propagation directive expressions from simpler ones.

7.7.1 Join Operator

Consider the two propagation directives

`*from* Country *to* Household`

`*from* Household *to* Dog`

---

[8]Propagation directive abstraction, page 447 (60).

7.7. OPERATIONS ON PROPAGATION DIRECTIVES

Since the target of the first propagation directive coincides with the source of the second propagation directive, it is natural to join the two propagation directives. We get the equation:

```
*join* (*from* Country *to* Household,
       *from* Household *to* Dog)
=
*from* Country *via* Household *to* Dog
```

The join expresses concatenation of the set of paths in the high-level interpretation and union of graphs in the low-level interpretation.

Notice that the following two propagation directives are different since the second one also catches the wild dogs and other dogs not associated with a **Household**-object.

```
*from* Country *via* Household *to* Dog

*from* Country *to* Dog
```

7.7.2 Merge Operator

Now consider the two directives

```
*from* Household *to* Dog

*from* Household *to* Cat
```

Since they both have the same source, it is natural to merge the two propagation directives. We get the equation:

```
*merge* (*from* Household *to* Dog,
        *from* Household *to* Cat)
=
*from* Household *to* {Dog, Cat}
```

7.7.3 Restrict Operator

There is a third operator for propagation directives that is useful: restriction.

For an example for restriction, we consider named propagation directives. It is useful to name propagation directives so that the same propagation directive has a short name that can conveniently be used many times.

Consider the following propagation directives:

```
PhysicalPartStructureCar = *from* Automobile ...
CarScrewsOnly = *restrict* (
  *from* Automobile *to* Screw,
  PhysicalPartStructureCar)
```

Propagation directive **CarScrewsOnly** selects only the part structure that contains all car screws. If there is a lawn mower in the trunk of the car then the screws in the lawn mower will not be selected since the lawn mower is not a physical part of the car.

Consider the following propagation directives:

```
PhysicalPartStructureCar = *from* Automobile ...
CarChipsOnly = *restrict* (
  *from* Automobile
    *bypassing* -> AirConditioning,*,*
  *to* Chip,
  PhysicalPartStructureCar)
```

Propagation directive **CarChipsOnly** selects only the chips used in the car itself, except the ones in the air conditioning system. If the car belongs to a computer repair person and it is full of repair chips, they will not be selected since they are not a physical part of the car.

One application of propagation directives is to define traversals. We can summarize the meaning of the propagation directive operations in terms of traversals as follows.

```
Operation          Interpretation
-----------------------------------------------------------

merge              Union of sets of knowledge paths

join               Concatenation of sets of knowledge paths

restrict           Restriction of sets of knowledge paths

*from* A
*to* B             The set of knowledge paths from A to B
```

7.7.4 Propagation Graph Calculus

To define the propagation directive operations more precisely, we first define the merge and join operation for propagation graphs. Later we generalize both operations to propagation directives. The restriction operator is directly defined for propagation directives by using the propagation operator twice.

It is quite useful to use existing propagation graphs to compose new propagation graphs. We introduce two operators on propagation graphs: **merge** and **join**. The merge operator merges its two operands; the join operator "joins" its two operands. Recall that a propagation graph is a triple S, F, T, where S is a subgraph, F the "from" vertices, and T the "to" vertices.

Definition 7.1 For two given propagation graphs

$$PS_1 = (S_1, F_1, T_1) \text{ and } PS_2 = (S_2, F_2, T_2),$$

we define two operators as follows:

7.7. OPERATIONS ON PROPAGATION DIRECTIVES

1. $merge(PS_1, PS_2) = \begin{cases} (S_1 \cup S_2, F_1 \cup F_2, T_1) & \text{if } T_1 = T_2 \\ (S_1 \cup S_2, F_1, T_1 \cup T_2) & \text{if } F_1 = F_2 \\ empty & \text{otherwise} \end{cases}$

2. $join(PS_1, PS_2) = \begin{cases} (S_1 \cup S_2, F_1, T_2) & \text{if } T_1 = F_2 \\ empty & \text{otherwise} \end{cases}$

The two operators are illustrated in Fig. 7.9. Each propagation graph is a unit with a source port and a target port. Each port is defined by a nonempty set of vertices. The merging of PS_1 and PS_2 is the union of source ports, target ports, and knowledge paths separately. The join of PS_1 and PS_2 is to plug PS_2 into PS_1, when the target port of PS_1 is the same as the source port of PS_2.

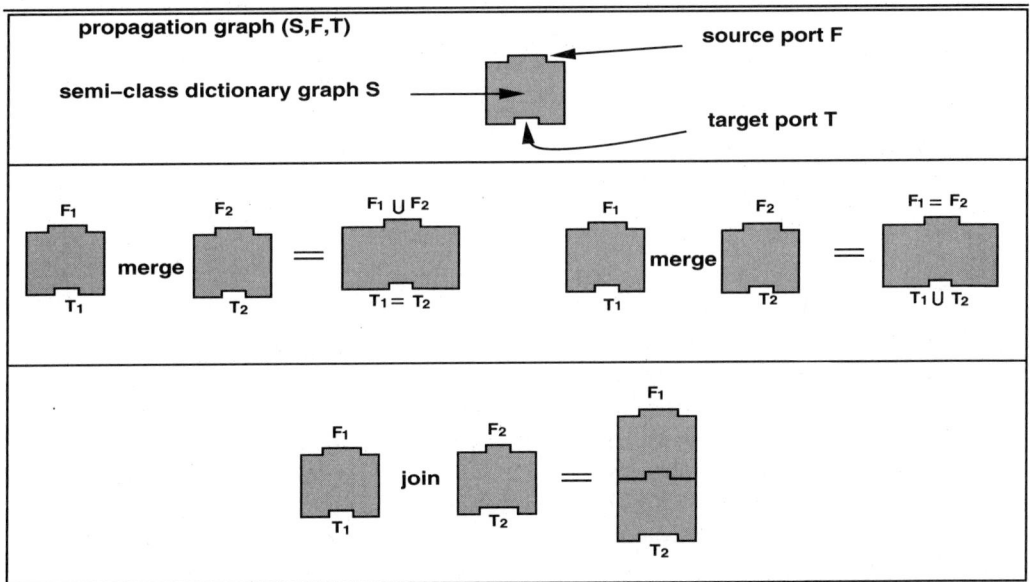

Figure 7.9: Propagation graph calculus

7.7.5 Propagation Directive Expressions

Suppose that we have a large complex semi-class dictionary graph S and we want to apply different propagation directives to S to have various propagation graphs for different purposes. Sometimes we may first want to use a propagation directive on S to trim S to a simpler propagation graph, and then we can more easily write propagation directives that will be applied to the simpler propagation graph to obtain the desired result. For the same reasons that we need a propagation graph calculus, we need a propagation directive calculus to compose propagation directives.

Three operators are introduced below to compose propagation directives. The operators, *merge* and *join* correspond to the operators, *merge* and *join* in the propagation graph calculus. The *restrict* operator is defined in terms of *propagate*.

Definition 7.2 *PDE* is the set of **propagation directive expressions**, defined as

1. $PD \in PDE$ (PD is the set of propagation directives),

2. $merge(d_1, d_2) \in PDE$ if $d_1, d_2 \in PDE$,

3. $join(d_1, d_2) \in PDE$ if $d_1, d_2 \in PDE$

4. $restrict(d_1, d_2) \in PDE$ if $d_1, d_2 \in PDE$

We use the propagate operator to generalize merge and join to propagation directives. Suppose (S', F, T) is a propagation graph, S is a semi-class dictionary graph or a propagation graph. We define (d_1 and d_2 are propagation directive expressions)

1. $propagate(d_1, (S', F, T)) = propagate(d_1, S')$

2. $propagate(merge(d_1, d_2), S) = merge(propagate(d_1, S), propagate(d_2, S))$

3. $propagate(join(d_1, d_2), S) = join(propagate(d_1, S), propagate(d_2, S))$

4. $propagate(restrict(d_1, d_2), S) = propagate(d_1, propagate(d_2, S))$

The *restrict* operator defines what it means to apply propagation directives in sequence. The second argument restricts the first in the sense that the first argument operates only on what is left by the second argument.

Not all propagation directive expressions can be meaningfully applied to a semi-class dictionary graph. A propagation directive expression d is **compatible** with a semi-class dictionary graph S if $propagate(d, S)$ is not the empty graph. A propagation directive expression d is **compatible** with a propagation graph (S, F, T) if d is compatible with S.

The merge and join operators are very useful for defining propagation directives. They are needed to improve expressiveness. For example,

```
*merge* (*from* Country *via* Metropolitan *to* Cat,
         *from* Country *via* Rural *to* Dog)
```

cannot be expressed without the merge operator.

Sometimes, propagation directives can be simplified before they are applied to a semi-class dictionary graph. For an example, the propagation directive

```
*from* Household
  *bypassing* -> LivingRoom,*,*
  *bypassing* -> DiningRoom,*,*
*to* VCR
```

and

```
*restrict*(
  *from* Household
    *bypassing* -> LivingRoom,*,*
  *to* VCR,
  *from* Household
    *bypassing* -> DiningRoom,*,*
  *to* VCR)
```

are equivalent. The first one is simpler.

7.7.6 Customization Space

If a propagation directive is compatible with one semi-class dictionary graph, then there are infinitely many semi-class dictionary graphs compatible with it. Given a semi-class dictionary graph compatible with a propagation directive, we can always find a larger semi-class dictionary graph that is also compatible with the propagation directive. The basic idea is that we can take any edge in the semi-class dictionary graph and add a new vertex in the middle of the edge.

7.8 SUMMARY

This chapter introduced propagation directives which are used extensively during object-oriented software development. The main application of propagation directives is to express design patterns for groups of collaborating classes.

We introduced a metric for propagation directives and semi-class dictionary graphs that is useful for designing and testing propagation patterns. Given a propagation directive, the metric helps to find a good semi-class dictionary graph for testing the directive, and given a semi-class dictionary graph, the metric helps to properly formulate a propagation directive.

When developing software with propagation patterns, we recommend that semi-class dictionary graphs and propagation directives be used so that the dependency between all propagation directives and the corresponding semi-class dictionary graphs is 0 unless an exception is motivated by robustness.

7.9 EXERCISES

Exercise 7.1 Remark:

At = Bt Ct.

is an abbreviation for

At = <bt> Bt <ct> Ct.

Consider the following class dictionary:

```
-------------------------------------------
Class Dictionary
-------------------------------------------
    1  Example = B1.
```

```
 2   A1 : B1 | B2 *common* [A2] .
 3   A2 : B3 | B4 *common* [A3] .
 4   A3 : B5 | B6.
 5   B1 =  [C1] [B2].
 6   B2 : C1 *common* [B3] .
 7   B3 =  [C2] [B4].
 8   B4 : C2 *common* [B5] .
 9   B5 =  [C3] [B6].
10   B6 : C3.
11   C1 = .
12   C2 = .
13   C3 = .
```

Alphabetically Sorted Cross Reference List

```
A1          :2
A2          :3      2
A3          :4      3
B1          :5      1       2
B2          :6      2       5
B3          :7      3       6
B4          :8      3       7
B5          :9      4       8
B6          :10     4       9
C1          :11     5       6
C2          :12     7       8
C3          :13     9       10
Example             :1
```

Find the unknowns in the following propagation directives and propagation graphs:
   Propagation directive:

```
*traverse*
  *from* Example
    *bypassing* -> B3,*,UNKNOWN1,
                -> *,a3,*,
                -> *,*,UNKNOWN2
  *to* C3
```

   Equivalent propagation directive, expanded for class dictionary:

```
*from* Example
  *bypassing*
    -> B3 , c2 , C2 ,
    -> B3 , b4 , B4 ,
```

7.9. EXERCISES

```
        -> A2 , a3 , A3 ,
        -> B5 , c3 , C3
*to* C3
```

Propagation graph:

```
    Example = < b1 > UNKNOWN3 (*inherits* ) .
    A1 : UNKNOWN4 *common* UNKNOWN5.
    A2 : UNKNOWN6 *common* (*inherits* ) .
    B1 = UNKNOWN7 (*inherits* UNKNOWN8 ) .
    B2 : UNKNOWN9 *common* (*inherits* UNKNOWN10 ) .
    UNKNOWN11 : UNKNOWN12
       *common* [ < UNKNOWN13 > UNKNOWN14 ] (*inherits* ) .
    B5 = UNKNOWN15 (*inherits* ) .
    B6 : UNKNOWN16 *common* (*inherits* ) .
    C1 = (*inherits* UNKNOWN17 ) .
    C2 = (*inherits* UNKNOWN18 ) .
    C3 = (*inherits* UNKNOWN19) .
```

```
//    There are 13 classes in total
//    There are 11 classes in the propagation schema
//     There are 2 classes not in the propagation graph
//      They are   UNKNOWN20  UNKNOWN21
```

Propagation directive:

```
  *traverse*
   *from* Example
     *bypassing* -> A1,*,*,
                 -> A2,*,*,
                 -> *,*,C1,
                 -> *,*,C2,
                 -> *,*,C3
   *to* C3
```

Equivalent, expanded propagation directive:

```
*from*   Example
  *bypassing*
    -> A1 , a2 , A2 ,
    -> A2 , a3 , A3 ,
    -> B1 , c1 , C1 ,
    -> B3 , c2 , C2 ,
    -> B5 , c3 , C3
*to* C3
```

Propagation graph:

```
Example = < b1 > B1 (*inherits* ) .
UNKNOWN22 = UNKNOWN23 (*inherits* ) .
B2 : UNKNOWN24 *common* UNKNOWN25 (*inherits* ) .
B3 = UNKNOWN26 (*inherits* ) .
B4 : C2 *common* UNKNOWN27 (*inherits* ) .
B5 = UNKNOWN28 (*inherits* ) .
UNKNOWN29 : UNKNOWN30 *common* (*inherits* ) .
C1 = (*inherits* UNKNOWN31 ) .
C2 = (*inherits* UNKNOWN32 ) .
C3 = (*inherits* UNKNOWN33) .


//    There are 13 classes in total
//    There are 10 classes in the propagation schema
//     There are 3 classes not in the propagation graph
//     They are UNKNOWN34 UNKNOWN35 UNKNOWN36
```

Exercise 7.2 Find algorithms to test the following properties:

- A propagation directive is an all-loser or contradictory if all compatible customizers have information loss.

    Examples:

```
*from* A
    *via* B
        *through* ->X,y,Y
            *via* C
                *through* ->W,v,V
                    *via* B
                        *through* ->E,f,F
                            *to* T

*from* A
    *through* -> B,a,A,
              -> C,b,B
                *to* C
```

- A propagation directive is an all-winner if no compatible customizer has information loss.

    Examples:

```
*from* A *to* Z
*from* A *bypassing* ->K,l,L *to* Z
```

7.9. EXERCISES

- A propagation directive is a winner/loser if it is neither an all-winner nor an all-loser. Most propagation directives are in this category.

  Examples:

  ```
  *from* A *via* B *to* Z
  *from* A *through* -> K,1,L *to* Z
  ```

- A propagation directive is a failure if it has no compatible customizer at all.

  Examples:

  ```
  *from* A
    *through* -> K,1,L
    *bypassing* -> K,1,L
  *to* Z

  *from* A
    *bypassing* => *,B,
                -> *,*,B
    *via* B
  *to* Z
  ```

What is the complexity of deciding whether a propagation directive is all-loser, all-winner, winner/loser, failure?

Exercise 7.3 Contributed by Jens Palsberg.

Is the following true or false?

For a given propagation directive that uses the class-valued variables CV and relation-valued variables RV, there is always a compatible customizer with property X that uses only vertices with names in CV and edges with label names in RV. For X choose:
no information loss (that is, consistent),
inductive,
no information loss and inductive.

For the case X = inductive there is a counter-example: The propagation directive

```
*from* A
  *through* -> B,a,A
*to* B
```

has no inductive customizer using only B and A.

Example:

```
A : B.
B = <a> A.
```

is noninductive. Noninductive customizers have to be avoided since they produce programs with infinite loops.

An inductive extension would be:

```
A : B | C.
B = <a> A.
C = .
```

Exercise 7.4 Contributed by Jens Palsberg.
Is the following true or false: If a propagation directive is not a failure and does not use edge patterns, it has a customizer with the same number of vertices as the propagation directive contains class-valued variables.

Exercise 7.5 Contributed by Jens Palsberg.
Prove that adding vertices and edges to a customizer never eliminates information loss.

Exercise 7.6 Is the following true? If we have a propagation directive without edge patterns and use only

```
*from*
*to*
*via*
*bypassing*
*through*
```

the only failures are propagation directives that contain the pattern:

```
*bypassing* edge
*through* edge
```

Exercise 7.7 Consider propagation directives that use only *from* A *to* B, join and merge. Find an algorithm that checks for a given class dictionary graph G and propagation directive pd whether the propagation graph $propagate(pd, G)$ has information loss.

Find an algorithm that checks for a given propagation directive whether it has a customizer without information loss.

Hint: use a compositional definition of information loss; see [PXL95] and Chapter 15 for a solution.

Exercise 7.8 Can we eliminate semi-class dictionary graphs, inheritance edges, and the regular expression for knowledge paths by working with flattened customizers only?

Assume you have a propagation directive that does not mention inheritance edges. Before you apply a customizer you flatten the customizer by distributing all common parts to concrete subclasses. After you have applied the propagation directive to the flattened customizer, you abstract the common parts, if any, that were distributed before.

Does this approach give the same propagation graph as the one described in the text? How can we simplify the treatment in the text, if we apply propagation directives to flattened customizers only? Can we eliminate semi-class dictionary graphs and work with class dictionary graphs only? Can we eliminate the restriction on knowledge paths?

Exercise 7.9 Propagation directive abstraction algorithm
Find an algorithm that solves the following problem: Given a class dictionary and a propagation graph, find a propagation directive that defines the propagation graph.

Hint: [SL94] Use strongly-connected components to compute a vertex basis for the propagation graph. The vertex basis defines the set of sources of the propagation directive. The set of targets of the propagation directive consists, in a first approximation, of the vertices that have no outgoing edges in the propagation graph. Use a set of bypassing constraints if the set of all paths from the sources to the targets should be too big.

Exercise 7.10 Introduce an intersection operator for propagation directives so that identities such as the following hold:

```
*from* A
  *bypassing* -> B,c,C
  *through* -> D,e,E
*to* F
```

is equivalent to

```
*from* A
  *bypassing* -> B,c,C
*to* F
```

intersection

```
*from* A
  *through* -> D,e,E
*to* F
```

Exercise 7.11 Given a C++ program, how can you identify the traversal parts and express them as propagation directives?

Hint: See [SL94].

7.10 BIBLIOGRAPHIC REMARKS

- Path sets are regular

  Kleene's Theorem for Digraphs is relevant to the study of propagation directives: Let G be a directed graph. The set of paths in G with origin i and destination k is a regular set of paths [FB94]. The set of paths can be computed using dynamic programming.

  Example: For the graph

  ```
  B = [<a> A].
  A = [<b> B] [<d> A].
  ```

  the regular expression describing all paths from B to A is: $a(d \cup ba)*$.

  In formal language theory, Kleene's theorem is used to show that the language defined by a nondeterministic finite automaton is regular.

- Modeling programs as regular expressions

  Regular expressions have been used for a long time to study programs. For example, [Kap69] uses regular expressions to model the flow of control in simple programs. This program modeling allows us to reason about the equivalence of the programs. Adaptive software also uses regular expressions to model programs. The differences are one, the regular expressions described by adaptive programs are tied to flow of control prescribed by object traversals and most importantly two, the regular expressions are described in two steps. The first step yields a propagation specification and the second one a class graph. Together, both define a regular expression.

  Therefore, a propagation specification can be viewed in two ways: it defines a family of regular expressions, and it defines a family of graphs. From both kinds of families we can select an element by giving a class graph.

- Checking for information loss (inconsistency)

  [PXL95] studies propagation directives that use only *from* A *to B, *merge* and *join*. An algorithm is presented to check conservatively for information loss. [PXL95] is in annotated form in chapter 15.

- Propagation directive abstraction

  [SL94] studies various aspects of propagation directives. It includes identities between propagation directives, abstracting propagation directives from propagation graphs and from object-oriented call graphs, and complexity of propagation directive design.

- Opportunistic parameterization

  An application of propagation directives to parameterizing class dictionaries is given in [FL94].

7.11 SOLUTIONS

Solution to Exercise 7.1

```
UNKNOWN1 = *
UNKNOWN2 = C3
UNKNOWN3 = B1
UNKNOWN4 = NOTHING
UNKNOWN5 = [<a2> A2]
UNKNOWN6 = B4
UNKNOWN7 = [<c1>C1] [<b2>B2]
UNKNOWN8 = A1
UNKNOWN9 = C1
UNKNOWN10 = A1
UNKNOWN11 = B4
UNKNOWN12 = C2
UNKNOWN13 = b5
```

7.11. SOLUTIONS

```
UNKNOWN14 = B5
UNKNOWN15 = [<b6>B6]
UNKNOWN16 = C3
UNKNOWN17 = B2
UNKNOWN18 = B4
UNKNOWN19 = NOTHING
UNKNOWN20 = A3 *CHOICE*
UNKNOWN21 = B3 *CHOICE*
UNKNOWN22 = B1
UNKNOWN23 = [<b2>B2]
UNKNOWN24 = C1
UNKNOWN25 = [<b3>B3]
UNKNOWN26 = [<b4>B4]
UNKNOWN27 = [<b5>B5]
UNKNOWN28 = [<b6>B6]
UNKNOWN29 = B6
UNKNOWN30 = C3
UNKNOWN31 = B2
UNKNOWN32 = B4
UNKNOWN33 = NOTHING
UNKNOWN34 = A1 *CHOICE*
UNKNOWN35 = A2 *CHOICE*
UNKNOWN36 = A3 *CHOICE*
```

Chapter 8

Propagation Patterns

With propagation patterns we describe adaptive design patterns for groups of collaborating classes. The adaptiveness of propagation patterns comes from the specification of implementations without hardwiring them to a class structure (see Fig. 8.1). An implementation is specified in terms of a few class specifications and relationship specifications that serve as hooks into the class structure. But the classes and relationships between the class specifications are not mentioned in the implementation; code for them is generated from the class dictionary graph. In other words, implementations are parameterized by constraints on class dictionary graph information. An adaptive program contains only hooks into the class structure and normally does not fully encode the details of the class structure. This idea of not duplicating the class structure is an application of the key idea behind the Law of Demeter.

8.1 CONNECTION TO LAW OF DEMETER

The Law of Demeter[1] avoids the encoding of details of the class structure in individual methods whereas adaptive programming attempts to keep the details of the class structure out of the entire program. The Law of Demeter leads to a programming style where lots of tiny methods are produced. Using the Demeter Tools/C++, we don't actually write the tiny methods.

The Law of Demeter (class form) says that inside an operation O of class C we should call only operations of the following classes, called preferred supplier classes:

- The classes of the immediate subparts (computed or stored) of the current object
- The classes of the argument objects of O (including the class C itself)
- The classes of objects created by O.

The Law of Demeter leads to a programming style that follows the part-of structure of classes closely and is generally considered beneficial. In the bibliography section at the end of this chapter (Section 8.10, page 253) you will find quotes about the Law of Demeter

---

[1] Law of Demeter for functions, page 445 (56).

8.1. CONNECTION TO LAW OF DEMETER

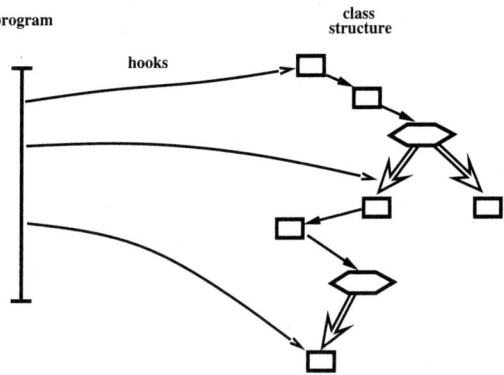

Figure 8.1: Programming by hooks

in popular textbooks. The Law of Demeter essentially says that you should only talk to yourself (current class), to close relatives (immediate part classes), and friends who visit you (argument classes). But you never talk to strangers.

The Law of Demeter might be violated in a method that contains nested function calls.

```
class A { public:   void m(); P* p(); B* b; };
class B { public:   C*c; };
class C { public:   void foo(); };

class P { public:   Q* q(); };
class Q { public:   void bar(); };

void A::m() {
    this → b → c → foo();
    this → p() → q() → bar();
}
```

The above program contains violations that are highlighted in Fig. 8.2. The calls of foo() and bar() are violations.

However, violations can always be eliminated by introducing small methods, as shown below. We introduce two small methods: B::foo() and P::bar().

```
class A { public:   void m(); P* p(); B* b; };
class B { public:   void foo(); C*c; };
class C { public:   void foo(); };

class P { public:   void bar(); Q* q(); };
class Q { public:   void bar(); };
```

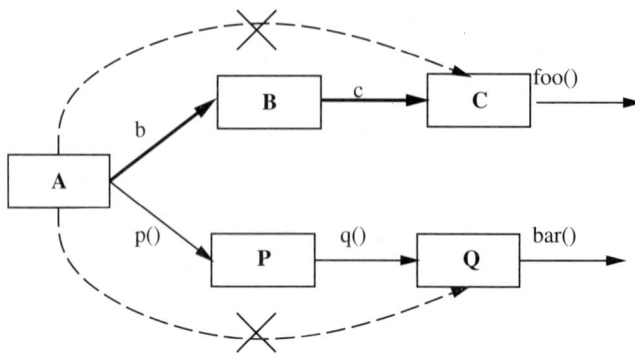

Figure 8.2: Violations of the Law of Demeter

```
void A::m() {
   this → b → foo();
   this → p() → bar();
}

void B::foo() { this → c → foo(); }

void P::bar() { this → q() → bar(); }
```

Therefore, the Law of Demeter is not restricting what we can express; it restricts only the form we use for expression.

The Law of Demeter, although a simple rule, has a positive impact on program structure as the following informal experiment shows. A graduate class had a homework assignment to write a C++ program for evaluating expressions defined by the class dictionary graph in Fig. 8.3. Without any instruction on the Law of Demeter, some students turned in programs that are summarized in Fig. 8.4. The C++ code is not shown directly; only a summary of it is shown. An additional kind of edge, called call dependency edge, shows call relationships. A call edge from class A to class B means that some function of class A calls some function of class B. We then taught the Law of Demeter and asked again for a problem solution. Now the programs looked a lot nicer and are summarized in Fig. 8.5. By nicer we mean that there are fewer dependencies between the classes. Nicer also means that call dependencies are often parallel to structural dependencies.

The Law of Demeter promotes **information restriction** (a generalization of information hiding). The public interface of a class C may be used only in classes that are closely related to C. A set of operations that comply with the Law of Demeter will span a class

8.1. CONNECTION TO LAW OF DEMETER

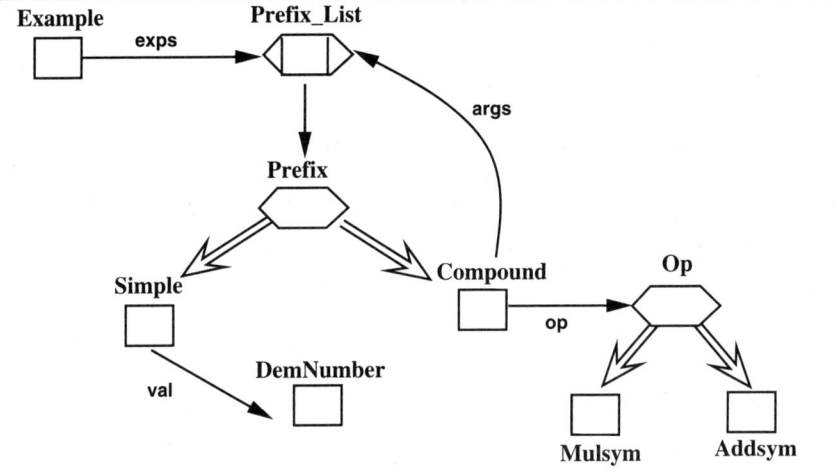

Figure 8.3: Class dictionary graph to discuss Law of Demeter

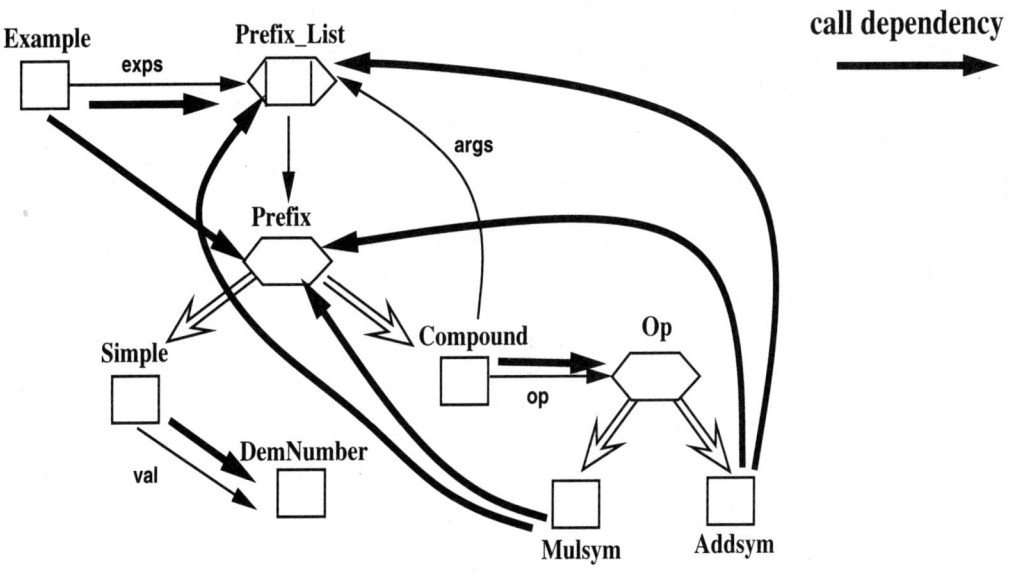

Figure 8.4: Before the Law of Demeter

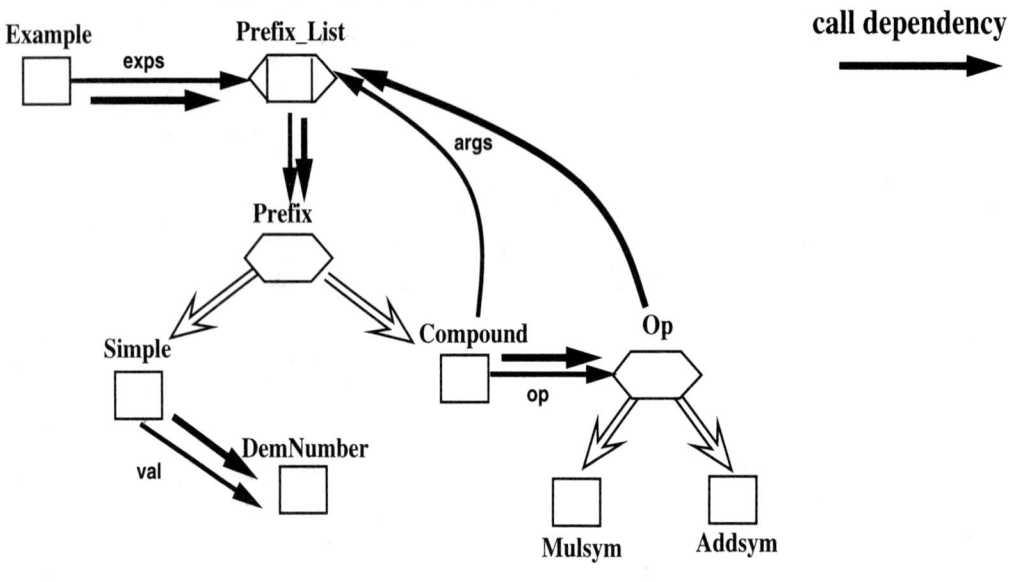

Figure 8.5: After the Law of Demeter

dictionary subgraph where much of the activity is irrelevant to the core of the algorithm being implemented. The regularity in the flow of messages implied by following the Law of Demeter can and should be exploited.

Propagation patterns promote the Law of Demeter since for a given class C, the implementation generated for a propagated operation, calls the same-named operation for some or all of the classes of the immediate subparts of C. Class C becomes dependent only on the classes of those parts to which the operation is propagated. Propagation introduces no undesirable interclass dependencies, and may avoid those that might result from direct user implementation.

The analysis of object-oriented systems confirms the fact that small methods, as suggested by the Law of Demeter, abound in object-oriented software. For example, in [PB92] we read: "A further problematic factor appearing in the Smalltalk system, the dispersal of operations across tiny procedures, ... stems from the language's object-oriented nature. This problem exacerbates the difficulty inherent in understanding a large software system ..."

Wilde et al. report that in their tests 80% of all C++ member functions consisted of two executable statements or less [WH92].

Violating the Law of Demeter, on the other hand, creates larger methods but at the price of a significant maintenance problem. Propagation patterns were invented to eliminate the disadvantage of the many small methods produced when following the Law of Demeter.

Propagation patterns grew out of the observation that object-oriented software encodes the same class relationships repeatedly into the programs. Therefore, the programs become very redundant. Objects of a given class A need to be traversed often for many different reasons and for any such reason, the composition of class A is encoded into the program. Should the composition of class A change, all those traversals would have to be changed manually.

As a first, nonoptimal solution we developed a code generator that produced the traversal code which was then edited by hand. The manual editing was not satisfactory since after a change to the class structure, the traversal had to be regenerated and manually reedited. A natural second solution was to use the wrapper fragments for enhancing the traversal code. The wrappers are essentially editing instructions that say how the traversal code has to be modified. The wrappers have the key advantage that they can be applied to many different class structures.

A wrapper has a prefix part and a suffix part, at least one of which must be present. The wrapper code is wrapped around the traversal code: the prefix part comes first, followed by the suffix part.

8.2 OBJECT-ORIENTED IMPLEMENTATION

When working with adaptive software it is important to use two views to look at class dictionary graphs. A class dictionary graph has a C++ view in the form of a C++ class library, and it has, after being flattened, a traversal view in the form of C++ member functions.[2]

- Class library view of a class dictionary graph. This view was discussed in Chapter 6.

```
edges

    Demeter               C++

    construction          data member
    repetition            data member
    alternation           subclassing

vertices

    Demeter               C++

    construction          instantiable class
    repetition            instantiable class
    alternation           abstract class, virtual functions
```

The class library provides generic functionality for manipulating objects. The class library view is a permanent architectural view that provides a scaffold to build functionality.

- Traversal view of a class dictionary graph

---

[2]Propagation pattern partial evaluation, page 448 (64).

This view is very important for understanding propagation patterns. For a given propagation directive pd and a class dictionary graph G, we compute the propagation graph $pg = propagate(pd, G)$. The propagation graph pg is the union of all knowledge paths from a source to a target. The propagation graph determines the meaning of the propagation pattern. It is best understood by a translation to C++. In Chapter 9 we give more general semantics. Here we make the simplifying assumption that we only have wrappers at construction classes. The propagation graph is flattened and mapped into a set of C++ member functions as follows.

```
function definitions: edge

    Demeter               C++

    construction          call to parts
      optional              if statement
    repetition            call to parts (loop)
    alternation           late binding (virtual function)

    does a wrapper exist for a construction edge?
      yes: wrap around edge traversal code

function definitions: vertex

    does a wrapper exist for vertex?
      no : use traversal code
      yes: wrap around vertex traversal code
```

The traversal view of a class dictionary graph is a short-term interpretation used to define a specific functionality. We first assume that vertex wrappers are attached only to construction vertices.

A simple example explains 80% of the semantics of propagation patterns. We give a class dictionary that uses all features of the notation and we show the code generated for a propagation pattern that traverses everything. The class dictionary graph is

```
A = <b> B [<c> C].
B ~ Identifier {Identifier}.
C : A | D *common* <e> B.
D = .
Identifier = <i> DemIdent.
```

The corresponding graphical form is in Fig. 8.6.

"Traverse everything" is specified by the following propagation pattern:

8.2. OBJECT-ORIENTED IMPLEMENTATION

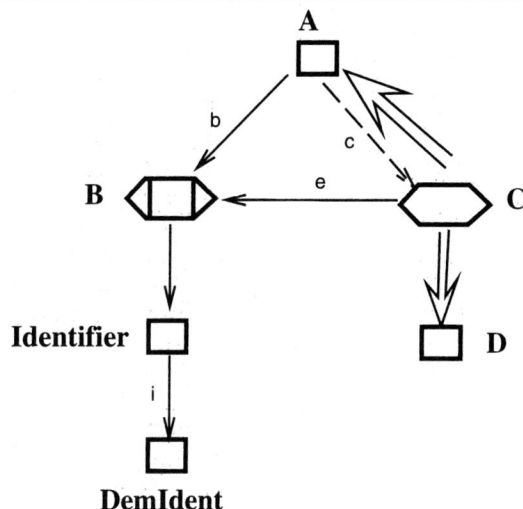

Figure 8.6: Class dictionary graph using all features

```
*operation* void traverse() // signature
  // traverse all subparts of an A-object
  *traverse*
    *from* A
  *wrapper*    * // all classes in propagation graph
    *prefix*
      (@ cout << " prefix " << this << endl; @)
    *suffix*
      (@ cout << " suffix " << this << endl; @)
```

The first line specifies the signature of the propagation pattern. The propagation graph is the complete class dictionary graph, flattened for the purpose of code generation. For objects of class A we need to traverse the b, c, and e parts. Part c is optional and therefore we need to first check whether the part exists. The e part is inherited from class C.

```
void A::traverse( )
{
  // prefix wrappers
  cout << " prefix " << this << endl;

  // outgoing calls
  this->get_b()->traverse( );
  if ( this->get_c() != NULL )
  {
```

```
      this->get_c()->traverse( );
   }
   this->get_e()->traverse( );

   // suffix wrappers
   cout << " suffix " << this << endl;
}
```

Class B is a repetition class. We use an iterator object, called next_Identifier, to visit all elements of a list of Identifier-objects. The iterator object has the function call operator () overloaded to retrieve the next element from the list.

```
void B::traverse( )
{
   // prefix wrappers
   cout << " prefix " << this << endl;

   // outgoing calls
   Identifier_list_iterator   next_Identifier(*this);
   Identifier*                each_Identifier;

   while ( each_Identifier = next_Identifier() )
   {
      each_Identifier->traverse( );
   }

   // suffix wrappers
   cout << " suffix " << this << endl;
}
```

Traversing a C-object means to traverse either a A- or D-object. Since the propagation graph is flattened for code generation, no code is needed for this class. The traversal is made by the subclasses.

```
void C::traverse( )
{
}
```

Traversing a D-object means to traverse its inherited part.

```
void D::traverse( )
{
   // prefix wrappers
   cout << " prefix " << this << endl;

   // outgoing calls
   this->get_e()->traverse( );
```

```
  // suffix wrappers
  cout << " suffix " << this << endl;
}
```

Traversing an Identifier-object means to traverse nothing (terminal objects, such as DemIdent-objects are not involved in a traversal).

```
void Identifier::traverse( )
{
  // prefix wrappers
  cout << " prefix " << this << endl;

  // suffix wrappers
  cout << " suffix " << this << endl;
}
```

This example has shown how objects are traversed for a class dictionary graph that uses all features of the notation.

The kind of code generation we just learned is called flat code generation since the propagation graph is flattened before code generation. This leads to the most straightforward and easy-to-understand approach to generating code. However, there are nonflat, more sophisticated ways to generate the code. For example, we could put the traversal code for the e edge into class C and call it from classes A and D. This would be advantageous if C has many outgoing edges that need to be traversed.

When we show examples of code generation we use either flat code generation or a variant of nonflat code generation.

8.3 SYNTAX SUMMARY FOR PROPAGATION PATTERNS

The basic syntax for propagation patterns[3] (without transportation patterns) is summarized below.

```
*operation* void f() // signature
*traverse*  // traversal part is optional
  // propagation-directive
  // vertex wrapper
  *wrapper* C
    *prefix*
      (@ statements before traversal code @)
    *suffix*
      (@ statements after traversal code @)
  // construction edge wrapper
  *wrapper* -> D,e,E
      *prefix* (@ statements in D
```

---

[3]Legal propagation patterns, page 447 (61).

```
              before edge traversal of e @)
    *suffix* (@ statements in D
              after edge traversal of e @)
// repetition edge wrapper
*wrapper* ~> D,E
    *prefix* (@ statements in D
              before traversal of list element @)
    *suffix* (@ statements in D
              after traversal of list element @)
```

We have seen many examples of vertex wrappers. Edge wrappers are used to attach code to edges. Traversal code for an edge starting at vertex A may be wrapped with a prefix and suffix code fragment. This code will be put before or after the edge traversal call in class A.

8.4 EXAMPLES

We present several examples of propagation patterns.

8.4.1 Graph Algorithms

Next we look at a more complex example. We implement the depth-first traversal (DFT) algorithm for graphs. As the name implies, it traverses a directed graph in a depth-first manner. See Fig.8.7 for an example where the alphabetical order indicates the DFT order.

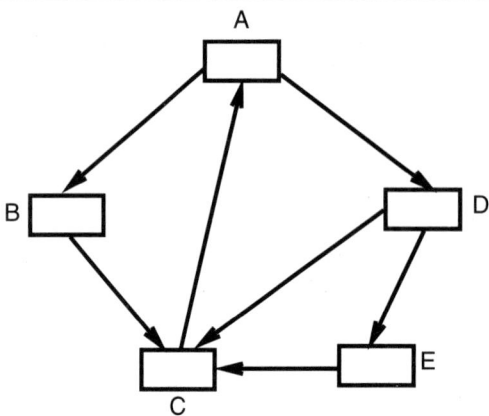

Figure 8.7: Graph example

First we need a class dictionary graph for graphs. Since we want to traverse graphs, an adjacency list representation makes sense; the class dictionary graph in Fig. 8.8 serves this purpose. Where did the classes come from? How did we find them? Later we will learn (Chapter 11) how we can derive such class definitions from a stylized English description of adjacency lists. The graph is represented as a list of vertices with the neighbors given for

8.4. EXAMPLES

each vertex. In addition, every adjacency, that is, every vertex with its successors, has a part called **marked** to store whether a vertex has already been visited during the traversal.

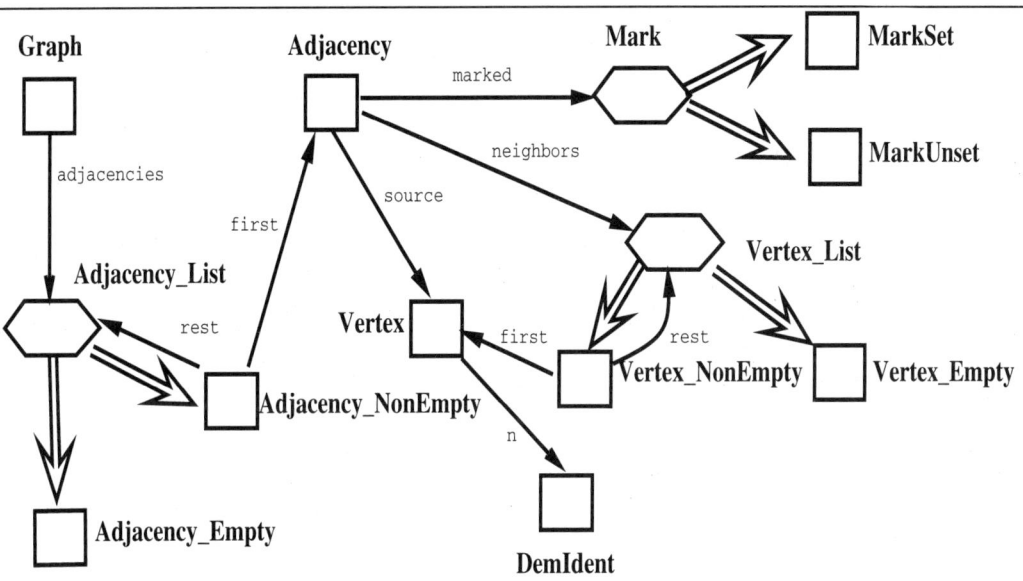

Figure 8.8: Graph class dictionary graph

We assume that the algorithm starts at a vertex from which all other vertices can be reached. The propagation patterns in Fig. 8.9 implement the depth-first traversal algorithm in terms of the data model in Fig. 8.8. We assume that the input graph object is properly initialized.

The algorithm is activated by calling function **dft** for an **Adjacency**-object. This function will eventually call the unconditional version of **dft** (called **uncond_dft**), if the adjacency is not marked. The reason we use two operations, **dft** and **uncond_dft**, is that we need two different methods at class **Adjacency**. Otherwise we could have used a longer traversal with one operation name. The collaboration of the classes **Mark** and **MarkUnset** is used (see Fig. 8.10; **Adjacency** is also included since it has a function with name **dft**). Whether or not an adjacency is marked is not checked explicitly by the algorithm. Instead an **Adjacency**-object is passed to **Mark** and **MarkUnset**, and the unconditional version of **dft** is called only in **MarkUnset**. To accomplish the unconditional traversal, we need classes from **Adjacency** to **Vertex** to cooperate (see Fig. 8.11). It is important to exclude the source part of **Adjacency**, and therefore we formulate the propagation directive with a **through** clause.

To implement the **find** operation, we need the cooperation of classes from **Graph** to **Adjacency** (see Fig. 8.12).

How were the propagation patterns in Fig. 8.9 found? Which approach was used to derive the algorithm? The algorithm was broken into three parts and for each part one or two propagation patterns were developed. In the first part we had to test whether an

```
*operation* void dft(Graph* g)
  *wrapper* Adjacency
    (@ marked->dft(g, this); @)
*operation* void dft(Graph* g,
    Adjacency* adj)
*traverse*
  *from* Mark *to* MarkUnset
  *wrapper* MarkUnset (@ adj->g_print();
    adj->set_marked(new MarkSet());
    adj->uncond_dft(g); @)
*operation* void uncond_dft(Graph* g)
*traverse*
  *from* Adjacency
    *through* -> *,neighbors,*
  *to* Vertex
  *wrapper* Vertex (@ g->find(this)->dft(g); @)
*operation* Adjacency* find(Vertex* v)
*traverse*
  *from* Graph *to* Adjacency
  *wrapper* Adjacency
    (@ if (v->g_equal(source))
      return_val=this; ; @)
```

Figure 8.9: Depth-first traversal

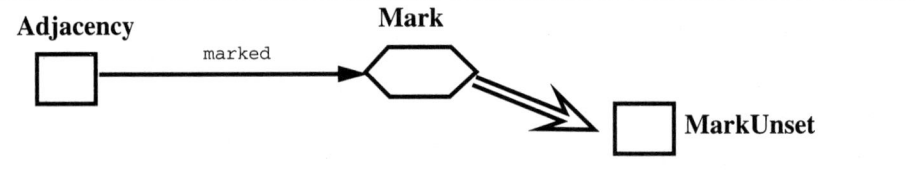

Figure 8.10: Propagation graph dft (extension at Adjacency)

8.4. EXAMPLES

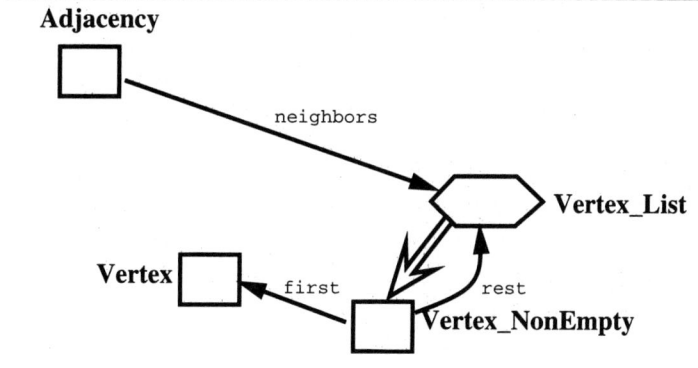

Figure 8.11: Propagation graph uncond_dft

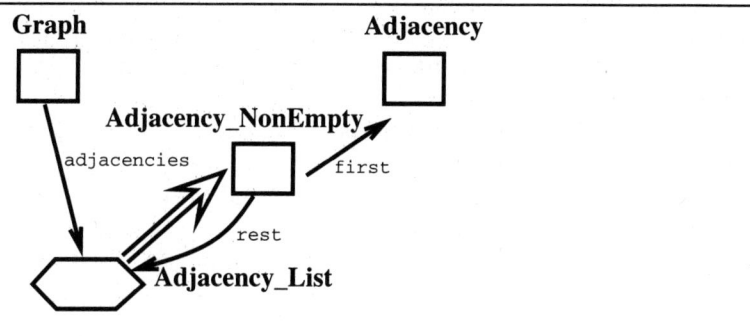

Figure 8.12: Propagation graph find

Adjacency-object has been marked. If it was unmarked, it became marked and the function of part two was called. The first part required the collaboration of three classes in two propagation patterns.

In the second part we had to find all neighbors of an Adjacency-object. This required the collaboration of four classes that we captured with

```
*from* Adjacency
  *through* -> *,neighbors,*
*to* Vertex
```

Why do we need the *through* keyword? If we omit it, we get a propagation graph that is too big. It would also include the edge from Adjacency to Vertex with label source. Why are we using a through clause and not a bypassing clause such as

```
*from* Adjacency
  *bypassing* -> *,source,*
*to* Vertex
```

This is a matter of taste, but our goal is to write the propagation directives so that they are robust under evolution of the class dictionary. It appears that the *through* -> *,neighbors,* constraint is the best choice since we really want to find all neighbors.

For the third part we have to find all Adjacency-objects contained in a Graph-object. This requires the collaboration of four classes that we can elegantly capture with

```
*from* Graph *to* Adjacency
```

It is interesting to notice here how we can make four classes out of mentioning only two. This is the magic of adaptive software that allows us to describe many classes in terms of a few. This makes the software shorter and, more importantly, it becomes easier to maintain. The maintenance phase is the most expensive part of the entire development process. Fortunately, adaptive programs are more amenable to changes late in the software development life-cycle than ordinary object-oriented programs. Adaptive programs will help to solve the maintenance backlog.

Next we generalize the depth-first traversal algorithm to a graph cycle-checking algorithm. It maintains a path of vertices from the start vertex to the current vertex. If the next vertex during the traversal is a vertex already on the path, a cycle has been found. We use a parameterized Stack class that keeps track of the path. To get the cycle checker, we enhance the depth-first-traversal propagation patterns as follows (we omit the implementation of the push, pop, and contains_duplicate functions of the stack class):

```
*reuse-pp* DFT
  // we reuse the propagation patterns we already have
  // and change them as follows
  *code-change*
    *operation* void dft(Graph* g)
      *add-arguments*   Stack<Adjacency>* s
      *add-fragments*
```

8.4. EXAMPLES

```
Adjacency
// add to the member function for Adjacency
*prefix*
  (@ s->push(this);
      if (s->contains_duplicate(this)){
        s->g_print();
        cout << "cycle found";} @)
*suffix*
  (@ s->pop(); @)
```

This means that

operation void dft(Graph* g)

becomes

operation void dft(Graph* g, Stack<Adjacency>* s)

In the above dft function we changed only the signature of dft(Graph* g) and we added a wrapper for Adjacency with a prefix and a suffix code fragment. Extra formal and actual arguments for the definitions and calls of the other functions are provided automatically. This is an elegant reuse of the basic traversal algorithm and compares favorably with corresponding discussions in algorithm textbooks. One key advantage of the approach given here is that no parameterization of the dft algorithm is needed; we just add new information and replace the old.

Robustness of Propagation Patterns

Propagation patterns are more reusable than standard object-oriented software. We demonstrate their flexibility by changing the class structure for the traversal problem. Instead of traversing graphs with only one kind of edge, we now traverse graphs with two kinds of edges, and we want the traversal to be done with respect to both kinds of edges. The new graph data model is shown in the class dictionary graph in Fig. 8.14. It includes an a_neighbors construction edge but no b_neighbors construction edge. However, there are two kinds of neighbors, A_Neighbors and B_Neighbors, that express the two kinds of edges. B_Neighbors may have only neighbors parts but A_Neighbors may have both neighbors and a_neighbors parts.

The propagation directive

from Adjacency
  through -> *,neighbors,*
to Vertex

will select the propagation graph shown in Fig. 8.13.

To adjust the algorithm to the new requirements, nothing needs to be changed; that is, the propagation patterns in Fig. 8.9 stay invariant. Although we have introduced the new classes Neighbors, A_Neighbors, and B_Neighbors, we do not have to write code for them. The propagation patterns will do it for us.

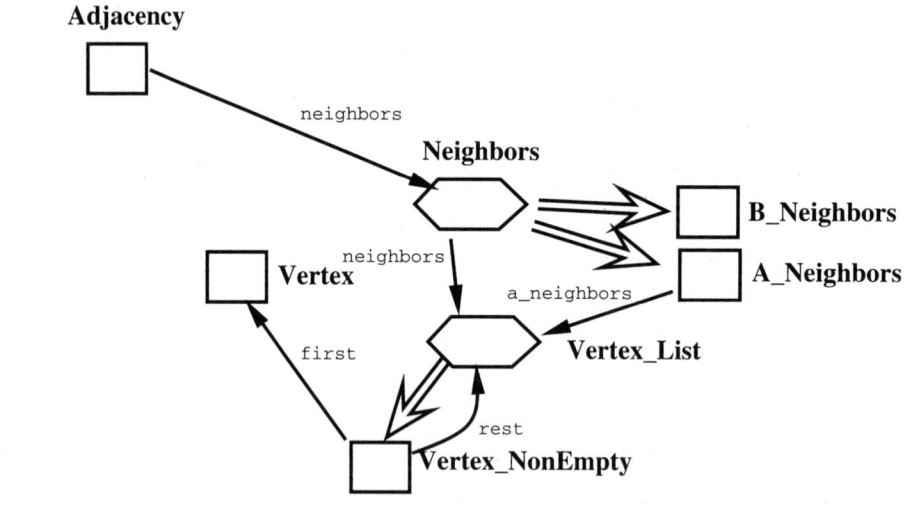

Figure 8.13: Propagation graph for extended graph data model

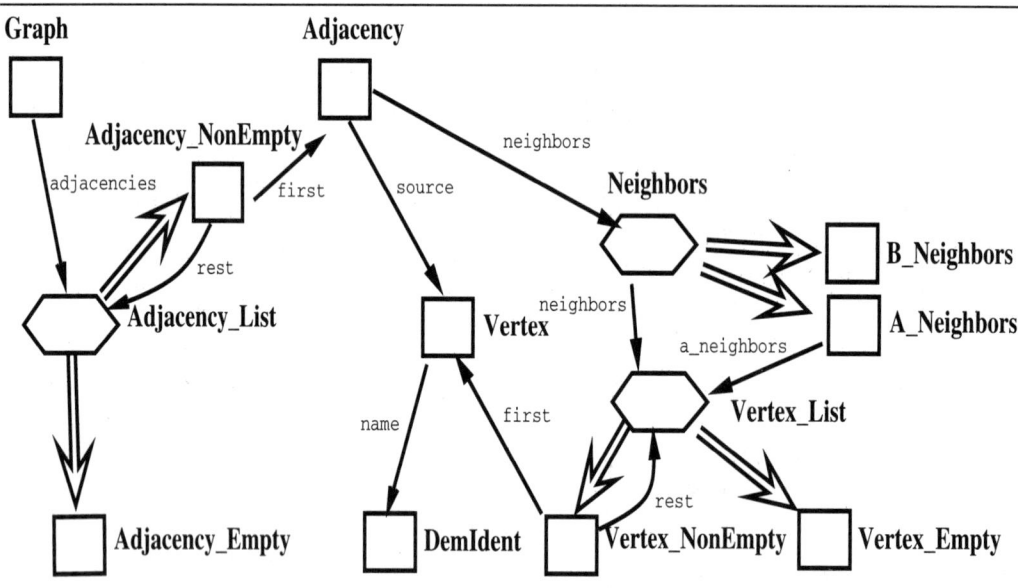

Figure 8.14: Extended graph data model

8.4.2 Chess Board

The next example deals again with a counting problem: consider the class dictionary graph for a chess board in Fig. 8.15. The propagation pattern in Fig. 8.16 computes the number

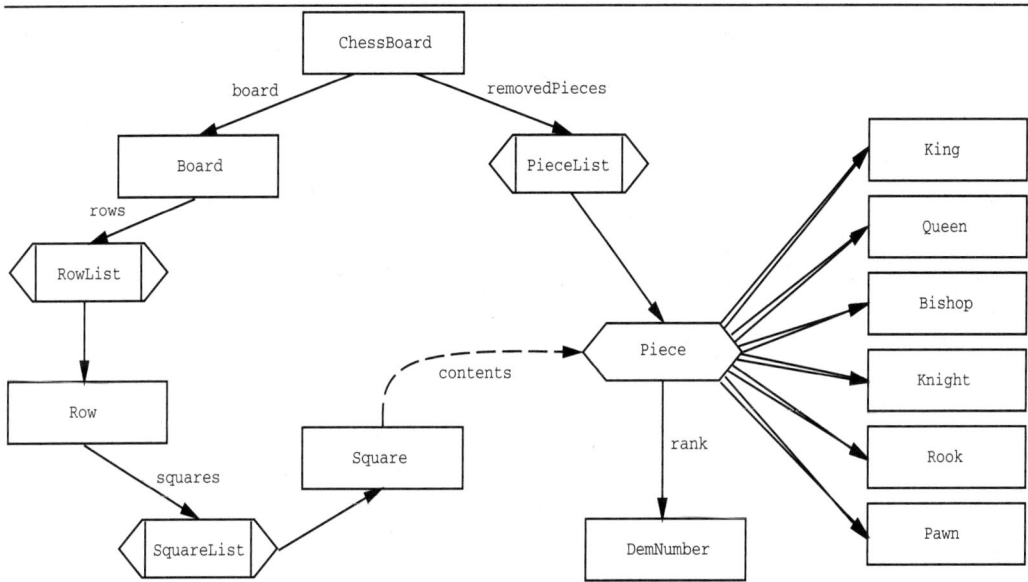

Figure 8.15: Chess board class dictionary graph

of pawns on the board. The generated code and the propagation graph is given in Fig. 8.17.

```
*operation* void countPawns( int& pawnCount )
*traverse*
  *from* ChessBoard
    *through* -> *,board,*
  *to* Pawn
*wrapper* Pawn
  (@ pawnCount++; @)
```

Figure 8.16: Count pawns

A chessboard should always have two kings on it. We could check for this with a propagation pattern that traverses from Chessboard through board to King. Such cardinality constraints are expressed by propagation patterns.

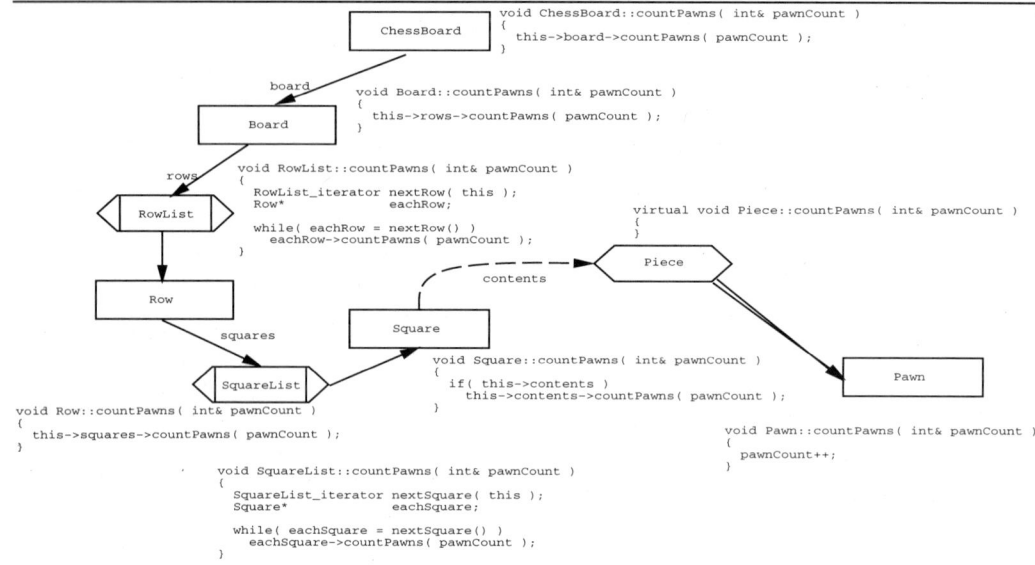

Figure 8.17: Annotated propagation graph

8.4.3 Painting a Car

A propagation pattern is like a guideline for specifying patterns for painting objects. A propagation pattern together with a class dictionary graph is a pattern for painting objects defined by the class dictionary graph.

A good example to illustrate the idea of propagation patterns is the automobile painting problem. It consists of painting the appropriate parts of a car. We write a family of painting implementations for the following signature:

operation void paint(Color* c)

We assume only minimal knowledge about cars. We assume that the class structure is organized in such a way that each paintable part has a part of class **Colored** that contains the color of the part. Therefore, the propagation pattern has to find only all **Colored**-objects in an **Automobile**-object, which is accomplished by the propagation pattern in Fig. 8.19. This propagation pattern is like a guideline for specifying patterns for painting cars. Next we customize this propagation pattern for painting cars of a specific class **Automobile**.

Consider the class dictionary graph in Fig. 8.18. Recall the rule that A = Bcde. is equivalent to A = <bcde> Bcde.

The propagation pattern in Fig. 8.19 is much shorter than the generated C++ program. The propagation pattern finds the set P of all vertices on some path from vertex **Automobile** to vertex **Colored**. For each vertex in P an operation **paint** with the given signature is generated, which calls operation **paint** for all the part classes in P that contain a **Colored** part.

8.4. EXAMPLES

```
Automobile = Roof Hood Trunk Windshield <windows> List(Window)
  <body_side_moldings> List(Body_side_molding)
  <doors> List(Door) Colored.
Roof = Colored.         Hood = Emblem Colored.        Emblem = .
Trunk = <trunk_lock> Lock Colored.
Body_side_molding =  Colored.
Door = <door_lock> Lock <door_handle> Handle Colored.
Lock = .                Handle = .                    Windshield = .
Window = .              Colored = <color> Color <thickness> DemNumber.
Color : Red | Blue.     Red = "red".                  Blue = "blue".
List(S) ~ {S}.
```

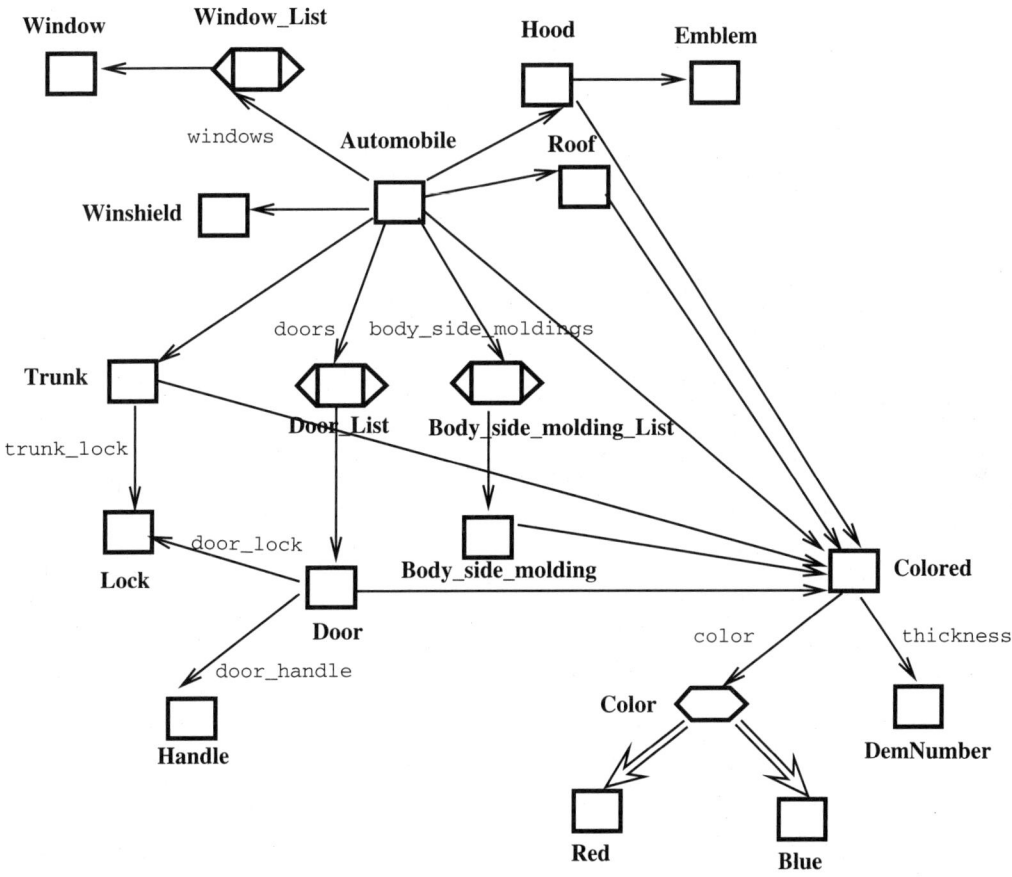

Figure 8.18: Car

```
*operation* void paint(Color* c)
  *traverse*
    *from* Automobile
    *to* Colored
*wrapper* Colored
  *prefix* (@ this->set_color(c); @)
```

Figure 8.19: Painting a car

In Fig. 8.20, we give a propagation pattern that paints the car, except the doors. We bypass the doors by using a bypassing directive in the propagation directive. We bypass any construction edge with label **doors**. Finally, we paint only the doors of a car with the

```
*operation* void paint_except_doors(Color* c)
  *traverse*
    *from* Automobile
      *bypassing* -> *,doors,*
    *to* Colored
*wrapper* Colored
  *prefix* (@ this->set_color(c); @)
```

Figure 8.20: Painting a car, except doors

propagation pattern in Fig. 8.21.

```
*operation* void paint_doors(Color* c)
  *traverse*
    *from* Automobile
      *via* Door
    *to* Colored
*wrapper* Colored
  *prefix* (@ this->set_color(c); @)
```

Figure 8.21: Painting car doors only

8.4. EXAMPLES

Programming tasks can be broken down into simpler tasks, some of which consist of mostly systematic object traversal tasks. Therefore it is important to provide support for describing an object traversal mechanism. Traversal-like tasks can be formulated very succinctly by using propagation patterns.

8.4.4 Meal

Propagation patterns focus on groups of cooperating classes that collaborate primarily by object traversal. The classes involved in the cooperation are specified by a graph notation that allows us to select all the paths from a set of start classes to a set of zero or more target classes, including only paths that use either at least one of a set of *through* edges or none of a set of *bypassing* edges.

Objects of the selected classes collaborate by calling an operation with a fixed signature for all immediate subparts whose edge is also selected. The operations for the parts are called in the order the parts are given in the textual form of the class dictionary graph.

The simplest examples for propagation patterns are generic task propagation patterns. Consider a class dictionary graph G which has only one start class S and which contains a class X. You would like to write an operation that counts the instances of class X an S-object contains. This task is easily solved by the propagation pattern in Fig. 8.22. The classes selected by the propagation pattern are all the classes that have a part class X, directly or indirectly. In other words, it selects all classes whose collaboration is needed to find all the X-objects in a given S-object.

```
*operation* int count_x() *init* (@ 0 @)
  *traverse*
    *from* S *to* X
*wrapper* X
  *prefix* (@ return_val += 1; @)
```

Figure 8.22: Simple counting of X-objects

Consider again the example of computing the cost of a meal. We want to traverse the parts of a meal object while summing all the costs of the parts.

We use the class dictionary graph in Fig. 8.23.

To compute the cost of a meal we write the following propagation pattern:

```
*operation* float cost()
*traverse*
*from* Meal
*to*
 {Melon,                // 3.75
  Shrimp,               // 1.65
  CocktailSauce,        // 1.15
```

```
Meal = Appetizer Entree Dessert.
Appetizer : Melon | ShrimpCocktail.
ShrimpCocktail = Shrimps Lettuce [CocktailSauce].
CocktailSauce = Ketchup HorseRadish.
Entree : SteakPlatter | BakedStuffedShrimp.
SteakPlatter = Steak Trimmings.
BakedStuffedShrimp = StuffedShrimp Trimmings.
Trimmings = Potato <veggie1> Vegetable <veggie2> Vegetable.
Vegetable : Carrots | Peas | Corn.
Dessert : Pie | Cake | Jello.
Shrimps ~ Shrimp {Shrimp}.

Shrimp = .
Melon = .
Lettuce = .
Ketchup = .
Steak = .
Potato = .
Carrots = .
Peas = .
Cake = .
Pie = .
Jello = .
Corn = .
StuffedShrimp = .
HorseRadish = .
```

Figure 8.23: Meal example

```
    SteakPlatter,         // 9.00
    BakedStuffedShrimp,   // 9.10
    Pie,                  // 3.60
    Dessert}              // 1.50 (default)
```

We need the following hand-coded wrappers:

```
*wrapper* Melon
   *prefix* (@ return_val += 3.75; @)
*wrapper* Shrimp
   *prefix* (@ return_val += 0.65; @)
*wrapper* CocktailSauce
   *prefix* (@ return_val += 1.15; @)
*wrapper* SteakPlatter
   *prefix* (@ return_val += 9.00; @)
*wrapper* BakedStuffedShrimp
   *prefix* (@ return_val += 9.10; @)
*wrapper* Pie
   *prefix* (@ return_val += 3.60; @)
*wrapper* Dessert
   *prefix* (@ return_val += 1.50; @)
```

The expansion rules are best explained graphically. A propagation pattern defines a subgraph of the original class dictionary graph that includes all edges and vertices on paths from the source vertices to the target vertices. Paths in class dictionary graphs have a precise meaning that is slightly different than the meaning of an ordinary path.[4]

8.4.5 Compiler

Propagation patterns often protect against changes in the structure of classes. This robustness of propagation patterns is a clear help during the maintenance process. A good example of the use of propagation patterns is a propagation pattern for a simple compiler for postfix expressions. The class dictionary is given in Fig. 8.24. We need only one simple propagation pattern that defines the signature and body for ten functions. We provide wrappers for three of these functions (Fig. 8.25). The same propagation pattern will also work on many other class dictionary graphs.

Of course, a change in the class dictionary may invalidate wrapper code fragments. But updating a few functions is much simpler than potentially having to rewrite all the functions.

8.5 COMPONENTS: SETS OF PROPAGATION PATTERNS

We introduce components that encapsulate groups of collaborating propagation patterns. Components are software packages that are easy to maintain and reuse for different applications. Components are a generalization of ordinary application frameworks. An example

---

[4]Semi-class dictionary graph reachability, page 431 (8).

```
Example = <exps> Postfix_List.
Postfix : Numerical | Compound.
Numerical = <val> DemNumber.
Compound = "(" <args> Args <op> Op ")".
Args = <arg1> Postfix <arg2> Postfix.
Op : Mulsym | Addsym.
Mulsym = "*".
Addsym = "+".
Postfix_List ~ Postfix {Postfix }.
```

Figure 8.24: Expressions

```
*operation* void gen_code()
  *traverse*
  *from* Example
  *to* {Numerical, Mulsym, Addsym}

*wrapper* Addsym
  *prefix*
  (@
    cout << " ADI \n";
    // adds two top-most elements
    // and leaves result on stack
  @)

*wrapper* Mulsym
  *prefix*
  (@
    cout << " MLI \n"; @)

*wrapper* Numerical
  *prefix*
  (@
    cout << " LOC " << val << "\n";
    // loads constant on stack
  @)
```

Figure 8.25: Compiler

8.5. COMPONENTS: SETS OF PROPAGATION PATTERNS

of a framework is a group of classes that define generic dialogs in a graphical user interface. Such an application framework can be specialized for specific dialogs, such as question dialogs. For a discussion of frameworks and patterns, see [GHJV95].

There are several differences between application frameworks and components.

- Application frameworks reuse object code but components rely on the reuse of source code. A component usually implements an interface in terms of propagation which will affect the implementation in the new class structure.

- Components are written in terms of approximate information on a class dictionary graph. A class dictionary graph acts as a generator of generators, the generators being propagation patterns. Components are at a higher level of abstraction than application frameworks.

- Application frameworks are rigid artifacts, but components are flexible structures that adjust more easily to change. In components, interfaces are strongly localized.

A component consists of two parts, a constraint part and an implementation part. The constraint part defines all the assumptions made about customizing class dictionaries. The assumptions fall into the following categories:

- Existence of classes

    A list of class-valued variables determines which classes have to be present. A renaming mechanism is provided to change class and relation names when the component is customized.

- Partial information on class dictionary

    A list of edge patterns specifies the existence of properties.

    Examples:

    ```
    -> A,*,*              A has an outgoing construction edge
    -> *,b,*              There exists a construction edge b
    -> *,*,B              B has an incoming construction edge

    => A,*                A is an alternation class
    -> A,b,*              A has part b
    -> A,*,B              There is a construction edge from A to B
    -> *,b,B              B has an incoming construction edge b
    ```

    In addition, we use

    ```
    =>* A,B               B is alternation-reachable from A
    ```

    For example, a wrapper of the form

    ```
    A* a = new B(...);
    ```

implies that B is alternation reachable from A. Otherwise, the wrapper would not compile.

A renaming mechanism is provided for edge labels.

- Path constraints

  Propagation directives are used to specify the existence of paths in the customizers. The path constraints serve several purposes. Besides constraining the customizers of a component, they are used to specify traversal and transportation code. The path constraints also specify some cardinality constraints. For example, AZ = *from* A *to* Z means that an A-object is in relationship with zero or more Z-objects. We can write this as 0+: AZ. But other cardinality constraints cannot be expressed with the propagation directive notation.

- Cardinality constraints

  Some propagation patterns work only under certain cardinality constraints. The following constraints may be used. AZ is a directive with one source and one target.

  ```
  1+: AZ       one or more
  1 : AZ       exactly one
  0/1: AZ      zero or one
  ```

- Invariants

  Invariants may also be needed to express how a component may be used. The invariants may be checked when the component is customized or when it is executed.

The implementation part provides the propagation patterns. Propagation patterns local to the component are introduced with the *private* ! keyword.

The syntax of components follows the following example:

```
*component* component_name
  // a group of collaborating propagation patterns
  *customizers* // sample customizers
    // first sample customizer
    A = B.
    B : C | D.
    C = .
    D = E.
    E ~ {DemIdent}.
    ,
    // second sample customizer
    A = B.
    B = .
  *constraints*
    // in this constraints section we summarize the assumptions
```

```
    // made by the propagation patterns
    *classes* // class-valued variables
      A, B, C, ...
    *edge* *patterns* // relation-valued variables
      a, b, c, ...
      // further constraints as comments
      // -> A,b,C
    *class-set* // variables for sets of classes
      AB = {A, B};
    *directives* // named propagation directives
      CAB = *from* C *to* *class-set* AB;
        // equivalent to
        // CAB = *from* C *to* {A, B};
      AZ = *from* A *to* Z;
    *cardinality*
      1+  : AZ; 1   : AZ; 0/1 : AZ
*end*

// propagation patterns

//public function
*operation* ...

// function only for this component
*private* *operation* ...

*require* //functions which are needed by this component
  A::*operation* void f(A* a);
    // function f for class A is needed
*end* component_name
```

The syntax for instantiating components is

```
    *comp-path* // directory where components are located
      "component_library"
        *component* ABC
          *rename* // rename vocabulary
            ABC_K => new_K,
            ABC_L => new_L
          *end*
        *component* DEF // no renaming needed
        *component* GHI ...
```

8.6 EDGE WRAPPERS AND VERTEX WRAPPERS

Edge wrappers (for construction and repetition edges only) serve to wrap code around traversal edges. The code will be called in the source classes of the edges. Edge wrappers are described either by

```
*wrapper* -> Source, label, Target
  *prefix* (@ code @)
  *suffix* (@ code @)
```

for construction edges or by

```
*wrapper* ~> Source, Target
  *prefix* (@ code @)
  *suffix* (@ code @)
```

for repetition edges.

Some overlap exists in expressiveness between vertex wrappers and edge wrappers, but both are needed. At first it appears that edge wrappers are more expressive since they allow us to control code on individual edges whereas vertex wrappers cannot discriminate between different incoming edges.

Some vertex wrappers can easily be expressed by edge wrappers. Consider a class dictionary graph that contains only construction classes. Consider the two operations test1 and test2 in Fig. 8.26. They are equivalent (if there are no alternation classes) since we simply push the prefix code fragment back through the construction edges.

The produced code is given in Figs. 8.27 and 8.28.

Now consider the line with the comment for the suffix vertex wrapper in the propagation pattern **test1**. There is no elegant way of expressing this vertex wrapper with edge wrappers! You are invited to try. Of course, for a specific class dictionary it is easy to simulate vertex wrappers with edge wrappers. A prefix wrapper becomes a prefix wrapper of the first edge and a suffix wrapper becomes a suffix wrapper of the last edge.

Another example shows that vertex wrappers are sometimes more generic than edge wrappers because they make less assumptions of the class dictionary graph.

Consider the class dictionary graph

```
K = C.
L = C.
C : B.
B = M N.
M = .
N = .
```

and the propagation patterns

```
KLMN = *from* {K,L} *via* B *to* {M,N}

  *operation* void test1()
    *traverse* KLMN
    *wrapper* B
      *prefix* (@ cout << 1; @)

  *operation* void test2()
```

8.6. EDGE WRAPPERS AND VERTEX WRAPPERS

```
*component* equiv_wrappers
  *constraints* // describes assumptions
        // made on customizing cd
        // and defines suitable abbreviations
    *classes* K, L, M, N, B
    *directives*
      KLMN = *from* {K,L} *via* B *to* {M,N}
  *end*
  *operation* void test1()
    *traverse* KLMN
    *wrapper* B
      *prefix* (@ cout << 1; @)
//    *suffix* (@ cout << 0; @)

  *operation* void test2()
    *traverse* KLMN
    // before entering B
    *wrapper* -> *,*,B
      *prefix* (@ cout << 1; @)

*end* equiv_wrappers
```

Figure 8.26: Equivalent wrappers

```
void K::test1( )
{ // outgoing calls
  b ->test1( ); }

void L::test1( )
{ // outgoing calls
  b ->test1( ); }

void B::test1( )
{ // prefix wrappers
 cout << 1;
  // outgoing calls
  m ->test1( );
  n ->test1( );
  //          suffix wrappers
  //          cout << 0;

}

void M::test1( ) { }

void N::test1( ) { }
```

Figure 8.27: Code for test1 in edge wrapper example

8.6. EDGE WRAPPERS AND VERTEX WRAPPERS

```
void K::test2( )
{ // outgoing calls
 cout << 1;
  b ->test2( ); }

void L::test2( )
{ // outgoing calls
 cout << 1;
  b ->test2( ); }

void B::test2( )
{ // outgoing calls
  m ->test2( );
  n ->test2( ); }

void M::test2( ) { }

void N::test2( ) { }
```

Figure 8.28: Code for test2 in edge wrapper example

```
*traverse* KLMN
*wrapper* -> *,*,C //!!
  *suffix* (@ cout << 1; @)
```

Operation test1 expresses a traversal with a vertex wrapper. The same traversal can be expressed only by encoding some detail of the class structure, namely that a class C exists.

In summary, both vertex wrappers and edge wrappers (both prefix and suffix) are needed to conveniently express adaptive programs.

8.7 PROGRAMMING WITH PROPAGATION PATTERNS

Programming with propagation patterns involves searching for the really important class structure aspects of a program. The starting point is a potentially big class dictionary that describes the static class relationships. The class dictionary does not have to be good or complete. Work on the class dictionary may continue in parallel with propagation pattern development.

The big class dictionary will be broken into partitions gradually as propagation patterns are developed. The goal is to partition the class dictionary so that not too many propagation paths are broken by the partitioning. For a broken propagation path, the propagation will stop in the first partition and start again in the second partition. We don't want to propagate directly from one partition to the next. A propagation pattern that works in one partition can call functions only from other partitions but can not propagate into them.

To develop elegant propagation patterns that work with many class dictionary graphs, it is important that systematic name conventions are used. For example, the class dictionary graph

```
Price = <v> DemNumber.
Salary = <m> Money.
Money = <v> DemNumber.
```

is not systematic since class Price is not expressed in terms of money. The following class dictionary graph is better:

```
Price = <v> Money .
Salary = <m> Money.
Money = <v> DemNumber.
```

If we want to find all the money information, we can propagate to Money with the second solution. There is an interplay between class dictionaries and propagation patterns.

8.7.1 Evolution Histories

When developing software it is important to do it in layers by simplifying the problem first. Finding a minimal subset of a software system can be done in two ways: We can simplify with respect to the data or with respect to the functionality. Figure 8.29 gives an example. Suppose that we have to write a cycle checker for directed graphs which have two kinds of edges. Data simplification means that we consider only a subset of all possible inputs. A data simplification would be to consider first only graphs that have one kind of

8.7. PROGRAMMING WITH PROPAGATION PATTERNS

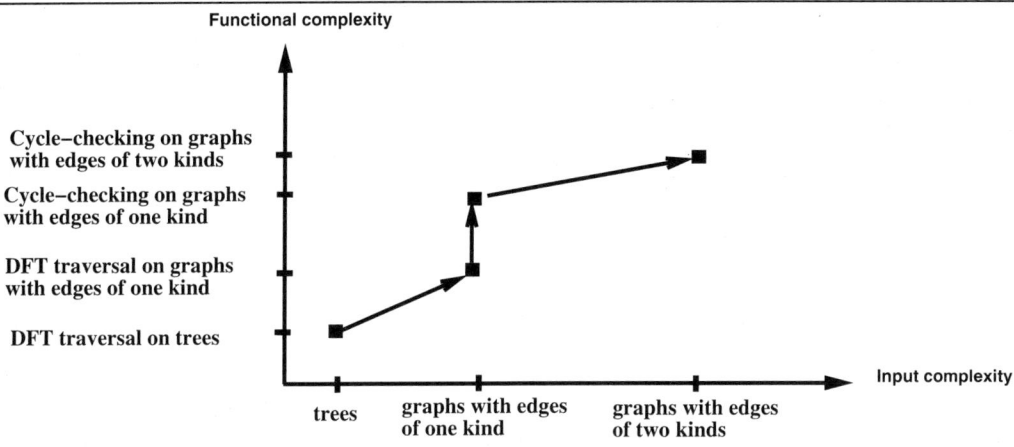

Figure 8.29: Simplifying the cycle checking problem

directed edge. Functionality simplification means that we keep the data the same, but we simplify the problem. For example, instead of writing a cycle checker directly, we first write a traversal algorithm for the graphs. Later this traversal algorithm will be enhanced to a cycle checker. Finally, further data simplification leads to the simple problem of writing a traversal algorithm on trees. Data simplification normally implies functionality simplification.

When one implements the four design phases shown in Fig. 8.29, at each phase the first step is to produce a class dictionary graph that describes the objects for the current phase. Figure 8.30 gives the statistics of the example. The application program is developed as a sequence of increasingly more complex components. Step by step, components are naturally enhanced. Each step has an executable program ready to be tested against the design requirements. When we write components, we try to make them minimally dependent on the specific class dictionary graph for which they are developed so that we can easily reuse them on other class dictionary graphs. Therefore the class dictionary graph for which a component is developed is just an example to explain and understand the program description. Later when we reuse the description for another class dictionary graph all the names of vertices and edge labels can be bound to the names in the new class dictionary graph. We call a collection of components with enhancement relationships an **evolution history**.

We summarize the evolution phases used in the evolution history for the cycle checking example. The first program formulates the basic depth-first traversal algorithm for a wide variety of tree structures. The second program adds additional knowledge to handle a wide variety of graph structures. The addition is about marking vertices when they have been visited and making sure that a marked vertex is not visited again. Program three adds additional knowledge to handle cycle checking for a wide variety of graph structures, including graphs with two kinds of edges.

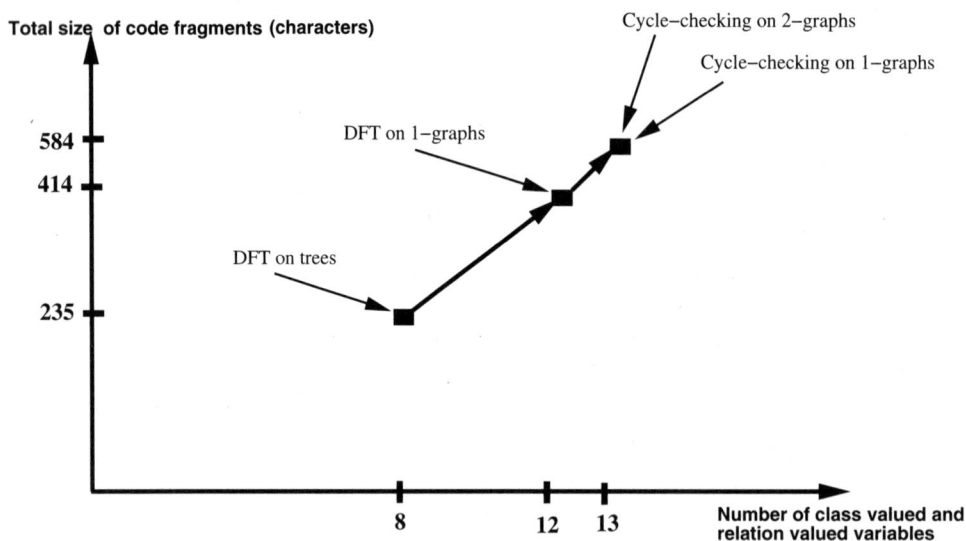

1-graphs: graphs with edges of one kind.
2-graphs: graphs with edges of two kinds.

Figure 8.30: Evolution history

8.7.2 Three-Stage Development

We recommend that propagation patterns be developed in three stages. First we focus on the correct traversal of objects. In the second stage we focus on which objects need to be assembled together at certain places during the traversal, and we use transportation directives to plan the routes along which the objects will travel. (Transportation is discussed in Chapter 10.) In the third stage, we express, using wrappers, what kind of acts the assembled objects need to perform during the various phases of the traversal.

When you develop propagation patterns, eventually you will focus on one subtask and choose a signature. To implement the subtask, we identify a group of collaborating classes. Although we have a class dictionary available for which we develop the software, we do not explicitly itemize the collaborators. Instead we describe the classes by a propagation directive using only minimal information about the class dictionary. The dependency metric *Dep* is a useful guide. When we write the propagation directive we take the evolution of the class dictionary into account.

A propagation directive is usually developed using the following steps:

- Start with *from* and *to* and *via*.

- Fine-tune with *through* and *bypassing*.

- Use *to-stop* if no recursion is desired.

- Use *merge* and *join* as needed (discussed later).

A propagation directive is used for traversal and transportation. During the first stage, we use a propagation directive as a traversal specification, and we debug the traversal code by running it. During the second stage, we use a propagation directives as transportation specifications and we debug the traversal and transportation code together. In the third stage, the detailed processing is addressed by vertex and edge wrappers. The wrappers are developed incrementally, using a growth plan.[5] The complete program (traversal, transportation, and wrappers) is debugged incrementally.

To summarize, adaptive software may be developed in three steps. First we focus on traversing the correct objects, then on transporting the correct objects, and finally on doing the detailed processing. Propagation pattern are naturally grouped into behavioral units, called components. A component should do only one thing.

8.7.3 Propagation and Alternation

Defining code for an alternation class can have several intentions: we want to select a subset of the alternatives, we want to build an inheritance hierarchy using overriding (redefinition) of methods, we want to combine code from several subclasses in construction classes associated with the alternation class. As we will see, the second intention is a special case of the third.

Each intention requires a different solution. In the following A is an alternation class. A positive answer to a question helps us select the appropriate solution.

---

[5] Growth plan, page 445 (54).

Subset of Alternatives

Question: Do I want to selectively choose one or a few alternatives?
    Example: Consider the class dictionary

```
Basket = "basket" <contents> SeveralThings.
SeveralThings ~ "(" {Thing} ")" .
Thing : Fruit | Basket.
Fruit : Apple | Orange.
Weight = <v> DemNumber.
Apple = "apple" <weight> Weight.
Orange = "orange" <weight> Weight.
```

The following propagation pattern computes the total weight of the apples only in a given fruit basket.

```
*operation* int add_weight() *init* (@ 0 @)
  *traverse*
    *from* Basket *via* Apple *to* Weight
  *wrapper* Weight
    *prefix* (@ return_val = return_val + *v ; @)
```

Inheritance Hierarchy

Question: Am I using A to provide functionality to subclasses; that is, am I building an inheritance hierarchy where the code of superclasses is inherited by subclasses?

In this case we do not use propagation, but instead standard object-oriented notation where each class gets code assigned.
    Example: Consider the class dictionary

```
Symbol :
  RegularSymbol | LabeledSymbol
    *common* <symbolName> DemIdent.
RegularSymbol = .
LabeledSymbol = ["<" <labelName> DemIdent ">"].
```

The following propagation pattern computes the slot name of a given symbol. No propagation is used in the propagation pattern.

```
*operation* DemIdent* slot_name()
  *wrapper* Symbol
    *prefix* (@ return_val = symbolName; @)
  *wrapper* LabeledSymbol
    *prefix* (@ return_val = labelName; @)
```

Method Combination

Question: Is all the functionality most easily defined at the classes associated with A? Are the superclasses contributing code incrementally? Do sets of classes have similar functionality although the set does not have an exclusive superclass?

In this context, we use the following design rule:

> Wrappers for sets of classes should be used to express method combination.

In this context of incremental code reuse, using wrappers is more flexible than multiple inheritance since the combination mechanism may change from operation to operation and is not frozen by a class structure.

Consider the following class dictionary graph:

```
Example = List(ABCD).
ABCD : AB | CD.
AB : A | B.
CD : C | D.

A = "a".
B = "b".
C = "c".
D = "d".

List(S) ~ "(" S {","S} ")".
```

The following propagation pattern simulates multiple inheritance. Classes B and C have some common behavior that they get by a wrapper not related to the classification structure. Classes B and C also get code from class ABCD. associated(A) is the set of construction classes alternation reachable from A.

```
*operation* DemString_List* test()
  *init* (@ new DemString_List() @)
  *traverse* *from* Example
  *wrapper* {B,C}
    *prefix* (@ return_val ->
      append(new DemString("common-BC")); @)
  *wrapper* {A,B,C,D} // associated(ABCD)
    *prefix* (@ return_val ->
      append(new DemString("top-level")); @)
  *wrapper* {A,B} // associated(AB)
    *prefix* (@ return_val ->
      append(new DemString("AB-middle-level")); @)
  *wrapper* {C,D} // associated(CD)
    *prefix* (@ return_val ->
      append(new DemString("CD-middle-level")); @)
```

On input

(a, b, c, d)

the propagation pattern produces the following list of strings:

```
(
"AB-middle-level" , "top-level" ,
"AB-middle-level" , "top-level" ,
"common-BC" , "CD-middle-level" , "top-level" ,
"common-BC" , "CD-middle-level" , "top-level"
)
```

This means that code of class A is a concatenation of code of classes AB and ABCD. Code of class C is a concatenation of code of class BC and classes CD and ABCD.

Area computation for squares, rectangles, circles, and ellipses is an application of method combination with wrappers. Consider the following class dictionary:

```
Example = <ex> List(Figure).
Figure: Rectangular | Elliptic .
Rectangular : Rectangle | Square.
Rectangle = "rectangle"
  <dim1> DemNumber
  <dim2> DemNumber.
Square = "square" <dim1 > DemNumber.
Elliptic : Ellipse | Circle.
Ellipse = "ellipse"
  <dim1> DemNumber
  <dim2> DemNumber.
Circle = "circle" <dim1> DemNumber.
List(S) ~ {S}.
```

The following propagation pattern computes the area of any of the four figures if the measures are given.

```
// simulating multiple inheritance with wrappers
// A circle inherits code for two reasons:
//   its area is determined by one side
//   its area is computed using PI
*operation* float area()
  *traverse* *from* Figure
*wrapper* {Rectangle, Ellipse}
  *prefix*
     (@ return_val = *dim1 * *dim2; @)
*wrapper* {Square, Circle}
  *prefix*
     (@ return_val = *dim1 * *dim1; @)
*wrapper* {Circle, Ellipse}
  *suffix*
     (@ float PI = 3.1415; return_val = return_val * PI; @)
```

8.7.4 Wrappers Simulating Inheritance

A classification hierarchy can be expressed with propagation and class-set wrappers. Therefore, in principle, we can do without traditional inheritance of methods to express incremental code composition. For each group G of classes that share some common code, we use a wrapper with class-set G. This has the advantage that we can group classes freely and define common functionality for them, without changing the inheritance structure.

Consider the class dictionary in Fig. 8.31. The operations t and t2 in Fig. 8.32

```
Example = List(ABCD).
ABCD : AB | CD.
AB : A | B.
CD : C | D.

A = "a".
B = "b".
C = "c".
D = "d".

List(S) ~ "(" S {","S} ")".
```

Figure 8.31: Classification hierarchy

have identical behavior. t is written in terms of propagation and t2 is an ordinary object-oriented program that relies on method overriding. Operation t explicitly says which method the construction classes get. Operation t2 uses inheritance to give functionality to the construction classes indirectly. The function **associated** makes it easier to express the method combination solution.

Both programs produce on input

(a, b, c, d)

the identical output

("A", "AB", "ABCD", "ABCD")

The method combination approach used by the first propagation pattern in Fig. 8.32 is more flexible. We could easily add more functionality. If classes A and D need to contribute some common code, we would write a wrapper

`*wrapper* {A,D} ...`

without changing the class structure.

It is interesting to reflect on the role of alternation edges. In the above example they are used to disseminate functionality to the classes A,B,C, and D. But the same dissemination role, although with some excess baggage, can be played by construction edges. The

```
// method combination
*operation* DemString_List* t()
  *init* (@ new DemString_List() @)
  *traverse* *from* ABCD
  *wrapper* {C,D} //associated(ABCD) - associated(AB)
    *prefix* (@ return_val -> append(new DemString("ABCD")); @)
  *wrapper* B //associated(AB) - associated(A)
    *prefix* (@ return_val -> append(new DemString("AB")); @)
  *wrapper* A
    *prefix* (@ return_val -> append(new DemString("A")); @)

// method overriding
*operation* DemString_List* t2()
  *init* (@ new DemString_List() @)
  *wrapper* ABCD
    *prefix* (@ return_val -> append(new DemString("ABCD")); @)
  *wrapper* AB
    *prefix* (@ return_val -> append(new DemString("AB")); @)
  *wrapper* A
    *prefix* (@ return_val -> append(new DemString("A")); @)
```

Figure 8.32: Simulating method inheritance

8.7. PROGRAMMING WITH PROPAGATION PATTERNS

propagation pattern with signature name t in Fig. 8.32 produces identical behavior if used with the class dictionary in Fig. 8.33.

```
Example = List(ABCD).
ABCD = [AB]   [CD].
AB = [A] [B].
CD = [C] [D].

A = "a".
B = "b".
C = "c".
D = "d".

List(S) ~ "(" S {","S} ")".
```

Figure 8.33: Classification with construction edges

Traditional object-oriented programming uses only inheritance edges to disseminate functionality. With class-set code wrappers we can use construction edges as well.

8.7.5 Readers and Writers

Propagation patterns can be partitioned into two kinds: readers and writers. A propagation pattern is a reader if the traversed object is invariant under the propagation pattern code. A propagation pattern is a writer if the traversed object gets modified by the propagation pattern code. Both readers and writers may create new objects from the traversed objects.

An example of a reader is

```
*operation* int sum()
  *init* (@ 0 @)
  *traverse*
    *from* Airplane *to* Weight
  *wrapper*
    *prefix*
      (@ return_val += *v; @)
```

The Airplane-object is invariant.

An example of a writer is

```
*operation* void update_phone_no(PersonName* pname, PhoneNo* phone)
  *traverse*
    *from* Company *to* Person
  *wrapper* Person
    *prefix*
```

```
(@ if (this -> get_name() -> g_equal(pname)) {
    this -> set_phone_number(phone);} @)
```

Here the traversed Company-object gets updated.

Propagation patterns are equally useful for reading as well as for modifying objects. Let's look at some typical propagation patterns that are writers.

- Change a part

```
*operation* void f(Q* update)
  *traverse*
    *from* A *to* ClassContainingQ
  *wrapper* ClassContainingQ
    *prefix*
      (@ this -> set_q(update); @)
```

To avoid memory leakage, we must use a function called rset_q, which returns the pointer to the old object so that we can delete it. For a part <q> Q of class Class, the rset_q function is implemented as

```
// Class = <q> Q.
Q* Class::rset_q(Q* new_q){
  Q* old_q = q;
  q = new_q;
  return (old_q);}
```

The wrapper for ClassContainingQ is replaced by

```
(@ delete(this -> rset_q(update)); @)
```

- Add element to list

```
*operation* void f(Q* new_element)
  *traverse*
    *from* A *to* ClassContainingList
  *wrapper* ClassContainingList
    *prefix*
      (@ partContainingList -> append(new_element); @)
```

An important consideration when building entirely new objects under program control is to avoid building the structure manually. It is better to create a skeleton of the structure with parsing (see Chapter 11) and then to fill in the terminal objects using writers as described above. In other words, we use a prototypical object that gets copied and filled in.

8.8 SUMMARY

We summarize propagation patterns (without transportation, which will be discussed in Chapter 10). Adaptive software is expressed as propagation patterns. There are two kinds of propagation patterns:

- Incremental inheritance propagation patterns

- Overriding inheritance propagation patterns

The incremental inheritance propagation patterns are the interesting ones and have a traversal directive. The overriding inheritance propagation patterns are like object-oriented programs and express the functions attached to classes explicitly.

The incremental inheritance propagation patterns can have several wrappers of two different kinds:

- Vertex wrappers

- Edge wrappers

Both kinds of wrappers are either prefix wrappers, suffix wrappers, or both. A vertex prefix wrapper of class A is called before an object of class A is entered and a vertex suffix wrapper is called after an object of class A is left.

Edge wrappers cannot be defined for alternation edges, but can be defined for construction and repetition edges. A prefix edge wrapper is called before the corresponding edge is traversed and a suffix edge wrapper is called after traversing the edge.

The implementation of propagation patterns is summarized in two phases. First we focus on the traversal property, without taking wrappers into account.

- Traversals

  The implementation of propagation patterns has to satisfy two important requirements:

  – traversal meaning of propagation patterns. The required traversals are done; that is, the subobjects selected by the propagation directive are properly traversed.

  – observes path constraints. Only the required traversals are done; that is, the traversal does not traverse paths disallowed by the propagation directive.

  Code generation:

  – edges:
    in flattened traversal graph
    construction, repetition : call part

  – alternation vertices: attached functions are virtual

- Wrappers

    When wrappers are present, they all must be called. This requires wrapper pushing consistent with the incremental use of inheritance in the presence of traversal.

    Code generation:

    – alternation vertices:
        wrapper pushing; if a vertex has an outgoing alternation edge distribute wrapper to target of alternation edge. Distribute further if rule applies again.

8.9 EXERCISES

Exercise 8.1 Consider a propagation pattern of the form

```
*operation* void f()
  *traverse*
    *from* A *via* B *to* C
  *prefix* C
    (@ cout << this; @)
```

Is the following true or false? Explain your answer. For all class dictionary graphs G in an equivalence class of object-equivalent class dictionary graphs and for every A-object of G, the above program will have identical behavior after a suitable mapping of A, B, and C to classes or class sets of G.

Exercise 8.2 Method combination allows us to combine code at the leaf classes of an inheritance hierarchy in a flexible way by rearranging the wrappers. How flexible is the approach? Can you think of a situation where the desired ordering cannot be achieved without manual expansion of the code? Which reorderings can be achieved?

Exercise 8.3 Is the following correct? Explain your answer.
    The two propagation patterns below, called f1 and f2, are equivalent.

```
*operation* void f1()
  *constraints*
    *class* A, B
  *traverse*
    *from* A *to* B
  *wrapper* B
    *prefix* (@ ... @)

*operation* void f2()
  *constraints*
    *class* A, B
    *class-set*
      Assoc_B = { ... }; // associated(B)
  *end*
  *traverse*
```

8.9. EXERCISES

```
    *from* A *to* Assoc_B
  *wrapper* B
    *prefix* (@ ... @)
```

Hint: In general, the knowledge paths in the second one are longer.

Exercise 8.4 Below you get a propagation pattern and the corresponding C++ code for two distinct class dictionaries. From the C++ programs, derive the information in the propagation pattern.

Propagation pattern:

```
*operation* void UNKNOWN1()
  *traverse*
    UNKNOWN2 // make it as small as possible
  *wrapper* UNKNOWN3
    *prefix*
      (@ cout << "in UNKNOWN4 " << endl; @)
  *wrapper* UNKNOWN5
    *suffix*
      (@ cout << "after UNKNOWN6-traversal " << endl; @)
```

Class dictionary 1

```
A = <b> B <f1> F.
B = <c> C <f2> F.
C = <d> D <f3> F.
D = <e> E.
E = <f> F.
F = .
```

and the corresponding C++ program

```
//   A   = <b > B
//         <f1 > F .
void A::fun( )
{ // outgoing calls
  this->get_b()->fun( );
  // suffix class wrappers
  cout << "after A-traversal " << endl; }

//   B   = <c > C
//         <f2 > F .
void B::fun( )
{ // outgoing calls
  this->get_c()->fun( ); }

//   C   = <d > D
```

```
//      <f3 > F .
void C::fun( )
{ // outgoing calls
  this->get_d()->fun( ); }

//   D  = <e > E .
void D::fun( )
{ // outgoing calls
  this->get_e()->fun( ); }

//   E  = <f > F .
void E::fun( )
{ // outgoing calls
  this->get_f()->fun( ); }

//   F  = .
void F::fun( )
{ // prefix class wrappers
 cout << "in F " << endl; }
```

Class dictionary 2

```
A = <b1> B1 <f1> F.
B1 = <c1> C1.
C1 = <b> B.
B = <c> C <f2> F.
C = <d> D <f3> F.
D = <e1> E1 <f4> F.
E1 = <f5> F1.
F1 = <e> E.
E = <f> F.
F = .
```

and the corresponding C++ program

```
//   A  = <b1 > B1
//      <f1 > F .
void A::fun( )
{ // construction edge prefix wrappers
  this->get_b1()->fun( );
  // suffix class wrappers
 cout << "after A-traversal " << endl; }

//   B1 = <c1 > C1 .
void B1::fun( )
{ // outgoing calls
```

8.9. EXERCISES

```
    this->get_c1()->fun( ); }

//  C1  = <b > B .
void C1::fun( )
{ // outgoing calls
    this->get_b()->fun( ); }

//  B   = <c > C
//        <f2 > F .
void B::fun( )
{ // construction edge prefix wrappers
    this->get_c()->fun( ); }

//  C   = <d > D
//        <f3 > F .
void C::fun( )
{ // outgoing calls
    this->get_d()->fun( ); }

//  D   = <e1 > E1
//        <f4 > F .
void D::fun( )
{ // outgoing calls
    this->get_e1()->fun( );
    this->get_f4()->fun( ); }

//  E1  = <f5 > F1 .
void E1::fun( )
{ // outgoing calls
    this->get_f5()->fun( ); }

//  F1  = <e > E .
void F1::fun( )
{ // outgoing calls
    this->get_e()->fun( ); }

//  E   = <f > F .
void E::fun( )
{ // outgoing calls
    this->get_f()->fun( ); }

//  F   = .
void F::fun( )
{ // prefix class wrappers
  cout << "in F " << endl; }
```

Exercise 8.5 Consider the following class dictionary, propagation pattern, and propagation graph. Find the UNKNOWNS.

Class dictionary

```
Cd_graph = <adjacencies> List(Adjacency).
Adjacency =
  <source> Vertex
  <ns> Neighbors ".".
Neighbors : Construct_ns | Alternat_ns
  *common* <construct_ns> List(Labeled_vertex).
Labeled_vertex =
  "<" <label_name> DemIdent ">" <vertex> Comma_list(Vertex).
  // vertex plays double role:
  // in cd: Part class (only one element in list)
  // in PartCluster: Cluster
Alternat_ns = ":" <alternat_ns> Bar_list(Vertex) [<common> Common].
Common = "*common*".
Construct_ns = "=".
Vertex = <vertex_name> DemIdent [ "*mark*" <mark> DemIdent ].

// parameterized classes
List(S)   ~ {S} .
Nlist(S)  ~ S {S}.
Comma_list(S) ~ S {"," S}.
Bar_list(S)   ~ S {"|" S}.

Cluster     = "*clusters*" <clusters> List(PartCluster) .
PartCluster = "*source*" <source> Vertex
              "(" <parts> List(Labeled_vertex) ")".

Dummy = List(Vertex).
```

Propagation Pattern

```
// computes the set of construction classes which are alternation-
// reachable from vertex v in class dictionary graph cd.
// alternation-reachable means by following only alternation edges.

*operation* Vertex_Comma_list* find_assoc
    (Vertex* v,  Cd_graph* cd)
  *init* (@ new Vertex_Comma_list(); @)
*traverse*
  *from* UNKNOWN1
    *bypassing* -> *,construct_ns,* ,
                -> *,UNKNOWN2,*
  *to* {UNKNOWN3, UNKNOWN4}
```

8.9. EXERCISES   251

```
*wrapper* Cd_graph
  *suffix* (@ cout << "\n assoc " << v << " is " << return_val << "\n"; @)
*wrapper* Adjacency
  *prefix* (@ if (source->g_equal(v)) { @)
  *suffix* (@ } @)

*wrapper* UNKNOWN5
  *prefix* (@ return_val -> append((Vertex *)(v -> g_copy()));
    cout << "\n Vertex appended in find_assoc " << v << "\n"; @)

*wrapper* UNKNOWN6
  *prefix*
    (@
      cout << "\n alternative of " << v << " is " << this << "\n";
      return_val ->
          concatenate(cd -> find_assoc(this, cd)); @)
          // concatenate combines two lists
```

Propagation schema for traversal

```
    Cd_graph = UNKNOWN7 .
    Adjacency = UNKNOWN8 .
    Neighbors : UNKNOWN9 .
    Alternat_ns = UNKNOWN10 .
    Construct_ns = UNKNOWN11 .
    Vertex = .
    UNKNOWN12 ~ { UNKNOWN13 } .
    UNKNOWN14 ~ UNKNOWN15 { UNKNOWN16 } .
//////////////////////////////////////////////////////////
//    There are 17 classes in total
//    There are 8 classes in the propagation schema
//    There are 9 classes not in the propagation graph
//////////////////////////////////////////////////////////
```

Trace output

```
    IN Cd_graph::find_assoc
     IN Cd_graph::find_assoc
      IN Adjacency_List::find_assoc
       IN Adjacency::find_assoc
       OUT Adjacency::find_assoc
       IN Adjacency::find_assoc
        IN Alternat_ns::find_assoc
         IN Vertex_Bar_list::find_assoc
          IN Vertex::find_assoc
```

```
alternative of O  is A
            IN Cd_graph::find_assoc
             IN Cd_graph::find_assoc
              IN Adjacency_List::find_assoc
               IN Adjacency::find_assoc
               OUT Adjacency::find_assoc
               IN Adjacency::find_assoc
               OUT Adjacency::find_assoc
               IN Adjacency::find_assoc
                IN Construct_ns::find_assoc

Vertex appended in find_assoc A
                OUT Construct_ns::find_assoc
               OUT Adjacency::find_assoc
               IN Adjacency::find_assoc
               OUT Adjacency::find_assoc
               IN Adjacency::find_assoc
               OUT Adjacency::find_assoc
               IN Adjacency::find_assoc
               OUT Adjacency::find_assoc
               IN Adjacency::find_assoc
               OUT Adjacency::find_assoc
               IN Adjacency::find_assoc
               OUT Adjacency::find_assoc
               IN Adjacency::find_assoc
               OUT Adjacency::find_assoc
              OUT Adjacency_List::find_assoc

assoc A  is A
                OUT Cd_graph::find_assoc
               OUT Cd_graph::find_assoc
             OUT Vertex::find_assoc
            OUT Vertex_Bar_list::find_assoc
           OUT Alternat_ns::find_assoc
         OUT Adjacency::find_assoc
         IN Adjacency::find_assoc
         OUT Adjacency::find_assoc
         IN Adjacency::find_assoc
         OUT Adjacency::find_assoc
         IN Adjacency::find_assoc
         OUT Adjacency::find_assoc
         IN Adjacency::find_assoc
         OUT Adjacency::find_assoc
         IN Adjacency::find_assoc
         OUT Adjacency::find_assoc
```

```
            IN Adjacency::find_assoc
            OUT Adjacency::find_assoc
            IN Adjacency::find_assoc
            OUT Adjacency::find_assoc
            OUT Adjacency_List::find_assoc
```

```
assoc O  is A
        OUT Cd_graph::find_assoc
    OUT Cd_graph::find_assoc
```

8.10 BIBLIOGRAPHIC REMARKS

- Pattern community

  Propagation patterns provide a polished mechanism for software development through formal patterns. Informal, but more general patterns, have been promoted for several years by Kent Beck, Ward Cunningham, and others [Bec87, Bec94]. In pattern software development, abstractors and elaborators do their work. A pattern consists of a problem, a context, and a solution. For more information on patterns, send mail to

  patterns-request@cs.uiuc.edu.

- Law of Demeter

  The Law of Demeter was introduced in [LHR88, LH89a, LHLR88, Sak88a].

  It is discussed in several theses (e.g., [Hol93, Cas91]) and several textbooks, for example,

  Rumbaugh/OMT Method [RBP+91]

  - Context

    Chapter: Programming Style; Section: Extensibility

  - Quote

    Avoid traversing multiple links or methods. A method should have limited knowledge of an object model. A method must be able to traverse links to obtain its neighbors and must be able to call operations on them, but it should not traverse a second link from the neighbor to a third class.

  Coleman/Fusion Method [Col94]

  - Context

    Chapter: Design; Section: Principles of Good Design; Subsection: Visibility Graphs

  - Quote

    Minimize data and functional dependencies. ... Following the Law of Demeter improves the modularity of a system. An object is dependent only on its immediate structure and makes no assumptions about the structure beyond the immediate references. Applying this law, one can achieve "loosely coupled" systems and localization of information.

Booch/Booch Method [Boo86]

- Context

    Chapter: Classes and Objects; Section: On Building Quality Classes and Objects; Subsection: Choosing Relationships

- Quote

    The basic effect of applying this Law is the creation of loosely coupled classes, whose implementation secrets are encapsulated. Such classes are fairly unencumbered, meaning that to understand the meaning of one class, you need not understand the details of many other classes.

8.11 SOLUTIONS

Solution to Exercise 8.4

```
UNKNOWN1 = fun()
UNKNOWN2 = *from* A   *via* D   *to* F
   or: (but longer):
      *from* A
         *bypassing* -> *,f1,*,
                     -> *,f2,*,
                     -> *,f3,*
      *to* F
UNKNOWN3 = F
UNKNOWN4 =  F
UNKNOWN5 = A
UNKNOWN6 = A
```

Solution to Exercise 8.5

```
UNKNOWN1 = Cd_graph
UNKNOWN2 = source
UNKNOWN3 = Vertex           CHOICE
UNKNOWN4 = Construct_ns     CHOICE
UNKNOWN5 = Construct_ns
UNKNOWN6 = Vertex
UNKNOWN7 = < adjacencies > Adjacency_List
UNKNOWN8 = < ns > Neighbors
UNKNOWN9 = Construct_ns | Alternat_ns *common*
UNKNOWN10 = < alternat_ns > Vertex_Bar_list
UNKNOWN11 = NOTHING
UNKNOWN12 = Adjacency_List
UNKNOWN13 = Adjacency
UNKNOWN14 = Vertex_Bar_list
UNKNOWN15 = Vertex
UNKNOWN16 = Vertex
```

Chapter 9

Propagation Pattern Interpretation

This chapter has a connection to Chapter 15. In this chapter we discuss many of the details of propagation pattern interpretation, and in Chapter 15 we focus on the essence of the interpreter. Chapter 15 also presents a compiler and proves the correctness of the compiler with respect to the interpreter.

There are two kinds of propagation patterns: those with a traversal directive and those without a traversal directive. This chapter explains the meaning and implementation of propagation patterns with traversal directives.

We explain propagation patterns by first giving an algorithm called TRAVERSE for propagation pattern execution in terms of object traversal, and wrapper execution as the side effect of the traversal. This algorithm uniquely prescribes in which order the wrappers are called for a given input object. The intent of the rules is to traverse only the object paths that are allowed by the constraints in the propagation patterns. However, the rules fail to give appropriate behavior if customizers that cause a misbehavior are used. Those customizers don't appear often in applications. Therefore, we introduce customizer restrictions that ensure that the rules result in correct behavior as specified in the propagation directives of the propagation patterns. An alternative solution would have been to generalize the implementation of propagation patterns to allow for the misbehaving customizers. But since those customizers are usually "strange" customizers, we have decided to exclude them.

The rules together with the customizer restrictions guarantee that the propagation patterns have a number of very useful properties for adaptive software development. Those properties can be viewed as requirements that the propagation pattern interpretation algorithm TRAVERSE satisfies. The algorithm is shorter than the discussion of all its properties and therefore we give the algorithm first.

Finally we discuss an object-oriented implementation of propagation patterns that is faithful to algorithm TRAVERSE and that has all the properties discussed. The core of algorithm TRAVERSE is given in Chapter 15.

9.1 HOW TO RUN A PROPAGATION PATTERN

Given a propagation pattern pp and a compatible, single-inheritance class dictionary graph G, the program $propagate(pp, G)$ has the behavior described below. First we compute the propagation graph $pg = propagate(d, G)$, where d is the propagation directive of pp. Wrappers can be attached only to vertices of the pg. We assume first that each vertex and each edge has at most one wrapper.

We use the following definitions. A **propagation vertex** contained in a propagation graph of a class dictionary graph is either a construction vertex in the propagation graph or a target vertex.

A **propagation object** of a propagation graph is an object of a propagation vertex of that graph.

A call of the propagation pattern pp on an object graph of one of the sources of propagation directive d of pp leads to a traversal of the object graph and to wrapper executions.[1] Essentially, the relevant parts of the object are traversed and as vertices and edges are traversed, the appropriate wrappers are executed. The interpreter TRAVERSE is given in Fig. 9.1.

Algorithm TRAVERSE is a high-level interpreter that treats the wrappers as black boxes.

The following explains the interpreter in more detail and allows for several wrappers per object or vertex. The interpreter follows these rules:

- Only-subobjects

    - inside propagation graph

        When an instance O of vertex V is traversed, only the part objects of O prescribed by the definition of V in the propagation graph pg, are traversed.

    - outside propagation graph

        When an object O of vertex V is traversed and the object is an instance of a vertex not in the propagation graph, no further traversal is done for O and no wrappers are called for O. In other words, objects that are not instances of classes in the propagation graph are not traversed unless they belong to a target class.

- Part-ordering

    - immediate-first

        The part objects described by the immediate parts of a subclass are visited before the part objects described by the immediate parts of the superclasses.

    - class dictionary graph order

        The part objects described by the immediate parts of a vertex are traversed in the order the parts are defined in the class dictionary graph.

---

[1] Propagation pattern interpretation, page 447 (63).

Input:
A propagation pattern pp containing a propagation directive d, a class dictionary graph G compatible with the propagation pattern pp, and an object O which is an object of a source vertex of d.

Output:
Traversal of O with sequence of wrapper executions.
Partial compilation: $pg = propagate(d, G)$

call TRAVERSE(O), where
TRAVERSE(O : object of class dictionary graph G)

1. If O is not a propagation object of pg then nothing happens.

2. Otherwise,

    (a) prefix wrappers of the class of O and its superclasses (alternation predecessors) in pg are executed in the least-specific to most-specific order.

    (b) part-objects prescribed by the inheritance and construction edges in pg are traversed next. For each part object O' of O, TRAVERSE(O') is called in the following order:

        i. part-objects of O prescribed by a subclass are traversed before the part-objects prescribed by its superclasses.
        ii. part-objects of O prescribed by a class are traversed in the order defined in the class dictionary graph.

        If a part has an edge wrapper, the prefix wrapper is executed immediately before the part is traversed and the suffix wrapper immediately afterwards.

    (c) suffix code fragments of the class of O and its superclasses (alternation predecessors) in pg are executed in the most-specific to least-specific order.

Figure 9.1: Interpreter TRAVERSE to run a propagation pattern

- Class-wrapper

    We describe which wrappers are executed and in what order.

    When an instance of construction vertex V is traversed, if the object is

    - a propagation object, then the wrappers of vertex V and its alternation predecessors or inheritance successors in the propagation graph are executed.
    - a non-propagation object, then none of the wrappers is executed and no traversal is done.

    The wrappers are called in the following order:

    - prefix-parts-suffix

        The prefix wrapper of a vertex is executed before traversing any part object and before executing the suffix wrapper. The suffix wrapper of a vertex is executed after executing the prefix wrapper and after traversing any part-object.

    - wrapper-extension

        When an instance of vertex V is traversed, the prefix wrappers of V as well as the prefix wrappers of all alternation predecessors or inheritance successors of V are executed.

        * prefix-super-sub

            Let V be either an immediate alternation predecessor or an immediate inheritance successor of W in the propagation graph. The prefix wrapper of V is executed before the prefix wrapper of W.

        * suffix-sub-super

            The suffix wrapper of V is executed after the suffix wrapper of W.

- Edge wrapper, prefix-edge-suffix

    When an object edge is traversed, we consider the corresponding construction edge. The prefix wrapper of the construction edge is executed immediately before the object edge is traversed. The suffix wrapper is executed immediately after the object edge is traversed.

If a vertex or edge has several wrappers

- pp-order-class

    If a vertex has two prefix wrappers pw_1, pw_2, and pw_1 is textually before pw_2 in the propagation pattern, then pw_1 is executed before pw_2.

    If vertex has two suffix wrappers sw_1, sw_2, and sw_1 is textually before sw_2 in the propagation pattern, then sw_2 is executed before sw_1.

- pp-order-edge

    Same as pp-order-class but now for edges instead of vertices.

9.1.1 Discussion of the Rules

The rules specify how to interpret an object in the context of a class dictionary graph and a propagation pattern. The rules provide an operational semantics for propagation patterns.

The immediate-first rule needs justification. It says that the immediate parts are traversed before the inherited parts. The main reason for the rule is that we would like to have robustness under flattening of common parts. When the common parts are flattened they are appended after the immediate parts. Therefore, due to the immediate-first rule, a small change to a customizer, such as flattening, will not change the order in which the wrappers are called.

The selection of the prefix-super-sub rule over the prefix-sub-super rule requires motivation. The prefix-super-sub rule has an important advantage over the prefix-sub-super rule: robustness of the superclass for the purpose of initialization. A superclass contains more general code than a subclass. The specific code could be dependent on the general code. But the general code should not depend on the specific code. This would be a violation of robustness of the superclass if it would be dependent on subclasses. Since a prefix wrapper often has the intention to initialize or to do some preliminary work, it is natural to call the most general code first.

If there is no dependency between the code of the superclass and the code of the subclass, we would be happy with either the prefix-super-sub or prefix-sub-super rule.

There is an apparent tension between the prefix-super-sub rule and the immediate-first rule. The prefix-super-sub rule asks for super-first, but immediate-first asks for sub-first. This is not a contradiction since wrappers and traversals are handled independently.

Below is an example that shows a dependency of the code of the subclass on the code of the superclass. The idea behind the example is: initialize at the superclass, use at the subclass.

For example, we want to print the cost of each dessert and entree for a **Banquet**-object. We reset a summation variable at the beginning of dessert and entree.

```
Banquet = List(Meal).
Meal = Entree Dessert.
Entree : Wienerschnitzel | Steak.
Dessert : Mousse | Cake.
Mousse = [ WhippedCream ].
Cake = .
Wienerschnitzel = TomatoSoup Peas Potatos Schnitzel.
TomatoSoup = [ WhippedCream ].

*operation* void partial_cost(int& c)
  // c should really be a variable local to the pp
  *traverse*
    *from* Banquet
  *wrapper* Dessert
    *prefix* (@ c =  3; @) // fixed cost of dessert
    *suffix* (@ cout << " dessert cost " << c; @)
  *wrapper* Mousse
```

```
    *prefix* (@ c = c +  4; @) // additional cost for mousse
*wrapper* Cake
    *prefix* (@ c = c +  2; @) // additional cost for cake

*wrapper* WhippedCream
    *prefix* (@ c = c + 1; @)  // additional cost for whipped cream

*wrapper* Entree
    *prefix* (@ c =   10; @) // fixed cost of entree
    *suffix* (@ cout << " entree cost " << c; @)
*wrapper* Wienerschnitzel
    *prefix* (@ c = c +  5; @) // additional cost for Wienerschnitzel
*wrapper* Steak
    *prefix* (@ c = c +  7; @) // additional cost for steak
```

9.2 CUSTOMIZER RESTRICTIONS

Several customizer restrictions are needed. Some of them simply make the program meaningful with respect to the customizer. Others are needed to enforce correct behavior.[2] Rather than generalizing the interpreter, we exclude the uninteresting borderline cases. Those situations that the customizer restrictions exclude occur with small probability in practice. Therefore, the reader may skip this section on first reading.

We summarize the customizer restrictions.

Name	Purpose
compatibility	vocabulary of propagation pattern matches vocabulary of customizer
propagation	no source is superfluous
information loss (synonym: consistency)	disallow traversal shortcuts and zigzag paths
delayed binding (synonym: subclass invariance)	disallow traversal shortcuts due to delayed binding (specific to object-oriented implementation)
inheritance	provide sufficiently many inheritance edges for every propagation alternation vertex to be on a completed knowledge path (needed only for nonflat class dictionaries)

The following restriction is implied
    (by inheritance and delayed binding restriction):

---
[2] Legal propagation pattern customization, page 447 (62).

```
alternation              provide sufficiently many alternation
                         edges for every propagation alternation
                         vertex to be on a completed knowledge path
```

9.2.1 Compatibility Restriction

It is important that the vocabulary of a propagation pattern matches the vocabulary of the customizer. For example, the propagation pattern cannot mention a class-valued variable A without indicating how A is mapped into a vertex of the customizer. In the simplest situation this means that a propagation pattern using A is not compatible with a customizer not using A. A propagation pattern pp is compatible with a semi-class dictionary graph G if the propagation directive of pp is compatible with G and if the vertices and edge patterns appearing in wrappers are compatible with G. The compatibility of a propagation directive or edge pattern with a semi-class dictionary graph is defined in the chapter on propagation directives. The compatibility restriction ensures properly defined propagation graphs.

9.2.2 Propagation Restriction

A fundamental customizer restriction covered by the compatibility restriction between a propagation directive and a semi-class dictionary graph is that there is at least one knowledge path from a source to a target. If there were no knowledge path, the propagation graph would be empty and no functionality would be defined. The **propagation restriction** addresses the issue that for every source some functionality is defined.

- No source is superfluous

  From every source vertex there is at least one path to some target vertex. More precisely, for a propagation directive (F, c, T) and semi-class dictionary graph S—For all images v of F (sources) in S there exists an image w of T (targets) in S such that there exists at least one knowledge path in S from v to w satisfying c.

What would happen without the propagation restriction? If we allowed superfluous source vertices, we would call functions that don't exist. We would have a type violation at the object-oriented level.

For the vertices in *via* clauses, we adopt the same rule as for *through*—at least one is used.

Consider the propagation pattern

```
*operation* void search()
  *traverse*
    *from* {Kitchen, House}
    *to* {Key, Hamster}
  *wrapper* {Key, Hamster}
    *prefix*
      (@ this -> return_to_its_place(); @)
```

The propagation directive

```
*from* {Kitchen, House} *to* {Key, Hamster}
```

is equivalent to

```
*merge*(
  *merge*(
    *from* Kitchen *to* Key,
    *from* Kitchen *to* Hamster),
  *merge*(
    *from* House *to* Key,
    *from* House *to* Hamster))
```

Some of the four paths may define the empty propagation graph. But at least two of the paths have to define a nonempty propagation graph. At least two paths are needed to cover both sources.

9.2.3 Information Loss Restriction

Sometimes information loss is also called inconsistency. This customizer restriction can be understood in the context of propagation directives. It disallows information loss in propagation directives, as discussed in the chapter on propagation directives. A propagation directive has **information loss** with respect to a class dictionary graph if the propagation graph contains a completed knowledge path that does not satisfy the propagation directive. A knowledge path from a source to a target is completed if every used alternation vertex on the path has an outgoing alternation edge.

We use the refrigerator example to illustrate propagation directive information loss. Consider the propagation pattern in Fig. 9.2. The customizer whose graphical represen-

```
*operation* void collect()
  *traverse*
    *from* Country
      *via* Family
    *to* {Refrigerator, Chessboard}
  *wrapper* {Refrigerator, Chessboard}
    *prefix* (@ this -> g_print(); @)
```

Figure 9.2: Refrigerator propagation pattern

tation is in Fig. 9.3 and whose textual representation is in 9.4 has information loss. The propagation graph is shown in Fig. 9.5.

The propagation directive information loss is demonstrated by the knowledge path **Country, ThingList, Thing, Refrigerator**. This is a completed knowledge path that does not satisfy the propagation directive.

The information loss causes things outside **Family**-objects to be printed. The reason is that the union of paths from **Country** to **Refrigerator** also contains paths that do not satisfy the propagation directive.

9.2. CUSTOMIZER RESTRICTIONS

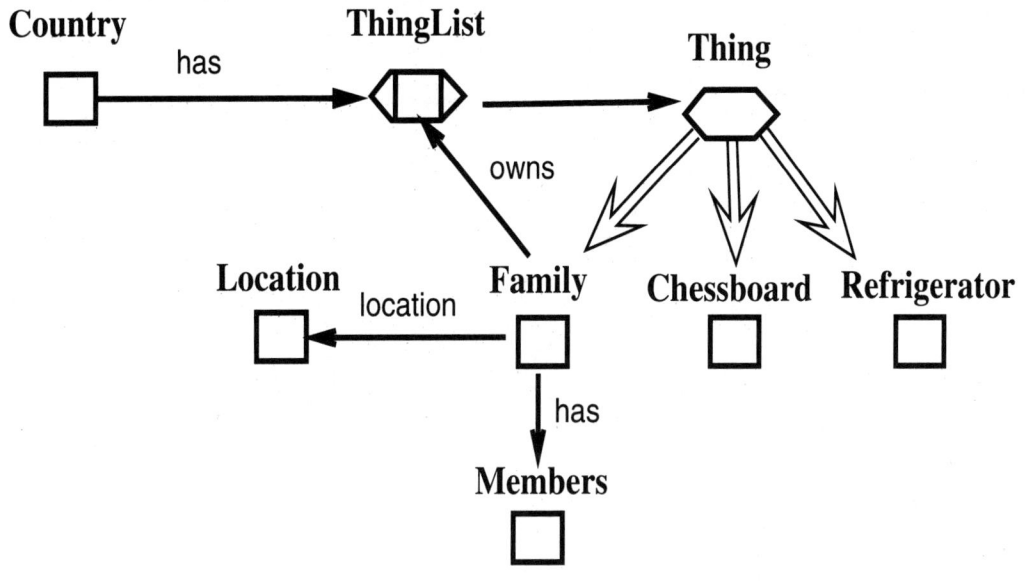

Figure 9.3: Propagation directive information loss

```
Country = <has> ThingList.
Family =
  <owns> ThingList
  <has> Members
  <location> Location.
Members = .
Location = .
Thing : Family | Chessboard | Refrigerator.
Refrigerator = .
Chessboard = .
ThingList ~ Thing {Thing}.
```

Figure 9.4: Customizer with information loss

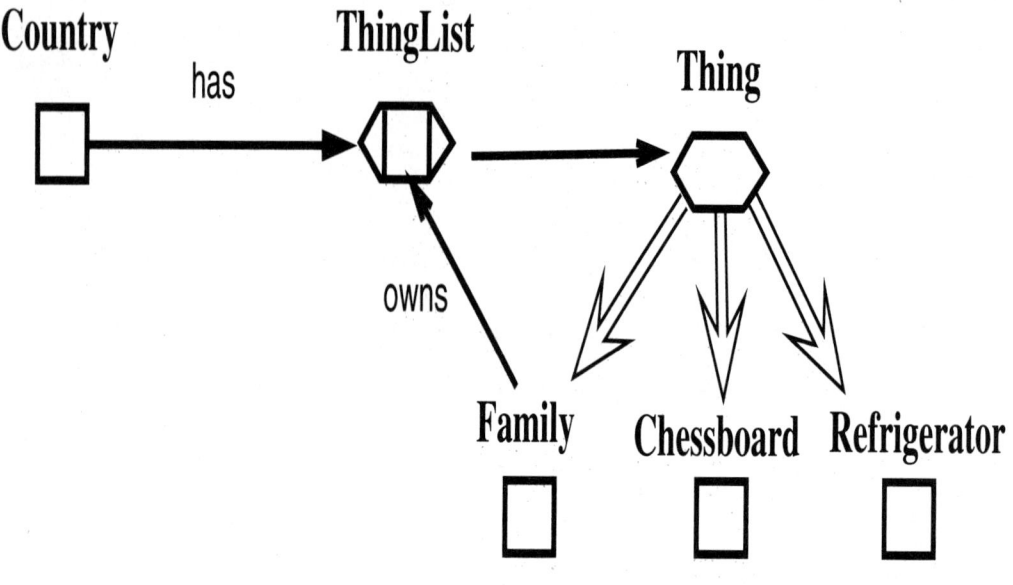

Figure 9.5: Propagation graph

Two solutions can avoid the information loss restriction. Either the propagation pattern is split into two or the class dictionary is slightly changed.

The customizer (in Fig. 9.4) contains both alternation and construction vertices. We could also give a customizer that demonstrates information loss by using construction vertices only.

As a second example consider the propagation directive

```
*from* A
  *via* K
*to* {X,Y}
```

and the class dictionary

```
A = "a" B.
B : K | C.
K = "k" B.
C = X Y.

X = "x".
Y = "y".
```

The propagation directive will traverse all X and Y objects, not just the ones that are subobjects of K-objects. This customizer creates information loss; therefore it is disallowed.

9.2.4 Delayed Binding Restriction

The delayed binding restriction is sometimes also called the Subclass Invariance Restriction. In a first approximation, the delayed binding restriction says that the propagation graph cannot contain an alternation vertex and an alternative of the alternation vertex, without containing the corresponding alternation edge. In this situation, delayed binding causes the propagation pattern to malfunction.

Consider again the refrigerator propagation pattern in Fig. 9.2. Now we use the class dictionary

```
Country = <has> RorSList.
RorS : Refrigerator | State.
State = <has> FamilyList.
Family =
   <owns> ThingList
   <members> Members
   <location> Location.
Members = .
Location = .
Thing : Kitchen | Chessboard.
Kitchen = <contains> Refrigerator.
Refrigerator = .
Chessboard = .
FamilyList ~ Family {Family}.
ThingList ~ Thing {Thing}.
RorSList ~ RorS {RorS}.
```

which is also shown in Fig. 9.6.

The propagation graph is in Fig. 9.7. In this example we have a violation of the delayed binding restriction because the alternation edge from **RorS** to **Refrigerator** is not in the propagation graph. Delayed binding will also print **Refrigerator**-objects, which are not contained in **Family**-objects. Two solutions can avoid the delayed binding restriction. Either the propagation pattern is split into two or the class structure is slightly changed.

As a second example, consider the class dictionary graph in Fig. 9.8 for the propagation directive

```
*from* A
  *via* K
*to* {X,Y}
```

If an X-object is in the b-part of A, it should not be traversed since the X-object is not a subobject of a K-object. But it will be traversed nevertheless because of late binding. Therefore, we disallow such customizers that create a propagation graph with "missing" alternation edges.

We give another example that discusses the delayed binding restriction from the information loss point of view. Two kinds of information loss play a role during adaptive

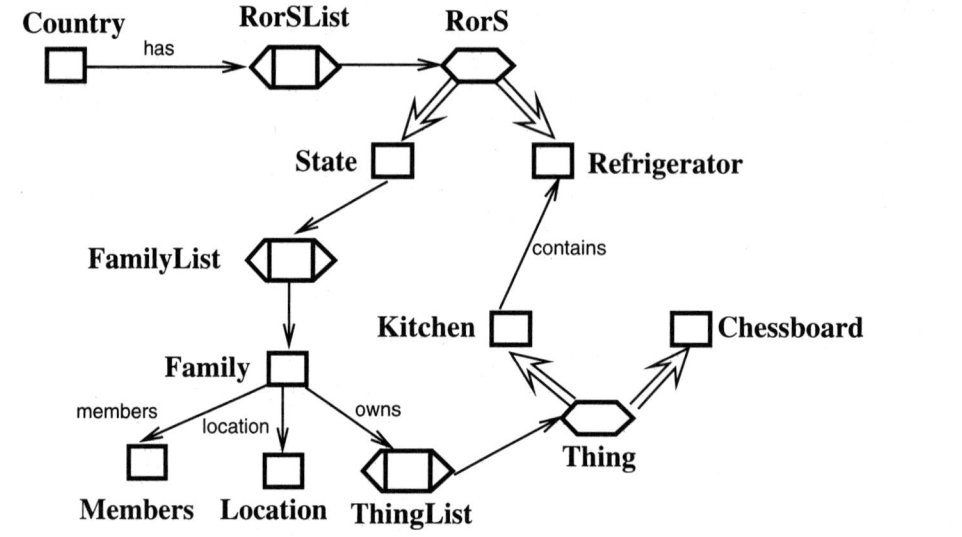

Figure 9.6: Delayed binding restriction violated

9.2. CUSTOMIZER RESTRICTIONS

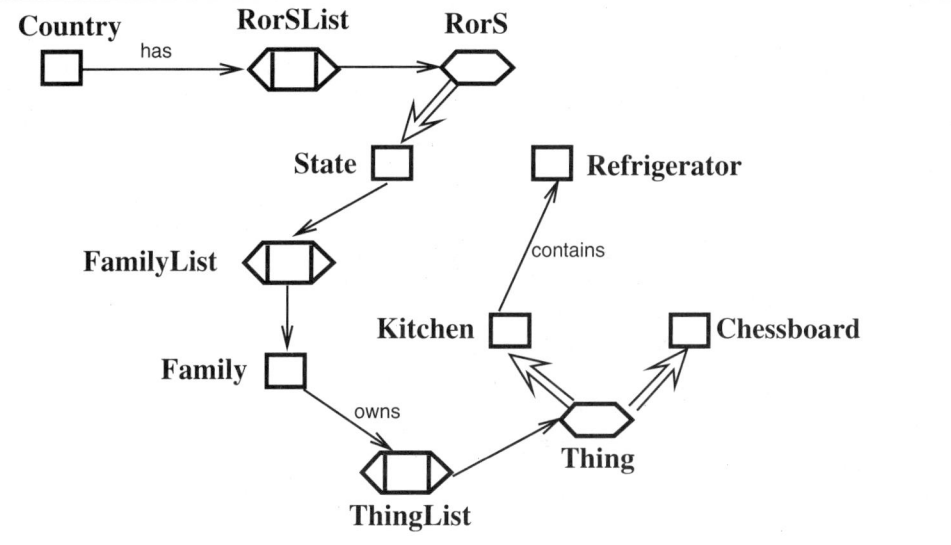

Figure 9.7: Propagation graph

```
A = B.
B : X | K.
C = X.
K = X Y.
X = "x".
Y = "y".
```

Figure 9.8: Bad customizer

software development. The first one, which we already discussed, is related to propagation directives. When knowledge paths are merged into a graph, new paths are introduced that are not allowed by the propagation directive. The second kind of information loss is related to delayed binding. There is an algorithm to test for both kinds of information loss and to appropriately inform the developer of adaptive software. (See Chapter 15.)

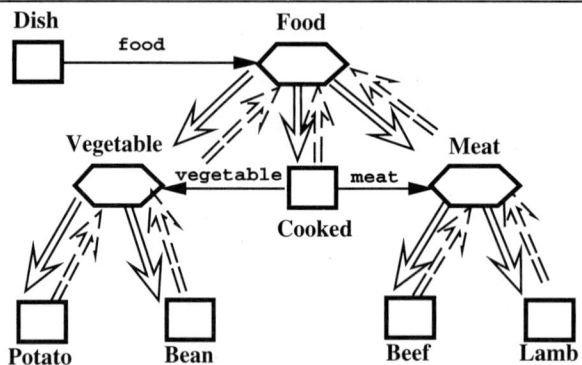

Figure 9.9: Class dictionary graph Dish

Consider the semi-class dictionary graph in Fig. 9.9. A dish may contain raw vegetables, raw meat, and cooked meat with some vegetables. There are two kinds of vegetables—potatoes and beans, and two kinds of meat—lamb and beef. We want to write a program that takes a dish and eats only cooked meat. First, we would like to write the propagation pattern in Fig. 9.10 to do the job. The corresponding C++ program is shown in Fig. 9.11.

```
*class-set* VM = {Vegetable, Meat};
  *operation* void eat()
    *traverse*
      *from* Dish
        *through* => Food, Cooked
      *to* *class-set* VM
    *wrapper* *class-set* VM
      *prefix* (@ this -> eat(); @)
```

Figure 9.10: A propagation pattern

In fact, the program will eat any food, whether it is raw or not. For example, class Vegetable is a subclass of class Food and method eat() of class Food is a virtual member function. If a piece of raw vegetable is in a dish, the program will eat it because of the late binding of methods eat() at run-time.

9.2. CUSTOMIZER RESTRICTIONS

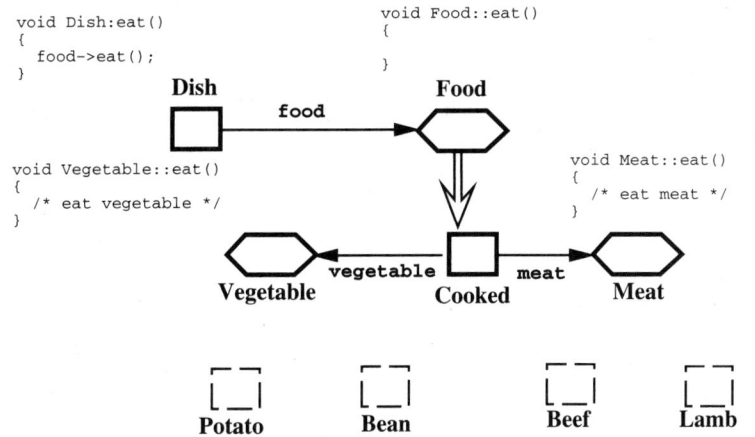

Figure 9.11: Propagation graph for eat/Dish

The **delayed binding restriction** enforces subclass invariance for the propagation graph with respect to the class dictionary graph and can be stated informally as follows. Any two vertices in the propagation graph have a subclass path between them if they do in the class dictionary graph. The formal definition is:

> For a propagation directive d and a semi-class dictionary graph S we compute the propagation graph $pg = propagate(d, S)$. There is a violation of the delayed binding restriction if there exist two vertices v and w such that v is used and v and w are in pg, but there is an alternation path from v to w which consists of alternation edges not in pg.

A vertex v is used in the propagation graph pg, if vertex v is a source vertex of the propagation directive d, or vertex v has at least one incoming alternation or construction edge.

It is straightforward to check such information loss due to delayed binding. To correct the information loss, the propagation pattern in Fig. 9.10 is decomposed into two propagation patterns with different signatures (see Fig. 9.12).

The information loss restriction (consistency restriction) and the delayed binding restriction (subclass invariance restriction) overlap in the sense that the information loss restriction already excludes cases that are also excluded by the delayed binding restriction. For an example see Fig. 9.13.

9.2.5 Inheritance Restriction

The purpose of the inheritance restriction is that there are no abandoned common parts. This restriction makes sure that there are enough inheritance edges in the propagation graph to guarantee that every alternation vertex in the propagation graph is on a completed knowledge path from a source to a target in the propagation graph.

```
*operation* void eat2()
  *traverse* *from* Dish *to* Cooked
  *wrapper* Cooked
    *prefix* (@ this -> eat_cooked(); @)
*operation* void eatCooked()
  *traverse*
    *from* Cooked *to* *class-set* VM
  *wrapper* *class-set* VM
    *prefix* (@ this -> eat(); @)
```

Figure 9.12: A propagation pattern

```
X = A.
A : D *common* B.
B : C | D.
C = A.
D = "d".

*operation* void f()
  *traverse*
    *from* X *via* C *to* D
  *wrapper* D
    *prefix*
      (@ cout << this; @)
```

Figure 9.13: Overlap of restrictions

The interpreter requires that an object is traversed based on information in the propagation graph. The propagation graph has to satisfy the inheritance restriction, otherwise there will be classes in the propagation graph whose objects are never visited.

The **inheritance restriction** requires:

If a nontarget alternation vertex has outgoing construction or inheritance edges, it must have at least one incoming inheritance edge.

In other words, if a nontarget vertex is contributing, it must have at least one incoming inheritance edge.

To motivate this customizer restriction, consider the following example:

```
Container = <fruit1> Fruit <fruit2> Apple.
Fruit : Apple | Orange *common* <w> Weight.
Apple = .
Orange = .
Weight = .

*operation* void f()
  *traverse*
    *from* Container
      *bypassing*
        :> Apple, Fruit,
        :> Orange, Fruit
    *to* {Apple, Weight}
  *wrapper* Weight
    *prefix* (@ cout << this; @)
```

The propagation graph is

```
Container = <fruit1> Fruit <fruit2> Apple.
Fruit : Apple *common* <w> Weight.
Apple = .
Weight = .
```

We note that the inheritance edge from **Apple** to **Fruit** is missing. In the propagation graph, **Fruit** is contributing. Therefore, **Fruit** should have an incoming inheritance edge. Since it does not, there is no completed knowledge path from **Container** to **Weight**. For no input, a **Weight**-object will be printed.

This is undesirable and therefore we exclude customizers that don't allow for completed knowledge paths from source to target.

9.3 PROPAGATION PATTERN PROPERTIES

The rules imply a unique operational semantics for propagation patterns. Together with the customizer restrictions, propagation patterns have many useful properties that are important for adaptive software development.

9.3.1 Alternation Property

If an alternation vertex in the propagation graph has no outgoing alternation edge in the propagation graph then there is no completed knowledge path that contains the alternation vertex. Therefore, the alternation vertex could not participate in a traversal. The inheritance and delayed binding restrictions imply the following property, which guarantees that every alternation vertex participates in a traversal.

> The **alternation property** requires that each used, nontarget vertex in a propagation graph has at least one outgoing alternation edge.

A vertex on a knowledge path from a source to a target vertex is used if it has incoming construction or alternation edges or if it is a source vertex. To motivate this customizer property, consider the following example:

```
Container = <fruit> Fruit.
Fruit : Apple *common* <w> Weight.
Apple = .
Weight = .

*operation* void f()
  *traverse*
    *from* Container
      *bypassing* => Fruit, Apple
    *to* {Weight}
  *wrapper* Weight
    *prefix* (@ cout << this; @)
```

The propagation graph consists only of

```
Container = <fruit> Fruit.
Fruit : *common* <w> Weight.
Weight = .
```

Unfortunately the only knowledge path contained in the propagation graph cannot be completed within the propagation graph. Therefore the interpreter TRAVERSE will not traverse any Fruit-object although the propagation directive allows such traversals. Therefore, customizers that violate the alternation property are disallowed.

9.3.2 Propagation Directive Satisfaction

We assume that the customizer restrictions hold. One of the primary objectives of a propagation pattern is to specify traversals of objects of a group of collaborating classes. When the code of those classes executes, objects will be traversed as specified in the directive of the propagation pattern.

In this section we will talk about class dictionary graphs and object graphs simultaneously. To avoid confusion, we use the following terminology:

9.3. PROPAGATION PATTERN PROPERTIES

```
Class Level
-----------
Graph              Object-oriented design

vertex             class
edge               relationship between classes
path               sequence of consecutive edges
                   derived class relationship


Object Level
------------
Graph              Object-oriented design

node               object
arc                binary relationship between objects
traversal          sequence of consecutive arcs
                   traversal of the object
```

A node in an object graph is a source node if it is an object of a source vertex of the propagation graph. A node in an object graph is a target node if it is an object of a target vertex of the propagation graph.

The traversals done by the interpreter TRAVERSE fall into two categories:

- Regular traversal

  A regular traversal from a source node to a target node of the object graph is a traversal going through propagation nodes only.

- Prematurely terminated traversal

  A prematurely terminated traversal is a traversal from a source node following zero or more propagation nodes and terminating in a nonpropagation node.

The concept of a completed knowledge path is important for defining properties of propagation patterns.

A completed knowledge path is a knowledge path from a source vertex to a target vertex of a propagation graph if all alternation vertices described here are followed by an outgoing alternation edge: any alternation vertex preceded by a construction or alternation edge on the path, and if the source vertex is an alternation vertex.

The traversals done by the interpreter TRAVERSE have the following important properties:

- Regular-completed

  If a class dictionary graph satisfies the customizer restrictions then every regular traversal is an instance of a completed knowledge path in the propagation graph. The completed knowledge path satisfies the propagation directive.

This follows essentially from the propagation directive information loss definition and the knowledge path instantiation definition: if there is no information loss then all completed knowledge paths that go from a source vertex to a target vertex of the propagation graph satisfy the directive.

- Completed-regular

  For every completed knowledge path in the propagation graph there is an object O so that TRAVERSE(O) makes a regular traversal, which is an instance of the knowledge path.

The two properties ensure that there is a one-to-one correspondence between regular traversals and completed knowledge paths.

This means that objects are properly traversed as defined in the propagation pattern. Consider the following propagation pattern:

```
*operation* void collect()
  *traverse*
    *from* A
      *via* K
    *to* {X, Y}
  *wrapper* {K, X, Y}
    *prefix* (@ this -> g_print(); @)
```

This propagation pattern should print all the K- and X- and Y-objects that are reachable from an A-object following the constraints expressed by the propagation directive. To define the constraints of a propagation directive at the object level, we use the concept of a traversal to be an instance of a knowledge path. A traversal is an instance of a knowledge path if the sequence of construction edges corresponding to the object graph arcs is a legal sequence with respect to the knowledge path. The knowledge path may contain additional edges.

More precisely, the meaning of the above propagation pattern is

For a given A-object print in preorder all objects of classes K, X, and Y that satisfy the following constraint: They are contained in an A-object along paths that are instances of the knowledge paths defined by the propagation directive.

For an object traversal starting from a source object of propagation directive d, the corresponding completed knowledge path p must satisfy one of the following rules:

- p satisfies d

- p is a prematurely terminated path

A knowledge path p is **prematurely terminated** if both of the following conditions hold:

- path p does not satisfy d

9.3. PROPAGATION PATTERN PROPERTIES

- after dropping the last vertex and its alternation predecessors from p, except the last one, the path can be extended to one satisfying d

For a given propagation directive, class dictionary graph, and corresponding propagation graph there are two possibilities: either there are prematurely terminated paths in the propagation graph or there are none. Both situations happen frequently. A good strategy when writing propagation patterns is to make them independent of the existence of prematurely terminated paths.

Instead of writing

```
*from* Person *to* Salary
*wrapper* Person
  *prefix*  (@ cout << "salary updated"; @)
*wrapper* Salary
  *prefix*  (@ this -> christmas_bonus(); @)
```

it is better to write

```
*from* Person *to* Salary
*wrapper* Person
*wrapper* Salary
  *prefix*  (@ this -> christmas_bonus(); @)
  *suffix*  (@ cout << "salary updated"; @)
```

The second solution has the advantage that it will also behave properly if a person does not have a salary part. Nothing will be done in this case for the second solution.

An example of premature path termination is shown by the following propagation directive and class dictionary graph:

```
*from* A *via* B *to* E

A = <b> B.
B : C | D.
C = E.
E = .
D : F | G.
F = .
G = .
```

B has one alternative outside the propagation graph. An A-object with a F-part leads to a prematurely terminated traversal (which is considered acceptable). We have the prematurely terminated path A, B, D, F. After deleting D and F from the path, the path can be completed to A, B, C, E, which satisfies the propagation directive.

Propagation graph satisfaction means that the traversed object paths are permitted by the propagation graph. For every traversed object path, the corresponding knowledge path is in the propagation graph (unless it is prematurely terminated). For example,

```
*operation* void f()
  *traverse*
    *from* A
      // constraint
    *to* Z
  *wrapper* Z
    *prefix* (@ cout << this; @)
```

prints at least all Z-objects that are reachable along object paths satisfying the constraint.

Constraint satisfaction means that for every object path traversed, there must exist a knowledge path in the class dictionary graph that satisfies the constraint so that the object path is an instance of the knowledge path.

9.3.3 Propagation Graph Properties

A propagation graph for a class dictionary graph has two kinds of outgoing alternation edges exiting from the propagation graph to the class dictionary graph.

- To nonpropagation vertices

  Such an alternation edge leads to a prematurely terminated traversal at the object level.

- To propagation vertices (i.e., vertices associated with a target vertex)

  Such alternation edges lead to a regular traversal at the object level.

9.3.4 Consistent Ordering

When writing a program that finds all B-objects properly contained in an A-object, we expect that the prefix wrapper of A is executed before the prefix wrapper of B. Such a local ordering property is useful for reasoning about the ordering of wrapper executions.

When an object edge from an A-object to a B-object is traversed, the activation of the wrappers of A and B and of the construction edge on the path from A to B is *always* done in the same order, independent of the customizer used.

More precisely, for the propagation pattern

```
*operation* void f()
  *traverse*
    *from* A
      *through* ->*,b,*
    *to* B
  *wrapper* A
    *prefix* (@ cout << " pA "; @)
    *suffix* (@ cout << " sA "; @)
  *wrapper* B
    *prefix* (@ cout << " pB "; @)
    *suffix* (@ cout << " sB "; @)
  *wrapper* -> *,b,*
```

9.3. PROPAGATION PATTERN PROPERTIES

```
*prefix* (@ cout << " pCE-b "; @)
*suffix* (@ cout << " sCE-b "; @)
```

the wrappers are always called in the following order (also see Fig. 9.14; the wrappers are called in order 1 through 6):

pA < pCE-b < pB < sB < sCE-b < sA

This will be guaranteed by any compatible customizer. p-CE stands for prefix wrapper of a construction edge. s-CE stands for suffix wrapper of a construction edge.

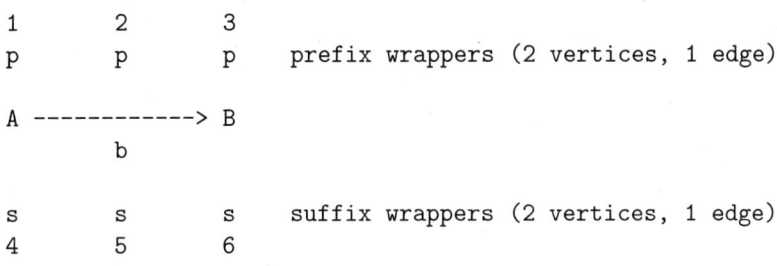

Figure 9.14: Ordering of wrapper calls

pA and pB are prefix wrappers for vertices A and B. pCE-b is a prefix wrapper for the construction edge labeled b. sA, sB, and sCE-b are corresponding suffix wrappers.

9.3.5 Robustness Under Class Dictionary Transformations

Robustness is an important property for the evolution of customized adaptive software. When we have a customized program running and we make a small change to the class dictionary, we don't want to have the behavior of the program changed in a big way.

Propagation patterns are robust in the following way. If a propagation pattern is applied to two class dictionaries that both define the same objects with the same ordering for part objects, and if the propagation pattern is compatible with both class dictionaries, then the activation of the wrappers is identical for both object-oriented programs when they execute on the same object.

Robustness essentially means that the calling order of customized adaptive programs is invariant under order-preserving, object-equivalent changes to the customizer. Of course, we make the assumption that the object-equivalent customizers that we consider are also compatible with the propagation pattern. For example, flattening of common parts should not change the sequence of wrapper calls as demonstrated in the example below.

Consider the following propagation pattern that will be customized by two object-equivalent class dictionaries.

```
*operation* void f()
  *traverse*
    *from* Ex *to* Common

    *wrapper* Base
      *prefix*
        (@ cout << " pBase " ; @)
      *suffix*
        (@ cout << " sBase " ; @)

    *wrapper* Derived
      *prefix*
        (@ cout << " pDerived " ; @)
      *suffix*
        (@ cout << " sDerived " ; @)

    *wrapper* Common
      *prefix*
        (@ cout << " pCommon " ; @)

    *wrapper* -> *,q,*
      *prefix*
        (@ cout << " pCE-q" ; @)
      *suffix*
        (@ cout << " sCE-q" ; @)
```

Next we show two object-equivalent customizers:

```
Ex = <r> Base.
Base : Derived .
Derived = "derived" <q> Common.
Common = "common".

Ex = <r> Base.
Base : Derived *common* <q> Common.
Derived = "derived".
Common = "common".
```

When we run both resulting programs on the object:

```
: Ex (
   < r > : Derived (
      < q > : Common ( ) ) )
```

`derived common`

we get the following output for both customizers:

```
pBase
pDerived
pCE-q
pCommon
sCE-q
sDerived
sBase
```

9.3.6 Access Independence

Independent of where a propagation starts, for an instance of class D, the wrappers of class D are activated in the same sequence when a D-object is traversed.

For example, D-objects may appear as named parts of a construction class or as elements of a heterogeneous list. In the following example we have D-objects in two different parts.

```
A = <c> C.
B = <d> D.
C : D *common* <e> E.
D = <e2> E.

*operation* void f()
  *traverse*
    *from* {A,B}
      *via* D
    *to* E
  *wrapper* C
    *prefix* (@ cout << " pC "; @)
  *wrapper* D
    *prefix* (@ cout << " pD "; @)
  *wrapper* -> *,e2,*
    *prefix* (@ cout << " pCE-e2 "; @)
```

Independent of whether an instance of class D is in the c or d part, the wrappers are called in the same order: pC, pD, pCE-e2, ...

9.3.7 Method Selection Rule

Propagation patterns with a traversal directive support a special kind of delayed binding: choose one of many alternatives. It is a special kind of delayed binding since no overriding is allowed. Overriding is expressed with propagation patterns without a traversal directive. The method selection takes place because in a part, we can have only objects that are instances of classes associated with the part class. For example,

```
*operation* void select()
  *traverse*
    *from* A
    *to* {B,C} // B,C are construction classes
```

```
                // which are alternation-reachable from A
*wrapper* {B,C}
  *prefix* (@ this -> visit(); @)
```

If the A-object is a B-object, the wrapper of B is called. If the A-object is a C-object, the wrapper of C is called.

9.3.8 Split Alternation Class

Alternation classes have wrappers and parts, and the activation of the two is treated separately. Between the call of a wrapper of an alternation class and the traversal of the parts of the alternation class, other code may be called.

For example, for the class dictionary graph in Fig. 9.15 and the propagation pattern

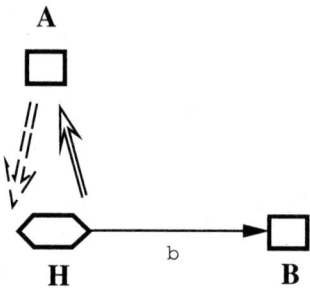

Figure 9.15: Class dictionary graph

```
*operation* void f()
  *traverse*
    *from* A
      *through* -> *,b,*
    *to* B
  *wrapper* A
    *prefix* (@ cout << " pA "; @)
  *wrapper* H
    *prefix* (@ cout << " pH "; @)
  *wrapper* -> *,b,*
    *prefix* (@ cout << " pCE-b "; @)
```

the wrappers are called in the order

pH
pA
pCE-b

The prefix wrapper of A is called between the wrappers of class H. There could be much more in between: if A has parts, they would be traversed first.

9.3.9 Symmetry

Prefix and suffix wrappers are called symmetrically. If the prefix wrapper of classes A and B are called in the order A, B, then the suffix wrappers are called in the order B, A.

For example, consider the class dictionary graph in Fig. 9.16, and the propagation

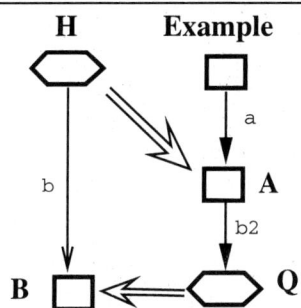

Figure 9.16: Class dictionary graph

```
pattern
*operation* DemString_List* test()
  *init* (@ new DemString_List() @)
  *traverse* *from* Example *to* B
  *wrapper* A
    *prefix* (@ return_val -> append(new DemString("pA")); @)
    *suffix* (@ return_val -> append(new DemString("sA")); @)
  *wrapper* H
    *prefix* (@ return_val -> append(new DemString("pH")); @)
    *suffix* (@ return_val -> append(new DemString("sH")); @)
  *wrapper* B
    *prefix* (@ return_val -> append(new DemString("pB")); @)
    *suffix* (@ return_val -> append(new DemString("sB")); @)
  *wrapper* -> *,b,*
    *prefix* (@ return_val -> append(new DemString("pCE-b")); @)
    *suffix* (@ return_val -> append(new DemString("sCE-b")); @)
  *wrapper* -> *,b2,*
    *prefix* (@ return_val -> append(new DemString("pCE-b2")); @)
    *suffix* (@ return_val -> append(new DemString("sCE-b2")); @)
      On input
Example(
  <a> A(
    <b> B()
    <b2> B())))
```

the output is (we show the derivation of the order in terms of the rules in comments)

```
// derivation
// pH < pA (prefix-super-sub)
("pH", "pA" ,
// pCE-b2 < pCE-b (immediate-first)
// pA < CE-b2 < pB (consistent-ordering)
// sB < sCE-b2 < sA (consistent-ordering)
"pCE-b2" , "pB" , "sB" , "sCE-b2" ,
// H < CE-b < B (consistent-ordering)
// sB < sCE-b < sA (consistent-ordering)
"pCE-b" , "pB" , "sB" , "sCE-b" ,
// sA < sH (suffix-sub-super)
"sA" , "sH" )
```

9.3.10 No Wrapper Shadowing

If a wrapper of class A is executed then all the wrappers of alternation predecessors of A (in the propagation graph) will be called.

Propagation patterns with a traversal specification employ incremental inheritance. There is no room for overriding of wrappers. If overriding inheritance for wrappers is needed, a propagation pattern without a traversal directive is used.

It is worth mentioning that shadowing for the purpose of traversal is possible.

Consider the propagation directive

```
*merge*(
  *from* Basket *to* Apple,
  *from* Basket *via* Orange *to* Weight)
```

This directive is useful for printing the weight of all orange objects and all information about apple objects. For the class dictionary graph

```
Container = <fruit> List(Fruit).
Fruit : Apple | Orange *common* <w> Weight.
Apple = .
Orange = .
Weight = <v> DemNumber.
```

we will traverse the weight-part of Orange-objects but not the weight-part of Apple-objects. So overriding for the purpose of traversal is possible.

9.3.11 Customizer Analysis

A given object edge can be an instance of one of five distinct knowledge path kinds. Consider an object edge from some object belonging to class A to some object belonging to class B. A and B are not necessarily construction classes; they may be alternation classes.

This object edge can be an instance of five different knowledge path kinds which we discuss in turn. We talk about knowledge path kinds since an alternation or inheritance edge may be replaced by several alternation or inheritance edges in the following discussion.

9.3. PROPAGATION PATTERN PROPERTIES

For all five cases we show the wrapper execution sequence. Since prefix and suffix wrappers are called symmetrically, it is sufficient to focus on the prefix wrappers. A prefix wrapper is described by the name of the class. For example, A B means that the wrappers are called in the following order: the prefix wrapper of A, the prefix wrapper of B, the suffix wrapper of B, the suffix wrapper of A.

We use CE-b to describe the wrapper of construction edge with label b. B may be a construction or an alternation class. The five class dictionary graphs are summarized in Fig. 9.17.

1. Knowledge path: only construction edge.

    A = <b> B. or A : *common* <b> B.

    A   CE-b   B

2. Knowledge path: alternation-construction

    A : H.
    H = <b> B.

    wrapper execution sequence

    A H CE-b B

3. Knowledge path: construction-alternation

    A = <b> H.
    H : B.

    wrapper execution sequence

    A CE-b H B

4. Knowledge path: inheritance-construction

    A = (*inherit* H). or A : *common* (*inherit* H).
    H : *common* <b> B.

    wrapper execution sequence

    H A CE-b B

5. Knowledge path: alternation-inheritance-construction

    A : H *common* <b> B.
    H = (*inherit* A).

    wrapper execution sequence

    A H CE-b B

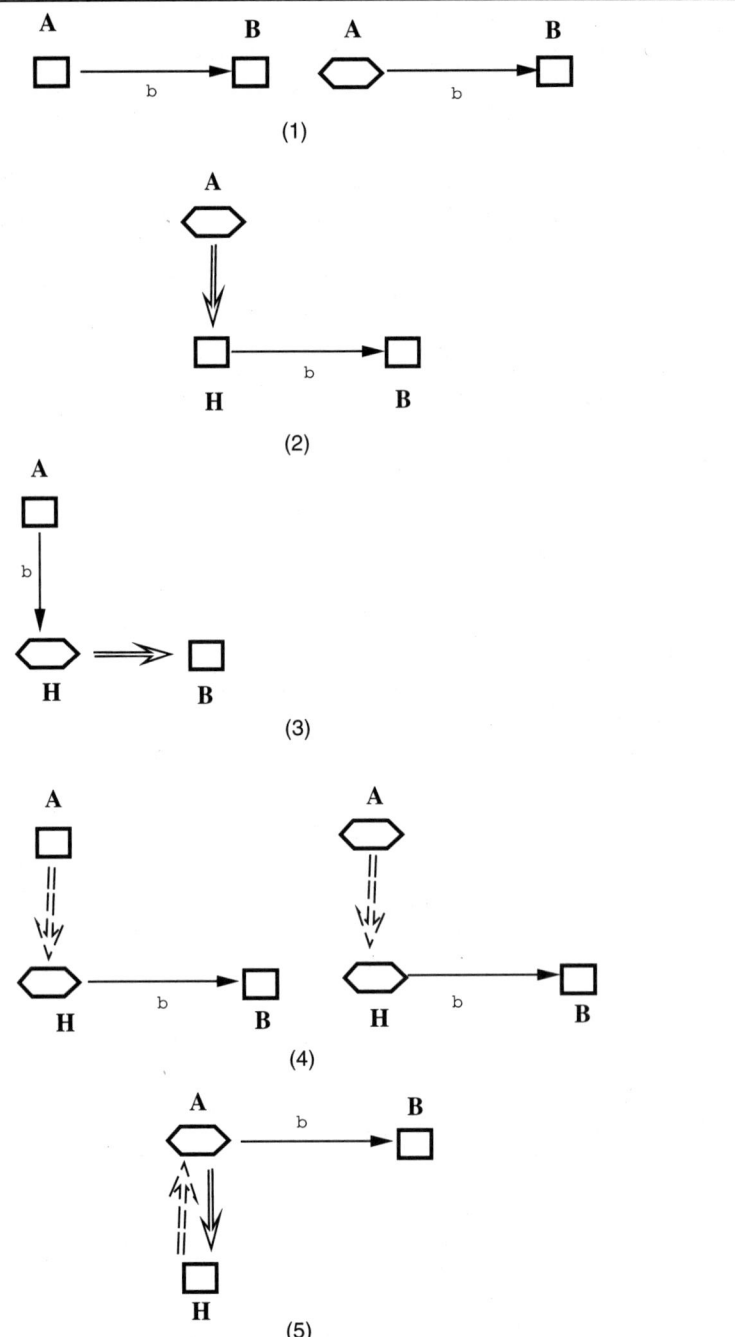

Figure 9.17: Knowledge paths for object path

9.4 OBJECT-ORIENTED IMPLEMENTATION

We summarize approaches to the translation of a propagation graph into C++ member functions. Two important possibilities are flat code generation[3] and nonflat code generation. Flat code generation flattens the propagation graph before the code is produced. This produces larger code, but it is very easy to understand.

Nonflat code generation does not flatten the propagation graph before code generation, and there are several ways to optimize the generated code. A straightforward way to nonflat code generation is to translate every inheritance edge into a call to the superclass.

We first assume that vertex wrappers are attached only to construction vertices and show the translation of a propagation graph into C++.

- Flat code generation

    The following rules govern the flat code generation (flat, no alternation wrappers).

    ```
    function definitions: edge

        Demeter            C++

        construction       call to parts
          optional           if statement
        repetition         call to parts (loop)
        alternation        late binding (virtual function)

        does a wrapper exist for a construction edge?
          yes: wrap around edge traversal code

    function definitions: vertex

        does a wrapper exist for vertex?
          no : use traversal code
          yes: wrap around vertex traversal code
    ```

- Nonflat code generation

    For nonflat code generation (nonflat, no alternation wrappers) there is one important additional rule:

    ```
        inheritance        call to super
                             for traversal only
    ```

    In addition, empty methods need to be generated as discussed in the following section on exiting alternation edges.

---
[3]Propagation pattern partial evaluation, page 448 (64).

To give an explanation of how propagation patterns work, we consider an example of a class dictionary graph that uses all features of the class dictionary graph notation and a simple propagation pattern, and then we show the generated code for nonflat code generation.

The code is produced in two steps. First a propagation graph is produced by computing all knowledge paths from the source to the targets. The resulting propagation graph is translated into the program according to the propagation graph translation rules.

The application is about creating a patchwork quilt by using a set of primitive designs that may be turned and sown together. We use the following propagation directive:

```
*operation* void traverse()
  *traverse*
    *from* Patchwork
      *to* Measure
  // no wrappers
```

The class dictionary graph is given in Figs. 9.18 and 9.19.

```
Patchwork =
  <primitives> PrimitiveExp_List
  <pattern> PatchworkExp.
PatchworkExp :
  PrimitiveExp | TurnExp | SewExp
  *common*
    [<length> Measure]
    [<width> Measure].
Measure = <v> DemNumber.
PrimitiveExp = <patternName> Name.
Name = <v> DemIdent.
TurnExp = <arg1> PatchworkExp .
SewExp  = <arg1> PatchworkExp <arg2> PatchworkExp .
PrimitiveExp_List ~ {PrimitiveExp}.
```

Figure 9.18: Patchwork class dictionary, textual

The propagation graph is given in Fig. 9.20. It is almost the original class dictionary graph. The generated C++ code is in Fig. 9.21.

9.4.1 Exiting Alternation Edges

This section applies only to nonflat code generation. It may be skipped. An exiting alternation edge is an alternation edge that exits the propagation graph. There are two kinds of exiting alternation edges:

9.4. OBJECT-ORIENTED IMPLEMENTATION

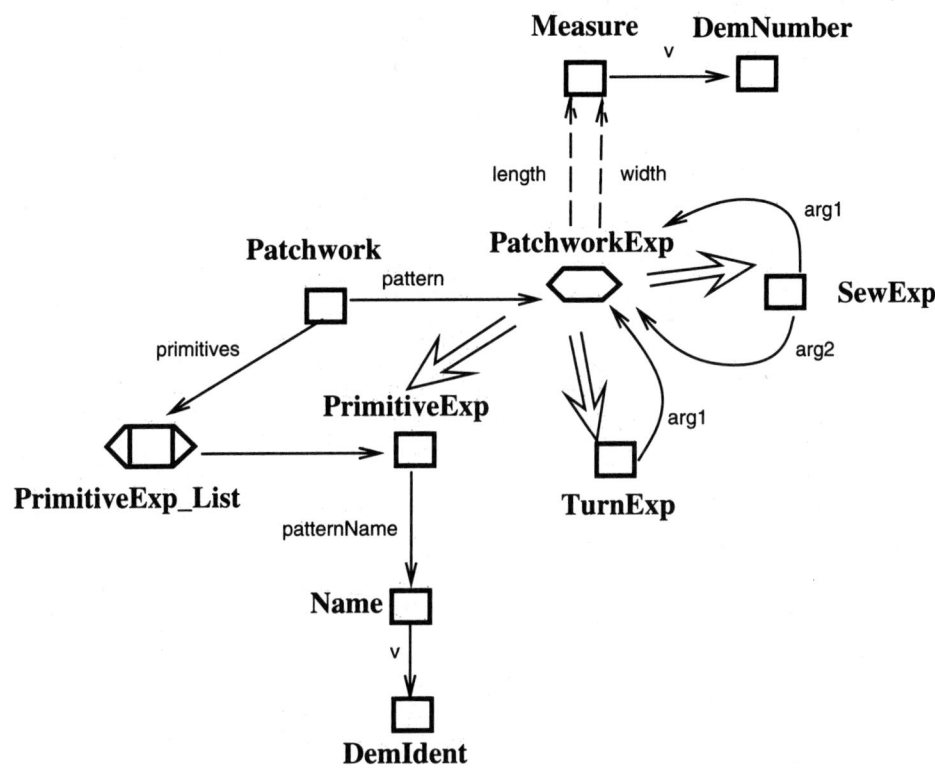

Figure 9.19: Patchwork class dictionary, graphical

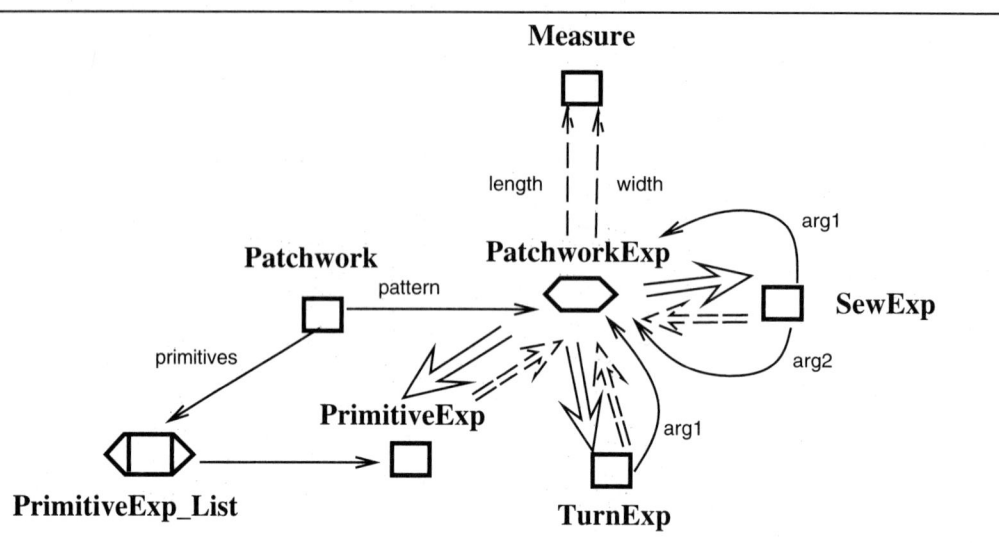

Figure 9.20: Propagation graph

- The target of the exiting edge is a vertex associated with a target vertex of the propagation directive.

  This means that the target is an alternation successor of a target vertex of the propagation directive.

- The target is a nonpropagation vertex.

  This means that the target is an alternation successor of an inner vertex of the propagation graph. An empty method is produced for the target vertex as described below.

This issue of code generation of empty methods is not covered by the patchwork example and will be addressed with another example. Propagation patterns define code for class structures and when those class structures contain inheritance then we have to distinguish between two kinds of classes: classes that get code defined directly and classes that get code defined through inheritance. This can cause unintended behavior in propagation patterns unless we limit the influence of the inheritance relations. Consider the semi-class dictionary graph in Fig. 9.23 and the propagation pattern in Fig. 9.22. The intention of this propagation pattern is to access only the `Maker`-objects belonging to some `HeavyTruck`-objects. This only works if classes `Car`, `Jeep`, and `LightTruck` do not inherit the code from class `Vehicle`. Otherwise, the propagation pattern has the same effect as the one in Fig. 9.22 if the *via* `HeavyTruck` clause is omitted.

This would be undesirable since we lost the information that the path is forced through `HeavyTruck`. Therefore the following rule, called the **empty-methods-rule**, is used for code generation:

9.4. OBJECT-ORIENTED IMPLEMENTATION

```
void Patchwork::traverse(){
    // <primitives> PrimitiveExp_List
    primitives->traverse();
    // <pattern> PatchworkExp
    pattern->traverse(); }

void PatchworkExp::traverse(){
    //[ < length > Measure ]
    if( length )
        length->traverse();
    //[ < width > Measure ]
    if( width )
        width->traverse(); }

void PrimitiveExp::traverse(){
    this->PatchworkExp::traverse(); }

void TurnExp::traverse(){
    // <arg1> PatchworkExp
    arg1->traverse();
    this->PatchworkExp::traverse(); }

void SewExp::traverse(){
    // <arg1> PatchworkExp
    arg1->traverse();
    // <arg2> PatchworkExp
    arg2->traverse();
    this->PatchworkExp::traverse(); }

void PrimitiveExp_List::traverse(){
        PrimitiveExp_list_iterator next_arg(*this);
        PrimitiveExp* each_arg;
        while ( each_arg = next_arg() )
            each_arg->traverse(); }

void Measure::traverse(){ }
```

Figure 9.21: Traversal code

```
*component* empty_methods
  *customizers*
    // terminals between " and " should be ignored.
    // this is external representation information
    // and will be explained later.
    CarDealer = <vehicles> List(Vehicle).
    List(S) ~ "(" {S} ")".
    Vehicle : Car | Jeep | Truck *common*
      <maker> Maker <price> DemNumber.
    Maker = <name> DemIdent.
    Truck : LightTruck | HeavyTruck.
    Car = "car".
    Jeep = "jeep".
    LightTruck = "light" "truck".
    HeavyTruck = "heavy" "truck".

  *operation* void report_HT()
    *traverse*
      *from* CarDealer
        *via*  HeavyTruck
      *to* Maker
    *wrapper* Vehicle
      *prefix*
        (@ cout << "Price" << this -> get_price(); @)
    *wrapper* Maker
      *prefix*
        (@ cout << "Make" << this -> get_name(); @)
*end* empty_methods
```

Figure 9.22: Coping with unintended inheritance

9.4. OBJECT-ORIENTED IMPLEMENTATION

For every alternation class C in a propagation graph such that there is at least one immediate subclass of class C not in the propagation graph, all the immediate subclasses of class C which are contained in the original graph but not in the propagation graph, get an empty operation generated.

A target class is a class used in the **to** clause in a propagation directive.

A shorter, equivalent formulation is

Every nonpropagation vertex with an incoming alternation edge exiting the propagation graph gets an empty method generated.

In the above example, classes Car, Jeep, and LightTruck will each get an empty method generated (see Fig. 9.24). Therefore, the information about cars, jeeps, and light trucks will not be reported.

With empty methods attached to classes Car, Jeep, and LightTruck, the program in Fig. 9.24 describes the same semantics described by the propagation pattern in Fig. 9.22.

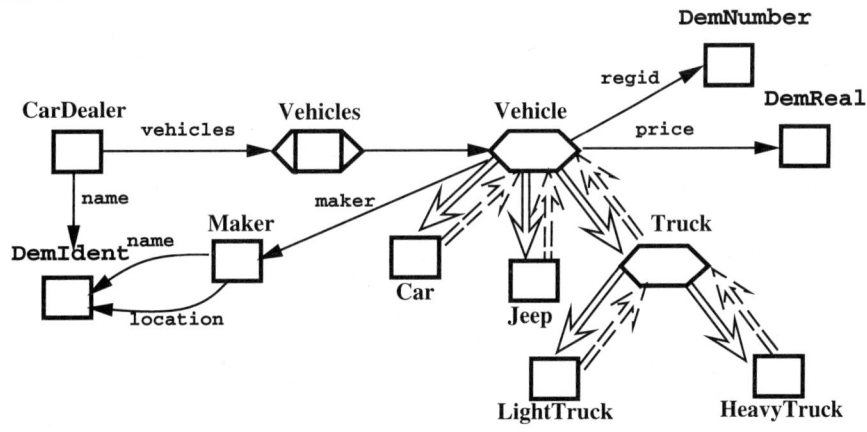

Figure 9.23: Car dealer semi-class dictionary graph with traversal code

9.4.2 Wrapper Pushing

When a wrapper is attached to an alternation class A it needs to be properly called when an instance of an associated class of A is traversed. One convenient implementation pushes the wrapper to the associated classes.

Consider the example in Fig. 9.25. If there is a wrapper at class Family, it will be pushed to class Urban.

Wrapper pushing is best described in terms of an extended flattening operation. Instead of flattening only all the common parts, the wrappers are also flattened. The prefix wrappers are concatenated in the the same order as the common parts would be concatenated. The suffix wrappers are concatenated in the opposite order.

If a class A has two wrapper specifications

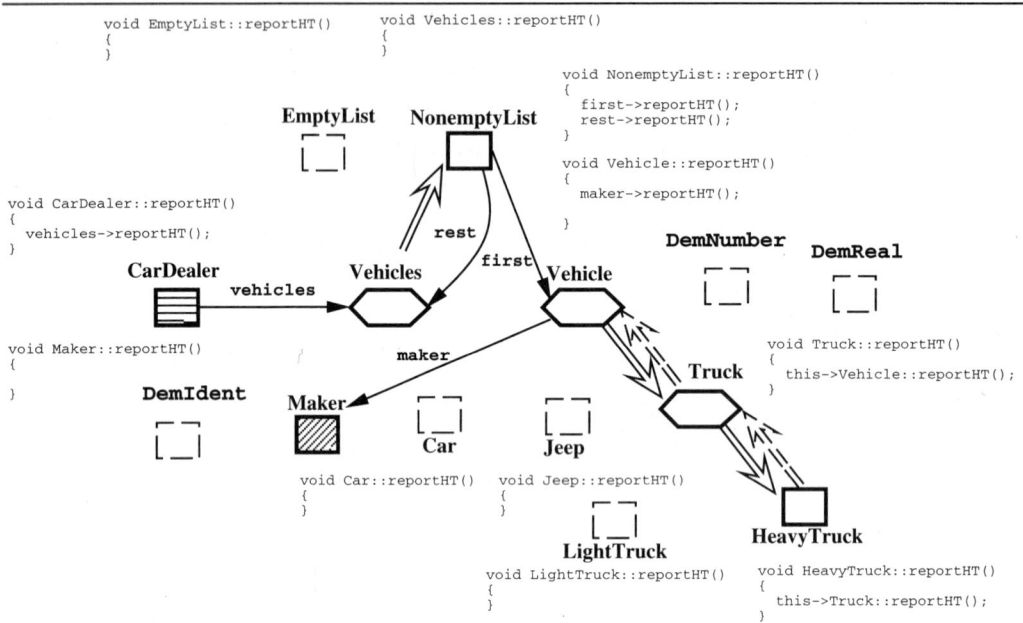

Figure 9.24: Propagation graph for car dealer semi-class dictionary graph

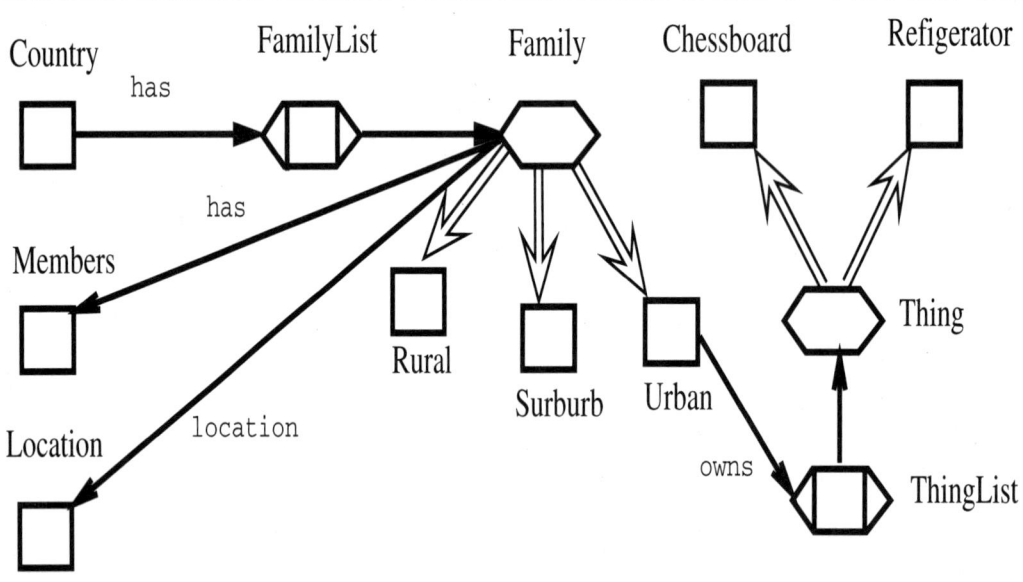

Figure 9.25: Wrapper pushing

9.4. OBJECT-ORIENTED IMPLEMENTATION

```
*wrapper* A
  *prefix* (@ pA1(); @)
  *suffix* (@ sA1(); @)

*wrapper* A
  *prefix* (@ pA2(); @)
  *suffix* (@ sA2(); @)
```

then the order is the same as if only the following wrapper were used

```
*wrapper* A
  *prefix* (@ pA1(); pA2(); @)
  *suffix* (@ sA2(); sA1(); @)
```

Multiple wrapper specifications for the same class are useful. Sometimes the same traversal implements two simple tasks, each with its own set of wrappers that might be defined for overlapping classes.

9.4.3 Propagation Patterns with Return Types

The operation signature may also use a return type: If we want to return an object of class R, we use

```
*operation* R* f() *init* (@ ... @)
```

As usual, we put all objects into the heap (free-store). Therefore, the * is used after R to indicate that we return a pointer to an object.

If we want to return an integer, for example, we use

```
*operation* int f() *init* (@ ... @)
```

This means that a variable called return_val will be defined throughout the traversal and may be used to accumulate information during the traversal. When the traversal is complete, the value of this variable will be returned. The variable may be initialized by the expression after the init keyword.

Let's compare propagation patterns with and without a return type. First we show a propagation pattern and associated code with return type and then without return type. As the customizing class dictionary we use

```
Basket = <contents> Apple_List.
Apple_List : Empty | Nonempty.
Empty = .
Nonempty = <first> Apple <rest> Apple_List.
Apple = "apple".

Refrigerator = "refrigerator".
```

The propagation pattern with return type is

```
*operation* int f1(Refrigerator* r)
    *init* (@ 0 @)
  *traverse*
    *from* Basket *to* Apple
    *wrapper* Apple
      *prefix*
        (@ r-> g_print(); return_val = return_val + 1; @)
```

The corresponding object-oriented program is

```
int Basket::f1( Refrigerator*   r   )
{ int return_val =   0 ;
  this->f1_( return_val, r   );
  return return_val; }

void Basket::f1_( int& return_val, Refrigerator*   r   )
{ contents ->f1_( return_val, r   ); }

void Apple_List::f1_( int& return_val, Refrigerator*   r   )
{ }

void Empty::f1_( int& return_val, Refrigerator*   r   )
{ }

void Nonempty::f1_( int& return_val, Refrigerator*   r   )
{ first ->f1_( return_val, r   );
  rest ->f1_( return_val, r   ); }

void Apple::f1_( int& return_val, Refrigerator*   r   )
{ r-> g_print(); return_val = return_val + 1; }
```

The propagation pattern without a return type is

```
*operation* void f2(Refrigerator* r)
  *traverse*
    *from* Basket *to* Apple
    *wrapper* Apple
      *prefix*
        (@ r-> g_print(); @)
```

The corresponding object-oriented code is

```
void Basket::f2( Refrigerator*   r   )
{ contents ->f2( r   ); }

void Apple_List::f2( Refrigerator*   r   )
```

```
{ }

void Empty::f2( Refrigerator*  r )
{ }

void Nonempty::f2( Refrigerator*  r )
{ first ->f2( r );
  rest ->f2( r ); }

void Apple::f2( Refrigerator*  r )
{ r-> g_print(); }
```

Operations f1 and f2 are analogous. They do the same work except that f1 also counts. The analogy is clearly reflected in the generated code. For f1 one additional function is created, called an initialization function. This function simply initializes the count and then calls the auxiliary function f1_. A one-to-one relationship exists between the functions with name f1_ and f2.

The reason why the function name f1_ and not f1 is used in the generated code is to hide the auxiliary functions. They are there to do the task of the propagation pattern and should not be called explicitly. The code generation rule implies that operation names should not end in _ to avoid conflicts.

The above example implies the following rule for working with wrappers. If the operation has a nonvoid return type, the body of the wrapper may use a variable **return_val** which is defined in the initalization function. The variable **return_val** is used to accumulate the return value of the operation. For a function with a void return type, variable **return_val** is not available.

It is very important that the meaning of wrappers is almost the same whether we have a nonvoid or a void return type. The reason is that with wrappers for operations with a void return type we can easily construct software by using several prefix and suffix wrappers. For operations with a nonvoid return type we want to do the same.

Imagine what would happen if we would implement f1 as

```
int Basket::f1( Refrigerator*  r)
{ return contents ->f1( r ); }

int Apple_List::f1( Refrigerator*  r)
{ return (0);}

int Nonempty::f1( Refrigerator*  r)
{
  return (first ->f1(r) + rest ->f1(r)); }

int Apple::f1( Refrigerator*  r)
{ r-> g_print(); return (1); }
```

This is considered good programming style by most programming communities, but it is not satisfactory from a reusability point of view. If we want to do some post processing for any of the classes, we could not write a suffix wrapper. Therefore, the return_val solution used by propagation patterns is much better and fosters unplanned software reuse.

9.5 SUMMARY

The traversal meaning of a propagation pattern, a customizing class dictionary graph, and an object on which the propagation pattern is invoked is controlled by a small set of rules:

```
pure-traversal
  only-subobject
  part-ordering
     immediate-first
     cdg-order
wrapper
  class
    prefix-parts-suffix
    extension
       prefix-super-sub
       suffix-sub-super
    pp-order-class
  edge
    prefix-edge-suffix
    pp-order-edge
```

There are a few unlikely situations where the rules don't create the right behavior. Since the situations are unlikely, we introduce customizer restrictions that exclude those situations.

The rules, together with the customizer restrictions imply a number of useful and interesting properties for propagation patterns.

```
propagation directive satisfaction
method selection
consistent ordering
access independence
symmetry
robustness
alternation class split
no wrapper shadowing
customizer analysis
```

An object-oriented implementation is introduced that satisfies the rules and properties discussed above. The implementation flattens the propagation graph and then generates code according to the following rules. All vertices in the propagation graph get a method. The bodies of the methods are determined by

- A construction edge in the propagation graph is translated to a call for the part.

9.5. SUMMARY

- An edge wrapper inserts code into the body of the method of the source of the edge. The prefix wrapper goes before the part call, the suffix wrapper goes after the part call.

- For an alternation vertex, which is not alternation-reachable from a target vertex, the body contains a statement: print "prematurely terminated path."

- Wrappers of alternation classes are pushed into the construction subclasses.

A method of an alternation vertex is virtual.

9.5.1 The Flat Demeter Method

The Demeter Method with its generality with semi-class dictionary graphs, knowledge paths, completed knowledge paths, etc. can be intimidating to a new user. We get a useful, very simple method, called the flat Demeter Method, if we make the following assumption:

> When we work with propagation directives we think in terms of flattened class dictionary graphs although we might present them in unflattened form for easier comprehension.

The flattening operation has to be learned anyway for understanding the object structure and for understanding the language structure defined by a class dictionary. Thinking in terms of flattened class dictionary graphs means that the inheritance edges disappear. This means that we get a method where we do the work with class dictionary graphs, eliminating the semi-class dictionary graphs. With the inheritance edges gone, we lose some of the expressiveness, but the lost expressiveness does not seem to be important for many applications

- We can no longer mention inheritance edges in propagation patterns.

- We get additional customizer restrictions:
    - we cannot use a customizer for which a propagation directive forces an inheritance edge. For example, *from* Apple *via* Fruit *to* Weight cannot be used together with

    `Fruit : Apple *common* Weight`

    - we cannot use customizers that attach wrappers to superfluous alternation classes after the flattening. An alternation class is superfluous if it is not contributing and not used.

- Construction edges should be written in the form

    `-> *,b,C`

    because if we write them in the form

    `-> A,b,C`

and A is an alternation class, the edge no longer exists after flattening.

The important benefit of the flat Demeter Method is that we need to learn fewer and simpler concepts; for example, we can work without semi-class dictionary graphs, knowledge paths, completed knowledge paths, etc. A summary of the flat Demeter Method is in Chapter 15.

9.6 EXERCISES

Exercise 9.1 Consider the following.

```
------------------------------
 Class Dictionary
------------------------------
      1   Example = <a1> A1.
      2   A1 : B.
      3   B = <c> C <h> H.
      4   D1 : C *common* <e> E.
      5   C = .
      6   E = <f> F <h> H.
      7   G1 : F *common* <g> G.
      8   F = .
      9   G = <h> H.
     10   H = .


------------------------------------------
 Alphabetically Sorted Cross Reference List
------------------------------------------
A1         :2      1
B          :3      2
C          :5      3       4
D1         :4
E          :6      4
Example            :1
F          :8      6       7
G          :9      7
G1         :7
H          :10     3       6       9
```

Find the unknowns in the following object. It corresponds to the empty sentence.

```
: Example (
   < UNKNOWN1 > : UNKNOWN2 (
      < UNKNOWN3 > : UNKNOWN4 (
         < UNKNOWN5 > : UNKNOWN6 (
            < UNKNOWN7 > : UNKNOWN8 (
               < UNKNOWN9 > : UNKNOWN10 (
```

9.6. EXERCISES

```
            < UNKNOWN11 > : H ( ) ) )
         < UNKNOWN12 > : UNKNOWN13 ( ) ) )
     < UNKNOWN14 > : H ( ) ) )
```

Find the unknowns in the following propagation pattern and corresponding C++ program.

Propagation pattern:

```
*operation* void fun()
  *traverse*
    *from* Example *via* E *to* H
  *wrapper* H
    *prefix* (@ cout << endl << "done" << endl; @)
```

C++ program (without flattening the propagation graph):

```
void Example::fun( )
{ this->UNKNOWN15()->fun( ); }

void A1::fun( )
{ UNKNOWN16}

void B::fun( )
{ this->UNKNOWN17()->fun( ); }

void D1::fun( )
{ this->UNKNOWN18()->fun( ); }

void C::fun( )
{ UNKNOWN19 }

void E::fun( )
{ this->UNKNOWN20()->fun( );
  this->UNKNOWN21()->fun( ); }

void G1::fun( )
{ this->UNKNOWN22()->fun( ); }

void F::fun( )
{ this->G1::fun( ); }

void G::fun( )
{ this->UNKNOWN23()->fun( ); }

void UNKNOWN24::fun( )
{ // prefix blocks
  cout << endl << "done" << endl; }
```

Exercise 9.2 This exercise uses class dictionaries covered in Chapter 11. Consider the following.

```
-----------------------------------------------------------------
Class Dictionary
-----------------------------------------------------------------
    1   RestaurantOrder =  <orders> OrderList.
    2   OrderList ~ {Order}.
    3   Order =   "ORDER:"
    4             [ "Appetizer:" <appetizer> Appetizer_List ]
    5             "Entree:" <entree> Entree
    6             "Salad" <salad> Salad
    7             [ "Dessert" <dessert> Dessert ]
    8             "Bon" "Appetit!".
    9   Appetizer_List ~ Appetizer { "and" Appetizer }.
   10   Entree : Beef | Chicken | Vegetarian | Fish .
   11   Dessert = "with" <calories> DemNumber "calories".
   12   Appetizer : Soup| Nachos |
   13           Potato_Skins | Stuffed_Mushrooms.
   14   Soup = "Soup".
   15   Nachos = "Nachos".
   16   Potato_Skins = "Potato" "Skins".
   17   Stuffed_Mushrooms = "Stuffed" "Mushrooms".
   18   Salad = <greens> Lettuce "with"
   19           <dressing> Salad_Dressing "dressing"
   20           "and" <garnish> Vegetable.
   21   Beef = "Beef".
   22   Chicken = "Chicken".
   23   Vegetarian = "Vegetarian Entree".
   24   Lettuce = .
   25   Salad_Dressing = <brandName> DemString "("
   26           <calories> DemNumber "calories )".
   27   Vegetable : Tomato| Carrot.
   28   Tomato = "tomatoes".
   29   Carrot = "carrots".
   30   Fish : OceanFish | LakeFish
   31     *common* "Fish -" <name> DemString.
   32   LakeFish = "Lake".
   33   OceanFish = "Ocean".

-----------------------------------------------------------------
Alphabetically Sorted Cross Reference List
-----------------------------------------------------------------
Appetizer        :12     9       9
Appetizer_List   :9      4
Beef      :21    10
```

9.6. EXERCISES

```
Carrot      :29      27
Chicken              :22      10
Dessert              :11       7
Entree      :10       5
Fish        :30      10
LakeFish             :32      30
Lettuce              :24      18
Nachos      :15      12
OceanFish            :33      30
Order       :3        2
OrderList            :2        1
Potato_Skins         :16      13
RestaurantOrder              :1
Salad       :18       6
Salad_Dressing       :25      19
Soup        :14      12
Stuffed_Mushrooms            :17      13
Tomato      :28      27
Vegetable            :27      20
Vegetarian           :23      10
```

Find the unknowns in the following propagation pattern, object, corresponding sentence, trace (for the object), and C++ program.

```
//
//      Print the UNKNOWN1 and UNKNOWN2 for the
//      orders which have UNKNOWN3 on the salad.
//

*operation* void f()
  *traverse*
    *from* RestaurantOrder *to* Salad
  *wrapper* Salad
    *prefix*
      (@ this -> f(dressing); @)

*operation* void f(Salad_Dressing* d)
  *traverse*
      *from* Salad *to* Carrot
  *wrapper* Carrot
    *prefix*
      (@ d->g_print();
         cout << "\n"; @)
```

Object:

: RestaurantOrder (

```
< orders > : UNKNOWN4 {
  : Order (
    < entree > : Beef ( )
    < salad > : Salad (
      < greens > : Lettuce ( )
      < dressing > : Salad_Dressing (
        < brandName > : DemString "UNKNOWN5"
        < calories > : DemNumber "UNKNOWN6" )
      < garnish > : UNKNOWN7 ( ) )
    < dessert > : Dessert (
      < calories > : DemNumber "UNKNOWN8" ) ) ,
  : Order (
    < appetizer > : Appetizer_List {
      : UNKNOWN9 ( ) ,
      : UNKNOWN10 ( ) ,
      : Soup ( ) }
    < entree > : UNKNOWN11 ( )
    < salad > : Salad (
      < greens > : Lettuce ( )
      < dressing > : Salad_Dressing (
        < brandName > : DemString "UNKNOWN12"
        < calories > : DemNumber "UNKNOWN13" )
      < garnish > : UNKNOWN14 ( ) ) ) ,
  : Order (
    < appetizer > : Appetizer_List {
      : UNKNOWN15 ( ) }
    < entree > : UNKNOWN16 (
      < name > : DemString "Native Swordfish" )
    < salad > : Salad (
      < greens > : Lettuce ( )
      < dressing > : Salad_Dressing (
        < brandName > : DemString "Italian"
        < calories > : DemNumber "250" )
      < garnish > : UNKNOWN17 ( ) )
    < dessert > : Dessert (
      < calories > : DemNumber "UNKNOWN18" ) ) } )
```

Sentence:

ORDER:
    Entree: Beef
    Salad with "Bleu Cheese" (1500 calories) dressing and carrots
    Dessert with 1000 calories
    Bon Appetit!
ORDER:
    Appetizer: Nachos and Potato Skins and Soup

9.6. EXERCISES   303

```
        Entree: Chicken
        Salad with "French" (550 calories ) dressing and tomatoes
        Bon Appetit!
ORDER:
        Appetizer: Stuffed Mushrooms
        Entree: Ocean Fish - "Native Swordfish"
        Salad with "Italian" (250 calories ) dressing and carrots
        Dessert with 5700 calories
        Bon Appetit!
```

Trace (object above is used as input):

```
>> void RestaurantOrder::f()
 >> void OrderList::f()
  >> void Order::f()
   >> void UNKNOWN19::f()
    >> void Salad::f(Salad_Dressing*  d)
     >> void UNKNOWN20::f(Salad_Dressing*  d)
UNKNOWN21
      << void UNKNOWN22::f(Salad_Dressing*  d)
     << void Salad::f(Salad_Dressing*  d)
    << void UNKNOWN23::f()
   << void Order::f()
  >> void Order::f()
   >> void Salad::f()
    >> void Salad::f(Salad_Dressing*  d)
     >> void Tomato::f(Salad_Dressing*  d)
     << void Tomato::f(Salad_Dressing*  d)
    << void Salad::f(Salad_Dressing*  d)
   << void Salad::f()
  << void Order::f()
  >> void Order::f()
   >> void UNKNOWN24::f()
    >> void Salad::f(Salad_Dressing*  d)
     >> void UNKNOWN25::f(Salad_Dressing*  d)
UNKNOWN26
      << void UNKNOWN27::f(Salad_Dressing*  d)
    << void Salad::f(Salad_Dressing*  d)
   << void UNKNOWN28::f()
  << void Order::f()
 << void OrderList::f()
<< void RestaurantOrder::f()
```

    C++ program:

```
void RestaurantOrder::f(  )
```

```
{ this->get_orders()->f( ); }

void OrderList::f( )
{ Order_list_iterator   next_Order(*this);
  Order*                each_Order;
  while ( each_Order = UNKNOWN29 )
  {
    each_Order->f( ); } }

void Order::f( )
{ this->UNKNOWN30()->f( ); }

void Salad::f( )
{ // prefix blocks
  this -> f(dressing); }

void Salad::f( Salad_Dressing* d )
{ this->UNKNOWN31()->f( d ); }

void Vegetable::f( Salad_Dressing* d )
{ UNKNOWN32 }

void Tomato::f( Salad_Dressing* d )
{ }

void Carrot::f( Salad_Dressing* d )
{ // prefix blocks
  d->UNKNOWN33();
         cout << "\n"; }
```

Exercise 9.3 Find a class dictionary graph G and two propagation directives pd_1 and pd_2 so that $propagate(pd_1, S)$ and $propagate(pd_2, S)$ define the same propagation graph and, so that pd_1 has information loss while pd_2 has not.

Exercise 9.4 Given two propagation patterns, determine whether they are traversal equivalent. That is, for all reasonable class dictionary graphs and inputs they have the same traversal and wrapper execution behavior. What is the complexity of this decision problem?

Exercise 9.5 Can you find two class dictionary graphs G and $G1$ and a propagation pattern pp so that $propagate(pp, G)$ has running-time $O(n)$ and $propagate(pp, G1)$ has running-time $O(n*n)$?

Exercise 9.6 Optimizing the code generation. One code generation mechanism calls the superclass code whenever an inheritance edge is present in the propagation graph. Sometimes, this superclass call is not needed resulting in faster execution and shorter code. Consider the propagation directive *from* A *to* C. The example

9.6. EXERCISES

```
Ex = A.
A : B *common* C.
B = (*inherits* A).
```

does not require the call to the superclass since inheritance provides the same functionality. However,

```
Ex = A.
A : B *common* C.
B = C (*inherits* A).
```

requires the call to the superclass. Does the following condition create correct code for a propagation graph?

Let A be an alternation class with alternative B. Assume that the inheritance edge from B to A is in the propagation graph. If there is a class C so that there is no knowledge path from B to C avoiding A, but there is a knowledge path from A to C, starting with a construction edge, then no call to the superclass A is generated in B.

Exercise 9.7 Assume a propagation pattern where wrappers are attached only to construction classes and construction edges of the form -> *,b,*.

Is the following true or false?

For a propagation pattern pp, a compatible class dictionary graph G, and a class dictionary graph $G1$ which is order-preserving and object-equivalent to G, if G and $G1$ are compatible with pp, then both $propagate(pp, G)$ and $propagate(pp, G1)$ execute wrappers in the same order.

Exercise 9.8 Consider the following five class dictionaries cd1, ... ,cd5 and the four propagation patterns f1, ... ,f4.

cd1:

```
Ex = PCList(A).
PCList(S) ~ "(" S { "," S } ")".
A = K Z.
K = L.
L = <z2> Z.
Z = .
```
----

cd2:

```
Ex = PCList(A).
PCList(S) ~ "(" S { "," S } ")".
A = D <z1> Z.
D = <z2> Z <k> K.
K = ["l" <l> L].
L = <a> A.
Z = .
```
----

cd3:

```
Ex = PCList(A).
PCList(S) ~ "(" S { "," S } ")".
A = <d1> D <z1> Z.
D = <k1> K <u1> U.
U = ["a" <a1> A].
K = <z2> Z ["l" <l> L].
L = <u2> U.
Z = .
```
----

cd4:

```
Ex = PCList(A).
PCList(S) ~ "(" S { "," S } ")".
A = <d1> D <z1> Z.
D = <k1> K.
K = L.
L = Z.
Z = .
V1 : D | U1 *common* <v2> V2.
V2 : U2 | Z.
U1 = "u1".
U2 = "u2".
```
----

cd5:

```
Ex = PCList(A).
PCList(S) ~ "(" S { "," S } ")".
A = D.
D : K | Z.
K = ["l" L].
L = Z.
Z = .
```

The four propagation patterns are:

```
*operation* void f1()
  *traverse*
    *from* Ex *to* Z
  *wrapper* Z
    *prefix*
      (@ cout << this << endl; @)
  *wrapper* A
```

9.6. EXERCISES

```
      *suffix*
        (@ cout << "f1 after traversing A ------------------" << endl; @)

*operation* void f2()
  *traverse*
    *from* Ex *via* K *to* Z
  *wrapper* Z
    *prefix*
      (@ cout << this << endl; @)
  *wrapper* A
    *suffix*
      (@ cout << "f2 after traversing A ------------------" << endl; @)

*operation* void f3()
  *traverse*
    *from* Ex
      *bypassing* -> K,1,L
    *to* Z
  *wrapper* Z
    *prefix*
      (@ cout << this << endl; @)
  *wrapper* A
    *suffix*
      (@ cout << "f3 after traversing A ------------------" << endl; @)

*operation* void f4()
  *traverse*
    *from* Ex
      *through* -> K,1,L
    *to* Z
  *wrapper* Z
    *prefix*
      (@ cout << this << endl; @)
  *wrapper* A
    *suffix*
      (@ cout << "f4 after traversing A ------------------" << endl; @)
```

For which combinations of class dictionary and propagation pattern is there information loss (= inconsistency) between the propagation directive in the propagation pattern and the class dictionary?

Put your answer for propagation directive f_i and class dictionary cd_j into

$$UNKNOWN_{i,j}.$$

For example, $UNKNOWN_{1,3}$ contains nothing if there is no information loss for f_1 and cd_3; otherwise $UNKNOWN_{1,3}$ contains a shortcut path.

9.7 BIBLIOGRAPHIC REMARKS

- The publications [WH91, WMH93, WH92] describe the tiny method problem in object-oriented programming. Propagation patterns provide a solution to this problem.

- Cun Xiao's thesis [Xia94] formally defines the semantics of propagation patterns.

9.8 SOLUTIONS

Solution to Exercise 9.2

```
UNKNOWN1 = salad dressing name  *CHOICE* brand name
UNKNOWN2 = number of calories     UNKNOWN3 = carrots
UNKNOWN4 = OrderList              UNKNOWN5 = Bleu Cheese
UNKNOWN6 = 1500                   UNKNOWN7 = Carrot
UNKNOWN8 = 1000                   UNKNOWN9 = Nachos
UNKNOWN10 = Potato_skins          UNKNOWN11 = Chicken
UNKNOWN12 = French                UNKNOWN13 = 550
UNKNOWN14 = Tomato                UNKNOWN15 = stuffed_Mushrooms
UNKNOWN16 = OceanFish             UNKNOWN17 = Carrot
UNKNOWN18 = 5700                  UNKNOWN19 = Salad
UNKNOWN20 = Carrot
UNKNOWN21 = "Bleu Cheese" (1500 calories)
UNKNOWN22 = Carrot                UNKNOWN23 = Salad
UNKNOWN24 = Salad                 UNKNOWN25 = Carrot
UNKNOWN26 = "Italian" (250 calories)   UNKNOWN27 = Carrot
UNKNOWN28 = Salad                 UNKNOWN29 = next_Order()
UNKNOWN30 = get_salad             UNKNOWN31 = get_garnish
UNKNOWN32 = NOTHING               UNKNOWN33 = g_print
```

Solution to Exercise 9.8

```
UNKNOWN11 = NOTHING               UNKNOWN12 = NOTHING
UNKNOWN13 = NOTHING               UNKNOWN14 = NOTHING
UNKNOWN15 = NOTHING               UNKNOWN21 = NOTHING
UNKNOWN22 = Ex A_PCList A Z
UNKNOWN23 = Ex A_PCList A D K Z
UNKNOWN24 = NOTHING               UNKNOWN25 = NOTHING
UNKNOWN31 = NOTHING               UNKNOWN32 = NOTHING
UNKNOWN33 = NOTHING               UNKNOWN34 = NOTHING
UNKNOWN35 = NOTHING               UNKNOWN41 = NOTHING
UNKNOWN42 = Ex A_PCList A Z
UNKNOWN43 = Ex A_PCList A D K Z
UNKNOWN44 = NOTHING               UNKNOWN45 = NOTHING
```

Chapter 10

Transportation Patterns

During execution, an object-oriented program may be compared to a play. The objects correspond to actors and the locus of control is on the stage. At any point in time, a group of actors will be on the stage to perform their act. Those actors correspond to objects participating in a function call. In this chapter we discuss how we can elegantly specify the sequence of actor sets we need on the stage.

10.1 SPECIFYING OBJECT TRANSPORTATION

Object transportation can be simulated with propagation patterns, but at the expense of a longer program, reduced maintainability, and reusability. Consider the following problem. For a given **Company**-object you have to find the **Customer**-objects it contains and for each such **Customer**-object you need all **Item**-objects that the customer ordered. For a given **Item**-object you need to know the containing **Customer**-object. This problem can be solved with the two propagation patterns in Fig. 10.1.

Although the propagation patterns in Fig. 10.1 are generic and work with many different class dictionary graphs, they contain redundant signature information, and their closely related assumptions on potential class structures are scattered into two propagation patterns instead of one. The two propagation patterns have the following evolution problems:

- Redundant signature

    Let's suppose we add an extra argument X* x to the signature. We have to add x to both signatures shown in Fig. 10.1 and we have to update the call.

- Inefficiency or structure dependency

    The two propagation patterns in Fig. 10.1 have another disadvantage: class **Customer** gets two methods with different signatures. The only way to avoid two methods for class **Customer** would be to encode more class structure into the program. We would have to mention the class that "follows" the **Customer** class.

To avoid the signature redundancy and the inefficiency or structure dependency problem, we replace the two propagation patterns with only one that uses a transportation pattern (Fig. 10.2). If we now add an extra argument X* x, we have to update only one

```
*operation* void itemsAndCustomers()
  *traverse*
    *from* Company *to* Customer
  *wrapper* Customer
    *prefix* (@ this -> itemsAndCustomers(this); @)

*operation* void itemsAndCustomers(Customer* c)
  *traverse*
    *from* Customer *to* Item
  *wrapper* Item
    *prefix* (@ c -> g_print(); this -> g_print(); @)
```

Figure 10.1: Redundant propagation patterns

signature. In addition, the extra call and structure dependency disappear. The solution in

```
*operation* itemsAndCustomers()
  *traverse*
    *from* Company *to* Item
  *carry* *in* Customer* c = (@ this @)
    *along* *from* Customer *to* Item
  *wrapper* Item
    *prefix* (@ c -> g_print(); this -> g_print(); @)
```

Figure 10.2: Nonredundant propagation pattern

Fig. 10.2 creates only one method for class **Customer** without encoding more class structure.

Transportation patterns solve the evolution problems mentioned above and most importantly, we get a reusable unit. The transportation pattern that starts with *carry* can be used in other contexts with other traversal directives and in combination with other transportation patterns.

Transportation allows us to distribute an object to a group of other objects specified through a subgraph in the class dictionary graph. We call such a subgraph a transportation graph. A transportation graph is described by a transportation directive that is like a propagation directive. Transportation can be simulated by pure propagation patterns at the expense of maintainability and reusability. Therefore, we consider transportation not just syntactic sugar since the same maintainability and reusability cannot be achieved without transportation.

10.1. SPECIFYING OBJECT TRANSPORTATION

A transportation pattern has the form

```
*carry*
  // transported variables
  // broadcasting
  *in* P* p
    = (@ ... @)   // optional, for initialization
  , // condensing
  *out* Q* q
    = (@ ... @)   // optional, for initialization
  , // broadcasting and condensing
  *inout* R* r
    = (@ ... @)   // optional, for initialization
  *along*
    // propagation directive, see above
    // defines transportation graph
  *at* A  // update transported variable
    p = (@ ... @)
  *at* B  // update transported variables
    q = (@ ... @), r = (@ ... @)
*carry* // several carry are allowed
  ...
  *along*
    ...
  *at*

  // wrappers which usually use the transported variables
  // both vertex and edge wrappers may be used
    ...
// end transportation pattern
```

This means that a group of variables p, q, r will be available along all vertices of the transportation graph defined by the first transportation directive of the transportation pattern. A similar set of variables is defined by the second and later carry statements. To make those variables available to other classes is in line with the Law of Demeter since it allows calling functions of method arguments.

A transportation pattern lives in the context of a propagation pattern that contains a propagation directive specifying a traversal graph. Therefore we call such a propagation directive a traversal propagation directive. The propagation directives inside a transportation pattern are called transportation propagation directives and each determines a transportation graph. This terminology is summarized as

```
propagation directive
   (generic: succinct subgraph definition)
```

```
    used for traversal:

        traversal propagation directive,
        determines a traversal graph


    used for transportation:

        transportation propagation directive,
        determines a transportation graph
```

An example of the embedding of a transportation pattern into a propagation pattern is:

```
*operation* void f()
  *traverse*
    *from* A *to* Z

// transportation pattern
// see above

// additional wrappers used for traversal
*wrapper* A
    ...
*wrapper* Z
    ...
// end propagation pattern
```

An *in* variable is used for broadcasting information to several objects. An *out* variable is used for condensing information from several objects. Alternatively, we can say that an *in* variable is used for transporting objects down the class dictionary graph and an *out* variable is used for transporting objects up the class dictionary graph.

Therefore, transportation variables are split into broadcasters and condensers. The same transportation pattern may contain broadcasters and condensers.

If down is used, the broadcasting starts from a source transportation object to target transportation objects. If up is used, the condensing starts from the target transportation objects back to a source transportation object.

An optional *at* clause may be used to update variables during the traversal.

10.2 TRANSPORTATION CUSTOMIZER RESTRICTIONS

This section may be skipped on first reading since the customizer restrictions rarely apply in practice.

The study of customizer restrictions for adaptive programs, whether they are propagation patterns or transportation patterns, has the following structure:

- Without a customizer

  Type-correctness: An adaptive program is type-correct if at least one customizer creates an executable program implementing the intent of the adaptive program. Type-correctness implies:

  Well-formedness: The adaptive program must satisfy simple structural constraints.

- With a customizer S

  - Compatibility: S must satisfy the customizer constraints; that is, the customization must generate a nonempty program.
  - Implementation correctness: the implementation of the customization might optimize the customized program. This optimization might destroy the intent of the adaptive program for some customizers, implying further customization restrictions.

Now we apply the above approach to transportation patterns.

- Without a customizer (traversal graph)

  Type-correctness: The transportation patterns allow for at least one customizer that satisfies all the restrictions. This implies:

  Well-formedness: The transportation variables are not defined more than once and the at-clauses contain only assignments to variables declared in a carry clause. Each propagation directive appearing in the transportation pattern must be well-formed.

- With a traversal graph

  - Compatibility

    The transportation directives must be compatible with the traversal graph; that is, the terminology used in the transportation pattern must be a subset of the terminology in the traversal graph.

    In addition, each transportation directive in the propagation pattern has to satisfy two transportation restrictions:

    * The Transportation Entry Restriction (discussed below) which limits how the transportation graph may be entered from the traversal graph.
    * The Transportation Recursion Restriction (discussed below) which limits the edges that go into a transportation source vertex.

    Without those restrictions, the customized program would not be meaningful.

  - Implementation correctness

    Those restrictions are analogous to the restrictions for propagation patterns.

    * The Consistency Restriction for Transportation which is analogous to the consistency restriction (information loss restriction) for traversal.
      Object transportation expresses object-flow, and when there are shortcut paths or zigzag paths in the transportation graph, the intent of the object flow would be violated.

* The Subclass Invariance Restriction for Transportation which is analogous to the Subclass Invariance Restriction (delayed binding restriction) for traversal.

The Transportation Entry Restriction and the Transportation Recursion Restriction ensure that the C++ code we generate is type-correct in the sense that each generated method invocation has a corresponding method definition.

If any of the restrictions occurs, a simple transformation either changes the adaptive program, or the class dictionary, or both to eliminate the restriction and to preserve the intent of the program.

We have discussed the situation when a transportation pattern is customized with a traversal graph. A transportation pattern will live in some propagation pattern and therefore we need to discuss the customization of propagation patterns that contain transportation patterns.

10.2.1 Type-Correctness

Given a propagation pattern containing a traversal propagation directive tv and a transportation propagation directive tp, the following type-correctness rule needs to hold true:[1]

- tv and tp are both type-correct; that is, there exists a customizing class dictionary graph that defines a nonempty propagation graph.

- $restrict(tp, tv)$ is type-correct; that is, there is a customizing class dictionary graph S such that $propagate(tp, propagate(tv, S))$ defines a nonempty propagation graph. This implies that the transportation graph must be contained in the propagation graph.

By definition, the transportation graph is always a subgraph of the traversal graph. A customizing class dictionary graph S for a pair (tp, tv) has to satisfy: $propagate(tv, S)$ is nonempty and $propagate(tp, propagate(tv, S))$ is nonempty.[2]

A negative example of two propagation directives that do not satisfy the type-correctness rule is

```
TV = *from* A *bypassing* -> *,k,* *to* Z
TP = *from* A *through* -> *,k,* *to* Z
```

Two positive examples are

```
TV = *from* A *to* Z
TP = *from* B *to* Q

TV = *from* A *via* B *to* Z
TP = *from* B *to* Z
```

Object transportation is naturally implemented by signature extension. The signature is extended for the vertices in the transportation graph as implied by the example in Figs. 10.1 and 10.2.

---

[1] Legal transportation patterns, page 448 (66).
[2] Legal transportation pattern customization, page 448 (67).

10.2.2 Traversal Restrictions

Traversal restrictions are discussed in Chapter 7.

10.2.3 Transportation Restrictions

Transportation patterns and their customizers need to follow two transportation customizer restrictions: the Transportation Entry Restriction and the Transportation Recursion Restriction. To formulate the transportation customizer restrictions, we use the following terminology. A transportation directive of a transportation pattern and the corresponding transportation graph are defined with respect to a bigger traversal graph. The edges in the transportation graph are said to be transportation edges. Edges in the traversal graph, but not in the current transportation graph, are said to be nontransportation edges. The sources of the transportation graph are said to be source-transportation vertices. The **Transportation Entry Restriction** is now formulated as follows:

> No vertices of a transportation graph, except its source vertices, can have incoming nontransportation edges.

A nontransportation edge is an edge that is not in the transportation graph we are currently considering; it may be contained in another transportation graph that is used with the same traversal graph.

A simple letter example is

```
// class dictionary
A = B C.
B = C.
C = .

// propagation pattern
*operation* void f()
  *traverse*
    *from* A *to* C
    // transportation pattern
    *carry* *in* B* b
      *along* *from* B *to* C
```

An appropriate error message is

```
propagate: error:
nontransportation construction edge '-> A,c,C' is not allowed,
since 'C' is in
the transportation graph but not a transportation source.
```

The reason for the restriction is to get a C++ program that compiles. We further explain the motivation by introducing the concept of a conflict vertex. If v is not a source-transportation vertex, we call it a conflict vertex. Consider the propagation pattern in Fig. 10.2. If **Customer** is not between **Company** and **Item**, the propagation pattern is not meaningful. The reason is that a conflict vertex would exist. A conflict vertex is a vertex that is reachable from a source of the traversal graph along paths requiring distinct numbers of arguments. This happens, for example, when a transportation graph can be entered from a source of the bigger traversal graph without going through a source of the transportation graph. Propagation patterns may be applied only to class dictionary graphs that do not create any conflict vertices. In other words, transportation directives limit the applicable class dictionary graphs.

To better understand the Transportation Entry Restriction more examples are shown. In the first example we need to print the names of all the self-employed people living in a given town.

```
*operation* void printNamesOfSelfEmployed()
  *traverse*
    *from* Town *to* SelfEmployed
  *carry*
    *in* DemIdent* person_name = (@ this -> get_name(); @)
    *along*
      *from* Person *to* SelfEmployed
  *wrapper* SelfEmployed
    *prefix* (@ person_name -> g_print(); @)
```

The customization with the class dictionary graph in Fig. 10.3 is legal, but the customization with the class dictionary graph in Fig. 10.4 is illegal. In Fig. 10.4, we transport an DemIdent-object from Person to SelfEmployed along the traversal from Town to SelfEmployed. When a SelfEmployed-object receives message printNamesOfSelfEmployed, it expects an argument, called person_name, of the message. But the dog catcher does not have the argument person_name well defined. The transportation customizer restriction is violated since the construction edge Town $\stackrel{dogCatcher}{\longrightarrow}$ SelfEmployed enters a vertex in the transportation graph, which is not a source-transportation vertex.

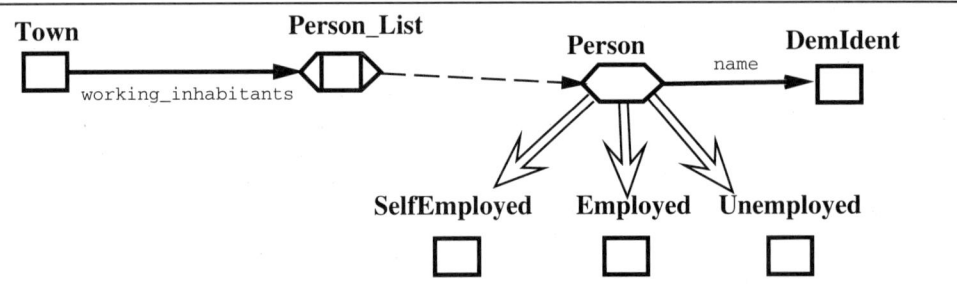

Figure 10.3: Town without a dog catcher

The customization with the class dictionary graph in Fig. 10.5 shows another violation of the Transportation Entry Restriction. There is a traversal-only edge entering the transportation graph at SelfEmployed that is not a transportation source.

10.2. TRANSPORTATION CUSTOMIZER RESTRICTIONS

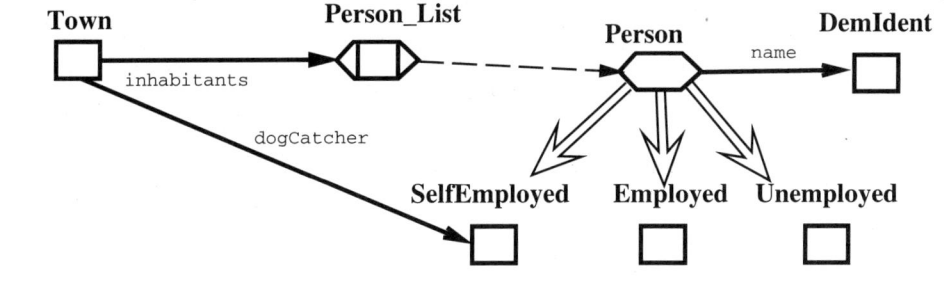

Figure 10.4: Town with a dog catcher

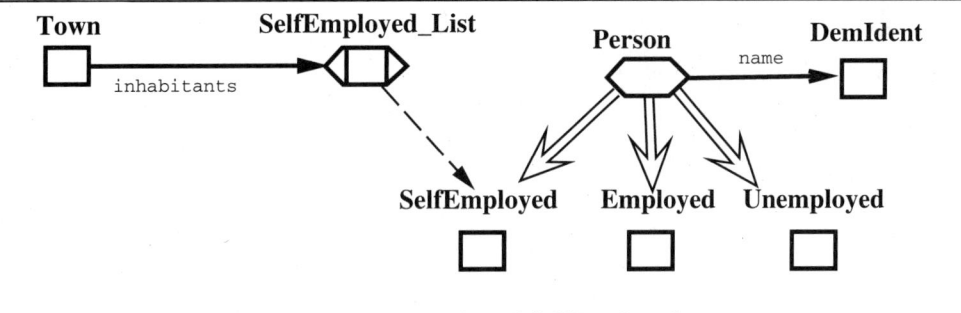

Figure 10.5: Town of SelfEmployed

The **Transportation Recursion Restriction** is defined as

A source vertex of a transportation graph cannot have incoming transportation edges.

The reason for the restriction is again to avoid compilation errors. Consider the following class dictionary:

```
Example = Expression.
Expression : Numerical | Compound.
Numerical = <val> DemNumber.
Compound = <op> Addition <arg1> Expression <arg2> Expression.
Addition = "+".
```

Let's write a transportation pattern that counts the number of addition operators in an Example-object. A first solution might be

```
*operation* void countAdditions()
  *traverse*
    *from* Example *to* Addition
  // transportation pattern
  *carry* *in* DemNumber* count = (@ new DemNumber(0); @)
    *along*
      *from* Expression *to* Addition
  *wrapper* Addition
    *prefix*
      (@ count -> set_val(*count + 1); cout << count << endl; @)
  // end transportation pattern
```

Class **Expression** is the source vertex of the transportation graph. But **Expression** has an incoming transportation edge and therefore the above transportation pattern and customizer are illegal.

To repair the violation, we start the transportation at **Example**; that is, we replace *from* Expression *to* Addition by *from* Example *to* Addition. Now class **Example** is the transportation start class and there is no transportation edge back to **Example**. Like in this example, customizer restrictions can always be repaired easily.

Fig. 10.6 summarizes the transportation customizer restriction discussed.

Note that the transportation edge going into a traversal source vertex is not explicitly excluded by a restriction. But its exclusion is implied by the Transportation Recursion Restriction. If there were a transportation edge into a traversal source then there would also be a transportation edge into a transportation source. The reason is that the transportation source is reachable along transportation edges from the traversal source.

10.3 TRANSPORTATION PATTERN EXAMPLES

Transportation patterns carry objects across graphs without knowing the detailed structure of the graphs. If those graphs contain alternation edges, then the transportation pattern simulates a conditional statement.

10.3. TRANSPORTATION PATTERN EXAMPLES

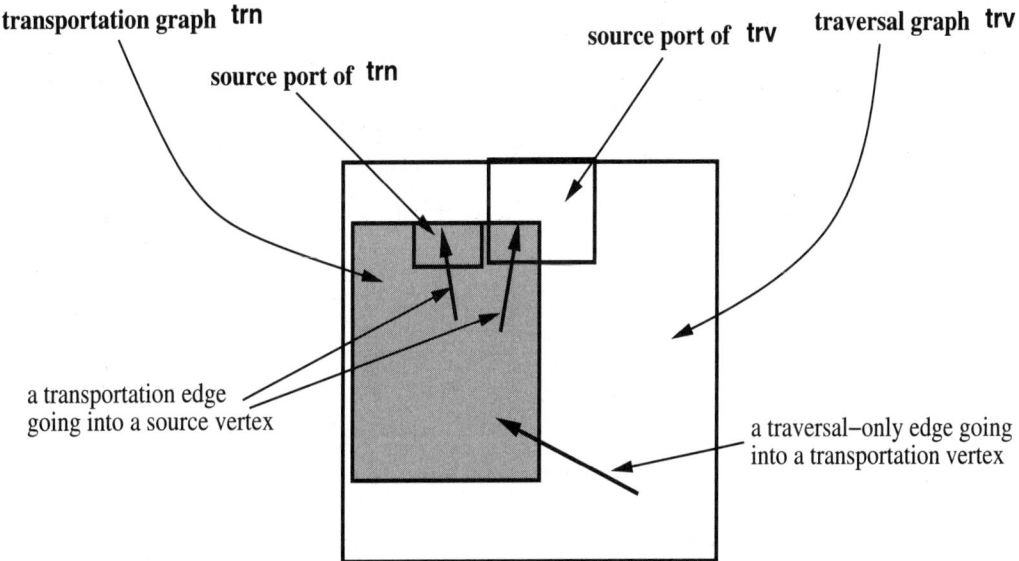

trv: traversal graph
trn: transportation graph
two upper thick arrows: Transportation Recursion Restriction
lower thick arrow: Transportation Entry Restriction

Figure 10.6: Transportation restrictions: Disallowed edges

10.3.1 Triples Example

We use an example to show how to design and write an adaptive and extensible object-oriented program.

Suppose we have a company that works with producers who manufacture product items that are sold by sales agents to customers. We would like to find all the triples of customers, producers, and sales agents who do business together (that is, they buy, produce, and sell the same items) and are located in the same location. In other words, we need to implement a function called `triples()` which finds the desired entities.

The standard object-oriented approach would next itemize a group of collaborating classes needed for implementing the `triples()` function. This has the disadvantage that the algorithm depends on this specific list of classes. Instead, we want to make only a minimal number of assumptions on the class dictionary and we then use those assumptions to describe the group of collaborating classes we need.

Assumptions about the class dictionary are expressed in terms of *class-valued variables* and *relation-valued variables*. The class-valued variables will be mapped to real classes later when we select a specific program from the infinite set of programs we are going to describe. We assume that we have class-valued variables `Company`, `Customer`, `Producer`, `Agent`, and `Item`, which will be mapped to classes with the same names. We also make the following additional assumptions about the class dictionary:

Company: From `Company` there is a path via `Customer` and via `Item` to `Producer` and `Agent`.

> That is, `Company`-objects contain `Customer`-objects, which in turn contain `Item`-objects, which in turn contain `Producer`- and `Agent`-objects.
>
> The following summarizes the assumed ordering of the classes:
>
>   Company
>   Customer
>   Item
> Producer Agent

Customer: We assume that a customer has a name and a location.

Item: The relations between `Item` and `Producer` and between `Item` and `Agent` are 1-1 relations.

Producer: We assume that a producer has a name and a location.

Agent: We assume that an agent has a name and a location.

With those assumptions we can now formulate a program that will work with any class dictionary that satisfies those assumptions. Therefore, we have now set up the right structure to write an infinite family of programs. We can later select specific programs from this family by applying the program to a class structure that satisfies the assumptions. To write the program, we first describe the group of collaborating classes needed to implement the `triples()` function. Since the details of the class structure are not known, a generic

10.3. TRANSPORTATION PATTERN EXAMPLES

```
*from* Company
  *via* Customer
  *via* Item
*to* {Producer, Agent}
```

Figure 10.7: Propagation directive

---

specification of the collaboration group is given, instead of an itemized list of collaborators. The generic specification is expressed in Fig. 10.7.

The propagation pattern needed for our example is given in Fig. 10.8. Fig. 10.10 shows how objects are transported to an **Item**-object where the bulk of the computation is done.

Component `triples` defines a family of programs that provide the `triples()` function implemented by the propagation pattern in Fig. 10.8.

Two class dictionary graphs will be given to customize the adaptive program and to select two different C++ programs from the family. The two class dictionary graphs have different structures and define different objects. We will explain the customization process in detail by using the class structure in Fig. 10.9. The customization interprets propagation pattern `triples` in the context of a class dictionary graph.

Figure 10.9 shows the first customizer, called **Company1**. It is a class structure in graphical form that satisfies the assumptions listed in Fig. 10.8.

The propagation directive (Figure 10.7) defines a set of paths from **Company** to **Producer** and **Agent**. Three examples are:

1. $\text{Company} \xrightarrow{customers} \text{Customer\_List} \Longrightarrow \text{Customer\_NonemptyList} \xrightarrow{first} \text{Customer} \xrightarrow{orders} \text{Item\_List} \Longrightarrow \text{Item\_NonemptyList} \xrightarrow{first} \text{Item} \xrightarrow{sold\_by} \text{Agent}$

2. $\text{Company} \xrightarrow{customers} \text{Customer\_List} \Longrightarrow \text{Customer\_NonemptyList} \xrightarrow{first} \text{Customer} \xrightarrow{orders} \text{Item\_List} \Longrightarrow \text{Item\_NonemptyList} \xrightarrow{first} \text{Item} \xrightarrow{made\_by} \text{Producer}$

3. $\text{Company} \xrightarrow{customers} \text{Customer\_List} \Longrightarrow \text{Customer\_NonemptyList} \xrightarrow{first} \text{Customer} \xrightarrow{orders} \text{Item\_List} \Longrightarrow \text{Item\_NonemptyList} \xrightarrow{rest} \text{Item\_List} \Longrightarrow \text{Item\_NonemptyList} \xrightarrow{first} \text{Item} \xrightarrow{sold\_by} \text{Agent}$

According to the first path, we locate the first **Customer**-object in a list of **Customer**-objects that belongs to a **Company**-object; then we follow part-of relation `orders` to locate its part-object, an `Item_List`-object; then we locate the first **Item**-object in the `Item_List`-object. The **Item**-object is the first item ordered by the customer. Finally we reach the **Agent**-object which is the part-object of the first **Item**-object.

The second path describes the same traversal as the first one except that finally we reach a **Producer**-object instead of an **Agent**-object.

```
*operation* void triples()
*constraints*
  *classes* Company, Producer, Agent, Item
  *directives*
    // introduce names for traversal and transportation graphs
    C_PA = *from* Company *to* {Producer,Agent};
    C_I  = *from* Customer *to* Item;
    I_P  = *from* Item *to* Producer;
    I_A  = *from* Item *to* Agent;
  *end*

*traverse* C_PA
  // begin transportation pattern
  *carry* *in* DemIdent* c_name, *in* DemIdent* c_location
    *along* C_I
    *at* Customer
      c_name = (@ get_name() @)
      c_location = (@ get_location() @)
  *carry* *out* DemIdent* p_name, *out* DemIdent* p_location
    *along* I_P
    *at* Producer
      p_name = (@ get_name() @)
      p_location = (@ get_location() @)
  *carry* *out* DemIdent* a_name, *out* DemIdent* a_location
    *along* I_A
    *at* Agent
      a_name = (@ get_name() @)
      a_location = (@ get_location() @)
  *wrapper* Item
    *suffix*
      (@ if ((c_location->g_equal(a_location)) &&
             (p_location->g_equal(a_location)))
           { c_name -> g_print();
             p_name -> g_print();
             a_name -> g_print(); } @)
  // end transportation pattern
```

Figure 10.8: Propagation pattern triples

10.3. TRANSPORTATION PATTERN EXAMPLES

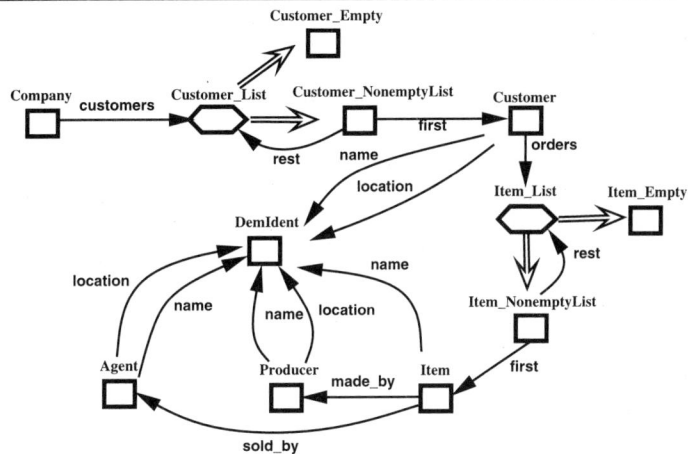

Figure 10.9: Customizer 1: Class dictionary graph Company1

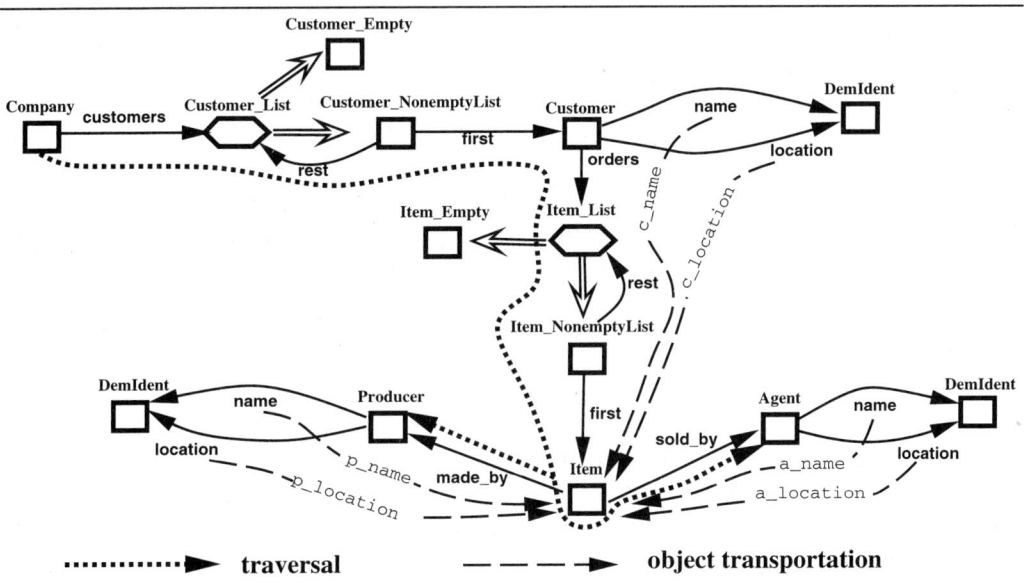

Figure 10.10: Bringing the actors on stage

The third path also describes the same traversal as the first one except that we choose the second `Item`-object from an `Item_List`-object instead of the first `Item`-object.

We call all such paths **knowledge paths**, since they follow the knowledge links between objects.

To solve the problem we posed, we need to transport objects during traversal from each `Customer`-object to the `Producer`- and `Agent`-objects (see Fig. 10.10). We want to transport two `DemIdent`-objects, which are the name and location of a `Customer`-object to each `Item`-object ordered by the customer. For each `Item`-object, we also want to transport the four `DemIdent`-objects, which are the names and locations of its producer and agent to the `Item`-object. Then, at each `Item`-object conditions can be checked, and desired actions can be taken. In other words, at an item object we need six actors, all identifier objects, to play the next scene. Recall that `&&` is the *and* operator of C++.

The object transportation is specified by transportation patterns that are implemented by adding arguments to the signatures of those classes that participate in the transportation. This implementation process is called **signature extension**. A transportation pattern consists of an argument declaration part, a transportation directive (after the keyword *along*), and an initialization part (after the keyword *at*). The arguments name the variables that will be transported, the transportation part specifies the transportation scope, and the initialization part defines initialization of the arguments. Similar to the argument modes in Ada, argument modes *in*, *out*, *inout* are provided. Argument mode *in* is used to pass down `DemIdent`-objects from each `Customer`-object to each `Item`-object contained by the `Customer`-object. Argument mode *out* is used to bring information to the `Item`-object from its subobjects.

The transportation pattern uses one wrapper at class `Item` to process all the transported objects. The wrapper checks a condition and if it holds, the names of the producer, the agent, and the customer who orders the item are printed. It is important that the wrapper is a suffix wrapper since some of the transported objects are available only *after* the traversal.

The C++ program selected by class dictionary graph `Company1` in Fig. 10.9 is in Fig. 10.11. The program is divided into four blocks due to the different signatures.

Component `triples` is adaptive since it works for many different class structures. Fig. 10.12 shows a second customizer that uses two repetition vertices (drawn as ⟨▷). `Customers`, `Items`, and a construction class `Warehouse` are introduced. The two repetition vertices are used to replace two alternation vertices and six construction vertices which are `Customer_List`, `Customer_Empty`, `Customer_NonemptyList`, `Item_List`, `Item_Empty`, and `Item_NonemptyList`. Despite these changes, propagation pattern `triples` can still be used on class dictionary graph `Company2`, because the propagation pattern does not depend on how list structures are specified, and what exactly the relation is between `Item` and `Producer`.

When we use class dictionary graph `Company2` to select a C++ program from the family of programs defined by propagation pattern `triples`, we will get a program different from the one in Fig. 10.11 because of the different class structure.

Propagation patterns are much more flexible software artifacts than traditional object-oriented programs. We have shown how a program adapts itself to different class structures. When there is a large change to a class structure, it is much easier to adjust the propagation pattern rather than the corresponding object-oriented program.

10.3. TRANSPORTATION PATTERN EXAMPLES

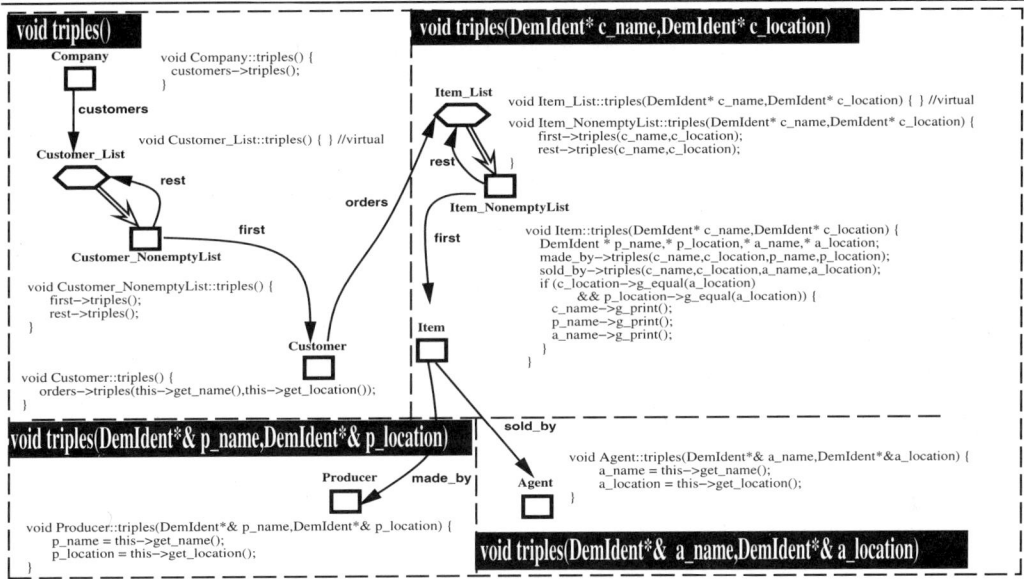

Figure 10.11: After customization of triples with class dictionary graph Company1

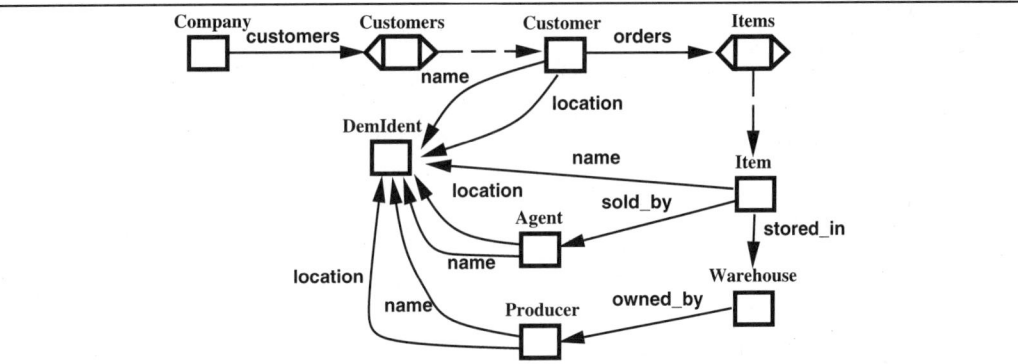

Figure 10.12: Customizer 2: Class dictionary graph Company2 with repetition vertices

10.3.2 Avoiding Conditional Statements

Consider the statements

```
A* a = ...;
if (a -> property())
  a -> do_it();
```

If property is defined by: "Is there a U-object in the A-object (under the assumption that there is at most one U-object in an A-object)" then the above statements can be implemented by the following, which avoids a conditional statement.

```
*operation* void do_it_property()
*traverse* *from* A *to* U
  *carry* *in* A* a
    *along*
      *from* A *to* U
    *at* A* a = (@ this @)
  *wrapper* U
    *prefix* (@ a -> do_it(); @)
```

Notice that when an A-object contains no U-object, a call of do_it_property on the A-object has no effect. The conditional is eliminated now:

```
A* a = ...;
a -> do_it_property();
```

The following component shows a more general solution of the transporting-down problem. The schema example shows a use case that applies the propagation pattern to a graph problem.

```
*component* test_subobjects
// tests whether an A-object contains a U-object
// and for each occurrence function
// g_print is called on a B-object which contains
// the U-object.
// The intention is usually that there is
// at least one alternation edge
// on the path from B to U.
// Can be generalized to several U-objects
*customizers*
  Graph = <adjs> List(Adjacency).
  Adjacency = <source> DemIdent <neighbors> Neighbors.
  Neighbors : A_Neighbors | B_Neighbors *common*.
  A_Neighbors = "a".
  B_Neighbors = "b".
// *rename*
```

```
//    Graph     => A,
//    Adjacency => B,
//    A_Neighbors => U
*constraints*
  *classes* A,B,U
  *class-set* Targets = {U}
  *directives*
    AU = *from* A *via* B *to* *class-set* Targets;
    BU = *from* B *to* *class-set* Targets
*end*

*operation* void do_it_property()
  *traverse* AU
    *carry* *in* B* b *along* BU
      *at* B b = (@ this @)
    *wrapper* *class-set* Targets
      *prefix* (@ b -> g_print(); @)
*require* *operation* void g_print()
*end* test_subobjects
```

In summary, checking for the existence of subobjects in a given object can be done without explicit conditional statements. The approach is to take advantage of delayed bind of calls to code (virtual functions in C++) and to express traversal and transportation succinctly.

10.3.3 DFT Example

The following component improves the earlier algorithm from the chapter on propagation patterns by now using a transportation directive.

```
*component* dft // a group of collaborating propagation patterns
              // group will be called with init()
  *constraints*
    // in this constraint section we summarize the assumptions
    // made by the propagation patterns
    *classes* // class-valued variables
      Graph, Adjacency, MarkUnset, Vertex
    *edge* *patterns* // relation-valued variables
           -> *,neighbors,*,
           -> *,marked,*,
           -> *,start,*,
           -> *,source,*
    *directives* // named propagation directives
      AMU = *from* Adjacency *to* MarkUnset;
      AcV = *from* Adjacency *through* -> *,neighbors,* *to* Vertex;
      GA  = *from* Graph *to* Adjacency;
```

    end

// propagation patterns for dft

operation void dft(Graph* g)
  traverse AMU
    // transportation pattern
    carry *in* Adjacency* adj = (@ this @)
      along AMU
    wrapper MarkUnset
     prefix
      (@ adj -> g_print();
         adj -> set_marked(new MarkSet());
         adj -> uncond_dft(g);
      @)
    // end transportation pattern

operation void uncond_dft(Graph* g)
  traverse AcV
  wrapper Vertex
   prefix
     (@ g->find(this)->dft(g);
        // find is a functional edge from Vertex to Adjacency
        // a computed part; o.k. with Law of D.
        // better to use propagation supporting derived edges
     @)

operation Adjacency* find(Vertex* v) *init* (@ NULL @)
  traverse GA
  wrapper Adjacency
   prefix
     (@ if (v -> g_equal(source)) return_val=this; @)

operation void init()
  traverse GA
  wrapper Adjacency
    prefix
      (@ this -> set_marked(new MarkUnset()); @)
  wrapper Graph
    suffix
      (@ this -> find(start) -> dft(this); @)
end dft

A component serves to group together several propagation patterns and forms a very reusable software unit. The dft component may be combined with several other components.

The collection of such components may be injected into the following class dictionary, for example.

```
Graph = <adjacencies> List(Adjacency) "*start*" <start> Vertex.
Adjacency =
  ":" <source> Vertex <neighbors> List(Vertex) <marked> Mark.
Mark : MarkSet | MarkUnset *common*.
MarkSet = "*set*".
MarkUnset = .
Vertex = <name> DemIdent.
List(S) : Empty(S) | NonEmpty(S) *common*.
Empty(S) = .
NonEmpty(S) = <first> S <rest> List(S).
```

It often happens that components are written with a conflicting vocabulary since they are developed by different people. For example, a graph algorithm might have been formulated for networks and now we want to reuse it for graphs. A renaming, such as,

```
Network => Graph,
Node => Vertex
```

takes care of the mapping of the vocabulary.

10.4 CODE GENERATION

The code generation for propagation patterns falls into the following steps.

1. Check whether the class dictionary graph is compatible with the propagation pattern.

    Class dictionary graph Company1 in Figure 10.9 is compatible with the propagation patterns in triples.

2. Apply the propagation directive of the propagation pattern to the class dictionary graph to get propagation graph Ω.

    Propagation graphs are constructed from the set of knowledge paths satisfying the propagation directive. Propagation graphs describe object traversals.

3. Extend signatures.

    When we apply component triples to class dictionary graph Company1 in Fig. 10.9, signatures are extended (Fig. 10.11 shows the result). Therefore during the traversal, objects are transported to desired locations.

4. Attach code fragments.

    Based on the traversal directive, member functions are created and wrappers are attached to various classes that participate in the traversal (see Fig. 10.11). The transportation graph influences the code generation for the traversal.

5. Generate a program in a target language. The compiler will do the detailed type-checking.

The executable program in C++ for our example is in Fig. 10.11.

To show how code generation works in detail, we use the class dictionary graph in Fig. 10.13. The propagation pattern under consideration is in Fig. 10.14. The generated code is in Fig. 10.15. This example does not show signature extension at an alternation class; it will be explained shortly.

10.4.1 Code Generation with Two Transportation Patterns

We consider four propagation patterns with two transportation patterns. The first transportation pattern uses a broadcasting variable, the other a condensing variable. We consider cases where the transportation starts at an alternation vertex, which makes the translation to C++ more interesting. We use the following class dictionary throughout:

```
Ex = <r> Base.
Base : Derived *common* <q> Common.
Derived = "derived" <d> DerivedPart.
DerivedPart = "part".
Common = "common".
Transport = "transported".
```

This class dictionary lets us discuss the four important kinds of transportations summarized in Fig. 10.16. They are determined by the combination of the following two cases, each having two possibilities:

- Transportation starting at alternation class **Base** or starting at nonalternation class **Ex**.

- Transportations where the traversal graph contains an inheritance edge or where it does not contain an inheritance edge. In both cases, wrappers are pushed down to subclasses.

To show how the wrappers are handled, we assume that **Base** has a prefix wrapper **pBase** and a suffix wrapper **sBase**, and **Derived** has a prefix wrapper **pDerived** and a suffix wrapper **sDerived**. In all four cases the wrappers for **Base** and **Derived** are called in the following order:

```
pBase
pDerived

sDerived
sBase
```

This means that the implementation of transportation satisfies the following rule. A prefix wrapper is called just after an object is entered; a suffix wrapper is called just before an object is left. If the class of an object has several superclasses, the following rule applies: for

10.4. CODE GENERATION

```
WorkFlowManagement =
  <tasks> List(Task).
Task = "timing" Timing
  "name" TaskName
  <description> DemText
  "prerequisites"
  <prerequisites> List(TaskName)
  "resources"
  <resources> List(Resource).
TaskName = <v> DemIdent.
Timing =
  <dueDate> Date
  <startDate> Date
  <completionDate> Date.
Date : DateOpen | DateSelected.
DateSelected =
  <day> DemNumber
  <month> DemNumber
  <year> DemNumber.
Resource = "sun4".
DateOpen = "open".
List(S) ~ "(" {S} ")".
```

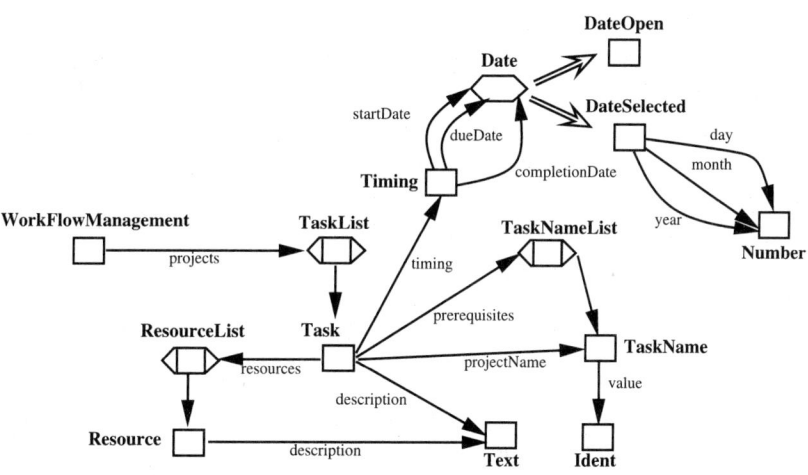

Figure 10.13: Work flow management

```
*operation* Resource_List* required_res()
  // print resources required by all started projects
  *init* (@ new Resource_List() @)
  *traverse*
    *from* WorkFlowManagement
      *via* Task
      *through* -> *,startDate,*
    *to* DateSelected
  // transportation pattern
    *carry* *in* Resource_List* r = (@ resources; @)
      *along* *from* Task *to* DateSelected
  *wrapper* DateSelected
    *prefix*
      (@ return_val -> concatenate(r); @)
```

Figure 10.14: Transporting resources

the prefix wrappers, the most specific prefix wrapper is called first. For the suffix wrappers, the most specific suffix wrapper is called last.

We want to write a program that traverses an Ex-object and transports a Transport-object from a Base-object to the Common-object. In the same traversal we want to transport the Common-object back to the Base-object.

Since C++ has the equal signature rule (the signature of a function f has to be identical at the base and derived class), for cases 1 and 2 we use two functions for each of the two classes Base and Derived.

```
Base::f()                Base::f( 2 arguments)
                              ^
                              |
                              | calls
                              |
Derived::f()   calls -> Derived::f( 2 arguments)
```

Case 1

If Base has a prefix wrapper pBase and a suffix wrapper sBase, and Derived has a prefix wrapper pDerived and a suffix wrapper sDerived, then the generated code will look like the example in Fig. 10.17 and will be called in the sequence: 1 through 6.

The propagation pattern consists of the traversal directive and two transportation patterns. The first transportation pattern uses a broadcasting variable that sends a Transport-object from a Base-object to a Common-object and prints it. This is achieved by the transportation pattern

```
Resource_List*  WorkFlowManagement::required_res(  )
{ Resource_List*  return_val = new Resource_List() ;
  // outgoing calls
  this->required_res_( return_val );
  return return_val;
}
void WorkFlowManagement::required_res_
  ( Resource_List* & return_val )
{ tasks ->required_res_( return_val );
}
void Task::required_res_
  ( Resource_List* & return_val )
{ // variables for carrying in and out
  Resource_List*  r ;
  // assignments for carrying in
  r = resources;
  // outgoing calls
  timing ->required_res_( return_val, r );
}
void Timing::required_res_
  ( Resource_List* & return_val, Resource_List*  r  )
{ startDate ->required_res_( return_val, r );
}
void Date::required_res_
  ( Resource_List* & return_val, Resource_List*  r  )
{ }
void DateSelected::required_res_
  ( Resource_List* & return_val, Resource_List*  r  )
{ // prefix blocks
 return_val -> concatenate(r);
}
void Task_List::required_res_
  ( Resource_List* & return_val )
{ // outgoing calls
  Task_list_iterator    next_Task(*this);
  Task*          each_Task;
  while ( each_Task = next_Task() )
  {
    each_Task->required_res_( return_val );
  }
}
```

Figure 10.15: Code for resource transportation

```
              with inheritance edge           without inheritance edge
                 (call to super)
     ----------------------------------------------------------------------
     A:      Case 1                           Case 2
             trv: Ex via Base to Common       trv: Ex via Base to DerivedPart
             trn: Base to Common              trn: Base to DerivedPart
     ----------------------------------------------------------------------
     B:      Case 3                           Case 4
             trv: Ex to Common                trv: Ex to DerivedPart
             trn: Ex to Common                trn: Ex to DerivedPart
     ----------------------------------------------------------------------

     A:   transportation starts at alternation class
              (transportation code pushing)
     B:   transportation starts at nonalternation class
     trv: traversal
     trn: transportation
```

Figure 10.16: Code generation with transportation

```
            |     0 args        |   2 arguments
   ---------|-------------------|--------------------
   Base     | (never called)    |   no function
   ---------|-------------------|--------------------
            |                   |   2 pBase
            |                   |   3 pDerived
   Derived  | 1 calls 2 args    |      4 call base
            |                   |   5 sDerived
            |                   |   6 sBase
```

Figure 10.17: Summary: Case 1

10.4. CODE GENERATION

```
/////////// BROADCASTING /////////////////
*carry* *in* Transport* trans
  *along* *from* Base *to* Common
    *at* Base
      trans = (@ new Transport(); @)
*wrapper* Common
  *prefix*
    (@ cout << endl << "TRANSPORTED "
          << trans << " TO " << this << endl ; @)
/// end transportation
```

The second transportation specification is a condenser and transports a **Common**-object back to a **Base**-object and prints it. This is achieved by

```
/////////// CONDENSING /////////////////
*carry* *out* Common* c
  *along* *from* Base *to* Common
    *at* Common
      c = (@ this ; @)
*wrapper* Base
  *suffix*
    (@ cout << endl << "TRANSPORTED "
          << c << " TO " << this << endl ; @)
/// end transportation
```

Note that in a condenser the transportation graph is specified in a forward manner *from* **Base** *to* **Common**, although the transported object flows in the reverse direction from **Common** to **Base**.

The condenser assumes that a **Base**-object contains at least one **Common**-object. Otherwise the program will fail when it tries to print in class **Base**.

The complete propagation pattern is shown below. It includes the sequence of wrappers in Fig. 10.18, called **Base/Derived**-wrappers, which will be used repeatedly.

```
*operation* void f()
  *traverse*
    *from* Ex *via* Base *to* Common
    /////////// BROADCASTING /////////////////
    *carry* *in* Transport* trans
      *along* *from* Base *to* Common
        *at* Base
          trans = (@ new Transport(); @)
    *wrapper* Common
      *prefix*
        (@ cout << endl << "TRANSPORTED "
              << trans << " TO " << this << endl ; @)
    /// end transportation
```

```
*wrapper* Base
  *prefix*
    (@ cout << endl << " pBase " << endl; @) // pBase
  *suffix*
    (@ cout << endl << " sBase " << endl; @) // sBase
*wrapper* Derived
  *prefix*
    (@ cout << endl << " pDerived " << endl; @) // pDerived
  *suffix*
    (@ cout << endl << " sDerived " << endl; @) // sDerived
```

Figure 10.18: Base/Derived-wrappers

```
//////////// CONDENSING ///////////////////
*carry* *out* Common* c
  *along* *from* Base *to* Common
    *at* Common
       c = (@ this ; @)
*wrapper* Base
  *suffix*
    (@ cout << endl << "TRANSPORTED "
            << c << " TO " << this << endl ; @)
/// end transportation
//==================
insert Base/Derived-wrappers
//==================
```

Next we translate the propagation pattern to C++ for the given class dictionary. Transportation specifications are implemented by signature extension. We will extend the signature at class **Base** with two arguments.

In this example we can observe a different kind of code pushing than the wrapper pushing we saw with traversals only. The code pushing in this example is related to transportation.

Now let's look at the code produced. We use **PUSHED T** to mark transportation code pushing and **PUSHED W** to mark wrapper pushing.

```
// Ex = <r> Base .
void Ex::f( )
{
  this->get_r()->f( );
}
```

10.4. CODE GENERATION

```
// Base   : Derived
//          *common* <q> Common .
void Base::f( )
{
   // PREMATURELY TERMINATED
}

void Derived::f( )
{
  // variable definitions for carrying in and out
  Transport* trans = new Transport(); // PUSHED T
  Common* c ;                          // PUSHED T
    this->f( trans , c );
}
```

Why is there no code at class **Base**? What happened to the suffix wrapper for class **Base**? It will be attached to class **Derived** *after* signature extension with two arguments.

The transportation code associated in the propagation pattern with class **Base** is pushed to class **Derived**, which has a function with zero arguments containing transportation declarations and initialization. Class **Derived** calls a function of **Derived** with two additional arguments. Pushing of transportation code is triggered by signature extension at an alternation class.

C++ has the equal-signature rule which requires that at **Base** and **Derived** we have the same signature with zero arguments.

```
// Derived = "derived"
//           <d> DerivedPart .
void Derived::f( Transport* trans,Common* & c )
{
  // prefix class wrappers
  cout << endl << " pBase " << endl; // PUSHED W
  cout << endl << " pDerived " << endl;
   this->get_q()->f( trans , c );
  // suffix class wrappers
  cout << endl << " sDerived " << endl;
  cout << endl << " sBase " << endl; // PUSHED W
  cout << endl << "TRANSPORTED "
              << c << " TO " << this << endl ;
}

// Common = "common" .
void Common::f( Transport* trans,Common* & c )
{
  // prefix class wrappers
  cout << endl << "TRANSPORTED "
              << trans << " TO " << this << endl ;
```

```
    // assignments for carrying out
    c = this ; ;
}
```

Class **Derived** has a function f with two arguments. The suffix block of class **Base** shows up at the end of the two-argument function of class **Derived**. This is important since the suffix block refers to one of the two arguments. The suffix block would not be well defined in the context of the zero-argument function of class **Derived**.

Case 2

Next we consider Case 2. It shows wrapper pushing in the absence of an inheritance edge.

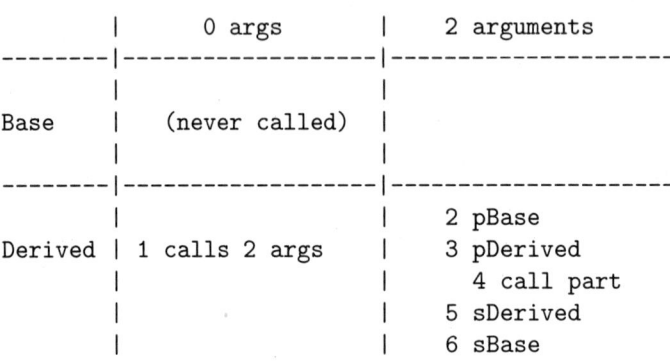

Figure 10.19: Summary: Case 2

The propagation pattern is now

```
*operation* void f()
  *traverse*
    *from* Ex *via* Base *to* DerivedPart
    //////////////////////////////
    *carry* *in* Transport* trans
      *along* *from* Base *to* DerivedPart
        *at* Base
          trans = (@ new Transport(); @)
      *wrapper* DerivedPart
        *prefix*
          (@ cout << endl << "TRANSPORTED "
              << trans << " TO " << this << endl ; @)
    /// end transportation
    //////////////////////////////
```

10.4. CODE GENERATION

```
        *carry* *out* DerivedPart* c
          *along* *from* Base *to* DerivedPart
            *at* DerivedPart
              c = (@ this ; @)
        *wrapper* Base
          *suffix*
            (@ cout << endl << "TRANSPORTED "
                    << c << " TO " << this << endl ; @)
        /// end transportation
        //===================
        insert Base/Derived-wrappers
        //===================
```

The corresponding C++ code is below and is summarized in Fig. 10.19.

```
//   Ex  = <r > Base .
void Ex::f( )
{
  this->get_r()->f( );
}

//  Base   : Derived
//          *common* <q > Common .
void Base::f( )
{
   // PREMATURELY TERMINATED
}

void Derived::f( )
{
  // variable definitions for carrying in and out
  Transport* trans =  new Transport(); // PUSHED T
  DerivedPart* c ;                     // PUSHED T
    this->f( trans , c );
}

//  Derived  = "derived"
//           <d > DerivedPart .
void Derived::f( Transport*  trans,DerivedPart* & c )
{
  // prefix class wrappers
 cout << endl << " pBase " << endl;  // PUSHED W
 cout << endl << " pDerived " << endl;

  // outgoing calls
  // construction edge prefix wrappers
```

```
  this->get_d()->f( trans , c  );
  // construction edge suffix wrappers

  // suffix class wrappers
 cout << endl << " sDerived " << endl;
 cout << endl << " sBase " << endl; // PUSHED W
 cout << endl << "TRANSPORTED "                       //PUSHED W
              << c << " TO " << this << endl ;        //PUSHED W
}

// DerivedPart  = "part" .
void DerivedPart::f( Transport*  trans,DerivedPart* &  c )
{
  // prefix class wrappers
 cout << endl << "TRANSPORTED "
              << trans << " TO " << this << endl ;
  // assignments for carrying out
  c =  this ;
}
```

Case 3

```
         |    2 arguments
---------|-------------------
 Base    |  4 call part
---------|-------------------
         |  1 pBase
         |  2 pDerived
 Derived |  3 call base
         |  5 sDerived
         |  6 sBase
```

Figure 10.20: Summary: Case 3

In Case 3 the transportation starts at a nonalternation vertex. The propagation pattern is

```
*operation* void f()
  *traverse*
    *from* Ex *to* Common
    /////////////////////////////
    *carry* *in* Transport* trans
```

10.4. CODE GENERATION

```
              *along* *from* Ex *to* Common
                *at* Ex
                  trans = (@ new Transport(); @)
         *wrapper* Common
           *prefix*
             (@ cout << endl << "TRANSPORTED "
                    << trans << " TO " << this << endl ; @)
      /// end transportation
      //////////////////////////////
      *carry* *out* Common* c
        *along* *from* Ex *to* Common
          *at* Common
            c = (@ this ; @)
         *wrapper* Ex
           *suffix*
             (@ cout << endl << "TRANSPORTED "
                    << c << " TO " << this << endl ; @)
      /// end transportation
      //==================
      insert Base/Derived-wrappers
      //==================
```

The corresponding C++ code is summarized in Fig. 10.20 and shown in detail below.

```
void Ex::f( )
{ // variables for carrying in and out
  Transport*  trans ;
  Common*  c ;

  // assignments for carrying in
  trans = new Transport(); ;

  // prefix blocks

  // outgoing calls
  r ->f( trans , c );

  // suffix blocks
 cout << endl << "TRANSPORTED "
               << c << " TO " << this << endl ; }
void Base::f( Transport*  trans,Common* &  c )
{
  // outgoing calls
  q ->f( trans , c );
}
```

```
void Derived::f( Transport* trans,Common* & c )
{
  // prefix blocks
  // pBase PUSHED W
  // pDerived

  // outgoing calls
  this->Base::f( trans , c );

  // suffix blocks
  // sDerived
  // sBase PUSHED W
}

void Common::f( Transport*  trans,Common* & c )
{ // prefix blocks
 cout << endl << "TRANSPORTED "
              << trans << " TO " << this << endl ;
  // assignments for carrying out
  c =  this ;}
```

Case 4

```
          |  2 arguments
 ---------|-------------------
 Base     |
 ---------|-------------------
          |  1 pBase
          |  2 pDerived
 Derived  |   3 call part
          |  4 sDerived
          |  5 sBase
```

Figure 10.21: Summary: Case 4

This case is the simplest since the transportation starts at a nonalternation vertex and since no inheritance edges are in the propagation graph. The propagation pattern is

```
*operation* void f()
  *traverse*
    *from* Ex *to* DerivedPart
    /////////////////////////////
```

10.4. CODE GENERATION

```
      *carry* *in* Transport* trans
        *along* *from* Ex *to* DerivedPart
          *at* Ex
            trans = (@ new Transport(); @)
      *wrapper* DerivedPart
        *prefix*
          (@ cout << endl << "TRANSPORTED "
                << trans << " TO " << this << endl ; @)
/// end transportation
////////////////////////////////
      *carry* *out* DerivedPart* c
        *along* *from* Ex *to* DerivedPart
          *at* DerivedPart
            c = (@ this ; @)
      *wrapper* Ex
        *suffix*
          (@ cout << endl << "TRANSPORTED "
                << c << " TO " << this << endl ; @)
/// end transportation
//====================
insert Base/Derived-wrappers
//====================
```

The C++ code is left as an exercise.

10.4.2 Combining Two Propagation Patterns

For efficiency reasons, it is often better to combine two independent traversals into one. To compute a sum and an average, we might start with two independent traversals.

```
*operation* void fsum(int& sum)
  *traverse*
    *from* B *to* X
  *wrapper* B
    *prefix* (@ sum = 0; @)
  *wrapper* X
    *prefix* (@ sum = sum + *v; @)
```

and

```
*operation* void fcount(int& count)
  *traverse*
    *from* B *to* Z
  *wrapper* B
    *prefix* (@ count = 0; @)
  *wrapper* Z
    *prefix* (@ count ++ ; @)
```

Then we call both functions and print their results.

```
*operation* call_them()
  *wrapper* B
    *prefix*
      (@ this -> fsum(s); this -> fcount(c);
         cout << s << c;
      @)
```

Instead of traversing B-objects in two sweeps, it is more efficient to traverse them in one sweep. This is especially the case if the paths to X and Z have a big overlap. The above three propagation patterns are equivalent to the following one; more precisely, the function call_them and combined produce the same output when called for a B-object.

```
*operation* void combined()
  *traverse*
    *from* B *to* {X, Z}
  // transportation pattern for fsum
  *carry* *out* int sum
    *along* *from* B *to* X
      *wrapper* B
        *prefix* (@ sum = 0; @)
      *wrapper* X
        *prefix* (@ sum = sum + *v; @)
  // end transportation for fsum
  // transportation pattern for fcount
  *carry* *out* int count
    *along* *from* B *to* Z
      *wrapper* B
        *prefix* (@ count = 0; @)
      *wrapper* Z
        *prefix* (@ count ++ ; @)
  // end transportation for fcount
  *wrapper* B
    *suffix*
      (@ cout << sum << count; @)
```

The strategy of the combination is to replace the two traversals by two transportations that collect the same information, and to embed the two transportations into a traversal that fits them both. The new traversal directive is the merge of the two original traversal directives.

10.5 SUMMARY

Transportation patterns simplify the transportation of objects. They allow us to group objects together without having to know the details of their structure.

A transportation pattern is a reusable unit that lives in the context of a propagation pattern containing a traversal directive. The same transportation pattern may be used with different traversals. A transportation pattern consists of several *carry* statements (containing transportation directives and initialization statements). Several transportation patterns may be used in a propagation pattern.

A class dictionary that customizes a propagation pattern containing transportation patterns has to satisfy additional customizer restrictions beyond those for the traversal. The terminology is summarized in Fig. 10.22.

```
propagation pattern (with traversal)
  propagation directive
    which determines traversal graph
  zero or more transportation patterns
  wrappers

transportation pattern
  carry statements (declare transportation variables)
  propagation directive
    which determines transportation graph
  initialization of transportation variables
  wrappers which use transported variables
```

Figure 10.22: Transportation pattern terminology

10.6 EXERCISES

Exercise 10.1 (contributed by Cristina Lopes)
The following statement is about the relationship between traversal and transportation graphs. Is it correct? If so, prove it; otherwise find a counterexample. If the traversal graph has a single source and a single target, all the paths from the source to the target in the traversal graph must pass through the source of the transportation graph.

Exercise 10.2 Write a propagation pattern which for a given A-object brings the X-object to the Y-object and prints them both in class Y. Write three different propagation patterns, one for each of the following class dictionaries.

- A = <x> X.
  X = <y> Y.
  Y = .
  Hint:

  traversal: *from* A *to* Y
  transportation: *from* X *to* Y

- A = <y> Y.
  Y = <x> X.
  X = .

  Hint:

  traversal: *from* A *to* X
  transportation: *from* Y *to* X

- A = <x> X <y> Y.
  X = .
  Y = .

  Hint:

  traversal: *from* A *to* Y
  transportation: *from* A *to* Y

How can the class dictionary graphs be generalized so that the propagation patterns don't need updating and still implement the same task?

Exercise 10.3 Consider the following class dictionary, called ES. (It is a grammar defining an equation language; see Chapter 11.)

```
1   EquationSystem = <eqs> List(Equation).
2   Equation =
3      <var> Variable "="
4      <exp> Exp "." .
5   Exp :
6      FunctionCall |
7      Variable |
8      Number.
9   FunctionCall = "*call*" <fn> Function
10     <args> CommaList(Exp) .
11  Variable = <variableName> DemIdent.
12  Function = <functionName> DemIdent.
13  Number = <n> DemNumber.
14  List(S) ~ {S}.
15  CommaList(S) ~ "(" S {"," S} ")".
```

Sorted cross reference list:

```
CommaList        :15     10
Equation         :2      1
EquationSystem   :1
Exp        :5    4       10
Function         :12     9
```

10.6. EXERCISES

```
FunctionCall    :9      6
List     :14    1
Number   :13    8
Variable        :11     3       7
```

All traversal and transportation graphs are with respect to ES.

- Consider the following propagation directive:

    from EquationSystem
      through -> * , var , *
    to   Variable

    Find the unknowns in the propagation graph:

        UNKNOWN1 = UNKNOWN2 .
        Equation = < UNKNOWN3 > UNKNOWN4 .
        UNKNOWN5 = .
        UNKNOWN6 ~ { UNKNOWN7 } .

- Consider the following propagation directive:

    from EquationSystem
      bypassing -> Equation , var , Variable
    to Variable

    Find the unknowns in the propagation graph:

        UNKNOWN8 = < UNKNOWN9 > UNKNOWN10 .
        UNKNOWN11 = < UNKNOWN12 > UNKNOWN13 .
        UNKNOWN14 : UNKNOWN15 | UNKNOWN16 .
        UNKNOWN17 = < UNKNOWN18 > UNKNOWN19 .
        UNKNOWN20 = .
        UNKNOWN21 ~ { UNKNOWN22 } .
        UNKNOWN23 ~ UNKNOWN24 .

- Consider the following propagation directive (for traversal):

    from   EquationSystem
      through -> Equation , var , Variable
    to   Variable

    and the corresponding transportation directive:

    from EquationSystem *to* Variable

    Find the unknowns in the following transportation graph:

```
UNKNOWN25 = < UNKNOWN26 > UNKNOWN27 .
Equation = < UNKNOWN28> UNKNOWN29 .
UNKNOWN30 = UNKNOWN31 .
UNKNOWN32 ~ { UNKNOWN33 } .
```

- Consider the following propagation directive (for traversal):

```
*from* EquationSystem
  *bypassing* -> Equation , var , Variable
*to* Variable
```

and the corresponding transportation directive:

```
*from* Equation *to* Variable
```

Find the unknowns in the following transportation graph:

```
UNKNOWN34 = < UNKNOWN35 > UNKNOWN36 .
UNKNOWN37 : UNKNOWN38 | UNKNOWN39 .
UNKNOWN40 = < UNKNOWN41 > UNKNOWN42 .
UNKNOWN43 = .
UNKNOWN44 ~ UNKNOWN45 .
```

Exercise 10.4 The class dictionary is ES (see previous exercise). Consider the propagation pattern:

```
*operation* void  f(ostream& strm)
  *traverse*
    *from* EquationSystem
      *through* -> *,var,*
    *to* Variable
     *carry*
        *in* EquationSystem* c
        *along* *from* EquationSystem
                *to* Variable
        *at* EquationSystem    c =(@ this @)
     *wrapper* Variable
     *prefix*
        (@ strm << this << "\t:" <<
        this->get_variableName()->get_line_number() << "\t";
        c->g(this,strm);
        strm << "\n";@)

*operation* void  g(Variable* v,ostream& strm)
  *traverse*
```

10.6. EXERCISES

```
    *from* EquationSystem
      *bypassing* -> *,var,*
    *to* Variable
    *carry* *in* Equation* eq
      *along* *from* Equation *to* Variable
        *at* Equation
          eq = (@ this @)

    *wrapper* ~> Equation_List, Equation
      *prefix*
        (@ cout << "going through next equation "
              << each_Equation << endl; @)
    *wrapper* Variable
      *prefix*
        (@
        cout << endl << this << " from " << eq <<
          " compared with " << v << endl;
        if (this->g_equal(v))
              {
              strm << "used on " <<
                this->get_variableName()->get_line_number() << "\n";
              }
        @)
```

and the following input object

```
: EquationSystem (
   < eqs > : Equation_List {
     : Equation (
       < var > : Variable (
         < variableName > : DemIdent "a" )
       < exp > : Number (
         < n > : DemNumber "1" ) ) ,
     : Equation (
       < var > : Variable (
         < variableName > : DemIdent "b" )
       < exp > : Number (
         < n > : DemNumber "2" ) ) ,
     : Equation (
       < var > : Variable (
         < variableName > : DemIdent "c" )
       < exp > : FunctionCall (
         < fn > : Function (
           < functionName > : DemIdent "f" )
         < args > : Exp_CommaList {
           : Variable (
```

```
                       < variableName > : DemIdent "a" ) ,
                    : FunctionCall (
                       < fn > : Function (
                          < functionName > : DemIdent "g" )
                       < args > : Exp_CommaList {
                          : Variable (
                             < variableName > : DemIdent "b" ) } ) } ) ) ,
            : Equation (
               < var > : Variable (
                  < variableName > : DemIdent "d" )
               < exp > : FunctionCall (
                  < fn > : Function (
                     < functionName > : DemIdent "h" )
                  < args > : Exp_CommaList {
                     : Number (
                        < n > : DemNumber "1" ) ,
                     : Variable (
                        < variableName > : DemIdent "c" ) ,
                     : Number (
                        < n > : DemNumber "6" ) } ) ) } )
```

Find the unknowns in the following sentence and trace. The object in sentence form

```
a = UNKNOWN1.
b = UNKNOWN2.
c = *call* UNKNOWN3 (UNKNOWN4,*call* g(UNKNOWN5)).
UNKNOWN6 = *call* UNKNOWN7(UNKNOWN8, UNKNOWN9, UNKNOWN10).
```

   The trace

```
>> void EquationSystem::f(ostream&  strm)
 >> void UNKNOWN11::f(ostream&  strm,EquationSystem*  c)
  >> void UNKNOWN12::f(ostream&  strm,EquationSystem*  c)
   >> void UNKNOWN13::f(ostream&  strm,EquationSystem*  c)
a       :2           >> void EquationSystem::g(Variable*  v,ostream& strm)
      >> void Equation_List::g(Variable*  v,ostream& strm)
going through next equation a = UNKNOWN14 .
       >> void UNKNOWN15::g(Variable*  v,ostream& strm)
        >> void Number::g(Variable*  v,ostream& strm,Equation* eq)
        << void Number::g(Variable*  v,ostream& strm,Equation* eq)
       << void UNKNOWN16::g(Variable*  v,ostream& strm)
going through next equation b = UNKNOWN17 .
       >> void UNKNOWN18::g(Variable*  v,ostream& strm)
        >> void Number::g(Variable*  v,ostream& strm,Equation* eq)
        << void Number::g(Variable*  v,ostream& strm,Equation* eq)
       << void UNKNOWN19::g(Variable*  v,ostream& strm)
```

10.6. EXERCISES

```
       going through next equation UNKNOWN20
             >> void Equation::g(Variable* v,ostream& strm)
              >> void FunctionCall::g(Variable* v,ostream& strm,Equation* eq)
               >> void Exp_CommaList::g(Variable* v,ostream& strm,Equation* eq)
               >> void Variable::g(Variable* v,ostream& strm,Equation* eq)

a    from UNKNOWN21 compared with a
used on 4
                 << void UNKNOWN22::g(Variable* v,ostream& strm,Equation* eq)
                 >> void UNKNOWN23::g(Variable* v,ostream& strm,Equation* eq)
                >> void UNKNOWN24::g(Variable* v,ostream& strm,Equation* eq)
                  >> void UNKNOWN25::g(Variable* v,ostream& strm,Equation* eq)

b    from UNKNOWN26 compared with a
                   << void UNKNOWN27::g(Variable* v,ostream& strm,Equation* eq)
                  << void UNKNOWN28::g(Variable* v,ostream& strm,Equation* eq)
                << void UNKNOWN29::g(Variable* v,ostream& strm,Equation* eq)
               << void UNKNOWN30::g(Variable* v,ostream& strm,Equation* eq)
              << void FunctionCall::g(Variable* v,ostream& strm,Equation* eq)
             << void Equation::g(Variable* v,ostream& strm)
going through next equation UNKNOWN31
             >> void Equation::g(Variable* v,ostream& strm)
              >> void FunctionCall::g(Variable* v,ostream& strm,Equation* eq)
               >> void Exp_CommaList::g(Variable* v,ostream& strm,Equation* eq)
                >> void Number::g(Variable* v,ostream& strm,Equation* eq)
                << void Number::g(Variable* v,ostream& strm,Equation* eq)
                >> void Variable::g(Variable* v,ostream& strm,Equation* eq)

c    from UNKNOWN32 compared with UNKNOWN33
                   << void Variable::g(Variable* v,ostream& strm,Equation* eq)
                  >> void Number::g(Variable* v,ostream& strm,Equation* eq)
                  << void Number::g(Variable* v,ostream& strm,Equation* eq)
                 << void Exp_CommaList::g(Variable* v,ostream& strm,Equation* eq)
                << void FunctionCall::g(Variable* v,ostream& strm,Equation* eq)
               << void Equation::g(Variable* v,ostream& strm)
              << void Equation_List::g(Variable* v,ostream& strm)
             << void EquationSystem::g(Variable* v,ostream& strm)

   << void Variable::f(ostream& strm,EquationSystem*   c)
   << void Equation::f(ostream& strm,EquationSystem*   c)
   >> void Equation::f(ostream& strm,EquationSystem*   c)
   >> void Variable::f(ostream& strm,EquationSystem*   c)
b        :3         >> void EquationSystem::g(Variable* v,ostream& strm)
     >> void Equation_List::g(Variable* v,ostream& strm)
going through next equation a = UNKNOWN34 .
```

```
        >> void Equation::g(Variable* v,ostream& strm)
         >> void Number::g(Variable* v,ostream& strm,Equation* eq)
         << void Number::g(Variable* v,ostream& strm,Equation* eq)
        << void Equation::g(Variable* v,ostream& strm)
going through next equation b = UNKNOWN35 .
        >> void Equation::g(Variable* v,ostream& strm)
         >> void Number::g(Variable* v,ostream& strm,Equation* eq)
         << void Number::g(Variable* v,ostream& strm,Equation* eq)
        << void Equation::g(Variable* v,ostream& strm)
going through next equation UNKNOWN36
        >> void Equation::g(Variable* v,ostream& strm)
         >> void FunctionCall::g(Variable* v,ostream& strm,Equation* eq)
          >> void Exp_CommaList::g(Variable* v,ostream& strm,Equation* eq)
           >> void Variable::g(Variable* v,ostream& strm,Equation* eq)

a   from UNKNOWN37 compared with b
           << void Variable::g(Variable* v,ostream& strm,Equation* eq)
          >> void FunctionCall::g(Variable* v,ostream& strm,Equation* eq)
           >> void Exp_CommaList::g(Variable* v,ostream& strm,Equation* eq)
            >> void Variable::g(Variable* v,ostream& strm,Equation* eq)

b   from  UNKNOWN38 compared with b
used on 4
            << void Variable::g(Variable* v,ostream& strm,Equation* eq)
           << void Exp_CommaList::g(Variable* v,ostream& strm,Equation* eq)
          << void FunctionCall::g(Variable* v,ostream& strm,Equation* eq)
         << void Exp_CommaList::g(Variable* v,ostream& strm,Equation* eq)
        << void FunctionCall::g(Variable* v,ostream& strm,Equation* eq)
       << void Equation::g(Variable* v,ostream& strm)
going through next equation UNKNOWN39
        >> void Equation::g(Variable* v,ostream& strm)
         >> void FunctionCall::g(Variable* v,ostream& strm,Equation* eq)
          >> void Exp_CommaList::g(Variable* v,ostream& strm,Equation* eq)
           >> void Number::g(Variable* v,ostream& strm,Equation* eq)
           << void Number::g(Variable* v,ostream& strm,Equation* eq)
           >> void Variable::g(Variable* v,ostream& strm,Equation* eq)

c   from UNKNOWN40 compared with b
           << void Variable::g(Variable* v,ostream& strm,Equation* eq)
           >> void Number::g(Variable* v,ostream& strm,Equation* eq)
           << void Number::g(Variable* v,ostream& strm,Equation* eq)
          << void Exp_CommaList::g(Variable* v,ostream& strm,Equation* eq)
         << void FunctionCall::g(Variable* v,ostream& strm,Equation* eq)
        << void Equation::g(Variable* v,ostream& strm)
     << void Equation_List::g(Variable* v,ostream& strm)
```

10.6. EXERCISES

```
         << void EquationSystem::g(Variable* v,ostream& strm)

      << void Variable::f(ostream& strm,EquationSystem*    c)
     << void Equation::f(ostream& strm,EquationSystem*    c)
     >> void Equation::f(ostream& strm,EquationSystem*    c)
      >> void Variable::f(ostream& strm,EquationSystem*    c)
c       :4            >> void EquationSystem::g(Variable* v,ostream& strm)
        >> void Equation_List::g(Variable* v,ostream& strm)
```

rest deleted

Exercise 10.5 Consider the following propagation patterns together with class dictionary ES (see previous exercise).

```
*operation* void  f(ostream& strm)
  *traverse*
    *from* EquationSystem
      *through* -> *,var,*
    *to* Variable
    *carry*
       *in* EquationSystem* c
       *along* *from* EquationSystem
              *to* Variable
       *at* EquationSystem   c =(@ this @)
     *wrapper* Variable
     *prefix*
        (@ strm << this << "\t:" <<
        this->get_variableName()->get_line_number() << "\t";
        c->g(this,strm);
        strm << "\n";@)

*operation* void  g(Variable* v,ostream& strm)
  *traverse*
    *from* EquationSystem
      *bypassing* -> *,var,*
    *to* Variable
    *carry* *in* Equation* eq
      *along* *from* Equation *to* Variable
        *at* Equation
          eq = (@ this @)

    *wrapper* ~> Equation_List, Equation
      *prefix*
        (@ cout << "going through next equation "
            << each_Equation << endl; @)
     *wrapper* Variable
```

```
        *prefix*
          (@
          cout << endl << this << " from " << eq <<
            " compared with " << v << endl;
          if (this->g_equal(v))
                  {
                  strm << "used on " <<
                     this->get_variableName()->get_line_number() << "\n";
                  }
          @)
```

Find the unknowns in the following C++ program:

```
void EquationSystem::f( ostream&  strm )
{ // variables for carrying in and out
  EquationSystem*  c ;

  // assignments for carrying in
  c =  UNKNOWN1 ;

  // outgoing calls
  eqs ->f( UNKNOWN2 , UNKNOWN3  ); }

void Equation::f( ostream&  strm, EquationSystem*  c )
{ // outgoing calls
  var ->f( UNKNOWN4 , UNKNOWN5  ); }

void Variable::f( ostream&  strm, EquationSystem*  c )
{ // prefix blocks
 strm << this << "\t:" <<
         this->get_variableName()->get_line_number() << "\t";
         c->g(this,strm);
         strm << "\n"; }

void Equation_List::f( ostream&  strm, EquationSystem*  c )
{ // outgoing calls
  Equation_list_iterator         next_Equation(*this);
  Equation*                each_Equation;

  UNKNOWN6 ( UNKNOWN7 = UNKNOWN8() )
  {
    UNKNOWN9->f( strm , c  ); } }

void EquationSystem::g( Variable*  v,ostream&  strm )
{ // outgoing calls
  eqs ->g( v ,  strm  ); }
```

10.6. EXERCISES

```
void Equation::g( Variable*  v,ostream&  strm )
{ // variables for carrying in and out
  UNKNOWN10

  // assignments for carrying in
  UNKNOWN11

  // outgoing calls
  exp ->g( UNKNOWN12 ,   UNKNOWN13 ,  UNKNOWN14  ); }

void Exp::g( Variable*  v,ostream&  strm, Equation*  eq )
{ }

void Number::g( Variable*  v,ostream&  strm, Equation*  eq )
{ UNKNOWN15 }

void FunctionCall::g( Variable*  v,ostream&  strm, Equation*  eq )
{ // outgoing calls
  args ->g( v ,   strm ,  eq  ); }

void Variable::g( Variable*  v,ostream&  strm, Equation*  eq )
{
        cout << endl << this << " from " << eq <<
           " UNKNOWN16 with " << v << endl;
        if (this->g_equal(v))
              {
              strm << "used on " <<
                 this->UNKNOWN17()->get_line_number() << "\n";
              }
}

void Equation_List::g( Variable*  v,ostream&  strm )
{ // outgoing calls
  Equation_list_iterator     next_Equation(*this);
  Equation*            each_Equation;

  UNKNOWN18 ( UNKNOWN19 = UNKNOWN20() )
   {
  cout << "UNKNOWN21"
            << each_Equation << endl;
    each_Equation->g( v ,  strm  );
  } }

void Exp_CommaList::g( Variable*  v,ostream&  strm, Equation*  eq )
```

```
{ // outgoing calls
  Exp_list_iterator   next_Exp(*this);
  Exp*                each_Exp;

  UNKNOWN22 ( UNKNOWN23 = UNKNOWN24() )
  {
    each_Exp->g( v , strm , eq );
  } }
```

10.7 BIBLIOGRAPHIC REMARKS

- The "bring actors on stage" metaphor was suggested by Sam Adams [Ada93].
- The triples example is from [LX93b].
- The DFT example is from [LX93c].

10.8 SOLUTIONS

Solution to Exercise 10.3

```
UNKNOWN1  = EquationSystem        UNKNOWN2  = < eqs > Equation_List
UNKNOWN3  = var                   UNKNOWN4  = Variable
UNKNOWN5  = Variable              UNKNOWN6  = Equation_List
UNKNOWN7  = Equation              UNKNOWN8  = EquationSystem
UNKNOWN9  = eqs                   UNKNOWN10 = Equation_List
UNKNOWN11 = Equation              UNKNOWN12 = exp
UNKNOWN13 = Exp                   UNKNOWN14 = Exp
UNKNOWN15 = FunctionCall *CHOICE* switch with UNKNOWN16
UNKNOWN16 = Variable              UNKNOWN17 = FunctionCall
UNKNOWN18 = args                  UNKNOWN19 = Exp_CommaList
UNKNOWN20 = Variable              UNKNOWN21 = Equation_List
UNKNOWN22 = Equation              UNKNOWN23 = Exp_CommaList
UNKNOWN24 = Exp                   UNKNOWN25 = EquationSystem
UNKNOWN26 = eqs                   UNKNOWN27 = Equation_List
UNKNOWN28 = var                   UNKNOWN29 = Variable
UNKNOWN30 = Variable              UNKNOWN31 = nothing
UNKNOWN32 = Equation_List         UNKNOWN33 = Equation
UNKNOWN34 = Equation              UNKNOWN35 = exp
UNKNOWN36 = Exp                   UNKNOWN37 = Exp
UNKNOWN38 = FunctionCall *CHOICE* swith with UNKNOWN 39
UNKNOWN39 = Variable              UNKNOWN40 = FunctionCall
UNKNOWN41 = args                  UNKNOWN42 = Exp_CommaList
UNKNOWN43 = Variable              UNKNOWN44 = Exp_CommaList
UNKNOWN45 = Exp { Exp }
```

Solution to Exercise 10.5

10.8. SOLUTIONS

```
UNKNOWN1 = this                  UNKNOWN2 = strm
UNKNOWN3 = c                     UNKNOWN4 = strm
UNKNOWN5 = c                     UNKNOWN6 = while
UNKNOWN7 = each_Equation         UNKNOWN8 = next_Equation
UNKNOWN9 = each_Equation         UNKNOWN10 = Equation*  eq ;
UNKNOWN11 = eq =  this ;         UNKNOWN12 = v
UNKNOWN13 = strm                 UNKNOWN14 = eq
UNKNOWN15 = nothing              UNKNOWN16 = compared
UNKNOWN17 = get_variableName     UNKNOWN18 = while
UNKNOWN19 = each_Equation        UNKNOWN20 = next_Equation
UNKNOWN21 = going through next equation
UNKNOWN22 = while                UNKNOWN23 = each_Exp
UNKNOWN24 = next_Exp
```

Chapter 11

Class Dictionaries

Class dictionaries are more sophisticated propagation pattern customizers than are class dictionary graphs. With a class dictionary we can choose not only the detailed structure of objects, but also an application-specific notation for describing the objects succinctly. This notation allows us to describe "input stories" for propagation patterns. For example, for a restaurant administration program we can write a story that describes today's menu.

Objects are important for object-oriented design and programming, but they are too bulky to look at or to produce by hand. An example of an object is

```
Compound(
  <op> MulSym()
  <args> ArgList{
    Variable(
      <v> DemIdent "a")
    Variable(
      <v> DemIdent "b")})
```

Can we find a more succinct way to describe objects than the textual object notation or, even worse, the statements of a programming language (e.g., constructor calls)? Which information is essential in the objects? We certainly need the values of the atomic objects and some information about how those atomic objects are grouped together into larger objects. In the above example we need to know that a and b are atomic objects of the expression. This grouping can be expressed with some extra strings that we put between the atomic objects to allow a program to recover an object from a sentence. We use the word sentence simply to mean a sequence of terminals. It can be a proper English or French sentence or a stylized sentence, or it can be anything. To make a complete sentence out of a b, we use a few extra terminals: (* a b). Although much shorter than the above object, it conveys the same information if we use a class dictionary to interpret (* a b).

We first study how we can assign a concise sentence to an object. The goal in the back of our mind is to make the sentences expressive enough so that we can recover the objects automatically.

Consider again the meal example. We would like to describe a meal with a sentence such as

```
Appetizer:
  Melon
Entree:
  Steak Potato Carrots Peas
Dessert:
  Cake
```

instead of using the object notation. We can achieve this with the class dictionary in Fig. 11.1. A sentence is like a story about an object. The stories can be concise, like the one above, or verbose, and it is the class dictionary designer who decides. For example, the above meal description could be given by the following sentence:

```
At Hotel Switzerland you will enjoy
  Melon as an appetizer
  Steak Potato Carrots Peas as entree
  and Cake as a delicious dessert.
You will enjoy a splendid view of the Alps during good weather.
```

It is easy to adjust the class dictionary in Fig. 11.1 so that meals are represented in the above verbose form as sentences. All we need is to replace the first class definition by

```
Meal = "At Hotel Switzerland you will enjoy"
  Appetizer "as an appetizer"
  Entree "as entree and"
  Dessert "as a delicious dessert."
  "You will enjoy a splendid view of the Alps during good weather.".
```

If sentences are like stories about objects, then class dictionaries are like templates for stories. A class dictionary prescribes precisely how we have to write the stories about the application objects. Class dictionary design is like designing story templates.

We can also look at a sentence as describing a family of objects. We select a specific object from the family by selecting a class dictionary that is compatible with the sentence. From this point of view a sentence is like a propagation pattern: both are customized by a class dictionary.

Conceptually, a class dictionary is very similar to a class dictionary graph. A class dictionary can be viewed as a class dictionary graph with comments required to define the input language.

Concrete syntax (also known as syntactic sugar) is used to "sweeten" the syntax of the sentences. Below are examples of construction, alternation, and repetition class definitions which show where concrete syntax may be used.[1] We call the concrete syntax elements **tokens**.

---

[1] Legal class dictionary, page 437 (32).

```
Meal =
  "Appetizer:" Appetizer
  "Entree:" Entree
  "Dessert:" Dessert.
Appetizer : Melon | ShrimpCocktail.
ShrimpCocktail = "Shrimp Cocktail" Shrimps Lettuce [CocktailSauce].
CocktailSauce = Ketchup HorseRadish.
Entree : SteakPlatter | BakedStuffedShrimp.
SteakPlatter = Steak Trimmings.
BakedStuffedShrimp = StuffedShrimp Trimmings.
Trimmings = Potato <veggie1> Vegetable <veggie2> Vegetable.
Vegetable : Carrots | Peas | Corn.
Dessert : Pie | Cake | Jello.
Shrimps ~ Shrimp {Shrimp}.

Shrimp = .
Melon = "Melon".
Lettuce = .
Ketchup = .
Steak = "Steak".
Potato = "Potato".
Carrots = "Carrots".
Peas = "Peas".
Cake = "Cake".
Pie = "Pie".
Jello = "Jello".
Corn = "Corn".
StuffedShrimp = "Stuffed Shrimp".
HorseRadish = .
```

Figure 11.1: Meal language

Construction class:

```
Info =
  "Demeter System" <t> Trademarked
  "followed" "by"
  ["Law of Demeter" NotTrademarked]
  "developed" "at" Northeastern.
```

Each part may have some syntax associated with it that can appear before or after the part.

Alternation class:

```
Fruit: Apple | Orange *common*
  "weight" <weight> DemNumber "end".
```

The alternatives of an alternation class may not contain syntax.

Repetition class:

```
List ~ "begin" "list"
  {"before-each" Element "after-each"}
  "end" "list".

List ~ "first" Element
  {"separator" "prefix" Element "suffix"}
  "terminator".
```

Syntax is not allowed between the first element and the repeated part. To specify the language defined by a class dictionary, we first translate a class dictionary into a class dictionary without common parts; that is, into a flat class dictionary. The class dictionary without common parts[2] is then used as a printing table to print a given object.[3] The collection of all printed legal objects constitutes the language of the class dictionary.

The expansion of common parts is best demonstrated with an example. Consider the class dictionary

```
Basket = <contents> Fruit_List.
Fruit_List ~ {Fruit}.
Fruit : Apple | Orange *common*
  "weight" <weight> DemNumber "end".
Apple = "apple".
Orange = "orange".
```

After expansion of common parts

---

[2]Class dictionary flattening, page 439 (33).
[3]Printing, page 439 (34).

```
// flat class dictionary
Basket = <contents> Fruit_List.
Fruit_List ~ {Fruit}.
Fruit : Apple | Orange.
Apple = "apple"
  "weight" <weight> DemNumber "end".
Orange = "orange"
  "weight" <weight> DemNumber "end".
```

The common parts are flattened out to all the construction classes; therefore we call the expanded class dictionaries flat. Flat class dictionaries are usually not written by the user but are produced from nonflat class dictionaries by tools. Flat class dictionaries are a useful intermediate form. Notice that the flattening operation is well defined since there can be no cycles of alternation edges in a class dictionary graph.

For flat class dictionaries it is straightforward to define a printing operation[4] that is applicable to any object. We determine the class of the object and look up the class definition. Then we print the object according to the class definition, including the concrete syntax. For example, to print an **Apple**-object, we first print **weight** followed by printing a **DemNumber**-object followed by printing **end**. The set of all legal objects in printed form for some class dictionary G is the language defined by G. The language defined by G is sometimes called the set of sentences defined by G.

To demonstrate the printing algorithm we use the above class dictionary for baskets. Consider the following **Basket**-object that we want to print.

```
Basket (
  < contents > Fruit_List {
    Apple (
      < weight >  DemNumber "2" ) ,
    Orange (
      < weight >  DemNumber "5" ) } )
```

When we print it, we get the following output:

```
// sentence describing a Basket-object
apple weight 2 end
orange weight 5 end
```

If we change the class dictionary to

```
Basket = "basket" <contents> Fruit_List.
Fruit_List ~ "(" {Fruit} ")".
Fruit : Apple | Orange *common*
  "weight" <weight> DemNumber.
Apple = "apple".
Orange = "orange".
```

---
[4]Printing, page 439 (34).

the same object appears as

```
basket
  ( apple weight 2 orange weight 5 )
```

11.1 PARSING

We know how a class dictionary defines a language by assigning a sentence to each object. An object represents the structure of a given sentence relative to a class dictionary. A class dictionary is closely related to a grammar, the main difference being that a grammar defines only a language and a class dictionary additionally defines classes. (Knowledge of grammars is *not* a prerequisite for understanding this section.) Examples of two grammars, using the Extended Backus-Naur Form (EBNF) notation are in Fig. 11.2.

```
// Grammar 1
Basket = {Apple | Orange}.
Apple = "apple" "weight" DemNumber "end".
Orange = "orange" "weight" DemNumber "end".

// Grammar 2, almost a class dictionary
Basket = Fruit_List.
Fruit_List = {Fruit}.
Fruit = Apple | Orange.
Apple = "apple" "weight" DemNumber "end".
Orange = "orange" "weight" DemNumber "end".
```

Figure 11.2: Two grammars defining the same language

The differences between a grammar and a class dictionary are

- A grammar is usually shorter than a class dictionary since it is not concerned about object structure.

- A grammar does not have labels to name parts.

- A grammar does not have common parts; it is like a flat class dictionary.

- The syntax for grammars and class dictionaries is different but grammars can be written in a form that is close to a class dictionary (see Grammar 2 in Fig. 11.2).

Normally we are interested in defining an object by reading[5] its description from a text file. We call such a description a sentence that defines an object. A special kind of object, called a **tree object**, is defined by a sentence. It is called a tree object since its

---
[5]Parsing, page 441 (38).

underlying graph structure, given by the reference relationships between the objects, is a tree. Not every object is a tree object for some sentence. There are also circular objects and objects that share subobjects. An object o is said to be a **tree object** for a sentence s if its structure is a tree and not a general graph. Tree objects o have the property that printing o and reading the sentence again returns an object identical to the original object o. Not every object needs to be a tree object since many objects are built under program control, and there is never a need to read them from a text file.

The class dictionary contains all the information that is usually put into a grammar for defining a language. Therefore standard parser generator technology can be used to generate a parser automatically from the class dictionary. The parser takes as input a sentence in some file and returns the corresponding tree object. The grammar given in the class dictionary defines how to build the tree object.

We want to restrict ourselves to a subset of all class dictionaries that promote good "object story writing". We want the stories to be easy to read and write and learn. We also want the stories to be unique so that no two different stories describe the same object.

Therefore we introduce the concept of an ambiguous class dictionary. A class dictionary is **ambiguous** if there exist two distinct objects that map to the same sentence when they are printed. An example of an ambiguous class dictionary is:

```
Basket = <fruits> Fruit_List.
Fruit_List ~ {Fruit}.
Fruit : Apple | Orange.
Apple = "apple".
Orange = "apple".
```

The sentence `"apple apple"` represents four different kinds of baskets:

- A basket with two apples

- A basket with one apple and one orange

- A basket with one orange and one apple

- A basket with two oranges.

Therefore, the class dictionary is ambiguous.

We want to avoid ambiguous class dictionaries; therefore we need an algorithm to check whether a class dictionary is ambiguous. Not all problems are algorithmically solvable and computer scientists have found many computational problems that are provably not algorithmically solvable. Indeed, the class dictionary ambiguity problem cannot be solved by an algorithm. This can be proved by a reduction that shows that if the class dictionary ambiguity problem is solvable, then one of the provably unsolvable problems (Post's correspondence problem) is solvable. This leads to a contradiction and therefore the class dictionary ambiguity problem is not algorithmically solvable.

We need to look for a work-around regarding the checking of a class dictionary for ambiguity. The solution is to restrict our attention to a subset U of all class dictionaries that are useful in practice and for which we can solve the ambiguity problem efficiently.

11.1. PARSING

We also need to find a subset U so that we can efficiently check whether a class dictionary belongs to U or not.

We choose U to be the set of LL(1) class dictionaries. We can efficiently check whether a class dictionary is LL(1), and in fact all LL(1) class dictionaries are not ambiguous. An LL(1) class dictionary has to satisfy two rules. We will learn Rule 1 shortly; Rule 2 is more technical and is explained in the next section and in the theory part of the book.

The LL(1) class dictionaries tend to define languages that are easy to learn and read. LL(1) class dictionaries are therefore very useful in practice especially in an environment where languages change frequently.

We parse class dictionaries by so-called recursive descent parsing, which will be explained next. This explains in detail how an object is constructed from a sentence. Recursive descent parsing is a standard concept from compiler theory; refer to your favorite compiler book (for example, [ASU86]) to learn how recursive descent parsing is used to build compilers.

A sentence is made up of terminals. There are two kinds of terminals, namely terminals with a value and terminals without a value. A number such as 123 is a terminal with a value and it represents an object of terminal class DemNumber. As a rule, terminals with values are representing objects belonging to a terminal class. Terminals without values correspond to the terminals appearing in the class dictionary. For example, apple orange are two terminals that correspond to the two terminals in the following class dictionary:

```
Fruits = Apple Orange.
Apple = "apple".
Orange = "orange".
```

We also call the terminals without value **tokens**. Notice that we overload the token concept since the syntax elements in a class dictionary are also called tokens.

Recursive descent parsing is best explained by mapping class dictionaries into **syntax graphs** (also called **syntax charts** or **syntax diagrams**) which are widely used for defining programming languages. In a syntax graph, classes are shown inside rectangles and tokens inside ovals. For every class there is one syntax graph. The syntax graph of a construction class

$$A = B_1[B_2]\ldots B_n.$$

is given in Fig. 11.3.

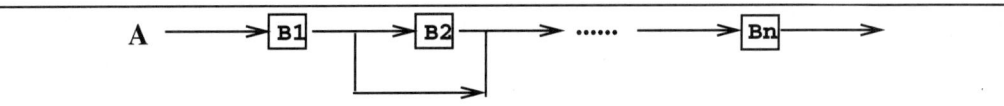

Figure 11.3: Syntax graph construction

The syntax graph of a repetition class

```
A ~ {S ";"}.
```

is given in Fig. 11.4.

The syntax graph of a repetition class

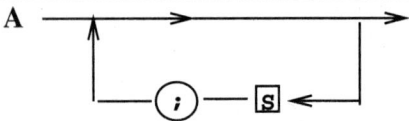

Figure 11.4: Syntax graph repetition

```
A ~ S { ";" S}.
```

is given in Fig. 11.5.

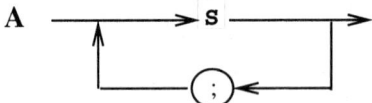

Figure 11.5: Syntax graph repetition (nonempty)

The syntax graph of an alternation class

$$A : B_1 | B_2 | \ldots | B_n.$$

is given in Fig. 11.6.

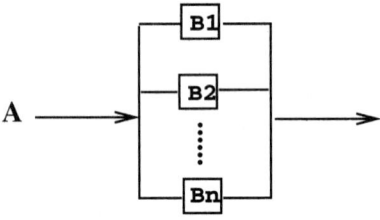

Figure 11.6: Syntax graph alternation

The parser works like a train that is trying to load a sentence while traversing the syntax graphs. (The sentence is broken into a sequence of terminals by a scanner.) The train enters the start syntax chart which corresponds to the start class of the class dictionary. Whenever the train enters a rectangle it moves to the syntax graph of the class in the rectangle. Whenever the train enters an oval it loads the token, provided it is the next terminal in the sentence to be parsed. The train stops and signals a syntax error if there is a different terminal in the input sentence.

The train has to make a decision whenever it comes to an intersection. We assume that the decision is made with a look-ahead of only one terminal and that no backtracking

11.1. PARSING

will be necessary. In a syntax graph that corresponds to a repetition class there is one branching point with a branching factor of 2. In a syntax graph that corresponds to a construction class there are as many branching points with branching factor 2 as there are optional elements. In a syntax graph that corresponds to an alternation class there is one branching point with a factor of n, where n is the number of classes on the right side of the alternation class definition.

To define the decision process more formally we have to define the **first set** $first(S)$ for every class S.[6] $first(S)$ is the set of all terminals that can appear as first terminal in a sentence of S. A branch gets labeled with the set $first(S)$. When S may derive the empty string, we define that $first(S)$ contains epsilon.

We give several representative examples of how to compute first sets. We describe first sets as sets of strings between quotes, epsilon, and terminal class names. *terminal-class* DemIdent is used for class DemIdent (similarly for other terminal classes) and epsilon stands for the empty string.

- Construction classes:

```
A = B C.
B = "is".
first(A) = first(B) = "is"

A = [B] [C] "is".
first(A) = first(B) union first(C) union "is"

A = [DemString] [DemNumber] DemIdent.
first(A) =
  {*terminal-class* DemString,
   *terminal-class* DemNumber, *terminal-class* DemIdent}

A = B C.
B = [DemIdent].
C = ["else" DemString].
first(A) = first(B) union first(C) union epsilon
        = {*terminal-class* DemIdent, epsilon, "else"}
```

epsilon is in the first set since the language of A contains the empty string as a legal sentence.

```
A = B C.
B = [DemIdent].
C = "else" DemString.
first(A) = first(B) union first(C) removing epsilon
        = {*terminal-class* DemIdent, "else"}
```

---
[6]First sets, page 439 (37).

- Repetition classes:

  ```
  A ~ {DemIdent}.
  first(A) = {*epsilon*, *terminal-class* DemIdent}

  A ~ "is" {DemIdent}.
  first(A) = "is"

  A ~ {DemIdent} "is".
  first(A) = first(DemIdent) union "is"
           = {*terminal-class* DemIdent, "is"}
  ```

- Alternation classes:

  ```
  A : B | C.
  B = "b".
  C = "c".
  first(A) = first(B) union first(C) = {"b", "c"}

  A : B | C.
  B ~ {DemIdent}.
  C = "c".
  first(A) = first(B) union first(C)
           = {*terminal-class* DemIdent, *epsilon*, "c"}
  ```

To simplify the decision process at a branching point we make the following assumption:

- We require that all the branches at a branching point in an alternation class definition have disjoint first sets (Rule 1).

With this restriction it is easy for the train to make these decisions. At an alternation class branching point, compare the next input terminal in the sentence to be parsed with the first sets of the branches. If the next input terminal is contained in any of those first sets we take that branch. Otherwise an error message is printed unless *epsilon* is in the first set of one branch, in which case this epsilon branch will be taken. According to Rule 1, only one branch may contain *epsilon*.

At a construction class branching point, we check whether the next input terminal is in the first set of what is inside the square brackets. If it is, we take the path that brings us to the optional terminal; otherwise, we take the other branch.

At a repetition class branching point, we check whether the next input terminal is in the first set of what is inside the curly brackets. If it is, we take the path through the loop, else we take the other branch.

This description implies that we have to compute the first function not only for classes, but for classes that might be preceded by terminals. This is a straightforward generalization. If the class is preceded by a string then the first set contains only that string.

We have seen that an error message can be generated at a branching point inside an alternation class definition. At a branching point inside a construction or repetition class definition we will never generate an error message. However, the parser generates an error message at nonbranching points, namely whenever a specific terminal is expected and that terminal is not the next input terminal.

We now extend the parser described above so that it returns a tree object for a given input string. This tree object stores the structural information about the string, but not all the details. None of the strings in the grammar definition will show up in the tree object.

Whenever the train starts a new syntax graph G that corresponds either to a construction or repetition class definition, a class instance is created. If G is defined by a construction class, the values of the parts will be assigned recursively when the syntax graphs of the classes on the right side are traversed. If G is defined by a repetition class, a list of objects will be created. It will be a list as long as the number of repetitions of objects of the class on the right side of the repetition class. Whenever the train starts a new syntax graph G that corresponds to an alternation class, the tree object remains unchanged.

The basket examples at the end of the last section also serve as examples for parsing.

11.2 LL(1) CONDITIONS AND LEFT-RECURSION

The LL(1) conditions for a class dictionary consist of two rules.[7] These conditions exclude ambiguous class dictionaries while being checkable efficiently. We have already discussed the first LL(1) rule since it is needed by the parsing algorithm. The first LL(1) rule requires that the first sets of the alternatives of an alternation class are disjoint. The second LL(1) rule is needed to make class dictionaries nonambiguous. To define Rule 2 we need to introduce follow sets.

$follow(A)$ for some vertex A consists of all terminals that can appear *immediately after* a sentence of $L(A)$. $L(A)$ is the set of all printed A-objects. The follow sets are computed with respect to the start class, which is the first class appearing in the class dictionary. For terminals of terminal sets, the corresponding terminal class name is given. If the end of file can appear after a sentence of $L(A)$, then $follow(A)$ contains eof.

Consider the example class dictionary

```
Basket = <contents> SeveralThings.
SeveralThings ~ {Thing}.
Thing : Apple | Orange *common* <weight> DemNumber.
Apple = "apple".
Orange = "orange".
```

Some of the follow sets are

$follow(\text{Thing}) = \{\ \text{eof},\ \text{"apple"},\ \text{"orange"}\ \}$,
$follow(\text{SeveralThings}) = \{\ \text{eof}\ \}$.

The follow set of **Thing** contains eof since a **Thing**-object can be the last thing in a basket. It contains "apple" since an apple may appear after a **Thing**-object.

---

[7]LL(1) conditions, page 442 (42).

Now we can formulate the second and last rule of the LL(1) conditions

Rule 2:

For all alternation classes

```
A : A1 | ... | An.
```

if an alternative, say $A1$, contains *empty* in its first set $first(A1)$, then $first(A2)$, $first(A3)$, ... have to be disjoint from $follow(A)$.

The following example motivates Rule 2. The class dictionary

```
Example = <l> List <f> Final.
List : Nonempty | Empty.
Nonempty = <first> Element <rest> List.
Empty = .
Element = "c".
Final : Empty | End.
End = "c".
```

violates Rule 2.

We choose A1 to be Empty and A2 to be Nonempty and A to be List. The relevant first and follow sets are

```
first(Empty) = {empty}.
first(NonEmpty) = {"c"}.
follow(List) = {"c", eof}.
```

Now first(NonEmpty) is not disjoint from follow(List) and therefore Rule 2 is violated.

The following two objects have the same corresponding sentence

```
object 1:

:Example(
  <l> :Empty()
  <f> :End())

object 2:

:Example(
  <l> :Nonempty(<first> :Element() <rest> :Empty())
  <f> :Empty())
```

In both cases, the sentence c is printed. For object 1, c is printed by the End-object. For object 2, c is printed by the Element-object.

Violation of the LL(1) conditions does not necessarily imply that the class dictionary is ambiguous. For example, the following class dictionary is not LL(1) but it is not ambiguous.

```
Example = <l> List <f> Final.
List : Nonempty | Empty.
```

```
Nonempty = <first> Element <rest> List.
Empty = .
Element = "c".
Final : End.
End = "c".
```

Rule two of the LL(1) conditions is violated. follow(List) contains "c" and so does first(Nonempty). But we cannot find two distinct objects that are mapped to the same sentence by the printing function *g_print*. This example however shows parsing ambiguity. When the parser sees the "c" terminal in the input while parsing an Example-object, it does not know whether to build a Nonempty or an Empty-object in part 1. The first "c" terminal has two different interpretations. We can represent it as an Element-object or as an End-object.

The LL(1) conditions force the object printing algorithm *g_print*() to have a useful property. We can always retrieve the object from the output of the printing algorithm. The LL(1) conditions are sufficient for *g_print* to be a **bijection** (i.e., onto and one-to-one) between tree objects and sentences. If a flat class dictionary G satisfies the LL(1) Rules 1 and 2 then the function $g\_print(G, \omega)$ is a bijection from C-objects in $TreeObjects(G)$ to $L(C)$. A flat class dictionary is a class dictionary where all common parts and terminals have been pushed down to the construction classes.

The inverse of *g_print* is function g_parse : $for\ all\ \omega \in TreeObjects(G)$

$$\omega = g\_parse(G, class\ of\ \omega, g\_print(G, \omega))$$

11.2.1 Left-Recursion

The LL(1) rules exclude a certain kind of left-recursion.

Informally, a class dictionary is left-recursive if it contains paths along which no input is consumed. An example of such a class dictionary is

```
Basket = <contents> Contents.
Contents : Fruit | Basket.
Fruit : Apple | Orange.
Apple = "apple".
Orange = .
```

There is left-recursion that involves the two classes

```
Basket = <contents> Contents .
Contents : Fruit | Basket .
```

We can go through the cycle Basket, Contents any number of times without consuming input.

This kind of left-recursion is a special case of LL(1) condition violation; specifically, a Rule 1 violation. Consider the first sets of the two alternatives of Contents:

```
first(Fruit) = {"apple", empty}.
first{Basket} = {"apple", empty}
```

The two first sets are not disjoint and therefore Rule 1 is violated.

Left-recursion can appear in a second form; consider the class dictionary graph

```
Mother = <has> Child.
Child  = <has> Mother.
```

Here the LL(1) conditions are satisfied but we still have left-recursion. This kind of left-recursion is excluded by the inductiveness axiom, which is discussed in the chapter on class dictionary design techniques (Chapter 12).

11.3 SUMMARY

A class dictionary D defines a language through the following mechanism. We consider all objects defined by the class dictionary graph G contained in D. This set is called $TreeObjects(D)$. We apply the print function which prints each object in $TreeObjects(D)$, and we call the resulting set $Sentences(D)$. This is the language defined by D.

To facilitate the writing, understanding, and learning of sentences, we use a subset of class dictionaries, called LL(1) class dictionaries. An LL(1) class dictionary is not ambiguous, and has other desirable properties. Specifically, different alternatives of an alternation class are introduced by different tokens.

This chapter explained the parsing process in detail, which takes a class dictionary and a sentence and constructs the corresponding object.

The relationships between class dictionaries and class dictionary graphs is summarized in Fig. 11.7. Four properties are considered in the figure: nonambiguous, LL(1), inductive,

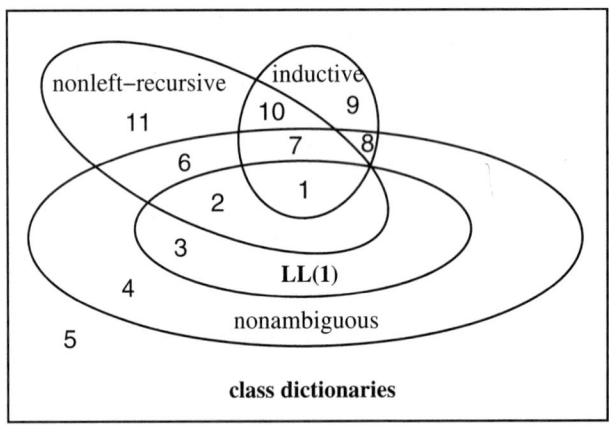

Figure 11.7: Venn diagram for class dictionaries

nonleft-recursive. Inductive class dictionaries are discussed in Chapter 12 but we give here the intuition: A class dictionary is inductive if it contains only good recursions; that is, recursions that terminate. Ideally, a class dictionary should satisfy all four properties. If the properties were independent, sixteen different sets would be defined by the four

11.3. SUMMARY

properties. However, there are only eleven because of the implication relationships between the properties (LL(1) implies nonambiguous, LL(1) and inductive imply nonleft-recursive).

We show example members for some of the eleven sets.

1. Nonambiguous, nonLL(1), noninductive, and left-recursive

   ```
   A = B C.
   B : E | C.
   C = "c".
   E = E.
   ```

2. LL(1), left-recursive, noninductive, Fig. 11.8

Figure 11.8: LL(1), left-recursive, noninductive

   ```
   A = B.
   B = A.
   ```

3. LL(1), nonleft-recursive, inductive, Fig. 11.9

Figure 11.9: LL(1), nonleft-recursive, inductive

   ```
   A = .
   ```

4. Nonambiguous, nonLL(1), left-recursive, inductive

   ```
   A = B.
   B : A | C.
   C = "c".
   ```

5. Ambiguous, nonLL(1), inductive

```
A = B C.
B : U | V.
C : G | H.
U = "c".
V = .
G = "c".
H = .
```

6. Ambiguous, nonLL(1), noninductive, left-recursive

```
A : B | C.
B = B.
C = .
```

11.4 EXERCISES

Exercise 11.1 (Design and implementation objective)
Write a class dictionary that defines Lisp lists, assuming that the atoms are only identifiers. Your language should handle the following examples:

```
()
(a b c)
(a (a b c) d)
(a (a b () c ( a b)) d)
etc.
```

> Write a program for the class dictionary that counts the number of atoms in a Lisp list. The answer for the above examples should be
> 0 3 5 7 etc.
> Verify that your class dictionary satisfies the LL(1) properties.

Exercise 11.2 Write an adaptive program so that it removes all while statements from a Modula-2 program. We assume that the class dictionary for Modula-2 contains the following class definitions:

```
StatementSeq ~ Statements {";" Statements}.
Statements = [Statement].
Statement : WhileStat | IfStat ...
WhileStat = "while" ...
```

You can assume that **Statements** is used only in **StatementSeq**.

Exercise 11.3 (Programming for given class dictionary objective)
The following class dictionary defines the data structures used by company Zeus Inc.

11.4. EXERCISES

```
CustomerList ~ {Customer}.

Customer =
  <customerNumber> DemNumber <customerName> DemString
  <customerAddress> Address <telephone> DemNumber
  <contracts> ContractList.

Address =
  <street> DemString <city>   DemString
  <state>  DemString <zip>    DemNumber
  <phone>  DemNumber.

ContractList ~ Contract {Contract}.

Contract =
  <contractNumber> DemNumber <deliveryAddress> Address
  <date> DemString <remarks> DemString
  ContractLines.

ContractLines ~ ContractLine {ContractLine}.

ContractLine =
  Part <quantity> DemNumber
  <discount> DemNumber <amount>   DemNumber.

Part =
  <partNumber> DemNumber <description> DemString
  <price> DemNumber.
```

The company Zeus Inc. has to send a letter to all customers who bought part number 4556. Write an adaptive program that prints out the addresses of all customers who ordered part 4556. The format of the addresses is unimportant, as long as the street, city, state, and ZIP code is contained in each address.

Exercise 11.4 (Design and implementation objective)

1. Invent a notation for describing any given position on a chess board, write a class dictionary for it, and write a program that prints the number of white pieces on a given board.

2. Give a sample input that describes a board with about five pieces on it.

3. Give the same board position in the object notation.

Exercise 11.5 Consider the following class dictionary:

```
A ~ {B}.
B : C | D .
C = "xxx" A ["if" B] "yyy".
D = .
```

Check the following inputs for syntactical correctness. For each input that is syntactically correct, give the object in the object notation.

- 1 2 3 xxx if 999 yyy

- a b c xxx 1 2 3 yyy

- xxx if yyy

Exercise 11.6 (Programming for given class dictionary objective)

A postfix expression is an expression where the operator comes after the arguments. For example, [3 4 *] is a postfix expression that evaluates to 12.

Consider the following postfix expression language:

```
Example = ExpressionList.
ExpressionList ~ { Expression }.
Expression : Simple | Compound.
Simple = <v> DemNumber.
Compound = "[" <argument1> Expression <argument2> Expression
            Operator "]".
Operator : MulSym | AddSym | SubSym.
MulSym = "*".
AddSym = "+".
SubSym = "-".
```

Write a program that returns the list of evaluations of the postfix expressions. For example, if the input contains 2 3 [3 4 *] then the program returns the list (2 3 12).

Exercise 11.7 (Programming for given class dictionary objective)

Write a program that operates on a grammar that satisfies the following class dictionary

```
Grammar ~ {Rule}.
Rule = <ruleName> DemIdent Body ".".
Body : Construct | Alternat | Repetit.
Construct = "=" <partsAndSyntax> List(AnySymbol).
Alternat = ":" <alternatives> BarList(DemIdent).
List(S) ~ {S}.
BarList(S) ~ S {"|" S}.
SandwichedSymbol = <first> AuxList Symbol <second> AuxList.
Repetit = "~" <first> AuxList [ <nonempty> DemIdent ]
            "{" SandwichedSymbol "}" <second> AuxList.
AnySymbol : Symbol | OptSymbol | Aux.
```

11.4. EXERCISES

```
Symbol = [ "<" <labelName> DemIdent ">" ] <symbolName> DemIdent.
OptSymbol = "[" SandwichedSymbol "]".
Aux : Token.
Token = <v> DemString.
AuxList ~ { Aux }.
```

Write a program that prints the list of all rules with a **Construct** body.
Write a program that prints out all label names.
Example:

```
A = <x> B <y> DemIdent.
B = <x> DemIdent.
```

The output should look like:

```
with Construct body = (A B)
labels = (x y x)
```

Your algorithm should be linear time and space in the length of the input grammar.

Exercise 11.8 (Programming for given class dictionary objective)
Consider the following class structure:

```
Tree = "proper" <root> DemNumber <left> TreeOrLeaf <right> TreeOrLeaf.
TreeOrLeaf : Tree | Leaf.
Leaf = "leaf" DemNumber.
```

All instances of class **Tree** are binary search trees. All numbers that occur in the left subtree are smaller than the root, and all numbers that occur in the right subtree are greater than the root.
Write a method **search** for class **Tree** that takes as argument a number, and returns 1 if the number is in the tree and 0 otherwise.

Exercise 11.9 (Programming for given class dictionary objective)
Write a translator for the following language:

```
Statement : ForStatement | PrintStatement.
ForStatement = "for" DemIdent ":=" <lower> DemNumber "to" <upper> DemNumber
   "do" Statement.
PrintStatement = "(print" IdentList ")".
IdentList ~ DemIdent { DemIdent}.
```

The purpose of the translator is to expand the for statements and produce a sequence of lists. They reflect the assignments made by the for statements. The following example should make the semantics of this language clear.
Example: The input

```
for i:=1 to 2 do
   for j :=3 to 4 do (print j i)
```

should output

(3 1)
(4 1)
(3 2)
(4 2)

Exercise 11.10 (Programming for given class dictionary objective)
Write a semantic checker for the language of the last problem. Verify that every variable that occurs in the print statement is assigned within a for statement.

Example:

```
for i:=1 to 3 do (print x)
```

is illegal.

Exercise 11.11 Consider the grammar

```
Person = "name" <name> DemIdent ["bittenBy" <bittenBy> DogList].
DogList ~ {Dog}
Dog =
  "dogName" <dogName> DemIdent
  <owner> Person.
```

Check the following three inputs for syntactical correctness. For those that are correct, draw the object.

```
name Peter
   bittenBy "dogName" Barry name Jeff
            "dogName" Bless name Linda

name Ana
   bittenby



name bittenby
```

Exercise 11.12 Consider the following class dictionary:

S = "a" [S] "b".

(Input finding objective) Give three distinct elements belonging to the language defined by this class dictionary.

(Language objective) Give a precise definition of the language defined by this class dictionary. Give a proof that the class dictionary defines exactly the described language.

11.5 BIBLIOGRAPHIC REMARKS

The meal example is from [LR88b].

- Compiler theory:

  The concepts of recursive descent parsing, first sets, follow sets, and the LL(1) conditions are reused from compiler theory. See for example [ASU86].

- Grammar-based programming:

  There are few papers about object-oriented programming using a grammar-based approach. An early paper that goes in this direction is [San82], which describes the Lithe language. In Lithe, class names are used as the nonterminal alphabet of a grammar. For manipulating objects, Lithe does not use message passing, but syntax-directed translation.

  A grammar-based approach to meta programming in Pascal has been introduced in [CI84]. [Fra81] uses grammars for defining data structures. [KMMPN85] introduces an algebra of program fragments. The POPART system treats grammars as objects [Wil83]. The synthesizer generator project also uses a grammar-based approach [RT84]. GEM described in [GL85b] is the predecessor of Demeter. The EBNF grammar notation is due to [Wir77].

- Program enhancement: [Bal86] proposes a frame-based object model to simplify program enhancement which has some similarities to the Demeter system.

- Knowledge engineering: Many papers in knowledge engineering propose an approach similar to the one used in the Demeter system. Minsky proposed an object-oriented approach to knowledge representation [Min75].

  The language KL-ONE [BS85] is an object-oriented knowledge representation language based on inheritance. KL-ONE was used in the late seventies. A class is called a *concept* in KL-ONE. Concepts are subdivided into primitive and defined concepts. Primitive concepts can be specified by a rich set of necessary conditions. A *role* belongs to a concept and describes potential relationships between instances of the concept and those of other closely associated concepts (i.e., its properties, parts, etc.). Roles are the KL-ONE equivalent to two-place predicates. The components of a KL-ONE concept are its *superconcepts* and the local internal structure expressed in 2.1 *roles* and 2.2 *constraints*, which express the interrelations among the roles. The roles and the constraints of a concept are taken as a set of restrictions applied to the superconcepts. Superconcepts are thought of as approximate descriptions, whereas the local internal structure expresses essential differences.

  There are several different kinds of roles, of which the *role set* is the most important. A role set captures the commonality among a set of individual role players. Role sets themselves have structure. Each role set has a value restriction (given by a type), and number restrictions to express cardinality information. KL-ONE supports role set restrictions that add constraints on the fillers of a role with respect to some concepts. KL-ONE uses a graphical language and the JARGON [Woo79] language to specify concepts. JARGON is a stylized, restricted, English-like language for describing objects and relationships. KL-ONE has been further developed in NIKL [KBR86], [Mor84], and KL-TWO [Vil84].

Classes defined by predicates (or generators [Bee87]) allow automatic classification of objects. This shifts an important burden from the user to the system (where it surely belongs), and it is very useful in knowledge acquisition and maintenance.

When classes are defined by predicates, it is necessary to study the complexity of the subsumption problem. The subsumption problem consists of deciding whether one class is a subclass of another class. It is well known that the subsumption problem can easily become intractable (for a summary see [PS88]; for the original article see [BL84]).

Frame-based description languages (including KL-ONE; a recent paper is [PS88]) are related to the Demeter system in the following way. A class dictionary defines a concept language that allows us to define concepts in terms of classes defined in the class dictionary and restrictions expressed in terms of instance variables. Such a concept language defines a subsumption algorithm that computes whether one concept is a subconcept of another.

Sheu [She87] proposes to put a logic-programming knowledge base as an interface between the user and an object-oriented system.

Object-oriented knowledge representation for spatial information is proposed in the paper [MK88].

- Object-oriented design:

  A good overview is given in [Weg87].

- Theory of program data:

  The work of Cartwright promotes a constructive approach to data specification, called domain construction, and is a precursor of our work on class dictionaries [Car84]. The idea of domain construction has its roots in the symbolic view of data pioneered by John McCarthy and embodied in the programming language Lisp. The domain construction approach to data specification views a data domain as a set of symbolic objects and associated operations satisfying the following three constraints:

    - Finite constructibility. Every data object is constructed by composing functions, called constructors.
    - Unique constructibility. No two syntactically distinct objects denote identical elements of the domain universe.
    - Explicit definability. Every operation, excluding a small set of primitive functions serving as building blocks, is explicitly defined by a recursive function definition.

  Cartwright uses subset definition to define noncontext-free types like height-balanced binary trees or nonrepeating sequences of integers. Quotient definitions are used to define types containing objects that are not uniquely constructible, such as finite sets and finite maps.

The Demeter approach also falls into the constructive method of data definition. At the moment we do not support subset and quotient definitions since they are difficult to handle at compile-time.

The constructors in the Demeter system come from construction and repetition classes. Alternation classes don't provide constructors.

11.6 SOLUTIONS

Solution to 11.12
3 inputs:

```
a b
a a b b
a a a b b b
```

This class dictionary defines the language $a^n b^n$. We prove this by induction on n:

Base For $n = 1$ it is true. When the optional symbol is missing, we get ab.

Step Induction hypothesis: Assume that the above class dictionary defines the language $a^n b^n$ for all $n = m - 1, n > 0$. We want to show this fact for $n = m$. Consider entering the optional symbol [S] one additional time. This adds one a and one b to $a^{m-1} b^{m-1}$ which by the induction hypothesis belongs to the language. Therefore we get that $a^m b^m$ also belongs to the language.

Chapter 12

Style Rules for Class Dictionaries

In this chapter we present several style rules related to the structural organization of classes. Defining the class dictionary for an application is a very important and interesting task. The class dictionary determines all the data structures, which in turn determine the efficiency of the algorithms. The class dictionary also influences the reusability of the resulting code.

There is a need to break large class dictionaries into modular pieces that are easier to manage. This topic of modularization will be discussed elsewhere. In this chapter we have collected a set of useful design techniques for those modular pieces of class dictionaries.

The style rules cover several topics: avoiding bad recursion in class structures, optimization of class structures, parameterization, systematic structuring and naming, functional dependency normalization, and notational issues such as viscosity.

12.1 LAW OF DEMETER FOR CLASSES

The class dictionary graphs of object-oriented applications often contain cycles which means that the class definitions are recursive. The goal of the Law of Demeter for classes is to avoid bad recursions in class structures; that is, recursions which cannot terminate.

If a class dictionary graph does not contain any cycle, we can build complex objects from simple objects inductively. The reason is obvious. We can topologically sort any acyclic directed graph, and the topological order tells us in what order to build the objects. As class dictionary graphs become more and more complex, which means there may be more and more cycles, we can still build objects inductively and incrementally as long as every cycle has a way out of cycles. We call such class dictionaries inductive. Otherwise we have to build finite cyclic objects for any vertex on those cycles. We argue that noninductive class dictionary graphs should be avoided most of the time.

Consider the class dictionary graph in Fig. 12.1a. When we construct a class dictionary graph slice anchored at vertex Nonempty, vertex Nonempty forces all the outgoing construction and inheritance edges to be included in the slice. Vertex List must have the only outgoing alternation edge List$\Longrightarrow$Nonempty, because it has an incoming construction

12.1. LAW OF DEMETER FOR CLASSES

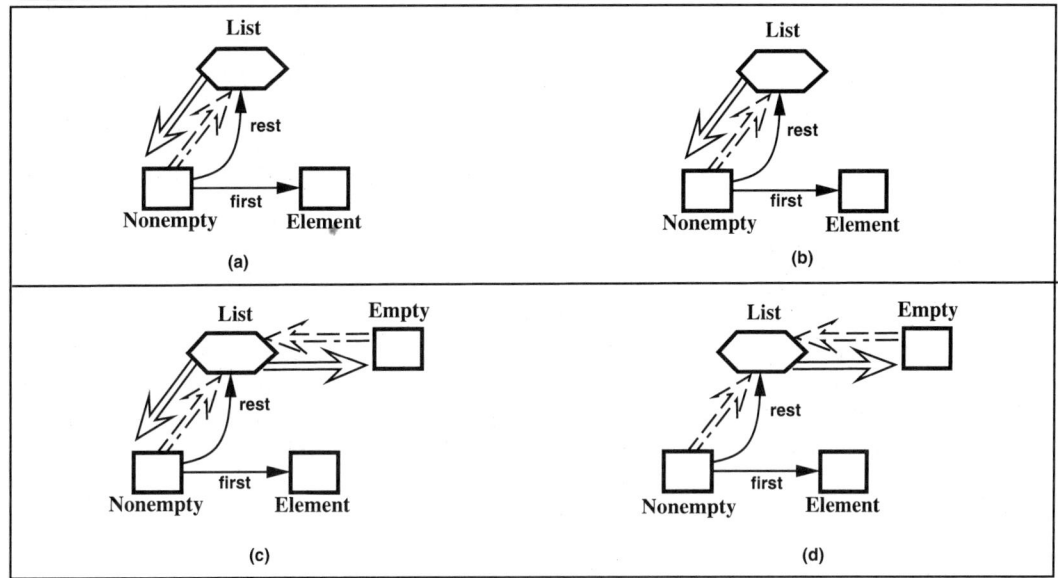

Figure 12.1: Illustration of class dictionary graph slices

edge. Fig. 12.1b shows the only class dictionary graph slice anchored at vertex Nonempty.

Consider the class dictionary graph in Fig. 12.1c. In Fig. 12.1d we show one of the class dictionary graph slices anchored at vertex Nonempty. The difference from the above case is that we can select alternation edge List$\Longrightarrow$ Empty instead of taking alternation edge List$\Longrightarrow$ Nonempty.

In the class dictionary graph of Fig. 12.1a, a Nonempty-object must contain an Element-object and a List-object. A List-object must always be a Nonempty-object—an infinite recursion. In Fig. 12.1b, this infinite recursion is expressed by the cycle formed by Nonempty$\xrightarrow{rest}$ List and List$\Longrightarrow$ Nonempty. This cycle is forced to be included.

In the class dictionary graph of Fig. 12.1c, a Nonempty-object must contain an Element-object and a List-object. But a List-object can be an Empty-object. In this case, we don't have an infinite recursion. We can have a Nonempty-object that is a list containing only one element, an Element-object. The Empty-object is used here for the end of the list.

Comparing the two class dictionary graphs in Fig. 12.1a and 12.1c, we can build only cyclic Nonempty-objects from the first class dictionary graph in Fig. 12.1a; but we can build acyclic Nonempty-objects of any size based on the Nonempty-objects of smaller size for the second class dictionary graph. We call the second class dictionary graph an **inductive** class dictionary graph. The first class dictionary graph is not inductive.

To introduce the Law of Demeter for classes, we reuse reachability concepts and the class dictionary graph slice concept introduced earlier.

A vertex w in a semi-class dictionary graph is said to be **reachable** from a vertex v by a path of length n, if there is a knowledge or an inheritance path of length n from v to w.

A semi-class dictionary graph is **cycle-free** if there is no $v \in V$ such that v is reachable from v by a path of at least length 1.

A semi-class dictionary graph is **inductive** if it satisfies the inductiveness rule. The inductiveness rule is: For all vertices v there exists at least one cycle-free class dictionary graph slice anchored at v.

The purpose of the inductiveness rule is

1. To make each recursion well defined and to guarantee that the inductive definitions of the objects associated with the vertices of the class dictionary graph have a base case. Informally, the rule disallows classes that have only circular objects.

2. To exclude certain useless symbols from the grammar corresponding to a class dictionary graph. There are two kinds of useless symbols: the ones that cannot be reached from the start symbol and the ones that are involved in an infinite recursion. The inductiveness rule excludes useless symbols of the infinite recursion kind.

3. To allow a tool to generate more code for groups of classes that satisfy this rule.

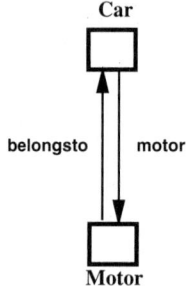

Figure 12.2: Car and motor

Sometimes, people may want to keep their class dictionary graphs noninductive for some purposes, as shown in Fig. 12.2. Every Car-object must have a Motor-object. Every Motor-object must have a Car-object on which it is installed. Therefore we propose an approximation of the inductiveness rule.

The Law of Demeter for Classes is:
Maximize the number of inductive vertices of a class dictionary graph[1].

Maximizing the number of inductive vertices in a class dictionary graph minimizes the complexity of building objects and the software associated with them. Fewer objects are forced to be cyclic. Further motivation for the Law of Demeter for classes includes

---

[1] The Law of Demeter for classes is different from the Law of Demeter (for functions) in class form discussed in Chapter 8.

12.1. LAW OF DEMETER FOR CLASSES

- The objects defined by noninductive vertices must all be cyclic. Classes that define only cyclic objects should be used only when absolutely needed. It is harder to reason about them.

- Cyclic objects are harder to manipulate because of the danger of infinite loops.

It is useful to discuss three dimensions of class dictionary design.

- C: number of common parts of abstract classes.

- F: number of vertices that are not inductive.

- L: LL(1) violations. Count the number of different violations of Rule 1 and Rule 2.

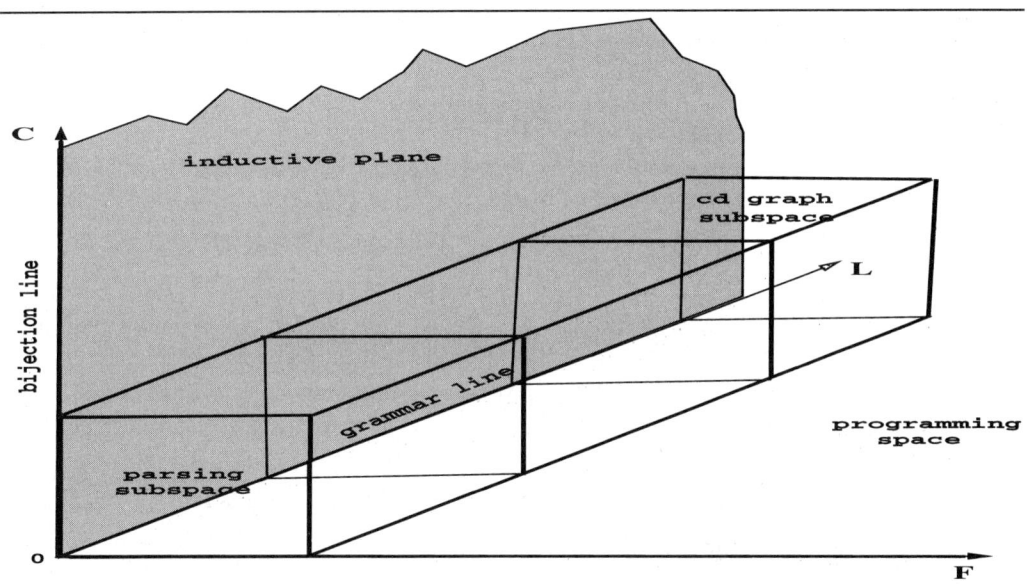

Figure 12.3: Three dimensions of class dictionary design

Figure 12.3 shows the design/programming space in the three dimensions.

- Pure data model subspace, class dictionary graphs (labeled as cd graph subspace in Fig. 12.3)

  Initially, when we develop a class structure, we put it into the class dictionary graph subspace. We will have many LL(1) violations and the class dictionary graph might not be inductive.

- Inductive class dictionaries plane

We improve the class dictionary graph and turn it into a class dictionary graph without noninductive vertices. This brings us into the inductive plane. We also maximize the common parts, which moves us away from the grammar line (traditional grammars don't have common parts).

- Parsing subspace

  We improve the class dictionary graph and turn it into a class dictionary with zero LL(1) violations. This moves us onto the bijection line. For class dictionaries on the bijection line, there is a bijection between sentences and tree objects.

12.2 CLASS DICTIONARY GRAPH OPTIMIZATION

The goal of class dictionary graph optimization is to improve the class organization while keeping the set of objects invariant. This involves "inventing" abstract classes to minimize the total size of the class dictionary graph.[2] Our algorithms are programming-language independent and are useful to programmers who use languages such as C++. Class dictionary graph optimization has applications to design, reverse engineering and optimization of programs.

We formalize the concept that two sets of class definitions define the same set of objects. A class dictionary graph $D1$ is **object-equivalent** to a class dictionary graph $D2$ if

$$Objects(D1) = Objects(D2)$$

The **size** of a class dictionary graph is the number of construction edges plus one quarter the number of alternation edges.

The constant one quarter is arbitrary. All that is important is that this constant is smaller than a half. The reason is that we want the class dictionary in Fig. 12.4a to be smaller than the class dictionary in Fig. 12.4b.

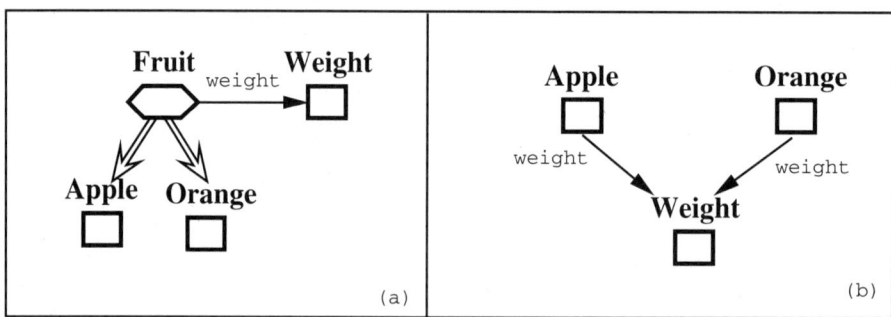

Figure 12.4: a has smaller size than b

---

[2]Class dictionary graph minimization, page 444 (50).

12.2. CLASS DICTIONARY GRAPH OPTIMIZATION

Anyway, we want alternation edges to be cheaper than construction edges since alternation edges express commonality between classes explicitly. This leads to better software organization through better abstraction and less code duplication.

The class dictionary graph minimization problem is defined as follows. Given a class dictionary graph, find an object-equivalent class dictionary graph of minimal size. Class dictionary graph minimization means more than moving common parts "as high as possible" in the class dictionary graph. It also minimizes the number of alternation edges.

In other words, we propose to minimize the number of edges in a class dictionary graph while keeping the set of objects invariant. Our technique is as good as the input it gets: If the input does not contain the structural key abstractions of the application domain then the optimized hierarchy will not be useful either, following the maxim: garbage in—garbage out.

However if the input uses names consistently to describe a class dictionary graph then our metric is useful in finding good hierarchies. However, we don't intend for our algorithms be used to restructure class hierarchies without human control. We believe that the output of our algorithms makes valuable proposals to the human designer who then makes a final decision.

Our current metric is quite rough: we just minimize the number of edges. We could minimize other criteria, such as the amount of multiple inheritance or the amount of repeated inheritance. A class B has repeated inheritance from class A, if there are two or more edge-disjoint alternation paths from A to B. The study of other metrics is left for future investigations.

12.2.1 Minimizing Construction Edges

Even simple functions cannot be implemented properly if a class dictionary graph does not have a minimal number of construction edges. By properly we mean with resilience to change.

Consider the class dictionary in Fig. 12.5, which is not minimized.

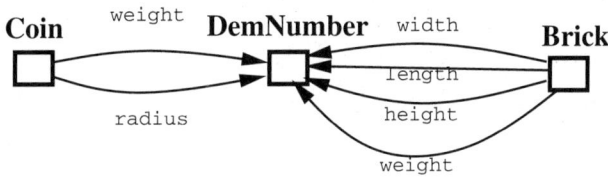

Figure 12.5: Class dictionary to be minimized

Suppose we implement a **print** function for **Coin** and **Brick**. Now assume that several hundred years have passed and that we find ourselves on the moon where the weight has a different composition: a gravity and a mass. We then have to rewrite our print function for both Coin and Brick.

After minimization of the number of construction edges in Fig. 12.5 we get the class dictionary in Fig. 12.6. In this minimized class dictionary we implement the print function

```
Coin = <radius> Number .
Brick = <width> Number <length> Number <height> Number .
Weight_related : Coin | Brick *common* <weight> Number.
```

Figure 12.6: Optimized class dictionary

for Coin with the method:

```
void Coin::print() {
  radius -> print(); Weight_related::print();}
```

The advantage of the optimization is that information about weights is now isolated to one class. If we change information about weights, we have to update only one class. For example, after the change of the weight composition, we get the new class

```
Weight_related : Coin | Brick *common* <mass> Number <gravity> Number.
```

We reimplement the print function for this new class and no change is necessary for classes Brick and Coin.

In summary, if the class dictionary graph has a minimal number of construction edges and the functions are written following the strong Law of Demeter (for functions), the software is more resilient to change. The strong Law of Demeter says that a function f attached to class C should call only functions of the *immediate* part classes of C, of argument classes of f including C, and of classes that are instantiated in f. A disadvantage of construction edge minimization is that it creates multiple inheritance. Therefore, it is not always strictly followed.

12.2.2 Minimizing Alternation Edges

Consider the following nonminimal class dictionary graph.

```
Occupation :
  Undergrad_student | TA | Professor | Adm_assistant
    *common* <ssn> Number.
Student : Undergrad_student | TA *common* <gpa> Real.
Faculty : Professor | TA *common* <course_assigned> Course.
Professor = .
TA = .
Adm_assistant = .
Course = .
Undergrad_student = <major> Area.
Area : Economics | Comp_sci.
```

12.2. CLASS DICTIONARY GRAPH OPTIMIZATION

```
Economics = .
Comp_sci = .
University_employee : TA | Professor | Adm_assistant
                    *common* <salary> Real.
```

Change the class definitions for Occupation and University_employee to

```
Occupation : Student | University_employee *common* <ssn> Number.
University_employee : Faculty | Adm_assistant *common* <salary> Real.
```

We have now reduced the number of alternation edges by three at the expense of adding repeated inheritance. By repeated inheritance we mean that a class is inherited several times in the same class. In the above example, class Occupation is inherited twice in class TA:

```
Occupation -> University_employee -> Faculty -> TA
           -> Student ->                        TA
```

However, not only alternation edges are reduced, but also the amount of multiple inheritance, which we propose as another metric to produce good schemas from the software engineering point of view.

Class dictionary graph minimization consists of two steps.

- Construction edge minimization. This is an easy task: we abstract out the common parts and attach them to an alternation class. If there is no appropriate alternation class, we introduce a new one.

- Alternation edge minimization. Alternation edge minimization is in general a computationally expensive problem (it is known to be NP-hard), but there is a special case, called the tree property[3] case, where there is an efficient algorithm.

To minimize the construction edges, we use the concept of a redundant part. In a first approximation a construction edge with label x and target vertex v is called **redundant** in a class dictionary graph, if there is more than one x-labeled construction edge going into v. This definition of redundant part is adequate for many practical situations. To cover all cases, it needs to be slightly generalized. A construction edge with label x and target vertex v is called **redundant** if there is a second construction edge with label x and target vertex w such that v and w have the same set of associated classes.

A class dictionary graph has a minimal number of construction edges if it does not contain any redundant construction edges.

Alternation edge minimization solves the following problem. Given a class dictionary graph D with a minimal number of construction edges, find a class dictionary graph D_1 such that the total number of alternation edges of D_1 is minimal, and so that D and D_1 are object-equivalent.

Next we consider a special case of the alternation edge minimization problem. This creates an interesting link between single inheritance and a property of class dictionary graphs, called the tree property.

---

[3]Tree property, page 444 (49).

Definition A class dictionary graph G is called a **single inheritance** class dictionary graph, if for each vertex v in G, v has at most one incoming alternation edge.

A class dictionary graph can become an object-equivalent, single inheritance class dictionary graph if and only if its sets of associated vertices satisfy the tree property. (The set of associated vertices of a vertex is the set of all the concrete subclasses.) The set of associated vertices of a vertex can be regarded as an inheritance cluster. If all inheritance clusters in a class dictionary graph are pairwise disjoint or in a proper subset relationship, then the class dictionary graph can become an object-equivalent single inheritance class dictionary graph. Furthermore, by checking whether the sets of associated vertices of a class dictionary graph satisfy the tree property, we are effectively transforming such a class dictionary graph into a single inheritance class dictionary graph.

Definition A collection of subsets of a set S has the **tree property** if for any pair of subsets of S one element of the pair is completely contained in the other, or if the two subsets are disjoint.

When a collection of subsets has the tree property, the graph having the subsets as vertices and the subset relationships as edges is a tree.

When the tree property is satisfied, it is easy to reorganize the class dictionary graph into a single inheritance class dictionary graph. The set inclusion relationships describe the inheritance structure.

Consider the following example. The class dictionary in Fig. 12.7 satisfies the tree property. The classes associated with **ChessPiece** are a superset of the classes associated with **Officer**. Therefore we can transform the class dictionary into the object-equivalent

```
ChessPiece : Queen | King | Rook | Bishop | Knight | Pawn.
Officer : Queen | King | Rook.
```

Figure 12.7: Class dictionary that satisfies tree property

class dictionary in Fig. 12.8, which is single inheritance.

```
ChessPiece : Officer | Bishop | Knight | Pawn.
Officer : Queen | King | Rook.
```

Figure 12.8: Single inheritance class dictionary

12.3 PARAMETERIZATION

Good abstractions in a class dictionary have numerous benefits. The class dictionary usually becomes cleaner and shorter, and an object-oriented program that uses the class dictionary

12.3. PARAMETERIZATION

will have less duplication of functionality. The goal of abstraction is to factor out recurring patterns and to make an instance of the recurring pattern where it is used.

Parameterization uses auxiliary parameterized classes for reinforcing the abstraction mechanism.

Consider the following class dictionary that introduces two classes (Department and Division) by using two parameterized classes (Organization and List). The parameters are used to express the degree of variability of the parameterized class.

```
Organization(SubOrganization, SuperOrganization) =
  <contains> List(SubOrganization)
  [<partOf> SuperOrganization]
  <managedBy> Employee.

List(P) ~ {P}.

Division = "Division"
  <org> Organization(Department, Company).
Department = "Department"
  <org> Organization(Employee, Division).
```

This class dictionary is much better than the following one, which does not use parameterized classes.

```
Division = "Division"
  <contains> DepartmentList
  [<partOf> Company]
  <managedBy> Employee.
DepartmentList ~ {Department}.

Department = "Department"
  <contains> EmployeeList
  [<partOf> Division]
  <managedBy> Employee.
EmployeeList ~ {Employee}.
```

The parameterized version is more flexible. It is a well known principle that solving a more general problem than the one under consideration often yields a better solution for the given problem. It is likely that the insight gained from the generalized problem will be of future benefit.

The following example shows how to define parameterized lists without a repetition class, using the terminology of the Lisp programming language.

```
List(E) : Nil | Cons(E).
Cons(E) = <car> E <cdr> List(E).
Nil = .
```

In the next example we use parameterization to personalize a language. We define a language **Sandwiched**, which encloses an instance sandwiched between two lists of strings. The following class dictionary (version 1)

```
Sandwiched(P) =
  <left> StringList <s> P <right> StringList.
Repetit = "~"
  <first>  StringList [ <nonempty> Instance ]
  "{" <s> Sandwiched(Instance) "}"
  <second> StringList.
OptionalInstance =
  "[" <s> Sandwiched(LabeledInstance) "]".
```

is better than (version 2)

```
SandwichedLabeledInstance =
    <left> StringList LabeledInstance <right> StringList.
Repetit = "~"
  <first>  StringList [ <nonempty> Instance ]
  "{" SandwichedLabeledInstance "}"
  <second> StringList.
OptionalInstance =
  "[" SandwichedLabeledInstance "]".
```

Both class dictionaries use

```
Instance = Vertex.
LabeledInstance = [<label> Label] Vertex.
```

A sentence for **Repetit**, version 1 is

`~ "start" { Family } "end"`

A sentence for **OptionalInstance**, version 1 is

`[ <arg1> Exp ]`

However, a sentence for **Repetit**, version 2 is

`~ "start" { <urban> Family } "end"`

which is not allowed by version 1.

Although we use abstraction, we cannot precisely formulate the recurring pattern. Therefore the language defined by the second class dictionary is larger. Version 1 is preferred since it defines exactly what we want.

It is acceptable to make the language larger if you can introduce a nice abstraction. It is much better to parameterize the abstraction and avoid enlarging the language. The right abstraction simplifies programming.

12.4 REGULARITY

Good label names, class names, and parameterized class names significantly improve the readability of the associated object-oriented programs. We have adopted the following conventions: class and parameterized class names always start with a capital letter. Label names start with a lowercase letter.

It is important that the instance variable names have a succinct mnemonic interpretation. Therefore it is often advisable to introduce labels for the purpose of better naming only.

To facilitate the writing of adaptive programs, it is advisable that terminal classes be buffered by construction classes. Instead of using

```
Order =
  <orderNumber> DemNumber
  <quantity> DemNumber
  <customerNumber> DemNumber
  <price> DemNumber.
```

it is better to use

```
Order =
  <orderNumber> OrderNumber
  <quantity> Quantity
  <customerNumber> CustomerNumber
  <price> Money.
OrderNumber = <v> DemNumber.
Quantity = <v> DemNumber.
CustomerNumber = <v> DemNumber.
Money = <v> DemNumber.
```

This leads to a more regular class structure for which it is easier to write adaptive software.

To summarize this section we propose the following design rule, called **Terminal-Buffer rule**:

> Usually, a terminal class should be used only as the *only* part class of a construction class. The label of the terminal class should be unimportant, for example, it could be always <v>. This leads to the desired buffering of terminal classes.

12.4.1 Regular Structures

We use the adjective regular in an informal way. We say that a class dictionary has a regular structure if similar classes are defined similarly. Regular definitions are without exception easier to learn, use, describe, and implement. They also make a class dictionary more reusable.

As an example we consider a fragment of the Modula-2 grammar, compare it with the corresponding fragment of the Pascal grammar and demonstrate that the Modula-2 grammar is more regular.

```
// Part of Modula-2 grammar

Statement = [Statements].
Statements : IfStatement | RepeatStatement.
StatementSequence ~ Statement {";" Statement}.
IfStatement =
  "if" <condition> Expression
  "then" <thenPart> StatementSequence
  "end".
RepeatStatement =
  "repeat"
    StatementSequence
  "until" <condition> Expression.
```

This Modula-2 grammar is better than the corresponding fragment of the Pascal grammar.

```
// Part of Pascal grammar

Statement : BeginEnd | IfStatement | RepeatStatement.
StatementSequence ~ Statement {";" Statement}.
BeginEnd = "begin" StatementSequence "end".
IfStatement =
  "if" <condition> Expression
  "then" <thenPart> Statement.
RepeatStatement =
  "repeat"
    StatementSequence
  "until" <condition> Expression.
```

Notice how the Modula-2 grammar is more systematic. Both if-statements and repeat-statements contain statement sequences and this is expressed in the same way for both kinds of statements. In the Pascal class dictionary, however, if-statements and repeat-statements are treated differently. A class, called **BeginEnd**, is needed, which turns several statements into one. This class is needed in the if-statement through class **Statement**.

12.5 PREFER ALTERNATION

Alternation classes should be used whenever possible. The reason is that a well designed object-oriented program will not contain an explicit conditional statement for the case analysis that needs to be done for an alternation class.

For example, one way to define a Prolog clause is

```
Clause = <head> Literal
  [":-" <rightSide> LiteralList] ".".
```

However, the following definition will give a cleaner object-oriented program.

12.5. PREFER ALTERNATION

```
Clause : Fact | Rule *common* ".".
Fact = "fact" <head> Literal .
Rule = "rule" <head> Literal ":-"
  <rightSide> LiteralList .
```

Although the concrete syntax is slightly different, both definitions of a Prolog clause store the same information. A program that processes a clause corresponding to the first definition will contain a conditional statement that tests whether **rightSide** is non-nil. A program that processes a clause corresponding to the second definition will delegate the conditional check to the underlying object-oriented system and it will not be explicitly contained in the program. In this case it was necessary to add the keywords `"fact"` and `"rule"` to the language because of the look-ahead of one symbol requirement.

There are other reasons, besides having shorter programs, for using alternation in a class dictionary:

- Modularity. The class dictionary is more modular. If we change the definition of a rule we don't have to change the definition of **Clause**.

- Space. The objects can be represented with less space since a fact will not have an instance variable **rightSide** that is always **nil**.

- Ease of adaptive programming.

Consider the following example: `A = B [C] [D]`. If C and D are mutually exclusive and exactly one is present, it is better to use `A = B X.  X : C | D`.

The object-oriented program for the second version will send a message to the object in instance variable X and the underlying object-oriented system will determine whether we have an instance of C or D. There is no need for an explicit conditional statement to distinguish between the two possible types of X.

However the program for the first version will contain at least one explicit conditional statement.

To compare the class dictionaries further, consider the following programming task: Given a **PrologProgram**-object, print the list of all the **Rule**-objects that are contained in the **PrologProgram**-object.

For the second class dictionary, we can use

```
*operation* void print_rules()
  *traverse*
    *from* PrologProgram *to* Rule
  *wrapper* Rule
    *prefix* (@ cout << this; @)
```

For the first class dictionary, we can use

```
*operation* void print_rules()
  *traverse*
    *from* PrologProgram
```

```
    *via* Clause
  *to LiteralList
*carry* *in* Clause* cin = (@ this @)
  *along* *from* Clause *to* LiteralList

*wrapper* LiteralList
  *prefix* (@ cout << cin; @)
```

12.6 NORMALIZATION

When defining the class dictionary for database type applications, the theory of normal forms is relevant. The class dictionary should be written in normalized form. Normalization will make it easier to extend the class dictionary and it enforces a more systematic and clean organization. The normalization is based on the concepts of **key** and **functional dependency**.

In the following we adopt definitions from the relational database field to class dictionaries that describe object-oriented databases. The adopted definitions serve in turn as style rules for class dictionaries. The motivation behind these definitions is to introduce the concept of a normalized class with respect to functional dependencies.

Definition: An instance variable $V1$ of some class C is **functionally dependent** on instance variable $V2$ if for all instances of class C each value of $V2$ has no more than one value of $V1$ associated with it. In other words, the value of the instance variable $V2$ determines the value of instance variable $V1$. We also use the terminology: $V2$ **functionally determines** $V1$. The concept of functional dependency is easily extended to sets of instance variables.

Definition: A **key** for a class C is a collection of instance variables that (1) functionally determines all instance variables of C, and (2) no proper subset has this property.

The concept of the key of a class is not a property of the class definition but rather a fact about an intended use of a class; that is, the intended set of instances.

Consider the class

```
Employee =
  <employeeNumber> DemNumber
  <employeeName> DemString
  <salary> DemNumber
  <projectNumber> DemNumber
  <completionDate> DemString.
```

The key is employeeNumber. Several problems with this class definition are:

- Before any employees are recruited for a project, the completion date of a project can be stored only in a strange way, by making an instance of class **Employee** with dummy employee number, name, and salary.

- If all employees should leave the project, all instances containing the completion date would be deleted.

- If the completion date of a project is changed, it will be necessary to search through all instances of class **Employee**.

12.7. COGNITIVE ASPECTS OF NOTATIONS

Therefore it is better to split the above class definition into two.

```
Employee =
  <employeeNumber> DemNumber
  <employeeName> DemString
  <salary> DemNumber
  <projectNumber> DemNumber.

Project =
  <projectNumber> DemNumber
  <completionDate> DemString.
```

The key for Employee is employeeNumber and for Project it is projectNumber.

The reason why the first Employee class has problems is that the project number determines the completion date, but projectNumber is *not* a part of the key of the Employee class. Therefore we define that a class is **normalized** if whenever an instance variable is functionally dependent on a set S of instance variables, S contains a key.[4] We recommend that classes be normalized.

It is often the case that there are no functional dependencies among the instance variables of a class. For example, the class Assignment, which is defined by

```
Assignment = <variable> DemIdent <assignedValue> Expression.
```

does not have a functional dependency among its two instance variables. In such classes all instance variables are a part of the key, and the concept of normalization is trivial.

12.7 COGNITIVE ASPECTS OF NOTATIONS

We want the notations defined by class dictionaries to be easy to read, write and modify. What is important in a notation to make it that way? Here is some advice from cognitive psychology.

- Opportunistic planning (which means to adapt the planning to circumstances without regard to principles): The notation must allow for opportunistic planning rather than require a fixed strategy. It has been repeatedly shown that users prefer opportunistic planning. High-level and low-level decisions are mixed; development in one area is postponed because potential interactions are foreseen; the descriptions are frequently modified.

  However, opportunistic planning can hinder reusability. The use of individual modeling approaches may lead to nontransferable models. A method for system design should provide enough flexibility to allow designers to make full use of their creative resources while guiding them towards uniform descriptions.

- Order independence: The descriptions should be order independent as much as possible. What is needed is to decouple the meaning of the description from the final text order as much as possible.

---
[4]This definition is a derivative of the Boyce-Codd normal form from relational database theory.

- **Viscosity:** A viscous notation resists local changes. Correspondingly, a viscous notation contains many dependencies between its parts, so that a small change requires several implied adjustments. The notation should have the right amount of viscosity. Viscous notations cause more work, yet they often have advantages. Their higher redundancy helps to detect certain errors and sweeping accidental changes are less likely. The extra work involved in using viscous notations may encourage users to think about their requirements more carefully.

- **Role-expressiveness:** The reader of a sentence must discover the role of each component of the sentence. Notations that show their structure clearly are called role-expressive.

Since the reader of a sentence has to recognize the intentions from the text, the presence of keywords reliably associated with particular intentions is helpful. This implies that each part of a class should be introduced by some keyword. This in turn implies that each alternative of an alternation class should start with a different keyword. Therefore the need for role-expressiveness is a strong motivator to use the LL(1) conditions for class dictionaries. The LL(1) conditions improve readability, a fact that is well known since the early days of Pascal in the late 1960s. Role-expressiveness also implies that keywords should not be overused; each keyword should indicate one intention. A rich set of keywords, however, also has disadvantages. It makes the language less uniform and increases the vocabulary to be learned.

To make a notation easier to use it is often necessary to provide tool support. These tools should keep track of dependencies that are expressed by a sentence, and the tools should make the dependencies easily accessible to the user (for example, by cross-referencing or browsing).

12.8 EXTENDED EXAMPLES

In this section we show some extended examples that have been designed with the techniques explained in this section.

12.8.1 VLSI Architecture Design

The functionality and structure that is put onto a chip is often naturally expressed in parameterized form: n-bit carry-look-ahead adder, n-bit multiplier, n-bit sorter, n-bit bus, n-processor array, etc. It is very natural to define the hardware on a chip in our class dictionary notation and then to express the functionality of the chip as an object-oriented program. The next class dictionary defines the structure of a Batcher sorting network in parameterized form. The structure of a sorting network is simple: The input consists of n numbers that are split into two parts of equal size. Each half is sorted in parallel by a sorting network of half the size. The output of the two half-sized sorting networks is sent through a merging network. The output from the merging network is the the desired sorted sequence. Such recursive structures have many applications. For example, a Batcher odd-even merging network has a similar structure. Therefore we parameterize the structure description and introduce the parameterized classes DivideAndConquerNetwork, Induction, and NonTrivial.

12.8. EXTENDED EXAMPLES

```
Merge = <network> DivideAndConquerNetwork(List(Comparator)).
Sort = <network> DivideAndConquerNetwork(Merge).
DivideAndConquerNetwork(Q) =
   "input" <input> List(DemNumber)
   "output" <output> List(DemNumber)
   "local" <local> Induction(Q).
Induction(Q) : NonTrivial(Q) | Trivial(Q).
NonTrivial(Q) =
   "left" <left> DivideAndConquerNetwork(Q)
   "right" <right> DivideAndConquerNetwork(Q)
   "postProcessing" <postProcessing> Q.
Trivial(Q) = .
List(S) ~ {S}.
Comparator = "c".
```

It is interesting that at this level of abstraction merging and sorting are almost identical. The only difference is that the sorting network uses a merger for post processing and the merging network uses a list of comparators. This class dictionary can be used in several ways for simulating, for example, sorting networks.

The parameterized class **DivideAndConquerNetwork** will be useful for many other applications.

An example sentence for a **Merge**-object is

```
input 1 2 3 4
output 5 6 7 8
local
  left
    input 9 10
    output 11 12
    local
  right
    input 13 14
    output 15 16
    local
  postProcessing
    c c
```

Indentation is used to show the recursive structure of the network.

In the next example we define the structure of a Newton-Raphson pipeline. The parameterized classes are: **ProcessorArray** and **List**.

```
NR = <array> ProcessorArray(NewtonRaphsonElement).
ProcessorArray(Processor) =
  "input" <input> Ports
  "local" <processors> List(Processor)
  "output" <output> Ports.
```

```
List(Processor) ~ {Processor}.

Register = "Register"
  "input" <i> DemReal
  "local" <store> DemReal
  "output" <o> DemReal.

NewtonRaphsonElement = "NewtonRaphsonElement"
  "input" <input> Ports
  "local"
    <argumentSave> Register
    <estimateSave> Register
  "output" <output> Ports.
Ports = <argument> DemReal <estimate> DemReal.
```

The parameterized class **ProcessorArray** will have many more applications than just defining a Newton Raphson pipeline.

12.8.2 Business Applications

We describe the example from [TYF86] in our class dictionary notation. The constraints are not formulated in the class dictionary. Instead, they are formulated as part of the object-oriented program that works on the data.

```
Company = <divisions> List(Division).
Organization(SubOrganization, SuperOrganization) =
  <contains> List(SubOrganization)
  [<partOf> SuperOrganization]
  <managedBy> Employee.
List(P) ~ {P}.

Division = "Division"
  <org> Organization(Department, Company).
Department = "Department"
  <org> Organization(Employee, Division).
Employee : Manager | Engineer |
           Technician | Secretary
  *common*
    [<belongsTo> Department]
    [<manages> Department]
    [<heads> Division]
    [<marriedTo> Employee]
    <skills> List(Skill)
    <assignedTo> List(Project).
Project =
  <requiredSkills> List(Skill)
```

```
      <location> Location.
Manager = "Manager".
Engineer = "Engineer"
  <hasAllocated> PC
  <belongsToProfAssoc> List(ProfAssoc).
Technician = "Technician".
Secretary = "Secretary".
Skill = "skill".
PC = "pc".
ProfAssoc = "assoc".
Location = "location".
```

Next we describe a class dictionary for an other company. The classes **Order**, **Customer**, and **Product** are normalized. This example shows the buffering of terminal classes.

```
Company =
  "orders" <orders> List(Order)
  "customers" <customers> List(Customer)
  "products" <products> List(Product).

Order = "Order" <orderNumber> OrderNumber
        <orderDate> Date
        <customer> Customer
        <quantityOrdered> DemNumber
        <product> Product.

Customer = "Customer" <customerNumber> CustomerNumber
           <customerName> Name
           <customerAddress> Address.

Product = "Product"
  <productNumber> ProductNumber
  <productName> Name
  <productPrice> Money.
Address = .
OrderNumber = DemNumber.
CustomerNumber = DemNumber.
ProductNumber = DemNumber.
Name = DemString.
Money = DemNumber.
Date = .
List(P) ~ {P}.
```

12.9 SUMMARY

This chapter used to play an important role in the Demeter Method. With the advent of adaptive software, the role of the chapter has diminished somewhat. The rules described here are still useful since a clean class dictionary is important.

12.10 EXERCISES

Exercise 12.1 What is the relationship between a noninductive vertex and a useless vertex? A vertex is useless, if it cannot be instantiated in a finite, noncyclic object.

12.11 BIBLIOGRAPHIC REMARKS

- Database design:

  A paper by John and Diane Smith [SS77] outlines some of the features of the Demeter system. Their aggregation/generalization concepts correspond to our construction/alternation concepts.

  Normalization of relational databases is explained in [Ull82] and [Sal86]. For interesting relationships between relational database design and object-oriented database design see [Kor86].

  Types and subtypes are discussed in [HO87].

- Complexity:

  Whether the language equivalence problem for deterministic context-free grammars is decidable or not is an open problem. Class dictionaries not using recursion define regular expressions of a restricted form (LL(1) restrictions). The equivalence problem for general regular expressions is NP-hard [GJ79].

- Transformations:

  The term "promotion of structure" is from [SB86].

- Predecessor:

  Since 1984 we have designed or participated in the design of numerous class dictionaries of various sizes, ranging from a couple of lines to a few hundred lines. Some of these class dictionaries were written for the predecessor of Demeter: GEM [GL85b]. The class dictionaries were used for applications such as silicon compilation for Zeus [GL85a], translation between intermediate forms for automatic test generation, translation of algebraic specifications into Prolog, programming language implementation, etc.

- Cognitive aspects:

  [Gre89] describes cognitive dimensions of notations.

Chapter 13

Case Study: A Class Structure Comparison Tool

In this chapter we go through the process of developing a simple programming tool for comparing class dictionaries. We use the Demeter Method for adaptive software development that we developed piece by piece in earlier chapters. The Demeter Method allows you to develop adaptive software, which is highly generic software that needs to be instantiated. The Demeter Method is a two-phase software development method. In phase one the adaptive software is developed and in phase two the adaptive software is instantiated by customizers. The phases are used iteratively.

Adaptive software consists of three parts:

- **succinct constraints** C on customizers

- **initial behavior specifications** expressed in terms of C

- **behavior enhancements** expressed in terms of C

The succinct constraints express the set of permissible customizers. A key ingredient to adaptiveness is that the constraints are succinct; that is, they are expressed in terms of partial knowledge about a larger structure. The initial behavior specifications express simple behavior. The behavior enhancements express in terms of the constraints, how the simple behavior is enhanced to get the desired behavior.

The constraints are graph constraints that are expressed, for example, in terms of edge patterns and propagation directives. The initial behavior specifications are propagation patterns, possibly with transportation directives, but without the wrappers. They define traversals and transportations. The enhancements are the vertex and edge wrappers.

13.1 THE DEMETER METHOD

We first give a summary of the method.

13.1.1 The Demeter Method in a Nutshell

The following artifacts are derived from the use cases.

- Derive a class dictionary.

  Start with requirements, written in the form of use cases and a high-level structural object model that describes the structure of application objects. The structural object model provides the vocabulary for expressing the use cases. A use case describes a typical use of the software to be built. From the high-level structural object model we derive a class dictionary to describe the structure of objects. The class dictionary has secondary importance since, after the project is complete, it is replaceable by many other class dictionaries without requiring changes or only a few changes to the rest of the software.

- Derive traversal and transportation patterns without wrappers.

  For each use case, focus on subgraphs of collaborating classes that implement the use case. Focus on how the collaborating classes cluster objects together. Express the clustering in terms of transportation patterns. Express the collaborations as propagation patterns that have minimal dependency on the class dictionary. The propagation patterns give an implicit specification of the group of collaborating classes, focusing on the classes and relationships that are really important for the current use case.

- Derive the wrappers.

  Enhance the propagation patterns by adding specific functionality through wrappers at vertices or at edges of the class dictionary. The wrappers use the object clusters. Derive test inputs from use cases and use them to test the system.

Next we describe the steps taken during adaptive software development and maintenance in more detail.

13.1.2 Design Checklist

We give a summary of the software engineering process for adaptive software. When applying the Demeter Method, the following activities are performed iteratively.

1. Develop/maintain use cases (and the high-level object structure)

   Use cases are used throughout adaptive software development and maintenance. Use cases are often described in English. Sometimes a class dictionary is developed to define a use case notation and a tool is used to test the software after development by driving it with use cases written in the use case notation. In other words, the use cases serve as test scripts.

   Use cases are used to develop and test class dictionaries and propagation patterns.

   Organize use cases into a list where the easy use cases are first and the most complex uses cases are last. Find relationships among the use cases such as when one use case calls another use case or when one use case is a refinement of another use case. The list of use cases you produce should contain a small set of functionally simplified use cases

13.1. THE DEMETER METHOD

that will be used to build a simple and interesting subsystem of the target system. We call this subsystem the system core.

Instead of use cases, a formal specification language could be used to define the behavior.

2. Develop/maintain class dictionaries

    (a) Finding classes through language design

    Derive/maintain stylized English descriptions (sentences) of objects mentioned in or implied by use cases, and develop preliminary class dictionary. The approach is to define a language for describing the objects and to express the language by a class dictionary. The classes are produced as a by-product. The classes are derived from the sentences in several steps. First a set of objects O is abstracted from the sentences. Then a simple algorithm is used to turn O into a class dictionary which defines O and similar objects. The class dictionary is optimized, preserving object equivalence, and finally the terminals are inserted into the class dictionary to make it a grammar that defines the original sentences.

    (b) Reuse

    Can existing class dictionaries be used and modified?

    (c) Testing

    Test class dictionaries against stylized English descriptions.

    (d) Robustness analysis

    Do a maintenance/robustness analysis of your class dictionaries. The adaptive software developer views information in class dictionaries as constantly changing. What kind of changes are likely to be made to the class dictionaries during maintenance? This information is valuable when the propagation directives are written. The succinct graph descriptions can be made more robust.

    (e) Growth plans

    The class dictionaries you produce should contain the subset of classes needed to build a simple, but interesting subsystem of the target system, the system core. Each class dictionary should have a corresponding growth plan consisting of growth phases of the class dictionary. A growth plan is defined by a sequence of propagation directives, each defining a class dictionary graph slice.

    Growth plans are used to describe structural simplifications. They are used to manage complexity during the debugging of adaptive programs.

3. Develop/maintain propagation patterns

Select a use case (the easy ones often come first) and translate it into a set of collaborating propagation patterns.

    (a) Functional decomposition

    Decompose a use case into simpler functions that are expressed as propagation patterns. (This is functional decomposition based on object structure.) Introduce new classes as needed. Decomposing a use case into simpler functions is a creative activity that involves knowledge of algorithms and data structures, and it takes performance requirements into account.

(b) Reuse

Can existing propagation patterns be used or modified? Can existing class libraries be used?

(c) Develop propagation patterns

The translation of a use case into propagation patterns is done in several steps:

   i. traversal directive

   Select a name of a function needed to implement a use case. Select a connected group of collaborating classes that need a function with the selected name for the implementation of the use case. Translate the group of name-equivalent functions into a propagation directive that will specify the traversal with minimal knowledge of the class dictionary. But take the robustness analysis of the class dictionary into account. Test the propagation directives by checking that they do the intended traversals on input objects.

   ii. transportation patterns

   Group objects into clusters that are needed to perform a task simultaneously. Write transportation patterns to produce object clusters with minimal dependency on the class dictionaries. If class dictionaries do not naturally support grouping the objects, change class dictionaries. Embed transportation directives into traversal directives. Test the traversal and transportation directives by checking that they bring the "intended actors on stage." Both steps, that is, finding traversal and transportation directives, require the abstraction of propagation graphs into propagation directives. First find suitable sources and then suitable targets. To make the propagation graph smaller, use either *via*, *bypassing*, or *through*. Use *to-stop* to control unwanted recursions. Use *merge* and *join* as needed.

   iii. wrappers

   Augment the traversal and transportation code with wrappers at vertices and edges. Write/modify wrappers that will call other propagation patterns.

(d) Testing

Test propagation patterns against use cases. This testing is done in layers by data simplification, using growth plans.

Do data simplifications for class dictionaries. What are the simplest class dictionaries to start with? What is the next phase of the class dictionaries to be selected? How are the inputs of those class dictionaries constrained? During testing, use inputs from the selected layer before you go to the next layer. Later layers usually activate more wrappers than early layers. This leads to incremental testing of the wrappers.

Software development methods frequently are decomposed into an analysis phase, a design phase, and an implementation phase.

13.1.3 Analysis/Design/Implementation

We may split analysis, design, and implementation as follows.

- Analysis (problem oriented)

  Developing and maintaining use cases and high-level object structure. What are the user's needs? Developing initial class dictionaries and partitioning them. Developing class interfaces. Robustness analysis for class dictionaries.

  Do cost/benefit considerations, cost and schedule estimations, risk analysis. Make a project plan.

- Design (solution-oriented, collaborating objects)

  Developing propagation directives for traversal and transportation. Refine the class dictionaries. Developing constraints for the customizers.

  Refine cost/benefit considerations, cost and schedule estimations, risk analysis. Refine project plan.

- Implementation (solution-oriented, details of collaboration)

  Developing the vertex and edge wrappers.

This subdivison assigns the different parts of an adaptive program to the three different software development stages. This is different from other software development methods where the analysis and design phases might produce a lot of paper that does not directly contribute to the executable program, and much of which usually counts as implementation, is done automatically.

13.2 GROWING ADAPTIVE SOFTWARE

Both class dictionaries and propagation patterns are building blocks for growing software. We need mechanisms to compose class dictionaries to get new class dictionaries, and to compose propagation patterns to get new propagation patterns. Also, we need a mechanism to customize propagation patterns with class dictionaries.

Developing a large software system is quite similar to building a large castle that consists of several partitions. The analogy is summarized in Fig. 13.1. The analogy refers to basic class libraries produced from a class dictionary. By this we mean the class library of a class dictionary in a specific programming language.

How do we build a new castle? We need to know which function it has to serve. Based on the function of the castle we will choose a suitable architecture and a suitable interior design. The architecture will partition the castle into several partitions and the interior design defines how to put the furniture and fixtures into each room.

> How do we build a new application using adaptive software? We need to know the functionality of the application, which will strongly influence the class dictionaries and propagation patterns we use. Each class dictionary corresponds to a partition of the castle and for each class dictionary a group of propagation patterns will decorate the classes with functions. The classes correspond to the

```
Castle construction          Adaptive software construction
================================================================
castle architecture          group of class dictionaries
empty castle                 group of basic class libraries
  with partitions              each produced from a
                               class dictionary
empty castle partition       basic class library produced from
                               class dictionary
castle with furniture        group of class libraries
  defined by                   with injected methods
  interior designs
room                         class
connections                  references
  between partitions           to external classes
  (doors, stairs)
minimize                     minimize
  connections                  references to external classes
furniture piece              method
interior design              propagation patterns
repository                   repository of propagation patterns
  of interior designs          (organized as components)
repository                   repository of
  of castle architectures    class dictionaries
```

Figure 13.1: Castle building analogy

rooms of the castle and the functions to the furniture. A propagation pattern is like an interior design that specifies how to arrange the furniture in the rooms.

Before we spend a lot of time developing an architecture and an interior design for the needed function of the castle, we browse through old architecture descriptions and interior designs that were developed for a related purpose.

We browse through our repository of class dictionaries and propagation patterns to find useful artifacts. This browsing may be assisted by tools that allow us to match partial class dictionaries and propagation patterns with information in the library.

When can the residents move in? How can I build a small functional subsystem of the castle? Do I need something from every partition of the castle? How can I get a development plan for the castle that lets us grow the small functional subsystem into the full castle in a well organized sequence of steps?

We identify a small subsystem through data and function simplification. Data simplification is guided by using class dictionary graph slices. This results in a functional subsystem with a plan (called an evolution history) on how to grow it. Growing means extending the class dictionaries and refining the propagation patterns.

When planning for the castle, we try to keep the partitions of the castle only loosely connected so that a change in one partition usually does not imply lots of changes in other partitions. Usually the interior design plans are related to one partition.

The architecture of the software can in principle be described by one huge class dictionary. But for many reasons, the class dictionary is partitioned into smaller class dictionaries referencing one another. We keep the number of those references small. Another important driving force for partitioning class dictionaries is the desire not to cut propagation paths. A propagation pattern may only propagate within the classes of one class dictionary and it may not propagate across class dictionary boundaries. The reason for this rule is that a change in a class dictionary should affect only the propagation patterns related to that class dictionary but not propagation patterns in other partitions. Similarly, a change in a propagation directive of a propagation pattern should affect only the classes of the current class dictionary and not classes in other partitions.

As we plan the castle, we have to make sure that there is a good match between the architecture and the interior design plans. If there is an inconsistency between the interior designs and the architecture, there is a need to adjust the two. There is an interplay between interior design and architecture.

A bad class dictionary makes it hard to design elegant propagation patterns, and a badly written propagation pattern can combine with only relatively few class dictionaries. There is an interaction between class dictionary design and propagation pattern design. The terminology of the class dictionary has to be chosen to make the propagation patterns easy to write.

Also, if the huge class dictionary is badly partitioned into class dictionaries, propagation patterns will be more difficult to write. The propagation patterns we need for an application have an influence on how we partition the huge class dictionary.

We write our interior designs so that they are loosely coupled with architecture. This allows us to apply the interior designs to many different architectures.

When we write the functionality in terms of propagation patterns, we use only minimal information from the class dictionary. This allows us to apply the same propagation pattern to many different class dictionaries.

13.3 PROBLEM FORMULATION

The problem solved by the case study has been chosen for the following reasons:

- It is an interesting self-contained problem that exercises many aspects of the Demeter Method.

- It uses concepts useful to adaptive software development, and the resulting tool is an important element of a tool suite.

Next we introduce the concepts.

13.3.1 Class Dictionary Graph Extension

The extension of class dictionary graphs can be viewed from primarily two perspectives. A fine-grained perspective considers the extension of a class dictionary graph at the primitive elements of the data model, such as adding a new class, renaming a class, adding a part to a class, and so forth. Another perspective is more coarse grained, capturing transformations of class dictionary graphs as a whole. In particular, one analyzes the set of objects that can be modeled by the class dictionary graph. In this section, three coarse-grained extensions are defined.

All extensions are expressed as relations on class dictionary graphs. Every relation is naturally associated with a transformation of a class dictionary graph. The three key extension relations are: object-equivalence, weak-extension, and extension. Object-equivalence preserves the set of objects modeled by the class dictionary graph, weak extension enlarges the set of objects, and extension enlarges and augments the set of objects. The extension relations represent a sequence of increasingly stronger transformations and form the basis of fundamental relations for software reuse.

Before we present the extension relations in more detail, we need a succinct way to specify the set of all classes whose instances can be assigned to a part of a given class. This is described by the notion of PartClusters defined below.[1] Informally, the PartClusters of a class v is a list of pairs, one for each part of v. Each pair consists of the part name and

---
[1] Part clusters, page 433 (20).

13.3. PROBLEM FORMULATION

the set of construction classes whose instances can be assigned to the part. Note that only instances of construction classes can be assigned to any part. Since alternation classes are abstract and cannot be instantiated, they need not be considered. Consider for example the class Furnace in Figure 13.2. The actual class of part norm is NormSensor, an alternation class, but only instances of either class OilSensor or class FaultSensor can be assigned to norm.

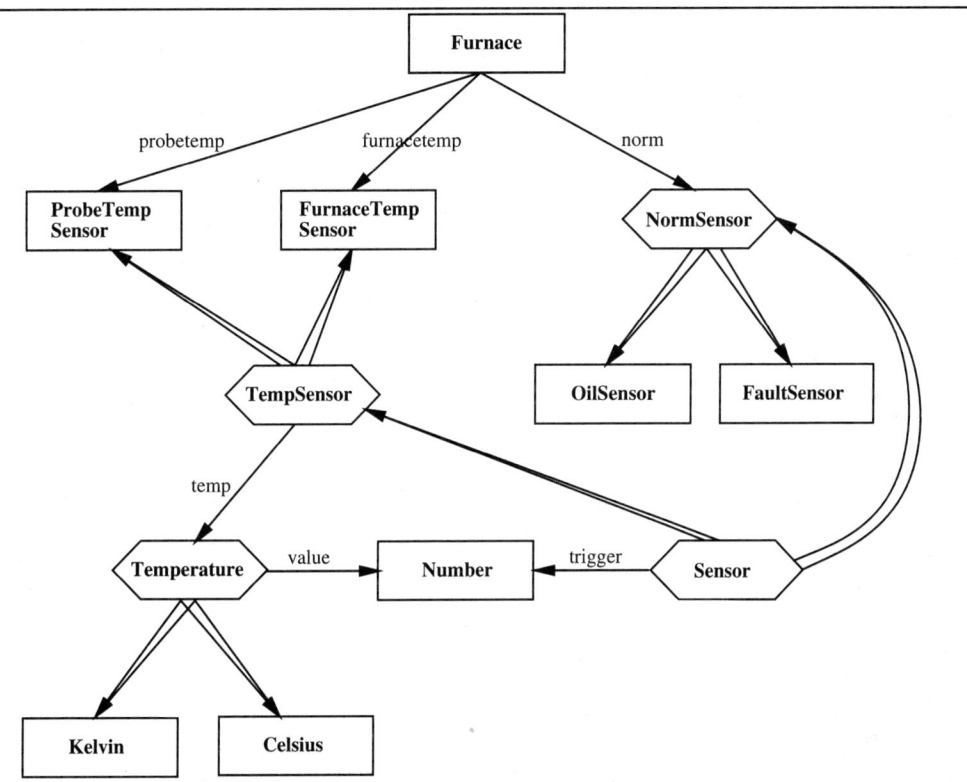

Figure 13.2: Experimental heating system: class dictionary graph Furnace

Example 13.1 *We give the PartClusters for some vertices of the class dictionary graph* Furnace *depicted in Figure 13.2.*

- $PartClusters_{Furnace}(\mathsf{ProbeTempSensor}) =$
  $\{(\mathit{temp},\{\mathsf{Kelvin},\mathsf{Celsius}\}), (\mathit{trigger},\{\mathsf{Number}\})\}$.
  Both parts of class ProbeTempSensor *are inherited:* temp *from class* TempSensor *and* trigger *from class* Sensor. *Only objects of classes* Kelvin *and* Celsius *can be assigned to part* temp.

- $PartClusters_{Furnace}(\mathsf{Furnace}) = \{\ (\mathit{probetemp},\{\mathsf{ProbeTempSensor}\}), (\mathit{furnacetemp},\{\mathsf{FurnaceTempSensor}\}), (\mathit{norm},\{\mathsf{OilSensor},\mathsf{FaultSensor}\})\}$.

Class Furnace *has three parts:* probetemp, furnacetemp, *and* norm. *To* probetemp, *objects of class* ProbeTempSensor *can be assigned, to* furnacetemp, *objects of class* FurnaceTempSensor, *and to* norm, *objects of classes* OilSensor *and* FaultSensor.

- $PartClusters_{Furnace}(\mathsf{Kelvin}) = \{$ *(*value,{Number}*)*$\}$.
  Part value *is inherited and can have objects of class* Number *assigned to it.*

If two class dictionary graphs Γ_1 and Γ_2 are object-equivalent, then both describe the same set of objects.[2] In other words, they must have the same PartClusters. If they are in a weak-extension relation then all objects have the same number of parts, but possibly different ones. If they are in an extension relation then the number of parts may be different also.

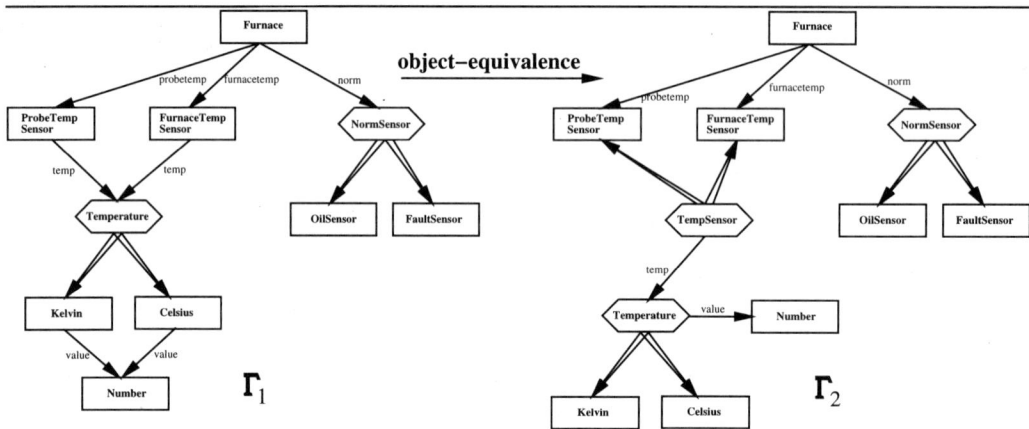

Figure 13.3: Example of object-equivalence: $\Gamma_1 \equiv \Gamma_2$

Example 13.2 *Figures 13.3 through 13.5 give an example of a class dictionary graph in object-equivalence, weak-extension, and extension relation. They represent the following changes to the class dictionary graph structure and hence to the model of the application domain:*

1. *Object-equivalence (Figure 13.3)*
   The designer abstracted out the common structure of the two temperature sensors into a common superclass called TempSensor. *She also realized that both units of temperature have a value to denote the magnitude, so she abstracted the part value up into the common superclass* Temperature.

2. *Weak-extension (Figure 13.4)*
   The basic unit of the system has changed to a set of two furnaces, a normal furnace and a high temperature furnace with only two temperature sensors. A furnace still has

---

[2] Object equivalence and class dictionary graph extension, page 435 (21).

13.3. PROBLEM FORMULATION

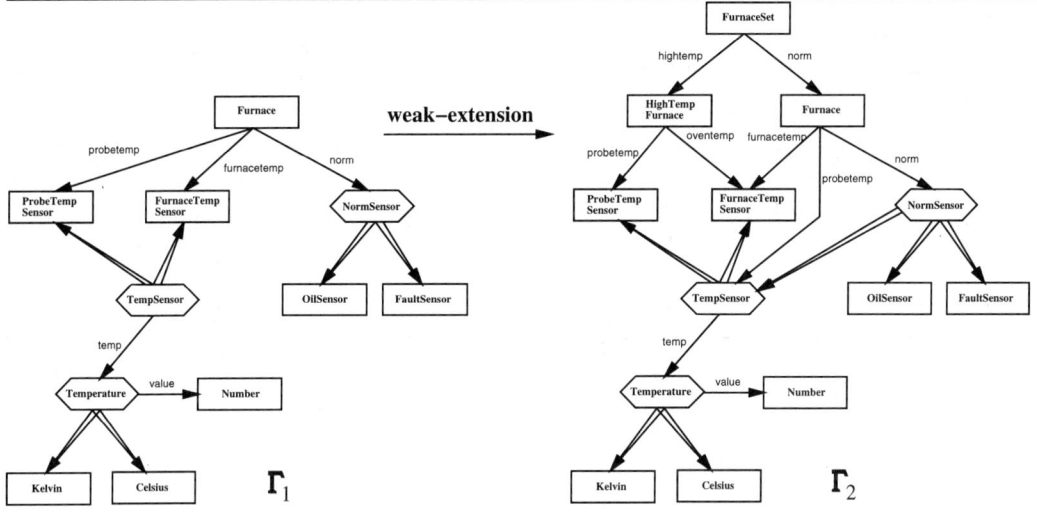

Figure 13.4: Example of weak-extension: $\Gamma_1 \preceq \Gamma_2$

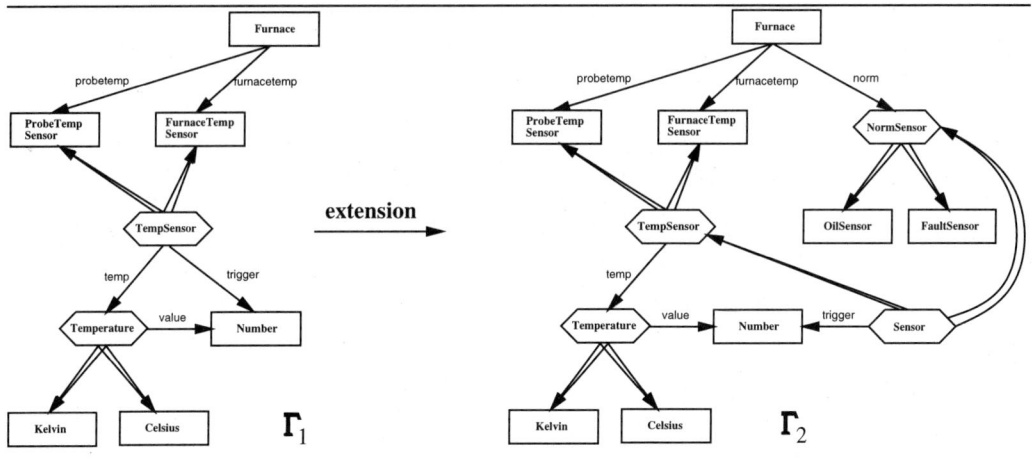

Figure 13.5: Example of extension: $\Gamma_1 \leq \Gamma_2$

three sensors but the first one (probetemp) can be both a ProbeTempSensor as well as a FurnaceTempSensor, and the third one (norm) can be one of the TempSensors also.

3. Extension *(Figure 13.5)*
   The furnace has a new sensor, a NormSensor, which can be either an OilSensor or a FaultSensor, both also having a trigger.

The $PartClusters(v)$ of a class v is a list of pairs, one for each part of v. Each pair consists of the part name and the set of construction classes whose instances can be assigned to the part. With the PartCluster definition, we can now give a definition of object-equivalence without referring to the set of objects defined by the two class dictionary graphs.

13.3.2 Precise Problem Statement

- Let G_1 and G_2 be two class dictionary graphs, where for $i = 1, 2$:

$$G_i = (VC_i, VA_i, \Lambda_i;\ EC_i, EA_i).$$

Class dictionary graph G_1 and G_2 are **object-equivalent** if $VC_1 = VC_2$ and for all $v \in VC_1$:

$$PartClusters_{G_1}(v) = PartClusters_{G_2}(v).$$

We now focus on object-equivalence only. The task is to implement the following use cases:

1. Given two object-equivalent class dictionary graphs G_1, G_2, the program will report: G_1 is object-equivalent to G_2. An example input is in Fig. 13.3.

2. Given two not object-equivalent class dictionary graphs G_1, G_2, the program will report: G_1 is not object-equivalent to G_2. One of the following reasons will be given:

   G_1 weakly extends G_2 (see Fig. 13.4), G_1 extends G_2 (see Fig. 13.5), G_1 and G_2 are not in any extension relation.

3. If an input file that is supposed to contain a class dictionary graph contains

   (a) a *syntactically* incorrect class dictionary graph, a syntax error and line number will be given for the first error.

   (b) a *semantically* incorrect class dictionary graph (e.g., a violation of the unique label rule), an error message will be given for each kind of error.

13.4 PROBLEM SOLUTION

Since we will test the program in layers, we simplify the problem by simplifying the data and the behavior. (This simplification is done in parallel with the class structure generalization. We write the algorithms for the simplified problem for a family of class structures.)

The intent of the simplification is to start with a simple working subsystem and to gradually extend it. Our hope is that as we generalize the class structure later, our propagation patterns will faithfully implement our intent for the more general class dictionaries

13.4. PROBLEM SOLUTION

also. This hope is often fulfilled due to the analogical generalization capabilities of properly designed propagation patterns.

Two kinds of simplifications are:

- Simplify data

    In the context of the object-equivalence problem, this means that initially we can focus just on class dictionaries with only construction and alternation vertices and edges. We ignore things like optional parts, syntax, and repetition vertices. We could go further in simplification and use only construction vertices and edges initially.

- Simplify behavior

    The data simplifications also lead to behavior simplifications. But we can simplify the functionality further. For example, for two class dictionaries to be object-equivalent, they must have the same set of construction classes. So first we could check the construction classes.

    We already noticed that computing the PartClusters is an important subcomputation. Testing object-equivalence means: find part clusters for construction classes of both class dictionaries, and check that name-equivalent construction classes have the same part clusters.

    To compute the PartClusters we need to find all the inherited parts of a class, which in turn means that we need to compute all the superclasses of a class.

    Simplifying the behavior is problem decomposition: we simplify until we get to tasks we know how to implement.

What is the difference between this kind of problem decomposition and stepwise refinement widely used in procedural programming? It is quite similar, but we are defining the behavior for class dictionaries.

The PartCluster problem can be decomposed as follows:

```
part clusters of a class
  compute parts
    compute super classes
    compute all parts
      immediate parts +
      parts of all super classes
  for each part class compute
    set of associated classes
```

In terms of packaging, we are developing three components, each describing a group of collaborating propagation patterns:

- partclusters

- superclasses

- associated

If we developed an air traffic controller, we would develop a class dictionary for air traffic control. Since we develop a tool for class dictionary graphs, we develop a class dictionary for class dictionary graphs.

13.4.1 Finding the Class Dictionary

How do we find the objects we need? We are going to need objects to define classes and PartClusters. The class definitions look like

```
A = <b> B <c> C.
B : C | D *common* <x> X.
```

The PartClusters will have the appearance

```
*clusters*
*source* A ( < b > C , D < c > C , H )
*source* B ( < x > X )
*source* E ( < y > Y )
*source* C ( < x > X < y > Y )
*source* D ( < x > X )
*source* H ( < y > Y )
```

Since labeled vertices are used by class definitions as well as by PartClusters, there is some sharing between the class dictionary for class definitions and the one for clusters. We now give a class dictionary for the above notations.

```
Cd_graph = <adjacencies> List(Adjacency).
Adjacency =
  <source> Vertex
  <ns> Neighbors ".".
Neighbors : Construct_ns | Alternat_ns
  *common* <construct_ns> List(Labeled_vertex).
Labeled_vertex =
  "<" <label_name> DemIdent ">"
  // for input, the comma list has only one element
  <vertex> Comma_list(Vertex).
Alternat_ns = ":"
  <alternat_ns> Bar_list(Vertex) "*common*".
Construct_ns = "=".
Vertex = <vertex_name> DemIdent.
// parameterized classes
List(S) ~ {S} .
Comma_list(S) ~ S {"," S}.
Bar_list(S) ~ S {"|" S}.

// representing results
Cluster = "*clusters*" <clusters> List(PartCluster) .
```

13.4. PROBLEM SOLUTION

```
PartCluster = "*source*" <source> Vertex
              "(" <parts> List(Labeled_vertex) ")".
// Labeled_vertex.vertex contains associated sets

// auxiliary list class
Dummy = List(Vertex).
// Needed for return type of functions.
```

We debug this class dictionary by feeding it sentences. This is all accomplished without writing a line of C++ code. With the class dictionary now in a reasonably good state, we move on to develop the behavior. We develop the behavior in phases based on the functional decomposition we did earlier.

13.4.2 Component superclasses

The component **superclasses** defines a family of algorithms for computing the superclasses of a given class. The component is developed in three phases. In the first phase, the traversal graph is determined. We need to find all **Vertex**-objects that are alternatives of alternation classes in the class dictionary graph. This is achieved by the propagation directive

```
*from* Cd_graph
  *via* Adjacency
  *through* -> *,alternat_ns,*
*to* Vertex
```

How did we find this directive? The source and the target are very easy to find in this case. But the propagation graph defined by

```
*from* Cd_graph
*to* Vertex
```

is too big. We can cut it down in several ways. For example,

```
*from* Cd_graph
  *bypassing* -> *,source,*,
              -> *,construct_ns,*
*to* Vertex
```

would also give the right propagation graph. Or we could use

```
*from* Cd_graph
  *via* Vertex_Bar_list
*to* Vertex
```

to get the right propagation graph.

We think that the propagation directive

```
*from* Cd_graph
  *through* -> *,alternat_ns,*
*to* Vertex
```

is the most natural way to specify the subgraph since it directly says that we are interested in the neighbors of alternation classes (ns stands for neighbors). This is likely to be a robust specification as the class dictionary changes during the life-cycle of the application.

Why did we add *via* Adjacency? Because we know that it is important for Adjacency to be on the path from Cd_graph to Vertex. This is the case for the current class dictionary, but it might not be the case for others. Remember that when we develop propagation patterns, we write constraints that limit the permissible customizers.

After this discussion of design alternatives, we continue with the algorithm. At class Vertex we check whether we have found the right vertex and if so, we recursively compute the superclasses. At vertex v we need to know the name of the alternation class containing v. Therefore, we transport the class name from Adjacency to Vertex.

```
*component* superclasses
  // a group of collaborating propagation patterns
  *constraints*
    // in this constraints section we summarize the assumptions
    // made by the propagation patterns
    *classes* // class-valued variables
      Cd_graph, Vertex, Adjacency, Vertex_List
    *edge* *patterns* // edge constraints
      -> *,alternat_ns,*,
      -> Adjacency, source, *
    *directives* // named propagation directives
      CV =
        // classes which have a superclass
        *from* Cd_graph
          *via* Adjacency
          *through* -> *,alternat_ns,*
        *to* Vertex;
      AV = *from* Adjacency *to* Vertex;
  *end*

// propagation patterns

*operation* Vertex_List* find_super
  (Vertex* v)
    *init* (@ new Vertex_List() @)
  *traverse* CV // find all alternatives
    // transportation directive
    *carry* *in* Cd_graph* cd = (@ this @)
      // needed at Vertex to compute superclasses
      // recursively
      *along* CV
    *carry* *in* Vertex* sv = (@ this -> get_source() @)
      *along* AV
```

13.4. PROBLEM SOLUTION

```
    *wrapper* Vertex
      *prefix*
        (@ if (this -> g_equal(v)) {
          // found super class sv
          return_val -> append(sv);
          // recursively compute superclass of sv
          return_val -> concatenate
             (cd -> find_super(sv)); } @)
    // debugging
    *wrapper* Cd_graph
      *suffix*
        (@ cout << endl << "super_classes of "
           << v << "are" << endl
           << return_val << endl; @)
  *require*
    // standard generic library, standard generation
*end* superclasses
```

At run-time, a call to find_super for a Cd_graph-object and a Vertex-object as argument, will traverse the CV subgraph. At class Cd_graph we load the Cd_graph-object, since we need it at class Vertex to call find_super recursively. At class Adjacency we load the source vertex object, since we need it at class Vertex to know which superclass we found.

We can test component superclasses independently by injecting it into the class dictionary.

13.4.3 Component partclusters

Next we focus on component partclusters. It introduces function part_clusters() for class Cd_graph. This function collects all the immediate parts for all class definitions and with the help of find_super it also collects the inherited parts.

Component partclusters is developed in three phases. For the traversal part we need to find all the Adjacency-objects contained in a Cd_graph-object. This is achieved by the propagation directive

from Cd_graph *to* Adjacency

At class Adjacency we need to know the class dictionary (for computing the superclasses and for computing the inherited parts). Therefore, we transport the class dictionary from Cd_graph to Adjacency.

At class Adjacency we must also collect all the PartClusters into a list. Therefore, we transport the PartCluster_List-object contained in a Cluster-object from Cd_graph to Adjacency.

Now we are ready to fill in the detailed processing in terms of wrappers. The prefix wrapper for Adjacency computes all the parts of the class definition. The suffix wrapper for Adjacency calls an auxiliary function to fill in the associated classes for the part classes.

Function find_inh_parts needs to collect all the parts for every superclass. Unfortunately we cannot propagate from Vertex_list to Labeled_vertex because there is no such path. Instead, we propagate from Vertex_List to Vertex and at Vertex we use function find to get the corresponding Adjacency-object. Finally we propagate from Adjacency to Labeled_vertex to collect all the inherited parts.

This example shows the need for derived edges. If we could introduce a derived edge from Vertex to Adjacency with label find, then we could propagate directly from Vertex to Labeled_vertex.

In function find_inh_parts we kept (in comments) a bug that appeared during initial development of this software. The bug resulted in the wrong output when all parts of the algorithm were used.

The bug was found through testing. When a class dictionary with two levels of inheritance was used, the results were wrong.

How was the bug localized? The bug must be related to collecting the inherited parts. First component superclasses was thought to be the suspect. It was tested but it worked fine. Then the function find_inh_parts was tested in isolation (together with function find) and it produced the wrong results.

A nice property of propagation patterns is that they can be tested incrementally by injecting them one-by-one into the classes. Also, during the debugging phase it is necessary to add print statements. Those print statements can be added as *additional* wrappers, minimizing the need to modify existing program text.

```
*component* partclusters
  // a group of collaborating propagation patterns
  *constraints*
    // in this constraints section we summarize the assumptions
    // made by the propagation patterns
    *classes* // class-valued variables
      Cd_graph, Adjacency,
      Vertex, Labeled_vertex,
      Cluster, PartCluster_List,
      PartCluster, Vertex_list, Labeled_vertex_List
    *edge* *patterns* // constraints on edges
      -> Adjacency,source,Vertex,
      -> Adjacency,ns,*,
      -> Neighbors, construct_ns, *
    *directives* // named propagation directives
    // *directives*
      CA = *from* Cd_graph *to* Adjacency;
  *end*

// propagation patterns

*operation* Cluster* part_clusters()
  *init* (@ new Cluster( new PartCluster_List()) @)
```

13.4. PROBLEM SOLUTION

```
    *traverse* CA
    *carry* *in* Cd_graph* cd = (@ this @)
      // needed at Adjacency to compute superclasses
      // and inherited parts
      *along* CA
    *carry* *in* PartCluster_List* pcl =
      (@ return_val -> get_clusters(); @)
      // needed at Adjacency to add part cluster
      *along* CA
    *wrapper* Adjacency
      *prefix*
        (@
          Vertex_List* l  = cd->find_super(this->get_source());
          // immediate parts
          Labeled_vertex_List* lvl =
            ((Labeled_vertex_List *)
              this -> get_ns() -> get_construct_ns() -> g_copy());
          // inherited parts
          lvl -> concatenate(l -> find_inh_parts(cd));
          PartCluster* pc =
            new PartCluster(this->get_source(), lvl);
          pcl -> append(pc); @)
    *wrapper* Cd_graph
      *suffix* (@ return_val -> insert_assoc(this); @)

*private* *operation* Labeled_vertex_List*
    find_inh_parts(Cd_graph* cd)
        *init* (@ new Labeled_vertex_List(); @)
    *constraints* // assumptions
      *directives*
        VV = *from* Vertex_List *to* Vertex;
    *end*
    *traverse* VV
    *wrapper* Vertex
      *prefix*
        (@
          // initial bug :
          // return_val =
          // cd->find(this)->find_inh_parts2();
          // corrected :
           return_val -> concatenate(
              cd->find(this)->find_inh_parts2());
        @)

    // debugging
```

```
     *wrapper* Vertex_List
       *suffix*
         (@
           // return_val -> g_check("Labeled_vertex_List");
           cout << endl << "inherited parts collected from " << this <<
           " are" << endl << return_val << endl; @)

*private* *operation* Labeled_vertex_List* find_inh_parts2()
     *init* (@ new Labeled_vertex_List() @)
  *constraints*
     *directives*
       AL = *from* Adjacency *to* Labeled_vertex;
  *end*
  *traverse* AL
  *wrapper* Labeled_vertex
     *prefix*
       (@
         return_val->
           append((Labeled_vertex*) this -> g_copy());
       @)

     *private* *operation* void insert_assoc(Cd_graph* cd)
       *traverse*
         *from* Cluster *to* Labeled_vertex
       *wrapper* Labeled_vertex
         *prefix*
           (@ this -> set_vertex
                (cd->associated(this->get_vertex() -> car())); @)
     *require*
       // dependency on external functions
       // Cd_graph
       *operation* Vertex_List* find_super (Vertex* v)
       // Cd_graph
       *operation* Vertex_Comma_list* associated (Vertex* v)
       // Cd_graph
       *operation* Adjacency* find(Vertex* v)
*end* partclusters
```

Component partclusters refers to a function associated, which is implemented in component associated.

13.4.4 Component associated

The idea of the algorithm in component associated is to find all Vertex-objects that are alternatives of an alternation class with the appropriate name. While we search for suitable Vertex-objects, we also go after construction class bodies (Construct_ns-objects).

13.4. PROBLEM SOLUTION

This simultaneous searching could be expressed by a merge operation.

```
*merge*(
  *from* Cd_graph
    *through* -> *,alternat_ns,*
  *to* Vertex,
  *from* Cd_graph
  *to* Construct_ns)
```

Instead, we use

```
    *from* Cd_graph
      *bypassing* -> *,construct_ns,* ,
                  -> *,source,*
    *to* {Vertex, Construct_ns}
```

which defines the same graph for the present class dictionary. The transportation pattern carries the class dictionary around since it is needed for a recursive call at class **Vertex**.

```
*component* associated
  // a group of collaborating propagation patterns
  // to compute the set of all instantiable subclasses
  // of a given class.
  *constraints*
    // in this constraints section we summarize the assumptions
    // made by the propagation patterns
    *classes* // class-valued variables
      Cd_graph, Vertex,
      Construct_ns, Vertex_Comma_list
    *edge* *patterns* // edge constraints
      -> *,construct_ns,*,
      -> Adjacency, source, Vertex
    *class-set*
      VC = {Vertex, Construct_ns};
    *directives* // named propagation directives
      CVC =
        *from* Cd_graph
          *bypassing* -> *,construct_ns,* ,
                      -> *,source,*
        *to* *class-set* VC;
*end*

// propagation patterns

*operation* Vertex_Comma_list* associated
    (Vertex* v)
  *init* (@ new Vertex_Comma_list(); @)
```

```
*traverse* CVC
  // transportation directive
  *carry* *in* Cd_graph* cd = (@ this @)
    *along* CVC
  *wrapper* Vertex
    *prefix*
      (@ return_val ->
          concatenate(cd ->
            associated(this)); @)
  *wrapper* Adjacency
    *prefix* (@ if (this->get_source()->g_equal(v)) { @)
    *suffix* (@ } @)

  *wrapper* Construct_ns
    *prefix*
      (@ return_val ->
          append((Vertex *)(v -> g_copy())); @)
  // end transportation directive
*end* associated
```

We can now run the application after we have injected the components into the class structure. For example, on input

```
A = <b> B <c> E.
B : C | D *common* <x> X.
E : G | H *common* <y> Y.
C = .
D = .
G = .
H = .
X = .
Y = .
```

we get the output:

```
*clusters*
*source* A ( < b > C , D < c > G , H )
*source* B ( < x > X )
*source* E ( < y > Y )
*source* C ( < x > X )
*source* D ( < x > X )
*source* G ( < y > Y )
*source* H ( < y > Y )
*source* X ( )
*source* Y ( )
```

The next step in the implementation is to write propagation patterns for comparing the PartClusters. This is left as an exercise; the bibliography section points to further literature on class dictionary extension relations.

13.5 SUMMARY

We outlined the Demeter Method for developing adaptive programs. Adaptive programs are programs where class structures are described only partially, by giving constraints that must be satisfied by a customizing class dictionary.

The Demeter Method works with use cases, class dictionaries, and propagation patterns. Groups of collaborating propagation patterns are encapsulated into components.

The Demeter Method is scalable to large systems. The idea of using succinct subgraph specifications is most effective for large systems with thousands of classes. Such a system is represented by several collaborating class dictionaries, each one containing not more than one hundred classes to keep compile and link times manageable.

13.6 EXERCISES

Exercise 13.1 Complete the implementation of the class dictionary comparator outlined in this chapter. Add a graphical user interface using Tcl/Tk.

Exercise 13.2 In [GHJV95] a proposal is made to use design patterns to help designers to apply existing methods. Apply this idea to the Demeter Method. Reuse patterns from [GHJV95] as appropriate. Below is a discussion of some of their patterns.

The authors of [GHJV95] have figured out, at the level of object-oriented software, what new concepts (i.e., design patterns) are necessary to get flexible software. In this book, we step outside object-oriented software and use adaptive object-oriented software to express flexible software. The difference is that the kinds of flexibility addressed by adaptive software is focused towards letting programmers talk in concepts they already had rather than in artificial concepts. Therefore, flexible design at the adaptive level is much easier than design at the object-oriented level.

Visitor This pattern stresses the importance of traversals in object-oriented software. In [GHJV95], the structural design pattern **Composite** and the behavioral design pattern **Visitor** are introduced. The purpose of the design pattern book is not to invent new patterns but to document widely used design patterns. The Composite pattern describes how to compose objects into tree structures to represent part-whole hierarchies and the Visitor pattern serves to traverse a part-whole hierarchy. With respect to the traversal operations, we read in [GHJV95]: "The problem here is that distributing all these operations across the various node classes leads to a system that is hard to understand, maintain and change."

The idea of the Visitor pattern is to code a traversal once and then to use it several times. The consequences of using the Visitor pattern are:

- Adding new operations that use the same traversal is easy. You do not have to change each class in the traversal domain.

- Related operations are gathered together. Related behavior is localized in a visitor and not spread over the classes defining the object structure.

- Adding a new class that participates in the traversal is hard. In [GHJV95] we read: when new classes that participate in the traversal are added frequently, "it is probably easier just to define the operations on the classes that make up the structure."

With adaptive software we achieve the goals of the Visitor pattern more effectively. We define the pattern **Adaptive Visitor** which is fundamental to adaptive software development:

- Intent

  Represent an operation to be performed on the elements of an object structure. Adaptive Visitor gathers the code describing the traversal in one place with minimal dependency on the class structure.

- Motivation

  For an operation to be performed on an object structure, usually many of the objects involved are accidental and not of inherent importance. Those objects have only simple traversal behavior and their methods are quite small. Statistics of object-oriented systems show that a large fraction of the methods in an application are very short. Those short methods are usually for object traversal.

  When several operations have to be performed on an object structure, the tiny methods become a nuisance since they encode the details of the class structure into the methods.

- Applicability

  Use the Adaptive Visitor pattern when

    – An object structure contains at least two classes of objects and you want to perform operations on those objects that depend on the classes of the objects. You want to avoid polluting the classes with many simple methods. The Adaptive Visitor pattern lets you keep related behavior together in a group of propagation patterns.

    – The classes defining the object structure may change often and you may often want to define new operations over the structure. (Notice here the difference from the Visitor pattern, where changes to the class structure are costly.)

- Consequences

    – Adaptive Visitor makes adding new operations easy, even with modified traversals.

      You write a new propagation pattern that adjusts the previous propagation directive by using one of the propagation directive primitives, such as join and merge.

13.6. EXERCISES 427

- Visiting across class hierarchies is easy. A propagation directive is like a powerful iterator that not only iterates through lists but through any kind of object structure.

- Implementation

    The implementation of the Adaptive Visitor pattern is done with propagation patterns. The propagation directive defines the traversal domain and the wrappers are like editing instructions that influence what needs to be done during the traversal. Both edge wrappers and vertex wrappers are used.

- Known Uses

    The Adaptive Visitor pattern is used extensively in the implementation of the Demeter Tools/C++.

- Sample Code

    A propagation pattern with transportation pattern

```
// print names of all employees who earn more than $100000
*operation* void select_more_than_100000
   *traverse*
     *from* Company
        *via* Employee
        *via* Salary
     *to* Money
   *carry* *in* Name* n = (@ name @)
     *along*
        *from* Employee *to* Money
   *wrapper* Money
     *prefix*
        (@ if (*val > 100000) cout << n; @)
```

Builder Builder is a creational pattern with the intent to separate the construction of an object from the representation.

Adaptive software uses a corresponding Adaptive Builder pattern that relies on parsing an object description to create an object.

Interpreter Interpreter is a behavioral pattern which for a given language defines a representation of the grammar that is used to interpret the sentences of the language.

Adaptive software uses a corresponding Adaptive Interpreter pattern that uses a class dictionary to express the grammar and an adaptive program to do the interpretation.

Iterator Iterator provides a way to access the elements of an aggregate object sequentially without exposing the implementation of the object.

Adaptive software uses a corresponding Adaptive Iterator pattern that uses a *from* ... *to* expression to express the iterator. Important aspects of the implementation may be exposed at the discretion of the designer to make the software more reusable.

13.7 BIBLIOGRAPHIC REMARKS

- Class dictionary transformations

    Object-preserving class transformations are discussed in [Ber91, Ber94].

    Object-extending class transformations are discussed in [BH93, HLM93, LHX94, Ber94, Hür95].

- Use cases

    They were introduced in [JCJO92, Jac87].

- Other methods

    The Demeter Method is unique as the first adaptive object-oriented method. As an object-oriented method only, it is related to many other methods, including: [RBP[+]91, JCJO92, WBWW90, Boo91, CY90, Col94, HSE94, SM92].

The castle analogy was suggested by George McQuilken.

Chapter 14

Instructional Objectives

An instructional objective (objective, for short) is a description of a performance we want you to exhibit; it describes an intended result of an instruction. Objectives are useful for designing instructional content, for evaluating the success of the instruction, and for organizing your efforts.[1]

Our method includes an ordered set of objectives designed to guide the uninitiated user from zero knowledge about adaptive object-oriented programming through class definitions to propagation patterns and transportation patterns. The method of teaching by objectives is valuable since it provides a metric by which you can gauge your progress. In addition to providing a useful metric, this method provides a facility through which you can begin your studies at a level commensurate with your experience.

We divide the study of adaptive object-oriented programming into structural and behavioral concepts. The structural concepts include objects and class dictionaries. Class dictionaries themselves are learned in stages, first just focussing on construction and alternation vertices and edges and later, on optional parts, repetition classes, and edges, and finally on parameterized classes. The behavioral concepts include propagation directives, propagation patterns, and transportation patterns.

This chapter is the nerve center of the book. It summarizes what you will learn. Each objective contains pointers to other parts of the book where more related information is available. Conversely, most parts of the book point back to this nerve center through footnotes. A footnote consists of an objective name, a page number, and the objective number.

Each objective consists of several parts pointing to other parts of the book. The prerequisite part lists other objectives you have to master for the current objective. The index part of an objective points to entries in the book's index, from where further information can be gathered about the objective. For example, you can find relevant glossary entries through the index. If you need very precise, but formal definitions, the formal definition part contains pointers to formal definitions, either in the book, or in published papers.

---

[1] For a course on cryptography which I prepared for Sandia Laboratories in Albuquerque, New Mexico, I was required to use an instructional objectives approach as described in [Mag62]. I found this approach useful; therefore, I apply it to this book.

Object Example Graphs

1. **Objective:** Object example graph recognition.

   Behavior: Given a graph, determine whether it has the structure of an object example graph.

   Prerequisites: Basic mathematics.

   Negative examples: An edge is labeled by a vertex.

   Formal definition: [LBSL91, Ber94, SL94].

2. **Objective:** Object example graph textual representation.

   Behavior: Given a graph with the structure of an object example graph, write its textual description.

   Prerequisites: Object example graph recognition (1).

   Index: learning.

   Formal definition: [LBSL91, Ber94, SL94].

3. **Objective:** Legal object example graphs.

   Behavior: Given a list of object example graphs, decide whether they are legal.

   Prerequisites: Object example graph recognition (1).

   Formal definition: [LBSL91, Ber94, SL94].

4. **Objective:** Object example finding.

   Behavior: Given a use case, find a representative list of object example graphs for input objects, output objects, and intermediate objects.

   Prerequisites: Understanding of use case, Object example graph recognition(1).

Class Dictionary Graphs

5. **Objective:** Class dictionary graph recognition.

   Behavior: Given a graph, determine whether it has the structure of a class dictionary graph.

   Prerequisites: Basic mathematics.

   Negative examples: An alternation vertex has no outgoing alternation edge. An edge is labeled by a vertex.

   Index: class dictionary graph, construction, alternation, repetition.

   Formal definition: 501.

6. **Objective:** Class dictionary graph graphical representation.

   Behavior: Given a mathematical description of a class dictionary graph, draw a picture of the graph and vice versa.

   Prerequisites: Class dictionary graph recognition (5).

   Index: graphical.

   Formal definition: 501.

7. **Objective:** Class dictionary graph textual representation.

   Behavior: Given a graph with the structure of a class dictionary graph, write its textual description.

   Prerequisites: Class dictionary graph recognition (5).

   Index: textual.

   Formal definition: 529.

8. **Objective:** Semi-class dictionary graph reachability.

   Behavior: Given a semi-class dictionary graph and a vertex v, list all vertices that are alternation-reachable, construction-reachable, inheritance-reachable, and reachable by a knowledge path from v.

   Prerequisites: Class dictionary graph recognition (5) .

   Index: knowledge path, alternation-reachable, cycle-free.

   Formal definition: 498.

9. **Objective:** Legal class dictionary graph.

   Behavior: Given a class dictionary graph, determine whether it is legal.

   Prerequisites: Class dictionary graph recognition (5) .

   Negative examples: The class dictionary in Fig. 14.1, page 432 violates the Cycle-Free Alternation Axiom since the path from **Fruit** to **Apple** and back forms an alternation cycle. It also violates the Unique Label Axiom since class **Military** has two parts labeled **orbit** (one immediate and one inherited).

   Index: unique label rule, cycle-free alternation rule.

   Formal definition: 501.

10. **Objective:** Class dictionary graph slice.

    Behavior: Given a class dictionary graph D and a subgraph S of D, determine whether S is a class dictionary graph slice of D.

    Prerequisites: Class dictionary graph recognition (5) .

    Negative examples: A construction vertex of the subgraph does not have all outgoing construction edges in the subgraph.

    Index: class dictionary graph slice.

    Formal definition: 500.

```
Satellite :
  Military |
  Civilian
    *common* <orbit> Orbit.
Military = <orbit> Low_orbit.
Civilian = <c> Country.
Country = <x> Civilian.
Fruit : Apple.
Apple : Fruit.
```

Figure 14.1: Class dictionary

11. **Objective:** Inductive class dictionary graph.

    Behavior: Given a class dictionary graph D, determine whether it is inductive.

    Prerequisites: Legal class dictionary graph (9), Class dictionary graph slice (10).

    Index: inductive, useless class definitions.

    Formal definition: 508.

12. **Objective:** Making class dictionary graph inductive.

    Behavior: Given a class dictionary graph D that violates the Inductiveness Axiom, find a minimum class dictionary graph that satisfies the Inductiveness Axiom and whose objects include the objects of D.

    Prerequisites: Inductive class dictionary graph (11).

13. **Objective:** Law of Demeter for classes.

    Behavior: Given a class dictionary graph D, determine the number of vertices that are not inductive.

    Prerequisites: Legal class dictionary graph (9), Class dictionary graph slice (10).

    Index: Law of Demeter for classes.

14. **Objective:** Class dictionary graph learning.

    Behavior: Given a set of object example graphs, find a class dictionary graph D so that $Objects(D)$ contains only objects similar to the example graphs.

    Prerequisites: Legal object example graphs (3), Legal class dictionary graph (9).

    Index: learning.

    Formal definition: [Ber94, SL94, LBSL91].

15. **Objective:** Incremental class dictionary graph learning.

    Behavior: Given a class dictionary graph and a legal object example graph, extend the class dictionary graph so that it defines all objects that it defined before, as well as the new example object and objects similar to the example graph.

    Prerequisites: Class dictionary graph learning (14).

    Formal definition: [BL91, Ber94].

16. **Objective:** Class dictionary graph development.

    Behavior: Write a legal class dictionary graph for a given application domain.

    Prerequisites: Legal class dictionary graph (9), Legal object graph (27).

17. **Objective:** Class dictionary graph checking with objects.

    Behavior: Given a class dictionary graph and an object graph, decide whether the object is legal with respect to the class dictionary graph. If it is illegal, propose a change to either the class dictionary graph or the object graph to make the object graph legal with respect to the class dictionary graph.

    Prerequisites: Legal object graph (27), Part clusters (20).

    Index: class dictionary graph design.

18. **Objective:** Class dictionary graph translation.

    Behavior: Given a class dictionary graph, give a list of the generated C++ classes (interfaces and implementations).

    Prerequisites: Legal class dictionary graph (9), C++.

    Positive examples: See Fig. 14.2.

    Index: legal object, translation to C++.

19. **Objective:** Class dictionary graph parts.

    Behavior: Given a class dictionary graph, list all its parts.

    Prerequisites: Legal class dictionary graph (9) .

    Index: flat, parts.

    Formal definition: 503.

20. **Objective:** Part clusters.

    Behavior: Given a class dictionary graph and a class, write down the part clusters of the class.

    Prerequisites: Legal class dictionary graph (9).

    Index: part cluster.

    Formal definition: 504.

```
A = <b> B <c> C.
B : C | D.
C = .
D = .

translation:
class A {
  private:
  B* b;
  C* c;
  // ...
  public:
  B* get_b() {return b;}
  void set_b(B* b_in) {b = b_in;}
  C* get_c() {return c;}
  void set_c(C* c_in) {c = c_in;}
  A(B* b_in = 0, C* c_in = 0){
    b = b_in;
    c = c_in;}
  // ...
}
```

Figure 14.2: C++ translation

21. **Objective:** Object equivalence and class dictionary graph extension.

    Behavior: Given two class dictionary graphs, decide whether they define the same set of objects or whether they are in an extension or weak extension relationship.

    Prerequisites: Legal class dictionary graph (9), Legal object graph (27).

    Positive examples: The two class dictionaries in Fig. 14.3 define the same set of objects.

    Index: object equivalence.

    Formal definition: 414.

```
A : B | C | D.
B_or_c : B | C.
B = .
C = .
D = .


A : B_or_c | D.
B_or_c : B | C.
B = .
C = .
D = .
```

Figure 14.3: Object-equivalence

---

22. **Objective:** Class dictionary graph flattening.

    Behavior: Given a class dictionary graph, compute an object-equivalent class dictionary graph without common parts. .

    Prerequisites: Object equivalence and class dictionary graph extension (21).

    Index: flat.

    Formal definition: 469.

23. **Objective:** Parameterized class dictionary graph expansion.

    Behavior: Given a parameterized class dictionary graph, check whether it is legal and expand it into an equivalent (with respect to objects and sentences) nonparameterized class dictionary graph.

    Prerequisites: Legal class dictionary (32).

    Index: parameterized class dictionary.

Object Graphs

24. **Objective:** Object graph recognition.

    Behavior: Given a graph, determine whether it has the structure of an object graph with respect to a class dictionary graph.

    Prerequisites: Legal class dictionary graph (9).

    Negative examples: A vertex is labeled with a class that does not exist in the class dictionary graph. An edge is not labeled.

    Index: object.

    Formal definition: 505.

25. **Objective:** Object graph graphical representation.

    Behavior: Given an object graph, draw a picture of it.

    Prerequisites: Object graph recognition (24).

26. **Objective:** Object graph textual representation.

    Behavior: Given an object graph, write its textual description.

    Prerequisites: Object graph recognition (24).

    Index: object graph: syntax.

    Formal definition: 506.

27. **Objective:** Legal object graph.

    Behavior: Given an object graph, determine whether it is legal with respect to a given class dictionary graph.

    Prerequisites: Legal class dictionary graph (9).

    Negative examples: The object graph with respect to the class dictionary graph shown in Fig. 14.4 is illegal since b cannot contain an F-object (only D- or E-objects are allowed) and since c cannot contain a D-object.

    There cannot be a d-part.

    Index: atomic object, terminal object, associated, legal object.

    Formal definition: 505.

28. **Objective:** Object graph finding.

    Behavior: Given a class dictionary graph, find five different objects that are legal with respect to the class dictionary graph.

    Prerequisites: Legal class dictionary graph (9), Legal object graph (27).

29. **Objective:** Object construction.

    Behavior: Given a class dictionary graph and an object graph, write a C++ program that creates a C++ object corresponding to the object graph.

```
A = <b> B <c> C.
B : D | E *common* <f> F.
C = .
D = .
E = .
F = .

object graph:

:A(
  <b> :F()
  <c> :D()
  <d> E())
```

Figure 14.4: Class dictionary and object graph

Prerequisites: Legal class dictionary graph (9), Legal object graph (27), C++.

Positive examples: See Fig. 14.5.

Index: object graph translation.

Class Dictionaries

30. **Objective:** Class dictionary recognition.

    Behavior: Given a mathematical structure, recognize whether it is a class dictionary.

    Prerequisites: Class dictionary graph recognition (5).

    Negative examples: The class dictionary in Fig. 14.6 is illegal since elements of *VT* cannot occur as alternatives.

    Index: terminal, class dictionary.

    Formal definition: 509.

31. **Objective:** Class dictionary textual representation.

    Behavior: Given a class dictionary, write its textual description.

    Prerequisites: Class dictionary recognition (30).

    Index: textual representation.

    Formal definition: 529.

32. **Objective:** Legal class dictionary.

    Behavior: Given a class dictionary, determine whether it is legal.

```
A = <b> B <c> C.
B : C | D.
C = .
D = .
```

object graph:

```
:A(
  <b> :C()
  <c> :C())
```

C++ program:

```
i = new A(new C(), new C());
```

Figure 14.5: Object construction

```
Prefix : Ident | Number | Compound.
Compound = .
*terminal_sets* Ident, Number.
```

Figure 14.6: Class dictionary

Prerequisites: Legal class dictionary graph (9).

Formal definition: 511.

33. **Objective:** Class dictionary flattening.

    Behavior: Given a class dictionary, compute the flattened, object-equivalent class dictionary that does not have common parts.

    Prerequisites: Class dictionary graph flattening (22).

    Index: flat.

    Formal definition: 512.

34. **Objective:** Printing.

    Behavior: Given a class dictionary and an object graph, write the sentence that represents the object in the language defined by the class dictionary.

    Prerequisites: Legal class dictionary (32), Legal object graph (27).

    Give an English explanation of the language defined by a class dictionary.

    Positive examples: See Fig. 14.7.

    Index: language.

    Formal definition: 516.

35. **Objective:** Language design.

    Behavior: Given an English description of a language, find a class dictionary that defines that language.

    Index: class dictionary design.

    Prerequisites: Printing (34).

36. **Objective:** Scanning.

    Behavior: Given a class dictionary and a character sequence, transform the characters into a terminal sequence (consisting of elements of τ and elements of the terminal sets in VT).

    Prerequisites: Class dictionary recognition (30).

    Index: scanning a sentence.

37. **Objective:** First sets.

    Behavior: Given a class dictionary, compute the first sets.

    Prerequisites: Legal class dictionary (32), Printing (34) .

    Positive examples: See Fig. 14.8.

    Index: first.

    Formal definition: 517.

```
A = "*" <b> B "+" "end".
B : C | D.
C = "is" <s> String.
D = "d" <i> Ident.

object graph:
A(
  <b> C(
    <s> String "*common*"))

sentence:
* is "*common*" + end

object graph:
:A(
  <b> :D(
    <i> :Ident "common"))

sentence:
* d common + end
```

Figure 14.7: Objects and sentences

```
A = <b> B <c> C <d> D.
B : Empty | B1.
C : Empty | B2.
D = "end".
Empty = .
B1 = "b1".
B2 = "b2".

First sets:
first(A) = {"b1", "b2", "end"},
first(B) = {empty, "b1"},
first(C) = {empty, "b2"},
first(D) = {"end"},
first(Empty) = {empty},
etc.
```

Figure 14.8: First sets

38. **Objective:** Parsing.

    Behavior: Given a class dictionary and a sentence belonging to the language defined by the class dictionary, give the corresponding object graph. Recognize syntax errors.

    Prerequisites: Legal class dictionary (32), First sets (37).

    Positive examples: See Fig. 14.9.

    Index: parsing.

    Formal definition: 524.

39. **Objective:** Sentence finding.

    Behavior: Given a class dictionary, find five different sentences that are legal with respect to the class dictionary.

    Prerequisites: Legal class dictionary (32), Parsing (38).

40. **Objective:** Class dictionary checking with sentences.

    Behavior: Given a class dictionary and a sentence, decide whether the sentence is legal with respect to the class dictionary. If it is not legal, propose a change to the class dictionary or the sentence to make the sentence legal with respect to the class dictionary.

    Prerequisites: Legal class dictionary (32), Legal object graph (27).

41. **Objective:** Follow sets.

The sentence

```
b1 end
```

is syntactically correct and defines the object graph

```
:A(
  <b> :B1()
  <c> :Empty()
  <d> :D())
```

The sentence

```
b2 b1 end
```

is syntactically incorrect since b1 must be before b2.

Figure 14.9: Syntax analysis

Behavior: Given a class dictionary, compute the follow sets.

Prerequisites: Legal class dictionary (32), First sets (37).

Positive examples: See Fig. 14.10.

Index: follow.

Formal definition: 519.

42. **Objective:** LL(1) conditions.

    Behavior: Given a single-inheritance class dictionary, determine whether or not it is LL(1). Given a multiple-inheritance class dictionary, prove that it satisfies the multiple-inheritance LL(1) conditions.

    Prerequisites: Legal class dictionary (32), Follow sets (41).

    Positive examples: The class dictionary in Fig. 14.10 is LL(1) since first(Empty) is disjoint from first(B1) and from first(B2), and since follow(B) and first(B1) are disjoint, and since follow(C) and first(B2) are disjoint.

    Index: LL(1) conditions.

    Formal definition: 519.

43. **Objective:** LL(1) correction.

    Behavior: Given a single-inheritance class dictionary, add concrete syntax to make it LL(1). Given a multiple-inheritance class dictionary, add concrete syntax to make it satisfy the multiple-inheritance LL(1) conditions.

    Prerequisites: Legal class dictionary (32), (42).

```
A = <b> B <c> C <d> D.
B : Empty | B1.
C : Empty | B2.
D = "end".
Empty = .
B1 = "b1".
B2 = "b2".

Follow sets:
follow(A) = {eof},
follow(B) = {"b2", "end"},
follow(C) = {"end"},
follow(D) = {eof},
follow(Empty) = {"b2", "end"},
etc.
```

Figure 14.10: Follow sets

44. **Objective:** Class dictionary development.

    Behavior: Given a project specification (a set of use cases), develop a class dictionary for it.

    Prerequisites: Legal class dictionary (32), LL(1) correction (43).

Class Dictionary Optimization

45. **Objective:** Equivalent parts.

    Behavior: Given a class dictionary graph, determine all pairs of parts that are equivalent. Given a class dictionary graph, transform it to an object-equivalent class dictionary graph where each part is only equivalent to itself.

    Prerequisites: Legal class dictionary graph (9).

    Index: redundant part.

    Formal definition: [LBSL91, Ber94, SL94].

46. **Objective:** Redundant parts.

    Behavior: Given a class dictionary, find all redundant parts.

    Prerequisites: Equivalent parts (45).

    Index: redundant part.

47. **Objective:** Common normal form.

    Behavior: Given a class dictionary graph, bring it to common normal form while preserving object-equivalence. Given a class dictionary, bring it to common normal form while preserving object-equivalence and language.

    Prerequisites: Redundant parts (46).

    Positive examples: See Fig. 14.11. The second class dictionary is in CNF.

    Index: minimize construction edges.

```
A = <b> B.
B = .
C = <b> B.

A_or_C : A | C *common* <b> B.
A = .
B = .
C = .
```

Figure 14.11: Common normal form

---

48. **Objective:** Consolidation of alternatives.

    Behavior: Given a class dictionary graph in CNF, minimize it while preserving object-equivalence.

    Prerequisites: Common normal form (47).

    Index: minimize alternation edges.

49. **Objective:** Tree property.

    Behavior: Given a class dictionary graph, determine whether it has the tree property. If it has the tree property, transform it to an object-equivalent single-inheritance class dictionary graph.

    Prerequisites: Object equivalence and class dictionary graph extension (21).

    Index: tree property.

    Formal definition: [SL94].

50. **Objective:** Class dictionary graph minimization.

    Behavior: Given a class dictionary graph, find a minimal object-equivalent class dictionary graph.

    Prerequisites: Common normal form (47), Consolidation of alternatives (48).

    Index: minimize alternation edges, minimize construction edges.

Formal definition: [LBSL91, Ber94, SL94].

Design

51. **Objective:** Use case decomposition.

    Behavior: Given a requirement specification (set of uses cases for initial design or maintenance), decompose them into a list of simpler use cases needed for the implementation of subsystems.

    Prerequisites: Experience.

52. **Objective:** Use case translation.

    Behavior: Given a use case, translate it into a sequence of collaborating propagation patterns.

    Prerequisites: Legal class dictionary (32).

53. **Objective:** Library objective.

    Behavior: Given a class dictionary and a specification (set if use cases), decide which library to use (e.g., NIHCL, Interviews, C++ tasks) and select an appropriate group of classes for reuse.

    Prerequisites: Knowledge of libraries, Legal class dictionary (32).

54. **Objective:** Growth plan.

    Behavior: Given a class dictionary graph and a growth plan, check whether it is legal and compute the growth plan complexity. Identify incomplete phases. Give a minimally adequate set of inputs for each phase.

    Prerequisites: Legal class dictionary graph (9).

    Positive examples: See Fig. 14.12.

    Index: growth plan.

55. **Objective:** Adaptive program test growth plan.

    Behavior: Given an adaptive program, find a growth plan for testing the adaptive program.

    Prerequisites: Growth plan (54) .

56. **Objective:** Law of Demeter for functions.

    Behavior: Given an object-oriented program, decide whether it satisfies the Law of Demeter for functions. If it does not, rewrite it.

    Prerequisites: Object-oriented programming language.

    Index: Law of Demeter.

    Formal definition: [Hol93, LHR88].

```
A : B | C.
B : D | E.
D : F | G.
F = <g> G.
C = .
E = .
G = .

Phases:

0: A, C.
1: B, E.
2: D, G.
3: F.

growth complexity: 7/4
```

Figure 14.12: Growth plan

---

57. **Objective:** Legal propagation directive.

    Behavior: Given a propagation directive, check whether it is syntactically and semantically correct.

    Prerequisites: Legal class dictionary graph (9).

    Index: propagation directive.

58. **Objective:** Legal propagation directive customization.

    Behavior: Given a class dictionary graph and a propagation directive, check whether the propagation directive is compatible with the class dictionary graph. If the class dictionary graph violates the information loss customizer restriction, show why it is violated.

    Prerequisites: Legal class dictionary graph (9).

    Index: compatible, information loss, customizer restrictions.

    Formal definition: [LX93b, PXL95, Xia94].

59. **Objective:** Propagation operator.

    Behavior: Given a propagation directive pd and a compatible class dictionary graph G, compute the propagation graph

    $$propagate(pd, G) = pg$$

by merging the paths into a graph.

Prerequisites: Legal propagation directive (57).

Index: propagate.

Formal definition: [LX93c, Xia94].

60. **Objective:** Propagation directive abstraction.

    Behavior: Given a class dictionary graph G and a propagation graph pg contained in the class dictionary graph G, find a propagation directive pd so that $propagate(pd, G) = pg$. Depending on the set of primitives used in the propagation directive, the answer will be different. The goal is to find a "small" propagation directive with dependency on the class dictionary graph close to minimum. Available primitives are: *from*, *to*, *bypassing*, *through*, *to-stop*, *via*, *join*, *merge*, *restrict*.

    Prerequisites: Legal propagation directive (57).

    Index: propagation pattern design.

    Formal definition: [SL94].

61. **Objective:** Legal propagation patterns.

    Behavior: Given a set of propagation patterns, check whether they are syntactically and semantically correct.

    Prerequisites: Legal class dictionary graph (9).

    Index: propagation pattern.

    Formal definition: [LX93c, Xia94].

62. **Objective:** Legal propagation pattern customization.

    Behavior: Given a class dictionary graph and a propagation pattern, check whether the propagation pattern is compatible with the class dictionary graph, and give the propagation graphs (traversal graph and the transportation graphs, if any). If the class dictionary graph violates a customizer restriction, name it and show why it is violated.

    Prerequisites: Legal class dictionary graph (9).

    Index: customizer restrictions, compatible.

    Formal definition: [Xia94].

63. **Objective:** Propagation pattern interpretation.

    Behavior: Given a class dictionary graph G, a propagation pattern pp compatible with G, and an object O of the class dictionary graph, give the output produced by pp on O.

    Prerequisites: Legal propagation patterns (61).

    Index: propagation patterns: operational semantics.

    Formal definition: [Xia94].

64. **Objective:** Propagation pattern partial evaluation.

    Behavior: Given a class dictionary graph G and a propagation pattern pp compatible with G, translate pp into a correct object-oriented program with respect to G.

    Prerequisites: Legal propagation patterns (61).

    Index: translation to C++: propagation patterns.

    Formal definition: [Xia94].

65. **Objective:** Object-oriented design.

    Behavior: Given a project specification, develop a class dictionary and a list of tasks with their task designs and growth plans. Satisfy the Law of Demeter.

    Prerequisites: Class dictionary development (44), Library objective (53), Use case decomposition (51), Adaptive program test growth plan (55), Use case translation (52), Law of Demeter for functions (56).

Programming

66. **Objective:** Legal transportation patterns.

    Behavior: Given a set of transportation patterns embedded in a propagation pattern, check whether they are syntactically and semantically correct.

    Prerequisites: Propagation operator (59).

    Index: transportation pattern: syntax, consistent: transportation pattern.

67. **Objective:** Legal transportation pattern customization.

    Behavior: Given a transportation pattern (embedded in a propagation pattern) and a class dictionary graph, check whether the transportation pattern is compatible with the class dictionary graph, and give the transportation graph and associated C++ code. If the class dictionary graph violates a customizer restriction related to the transportation patterns, name it and show why it is violated.

    Prerequisites: Legal transportation patterns, page 448 (66).; Propagation operator, page 446 (59)..

    Index: customizer restriction: transportation patterns.

    Formal definition: [Xia94].

68. **Objective:** Transportation pattern interpretation.

    Behavior: Given a class dictionary graph G, a propagation pattern pp compatible with G and containing several transportation patterns, and an object O of the class dictionary graph, give the output produced by pp on O.

    Prerequisites: Legal propagation patterns (61).

    Index: translation to C++: transportation patterns.

69. **Objective:** Transportation pattern partial evaluation.

   Behavior: Given a class dictionary graph G and a propagation pattern pp compatible with G and containing transportation patterns, translate pp into a correct object-oriented program with respect to G.

   Prerequisites: Legal propagation patterns (61).

   Index: signature extension, translation to C++: transportation patterns, wrapper pushing.

   Formal definition: [Xia94].

70. **Objective:** Propagation pattern development.

   Behavior: Given a task design, find a collection of propagation patterns that implement the task.

   Prerequisites: Propagation directive abstraction (60).

71. **Objective:** Virtual function table.

   Behavior: Given a single-inheritance class dictionary graph that is decorated with virtual functions at the alternation classes, produce the virtual function tables needed for all construction classes that are alternation-reachable from an alternation class with virtual functions.

   Prerequisites: Legal class dictionary graph (9).

72. **Objective:** Programming in C++.

   Behavior: Write a C++ program for a given project specification.

   Prerequisites: C++, Legal class dictionary graph (9), Legal object graph (27), Object construction (29), Class dictionary graph translation (18), Law of Demeter for functions (56), Virtual function table (71), Growth plan (54), Object-oriented design (65), Propagation pattern development (70).

73. **Objective:** Generic Programming.

   Behavior: Write a C++ program for a function that is defined for all applications; that is, implement a function that performs some action regardless of the class dictionary used.

   Prerequisites: Programming in C++ (72).

Course Specific Objectives

74. **Objective:** Programming language implementation.

   Behavior: Given a class dictionary for a programming language, implement an interpreter or a compiler for the language.

   Prerequisites: Knowledge of a subset of a programming language (e.g., Scheme, Pascal, C, Prolog), Programming in C++ (72), Developing an application in existing environment (89), Generation (90).

75. **Objective:** EER diagram to object-oriented program.

    Behavior: Given an extended entity-relationship diagram, translate its information content into a class dictionary and a C++ constraints checker.

    Prerequisites: EER.

76. **Objective:** Data model implementation.

    Behavior: Given a class dictionary for a data model, implement a schema checker, and a schema compiler.

    Prerequisites: ER, EER, Relational model, Programming in C++ (72), Developing an application in existing environment (89), Generation (90).

77. **Objective:** Data model translation.

    Behavior: Given two class dictionaries for two data models, implement a translator.

    Prerequisites: Programming in C++ (72), Developing an application in existing environment (89).

78. **Objective:** Data model as class dictionary.

    Behavior: Given a data model definition, write a class dictionary that defines the structure and the language of the data model (for the structures, constraints, and operations).

    Prerequisites: Class dictionary development (44).

Demeter System

79. **Objective:** Setting up your account for Demeter.

    Behavior: Give the commands to set up your account to use Demeter.

    Prerequisites: UNIX.

80. **Objective:** Semantic checking and class dictionary debugging.

    Behavior: Given a class dictionary, check it for semantic errors and correct it until no errors are reported.

    Prerequisites: Legal class dictionary (32).

81. **Objective:** Graphical, textual representation.

    Behavior: Show the structure of a class dictionary by producing a graphical representation.

82. **Objective:** Miscellaneous class dictionary tools.

    Behavior: Summarize all the class dictionary design tools available and how they can be called; for example, single inheritance checking, English translation, etc.

Using an Existing Environment

83. **Objective:** Available functions in generated environment.

    Behavior: Given a class dictionary, list all the classes and their functions that are available in the generated environment.

    Prerequisites: Legal class dictionary (32).

84. **Objective:** Implementation files.

    Behavior: Given a generated environment, give the directories where you can write your code and describe what kind of code you can put in each file and how you have to name the files.

    Prerequisites: Legal class dictionary (32), Available functions in generated environment (83).

85. **Objective:** Propagation/Compilation/Linking.

    Behavior: Describe how you can influence the compilation and linking process through changes to the Imakefile. Explain the gen-make and make commands.

86. **Objective:** Interface files.

    Behavior: Given a class dictionary and a set of C++ function implementations, give the set of generated function interfaces.

    Prerequisites: Legal class dictionary (32).

87. **Objective:** Compilation Error.

    Behavior: Given a compilation error, find the file where the error is located.

    Prerequisites: UNIX, C++.

88. **Objective:** Debugging.

    Behavior: If your program produces a core dump, use the system to find the problem.

    Prerequisites: Unix, C++.

89. **Objective:** Developing an application in existing environment.

    Behavior: Given a class dictionary and an environment, write application code in the environment.

    Prerequisites: Legal class dictionary (32), Setting up your account for Demeter (79), Available functions in generated environment (83), Implementation files (84), Interface files (86), Propagation/Compilation/Linking (85), Compilation Error (87), Debugging (88).

Generating Your Own Environments

90. **Objective:** Generation.

    Behavior: Given a class dictionary, give the commands to generate your own environments. Explain the gen-imake command.

    Prerequisites: Semantic checking and class dictionary debugging (80).

91. **Objective:** Lex.

    Behavior: Describe where and how to change a lex input file to get the desired scanner. The comment definitions, the white space definitions, and the terminal set definitions may be changed.

    Prerequisites: Generation (90).

Chapter 15

Core Concepts and Implementation

This chapter is an annotated version of [PXL95]. That paper was written for the ACM TOPLAS Journal (*Transactions on Programming Languages and Systems* published by the Association for Computing Machinery) and uses a style common in the programming language theory community. This style is very elegant and precise but may be difficult to read by people outside the programming language theory community. The purpose of the annotations is to make the chapter available to a wider audience. With those annotations it serves as a brief introduction to adaptive software for advanced undergraduate and graduate students. This chapter does not intend to fully model the Demeter system. However, the treatment is very precise and gives a reasonable first approximation to what propagation patterns are intended to do.

Adaptive programs compute with objects, just like object-oriented programs. Each task to be accomplished is specified by a so-called propagation pattern that traverses the receiver object.[1] The object traversal is a recursive descent via the instance variables where information is collected or propagated along the way.[2] A propagation pattern consists of a name for the task, a succinct specification of the parts of the receiver object that should be traversed, and code fragments to be executed when specific object types are encountered. The propagation patterns need to be complemented by a class graph that defines the detailed object structure. The separation of structure and behavior yields a degree of flexibility and understandability not present in traditional object-oriented languages. For example, the class graph can be changed without changing the adaptive program at all.

We present an efficient implementation of adaptive programs. Given an adaptive program and a class graph, we generate an efficient object-oriented program, for example in C++. Moreover, we prove the correctness of the core of this translation. A key assumption in the theorem is that the traversal specifications are consistent with the class graph. We

---

[1] The propagation pattern will be called on an object and that object is called the receiver object.

[2] Recursive descent does not mean that the structure is necessarily recursive. It means that the traversal is depth-first.

prove the soundness of a proof system for conservatively checking consistency, and we show how to implement it efficiently.[3]

15.1 INTRODUCTION

15.1.1 Background

One goal of object-oriented programming is to obtain flexible software through such mechanisms as inheritance and late binding. For example, flexibility was one of the goals in the project led by Booch [Boo90] where an Ada package was converted to a C++ component library. He used templates to parameterize certain components so that local substitutions are possible. But the degree of variability of such components is limited. Later he stated [Boo94]: "Building frameworks is hard. In crafting general class libraries, you must balance the needs for functionality, flexibility, and simplicity. *Strive to build flexible libraries, because you can never know exactly how programmers will use your abstractions.* Furthermore, it is wise to build libraries that make as few assumptions about their environments as possible so that programmers can easily combine them with other class libraries."

A key feature of most popular approaches to object-oriented programming is to explicitly attach every method of a program to a specific class. As a result, when the class structure changes, the methods often need modifications as well. In [GTC+90], we read "... the class hierarchy may become a rigid constraining structure that hampers innovation and evolution."

The idea of *adaptive* programs has been presented in [LX93c, LHSLX92, Lie92, LX93b, LSLX94, Kes93]. The basic idea is to *separate* the program text and the class structure. The result is called an adaptive program. It is a collection of *propagation patterns* and it computes with objects, just like object-oriented programs. Each propagation pattern accomplishes a specific task by traversing the receiver object. In a corresponding object-oriented program, the same task may require a family of methods specified in several classes. The object traversal is a recursive descent via the instance variables where information is collected or propagated along the way. A propagation pattern consists of

1. Name for the task

2. Succinct specification of the parts of the receiver object that should be traversed

3. Code fragments to be executed when specific object types are encountered

The separation of structure and behavior yields a degree of flexibility and understandability not present in traditional object-oriented languages. For example, the class graph can be changed without changing the adaptive program at all. Moreover, with adaptive software, it is possible to make a first guess on a class graph, and later with minimal effort change to a new class graph. In contrast, if we write a C++ program for example, then it usually needs significant updates to work on another class graph.[4]

---

[3] It is not necessary to have an algorithm that detects exactly which traversal specifications are inconsistent with a class graph. It is sufficient to have an algorithm that labels some consistent, but "unimportant" class graphs as inconsistent, as long as all inconsistent class graphs are labeled as inconsistent. This is what conservatively checking for inconsistency means. The algorithm for checking inconsistency is formulated so that it is easy to prove properties of it. It is formulated as a proof system consisting of a few rules.

[4] The C++ program generated from an adaptive program and a class graph is several factors larger than

15.1.2 Our Results

We present an efficient implementation of adaptive programs. Given an adaptive program and a class graph, we generate an object-oriented program, for example, in C++. Moreover, we prove the correctness of the core of this translation. A key assumption in the theorem is that the traversal specifications are consistent with the class graph. We prove the soundness of a proof system for conservatively checking consistency, and we show how to implement it efficiently.

The translation of an adaptive program and a class graph into a C++ program is implemented in the Demeter system. The Demeter system itself is an adaptive program, compiled by itself to C++.

15.1.3 Example

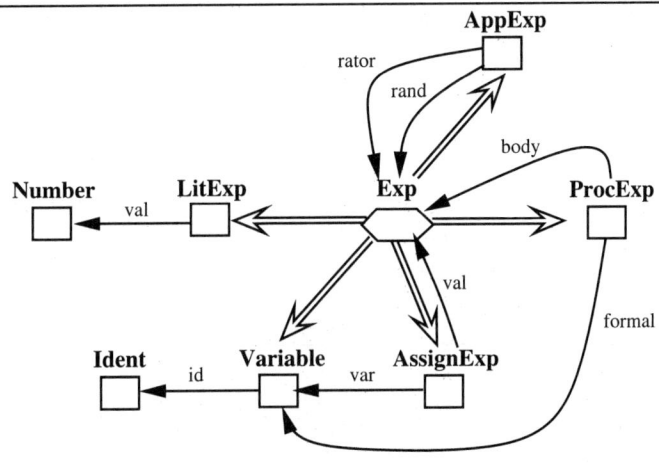

Figure 15.1: Class graph

We now give an example of adaptive programming. Along the way, we informally introduce the concepts that will be defined and reasoned about in Sections 15.2 through 15.4. Suppose we want to write a C++ program to print out all free variables in a Scheme expression. We will do that by first writing an adaptive program and then generating the C++ program.

While analyzing the problem, we identify several classes and relationships, yielding the class graph shown in Fig. 15.1.[5] (For simplicity, the example does not cover all of Scheme.) We take this graph as our first guess on a class graph for solving the problem. The figure uses two kinds of classes: **concrete** classes (drawn as □) which are used to instantiate objects, and **abstract** classes (drawn as ⬡) which are not instantiable. The figure uses two kinds

---

the adaptive program and class graph on a regular basis. This holds true for the Demeter system implementation of adaptive software. The factor is a possible quantitative measure of flexibility and understandability.

[5]Class graph is shorter than class dictionary graph, but has a similar meaning. Class graphs model both class dictionary graphs and propagation graphs.

```
void Exp::findFreeVars(VariableList * boundVars) {      void ProcExp::findFreeVars(VariableList* boundVars) {
  // virtual member function                              boundVars->push(formal);
}                                                         body->findFreeVars(boundVars);
void AssignExp::findFreeVars(VariableList* boundVars)     boundVars->pop();
{                                                       }
  val->findFreeVars(boundVars);
  var->findFreeVars(boundVars);                         void Variable::findFreeVars(VariableList* boundVars) {
}                                                         if (!boundVars->contains(this))  this->g_print();
void AppExp::findFreeVars(VariableList* boundVars) {    }
  rator->findFreeVars(boundVars);
  rand->findFreeVars(boundVars);
}
```

Figure 15.2: C++ program

```
1   operation void findFreeVars(VariableList* boundVars)
2     traverse
3       [Exp, Variable]
4     wrapper ProcExp
5       prefix
6         { boundVars->push(formal); }
7       suffix
8         { boundVars->pop(); }
9     wrapper Variable
10      prefix
11        { if (!boundVars->contains(this)) this->g_print(); }
```

Figure 15.3: Adaptive program

15.1. INTRODUCTION

of edges: **subclass** edges (drawn as $\Longrightarrow$) representing kind-of relations, and **construction** edges (drawn as $\longrightarrow$ and with labels) representing has-a relations. For example, the subclass edge Exp$\Longrightarrow$ LitExp means that class Exp is a superclass of class LitExp; the construction edge LitExp$\xrightarrow{\text{val}}$ Number means that class LitExp has a part called val of type Number.

If we write this program directly in C++ (see Fig. 15.2), a natural solution is to write methods first, all called `findFreeVars`, for the following classes: Exp, Variable, AssignExp, ProcExp, and AppExp. (An explanation of C++ terminology and syntax is given in Appendix A.) The C++ program has two ingredients: traversal and processing. The traversal is specified by the C++ code not in boldface in Fig. 15.2. It finds all Variable-objects in an Exp-object. The processing is the code in boldface that maintains a stack of bound variables and checks whether a variable found is a free variable by using the stack.

We use the adaptive program in Fig. 15.3 to specify an equivalent C++ program. Compared with the C++ program, the adaptive program is shorter than the one in Fig. 15.2. (Later, we will demonstrate how the adaptive program can be combined with class structures other than the one in Fig. 15.1).

The adaptive program in Fig. 15.3 contains just one propagation pattern (because the problem to be solved is simple). The propagation pattern consists of a signature, a traversal specification, and some code wrappers. The propagation pattern specifies a collection of collaborating methods, as described in the following.

Informally, the traversal specification, [Exp, Variable], describes a traversal of Exp-objects: traverse an Exp-object, locate all Variable-objects nested inside. We call this specification fragment a **traversal specification**. The code fragments to be executed during traversals are called wrappers, and they are written in C++.

We interpret this traversal specification as specifying the set of paths from Exp to Variable. A path is described by an alternating sequence of nodes and labels. The set of paths can be described by the regular expression shown in Fig. 15.4.[6]

((Exp,⋄,AppExp,rator) +
(Exp,⋄,AppExp,rand) +
(Exp,⋄,ProcExp,body) +
(Exp,⋄,AssignExp,val))* ((Exp,⋄,Variable) +
(Exp,⋄,AssignExp,var,Variable) +
(Exp,⋄,ProcExp,formal,Variable))

Figure 15.4: A regular expression

The regular expression is a concatenation of two subexpressions. The first half is a Kleene-closure of a union of four expressions. The second half is a union of three expressions. A sentence of the regular language is an alternating sequence of nodes and labels

---

[6]The set of paths in a graph from A to B can always be described by a regular expression. This is a theorem in graph theory.

(construction edge labels or ⋄).[7] A diamond between two vertices means that the second vertex is a subclass of the first vertex. For example, the sentence

$$\text{Exp}, \diamond, \text{Variable}$$

corresponds to the path

$$\text{Exp} \Longrightarrow \text{Variable} \ ;$$

and the sentence

$$\text{Exp}, \diamond, \text{AssignExp}, \text{val}, \text{Exp}, \diamond, \text{AssignExp}, \text{var}, \text{Variable}$$

corresponds to path

$$\text{Exp} \Longrightarrow \text{AssignExp} \xrightarrow{\text{val}} \text{Exp} \Longrightarrow \text{AssignExp} \xrightarrow{\text{var}} \text{Variable} \ .$$

We use the set of paths to guide the traversal of an Exp-object. Consider the object graph in Fig. 15.5a. There are five object nodes in the graph. i1, i2, i3, i4, and i5 are object identifiers. The names after colons are the classes of the objects. The edges with labels are part-of relationships between the objects. We want to traverse the object graph starting from node i1, being guided by the set of paths above. Since the class of node i1 is AssignExp, we first select all the paths from the set that begin with Exp,⋄,AssignExp. These paths are described by the following regular expression.

(Exp,⋄,AssignExp,val)((Exp,⋄,AppExp,rator) +
                (Exp,⋄,AppExp,rand) +
                (Exp,⋄,ProcExp,body) +
                (Exp,⋄,AssignExp,val))*((Exp,⋄,Variable) +
                                            (Exp,⋄,AssignExp,var,Variable) +
                                            (Exp,⋄,ProcExp,formal,Variable)) +
(Exp,⋄,AssignExp,var,Variable)

Moreover, we remove the prefix Exp,⋄ from the paths, since this prefix gives only the insignificant information that AssignExp is a subclass of Exp. We are then left with a set of paths described by the following regular expression, which we denote E.

(AssignExp,val)((Exp,⋄,AppExp,rator) +
                (Exp,⋄,AppExp,rand) +
                (Exp,⋄,ProcExp,body) +
                (Exp,⋄,AssignExp,val))*((Exp,⋄,Variable) +
                                            (Exp,⋄,AssignExp,var,Variable) +
                                            (Exp,⋄,ProcExp,formal,Variable)) +
(AssignExp,var,Variable)

After visiting the object i1, we continue by visiting the part objects of i1. There are two such parts, called val and var. To visit the val part, which is the object i4, we first select all those paths that begin with AssignExp,val,Exp, and we remove the prefix AssignExp,val, yielding:

---

[7]The use of ⋄ simplifies the theory.

15.1. INTRODUCTION

((Exp,◇,AppExp,rator) +
(Exp,◇,AppExp,rand) +
(Exp,◇,ProcExp,body) +
(Exp,◇,AssignExp,val))* ((Exp,◇,Variable) +
                              (Exp,◇,AssignExp,var,Variable) +
                              (Exp,◇,ProcExp,formal,Variable))

Since the class of the object i4 is LitExp, we will select paths from the set described by the preceding regular expression that begin with (Exp,◇,LitExp). However, there is none. Therefore, the traversal stops at node i4.[8] Notice that we let the set of paths guide the traversal as long as possible. This is the reason why the traversal visits node i4; whether or not we should continue the traversal can only be determined from the run-time information about the contents of the val-part. For example, we could have a ProcExp-object in the val part. In that case we would have to traverse further. When the traversal meets i4, it simply abandons that path.

To visit the var part of i1, which is the object i2, we first select those paths described by the regular expression E that begin with Exp,◇,Variable, and we remove the prefix Exp,◇, yielding just Variable. After visiting the object i2, we check how many part objects that need to be visited further. Since no outgoing edge from Variable is on the path, the traversal stops at node i2.

The nodes which are visited are marked black in Fig. 15.5b.

Cycles in the object graph may lead to a nonterminating traversal. In the Demeter system, one can handle such situations by inserting appropriate code into the code wrappers. This possibility will not be discussed further in this chapter.

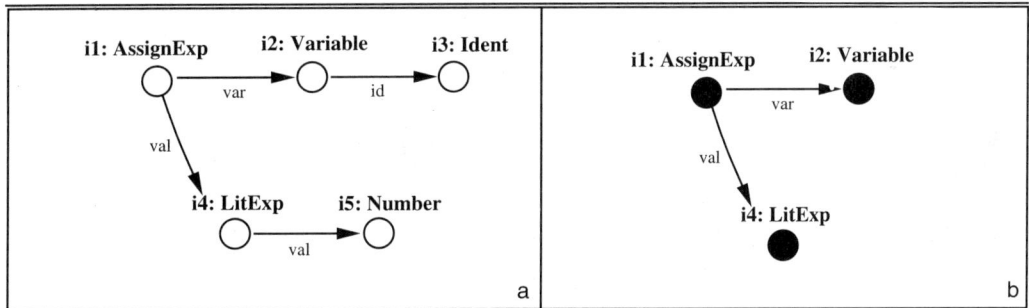

Figure 15.5: Exp-object

We now indicate how to implement the preceding traversal efficiently. The set of paths described by the traversal specification forms a graph called the **propagation graph**; see Fig. 15.6. This graph is a subgraph of the class graph in Fig. 15.1. The propagation pattern in Fig. 15.3 is then translated into C++ as follows.

---

[8]This is a special kind of node visit due to a prematurely terminated path. A prematurely terminated path occurs whenever the object leads the traversal to a node from which it is impossible to reach the target.

- Each class in the propagation graph gets a method with the interface specified on line 1 in Fig. 15.3. Methods of abstract classes are virtual (for an explanation of the term virtual, see Appendix A).
- If a class has an outgoing construction edge in the propagation graph, then the method will contain a method invocation through the corresponding part.

Notice that the subclass edges in the propagation graph do not cause generation of code; the late binding of C++ gives the right behavior.

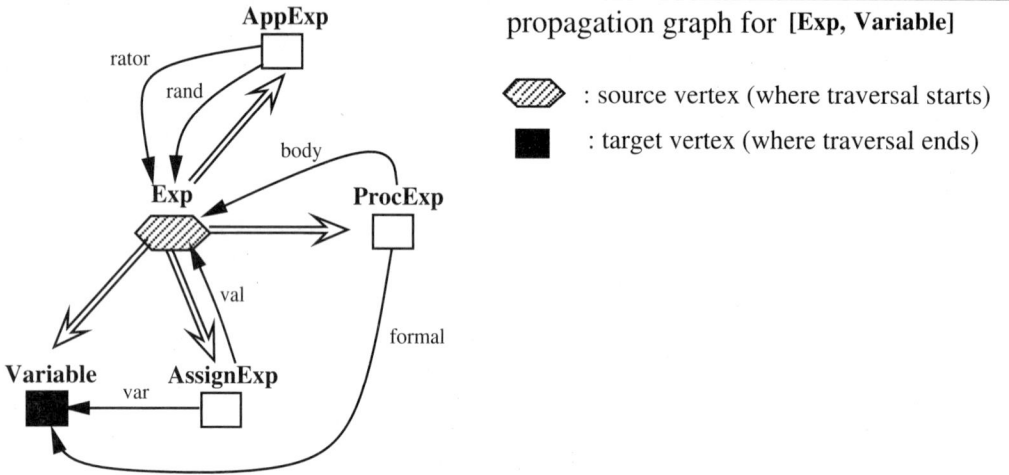

Figure 15.6: Propagation graph

```
void Exp::findFreeVars(VariableList * boundVars) {
  // virtual member function
}
void AssignExp::findFreeVars(VariableList* boundVars)
{
  val->findFreeVars(boundVars);
  var->findFreeVars(boundVars);
}
void AppExp::findFreeVars(VariableList* boundVars) {
  rator->findFreeVars(boundVars);
  rand->findFreeVars(boundVars);
}
```

```
void ProcExp::findFreeVars(VariableList* boundVars) {

  body->findFreeVars(boundVars);

}
void Variable::findFreeVars(VariableList* boundVars) {

}
```

Figure 15.7: Traversal skeleton

Based on these rules, the propagation graph in Fig. 15.6 is translated into the program skeleton in Fig. 15.7.

The code wrappers in lines 4–11 of Fig. 15.3 enhance the traversal specification to print out free variables. The **wrapper** clause attached to class ProcExp adds one statement at

15.1. INTRODUCTION

```
void Exp::findFreeVars(VariableList * boundVars) {
    // virtual member function
}
void AssignExp::findFreeVars(VariableList* boundVars)
{
    val->findFreeVars(boundVars);
    var->findFreeVars(boundVars);
}
void AppExp::findFreeVars(VariableList* boundVars) {
    rator->findFreeVars(boundVars);
    rand->findFreeVars(boundVars);
}
```

```
void ProcExp::findFreeVars(VariableList* boundVars) {
    boundVars->push(formal);
    formal->findFreeVars(boundVars);
    body->findFreeVars(boundVars);
    boundVars->pop();
}

void Variable::findFreeVars(VariableList* boundVars) {
    if (!boundVars->contains(this)) this->g_print();
}
```

Figure 15.8: Generated C++ program

the beginning and the end of the method of class ProcExp in Fig. 15.7. The **wrapper** clause attached to class Variable adds one statement at the beginning of the method of class Variable in Fig. 15.7. The resulting enhanced program is the one in Fig. 15.8, where the statements in boldface are from the wrappers.

The automatically generated program in Fig. 15.8 differs from the handwritten one in Fig. 15.2 in just one way, as follows. The ProcExp method in Fig. 15.8 contains an *extra* method invocation. The reason is simply that *every* outgoing construction edge causes the generation of a method invocation. For this particular example, the extra method invocation has no effect, so it does no harm. It does make the program less efficient, of course. In general, we may be interested in writing in the traversal specification that certain edges should be bypassed. For example, if we write that the edge from ProcExp to Variable should be bypassed, then the generated code should be exactly that of Fig. 15.2. This is possible in our Demeter system, but it will not be discussed further in this chapter.

Suppose we change the class graph by adding two new classes IfExp and VarExp as subclasses of Exp, letting the class Variable be a part class of VarExp, and renaming the labels var and val to rvalue and lvalue respectively. The resulting class graph is in Fig. 15.9. Had we written the C++ program by hand, it would need considerable change. In contrast, the adaptive program needs no change at all. The C++ program generated from the adaptive program for the new class graph is in Fig. 15.10. The example indicates that compared to object-oriented software, adaptive software can be shorter and more flexible, and therefore easier to understand and maintain.[9]

15.1.4 Compatibility, Consistency, and Subclass Invariance

When generating an object-oriented program from an adaptive program and a class graph, we require the traversal specifications to be **compatible** and **consistent** with the class graph, and we require the propagation graph determined by the traversal specification to be

---

[9]Adaptiveness has several applications including an application to building layered systems. When we write programs for a layer it is advisable not to rely on the detailed functionality of earlier layers. With adaptive software we can provide this independence. We deal with only two layers. The first layer provides very simple functionality based on the structure of objects. The second layer expresses new behavior in terms of the simple behavior. For the generalization to work, we need to add functional (also called derived) edges to the class graph.

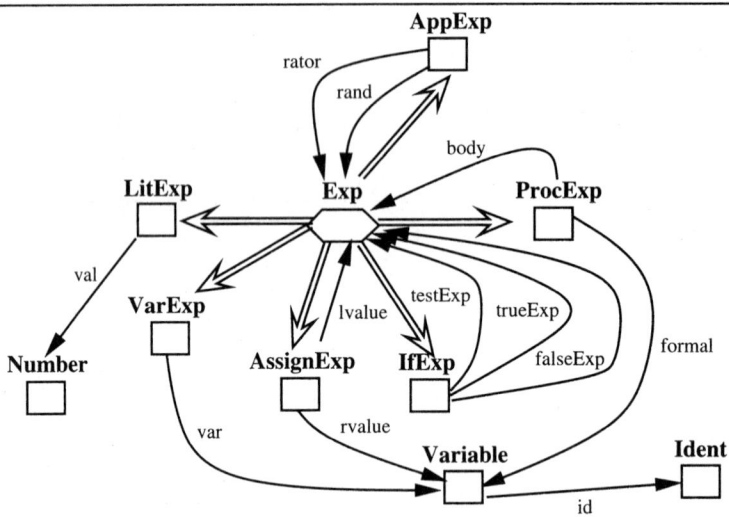

Figure 15.9: Another class graph

```
void Exp::findFreeVars(VariableList * boundVars) {
  // virtual member function
}
void VarExp::findFreeVars(VariableList* boundVars) {
  var->findFreeVars(boundVars);
}
void AssignExp::findFreeVars(VariableList* boundVars)
{
  lvalue->findFreeVars(boundVars);
  rvalue->findFreeVars(boundVars);
}
void IfExp::findFreeVars(VariableList* boundVars)
{
  testExp->findFreeVars(boundVars);
  trueExp->findFreeVars(boundVars);
  falseExp->findFreeVars(boundVars);
}
```

```
void AppExp::findFreeVars(VariableList* boundVars) {
  rator->findFreeVars(boundVars);
  rand->findFreeVars(boundVars);
}
void ProcExp::findFreeVars(VariableList* boundVars) {
  boundVars->push(formal);
  body->findFreeVars(boundVars);
  boundVars->pop();
}
void Variable::findFreeVars(VariableList* boundVars) {
  if (!boundVars->contains(this))   this->g_print();
}
```

Figure 15.10: Adapted C++ program

15.1. INTRODUCTION

a **subclass invariant** subgraph of the class graph. This section gives an informal motivation for these concepts.

The notions of compatibility, consistency, and subclass invariance are tied to the concept of a propagation graph which was briefly mentioned in the previous section. The propagation graph is the starting point when generating code from a traversal specification. Thus, when given a propagation pattern and a class graph, the first task is to compute the propagation graph. The propagation graph represents the paths to be traversed. This set of paths may be infinite, yet the propagation graph represents it compactly. Intuitively, compatibility, consistency, and subclass invariance can be understood as follows.

- *Compatibility.* The propagation graph represents at least some paths.[10]

- *Consistency.* The propagation graph represents at most the specified paths.[11]

- *Subclass invariance.* Any two nodes in the propagation graph have a subclass path between them if they do in the class graph.[12]

These three conditions ensure the correctness of the informal code-generation rules from the previous section for generating efficient traversal code. If the specification is not compatible with the class graph, then the traversals may not reach the specified subobjects. If the specification is not consistent with the class graph, or the propagation graph is not a subclass invariant subgraph of the class graph, then the traversals would go wrong as illustrated below.

We might attempt to compile adaptive programs without the preceding three conditions. This would require another representation of the paths. Currently, we do not know how to do that efficiently, so we prefer to outlaw class graphs that lead to violation of the preceding conditions. Our experience with the Demeter system indicates that the three conditions are met by typical programs. Moreover, in cases where the conditions are violated, it is usually straightforward to decompose the traversal specification such that each of the components meets the conditions.

Checking compatibility is straightforward: compute the propagation graph and check if it represents some paths. Checking subclass invariance is also straightforward: compute the propagation graph, and for each node pair in the propagation graph, check that if they are connected by subclass edges in the original graph, then they are also connected by subclass edges in the propagation graph. Checking consistency, however, is nontrivial, and Section 15.4 is devoted to this problem.

Traversal specifications can be combined in several ways, for example, by "concatenation of paths" and "union of sets of paths". In an analogy with type checking, we want **compositional** consistency checking. Thus, when we combine two specifications that are

---

[10] This is different than saying the propagation graph contains at least one path. The compatibility restriction says that for each subspecification there must be at least one path and therefore, compatibility may require several paths. An example where compatibility requires two paths is: $[A,B]\cdot[B,Z]+[A,C]\cdot[C,Z]$. By "at least some paths" we mean at least a constant number of paths where the constant depends on the traversal specification.

[11] Equivalently, the propagation graph contains no more paths than the ones allowed by the traversal specification.

[12] In other words, if class B is a subclass of class A and both A and B are in the propagation graph, then the propagation graph must include a path of subclass edges from A to B.

both consistent with a graph, we want to check that their combination is consistent with that graph also. In Section 15.4 we present a compositional proof system for checking that, and we prove it sound.[13] We also give an efficient algorithm for checking compositional consistency. Here, we give an informal outline of the system.

Consider the class graph in Fig. 15.11(a). The traversal specification on the left bottom describes a traversal of an Expression-object. This traversal visits all the Numerical-objects nested in Compound-objects in an Expression-object. Fig. 15.11(b) is the corresponding propagation graph. Unfortunately, this propagation graph has a path from Expression to Numerical that does not go through Compound. We call such a path a **shortcut**. The efficient traversal code generated from the propagation graph will visit a Numerical-object even if it is not nested in a Compound-object.

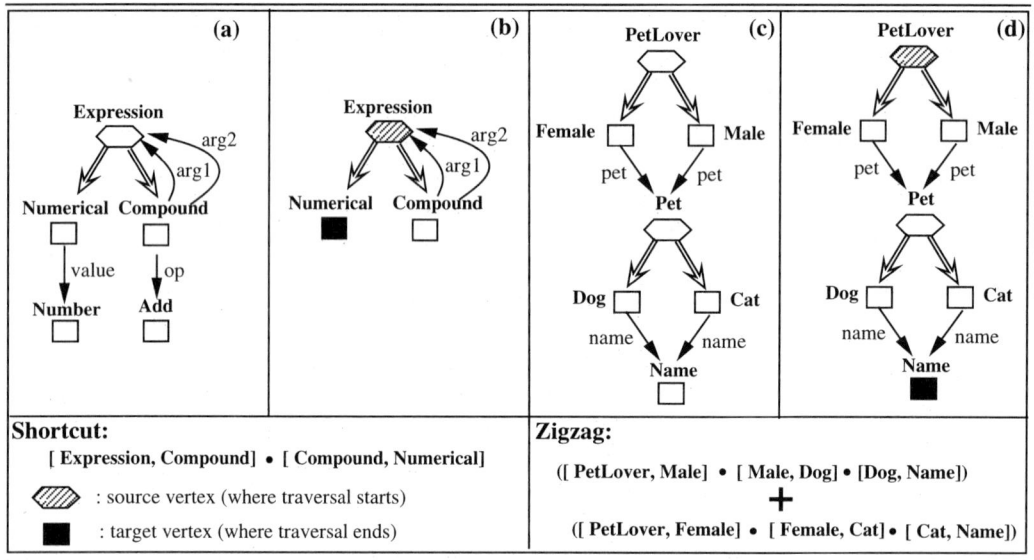

Figure 15.11: Inconsistency

Consider then the class graph in Fig. 15.11(c). The propagation specification on the right bottom describes a traversal of a PetLover-object. This specification says that we want to visit a Name-object which is nested in a Cat-object owned by a female pet lover, or nested in a Dog-object owned by a male pet lover. Fig. 15.11(d) is the corresponding propagation graph. Unfortunately, this propagation graph has two paths that do not satisfy the specification: PetLover$\Longrightarrow$ Male $\xrightarrow{pet}$ Pet$\Longrightarrow$ Cat$\xrightarrow{name}$ Name and PetLover$\Longrightarrow$ Female $\xrightarrow{pet}$ Pet$\Longrightarrow$ Dog$\xrightarrow{name}$ Name. We call such paths **zigzag paths**. The efficient traversal code generated from the propagation graph will visit all Name-objects no matter what.

In these cases, the traversal specifications are not **consistent** with the class graphs. Our soundness theorem states that for conservatively checking for consistency, it is sufficient to be able to rule out shortcuts and zigzag paths.

[13]Soundness means that compositionally consistent directives are consistent.

15.1. INTRODUCTION   465

Finally we show an example of the significance of the subclass invariance condition. The program in Fig. 15.13 prints out all refrigerators owned by families. Fig. 15.12(b) illustrates the propagation graph when the program is applied to the class graph in Fig. 15.12(a). Notice that Refrigerator is a subclass of Thing in the class graph of Fig. 15.12(a), but not in the propagation graph of Fig. 15.12(b). Fig. 15.12(c) shows the C++ code generated from the propagation graph. In the C++ code, the method attached to Thing is a virtual method. Because of late binding, any Refrigerator-object, whether it is a part-object of a Family-object or not, will be printed out. Subclass invariance rules out this program. Notice that we can decompose the traversal specification into [Country, Family] and [Family, Refrigerator], and it is easy to see that the propagation graphs for both of these satisfy the subclass invariance condition. Hence, the programmer can rewrite the program using *two* propagation patterns to solve the problem once it is detected.

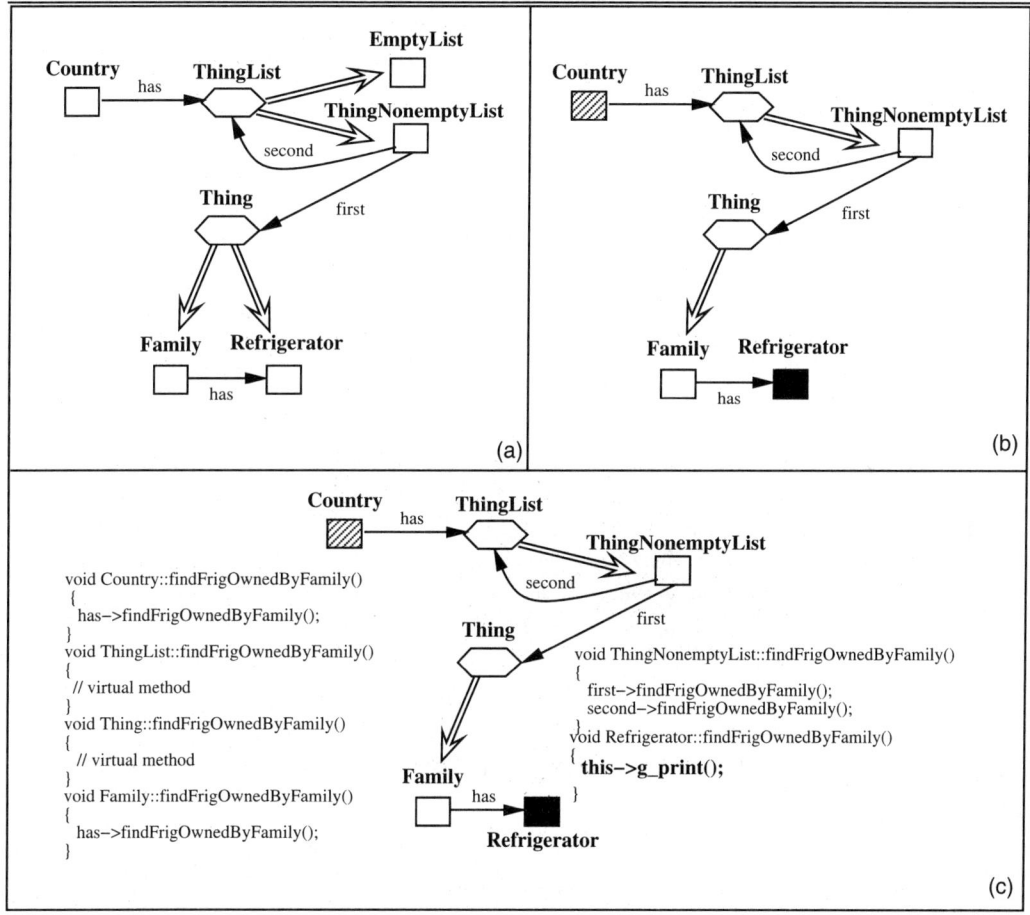

Figure 15.12: Violation of subclass invariance

> **operation** void findFrigOwnedByFamily()
>   **traverse**
>   [Country, Family] · [Family, Refrigerator]
>   **wrapper** Refrigerator
>   **prefix**
>   { this->g_print(); }

Figure 15.13: Find refrigerators owned by families

We will now turn to the formal presentation of our results. In the following section we present the syntax and semantics of adaptive programs. In Section 15.3 we show the core part of the efficient implementation of adaptive programs, and we prove the corresponding correctness theorem. In Section 15.4 we prove the soundness of a proof system for conservatively checking consistency, and we show how to implement it efficiently. Finally, in Section 15.5 we compare our approach to previous work.

15.2 THE SEMANTICS OF ADAPTIVE PROGRAMS

In the following we first define the concepts of graphs, paths, class graphs, object graphs, traversal specifications, and wrappers, and then present the semantics of adaptive programs and the semantics of an object-oriented target language.[14]

15.2.1 Graphs

We will use graphs for three purposes: to define classes (class graphs), objects (object graphs), and propagation graphs (subgraphs of class graphs). A directed graph is a pair (N, E) where N is a set of nodes, and E is a set of edges where $E \subseteq N \times N$. If $(v_1, v_2) \in E$, then v_1 is the source and, v_2 is the target of (v_1, v_2).

We will use the operation $\cup$ on graphs, defined as follows. If $G_1 = (N_1, E_1)$ and $G_2 = (N_2, E_2)$, then $G_1 \cup G_2 = (N_1 \cup N_2, E_1 \cup E_2)$.

Let $(L, \leq)$ be a totally ordered set of labels, such that $\diamond \notin L$. Define $\mathcal{L} = L \cup \{\diamond\}$.[15]

We will consider only graphs where each edge has a label from $\mathcal{L}$. An edge (u, v) with label l will be written $u \xrightarrow{l} v$.

If G is a graph and u is a node of G, $\mathsf{Edges}_G(u)$ denotes the set of edges from u.[16]

---

[14]See Appendix B for the list of concepts that are important for adaptive software development.

[15]The total order will be used to define the order of edges going out from each vertex. This is important to define object traversals. In the Demeter system, the ordering of edges is done more flexibly on a per-vertex basis.

The $\diamond$ is used for subclass edges.

A total order on a set S is a partial order R such that any two elements are comparable; that is, for all a and b, either aRb or bRa. A partial order has to be reflexive, transitive and antisymmetric.

[16]A directed labeled graph is a pair $(N, \mathcal{L}, E)$ where N is a set of nodes and E is a set of edges where $E \subseteq N \times \mathcal{L} \times N$ and $\mathcal{L}$ is a set of edge labels. All graphs used in this chapter are directed labeled graphs.

15.2.2 Paths

A **path** in a graph is a sequence $v_1 l_1 v_2 l_2 \ldots v_n$ where $v_1, \ldots, v_n$ are nodes of the graph; $l_1, \ldots, l_{n-1}$ are labels; and $v_i \xrightarrow{l_i} v_{i+1}$ is an edge of the graph for all $i \in 1..n-1$. We call v_1 and v_n the source and the target of the path, respectively. If $p_1 = v_1 \ldots v_i$ and $p_2 = v_i \ldots v_n$, then we define the concatenation $p_1 p_2 = v_1 \ldots v_i \ldots v_n$.[17]

Suppose P_1 and P_2 are sets of paths where all paths in P_1 have the target v and where all paths of P_2 have the source v. Then we define[18]

$$P_1 \cdot P_2 = \{p \mid p = p_1 p_2 \text{ where } p_1 \in P_1 \text{ and } p_2 \in P_2\}.$$

Next we introduce the Reduce function which is used in the definition of several other functions. Reduce is an operator that removes zero or more leading subclass edges from a set of paths. If R is a path set, then

$$\mathsf{Reduce}(R) = \{v_n \ldots v_{n+m} \mid v_1 l_1 v_2 \ldots v_n \ldots v_{n+m} \in R, l_i = \diamond, i \in 1..n-1, m \geq 0\}$$

$$\mathsf{Head}(R) = \{v_1 \mid v_1 \ldots v_n \in \mathsf{Reduce}(R)\}.$$

Intuitively, each path in $\mathsf{Reduce}(R)$ can be obtained from a path in R by removing a prefix where all labels are $\diamond$. Note that the prefix does not have to be maximal: we can remove zero or more subclass edges. Moreover, $\mathsf{Head}(R)$ is the set of classes we can get to in R when following zero or more $\diamond$-labels.

For example, consider the graph in Fig. 15.1, and denote the set of paths from Exp to Variable as R'; see Fig. 15.4.

$$\mathsf{Head}(R') = \{\texttt{Exp}, \texttt{Variable}, \texttt{AssignExp}, \texttt{ProcExp}, \texttt{AppExp}\}$$

If R is a path set, u is a node, and l is a label, then

$$\mathsf{Select}(R, u) = \{v_1 \ldots v_n \mid v_1 \ldots v_n \in \mathsf{Reduce}(R), v_1 = u\}$$

$$\mathsf{Car}(R, u) = \{v_1 \xrightarrow{l_1} v_2 \mid v_1 l_1 v_2 \ldots v_n \in \mathsf{Select}(R, u)\}$$

$$\mathsf{Cdr}(l, R, u) = \{v_2 \ldots v_n \mid v_1 l_1 v_2 \ldots v_n \in \mathsf{Select}(R, u), l_1 = l\}$$

Intuitively, $\mathsf{Select}(R, u)$ is the set of postfixes of paths in R where each postfix begins with u and where $u \in \mathsf{Head}(R)$. Moreover, $\mathsf{Car}(R, u)$ is the set of the first edges on such postfixes. Finally, $\mathsf{Cdr}(l, R, u)$ is the set of tails of postfixes where the head has label l.[19]

For the same example,

$\mathsf{Select}(R', \texttt{AssignExp}) =$
$\qquad$ Language(
$\qquad$ (AssignExp,val)((Exp,$\diamond$,AppExp,rator) +

---

[17] The v_i in a path don't have to be distinct. v_1 is a path from source v_1 to target v_1 where $n = 1$.

[18] $P_1 \cup P_2$ is the set union of the paths in P_1 and P_2.

[19] If u is a concrete class, then $\mathsf{Car}(R, u)$ consists of construction edges only. If none of the paths in R starts in u then $\mathsf{Car}(R, u)$ is empty. If u is an abstract class, then $\mathsf{Car}(R, u)$ may contain both construction and subclass edges.

$$(\text{Exp},\diamond,\text{AppExp},\text{rand}) +$$
$$(\text{Exp},\diamond,\text{ProcExp},\text{body}) +$$
$$(\text{Exp},\diamond,\text{AssignExp},\text{val}))^*(\ (\text{Exp},\diamond,\text{Variable}) +$$
$$(\text{Exp},\diamond,\text{AssignExp},\text{var},\text{Variable}) +$$
$$(\text{Exp},\diamond,\text{ProcExp},\text{formal},\text{Variable})) +$$
$$(\text{AssignExp},\text{var},\text{Variable}))$$

$$\textsf{Car}(R',\text{AssignExp}) = \{\text{AssignExp} \stackrel{\text{val}}{\to} \text{Exp}, \text{AssignExp} \stackrel{\text{var}}{\to} \text{Variable}\}$$

$$\textsf{Cdr}(\text{var}, R', \text{AssignExp}) = \{\text{Variable}\}$$

where $\textsf{Language}(E)$ denotes the language generated by the regular expression E.

The operator **Graph** maps a set of paths to the smallest graph that contains all the paths.

The set $\textsf{Paths}_G(A, B)$ consists of all paths from A to B in the graph G.

A set R of paths is **convex** over a graph G if R is nonempty and of the form $\textsf{Paths}_G(A, B)$. We write $\textsf{Root}(R) = A$ and $\textsf{Leaf}(R) = B$.

Lemma 15.1 *If R is a convex path set over G, $u \in \textsf{Head}(R)$, and $\textsf{Car}(R, u) = \{u \stackrel{l_i}{\to} v_i \mid i \in 1..n\}$, then $\textsf{Cdr}(l_i, R, u) = \textsf{Paths}_G(v_i, \textsf{Leaf}(R))$ for all $i \in 1..n$.*

Proof. Immediate.[20] □

15.2.3 Class Graphs

The following notion of class graph is akin to those presented in [LX93c, PS93].[21] A **class graph** is a finite directed graph. Each node represents either an abstract or a concrete class. The predicate **Abstract** is true of nodes that represent abstract classes, and it is false otherwise. Each edge is labeled by an element of $\mathcal{L}$. If $l \in L$, then the edge $u \stackrel{l}{\to} v$ indicates that the class represented by u has an instance variable with name l and with a type represented by v. Such an edge is called a **construction** edge. If $l = \diamond$, then the edge $u \stackrel{l}{\to} v$ indicates that the class represented by u has a subclass represented by v. Such an edge is called a **subclass** edge. If not $\textsf{Abstract}(u)$, then there are only construction edges from u. Moreover, for each $l \in L$, there is at most one outgoing construction edge from u with label l.[22]

If Φ is a class graph and u, v are nodes of Φ, then $\textsf{Subclass}_\Phi(u, v)$ is true if $v \in \textsf{Head}(\textsf{Paths}_\Phi(u, v))$ and false otherwise. Intuitively, there is at least one path in Φ from u to v that consists of only subclass edges.[23]

---

[20]Let's assume u is a concrete class. Then $\textsf{Car}(R, u)$ is the set of construction edges exiting from u. The Cdrs are the paths from the targets of the construction edges to $\textsf{Leaf}(R)$). In a Lisp list, a car (first element) has one corresponding cdr (rest of the list); here each car has several corresponding cdrs.

[21]It is closely related to the semi-class dictionary graphs in [LX93c].

[22]Later, we will also exclude cycles of subclass edges.

The binary equality predicate on classes will be written $=_{\text{nodes}}$.

We don't require here that each abstract class has at least one outgoing subclass edge. The reason is that class graphs will also be used in the role of propagation graphs.

[23]This is an interesting definition of the subclass relationship. The first argument is the superclass, the second one the subclass. If u is a construction class then $\textsf{Subclass}_\Phi(u, v)$ is always false for v different from u. $\textsf{Subclass}_\Phi(u, u)$ is true for all u.

If Φ and Φ' are class graphs, then Φ' is a **subclass invariant** subgraph of Φ, if Φ' is a subgraph of Φ, and for $u,v \in \Phi'$, if $\mathsf{Subclass}_\Phi(u,v)$ then $\mathsf{Subclass}'_\Phi(u,v)$.

A node v is a **Rome-node**[24] of a class graph Φ if for every node u in Φ, $\mathsf{Paths}_\Phi(u,v) \neq \emptyset$. Clearly, if u is a node and v is a Rome-node, then for every $u' \in \mathsf{Head}(\mathsf{Paths}_\Phi(u,v))$,

$$\mathsf{Car}(\mathsf{Paths}_\Phi(u,v), u') = \mathsf{Edges}_\Phi(u') \ .$$

The notion of Rome-node is central in the proof of correctness of the implementation of adaptive programs.

A class graph is **flat** if for every node u where $\mathsf{Abstract}(u)$, all outgoing edges are subclass edges. We are only interested class graphs for which there exists an object-equivalent flat one. Two class graphs are **object-equivalent** if they define the same set of objects. Given a class graph, it is straightforward to generate an object-equivalent flat one, provided the class graph satisfies two additional rules. Such a restricted class graph is called a class dictionary graph. The first rule requires that each abstract class has at least one outgoing subclass edge. This in itself does not guarantee that every class graph can be flattened since we could have a cycle of subclass edges. Therefore, the second rule requires that there are no cycles consisting entirely of subclass edges. With those two rules added, every class graph, called a class dictionary graph, can be flattened into an object-equivalent flat one.[25] Object-preserving class transformations have been studied by Bergstein [Ber91]. We will henceforth assume that all class graphs are flat.

15.2.4 Object Graphs

An **object graph** is a finite directed graph. Each node represents an object, and the function **Class** maps each node to "its class"; that is, a concrete class in some class graph. Each edge is labeled by an element of L. The edge $u \xrightarrow{l} v$ indicates that the object represented by u has a part object represented by v. For each node u and each label $l \in L$, there is at most one outgoing edge from u with label l.

Given a class graph Φ and an object graph Ω, Ω **conforms** to Φ if for every node o of Ω, $\mathsf{Class}(o)$ is a node of Φ, and moreover

- If $\mathsf{Class}(o) \xrightarrow{l} v$ is in Φ, then there exists $o \xrightarrow{l} o'$ in Ω such that $\mathsf{Subclass}_\Phi(v, \mathsf{Class}(o'))$.[26]

15.2.5 Traversal Specifications

A **traversal specification** is generated from the grammar

$$D ::= [A,B] \mid D \cdot D \mid D + D$$

---

[24] All paths lead to Rome.

[25] Class dictionary graphs satisfy the abstract superclass rule; that is, all superclasses are abstract. For a discussion of the abstract superclass rule, see [Hür94].

[26] We allow class graphs for which there are no conforming object graphs. For example, `A = B. B : .` is a class graph that has no conforming object graph.

When an object conforms to a class graph, the object graph is not necessarily "legal" with respect to the class graph. It is possible that the object graph has extra edges that are disallowed by the class graph. For proving the theorems in this chapter we don't need the stronger legality definition.

The conformance definition says that we can put only objects whose class is a subclass of v in a part of class v.

where A and B are nodes of a class graph.[27]

Our slogan is: "This language is the λ-calculus of traversal specifications." The idea is that although this language can be extended in many ways to ease programming, it does contain the essential constructs. Possible extensions include the empty specification, notation for including or excluding certain edges, and boolean connectives. In the Demeter system, we use those extensions.

A traversal specification denotes a set of paths in a given class graph Φ, intuitively as follows.[28] [29]

Directive	Set of paths
$[A, B]$	The set of paths from A to B in Φ
$D_1 \cdot D_2$	Concatenation of sets of paths
$D_1 + D_2$	Union of sets of paths

For a traversal specification to be meaningful, it has to be well-formed. A traversal specification is well-formed if it determines a **source** node and a **target** node, if each concatenation has a meeting point, and if each union of a set of paths preserves the source and the target. Formally, the predicate WF is defined in terms of two functions, Source and Target, which both map a specification to a node.

$$\begin{aligned}
\mathsf{WF}([A,B]) &= \mathsf{true} \\
\mathsf{WF}(D_1 \cdot D_2) &= \mathsf{WF}(D_1) \wedge \mathsf{WF}(D_2) \wedge \\
& \quad \mathsf{Target}(D_1) =_{\mathrm{nodes}} \mathsf{Source}(D_2) \\
\mathsf{WF}(D_1 + D_2) &= \mathsf{WF}(D_1) \wedge \mathsf{WF}(D_2) \wedge \\
& \quad \mathsf{Source}(D_1) =_{\mathrm{nodes}} \mathsf{Source}(D_2) \wedge \mathsf{Target}(D_1) =_{\mathrm{nodes}} \mathsf{Target}(D_2)
\end{aligned}$$

$$\begin{aligned}
\mathsf{Source}([A,B]) &= A & \mathsf{Target}([A,B]) &= B \\
\mathsf{Source}(D_1 \cdot D_2) &= \mathsf{Source}(D_1) & \mathsf{Target}(D_1 \cdot D_2) &= \mathsf{Target}(D_2) \\
\mathsf{Source}(D_1 + D_2) &= \mathsf{Source}(D_1) & \mathsf{Target}(D_1 + D_2) &= \mathsf{Target}(D_1)
\end{aligned}$$

Source(D) is the source node determined by D, and Target(D) is the target node determined by D.[30]

Moreover, D is **compatible** with Φ, if for any subspecification D' of D, there is a path in Φ from Source(D') to Target(D').[31]

---

[27]An alternative view is that A and B are class-valued variables that will be mapped later to specific classes when the specification is customized. Adaptive software is written in terms of class-valued variables without reference to a class graph.

[28]A traversal specification is like an algebraic expression: it is abstract. Only when we substitute numbers for the variables, do we get a value. Similarly, when we provide a class graph, we get a set of paths from the traversal specification.

[29]Directive is a synonym for traversal specification. The operator $\cdot$ is called the join operator, $+$ is called the merge operator.

[30]Well-formedness is a concept at the adaptive level without a reference to a class graph.

The well-formedness definition given here is very restrictive since each traversal specification can have only one source and one target. In the Demeter system we allow several sources and targets and a more general well-formedness concept.

[31]Compatibility may require the existence of several paths. Consider: A = B D. B = . D = C. and the specification $([A,B] \cdot [B,C]) + ([A,D] \cdot [D,C])$. Compatibility requires the existence of two paths.

If D is well-formed and compatible with Φ, then $\mathsf{PathSet}_\Phi(D)$ is a set of paths in Φ from the source of D to the target of D, defined as follows:[32]

$$\begin{aligned}
\mathsf{PathSet}_\Phi([A,B]) &= \mathsf{Paths}_\Phi(A,B) \\
\mathsf{PathSet}_\Phi(D_1 \cdot D_2) &= \mathsf{PathSet}_\Phi(D_1) \cdot \mathsf{PathSet}_\Phi(D_2) \\
\mathsf{PathSet}_\Phi(D_1 + D_2) &= \mathsf{PathSet}_\Phi(D_1) \cup \mathsf{PathSet}_\Phi(D_2)
\end{aligned}$$

Lemma 15.2 *If* $\mathsf{WF}(D)$ *and D is compatible with Φ, then* (i) $\mathsf{PathSet}_\Phi(D)$ *is well defined and* (ii) *each path in* $\mathsf{PathSet}_\Phi(D)$ *starts in* $\mathsf{Source}(D)$ *and ends in* $\mathsf{Target}(D)$.

Proof. By induction on the structure of D.[33] □

15.2.6 Wrappers

A **wrapper map** is a mapping from concrete classes in some class graph to **code wrappers**; that is, statements in some language, for example C++.[34] The idea is that when an object is processed by an adaptive program, the code wrapper for the class of that object will be executed. To ease programming, it is convenient to have both prefix and suffix wrappers, as indicated by the example in Section 15.1. The Demeter system supports both vertex wrappers and construction edge wrappers, but in this chapter we consider only vertex prefix wrappers.

The intuition behind compatibility is that the class graph uses the vocabulary of the specification. In the Demeter system we allow renaming of class-valued variables in a specification.

Why is the following definition not appropriate? D is **compatible** with Φ, if there is a path in Φ from $\mathsf{Source}(D)$ to $\mathsf{Target}(D)$.

[32] PathSet is a concept at the object-oriented level where a class graph is given for customizing the specification. Paths is defined for a pair of vertices and PathSet is defined for traversal specifications. Since both define sets of paths, we could have overloaded PathSet but we have chosen not to do so for clarity.

[33] The proof does not need the assumption that D is compatible with Φ. If D is not compatible with Φ the path set is empty and the lemma holds.

[34] In this chapter, wrappers can be attached only to concrete classes. In the Demeter system they also can be attached to abstract classes. This is convenient if the target of a specification is an abstract class. This chapter would force us to attach the code to subclasses of the abstract class. An alternative approach (taken by the Demeter system) is to flatten the wrappers to subclasses. The Demeter system supports two kinds of propagation patterns:

- With traversal specification

  They support incremental inheritance in that wrappers of superclasses add to the behavior of subclasses.

- Without traversal specification

  They support overriding inheritance in that wrappers of subclasses override wrappers of superclasses. They also support ordinary object-oriented programming with the additional benefit of interface localization.

In this chapter, the wrappers themselves need to be syntactically correct statements in some programming language. In the Demeter system, the wrappers together with the traversal code need to be syntactically correct. This allows for more flexibility like expressing conditional traversal.

In this chapter, a wrapper is attached to one class-valued variable. In the Demeter system, a wrapper may be attached to a set of class-valued variables. This is very useful to bring behavior into several classes without relying on the subclass structure.

15.2.7 Adaptive Programs

In general, an adaptive program is a collection of propagation patterns. For simplicity, here we consider the case where there is just one propagation pattern and where the execution of code wrappers does not affect the course of an ongoing traversal.[35] Such an adaptive program (D, W) consists of a well-formed traversal specification D, and a wrapper map W. Given class graph Φ, an object graph Ω, and a node o in Ω, the semantics of (D, W) is given by the function Run[36]:

$$\mathsf{Run}(D, W)(\Phi, \Omega, o) = \mathsf{Execute}_W(\mathsf{Traverse}(\mathsf{PathSet}_\Phi(D), \Omega, o))$$

$$\mathsf{Traverse}(R, \Omega, o) = \begin{cases} H & \text{if exists } H \text{ such that } \Omega \vdash_s o : R \triangleright H \\ \bot & \text{otherwise} \end{cases}$$

If Ω is an object graph, o is a node in Ω, R is a path set over Φ, and H is a sequence of objects, then the judgement

$$\Omega \vdash_s o : R \triangleright H$$

means that when traversing the object graph Ω starting in o, and guided by the path set R, then H is the **traversal history**; that is, the sequence of objects that are traversed.[37]

Formally, this holds when the judgement is derivable using the following rule:

$$\frac{\Omega \vdash_s o_i : \mathsf{Cdr}(l_i, R, \mathsf{Class}(o)) \triangleright H_i \quad \forall i \in 1..n}{\Omega \vdash_s o : R \triangleright o \cdot H_1 \cdot \ldots \cdot H_n}$$

if $\mathsf{Car}(R, \mathsf{Class}(o)) = \{\mathsf{Class}(o) \xrightarrow{l_i} w_i \mid i \in 1..n\}$,
$o \xrightarrow{l_i} o_i$ is in $\Omega, i \in 1..n$, and
$l_j < l_k$ for $1 \leq j < k \leq n$.

The label s of the turnstile indicates semantics.[38]

---

[35] In this section a formal operational semantics of adaptive programs is given. Essentially, the meaning of an adaptive program is a function that maps an object graph belonging to some class graph into a traversal history that is a sequence of traversed objects.

[36] Later, we will call the function Run only when

$$\mathsf{Subclass}(\mathsf{Source}(D), \mathsf{Class}(o)).$$

This will be mentioned in the correctness theorem for the implementation.

[37] A synonym for judgement would be: statement. The statement contains some nice looking symbols such as $\vdash_s$ and $\triangleright$ but those symbols are there only to make the statement more readable. You could replace those symbols by anything you like or you could drop them altogether. For example, we could use instead the notation

$$Statement(\Omega, o, R, H)$$

[38] This rule is read as follows: if the statements, called premises, above the horizontal bar have already been derived then we can derive the statement, called conclusion, under the bar provided the condition on the right (four lines beginning with if) holds. The condition on the right essentially labels the construction edges outgoing from $\mathsf{Class}(o)$. Since $\mathsf{Class}(o)$ is a concrete class, $\mathsf{Car}(R, \mathsf{Class}(o))$ consists only of construction edges. w_i is defined in the condition on the right but it is never used. From the context we can infer that w_i is a superclass of $\mathsf{Class}(o_i)$; i.e., $\mathsf{Subclass}(\mathsf{Class}(o_i), w_i)$.

The semantics works in the opposite direction than the program execution would.

The derivation rule says essentially: to get the traversal history of an object with respect to path set R, traverse the subobjects permitted by path set R and then concatenate the traversals of those subobjects.

15.2. THE SEMANTICS OF ADAPTIVE PROGRAMS

The functions Car and Cdr perform the operations on sets of paths that were informally described in the example in Section 15.1. Notice that for $n = 0$, the rule is an axiom; it is then simply

$$\frac{}{\Omega \vdash_s o : R \triangleright o} \quad \text{if } \mathsf{Car}(R, \mathsf{Class}(o)) = \emptyset$$

$\mathsf{Car}(R, \mathsf{Class}(o)) = \emptyset$ can hold for two reasons:

- The paths in R start with $\mathsf{Class}(o)$ but $\mathsf{Class}(o)$ has no outgoing construction edges. ($R = \{\mathsf{Class}(o)\}$).

- None of the paths in R start with $\mathsf{Class}(o)$.

The second reason is used when a dead end is reached during traversal.

Notice that Traverse is well defined: if both $\Omega \vdash_s o : R \triangleright H_1$ and $\Omega \vdash_s o : R \triangleright H_2$, then $H_1 = H_2$. This can be proved by induction on the structure of the derivation of $\Omega \vdash_s o : R \triangleright H_1$.

The call $\mathsf{Execute}_W(H)$ executes in sequence the wrappers for the class of each object in H. We leave $\mathsf{Execute}_W$ unspecified, since its definition depends on the language in which the code wrappers are written.

15.2.8 The Target Language

We will compile adaptive programs into an object-oriented target language.[39] Given that the source language contains only adaptive programs consisting of one propagation pattern, we make the target language correspondingly simple. A program in the target language is a partial function from nodes in a class graph to methods.[40] All of those methods have the *same* name. In the semantics below, that name is not made explicit, but for clarity we will call it M in the following discussion. A method is a tuple of the form $\langle l_1 \ldots l_n \rangle$, where $l_1 \ldots l_n \in L$. When invoked, such a method executes by sending the message M to each of the subobjects labeled $l_1 \ldots l_n$.

H_i is a sequence of object nodes that describes how object o_i is traversed. For example, the traversal history for the traversal described in the context of Fig. 15.5 is the sequence i1, i4, i2. $\mathsf{Subclass}(\mathsf{Class}(o_i), w_i)$ holds for $i \in 1..n$ although not explicitly mentioned in the rule.

The traversal history concatenation operator is not defined formally, but is straightforward. It concatenates sequences of object nodes.

It is interesting that in the derivation rule Car is used only when the second argument is a concrete class. Therefore, the Cdrs start "after" a construction edge.

Here we use the total order of the labels to express the traversal.

The axiom allows judgements that are not intended by the programmer. Consider the class graph X = A B. A = . B = . For traversal specification $[X, A]$ and an X-object, the traversal history for the B-object is well defined, although B-objects are not traversed. But this is not a problem. It is common that semantics is defined for more than the correct programs. Here, we are only interested in what is referenced in Theorem 15.1. If the definitions work for other cases, we don't care. To better understand the context of the semantics it is worthwhile to look at the premises of Theorem 15.1.

[39] In this section we give an operational semantics of the target language to which we compile adaptive programs. This language does not include wrappers since traversal and wrapper execution are treated separately.

[40] Below we use P to denote such a partial function. It is partial since usually a traversal is concerned with only a subset of the class graph.

If Ω is an object graph, o is a node in Ω, P is a program in the target language, and H is a sequence of objects, then the judgement

$$\Omega \vdash_t o : \mathsf{P} \triangleright H$$

means that when sending the message M to o, we get a traversal of the object graph Ω starting in o so that H is the traversal history. Formally, this holds when the judgement is derivable using the following rule:

$$\frac{\Omega \vdash_t o_i : \mathsf{P} \triangleright H_i \quad \forall i \in 1..n}{\Omega \vdash_t o : \mathsf{P} \triangleright o \cdot H_1 \cdot ... \cdot H_n} \quad \begin{array}{l} \text{if } \mathsf{P}(\mathsf{Class}(o)) = \langle l_1 \ldots l_n \rangle, \\ o \xrightarrow{l_i} o_i \text{ is in } \Omega, i \in 1..n, \text{ and} \\ l_j < l_k \text{ for } 1 \leq j < k \leq n. \end{array}$$

The label t of the turnstile indicates "target." Notice that for $n = 0$, the rule is an axiom; it is then simply

$$\frac{}{\Omega \vdash_t o : \mathsf{P} \triangleright o} \quad \text{if } \mathsf{P}(\mathsf{Class}(o)) = \langle \rangle.$$

Intuitively, the rule says that when sending the message M to o, we check to see if o understands the message, and if so, then we invoke the method.

Given a program in the target language, it is straightforward to generate, for example, a C++ program.

15.3 IMPLEMENTATION OF ADAPTIVE PROGRAMS

We will implement adaptive programs efficiently by representing $\mathsf{PathSet}_\Phi(D)$ as

$$\mathsf{Graph}(\mathsf{PathSet}_\Phi(D)),$$

the **propagation graph**.[41] The advantage of this representation is that the function $\mathsf{Graph}(\mathsf{PathSet}_\Phi(D))$ can be efficiently computed by the function PG_Φ, defined as follows:[42]

$$\begin{aligned} PG_\Phi([A, B]) &= \mathsf{Graph}(\mathsf{Paths}_\Phi(A, B)) \\ PG_\Phi(D_1 \cdot D_2) &= PG_\Phi(D_1) \cup PG_\Phi(D_2) \\ PG_\Phi(D_1 + D_2) &= PG_\Phi(D_1) \cup PG_\Phi(D_2) \end{aligned}$$

Lemma 15.3 *If* $\mathsf{WF}(D)$ *and* D *is compatible with* Φ*, then* $PG_\Phi(D) = \mathsf{Graph}(\mathsf{PathSet}_\Phi(D))$ *and*
$\mathsf{PathSet}_\Phi(D) \subseteq \mathsf{Paths}_{PG_\Phi(D)}(\mathsf{Source}(D), \mathsf{Target}(D)).$

Proof. By induction on the structure of D.[43] □

---

[41]Recall that **Graph** defines the smallest graph containing a set of paths.

[42]Function PG returns a class graph called a propagation graph. A propagation graph might not have any conforming objects. This is appropriate since propagation graphs are used to define programs and not objects.

[43]Can you find a D and Φ such that
$$\mathsf{PathSet}_\Phi(D) \subset \mathsf{Paths}_{PG_\Phi(D)}(\mathsf{Source}(D), \mathsf{Target}(D)).$$
To detect this situation is the purpose of the consistency concept.

15.3. IMPLEMENTATION OF ADAPTIVE PROGRAMS

Intuitively, we may view
$$\mathsf{PathSet}_\Phi(D)$$
as a high-level interpretation of the traversal specification D. It describes the intent of the programmer. In contrast,
$$\mathsf{Paths}_{PG_\Phi(D)}(\mathsf{Source}(D), \mathsf{Target}(D))$$
is a low-level interpretation of D. It describes those paths the implementation will consider.

The drawback of the low-level interpretation is that $\mathsf{Graph}(\mathsf{PathSet}_\Phi(D))$ may contain paths from $\mathsf{Source}(D)$ to $\mathsf{Target}(D)$ that are not in $\mathsf{PathSet}_\Phi(D)$. Given a well-formed specification D and a class graph Φ, a well-formed specification D is **consistent** with a class graph Φ, written $\Phi \models D$, if
$$\mathsf{PathSet}_\Phi(D) = \mathsf{Paths}_{PG_\Phi(D)}(\mathsf{Source}(D), \mathsf{Target}(D)) \ .$$

Intuitively, a well-formed specification is consistent with a class graph if the high-level interpretation and the low-level interpretation coincide. The following translation of adaptive programs into the target language requires compatibility, consistency, and subclass invariance.

Given a class graph Φ and a traversal specification D, we define the target program $\mathsf{Comp}(D, \Phi)$ by $\mathsf{Comp}(D, \Phi) = \mathsf{P}_{PG_\Phi(D),\Phi}$. For any two class graphs Φ, Φ' where Φ' is a subgraph of Φ, $\mathsf{P}_{\Phi',\Phi}$ is the partial function from nodes in Φ to methods, such that:

- For a concrete class $v \in \Phi'$, $\mathsf{P}_{\Phi',\Phi}(v) = \langle l_1 \ldots l_n \rangle$, where $\mathsf{Edges}_{\Phi'}(v) = \{v \xrightarrow{l_i} w_i \mid i \in 1..n\}$ and $l_j < l_k$ for $1 \leq j < k \leq n$.[44]

- For a concrete class $v \in (\Phi \setminus \Phi')$ where $\mathsf{Subclass}_\Phi(u, v)$ for some $u \in \Phi'$, $\mathsf{P}_{\Phi',\Phi}(v) = \langle\rangle$.[45]

- For all other classes $v \in \Phi$, $\mathsf{P}_{\Phi',\Phi}(v)$ is undefined.

In the Demeter system, the compiler generates empty *virtual* C++ methods for the abstract classes of Φ'. Here, we use a target language *without* inheritance, so to model empty virtual methods, we generate empty methods for all concrete classes outside Φ' that are subclasses of some class in Φ'.[46]

The correctness of the preceding translation is proved as follows.

Lemma 15.4 *If* $\mathsf{WF}(D)$, $\Phi \models D$, *and* D *is compatible with* Φ, *then* (i) $\mathsf{PathSet}_\Phi(D)$ *is convex over* $PG_\Phi(D)$, (ii) $\mathsf{Source}(D) = \mathsf{Root}(\mathsf{PathSet}_\Phi(D))$, *and* (iii)
$$\mathsf{Target}(D) = \mathsf{Leaf}(\mathsf{PathSet}_\Phi(D)).$$

---

[44]Intuitively, a call to M is generated for each construction edge in the propagation graph.

[45]All concrete classes in Φ but not in Φ' which are a subclass of a class in Φ', get an empty method. This is used to simulate virtual functions.

[46]It is interesting to notice how the compiler $\mathsf{P}_{\Phi',\Phi}$ is defined. Although it will be used only when the first argument is a propagation graph, it is formulated in a more general form. Why? We see here the roots of adaptiveness in mathematics. It is often easier to prove a more general theorem. In Lemma 15.6 we use this idea and state the lemma in a more general form to facilitate the proof.

In adaptive programming we use the same idea. Instead of writing a specific program, we write a generic program that is shorter and easier to maintain. In adaptive programming we generalize the data structures by expressing the adaptive program in terms of class-valued variables.

Proof. Immediate, using Lemma 15.2. □

Lemma 15.5 *If* WF(D), *and D is compatible with Φ, then* Target(D) *is a Rome-node of* $PG_\Phi(D)$.

Proof. By induction on the structure of D. □

Lemma 15.6 *For two class graphs Φ, Φ' such that Φ' is a subclass invariant subgraph of Φ, an object graph Ω conforming to Φ, a convex path set R over Φ', a node o in Ω such that* Subclass$_\Phi$(Root(R), Class(o)), *where* Leaf(R) *is a Rome-node of Φ', and a traversal history H, we have*

$$\Omega \vdash_s o : R \triangleright H \quad \text{iff} \quad \Omega \vdash_t o : \mathsf{P}_{\Phi',\Phi} \triangleright H .$$

Proof. Suppose first that $\Omega \vdash_s o : R \triangleright H$ is derivable. We proceed by induction on the structure of the derivation of $\Omega \vdash_s o : R \triangleright H$. Since $\Omega \vdash_s o : R \triangleright H$ is derivable, we have that Car(R, Class(o)) = {Class(o) $\overset{l_i}{\to} w_i \mid i \in 1..n$}; $o \overset{l_i}{\to} o_i$ is in $\Omega, i \in 1..n$, $l_j < l_k$ for $1 \leq j < k \leq n$; and that $\Omega \vdash_s o_i : $ Cdr(l_i, R, Class(o)) $\triangleright H_i$ is derivable for all $i \in 1..n$. There are two cases.

First, if Class(o) $\notin \Phi'$, then Car(R, Class(o)) = $\emptyset$. Moreover, since

$$\mathsf{Subclass}_\Phi(\mathsf{Root}(R), \mathsf{Class}(o)),$$

we have $\mathsf{P}_{\Phi',\Phi}$(Class(o)) = $\langle \rangle$, so $H = o$, and $\Omega \vdash_t o : \mathsf{P}_{\Phi',\Phi} \triangleright H$ is derivable.

Second, if Class(o) $\in \Phi'$, then since Leaf(R) is a Rome-node of Φ', there is a path p in Φ' from Class(o) to Leaf(R). Moreover, since Subclass$_\Phi$(Root(R), Class(o)), and Φ' is a subclass invariant subgraph of Φ, we have Subclass$_{\Phi'}$(Root(R), Class(o)) and thus a path p' in Φ' from Root(R) to Class(o) consisting of only subclass edges. Since R is convex over Φ', we get that $p'p \in R$, and hence Class(o) $\in$ Head(R). Since Leaf(R) is a Rome-node of Φ', we then have Car(R, Class(o)) = Edges$_{\Phi'}$(Class(o)). Thus, $\mathsf{P}_{\Phi',\Phi}$(Class(o)) = $\langle l_1 \ldots l_n \rangle$. Using Lemma 15.1 we get that Cdr(l_i, R, Class(o)) is convex and that Leaf(Cdr(l_i, R, Class(o))) is a Rome-node of Φ'. Since Ω conforms to Φ, we also have that Subclass$_\Phi$(Root(Cdr(l_i, R, Class(o))), Class(o_i)) for all $i \in 1..n$. By the induction hypothesis, $\Omega \vdash_t o_i : \mathsf{P}_{\Phi',\Phi} \triangleright H_i$ is derivable for all $i \in 1..n$. Hence, $\Omega \vdash_t o : \mathsf{P}_{\Phi',\Phi} \triangleright H$ is derivable.

The converse is proved similarly. □

Theorem 15.1 (Correctness) *For a class graph Φ, a well-formed specification D, an object graph Ω conforming to Φ, a node o in Ω such that* Subclass$_\Phi$(Source(D), Class(o)), *and a traversal history H, if $\Phi \models D$, D is compatible with Φ, and $PG_\Phi(D)$ is a subclass invariant subgraph of Φ, then*

$$\Omega \vdash_s o : \mathsf{PathSet}_\Phi(D) \triangleright H \quad \text{iff} \quad \Omega \vdash_t o : \mathsf{Comp}(D, \Phi) \triangleright H .$$

Proof. By Lemma 15.4, PathSet$_\Phi(D)$ is convex over $PG_\Phi(D)$,

$$\mathsf{Source}(D) = \mathsf{Root}(\mathsf{PathSet}_\Phi(D)),$$

and

$$\mathsf{Target}(D) = \mathsf{Leaf}(\mathsf{PathSet}_\Phi(D)).$$

By Lemma 15.5 we obtain that Target(D) is a Rome-node of $PG_\Phi(D)$. Finally, Comp(D, Φ) = $\mathsf{P}_{PG_\Phi(D),\Phi}$. The conclusion then follows from Lemma 15.6. □

15.4 COMPOSITIONAL CONSISTENCY

We now present an algorithm that does compositional consistency checking. First we present a specification of the algorithm, in the form of three inference rules.

Given class graphs Φ_1 and Φ_2 and nodes A, B, and C, we write

$$\mathsf{NoShortcut}(\Phi_1, \Phi_2, A, B, C)$$

if it is the case that $\mathsf{Paths}_{\Phi_1 \cup \Phi_2}(A, C) \subseteq \mathsf{Paths}_{\Phi_1}(A, B) \cdot \mathsf{Paths}_{\Phi_2}(B, C)$.[47] To better understand the shortcut property we study the three minimal examples involving three nodes. The specification we use in all three cases is $[A, B] \cdot [B, C]$. Φ_1 is the class graph determined by $[A, B]$. Φ_2 is the class graph determined by $[B, C]$. The propagation graph is the entire graph that contains a direct edge from A to C leading to a shortcut. The three examples are in Figs. 15.14, 15.15, and 15.16. In Fig. 15.14, the propagation graph of $[B, C]$ contains

---

```
A = B C.
B = [A].
C = .
```

Figure 15.14: Shortcut 1

---

the edge from A to C. In Fig. 15.15, the propagation graphs of $[A, B]$ and $[B, C]$ contain

---

```
A = B C.
B = C.
C = [A].
```

Figure 15.15: Shortcut 2

---

the edge from A to C. In Fig. 15.16, the propagation graph of $[A, B]$ contains the edge from A to C.

Given Φ_1 and Φ_2 and nodes A and B, we write

$$\mathsf{NoZigzag}(\Phi_1, \Phi_2, A, B)$$

if $\mathsf{Paths}_{\Phi_1 \cup \Phi_2}(A, B) \subseteq \mathsf{Paths}_{\Phi_1}(A, B) \cup \mathsf{Paths}_{\Phi_2}(A, B)$.[48]

---

[47] A shortcut inconsistency can occur only in a specification that contains at least one join ($\cdot$). It would be equivalent and maybe more intuitive to use $=$ instead of $\subseteq$ in the NoShortcut predicate definition.

[48] A zigzag inconsistency can occur only in a specification that contains at least one merge ($+$). It would be equivalent and maybe more intuitive to use $=$ instead of $\subseteq$ in the NoZigzag predicate definition.

```
A = B C.
B = C.
C = [B].
```

Figure 15.16: Shortcut 3

The judgement $\Phi \vdash D$ means that D is compositionally consistent with Φ. The judgement is conservative in the sense that for well-formed specifications, $\Phi \vdash D$ implies $\Phi \models D$, but not necessarily vice versa. There are three rules:[49]

$$\Phi \vdash [A, B]$$

$$\frac{\Phi \vdash D_1 \quad \Phi \vdash D_2}{\Phi \vdash D_1 \cdot D_2} \text{ if } \mathsf{NoShortcut}(PG_\Phi(D_1), PG_\Phi(D_2), \mathsf{Source}(D_1), \mathsf{Target}(D_1), \mathsf{Target}(D_2))$$

$$\frac{\Phi \vdash D_1 \quad \Phi \vdash D_2}{\Phi \vdash D_1 + D_2} \text{ if } \mathsf{NoZigzag}(PG_\Phi(D_1), PG_\Phi(D_2), \mathsf{Source}(D_1), \mathsf{Target}(D_1))$$

Theorem 15.2 (Soundness) *If* $\mathsf{WF}(D)$, *then* $\Phi \vdash D$ *implies* $\Phi \models D$.[50]

Proof. We proceed by induction on the structure of the derivation of $\Phi \vdash D$. In the base case, consider $\Phi \vdash [A, B]$. We must prove $\Phi \models [A, B]$, which amounts to proving $\mathsf{PathSet}_\Phi([A, B]) = \mathsf{Paths}_{PG_\Phi([A,B])}(A, B)$, which is immediate.

In the induction step, consider first $\Phi \vdash D_1 \cdot D_2$. We must prove $\Phi \models D_1 \cdot D_2$, which amounts to proving $\mathsf{PathSet}_\Phi(D_1 \cdot D_2) = \mathsf{Paths}_{PG_\Phi(D_1 \cdot D_2)}(\mathsf{Source}(D_1), \mathsf{Target}(D_2))$, which in turn amounts to proving

$$\mathsf{PathSet}_\Phi(D_1) \cdot \mathsf{PathSet}_\Phi(D_2) = \mathsf{Paths}_{PG_\Phi(D_1) \cup PG_\Phi(D_2)}(\mathsf{Source}(D_1), \mathsf{Target}(D_2)).$$

By the induction hypothesis we have $\Phi \models D_1$ and $\Phi \models D_2$ so we need to prove

$\mathsf{Paths}_{PG_\Phi(D_1)}(\mathsf{Source}(D_1), \mathsf{Target}(D_1)) \cdot \mathsf{Paths}_{PG_\Phi(D_2)}(\mathsf{Source}(D_2), \mathsf{Target}(D_2)) = \mathsf{Paths}_{PG_\Phi(D_1) \cup PG_\Phi(D_2)}(\mathsf{Source}(D_1), \mathsf{Target}(D_2)).$

---

[49] A from-to specification is always compositionally consistent.

[50] Soundness means that compositional consistency is a specialization of consistency. We see here a common pattern in computer science: if we cannot easily check a property P, we invent a more specialized property Q which we can check easily and which implies Q. Of course, there will be elements for which property Q does not hold although P holds for the same element. Property Q is chosen in such a way that the preceding situation does not hold for too many elements.

An application of the preceding pattern is: P = consistent. Q = compositionally consistent.

Another application is in grammar theory: P = the grammar is ambiguous. P is even undecidable. Q = the grammar is LL(1).

Compositional consistency is a good specialization of consistency, and does not exclude too many cases of consistency. If compositional consistency holds for a specification and a class graph, we know that it will also hold for the subspecifications. This nice property does not hold for consistency as we will show shortly.

15.4. COMPOSITIONAL CONSISTENCY

From $\mathsf{WF}(D_1 \cdot D_2)$ we get that $\mathsf{Target}(D_1) = \mathsf{Source}(D_2)$ and clearly

$$\mathsf{Paths}_{PG_\Phi(D_1)}(\mathsf{Source}(D_1), \mathsf{Target}(D_1)) \cdot \mathsf{Paths}_{PG_\Phi(D_2)}(\mathsf{Source}(D_2), \mathsf{Target}(D_2)) \subseteq \mathsf{Paths}_{PG_\Phi(D_1) \cup PG_\Phi(D_2)}(\mathsf{Source}(D_1), \mathsf{Target}(D_2)).$$

The reverse inclusion follows from

$$\mathsf{NoShortcut}(PG_\Phi(D_1), PG_\Phi(D_2), \mathsf{Source}(D_1), \mathsf{Target}(D_1), \mathsf{Target}(D_2)).$$

Consider then $\Phi \vdash D_1 + D_2$. We must prove $\Phi \models D_1 + D_2$ which amounts to proving $\mathsf{PathSet}_\Phi(D_1 + D_2) = \mathsf{Paths}_{PG_\Phi(D_1 + D_2)}(\mathsf{Source}(D_1), \mathsf{Target}(D_1))$ which in turn amounts to proving $\mathsf{PathSet}_\Phi(D_1) \cup \mathsf{PathSet}_\Phi(D_2) = \mathsf{Paths}_{PG_\Phi(D_1) \cup PG_\Phi(D_2)}(\mathsf{Source}(D_1), \mathsf{Target}(D_1))$. By the induction hypothesis we have $\Phi \models D_1$ and $\Phi \models D_2$ so we need to prove

$$\mathsf{Paths}_{PG_\Phi(D_1)}(\mathsf{Source}(D_1), \mathsf{Target}(D_1)) \cup \mathsf{Paths}_{PG_\Phi(D_2)}(\mathsf{Source}(D_2), \mathsf{Target}(D_2)) = \mathsf{Paths}_{PG_\Phi(D_1) \cup PG_\Phi(D_2)}(\mathsf{Source}(D_1), \mathsf{Target}(D_1)).$$

From $\mathsf{WF}(D_1 \cdot D_2)$ we get that $\mathsf{Source}(D_1) = \mathsf{Source}(D_2)$ and $\mathsf{Target}(D_1) = \mathsf{Target}(D_2)$, and clearly

$$\mathsf{Paths}_{PG_\Phi(D_1)}(\mathsf{Source}(D_1), \mathsf{Target}(D_1)) \cup \mathsf{Paths}_{PG_\Phi(D_2)}(\mathsf{Source}(D_2), \mathsf{Target}(D_2)) \subseteq \mathsf{Paths}_{PG_\Phi(D_1) \cup PG_\Phi(D_2)}(\mathsf{Source}(D_1), \mathsf{Target}(D_1)).$$

The reverse inclusion follows from

$$\mathsf{NoZigzag}(PG_\Phi(D_1), PG_\Phi(D_2), \mathsf{Source}(D_1), \mathsf{Target}(D_1)).$$

$\square$

In general, the converse of Theorem 15.2 is false. For example, consider the specification $D = ([A, B] \cdot [B, C]) + [A, C]$ and the graph $\Phi = (\{A, B, C\}, \{A \xrightarrow{l} B, B \xrightarrow{m} A, A \xrightarrow{m} C\})$. Clearly, $\mathsf{WF}(D)$ and $\Phi \models D$, but $\Phi \nvdash D$ because $\Phi \nvdash ([A, B] \cdot [B, C])$. To see $\Phi \nvdash ([A, B] \cdot [B, C])$, notice that $AmC \in \mathsf{Paths}_{PG_\Phi([A,B]\cdot[B,C])}(A, C)$, but $AmC \notin \mathsf{PathSet}_\Phi([A, B] \cdot [B, C])$.[51]

Given D and Φ, we can decide if $\Phi \vdash D$ by the following algorithm:

Input: A specification D and a graph Φ.
1: Check $\mathsf{WF}(D)$.
2: Check $\Phi \vdash D$ by
- building $PG_\Phi(D)$ recursively; and along the way
- computing the appropriate instances of NoShortcut and NoZigzag.

We can compute $\mathsf{WF}(D)$ in $O(|D|)$ time, we can build $PG_\Phi(D)$ in $O(|D| \, |\Phi|)$ time, and we can check each instance of NoShortcut and NoZigzag in $O(|\Phi|)$ time. Hence, the total running time is $O(|D| \, |\Phi|)$.

---

[51] This example shows that if a specification is consistent, the subspecifications are not necessarily consistent.

15.5 RELATED WORK

There are many approaches to making software flexible. In comparison, adaptive programming has a unique feature: succinct traversal specifications. In the following we briefly assess some of the approaches that are most closely related to the idea of adaptive programs.

Metaprogramming systems tend to spend considerable time doing recursive descents across program structures represented as data structures. In such systems, graph traversals are usually expressed either with attribute grammars [WG84] or other syntax-directed facilities such as code walkers [Gol89] (see also Wile [Wil86, Wil83]). With attribute grammars, detailing the traversal is necessary and laborious, and it is subject to the same maintenance problems as raw object-oriented methods containing explicit traversal code. With code walkers, the traversal is specified separately from the functionality, as in adaptive programs. Specifying the traversal is either more laborious than it is with our traversal specifications, or it uses defaults that are similar to what adaptive programming provides.

Object-oriented databases have been introduced to ease the development of database applications. Object navigation is a common activity of processing in hierarchical or object-oriented databases [Day89, CW91]. Queries can be specified in terms of navigating property value paths. However, as observed by Abiteboul and Bonner [AB91], the current object-oriented databases applications still demonstrate lack of flexibility. For example, restructuring object schemas often triggers a good amount of work in restructuring database applications accordingly. Markowitz and Shoshani [MS89, MS93] also observed the need to write adaptive database queries. They state: "In order to express database queries, users are often required to remember and understand large, complex database structures. It is important to relax this requirement by allowing users to express concise (*abbreviated*) queries, so that they can manage with partial or even no knowledge of the database structure" [MS89]. Kifer, Kim and Sagiv [KKS92] allow for similar abbreviated queries where a path expression can be bound to a sequence of attributes. Bussche and Vossen [VdBV93] use weights to help determine the meaning of certain abbreviated path expressions. Our use of succinct traversal specifications is intended to achieve such conciseness.

Rumbaugh [Rum88] proposed an operation propagation mechanism to specify object-oriented software. The motivation of his work was to increase the clarity of program specifications and to reduce the amount of code to be written. He found that lots of operations such as *copy*, *print*, and *save* always propagate to some objects in a collection. He proceeded by separating the propagation part out of an operation, and specified the propagation by attaching propagation attributes to classes involved in the operation. This is similar to the code walker approach. By doing so, the rules for propagating were clearly declared, easier to understand and modify, and the amount of code to be written is reduced. Rumbaugh's mechanism is run-time based, however, and appears to be less flexible than the succinct traversal specifications. Rumbaugh's mechanism requires explicitly attaching propagation attributes to each individual class involved in an operation. When the class structure evolves, programmers have to update propagation attributes. With an adaptive program, there may be no need to update the program even if the underlying class structure changes.

Harrison and Ossher [HO91] also found the need to separate the navigation responsibility from the processing responsibility, which simplifies system implementations and eliminates a good amount of explicit navigation code. They proposed a means of propagating messages between objects that are widely separated in a network based on routing specifications. A single, central navigator propagates messages according to routing specifications. They used default routing specifications to define how messages pass uninteresting objects. Their mechanism seems better than Rumbaugh's mechanism because routing specifications can be described relatively independent of object structures. The primary difference between their mechanism and ours is that theirs is run-time based.

Lamping and Abadi [LA94] discuss the methods-as-assertions view. This view generalizes object-oriented programming and helps the programmer express flexibly when a certain piece of code will correctly implement an operation. The methods-as-assertions view is consistent with the adaptive view, and moreover the two views are complementary and might be combined.

Wile and Balzer [WB94] discuss decontextualized components. In a decontextualized component, an architecture description language provides the usage context. Compilation decisions are delayed until the context information is available. Decontextualized components make fewer commitments to data and control decisions than do ordinary components. They do not use succinct traversal specifications, however.

In 1992, Kiczales and Lamping [KL92] wrote: "The problem then is how to say enough about the internal workings of the [class] library that the user can write replacement modules, without saying so much that the implementor has no room to work." While the metaobject protocol community addresses the problem with metaobject protocol programs, we address it with succinct subgraph specifications that exploit regularities in object-oriented software.

Object-oriented programs, especially those that follow such programming styles as the Law of Demeter [LH89a], have the small-methods problem [WH91, WMH93, WH92]. The small-methods problem results in dispersed program structure, hindering high-level and detailed understanding. To maintain object-oriented software, software developers have to trace how an operation is propagated along an object hierarchy and where the processing job is getting done. Experience shows that such tracing is time consuming and error prone [WMH93]. We could avoid the small methods by creating larger methods. This, however, would be at the price of a significant maintenance problem because in every method we would then encode more details of the class structure. Adaptive software solves the small-methods problem without introducing large methods and the associated maintenance problem.

Adaptive programs may be used as a succinct way to document object-oriented software. A large group of small cooperative methods can be summarized by a propagation pattern. As a result, the specification of the operation becomes localized and possibly shorter and easier to understand.[52]

In conventional object-oriented programming, object traversal may be specified using patterns. Gamma, Helm, Johnson, and Vlissides [GHJV95], introduce the structural design pattern **Composite** and the behavioral design pattern **Visitor**. The **Composite** pattern describes how to compose objects into tree structures to represent part-whole hierarchies, and

---

[52]There is also an interesting connection to robotics. Earlier approaches used detailed world models to control robots. This resulted in inflexible and slow robots. In 1986, Brooks [Bro86] introduced the subsumption architecture that avoids building and maintaining world models except for the need of individual behavior. In adaptive software we also avoid detailed world models when we express behavior.

the **Visitor** pattern serves to traverse a part-whole hierarchy. With respect to the traversal operations, we read in [GHJV95]: "The problem here is that distributing all these operations across the various node classes leads to a system that is hard to understand, maintain and change." The idea of the **Visitor** pattern is to code a traversal once and then to use it several times. The consequences of using the **Visitor** pattern are:

- Adding new operations that use the same traversal is easy. There is no need to change each class in the traversal domain.

- Related behavior is localized in a visitor and not spread over the classes defining the object structure.

- It is hard to add a new class as a participant in the traversal. In [GHJV95] we read: "When new classes which participate in the traversal are added frequently, it is probably easier just to define the operations on the classes that make up the structure."

With adaptive software we achieve the goals of the **Visitor** pattern more effectively. We can use a propagation pattern that gathers the code that describes the traversal together in one place. This makes it easy to add a new class as a participant in the traversal.

In deductive databases, searching is guided by logical rules. Current work [CTT93] addresses combining deductive databases and object technology. We believe that our succinct traversal specifications can help eliminate the need for at least some of the rules.

15.6 SUMMARY

Our implementation of adaptive programs has two main advantages. First, there is no loss of efficiency compared to conventional object-oriented programming. The generated object-oriented code is as efficient as equivalent handwritten traversal code. In the examples of this chapter, we use C++ as the target language. It is possible to use any typed language with classes, multiple inheritance, instance variables, methods, and late binding; for example, Eiffel [Mey88].

The second advantage is that our implementation scales well. Intuitively, the more classes a program contains, the longer the paths in the corresponding class graphs. Thus, larger programs often mean more traversal code. With our implementation of adaptive programs, the traversal code is automatically generated.

The usefulness of adaptive software hinges on two questions:

1. How much traversal happens in object-oriented programs?

2. If there is traversal, can it be specified succinctly?

Regarding the first question, statistics of object-oriented systems show that they contain many small methods. Those small methods tend to contain traversal code so their presence documents that traversal is common. The reason traversal is common is that, for each task we implement, there are often only a few worker classes that do interesting work, but many other bystanders that participate in the traversals only. Moreover, as we go from task to task, a class that was a worker may become a bystander, and vice versa.

15.6. SUMMARY

Regarding the second question, our experience with the Demeter system indicates that the forms of traversal that often appear in object-oriented programs can nicely be captured in our language of traversal specifications.[53]

If no traversal is going on, or if there is no succinct specification for the traversal we want, we may simply use the empty traversal specification in each propagation pattern. This leads to the generation of an object-oriented program with just one method for each propagation pattern.[54] We believe that both situations (no traversal and no succinct traversal specification) are rare in practice.

Notice that any object-oriented program can be reengineered into an adaptive program. The idea is to specify each method as a propagation pattern with the empty traversal specification. This demonstrates that an adaptive program at most needs to be as long as an object-oriented program for the same task.

Acknowledgment: We thank Mitchell Wand for numerous discussions and a wealth of suggestions for how to improve the ideas presented in this chapter. We also thank Jan Van den Bussche, William Clinger, Walter Hürsch, Linda Keszenheimer, and the anonymous referees for helpful comments on a draft of the chapter.

Appendix A: C++

This appendix is for readers who are not familiar with C++ [ES90].

C++ is an extension of C in that classes in C++ are a generalization of structures in C. Members of a class can be not only data (called data members) but also functions (member functions). Table 15.1 shows the different terminology used in C++, Smalltalk [GR83], and CLOS [Ste90].

C++	Smalltalk	CLOS
data member	instance variable	named slot
member function	method	function
virtual function	method	generic function
member function call	message send	function call

Table 15.1: Terminology

In C++ terminology, when a class A is inherited by a class B, class A is called a base class or superclass, and class B is called a derived class or subclass. Moreover, class A may be a **supertype** of class B. (This need not be the case in C++, e.g., when the inheritance is so-called private.) When class A is a supertype of class B, class B supports all member function interfaces that A supports. Furthermore, for a member function defined in A, the class B can have a member function with the same interface but with different implementation that overrides the implementation in A. Late binding of function calls is made possible by declaring the member function **virtual**, outlined as follows.

```
class A
```

---

[53] The bypassing and through specifications not covered in this chapter are important for expressing traversals.

[54] There might be several methods for each propagation pattern if several methods have the same signature.

```
{
  public:
    virtual void f();
};
```

The following code fragment gives a member function definition.

```
void A::f()
{
   // A's implementation goes here
}
```

The keyword void means that the method does not return any value. The syntax "::" resolves the function as a member function of class A. The fragment enclosed by braces is the implementation of the member function, which contains a line of C++ comment starting with "//" (double slash).

In C++, a variable v, which holds objects, can be of at least the following two kinds:

- Holding an object directly. Defined as

```
A v;
```

- Holding an address of an object. Defined as

```
A* v;
```

When class A is a supertype of B, the variable v with the second definition above can not only hold addresses of A-objects but also addresses of B-objects. To invoke the member function f() on the object pointed to by variable v, C++ uses the following syntax.

```
v->f();
```

Appendix B: Terminology Summary

We summarize the terminology used in this chapter. The terms listed below are needed for understanding the kernel of adaptive software. If you are interested in learning enough concepts to write adaptive programs, you need to focus only on the terms related to compilation (they are marked by +). You can ignore the terms needed to formulate the interpreter in terms of path sets and the terms needed for proofs only.

Class Graph Terms

This chapter	Synonyms
class graph +	class dictionary graph, semi class dictionary graph
node +	vertex
abstract class +	alternation class
concrete class +	construction class
subclass edge +	alternation edge
construction edge +	
propagation graph +	
Edges+	
Subclass+	alternation-reachable
path +	knowledge path
Paths+	
Graph+	
Reduce	
Head	
Select	
Car	
Cdr	
Root	
Leaf	
convex path set	
Rome-node	

Propagation Pattern Terms

This chapter	Synonyms
signature +	
traversal specification +	propagation directive
source, Source+	
target, Target+	
$[A, B]$, from-to +	*from* A *to* B
join +	
merge +	
wrapper +	
well-formed, WF+	legal

Object Graph and Class Graph Terms

This chapter	Synonyms
conform +	legal

Class Graph and Propagation Pattern Terms

This chapter	Synonyms
PathSet+	
PG+	propagate
P+	
Comp+	propagate
compatible +	
consistent +	information loss
compositionally consistent +	
shortcut, NoShortcut+	
zigzag, NoZigzag+	
subclass invariance +	delayed binding restriction

Concepts not covered in this chapter include: collaborating propagation patterns, propagation patterns for nonflat class graphs, transportation patterns, class dictionaries, etc.

15.7 EXERCISES

Exercise 15.1 Prove the following identities.

$$
\begin{aligned}
D_1 + D_1 &= D_1 \text{ idempotency of merge} \\
D_1 + (D_2 + D_3) &= (D_1 + D_2) + D_3 \text{ associativity of merge} \\
D_1 \cdot (D_2 \cdot D_3) &= (D_1 \cdot D_2) \cdot D_3 \text{ associativity of join} \\
D_1 \cdot (D_2 + D_3) &= (D_1 \cdot D_2) + (D_1 \cdot D_3) \text{ distributivity} \\
(D_2 + D_3) \cdot D_1 &= (D_2 \cdot D_1) + (D_3 \cdot D_1) \text{ distributivity} \\
D_1 + D_2 &= D_2 + D_1 \text{ commutativity of merge}
\end{aligned}
$$

$D_1 \subseteq D_2$ ($D_1 \subset D_2$) iff for all class graphs Φ compatible and consistent with D_1 and D_2 the propagation graph $PG_\Phi(D_1)$ is a (proper) subgraph of $PG_\Phi(D_2)$. $D_1 = D_2$ iff $D_1 \subseteq D_2$ and $D_2 \subseteq D_1$.

Can you find any other such identities that cannot be derived from the preceding identities? See [LX93c].

What is the complexity of deciding whether $D_1 \subseteq D_2$?

Exercise 15.2 Prove that if $\mathsf{Refine}(D_1, D_2)$ then $D_1 \subseteq D_2$. Does the converse hold? Refine is defined by the following equations:

$$
\begin{aligned}
\mathsf{Refine}(D_1 &, D_1) \\
\mathsf{Refine}([A, B] &, [A, C] \cdot [C, B]) \text{ for any class} - \text{valued variable } C \\
\mathsf{Refine}([A, B] &, [A, B] + D_1) \text{ provided } \mathsf{Source}(D_1) = A \text{ and } \mathsf{Target}(D_1) = B \\
\mathsf{Refine}(D_1 \cdot D_2 &, D_1 \cdot (D_3 \cdot D_2)) \text{ provided WF holds for second argument} \\
\mathsf{Refine}(D_1 + D_2 &, D_1 + (D_3 + D_2)) \text{ provided WF holds for second argument}
\end{aligned}
$$

See [LZHL94].

15.7. EXERCISES

Exercise 15.3 Representative class graph
Every traversal specification defines a class graph as follows:

$$\text{Repr}([A,B]) \quad is \quad A \ = \ <bs> \ \text{List}(B).$$
$$\text{Repr}(D_1 + D_2) \quad is \quad the \ union \ of \ \text{Repr}(D_1) \ and \ \text{Repr}(D_2).$$
$$\text{Repr}(D_1 \cdot D_2) \quad is \quad the \ union \ of \ \text{Repr}(D_1) \ and \ \text{Repr}(D_2).$$

Classes with the same name are merged.
The representative class graph of $([A,B] \cdot [B,C]) + ([A,D] \cdot [D,C])$ is

```
A = <bs> List(B) <ds> List(D).
B = <cs> List(C).
D = <cs> List(C).
List(S) : E(S) | N(S).
E(S) = .
N(S) = <first> S <rest> List(S).
```

Prove the following:

- Prove that the representative class graph is consistent with the specification or give a counterexample.

- Inequivalence of two propagation patterns can be tested with the representative class graph.

  If two propagation patterns without wrappers D_1, D_2 are different (i.e., they show different traversal histories for some class graph Φ and object graph Ω, more precisely,

  $$\text{Run}(D_1)(\Phi, \Omega, o) \neq \text{Run}(D_2)(\Phi, \Omega, o))$$

  and $\text{Repr}(D_1)$ is compatible and consistent with D_1 and D_2 then there exists an object graph Ω_1 conforming to $\text{Repr}(D_1)$ for which the two propagation patterns show different traversal histories for some node o_1 of Ω_1. More precisely:

  $$\text{Run}(D_1)(\text{Repr}(D_1), \Omega_1, o_1) \neq \text{Run}(D_2)(\text{Repr}(D_1), \Omega_1, o_1)$$

- Show that two propagation patterns without wrappers containing the specifications D_1 and D_2 are equivalent if $D_1 = D_2$. (See Exercise 15.1.)

Exercise 15.4 Restrict operator [LX93c]
Define $D_1 \triangleright D_2$ (the **restrict** operator) as follows:

$$PG_\Phi(D_1 \triangleright D_2) = PG_{PG_\Phi(D_2)}(D_1)$$

Given a traversal specification containing a restrict operator, can it be eliminated by expressing it in terms of from-to, merge, and join?
What kind of identities hold for traversal specifications containing the restrict operator? Are the following two directives equivalent?

```
*restrict* (
  *merge* (
    *join* ( *from LibrarySystem *to* Book,
             *from* Book *to* Title)
    *join* ( *from* LibrarySystem *to* CD,
             *from* CD *to* Publisher ))
  *from* LibrarySystem *through* -> *,ml,* *to* *)
```

and

```
  *merge* (
    *join* ( *from LibrarySystem
               *through* -> *,ml,*
             *to* Book,
             *from* Book *to* Title)
    *join* ( *from* LibrarySystem
               *through* -> *,ml,*
             *to* CD,
             *from* CD *to* Publisher ))
```

The restrict operator is important when you build layered adaptive software using derived or functional edges.

Exercise 15.5 Explain why traversal specifications contain a given node.

Let $\mathsf{Why}(E, \Phi, D)$ be the largest subgraph of $PG_\Phi(D)$ so that all paths from $\mathsf{Source}(D)$ to $\mathsf{Target}(D)$ contain node E.

Give an algorithm for computing Why and prove it correct. Hint: $\mathsf{Why}(E, \Phi, [A, B]) = PG_\Phi([A, E] \cdot [E, B])$.

Exercise 15.6 Need for negation [LSLX94, SL94]

Consider the class graph G:

```
A = B1 B2.
B1 = B.
B2 = B.
B = AOpt.
AOpt : A | NoA.
NoA = .
```

Try to find a specification that selects the following subgraph H

```
A = B1.
B1 = B.
B = .
```

so that the specification is consistent with G. Prove that it is impossible to find such a specification using from-to, join, and merge.

Introduce a new primitive $[X, \text{not } Y, Z]$ with the meaning for a class graph Φ to be

$$\text{Graph}(\text{Paths}_\Phi(X, \text{not } Y, Z)),$$

where $\text{Paths}_\Phi(X, \text{not } Y, Z)$ is the set of paths from X to Z not passing through Y.

Can you now express the preceding subgraph H? Can you make the specification shorter using the restrict operator?

Prove that the specification

$$[A, B1] \cdot [B1, B] + [A, B2] \cdot [B2, B]$$

is not compositionally consistent with G.

Exercise 15.7 Growth plans [LX93c]

A **class graph slice anchored at vertex** v is a class graph so that all abstract vertices have at least one outgoing subclass edge. All concrete classes must be reachable from v.

Prove that a class graph slice defines at least one object o with $\text{Class}(o) = v$ so that o conforms to the class graph slice. Also prove that no concrete class is superfluous; that is, it may be used in some conforming object.

For a **class graph** Φ, a **class graph slice** Π **anchored at vertex** v is a subgraph of Φ, which is a class graph slice anchored at vertex v so that for each vertex v of Π all construction edges outgoing from v in Φ are in Π.

Prove that if an object graph Ω conforms to a class graph slice of class graph Φ then it also conforms to Φ.

A **growth plan of a class graph** Φ **anchored at** v is a sequence $s_1...s_n$ of class graph slices of Φ which have the following properties:

- They are all anchored at vertex v.

- They increase in size; that is, slice s_{i+1} contains more edges than slice s_i.

- The last slice is the full graph; that is, $s_n = \Phi$.

Prove that there is an object graph that conforms to slice s_{i+1} but not to slice s_i. That is, the set of conforming object graphs gets larger as we move through the growth plan slices.

Exercise 15.8 Inductive class graphs [LX93a]

A vertex v of a class graph Φ is **inductive** if there is a cycle-free class graph slice of Φ anchored at v.

A class graph is **inductive** if all vertices of the class graph are inductive.

Prove the following: If vertex v is not inductive then all conforming objects with the following property are cyclic: they contain a node o such that $\text{Class}(o) = v$.

An example of a noninductive class graph is

```
A : B.
B = A.
```

Exercise 15.9 Time complexity

The **size** of an object is the number of edges of its object graph.

The **running time** $T(n)$ of a propagation pattern P on input objects of size n is the maximum length of the traversal history created by P on any Ω of size n starting at any node o of Ω.

Consider a propagation pattern containing the specification

```
*operation* void f()
  *traverse*
    *from* A *to* B
```

How does the customizing class graph influence the running time of the propagation pattern? The claim is that when object graphs with shared objects are allowed, the customizing class graph may force the running time from linear to exponential.

Prove the following: [Xia94] There is a customizing class graph for the preceding program P such that $T(n) = O(c^n)$ for some constant $c > 1$.

Hint: As class graph consider the directed complete graph $C(m)$ with m concrete vertices. $C(m)$ is constructed from $C(m-1)$ by adding a node and a directed construction edge from that node to every node in $C(m-1)$. As object graphs consider graphs with the same structure as the class graphs. Remember that even the Fibonacci numbers determined by the recurrence $F(n) = F(n-1) + F(n-2)$ grow exponentially.

Prove the following: There is a customizing class graph for the preceding program P such that $T(n) = O(n)$.

Exercise 15.10 Complete set of object-equivalence transformations

Given a class graph Φ and an object graph Ω, Ω is **legal** for Φ if Ω conforms to Φ and moreover

- If edge $o \xrightarrow{l} o'$ is in Ω then there exists a construction edge $\mathsf{Class}(o) \xrightarrow{l} v$ in Φ such that $\mathsf{Subclass}_\Phi(v, \mathsf{Class}(o'))$.

Define $\mathsf{Objects}(\Phi)$ to be the set of all legal objects of class graph Φ. Two class graphs Φ_1 and Φ_2 are **object-equivalent** if $\mathsf{Objects}(\Phi_1) = \mathsf{Objects}(\Phi_2)$.

Give an alternative definition of object-equivalence entirely in terms of class graphs without mentioning object graphs.

Find a set of complete object-preserving class graph transformations [Ber91, Ber94].

Exercise 15.11 Metric for structure-shyness [LX93b]

A specification D may be too dependent on the specifics of a class graph Φ. The function $Dep(D, \Phi)$ measures this dependency.

Define

$$\begin{aligned} size([A, B]) &= 2 \\ size(D_1 \cdot D_2) &= size(D_1) + size(D_2) + 1 \\ size(D_1 + D_2) &= size(D_1) + size(D_2) + 1 \end{aligned}$$

Define $D_{min}(D, \Phi)$ as a specification of minimal size among all specifications E for which $PG_\Phi(E) = PG_\Phi(D)$.

15.7. EXERCISES

Define $Dep(D, \Phi) = 1 - size(D_{min}(D, \Phi))/size(D)$. The closer to zero the function Dep, the more succinct the specification.

What is the complexity of computing Dep and D_{min}? Is the computation of D_{min} NP-hard? Hint: See the Ph.D. thesis of Ignacio Silva-Lepe [SL94].

Exercise 15.12 Generalize the theory in this chapter so that we can attach wrappers to alternation classes also.

Exercise 15.13 Adaptive sets of objects

Traversal specifications may be reused as adaptive set specifications. For a specification D, the adaptive set $\{D\}$ consists of the set of Target(D)-objects contained in a Source(D)-object. The adaptive set $\{D\}$ needs to be customized to an ordinary set $\{D\}_{\Phi,\Omega,o}$ with a class graph Φ, conforming object graph Ω and node o such that Class(o) = Source(D).

We also introduce the adaptive set $\{D \text{ where } D_1, D_2...D_n\}$. We assume that Target($D$) = Source($D_i$) for $i = 1...n$. $\{D \text{ where } D_1, D_2...D_n\}$ is the set of Target(D)-objects containing a D_i-object for all $i = 1...n$. The Target(D)-objects are contained in a Source(D)-object.

Introduce adaptive set union, intersection, and difference. Develop an algorithm to check that two adaptive sets are equivalent; that is, for all compatible and consistent customizers and conforming object graphs we get identical sets.

Given a set of adaptive sets all having the same source, at which vertex is it cheapest to have all sets available for a given class graph? This question is related to the efficient implementation of adaptive programs that use adaptive sets to specify resources.

Exercise 15.14 Prematurely terminated paths

A traversal in an object graph Ω of class graph Φ with respect to traversal specification D is prematurely terminated at node o if $[Source(d), Class(o)] \cdot [Class(o), Target(d)]$ is incompatible with $PG_\Phi(D)$. (We assume that D is consistent with Φ.)

Modify the semantics for traversals so that the traversal history contains a "prematurely terminated" marker after each node o where the traversal terminated prematurely.

Develop an algorithm that checks for a given class graph Φ and specification D that no object graph of Φ will create prematurely terminated paths during a traversal according to D.

Exercise 15.15 Asymptotic analysis of the benefits of adaptiveness

The key idea behind adaptive software is that we can benefit from the structure of a class graph Φ when we want to define subgraphs of Φ. To illustrate this point, let's consider the class graph C_n which consists of one cycle of construction vertices and edges. The class graph has n vertices and vertex i is connected to vertex $i+1$ by a construction edge. Vertex n is connected to vertex 1.

Now let's consider all connected subgraphs of this graph, except the entire C_n. Prove that the average number of vertices in those subgraphs is $n/2$. This means that on the average we need to write $n/2$ symbols to fully describe a subgraph.

But with succinct subgraph specifications we can do much better. Each of the subgraphs can be described with a constant number of symbols: $[i, stop\ j]$. The *stop* symbol means that no path exits vertex j. i is the first vertex and j is the last vertex in the subgraph.

This means that for this class of graphs we get an improvement by an arbitrary factor when we use succinct subgraph specifications. The larger the graph, the larger the improvement.

To consider another extreme graph, let's consider the complete graph. To describe a subgraph consisting of a single path is best done by a complete path specification such as $[1, direct\ 5][5, direct\ 7][7, direct\ 4]...$ which describes the path from 1 to 5 to 7 to 4, etc. So here the succinct subgraph specifications don't help. *direct* means that there must be a direct edge and that only that direct edge is selected as path.

The class graphs appearing in applications are somewhere "between" the cycle and the complete graph. As a general rule of thumb we can say that the larger the class graphs and the less connected they are, the more useful are the succinct subgraph specifications. But they can never make the subgraph specifications longer; they can only help.

Exercise 15.16 Adequate testing of propagation directives

When testing an adaptive program (white box testing; that is, we have access to the source of the program), we have to test the propagation directive. We define the following adequate testing rule: A class graph Φ is adequately testing a directive D, if D is compatible and consistent with Φ and if for each compound subdirective D_1 of D, the class graph Φ contains a path from $\mathsf{Source}(D_1)$ to $\mathsf{Target}(D_1)$ not satisfying D_1. A subdirective is called compound, if it is not of the form $[A, B]$.

1. Find a class graph that adequately tests $((([A, B] \cdot [B, C]) \cdot [C, D]) + ((([A, X] \cdot [X, Y]) \cdot [Y, D])$.

2. Develop an algorithm that, for a directive D as input, computes a class graph as output that adequately tests D. Find a directive D for which there is no class graph that tests it adequately.

3. Can you find a better condition for adequate testing of propagation directives?

4. Describe a family of propagation directive errors which a class graph that adequately tests a propagation directive is capable to detect.

Exercise 15.17 Forward path traversals (suggested by Michael Werner)

When dense, highly connected class graphs are used (e.g., graphs where for each construction edge from A to B there is also a construction edge from B to A), we need a stronger path concept to define subgraphs conveniently. One way to achieve this is to use forward paths.

A path is a forward path, if not both a forward and the corresponding reverse edge are contained in it. More precisely, a path p is a **forward** path if there is no pair of vertices X and Y in p such that p contains both a construction edge from X to Y and a construction edge from Y to X.

Develop a theory of traversal specifications for forward paths. There is a need for the concept of a forward consistent traversal specification with respect to a class graph.

Exercise 15.18 Contradicting traversal specifications (suggested by Jens Palsberg)

For the following three propagation patterns find a class dictionary that customizes all three of them.

15.7. EXERCISES

Check whether your class dictionary has a shortcut. A class dictionary has a shortcut with respect to a propagation directive if the propagation graph contains a path that violates the propagation directive by taking a shortcut.

```
*operation* void f1()
  *traverse*
    *from* A *via* B *to* C
    *wrapper* C
      (@ cout << this; @)

*operation* void f2()
  *traverse*
    *from* C *via* B *to* D
    *wrapper* D
      (@ cout << this; @)

*operation* void f3()
  *traverse*
    *from* A *via* C *to* D
    *wrapper* D
      (@ cout << this; @)
```

Show that all class dictionaries compatible with the preceding three propagation directives for the three propagation patterns must have a shortcut with one of the propagation directives.

A set of traversal specifications is **contradictory** if there is no customizing class graph compatible and consistent with all of the specifications in the set. For example, the directive set

$$[A, B] \cdot [B, C] \wedge [C, B] \cdot [B, D] \wedge [A, C] \cdot [C, D]$$

is contradictory.

Find an algorithm which for a given a set of traversal specifications decides whether it is contradictory. Call your algorithm "satisfiability checker for traversal specifications".

When writing adaptive software, we find that sets of traversal specifications are rarely contradictory and that the following algorithm shows that they are not contradictory.

An algorithm for finding a compatible and consistent class dictionary for a set of traversal specifications is: For each traversal specification find the representative class graph (introduced in an earlier exercise). Take the union of the representative class graphs. We call the class graph we obtain by this construction the representative class graph for the set of traversal specifications. We call a set of traversal specifications **natural** if their representative class graph is compatible and consistent with each traversal specification in the set.

A natural set of traversal specifications is obviously not contradictory. Discuss the adequacy of the concept of natural sets of traversal specifications for composing adaptive software. Does naturalness exclude too many sets that are not contradictory? Find examples of nonnatural sets of traversal specifications that are not contradictory.

Hint (reduction proposed by Boaz Patt-Shamir): Checking whether a set of propagation directives D is not contradictory can be reduced to checking whether for D there is a class graph G with at most $|CV(D)|$ nodes that is compatible and consistent with every directive in D. $CV(D)$ means the set of class-valued variables mentioned in D.

The reduction is achieved as follows: Let's assume we have a class graph G' which is consistent with all directives in D, and let's further assume that G' contains a node X not in $CV(D)$. We can find a graph G that is compatible and consistent with all directives in D and that has X eliminated. In graph G we replace vertex X with a complete bipartite graph. Let X have m incoming edges and n outgoing edges. We replace X by the complete bipartite graph $K(m,n)$. $K(m,n)$ has an edge from each of the m vertices on the "left" to each of the n vertices on the "right."

Since X is not mentioned in any of the directives in D, the removal of X does not change the consistency and compatibility property with each of the directives in D. We repeat the preceding process until there are only nodes in $CV(D)$ left in the graph.

A further reduction is useful: Checking whether a set of propagation directives D is not contradictory can be reduced to checking whether for D there is a class graph G that is compatible and consistent with every directive in D and that has at most one edge between any pair of nodes.

Combining the two reductions, in order to check that D is not contradictory we have only to search through all class graphs with at most $|CV(D)|$ nodes and at most $|CV(D)|^2$ edges. This is a finite number of graphs to search. For each class graph we check for compatibility and consistency using the algorithms described earlier. Can this algorithm be made more efficient?

Exercise 15.19 Propagation graphs and reducible flow graphs (suggested by John Reif)

Since propagation graphs summarize the structure of programs that use structured flow-of-control statements, they must be reducible flow graphs. The concept of reducible flowgraphs is studied in compiler theory with the purpose of loop optimization [ASU86].

Define the concept of a reducible class graph using the concept of dominator. Discuss whether class graphs in general should be reducible or whether only propagation graphs should be reducible. Give an example of a nonreducible class graph and a propagation directive that selects a reducible propagation graph. Implement a tool that efficiently checks whether a propagation graph is reducible. (This tool would be useful for checking whether a propagation directive selects a "reasonable" propagation graph.)

Exercise 15.20 Identity

Prove or disprove the following identity (suggested by Boaz Patt-Shamir)

$$([A,B] \cdot [B,C]) \cdot ([C,D] \cdot [D,E]) + ([A,F] \cdot [F,C]) \cdot ([C,G] \cdot [G,E]) =$$

$$([A,B] \cdot [B,C] + [A,F] \cdot [F,C]) \cdot ([C,D] \cdot [D,E] + [C,G] \cdot [G,E])$$

Exercise 15.21 Propagation directive abstraction

Given a set of pairs of class graphs (cd_i, pg_i) for $i = 1...n$, find a propagation directive D (if there is one), such that D and cd_i are compatible and consistent and $PG_{cd_i}(D) = pg_i$ for all $i = 1...n$. Under which circumstances is D unique if viewed as a function from class

15.7. EXERCISES

graphs to class graphs? (This problem can be viewed as propagation directive interpolation in analogy to polynomial interpolation.)

Exercise 15.22 Code generation for sets of directives

A current deficiency of adaptive software is that the presence of inconsistency requires manual intervention by the programmer. The goal is to automatically handle inconsistency and still generate the correct traversal code.

Given a set of directives $\{d_i\}$ and a class graph G compatible with each of the directives, find a correct traversal implementation for each of the directives.

A traversal implementation of directive d is correct for graph G, if all the traversals satisfy the directive; that is, at run-time no traversal will be made that violates the directive.

We ask for a correct traversal implementation even in the case of inconsistency as shown in the following example.
Directive $d = [A, B] \cdot [B, C]$.
Graph G:

```
A = X.
X = B C.
B = X.
X = .
```

G is compositionally inconsistent with d because of the shortcut from A via X directly to C. But still we can create a correct implementation by using two traversal functions: f for the traversal of $[A, B]$ and f_{red} for the traversal of $[B, C]$.

The compositional consistency checking algorithm is useful for controlling the code generation in the presence of inconsistency.

Some forms of inconsistency require that the target of the directive has an interface supporting several functions. For example, for $d = [A, B] \cdot [B, D] + [A, C] \cdot [C, D]$, and class graph

```
A = X.
X = B C D.
B = X.
C = X.
```

we need two functions at A to address the inconsistency.

This is an interesting code generation problem; the goal is not only to generate provably correct code but also tight code, which runs efficiently.

Exercise 15.23 Computing propagation graphs (proposed by Boaz Patt-Shamir)

Implement the following algorithm to compute the propagation graph of $[A, B]$ in graph G.

1. Do a breadth-first traversal from A and mark blue all nodes and edges that are reached.

2. Do a breadth-first traversal from B on reversed graph and mark red all nodes and edges that are reached. In the reversed graph all edges have been reversed.

3. The propagation graph consists of the nodes and edges marked both blue and red.

What is the running-time of your algorithm?

Exercise 15.24 Proof system for compositional satisfiability.

A directive D is **compositionally satisfiable** if there is a graph G so that directive D is compositionally consistent with the class graph G. Find a proof system for compositional unsatisfiability for directives that are in sum-of-product form.

A directive is in **sum-of-product form** (SOPF), if it is of the form $\sum_{i=1}^{n} D_i$, where each D_i is a product of the form $[A, B] \cdot [B, C] \cdot ...$; that is, a join of primitive directives of the form $[X, Y]$. The summation is used to describe merging of directives.

Hint: Use the following analogy to the propositional calculus (boolean expressions). The directives correspond to propositional formulas in conjunctive normal form (CNF). A boolean formula is in **conjunctive normal form** if it is of the form $\prod_{i=1}^{n} C_i$, where each C_i is a disjunction (or-operation) of literals. A **literal** is either a boolean variable v or its negation v'. The product describes a conjunction (and-operation) of clauses. Each product of a directive in SOPF corresponds to a clause of a boolean formula in CNF.

Let $x_1, x_2, ..., x_n$ be the variables that appear in a boolean formula S. An **interpretation** I of S is a mapping of the variables $x_1, x_2, ..., x_n$ to $true$ or $false$. We say that an interpretation I is a **model** of S if S is true under the interpretation I. A formula that has a model is satisfiable.

Consider the following analogies

```
boolean algebra                directives

formula in CNF                 directive in SOPF
clause                         product (join of primitives)
interpretation                 compatible class graph
model                          compositionally consistent
                                 and compatible class graph
satisfiable                    compositionally satisfiable
```

A well-known proof system, called **resolution** for unsatisfiability of boolean formulas in CNF [Rob65], allows us to prove that a formula is unsatisfiable. Two clauses c_1 and c_2 **clash** if there is exactly one literal in c_1 that is complemented in c_2. If the clauses $c_1 \cup \{x\}$ and $c_2 \cup \{x\}$ clash, then $c_1 \cup c_2$ is the **resolvent** of the two clauses. A **resolution proof** for the unsatisfiability of a boolean formula S in CNF is a sequence of clauses $c_1, c_2, ..., c_k$ so that c_k is the empty clause. For $1 \leq i \leq k-1$ the clause c_{i+1} must be a resolvent of $S \cap c_1 \cap c_2 \cap ... \cap c_i$. It can be shown that a formula is unsatisfiable if and only if it has a resolution proof. Such a proof system is called complete.

Can you find a complete proof system for compositional satisfiability? What kind of additional products can we add to a given a directive without disturbing the compositional satisfiability?

15.8 BIBLIOGRAPHIC REMARKS

This chapter is an annotated version of [PXL95] extended with exercises and a terminology summary. It is reprinted with permission of ACM.

Chapter 16

Theory of Class Dictionaries

This chapter is for intermediate and expert users of adaptive software technology after they have refreshed their knowledge of discrete mathematics. You can successfully use adaptive software without knowing about any of the formalisms used in this chapter.

In earlier chapters you get an intuitive, informal definition of the concepts with plenty of motivation. This informal style is a good way to learn the technology, but is bound not to answer all the questions that arise when the technology is applied to big projects. In this chapter we compensate for the earlier informality by giving a formal definition of the concepts. Motivation is minimal; a discussion of the theory is available in several journal papers.

This chapter serves the following purposes:

- Intuition is insufficient.

  For many applications, the intuitive explanations are sufficient. But when our intuition fails, we need to go back to formal definitions that contain all the details.

- Instructors need help.

  Instructors of adaptive software need to have a fall-back position in the form of a reference manual that defines the programming language and method they teach. This chapter serves as a formal reference manual.

- Implementors need help.

  Implementors of tools for adaptive software technology need a formal definition of what they have to implement.

16.1 CLASS DICTIONARY GRAPHS

We have introduced three kinds of vertices: construction, alternation, and repetition vertices. We also introduced six kinds of edges: required/optional construction, alternation, inheritance, and zero-more/one-more repetition edges. Since repetition vertices and optional construction edges can be represented by alternation and construction concepts, we deal with only construction, alternation vertices, (required) construction edges, alternation edges, and inheritance edges in the theoretical treatment of this chapter.

16.1.1 Semi-Class Dictionary Graphs

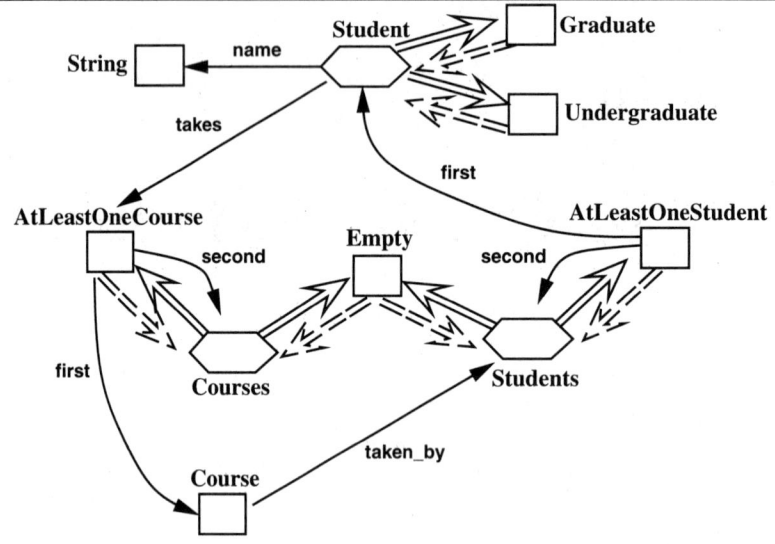

Figure 16.1: A semi-class dictionary graph

Fig. 16.1 shows a semi-class dictionary graph.

Definition 16.1 A **semi-class dictionary graph** is a tuple $\Phi = (VC, VA, \Lambda; EC, EA, EI)$ with finitely many labeled vertices in the disjoint sets VC and VA. We define $V = VC \cup VA$. VC is a set of vertices called construction vertices. VA is a set of vertices called alternation vertices. EC is a ternary relation on $V \times V \times \Lambda$, called construction edges. Λ is a finite set of construction edge labels. EA is a binary relation on $VA \times V$, called alternation edges. EI is a binary relation on $V \times VA$, called inheritance edges.

We also use $V(\Phi)$ to represent all the vertices in Φ. Next we define reachability concepts.[1]

Definition 16.2 In a semi-class dictionary graph $\Phi = (VC, VA, \Lambda; EC, EA, EI)$

- An **alternation path** is a path satisfying regular expression EA^*; that is, containing only alternation edges.

  Vertex w is **alternation-reachable** from vertex v if there is an alternation path from v to w or $v = w$.

  We write $v \overset{*}{\Longrightarrow} w$ if w is alternation-reachable from v. We write $v \overset{+}{\Longrightarrow} w$ if w is alternation-reachable from v via more than one alternation edge.

---
[1] Semi-class dictionary graph reachability, page 431 (8).

16.1. CLASS DICTIONARY GRAPHS

- An **inheritance path** is a path satisfying regular expression EI^*; that is, containing only inheritance edges.

  Vertex w **inherits** from vertex v if there is an inheritance path from v to w or $v = w$.

  We write $v \xdashrightarrow{*} w$ if v inherits from w. We write $v \xdashrightarrow{+} w$ if v inherits from w via more than one inheritance edge.

- A **knowledge path** is a path satisfying regular expression $(EA \mid (EI)^*EC)^*$; that is, a knowledge path is a sequence of construction, alternation, and inheritance edges such that an inheritance edge can be followed only by a construction edge or an inheritance edge, and the path cannot end with an inheritance edge.

The **length** of path p is the number of edges in p. We say that from vertex v back to vertex v there is always an alternation path of length zero, an inheritance path of length zero, and a knowledge path of length zero. A **cycle** in a semi-class dictionary graph is a path of length more than zero from some vertex v back to v.

If there is an alternation path from vertex v to vertex w, then vertex w is a subclass of vertex v, and any object of w is also an object of v. If there is an inheritance path from vertex v to vertex w, then vertex v inherits from vertex w. The relation **inherits** is the reflexive transitive closure of the relation EI. The relation **alternation-reachable** is the reflexive transitive closure of the relation EA.

Further explanation is needed for knowledge paths. The motivation behind the knowledge path concept is to define the set of classes needed to build objects of a given class. The set of vertices that are reachable (by a knowledge path) from a given vertex v, defines the set of classes whose instances may appear as (nested) part-objects of v-objects.

Alternation paths are a special kind of knowledge paths. Inheritance paths are not. When we refer to a path p, we mean a knowledge path, unless we explicitly mention that p is an inheritance or alternation path.

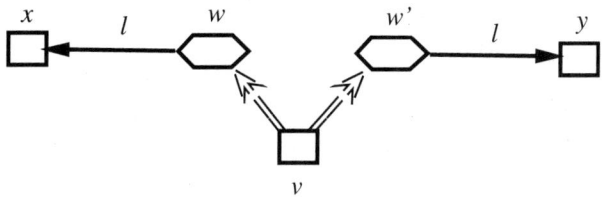

Figure 16.2: Forbidden graph

The semi-class dictionary graphs that appear in applications should always satisfy two independent axioms. We say a semi-class dictionary graph is **legal** if it satisfies two axioms called the **Cycle-Free Alternation and Inheritance Axiom** and the **Unique Label Axiom**.

Definition 16.3 A **legal** semi-class dictionary graph $\Phi = (VC, VA, \Lambda; EC, EA, EI)$ satisfies $(V = VC \cup VA)$:

Cycle-Free Alternation and Inheritance Axiom

There are no alternation cycles and no inheritance cycles; that is, $\not\exists v \in V : v \stackrel{+}{\Longrightarrow} v$ or $v \stackrel{+}{\dashrightarrow} v$;

Unique Label Axiom (see Fig. 16.2)

$\forall v, w, w', x, y \in V, l \in \Lambda$: if $v \stackrel{*}{\dashrightarrow} w$ or $w \stackrel{*}{\Longrightarrow} v$, and $v \stackrel{*}{\dashrightarrow} w'$ or $w' \stackrel{*}{\Longrightarrow} v$, then $w \stackrel{l}{\longrightarrow} x, w' \stackrel{l}{\longrightarrow} y \in EC$ implies $w \stackrel{l}{\longrightarrow} x = w' \stackrel{l}{\longrightarrow} y$ (i.e., $w = w'$ and $x = y$).

From now on, when we refer to a semi-class dictionary graph, we mean a legal semi-class dictionary graph.

16.1.2 Class Dictionary Graph Slices

Figure 16.3: A semi-class dictionary graph that cannot define objects

Some semi-class dictionary graphs are not meaningful for defining objects. For this purpose we use class dictionary graph slices.[2]

Definition 16.4 A **class dictionary graph slice** $P = (VC_P, VA_P, \Lambda_P; EC_P, EA_P, EI_P)$ **anchored at vertex** v_0 is a semi-class dictionary graph with the following four properties ($V_P = VC_P \cup VA_P$):

1. $v_0 \in V_P$ and $\forall w \in V_P \exists v \in V_P$: v is reachable from v_0 via a knowledge path and w is reachable from v via an inheritance path.

2. $\forall v \Longrightarrow w \in EA_P : w \stackrel{\ldots}{\dashrightarrow} v \in EI_P$.

   In other words, alternation edges imply inheritance edges.

3. $\forall v \in VA_P \exists w \in V_P : w \stackrel{\ldots}{\dashrightarrow} v \in EI_P$.

   In other words, there is no alternation vertex without an incoming inheritance edge.

4. $\forall v \in VA_P : v = v_0$ or $\exists w \Longrightarrow v \in EA_P$ or $\exists w \stackrel{l}{\longrightarrow} v \in EC_P$ implies $\exists v' \in V_P$ s.t. $v \Longrightarrow v' \in EA_P$.

   In other words, if an alternation vertex is "used" (i.e., it is v_0 or has some incoming construction or alternation edge in P), then this vertex must have at least one outgoing alternation edge in P.

The vertices incident with the edges are also in P.

The semi-class dictionary graph in Fig. 16.4 is a class dictionary graph slice.

---
[2]Class dictionary graph slice, page 431 (10).

16.1. CLASS DICTIONARY GRAPHS

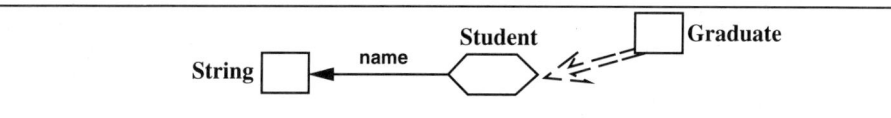

Figure 16.4: A class dictionary graph slice

16.1.3 Class Dictionary Graphs

Definition 16.5 A **class dictionary graph**[3] $\Phi = (VC, VA, \Lambda; EC, EA, EI)$ is a union of class dictionary graph slices such that

$$v \Longrightarrow w \in EA \; iff \; w \cdots\!\!\!\!\triangleright v \in EI.$$

We can also give a direct definition of class dictionary graphs without relying on class dictionary graph slices.

Definition 16.6 A **class dictionary graph** is a tuple $\phi = (VC, VA, VT, \Lambda; EC, EA)$ with finitely many labeled vertices in the disjoint sets VC and VA. We define $V = VC \cup VA$. VC is a set of vertices called construction vertices. VA is a set of vertices called alternation vertices. VT is a subset of VC, called terminal vertices. EC is a ternary relation on $V \times V \times \Lambda$, called construction edges. Λ is a finite set of construction edge labels. EA is a binary relation on $VA \times V$, called alternation edges.

In addition, a class dictionary graph defined this way must satisfy the cycle-free alternation and the unique label axiom. Those two axioms are similar to the ones we discussed for semi-class dictionary graphs.

The semi-class dictionary graph in Fig. 16.1 is a class dictionary graph. We use the following graphical notation[4] for drawing class dictionary graphs: squares for construction vertices, hexagons for alternation vertices, thin lines for construction edges, and double lines for alternation edges.

In class dictionary graphs, since the inheritance edge, say $v \cdots\!\!\!\!\triangleright w$, occurs whenever the alternation edge $w \Longrightarrow v$ occurs and vice versa, we usually do not draw inheritance edges in class dictionary graphs.

A class dictionary graph Φ defines objects for each vertex in Φ. Sometimes when we want to analyze or test a system, we need to find all the required vertices and associated edges to build objects for a certain vertex. Class dictionary graph slices of a given class dictionary graph provide such functionality. Informally, a class dictionary graph slice anchored at class C contains enough classes to build some C-object.

Definition 16.7 For a class dictionary graph $\Phi = (VC_\Phi, VA_\Phi, \Lambda_\Phi; EC_\Phi, EA_\Phi, EI_\Phi)$, a **class dictionary graph slice** $P = (VC_P, VA_P, \Lambda_P; EC_P, EA_P, EI_P)$ **of Φ anchored at vertex** v_0 is a class dictionary graph slice with the following three properties:

---

[3]Legal class dictionary graph, page 431 (9).
[4]Class dictionary graph graphical representation, page 431 (6).

1. $VC_P \subseteq VC_\Phi, VA_P \subseteq VA_\Phi, EC_P \subseteq EC_\Phi, EA_P \subseteq EA_\Phi, EI_P \subseteq EI_\Phi$ and $\Lambda_P \subseteq \Lambda_\Phi$

2. $\forall v \in VC_P \cup VA_P \forall v \dashrightarrow w \in EI_\Phi : v \dashrightarrow w \in EI_P$.

   In other words, if a (construction or alternation) vertex v is contained in V_P then all inheritance edges outgoing from v in Φ are in P.

3. $\forall v \in VC_P \cup VA_P \forall v \xrightarrow{l} w \in EC_\Phi : v \xrightarrow{l} w \in EC_P$.

   In other words, if a (construction or alternation) vertex v is contained in V_P then all construction edges outgoing from v in Φ are in P.

The vertices incident with the edges are also in P.

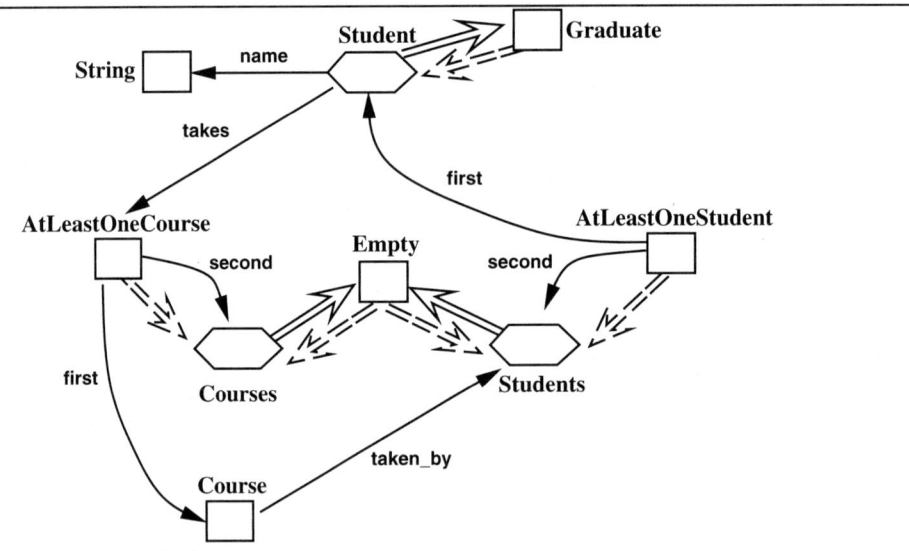

Figure 16.5: A class dictionary graph slice

Figure 16.5 is a class dictionary graph slice of the class dictionary graph in Fig. 16.1, anchored at `Graduate`.

Figure 16.6 shows the relations between the concepts we introduced so far.

16.1.4 Object Graphs

In this section we formally define a set of objects defined by a class dictionary graph slice and therefore also by a class dictionary graph. We first define three technical concepts: **associated, Parts,** and **PartClusters** before we define object graphs. An **associated** set of a class defines the set of instantiable subclasses of the class. Function *Parts* defines the set of parts of a class with their names and types. *PartClusters* is a generalization of *Parts* where the part types are given by a set of instantiable classes, using the definition of

16.1. CLASS DICTIONARY GRAPHS

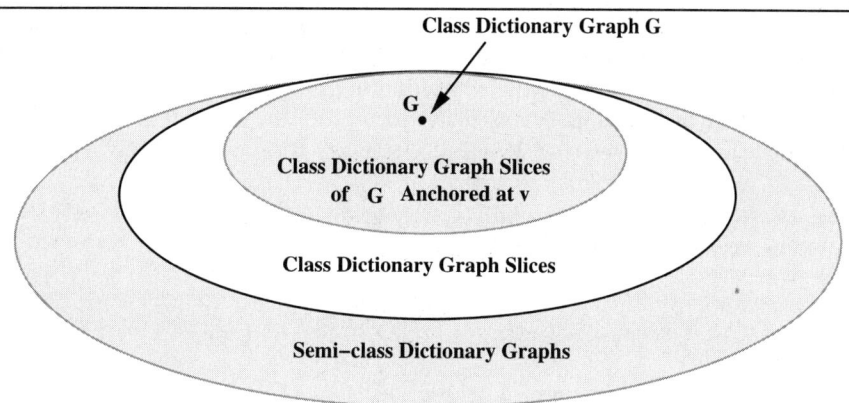

Figure 16.6: The relations between concepts

associated classes. The object graph definition is split into two parts: first we define the structure of object graphs without reference to a class dictionary graph slice and then we introduce the legality of an object-graph with respect to a class dictionary graph slice.

All the objects in this model are instantiated from construction vertices. For any vertex v in a class dictionary graph slice Φ, if we know the set S of all the construction vertices that are alternation-reachable from v, we will know all the possible classes of objects of vertex v. The set S is called the associated set of vertex v.

Definition 16.8 Let P be the class dictionary graph slice $(VC, VA, \Lambda; EC, EA, EI)$ anchored at some vertex. The **associated** set of a vertex $v \in VC \cup VA$ is

$$\mathcal{A}(v) = \{v' \mid v' \in VC \text{ and } v \stackrel{*}{\Longrightarrow} v'\}.$$

Next we introduce the *Parts* function. The construction edge $v \stackrel{l}{\longrightarrow} w$ describes a part-of relationship of vertex v with vertex w. The relation is called l. Such relationships can be inherited by inheritance descendants. It is convenient to have the pair (l, w), called a **part**, which means the relation with vertex w, called l. Therefore each vertex has the parts of its own or inherited from its inheritance ancestors.

Consider the class dictionary graph in Fig. 16.5. Vertex `Graduate` has two parts, (`name`, `String`) and (`takes`, `AtLeastOneCourse`). The two parts are inherited from vertex `Student`.

Definition 16.9 Let P be the class dictionary graph slice $(VC, VA, \Lambda; EC, EA, EI)$ anchored at some vertex. For any $v \in V$,[5]

$$Parts(v) = \{(l, w) \mid \exists v' : v \stackrel{*}{\dashrightarrow} v' \text{ and } v' \stackrel{l}{\longrightarrow} w \in EC\}.$$

---

[5]Class dictionary graph parts, page 433 (19).

The *PartClusters* function is a generalization of the *Parts* function. For an object of a given vertex, each immediate part-object corresponds to an object of a part class. The function *Parts* is not sufficient to define what kind of objects can be in each part. Therefore we replace w with $\mathcal{A}(w)$ in the previous definition to obtain the definition of part clusters. The result indicates the classes that may be instantiated for each part.

Definition 16.10 Let P be the class dictionary graph slice $(VC, VA, \Lambda; EC, EA, EI)$ anchored at some vertex. For any $v \in V$,[6]

$$PartClusters(v) = \{(l, \mathcal{A}(w)) \mid \exists v' : v \stackrel{*}{\dashrightarrow} v' \text{ and } v' \stackrel{l}{\longrightarrow} w \in EC\}.$$

Consider the class dictionary graph in Fig. 16.5.

$PartClusters(\texttt{AtLeastOneStudent}) = \{\ (\texttt{first}, \{\texttt{Graduate}\}),$
$\qquad\qquad\qquad\qquad\qquad\qquad\quad (\texttt{rest}, \{\texttt{Empty}\})\ \}.$

Figure 16.7 shows an object of vertex Graduate, usually called a Graduate-object. The graph is called an **object graph**. Each vertex in the object graph corresponds to an instantiation of a construction vertex. Each edge is an instance of a part-of relation. We use $\texttt{i1} \stackrel{name}{\longrightarrow} \texttt{i2}$ to represent the edge from vertex i1 to vertex i2 with label name. In the picture, i1 is the object identifier of the Graduate-object, and similarly for i2, i3, etc.

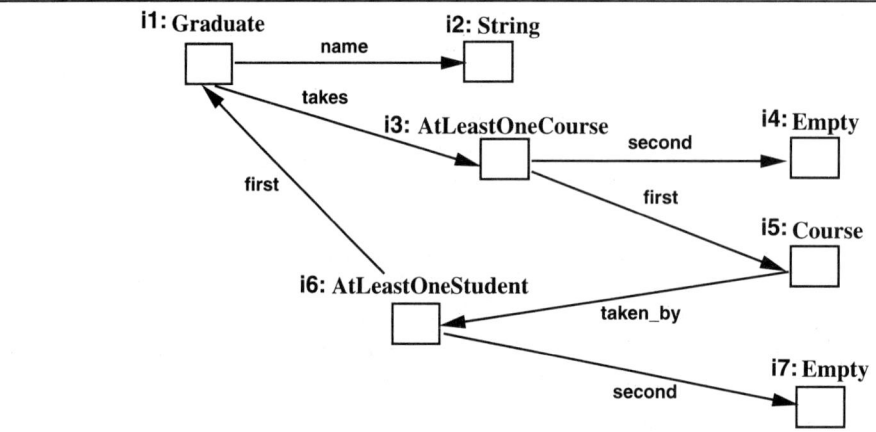

Figure 16.7: An object of vertex Graduate

An object graph defined below describes the structures of a group of objects mathematically. Each vertex in the object graph corresponds to an element in the group, called an instance/object of some vertex in a class dictionary graph slice.

---

[6]Part clusters, page 433 (20).

16.1. CLASS DICTIONARY GRAPHS

Definition 16.11 An **object graph**[7] is a graph $H = (W, S, \Lambda_H; E, \lambda)$ with vertex sets W, S satisfying the following properties:

1. The function $\lambda : W \to S$ maps each vertex of H to a vertex in S.

2. Λ_H is a set of edge labels.

3. E is a ternary relation on $W \times W \times \Lambda_H$.

All the elements in W are object identifiers. All the elements in S are the types of the vertices in the object graph.

In an object graph $H = (W, S, \Lambda_H; E, \lambda)$, a **path** P is a sequence of edges from E such that the end vertex of each edge in P is the start vertex of the next edge in P if there is one. The length of path P is the total number of edges in P.

If there is a path of length n from vertex v to vertex w, we can write $v \stackrel{n}{\mapsto} w$. For any vertex v, it is always true that $v \stackrel{0}{\mapsto} v$. We write $v \stackrel{*}{\mapsto} w$ when n can be zero; we write $v \stackrel{+}{\mapsto} w$ when n is larger than zero. We say that vertex w is **reachable** from vertex v when $v \stackrel{*}{\mapsto} w$.

In an object graph $H = (W, S, \Lambda_H; E, \lambda)$, if there exists a vertex w_0 in W such that every vertex in W is reachable from w_0, then we call object graph H an object graph **anchored** at w_0.

Not all object graphs with respect to a class dictionary graph slice are legal. Intuitively, the object structure has to be consistent with the class definitions and all the classes in S have to be construction classes.

Definition 16.12 An object graph $H = (W, S, \Lambda_H; E, \lambda)$ anchored at w_0 is a **legal**[8] v_0-object with respect to a class dictionary graph slice P anchored at v_0 where $P = (VC, VA, \Lambda; EC, EA)$, if H satisfies the following two rules.

Unique Label Axiom
$$\forall v, w, w' \in W \forall l \in \Lambda_H :$$

$$v \stackrel{l}{\longrightarrow} w, v \stackrel{l}{\longrightarrow} w' \in E \text{ implies } v \stackrel{l}{\longrightarrow} w = v \stackrel{l}{\longrightarrow} w' \text{ (i.e., } w = w').$$

Conformance Axiom

1. $S \subseteq VC \cup VA$ and
2. $v_0 \stackrel{*}{\Longrightarrow} \lambda(w_0)$,
3. $\forall \mu \in W \; \exists v \in S$ s.t. $\lambda(\mu) = v$ and
   (a) $\forall (\mu, \nu, l) \in E : \exists (l, A) \in PartClusters(v)$ s.t. $\lambda(\nu) \in A$
   (b) $\forall (l, A) \in PartClusters(v) : \exists \nu \in W$ s.t. $\lambda(\nu) \in A$ and $(\mu, \nu, l) \in E$.

---
[7] Object graph recognition, page 436 (24).
[8] Legal object graph, page 436 (27).

The Unique Label Axiom states that no two edges with the same label are outgoing from a vertex in an object graph. The Conformance Axiom enforces three properties. First, all the vertices in S have to be construction vertices in P. Therefore every vertex in W must be an instance of some construction vertex in P. Second, the anchor of the object graph must be an instance of a vertex in P which is alternation reachable from v_0. Third, if a vertex μ in W is an instance of a construction vertex v in P, then every part-object of the instance must conform to some part of vertex v, and every part of vertex v must have an instance as a part-object of instance μ. The third property is an application of the Unique Label Axiom. If this axiom is violated, we cannot identify the element (l, A) from $PartClusters(v)$, simply by the label l.

The object graph anchored at vertex i1 in Fig. 16.8 is not a legal Graduate-object of the class dictionary graph slice in Fig. 16.5, since vertex Graduate has two parts. But the object graph is a legal Graduate-object of the class dictionary graph slice in Fig. 16.4.

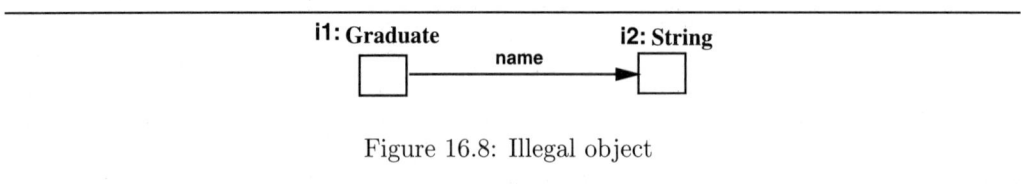

Figure 16.8: Illegal object

From now on, when we talk about object graphs we mean that they are legal object graphs, unless we explicitly mention illegality. Next we formally define all the object graphs of a class dictionary graph Φ. In database terminology, $Objects(\Phi)$ represents all instances of object base schema Φ. When we say C-object, where C is a construction vertex in the class dictionary graph, it means an instance of vertex C. For any alternation ancestor A of vertex C, we also say a C-object is an A-object.

We allow objects with several anchors. They are the union of objects with a single anchor.

We use a textual notation[9] for describing object graphs using an adjacency representation that also shows the mapping of object graph vertices to class dictionary graph vertices.

Definition 16.13 Let class dictionary graph Φ be $(VC, VA, \Lambda; EC, EA, EI)$.

- An η-*object graph* anchored at μ, where $\eta \in VC$, is an object graph anchored at μ with $\lambda(\mu) = \eta$.

- An η-*object graph*, where $\eta \in VA$, is a γ-object graph for some $\gamma \in VC$ s.t. $\eta \stackrel{*}{\Longrightarrow} \gamma$.

- $\forall \eta \in VC$, $Objects(\eta) = \{o | o \text{ is an } \eta\text{-object graph}\}$.

- $\forall \eta \in VA$, $Objects(\eta) = \bigcup_{u \in \mathcal{A}(\eta)} Objects(u)$.

- $Objects(\Phi) = \bigcup_{u \in VC} Objects(u)$.

16.1. CLASS DICTIONARY GRAPHS

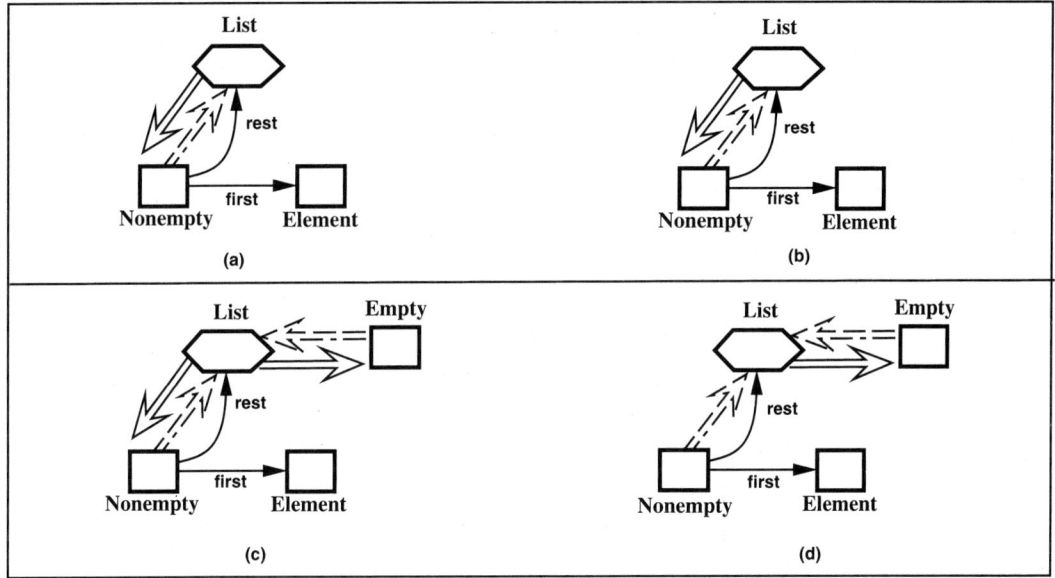

Figure 16.9: Illustration of class dictionary graph slices

16.1.5 Inductive Class Dictionary Graphs

Consider the class dictionary graph in Fig. 16.9a. When we construct a class dictionary graph slice anchored at vertex Nonempty, vertex Nonempty forces all the outgoing construction and inheritance edges. Vertex List must have the one outgoing alternation edge List$\Longrightarrow$ Nonempty, because it has an incoming construction edge. Figure 16.9b shows the only class dictionary graph slice anchored at vertex Nonempty.

Consider the class dictionary graph in Fig. 16.9c. Figure 16.9d shows one of the class dictionary graph slices anchored at vertex Nonempty. The difference from the preceding case is that we can select alternation edge List$\Longrightarrow$ Empty instead of taking alternation edge List$\Longrightarrow$ Nonempty.

In the class dictionary graph of Fig. 16.9a, a Nonempty-object must contain an Element-object and a List-object. A List-object is always a Nonempty-object — an infinite recursion. In Fig. 16.9b, this infinite recursion is expressed by the cycle formed by Nonempty$\xrightarrow{rest}$ List and List$\Longrightarrow$ Nonempty. This cycle is forced to be included.

In the class dictionary graph of Fig. 16.9c, a Nonempty-object must contain an Element-object and a List-object. But a List-object can be an Empty-object. In this case, we don't have an infinite recursion. We can have a Nonempty-object which is a list containing only one element, an Element-object. The Empty-object is used here for the end of the list.

Comparing the two class dictionary graphs in Fig. 16.9a and Fig. 16.9c, we can build only cyclic Nonempty-objects from the first class dictionary graph in Fig. 16.9a. We can

---

[9]Object graph textual representation, page 436 (26).

build acyclic `Nonempty`-objects of any size based on the `Nonempty`-objects of smaller size for the second class dictionary graph. We call the second class dictionary graph an **inductive** class dictionary graph. The first class dictionary graph is not inductive.

Definition 16.14 Inductiveness Axiom

A class dictionary graph is **inductive** if for all vertices v of the graph there exists at least one cycle-free class dictionary graph slice anchored at v.

If a class dictionary graph Φ is not inductive, we call each vertex v in Φ for which no cycle-free class dictionary graph slice is anchored at v, a **noninductive vertex**.

We conclude the discussion of the Inductiveness Axiom with the following comparison:

- If the Inductiveness Axiom is violated for a class dictionary graph Φ, then there is a vertex $v \in V_\Phi$ such that $Objects(v)$ contains only circular objects. A circular object is an object that contains cycles in its part-of relationships.

- If the Inductiveness Axiom is satisfied, then for all vertices $v \in V$, $Objects(v)$ contains inductively defined, noncircular objects as well as circular objects.

Law of Demeter for Classes

Minimize the number of noninductive vertices in a class dictionary graph.

We claim that when people minimize the number of noninductive vertices in a class dictionary graph, they minimize the difficulty of building objects and the associated software.

The Unique Label Axiom, Cycle-Free Alternation and Inheritance Axiom, and Inductiveness Axiom imply a mathematical theory; for example, the following theorem belongs to this theory.

Theorem 16.1 *There is no cyclic construction path in a class dictionary graph*

$$\Phi = (VC, VA, \Lambda; EC, EA, EI),$$

that is, for all $v \in VC \cup VA$ there is no construction path from v to v.

Proof: If there is a cyclic construction path then no vertex v on the path will have a cycle-free class dictionary graph slice since all construction edges leaving a vertex must be included in the class dictionary graph slice containing that vertex. Therefore, the Inductiveness Axiom is violated.

16.2 CLASS DICTIONARIES

So far we have considered class dictionary graphs as a mechanism of describing classes. But we also need a mechanism for describing objects in a succinct form. The object graph mechanism is not sufficient for this purpose. We extend class dictionary graphs to class dictionaries so that we can use them for describing objects succinctly at a high level of abstraction.

16.2. CLASS DICTIONARIES

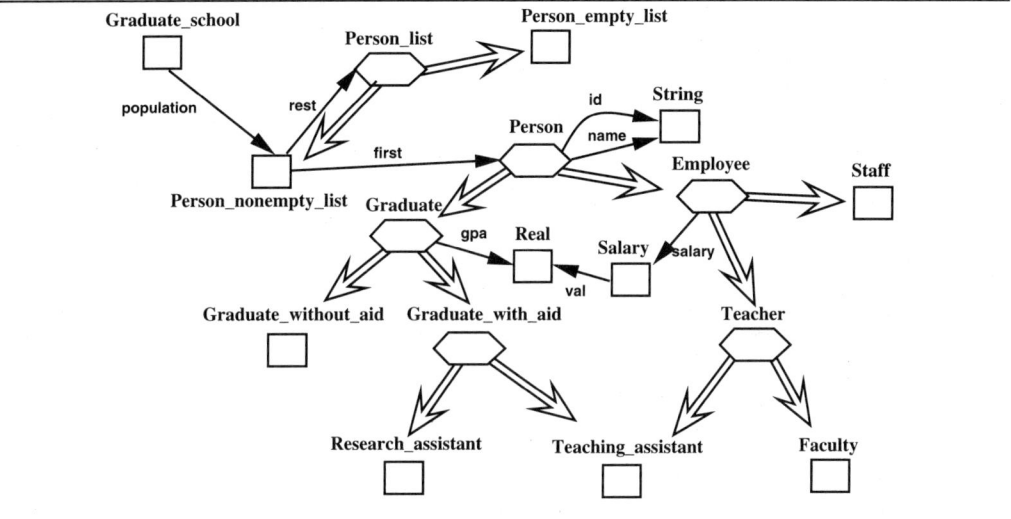

Figure 16.10: Class dictionary graph Graduate_school

16.2.1 Definitions

We use the textual adjacency list representation in Fig. 16.11 to describe the class structure in Fig. 16.10. It is called the **class dictionary notation**.

Each construction vertex is defined by a construction class definition that starts with the name of the source vertex followed by an equal sign. The equal sign is followed by a list of parts and syntax. The label of each part is enclosed between "<" and ">". The name after the label is the type of the part. The syntax is enclosed by double quotes.

Each alternation vertex is defined by an alternation class definition that starts with the name of the source vertex followed by a colon, which is in turn followed by a set of alternatives and a list of parts and syntax. The set and the list are separated by "*common*." The set comes first and its elements (vertices) are separated by "|."

Real and String are not shown on the left-hand sides of the class definitions, since they are predefined.

To define class dictionaries mathematically, we need four more components in addition to those of class dictionary graphs, namely VS, ES, Υ, and Σ.[10] VS is a set of **syntax vertices** used in a class dictionary, such as "Faculty" and "Staff" above. We use Faculty $\hookrightarrow$ "Faculty" to express that vertex "Faculty" has syntax "Faculty". We call the relationship a **syntax edge**. ES is the set of all syntax edges in a class dictionary. Υ is for ordering classes. Σ is for ordering the list of parts and syntax on the right-hand side of each class definition.

Definition 16.15 A **class dictionary** is a tuple $D = (\phi, VS; ES, \Upsilon, \Sigma, S)$ where ϕ is a class dictionary graph $(VC, VA, VT, \Lambda; EC, EA,)$. $V = VC \cup VA$ (disjoint union) is a finite

---
[10]Class dictionary recognition page 437 (30).

```
Graduate_school        = <population> Person_nonempty_list.
Person_nonempty_list   = <first> Person <rest> Person_list.
Person_list            : Person_nonempty_list | Person_empty_list.
Person_empty_list      = .
Person                 : Graduate |
                         Employee
                           *common* <id> String <name> String.
Graduate               : Graduate_without_aid |
                         Graduate_with_aid
                           *common* <gpa> Real.
Graduate_without_aid   = "Graduate_without_aid".
Graduate_with_aid      : Research_assistant | Teaching_assistant.
Research_assistant     = "Research_assistant".
Teaching_assistant     = "Teaching_assistant".
Employee               : Staff | Teacher *common* <salary> Salary.
Staff                  = "Staff".
Salary                 = <val> Real.
Teacher                : Teaching_assistant | Faculty.
Faculty                = "Faculty".
```

Figure 16.11: Class dictionary Graduate_school

nonempty set called the **class vertices**; VS is a finite set called the **syntax vertices**. ES is a binary relation on $V \times VS$, called **syntax edges**.

Function $\Upsilon : V \to \mathcal{N}$ maps each vertex in V to a unique natural number. Function $\Sigma : EC \cup ES \to \mathcal{N}$ maps each edge in $EC \cup ES$ to a unique natural number.

S is a vertex in $VC \cup VA$, called the **start vertex**.

The differences between class dictionary graphs and class dictionaries [Lie88] are as follows. A class dictionary has syntax for describing the syntax of the language. In a class dictionary, the ordering of classes and parts is relevant; that is, the order of the successors of a vertex along construction edges is relevant.

The order of class definitions and the order of syntax and parts are usually determined by the order in which they are written. In the preceding example, we have

$$\Upsilon(\texttt{Graduate\_school}) < \Upsilon(\texttt{Person\_nonempty\_list}) < ... < \Upsilon(\texttt{Faculty}),$$

and in the class definition of `Person_nonempty_list`

$$\Sigma(\texttt{Person\_nonempty\_list} \xrightarrow{first} \texttt{Person}) < \Sigma(\texttt{Person\_nonempty\_list} \xrightarrow{rest} \texttt{Person\_list}).$$

Before we discuss the legality of class dictionaries, we need to define the reachability concept.

Definition 16.16 Consider a class dictionary $D = (\phi, VS; ES, \Upsilon, \Sigma, S)$ with class dictionary graph $\phi = (VC, VA, VT, \Lambda; EC, EA)$. For any vertices v and w in $VC \cup VA$, w is **reachable** from v if

- v and w are the same vertex, or
- $v \Longrightarrow w \in EA$, or
- $\exists l \in \Lambda : v \xrightarrow{l} w \in EC$, or
- $\exists x \in VC \cup VA : x$ is reachable from v and w is reachable from x.

A class dictionary is a context-free grammar. To define a language properly, a class dictionary has to satisfy some additional properties with respect to a class dictionary graph.[11]

Definition 16.17 A class dictionary $D = (\phi, VS; ES, \Upsilon, \Sigma, S)$ is **legal** if

1. The class dictionary graph $\phi = (VC, VA, VT, EC, EA, \Lambda)$ is legal
2. For every vertex v in $VC \cup VA$, v is reachable from S
3. $\forall s \in VS \; \forall v \in VT : s \notin TerminalSet(v)$
4. $\forall v, w \in VT : TerminalSet(v) \cap TerminalSet(w) \neq \emptyset$ implies $v = w$

$TerminalSet(v)$ is the set of all the syntax terminals defined by terminal vertex v.

The set of all the syntax terminals in a class dictionary is the union of two sets of syntax terminals. The first set is defined by all the syntax vertices in the class dictionary; the second set is the union of all $TerminalSet(v)$ where v is ranging over all the terminal vertices in the class dictionary. The two sets should be disjoint.

---
[11] Legal class dictionary, page 437 (32).

16.2.2 Flat Class Dictionaries

To cope with parsing and printing of objects defined by a class dictionary, we have to transform a class dictionary into an equivalent one without common parts and syntax. This transformation is called **flattening** since the inheritance structure is flattened. The result is called a **flat class dictionary**. In a class dictionary, the order of class definitions as well as that of parts and syntax in a given class definition are relevant for the language.

We design an algorithm for the flattening transformation. Informally, when a construction vertex v inherits several parts and syntax from alternation ancestors, we append the inherited parts and syntax after the immediate parts and syntax of the construction vertex. If v inherits parts and syntax from several alternation ancestors, these parts and syntax are concatenated based on the order of the alternation ancestors.

Example 16.1 shows how the order of class definitions is relevant to the language defined by a class dictionary.

Example 16.1 Consider the class dictionary below (comments are prefixed with "//"):

```
MotorBoat    = "capacity"        // syntax vertex
               <c> Number.       // class vertex; part label is c
MotorPowered : MotorBoat *common* "horsepower" <hp> Number.
WaterVehicle : MotorBoat *common* "speed"      <speed> Number.
```

Its flat class dictionary is

```
MotorBoat    = "capacity"    <c> Number
               "horsepower"  <hp> Number
               "speed"       <speed> Number.
MotorPowered : MotorBoat.
WaterVehicle : MotorBoat.
```

If the class definitions is reordered as follows,

```
MotorBoat    = "capacity" <c> Number.
WaterVehicle : MotorBoat *common* "speed"      <speed> Number.
MotorPowered : MotorBoat *common* "horsepower" <hp> Number.
```

its flat class dictionary is

```
MotorBoat    = "capacity"    <c> Number
               "speed"       <speed> Number
               "horsepower"  <hp> Number.
MotorPowered : MotorBoat.
WaterVehicle : MotorBoat.
```

Whenever we consider the language of a class dictionary D, we first transform D into a flat class dictionary D', and then we consider the language of D'. Before formalizing the flattening transformation, we first define an ordering function Υ_D^v that orders all vertices in D from which vertex v is alternation-reachable.[12]

We may use any ordering function Υ_D^v that can be computed by a linear-time deterministic algorithm using only the following components of D: EA, V and Υ. One possible

---
[12]Class dictionary flattening, page 439 (33).

16.2. CLASS DICTIONARIES

algorithm is a Depth-First-Traversal algorithm. Starting from vertex v, the algorithm traverses the subgraph formed by a set S of all the vertices from which vertex v is alternation-reachable, assigning each vertex in S to a unique number along the way. When a vertex has several incoming alternation edges, the order in which immediate alternation ancestors are chosen to visit next is the increasing order determined by function Υ of D.

Consider the class structure in Fig. 16.12. The class structure contains all vertices from which vertex A is alternation-reachable in the class dictionary $D = (\phi, VS; ES, \Upsilon, \Sigma, S)$ where $\Upsilon(\text{A}) < \Upsilon(\text{D}) < \Upsilon(\text{C}) < \Upsilon(\text{B}) < \Upsilon(\text{E}) < \Upsilon(\text{F}) < \Upsilon(\text{G})$. We can have

$$\Upsilon_D^{\text{A}} = \{(\text{A}, 1), (\text{B}, 2), (\text{C}, 3), (\text{D}, 4), (\text{E}, 5), (\text{F}, 6), (\text{G}, 7)\}.$$

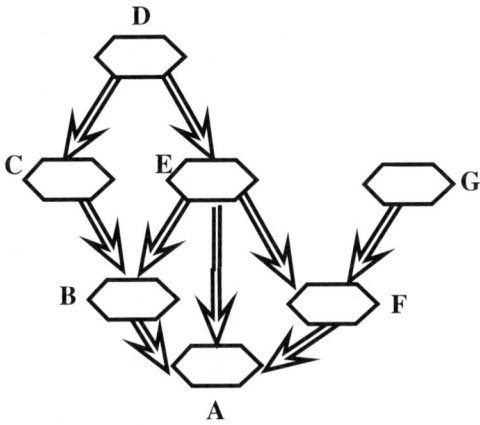

Figure 16.12: Order all vertices from which vertex A is alternation-reachable

- Please notice that the definition of function Υ_D^v is much simpler for single inheritance class dictionaries.

Next we use order function Υ_D^v to flatten a class dictionary $D = (\phi, VS; ES, \Upsilon, \Sigma, S)$. For a construction vertex v, function Υ_D^v together with function Σ determines the order of its outgoing construction edges and syntax edges in the flattened class dictionary.

Definition 16.18 Let D be class dictionary

$$(\phi, VS; ES, \Upsilon, \Sigma, S)$$

where $\phi = (VC, VA, VT, \Lambda; EC, EA)$. Its **flat** class dictionary is

$$D' = (\phi', VS; ES', \Upsilon, \Sigma', S)$$

where $\phi' = (VC, VA, VT, \Lambda; EC', EA)$ and

1. $\forall v \in VA \; \forall l \in \Lambda \; \forall w \in VC \cup VA \cup VS: v \xrightarrow{l} w \notin EC'$ and $v \hookrightarrow w \notin ES'$

    Alternation vertices do not have common parts and syntax.

2. Let n be the maximum number assigned by function Σ to the edges in $EC \cup ES$.
   For each construction edge $v \xrightarrow{l} w \in EC$ and for each construction vertex $x \in VC$ with $v \stackrel{*}{\Longrightarrow} x$, if $v = x$ we have

   $$x \xrightarrow{l} w \in EC' \text{ and } \Sigma'(x \xrightarrow{l} w) = \Sigma(v \xrightarrow{l} w),$$

   otherwise, we have

   $$x \xrightarrow{l} w \in EC' \text{ and } \Sigma'(x \xrightarrow{l} w) = \Upsilon_D^x(v) * n + \Sigma(v \xrightarrow{l} w)$$

   For each syntax edge $v \hookrightarrow w \in ES$ and for each construction vertex $x \in VC$ with $v \stackrel{*}{\Longrightarrow} x$, if $v = x$ we have

   $$x \hookrightarrow w \in ES' \text{ and } \Sigma'(x \hookrightarrow w) = \Sigma(v \hookrightarrow w),$$

   otherwise, we have

   $$x \hookrightarrow w \in ES' \text{ and } \Sigma'(x \hookrightarrow w) = \Upsilon_D^x(v) * n + \Sigma(v \hookrightarrow w)$$

An interesting remark is that the order of class definitions in a class dictionary affects the order of parts and terminals in its flat class dictionary (see Example 16.1). For single inheritance class dictionaries (i.e., class dictionaries where each vertex has at most one incoming alternation edge), the order of the class definitions does not affect the order of parts and terminals in the corresponding flat class dictionaries. Also it is obvious that D and D' define the same set of objects.

In the following discussion, we consider only flat class dictionaries. The flat class dictionary of the class dictionary in Fig. 16.11 is in Fig. 16.13.

16.2.3 Languages

There are two ways to associate a formal language with a class dictionary D. The first one, called the object approach, uses the set of objects of D, and the second more traditional approach in language theory, called the derivation approach, uses derivation trees. Here we study the object approach. We define a special set of objects called **tree-objects**. To each tree-object, we apply a printing function, called g_print, which assigns to each object its textual representation, called a **sentence**. The set of sentences we can generate by this mechanism is called the language defined by the class dictionary.

We consider sentences as declarative object definitions, and the object notations in object-oriented languages as imperative object definitions.

For talking about grammars and their languages we use the synonyms in Table 16.1.

We use special objects called **tree-objects** to define languages.

Definition 16.19 In a flat class dictionary $D = (\phi, VS; ES, \Upsilon, \Sigma, S)$ with class dictionary graph $\phi = (VC, VA, VT, \Lambda; EC, EA)$, for any vertex $\eta \in VC \cup VA$, an object graph t anchored at r is an η-**tree-object** if

- the object graph t has a tree structure,

16.2. CLASS DICTIONARIES

```
Graduate_school        = <population> Person_nonempty_list.
Person_nonempty_list   = <first> Person <rest> Person_list.
Person_list            : Person_nonempty_list | Person_empty_list.
Person_empty_list      = .
Person                 : Graduate | Employee .
Graduate               : Graduate_without_aid | Graduate_with_aid .
Graduate_without_aid   = "Graduate_without_aid"
                         <id> String <name> String  <gpa> Real.
Graduate_with_aid      : Research_assistant | Teaching_assistant.
Research_assistant     = "Research_assistant"
                         <id> String <name> String <gpa> Real.
Teaching_assistant     = "Teaching_assistant"
                         <id> String <name> String
                         <gpa> Real <salary> Salary.
Employee               : Staff | Teacher.
Staff                  = "Staff" <id> String <name> String
                         <salary> Salary.
Salary                 = <val> Real.
Teacher                : Teaching_assistant | Faculty.
Faculty                = "Faculty" <id> String <name> String
                         <salary> Salary.
```

Figure 16.13: Flat class dictionary Graduate_school

Class dictionary		*Grammar*	
vertex	class vertex	symbol(s)	nonterminal symbol
	terminal vertex		set of terminal symbols
	syntax vertex		terminal symbol

Table 16.1: The grammar interpretation of a flat class dictionary

- children in the tree are ordered,
- $\eta \stackrel{*}{\Longrightarrow} \lambda(r)$.

The anchor of the tree-object t is also called the **root**, written as $root(t)$.

The set of tree-objects of D **TreeObjects**$(D) = \{t \mid t \text{ is an } \eta\text{-tree-object for some } \eta \in VC\}$.

Tree-objects are drawn with the root at the top. For any inner vertex μ of a tree-object, its part-objects/children are drawn from left to right. The first child of μ is at the leftmost position. Figure 16.14 contains a tree-object with respect to the flat class dictionary in Fig. 16.13. Figure 16.15 shows a printing function called **g_print**.[13] *g_print* traverses its

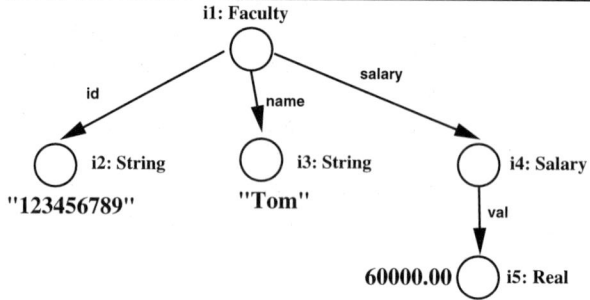

Figure 16.14: Faculty-tree object

argument tree-object ω in pre-order, and prints out the values of syntax terminals along the way by referring to the class definitions in the class dictionary D.

For example, the sentence with respect to the Faculty-object in Fig. 16.14 is

    Faculty 123456789 Tom 60000.00

We use *g_print* to define the language of a class dictionary.

Definition 16.20 For a vertex $u \in VC \cup VA$ in a class dictionary D with class dictionary graph $\phi = (VC, VA, VT, \Lambda; EC, EA)$, a u-**sentence** is the result of $g\_print(D, t)$, for some u-tree-object t.

Definition 16.21 For a vertex $u \in VC \cup VA$ in a class dictionary D with class dictionary graph $\phi = (VC, VA, VT, \Lambda; EC, EA)$,

$$\mathbf{L}(u) = \{s \mid s \text{ is a } u\text{-sentence}\}.$$

Definition 16.22 In a class dictionary D with class dictionary graph

$$\phi = (VC, VA, VT, \Lambda; EC, EA)$$

$$\mathbf{L}(D) = \{s \mid s \text{ is a } u\text{-sentence for some } u \in VC \cup VA\}.$$

---
[13]Printing, page 439 (34).

The g_print algorithm

Input   : Flat class dictionary D and D-object graph $\omega \in TreeObjects(D)$.
Output   : The sentence that describes the object graph ω.
Assumption   : When $NextPartorSyntax(\omega)$ is first called for ω,
                 it will return the reference of the first part or syntax vertex of ω.

g_print(D, ω)
1   **for** each construction and syntax edge e of $\lambda(\omega)$ ordered by Σ **do**
2   **if** $e \in ES$ and $e = v \hookrightarrow w$
3   **then** $print\_syntax(w)$
                (* print out the syntax represented by syntax vertex w. *)
4   **else** let e be $e = v \xrightarrow{l} w$
5   **if** $w \in VT$ (* w is a terminal vertex. *)
6   **then** $print\_terminal(NextPartorSyntax(\omega))$
                (* print out the value of the terminal. *)
7   **else** $g\_print(D, NextPartorSyntax(\omega))$

Figure 16.15: *g_print*

16.3 LL(1) RULES

A class dictionary D allows us to describe tree-objects in succinct form by writing a sentence in $L(D)$. For generality, it is important that sentences allow us to describe all legal tree-objects so that each tree-object has exactly one description as a sentence. The LL(1) conditions described below play an important role in the mapping process between tree-objects and sentences. We derive the LL(1) conditions for class dictionaries from the requirement that the *g_print* function must be one-to-one. We find the LL(1) parsing technology optimal for quickly changing languages.

The LL(1) conditions [ASU86] play an important role in the mapping process between derivation trees and sentences. Tree-objects are different from derivation trees, since they do not contain alternation vertices met during the parsing process; derivation trees contain all the nonterminals met during the derivation. We also extend the LL(1) rules to multiple inheritance. Therefore our LL(1) rules are not the same as the well-known LL(1) conditions [ASU86].

First, we give the definition of **first set** which is just a generalization of the one in [ASU86]. It is needed for our first LL(1) rule.[14]

Definition 16.23 In a flat class dictionary D with class dictionary graph

$$\phi = (VC, VA, VT, \Lambda; EC, EA)$$

---

[14]First sets, page 439 (37).

for any vertex $u \in VC \cup VA$ the **first set** of u, $first(u)$, is a set of syntax terminals that contains

- $empty^{15}$, if $\mathbf{L}(u)$ contains the empty sentence.
- All the syntax vertices or terminal vertices whose syntax terminal(s) may appear as the first element in an element of $\mathbf{L}(u)$.

First sets are computed based on Theorem 1.

Theorem 16.2 *In a flat class dictionary*

$$D = (\phi, VS; ES, \Upsilon, \Sigma, S) \text{ where } \phi = (VC, VA, VT, \Lambda; EC, EA)$$

*for any vertex $u \in VC \cup VA \cup VS$ the **first set** of u, $first(u)$, may be computed according to the following rules:*

1. *if $u \in VS$, then $first(u) = \{u\}$*

2. *if $u \in VT$, then $first(u) = \{u\}$*

3. *if $u \in VA$, then $\forall v$ s.t. $u \Longrightarrow v \in EA$, the following holds:*

   $$if\ e \in first(v),\ then\ e \in first(u)$$

4. *if $u \in VC$ and $e_1, ..., e_n$ are all the ordered construction and syntax edges outgoing from u,*

   (a) *if $n = 0$, then $empty \in first(u)$*

   (b) *otherwise $\forall e_i (1 \leq i \leq n)$ s.t. $i=1$ or first sets of all elements before e_i contain empty:*

       i. *if $e_i \in ES$ and $e_i = v_i \hookrightarrow w_i$, then $w_i \in first(u)$*

       ii. *if $e_i \in EC$ and $e_i = v_i \xrightarrow{l_i} w_i$, then one of the following holds:*
         A. $\forall s \in first(w_i) - \{empty\},\ s \in first(u)$
         B. $\forall s \in first(w_i),\ s \in first(u)\ if\ i = n$

Example 16.2 We illustrate the first sets of all the vertices in the following class dictionary.

```
Course              = <or> OptionalOrRequired
                      <dn> DayOrNight
                      ":" <name> String.
OptionalOrRequired : Optional | Required.
DayOrNight         : Day | Night.
Optional           = "optional".
Required           = .
Day                = "day".
Night              = .
```

---
[15] *empty* is called ϵ in [ASU86].

16.3. LL(1) RULES

$first(\text{Course}) = \{":", "day", "optional"\}$
$first(\text{OptionalOrRequired}) = \{empty, "optional"\}$
$first(\text{DayOrNight}) = \{empty, "day"\}$
$first(\text{Optional}) = \{"optional"\}$
$first(\text{Required}) = \{empty\}$
$first(\text{Day}) = \{"day"\}$
$first(\text{Night}) = \{empty\}$
$first(\text{String}) = \{\text{String}\}$

The LL(1) conditions are specified by two rules.[16]

Rule 1 *For each alternation class definition in a flat class dictionary*

$$D = (\phi, VS; ES, \Upsilon, \Sigma, S)$$

with $\phi = (VC, VA, VT, \Lambda; EC, EA)$, *say in textual form*

$$A : A_1 \mid ... \mid A_n.$$

and any two construction vertices C, C' *where* $A_i \overset{*}{\Longrightarrow} C$ *and* $A_j \overset{*}{\Longrightarrow} C'$ *and* $1 \le i, j \le n$, *if* $first(C) \cap first(C') \ne \emptyset$ *then* $C = C'$.

For example, the following class dictionary violates Rule 1.

```
AorB : A | B.
A    = "a".
B    = "a".
```

An A-object is an AorB-object. A B-object is also an AorB-object. But g_print maps both an A-object and a B-object to the sentence "a". Therefore g_print is not a bijection between $TreeObjects(\text{AorB})$ and $Sentences(\text{AorB})$.

In ordinary language theory, Rule 1 is simpler and only requires that $first(A_i) \cap first(A_j) = \emptyset$. The example in Fig. 16.10 motivates the generalization which is necessary due to multiple inheritance. Consider the example in Fig. 16.10, where $first(\text{Graduate})$ and $first(\text{Employee})$ are not disjoint, but the class dictionary in Fig. 16.10 still satisfies Rule 1.

The **follow set** concept, as the first set concept, is used to check our second LL(1) rule. It is a variant of the follow set concept in [ASU86]. Informally, $follow(u)$ is defined as the set of all terminals that may immediately follow a u-sentence in a sentence of $L(S)$.[17]

Definition 16.24 In a flat class dictionary

$$D = (\phi, VS; ES, \Upsilon, \Sigma, S) \text{ where } \phi = (VC, VA, VT, \Lambda; EC, EA)$$

for any vertex $u \in VC \cup VA$ the **follow set** of u, $follow(u)$, is the smallest set satisfying the following rules:

---

[16] LL(1) conditions, page 442 (42).
[17] Follow sets, page 441 (41).

1. If $u = S$, then $eof \in follow(u)$

2. $\forall v \Longrightarrow u \in EA$, the following holds:
$$\forall s \in follow(v), s \in follow(u)$$

3. $\forall w \in VC$ s.t. $e_1, ..., e_n$ are all the construction and syntax edges ordered by Σ, find i s.t. $e_i = w \xrightarrow{l} u$ and $1 \leq i \leq n$.

   (a) if i = n, then
   $$\forall s \in follow(w) : s \in follow(u)$$

   (b) otherwise

   i. if $e_{i+1} \in ES$ and $e_{i+1} = w \hookrightarrow y$, then $y \in follow(u)$

   ii. if $e_{i+1} \in EC$ and $e_{i+1} = w \xrightarrow{l} x$, then one of the following holds:

      A. if $empty \notin first(x)$, then $\forall s \in first(x) : s \in follow(u)$

      B. if $empty \in first(x)$, then $\forall s \in first(x) - \{empty\} : s \in follow(u)$ and $\forall s \in follow(x) : s \in follow(u)$

Example 16.3 The follow sets of the following class dictionary are shown below. Ident is a terminal vertex.

```
Tree    = <root> Ident <key> Number <left> TreeOpt "|" <right> TreeOpt.
TreeOpt : Tree | Empty.
Empty   = .
```

$follow(\text{Tree}) = \{eof,\ "|"\}$
$follow(\text{TreeOpt}) = \{eof,\ "|"\}$
$follow(\text{Empty}) = \{eof,\ "|"\}$
$follow(\text{Ident}) = \{\text{Number}\}$
$follow(\text{Number}) = \{"|",\ \text{Ident}\}$

Rule 2 For all alternation class definitions in a flat class dictionary
$$D = (\phi, VS; ES, \Upsilon, \Sigma, S)$$
with $\phi = (VC, VA, VT, \Lambda; EC, EA)$, say in textual form
$$A\ :\ A_1\ |\ ...\ |\ A_n.$$
if an alternative, say A_1, contains empty in its first set $first(A_1)$, then
$$first(A_i) \cap follow(A) = \emptyset$$
where $2 \leq i \leq n$.

For example, the following class dictionary violates Rule 2.

16.4. IMPLICATIONS OF LL(1) RULES

```
AorB_CorD  = <aorb> AorB <cord> CorD.
AorB       : A   | B.
CorD       : C   | D.
A          = "a".
B          = .
C          = "a".
D          = .
```

g_print is not a bijection between $TreeObjects$(AorB_CorD) and $Sentences$(AorB_CorD), because *g_print* maps the two different AorB_CorD-objects in Fig. 16.16a and Fig. 16.16b to the sentence "a". We prove soon that the LL(1) conditions imply that *g_print* is a bijection between tree-objects and sentences of a specific class.

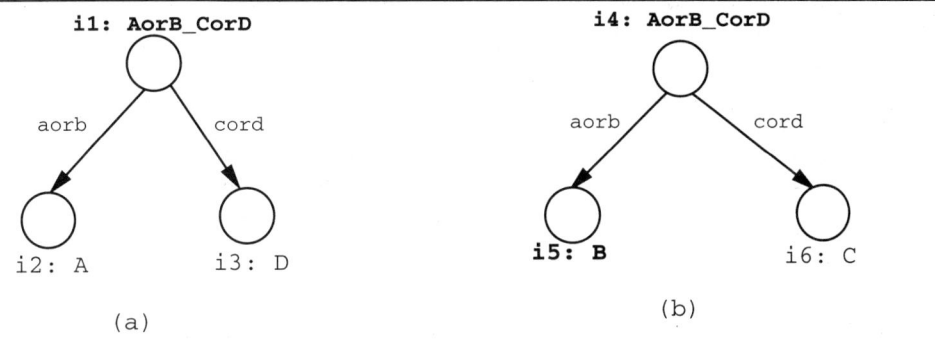

Figure 16.16: Two $AorB\_CorD$-objects

16.4 IMPLICATIONS OF LL(1) RULES

We discuss the role of the LL(1) rules played in printing and parsing of objects.

16.4.1 Printing

Next, we want to prove that if a class dictionary D satisfies the LL(1) rules and has the start symbol S, then *g_print* is a bijection between $TreeObjects(S)$ and $L(S)$. To make our discussion precise, we define the equality of sentences and tree-objects.

Definition 16.25 Two sentences s_1, s_2 are equal ($s_1 = s_2$), if they are the same sequence of syntax terminals.

Definition 16.26 For a flat class dictionary D with class dictionary graph

$$\phi = (VC, VA, VT, \Lambda; EC, EA)$$

tree-object t_1 anchored at r_1 and t_2 anchored at r_2 are equal ($t_1 = t_2$) if

1. $\lambda(r_1) = \lambda(r_2)$, and if $\lambda(r_1), \lambda(r_2) \in VT$ then $print\_terminal(r_1) = print\_terminal(r_2)$, or

2. r_1 and r_2 have the following properties:

    (a) r_1, r_2 have the same number of children.

    (b) if r_1, r_2 have n children($n \geq 1$) each, the tree-object rooted at the ith child in r_1 is equal to the tree-object rooted at the ith child in r_2, where $1 \leq i \leq n$.

Theorem 16.3 (One-to-One Property of g_print)
Consider a flat class dictionary $D = (\phi, VS; ES, \Upsilon, \Sigma, S)$ that satisfies the LL(1) rules where $\phi = (VC, VA, \Lambda; EC, EA)$. For any two T-tree-objects t_1 and t_2 where $T \in VC \cup VA$, $t_1 = t_2$ if $g\_print(D, t_1) = g\_print(D, t_2)$.

Proof. We proceed by induction on the maximum depth of tree-objects t_1 and t_2.

- Base case

  When the maximum depth of t_1 and t_2 is zero, we immediately have $t_1 = t_2$, since

  - If $T \in VA$ and $\lambda(root(t_1)) \neq \lambda(root(t_2))$, Rule 1 is violated.
  - If $T \in VC$, we can only have $\lambda(root(t_1)) = \lambda(root(t_2)) = T$.

- Induction step

  Assume that for any two T'-tree-objects t_1' and t_2' where $T' \in VC \cup VAS$ and $Depth(t_1'), Depth(t_2') \leq K$, they are equal if $g\_print(D, t_1') = g\_print(D, t_2')$.

  Consider any two T-tree-objects t_1 and t_2 that have the following properties:

  - $max(Depth(t_1), Depth(t_2)) \leq K + 1$,
  - $root(t_1)$ has n children ($n \geq 1$) which are the roots of objects $s_1, ..., s_i, ..., s_n$,
  - $root(t_2)$ has n children ($n \geq 1$) which are the roots of objects $s_1', ..., s_i', ..., s_n'$,
  - $g\_print(D, t_1) = g\_print(D, t_2)$.

  We know that $\lambda(root(t_1)) = \lambda(root(t_2))$ for the same reasons as those in the base step.

  Suppose that there exists j where $1 \leq j \leq n$ such that $g\_print(D, s_j) \neq g\_print(D, s_j')$ and $g\_print(D, s_k) = g\_print(D, s_k')$ for all $k < j$. Then one of the outputs of $g\_print(D, s_j)$ and $g\_print(D, s_j')$ must be *empty*. Otherwise the sentences for t_1 and t_2 cannot be the same. Suppose that $g\_print(D, s_j') = empty$, $g\_print(D, s_j) \neq empty$ and that the first syntax terminal of $g\_print(D, s_j)$ is s.

  In the class definition of $\lambda(root(t_1))$, let β be the jth part vertex that corresponds to s_j and s_j'. So, s_j and s_j' are β-tree-objects. From the preceding assumption, we have

  $$s \in first(\beta) \cap follow(\beta).$$

  Next we prove that the result is a contradiction since it leads to a violation of Rule 2. We consider the following two cases.

1. When $\lambda(root(s'_j)) \neq \lambda(root(s_j))$, β must be an alternation vertex, and there must be an alternation vertex A that is alternation-reachable from β, and A has two different alternatives, say A_1 and A_2, so that $\lambda(root(s_j)) \in A_1$, $\lambda(root(s_j)) \notin A_2$, $\lambda(root(s'_j)) \notin A_1$ and $\lambda(root(s'_j)) \in A_2$. Therefore, we have

$$s \in first(A_1) \cap follow(A) \text{ and } empty \in first(A_2).$$

Therefore, Rule 2 is violated.

2. Otherwise, we have $\lambda(root(s'_j)) = \lambda(root(s_j)) = \theta$ and $\theta \in VC$.
Since $g\_print(D, s'_j) = empty$ and $g\_print(D, s_j) \neq empty$, $root(s_j)$ and $root(s'_j)$ must have at least one child, and the right hand side of the class definition of θ contains *no syntax vertex*.
We also know that $s \in first(\theta) \cap follow(\theta)$, and $empty \in first(\theta)$.
Again $root(s'_j)$ and $root(s_j)$ have the same number of children, say m. Select the first subtree ss_l ($1 \leq l \leq m$) of s_j such that $g\_print(D, ss_l) \neq empty$ and $g\_print(D, ss'_l) = empty$ where ss'_l is the lth child of c'_j. Let the lth part vertex of θ be δ. We know that $s \in first(\delta)$, $empty \in first(\delta)$, and $s \in follow(\delta)$.
If $\lambda(root(ss_l)) \neq \lambda(root(ss'_l))$, then we have a violation of Rule 2 as reasoned above. Otherwise, we repeat such a process. Since the depth of each tree-object is finite, eventually we will meet a violation of Rule 2.

In other words, $g\_print(D, s_i) = g\_print(D, s'_i)$ for all $1 \leq i \leq n$. By the induction hypothesis, for all $1 \leq i \leq n$, we have $s_i = s'_i$. Therefore, $t_1 = t_2$.

$\square$

For any vertex T in $VC \cup VA$, by the definition of $L(T)$, g_print is a total functional from $TreeObjects(T)$ to $L(T)$ and satisfies the **onto property**. Therefore g_print is a bijection between $TreeObjects(T)$ and $L(T)$, if D satisfies the two LL(1) rules.

16.4.2 Parsing

Before presenting a simple table-driven parsing algorithm g_parse in Fig. 16.18 that allows us to map a sentence to a tree-object, we introduce the inductiveness concept for class dictionaries. A class dictionary is inductive if it does not contain useless class definitions. The useless terminology is borrowed from [HU79].

Definition 16.27 A class dictionary $D = (\phi, VS; ES, \Upsilon, \Sigma, S)$ with class dictionary graph $\phi = (VC, VA, VT, \Lambda; EC, EA)$ is **inductive**, if for all $v \in VC$ at least one v-tree-object exists.

Inductiveness plays a role in the parsing process, in the sense that inductiveness eliminates useless symbols. These useless symbols can never be used during parsing.

Example 16.4 The following class dictionary satisfies the LL(1) rules, but is not inductive. C and D can never be used in parsing, otherwise the input would be infinitely long.

```
C = "c" <d> D.
D : C.
```

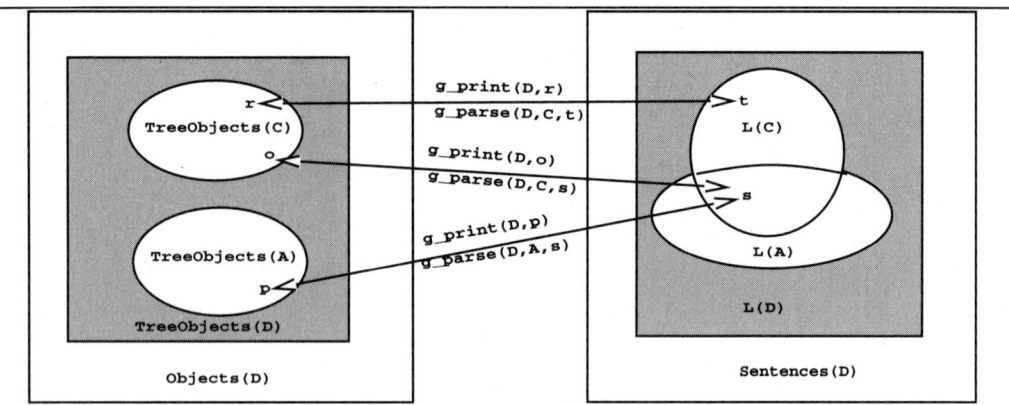

Figure 16.17: $g\_print(D)$ and $g\_parse(D)$ with D satisfying the LL(1) rules

Given an inductive class dictionary D with start symbol S and satisfying the LL(1) rules and an S-sentence s obtained by applying g_print to an S-tree-object t, by construction, $g\_parse(D, S)$ will create the S-tree-object t on reading s. In other words, if g_print is a bijection between $TreeObjects(S)$ and $L(S)$, g_parse is also a bijection between $TreeObjects(S)$ and $L(S)$. Therefore, g_parse is the inverse function of g_print by construction.[18] Software developers can have the parser quickly create objects by feeding sentences. In this way, they can debug their class dictionaries and programs. Remember that in our approach to programming we design a domain language for each program we write. Fig. 16.17 shows the relation between tree-objects and sentences when class dictionary D satisfies the LL(1) rules.

We have to guarantee that g_parse always halts on any input.

Theorem 16.4 (Halting Property of g_parse)
For a flat inductive class dictionary

$$D = (\phi, VS; ES, \Upsilon, \Sigma, S)$$

with $\phi = (VC, VA, VT, \Lambda; EC, EA)$ satisfying Rule 1, on any given finite string s,

$$g\_parse(D, s)$$

either reports an error or creates a unique finite S-tree-object t with $g\_parse(D, s) = t$ and $g\_print(D, t) = s$.

Proof. We know that VC, VA, VT, VS, EC, EA, and ES are finite sets. If $g\_parse(D, s)$ does not halt on reading the string s, $g\_parse(D, s)$ must repeatedly meet a sequence of

---
[18]Parsing, page 441 (38).

16.4. IMPLICATIONS OF LL(1) RULES

The g_parse algorithm
Input   : Flat class dictionary $D = (\phi, VS; ES, \Upsilon, \Sigma, S)$ with
              $\phi = (VC, VA, VT, \Lambda; EC, EA)$ and a string s.
Output   : S-object graph corresponding to s or error message.
Assumption : t is a global variable.
g_parse(D, s) (* parse sentence s as a S-object of D *)
1.1 $t = get\_token(s)$ (* removes t from s *)
1.2 $\omega = parse(D, S, s)$
1.3   **if** t is eof **then** return ω
1.4   **else** ReportError

parse(D, C, s)
2.1   **if** C is a terminal vertex (i.e., $C \in VT$)
2.2   **then if** $t \in TerminalSet(C)$
2.3   **then** $\omega = MakeTerminal(C, t); t = get\_token()$
2.4   **else** ReportError
2.5   **else if** $t \in first(C)$
2.6   **then** choose d in $\mathcal{A}(C)$ such that $t \in first(d)$
2.7   **else if** $empty \in first(C)$
2.8   **then** choose d in $\mathcal{A}(C)$ such that $empty \in first(d)$
2.9   **else** ReportError
2.10   build an empty d-object ω
               (* all parts are missing and will be set by the following statements *)
2.11   **for** each outgoing construction and syntax edge e from vertex d **do**
2.12   **if** e is a syntax edge (i.e., $e = v \hookrightarrow w$ and $e \in ES$)
2.13   **then if** $w \neq t$ **then** ReportError **else** $t = get\_token()$
2.14   **else** let e be $v \xrightarrow{l} w$
2.15   set the part of ω called l to the result of $parse(D, w, s)$
2.16   return ω

Figure 16.18: *g_parse*

---

vertices, say $A_1, ..., A_i, ..., A_n$, in a circular way without consuming any terminals in s. Therefore, $empty$ is in the first sets of all of them; that is,

$$empty \in first(A_1) \cap ... \cap first(A_i) \cap ... \cap first(A_n).$$

Otherwise g_parse will report an error on line 2.9. According to the existence of the cycle,

$$first(A_1) = ... = first(A_i) = ... = first(A_n).$$

Since D is inductive, the cycle must contain both construction and alternation vertices.

Further, by the first set definition, there must be a construction vertex v in $\mathcal{A}(A_k)$ for some alternation vertex on the cycle, where $1 \leq k \leq n$ such that v is not on the cycle and $empty \in first(v)$.

Since D is inductive and flat, there must be a construction vertex w on the cycle such that the alternation path from A_k to w is on the cycle.

We obtain that $v \neq w$ but $empty \in first(v) \cap first(w)$; that is, Rule 1 is violated.

Therefore the assumption at the beginning is not true. So $g\_parse(D, s)$ either reports an error or creates a unique finite S-tree-object.

Since g_parse is an inverse function of g_print, we have

$$g\_parse(D, s) = t \text{ and } g\_print(D, t) = s \text{ or}$$

$$g\_print(D, g\_parse(D, s)) = s$$

□

We will not discuss left-recursion [ASU86] in our case, because the LL(1) rules together with inductiveness eliminate left-recursion. For illustration, see Examples 16.5, 16.6, and 16.7.

Example 16.5 The following class dictionary contains left-recursion, and violates Rule 1, because $first(\mathsf{C}) = first(\mathsf{D}) = \{empty\}$.

```
A = <b> B.
B : C | D.
C = <a> A.
D = .
```

Example 16.6 The inductive class dictionary below contains left-recursion, and violates Rule 2, because $"e" \in follow(\mathsf{B})$, $empty \in first(\mathsf{D})$, and $"e" \in first(\mathsf{C})$.

```
A = <b> B <e> E.
B : C | D.
C = <a> A.
D = .
E = "e".
```

Example 16.7 The following class dictionary contains left-recursion and satisfies the LL(1) rules, but it is not inductive.

```
A = <b> B <e> E.
B : C .
C = <a> A.
E = "e".
```

16.4.3 LL(1) Rules and Ambiguous Context-Free Grammars

So far we have shown that if a class dictionary D satisfies the LL(1) rules, then g_print is a bijection between sentences and tree-objects of a vertex in D. We also know that if the LL(1) rules are violated then g_print might not be a bijection. An example is:

```
A : B | C.
B = "b".
C = "b".
```

But sometimes if the LL(1) rules are violated, we still have a bijection:

```
A : B | C.
B = "b" "x".
C = "b" "y".
```

Here g_print is a bijection. If for a class dictionary D the function g_print is not a bijection, we say that the class dictionary is ambiguous.

It would be useful to write a tool that tests whether a class dictionary is ambiguous. However the problem is undecidable by a reduction to Post's correspondence problem (see page 200 of [HU79]). Here, we see the role of LL(1) rules: ambiguity is too general, but the LL(1) conditions can be checked efficiently and they imply nonambiguity.

Of course, the LR(1) conditions (and others) also can be checked efficiently and they imply nonambiguity and we can efficiently parse the corresponding languages (see [HU79]). So why do we use the LL(1) conditions? The reason is psychological: they define languages that are easier to read and learn.

Based on the discussion above, Fig. 11.7, page 372 illustrates the inclusion relationships between sets of class dictionaries defined in terms of the four properties: nonambiguous, LL(1), nonleft-recursive, and inductive.

16.5 DEMETER DATA MODEL SUMMARY

Table 16.2 gives a summary of the six increasingly more specific axiomatic structures used in our method.

16.6 SELF APPLICATION

We suggest and demonstrate an alternative way to define mathematical objects other than using sets with relations and axioms (see Table 16.3). Instead we use a class dictionary to define a set of legal objects, and we use semantic rules to constrain those objects.

The advantages of the alternative approach are:

- We can easily introduce a convenient syntax for describing set elements and relations. A richer vocabulary is available.

- From the class dictionary we can generate an application-specific class library to speed up the implementation of algorithms operating on the objects.

- The class dictionary notation allows us to use propagation patterns easily to express the semantic rules.

Demeter Data Model Summary

Structure	Applications
semi-class dictionary graphs and **propagation schemas**	**programming with propagation patterns [LXSL91].** Propagation pattern specifications define semi-class dictionary graphs called propagation graphs. The propagation graphs are mapped into programs.
class dictionary graph slices	**growth plans [LH89b], inductiveness axiom, and object graphs.** A growth plan is a sequence of class dictionary graph slices. Inductiveness is defined in terms of existence of cycle-free class dictionary graph slices.
class dictionary graphs	**classes in some object-oriented programming language.** Alternation vertices correspond to abstract classes. Construction vertices correspond to concrete classes. Alternation edges correspond to inheritance relations. Construction edges correspond to part-of relations.
inductive class dictionary graphs	**inductive object graphs.** Objects are defined inductively.
class dictionaries	**application-specific object language.** A class dictionary defines both a class dictionary graph and a language.
LL(1) class dictionaries	**object construction from sentences.** An LL(1) class dictionary is not ambiguous; that is, the printing function is one-to-one.

Table 16.2: Demeter data model summary

Traditional	*Alternative*
sets(relations)	class dictionary
axioms	semantic rules

Table 16.3: The comparison

16.6. SELF APPLICATION

To demonstrate the usefulness of the class dictionary approach, we apply it now to define itself.

16.6.1 Self-Describing Class Dictionary Graphs

The following class dictionary, called DH-G, describes class dictionaries, and is also self-describing:[19] [20]

```
Cd_graph            = < adjacencies > Adjacency_List .
Adjacency           = < vertex > Vertex
                      < ns > Neighbors_wc "." .
Neighbors_wc        : Construct_ns | Alternat_ns
                        *common* < construct_ns > Any_vertex_List.
Construct_ns        = "=".
Alternat_ns         = ":"
                      < alternat_successors > Vertex_Bar_list "*common*".
Any_vertex          : Labeled_vertex | Syntax_vertex *common*.
Vertex              = < vertex_name > Ident .
Label               = "<" < label_name > Ident ">" .

Syntax_vertex       = < string > String .
Labeled_vertex      = < label > Label < vertex > Vertex .

Adjacency_List      : Empty_List | Adjacency_NList *common*.
Adjacency_NList     = <first> Adjacency <rest> Adjacency_List.
Any_vertex_List     : Empty_List | Any_vertex_NList *common*.
Any_vertex_NList    = <first> Any_vertex <rest> Any_vertex_List.
Vertex_Bar_list     = <first> Vertex <rest> Tvertex_Bar_list.
Tvertex_Bar_list    : Empty_List | Tvertex_Bar_NList *common*.
Tvertex_Bar_Nlist   = "|" <first> Vertex <rest> Tvertex_Bar_list.
Empty_List          = .
```

16.6.2 Parameterized Class Dictionaries

To make class dictionaries easier to use, we allow them to be parameterized.

Instead of writing

```
Adjacency_List     : Empty_List | NAdjacency_List *common*.
Adjacency_NList    = <first> Adjacency <rest> Adjacency_List.
Any_vertex_List    : Empty_List | Any_vertex_NList *common*.
Any_vertex_NList   = <first> Any_vertex <rest> Any_vertex_NList.
```

we want to use directly

---

[19] Class dictionary textual representation, page 437 (31).
[20] Class dictionary graph textual representation, page 431 (7).

```
            List(Adjacency)
            List(Any_vertex)
```

Therefore, we define:

```
     List(S)          : Empty_list(S) |Nonempty_list(S) *common*.
     Nonempty_list(S) = <first> S <rest> List(S).
     Empty_list(S)    = .
```

or with an abbreviation:

```
     List(S) ~ {S}.
```

A nonempty list is described by

```
     NList(S) ~ S { S } .
```

We call List(S) and NList(S) repetition vertices. We also introduce the abbreviation

```
     A = [<b> B].
```

for

```
     A     = <b> OptB.
     OptB  : B | Empty.
     Empty = .
```

We call [<b> B] an optional part of A. With these facilities we can now introduce the parameterized class dictionaries defined by the following class dictionary, called DH-P:

```
Cd_graph = < adjacencies > List(Adjacency).
Adjacency =
  < vertex > Vertex
  ["(" < parameters> Comma_list(Vertex) ")"]
  < ns > Neighbors "." .
Neighbors_wc : Construct_ns | Alternat_ns
  *common* < construct_ns > List(Any_vertex).
Neighbors : Neighbors_wc | Repetit_n *common*.
Construct_ns = "=".
Alternat_ns = ":"
  < alternat_ns > Bar_list(Term) "*common*".
Repetit_n = "~" <sandwiched> Sandwich(Kernel).
Kernel = [ <nonempty> Term ]
  "{" <repeated> Sandwich(Term) "}".
Any_vertex : Labeled_term | Optional_term |
  Syntax_vertex *common*.
Vertex = < vertex_name > Ident .
Label = "<" < label_name > Ident ">" .
Syntax_vertex = < string > String .
```

16.6. SELF APPLICATION

```
Labeled_term = < label > Label < vertex > Term.
Term = <vertex> Vertex
  ["(" <actual_parameters> Comma_list(Term) ")" ].
Optional_term = "[" <opt> Sandwich(Labeled_term) "]".
List(S) ~ {S}.
Bar_list(S) ~ S {"|" S}.
Comma_list(S) ~ S {"," S}.
Sandwich(S) =
  <first> List(Syntax_vertex) <inner> S
  <second> List(Syntax_vertex).
```

In DH-P we have added repetition classes and optional parts. We can restrict this class dictionary to describe only nonparameterized class dictionaries by disallowing a nonnull parameters part in an Adjacency and by disallowing that a Term has a nonnull actual_parameters part.

We didn't add repetition vertices and optional parts into our mathematical model in the main part of the chapter because we can simulate them by alternation and construction vertices.

Now we list the informal semantic rules for parameterized class dictionaries.

- The axioms of unparameterized class dictionary graphs.

- All alternatives on the right-hand side of an alternation class definition must have the same parameters.

- The scope of a formal parameter is the class definition in which it is defined.

- A formal or actual parameter cannot be a parameterized class.

- All parameterized class definitions must be bounded [CW85], [LR88b].

- The number of formal and actual parameters must match.

16.6.3 Object Graphs

We use a textual notation for describing object graphs using an adjacency representation. It also shows the mapping of object graph vertices to class dictionary graph vertices.

```
inst1:v1(
  <successor1> inst2:v2( ... )
  <successor2> inst3:v3( ... )
  ...
  <successorn> instn:vn( ... ))
```

The vertices correspond to the instance names, such as inst1, inst2 , ..., instn. The name after the instance name is preceded by a ":" and gives the label assigned by λ. The edge labels are given between the < and > signs.

For describing shared objects, we use the notation:

```
inst1:v1(
  <successor1> inst2)
```

where inst2 is an object identifier defined elsewhere. Each object identifier has to be defined exactly once.

The following class dictionary, called Object-CD, defines the structure of object graphs based on the preceding notation. We also allow repetition objects.[21]

```
Obj_graph = < adjacencies> List(Inst_or_adj).
Inst_or_adj : Named_adjacency | Adjacency.
Named_adjacency =
  <inst_name> Ident
  [<adjacency> Adjacency].
Adjacency =
  ":" <vertex> Vertex <neighbors> Constituents.
Constituents : Construction_parts | Repetition_parts |
Terminal_value.
Construction_parts = "(" <parts> List(Labeled_adjacency) ")".
Repetition_parts = "{" [ <parts> Comma_list(Inst_or_adj) ] "}".
Terminal_value = <terminal_value> String.
Labeled_adjacency =
  <objName> Label <objDescr> Inst_or_adj.
Label = "<" <objName> Ident ">".
Vertex = <vertex_name> Ident.
List(S) ~ {S}.
Comma_list(S) ~ S { "," S }.
```

Figure 16.19 summarizes how we use the different class dictionaries.

Structure	Class Dictionary
object graph	Object-CD
class dictionary graph	DH-G
class dictionary	DH-G
parameterized class dictionary	DH-P

Figure 16.19: Notations

16.6.4 Mapping to C++

Class dictionaries and object graphs can be mapped into a programming language, such as C++ or CLOS. Indeed, the translation can be adapted easily to any programming language that supports classes and objects, multiple inheritance, and delayed binding of calls to code.

---

[21]Object graph textual representation, page 436 (26).

Class Dictionaries

A class dictionary $DG = (VC, VA, VT, \Lambda; EC, EA)$ has an interpretation in C++: A class with a constructor corresponds to each element of VC and an abstract class corresponds to each element of VA. The mapping process allows multiple inheritance class dictionaries.

A predefined class Universal is the superclass of all classes. Class Universal provides generic functionality for parsing (g_parse), printing (g_print), drawing (using the object graph notation), copying, and comparing of objects. A predefined class Terminal is a subclass of class Universal. Class Terminal provides generic functions for terminal classes.

Each vertex is interpreted as a C++ class as follows:

- Data members

  A private data member is created for each outgoing construction edge. The label becomes the name of the data member. The type of the data member is a pointer type of the class corresponding to the target of the construction edge.

  A static data member stores the class name.

- Function members For construction vertices only, a constructor that has as many arguments as there are outgoing construction edges. The default value for all arguments is NULL.

  For each data member x, a writing function set_x (with one argument) and a reading function get_x.

  A cast-down function dealing with cast-down in multiple inheritance case.

- Inheritance

  All alternation vertices without alternation ancestors inherit from class Universal. Each class inherits from its alternation predecessors, which are virtual base classes.

```
Fruit_List = <first> Fruit <rest> Rest.
Rest    : None | Fruit_List.
None    = .
Fruit   : Apple | Orange *common* <weight> DemNumber.
Apple   = "apple" .
Orange  = "orange" .
```

Figure 16.20: Fruit_List

Example 16.8 Consider the class dictionary in Fig. 16.20. The following class definitions in C++ are automatically generated.

```cpp
class Rest : public Universal {
  private: static char *type;
  public: Rest();
          ~Rest();
          char     *get_type() { return( type ); }
          virtual void    DEM_abstract() = 0;
};
class Fruit_List : public Rest {
  private: Fruit *first;
           Rest *rest;
           static char *type;
  public:  Fruit_List( Fruit * = NULL, Rest * = NULL );
           ~Fruit_List();
           Fruit *get_first() { return( first ); }
           void set_first( Fruit *new_first ) { first = new_first; }
           Rest *get_rest() { return( rest ); }
           void set_rest( Rest *new_rest ) { rest = new_rest; }
           char     *get_type() { return( type ); }
           void     DEM_abstract() { }
};
class None : public Rest {
  private: static char *type;
  public:  None();
           ~None();
           char     *get_type() { return( type ); }
           void     DEM_abstract() { }
};
class Fruit : public Universal {
  private: DemNumber *weight;
           static char *type;
  public:  Fruit();
           ~Fruit();
           DemNumber *get_weight() { return( weight ); }
           void set_weight( DemNumber *new_weight ) { weight = new_weight; }
           char     *get_type() { return( type ); }
           virtual void    DEM_abstract() = 0;
};
class Apple : public Fruit {
  private: static char *type;
  public:  Apple( );
           ~Apple();
           char     *get_type() { return( type ); }
           void     DEM_abstract() { }
};
class Orange : public Fruit {
  private: static char *type;
  public:  Orange( );
           ~Orange();
           char     *get_type() { return( type ); }
```

```
            void       DEM_abstract() { }
};
class DemNumber : public Terminal {
   private: int val;
            static char *type;
   public:  DemNumber( int = 0 );
            ~DemNumber();
            char      *get_type() { return( type ); }
            int       get_val() { return( val ); }
            void      set_val( int new_val ) { val = new_val; }
};
```

The function DEM_abstract() is defined as a pure virtual function for alternation vertices, to make alternation classes uninstantiable.

Object Graphs

We describe how an object graph can be translated into a C++ program that produces the equivalent object in C++.

An object graph $H = (W, \Lambda_H; \; E, \lambda)$ with respect to a class dictionary graph $DG = (V, \Lambda; \; EC, EA)$ is mapped into a C++ object as follows:

For each vertex $v \in V_H$ we create an instance of class $\lambda(v)$ by calling the class constructor.

For the object graph in Fig. 16.7, we do the following.

```
Teacher *iTeacher = new Teacher( new DemNumber(40000));
//the argument is for salary
iTeacher->set_name(new DemIdent("John"));
iTeacher->set_ssn(new DemNumber(212011234));
//now iTeacher points to the legal Teacher-object.
```

The constructor call of **Teacher** has as many arguments as there are immediate parts of **Teacher**. The parts are constructed recursively. If a construction vertex has inherited parts from an alternation vertex, then we need to call the **set** functions to assign values to the inherited parts. The advantage is that we don't need to modify code when a class dictionary reorganization changes the order of parts.

16.7 KNOWLEDGE PATHS AND OBJECT PATHS

Relationships between knowledge paths and object paths are analyzed in this subsection. A knowledge path is a path in a class dictionary graph, whereas an object path is a path in an object graph. An object path has the standard graph-theoretic definition: it is a sequence of adjacent edges in an object graph. One important use of knowledge paths is to define the traversals of objects. A knowledge path is like a nondeterministic program that defines a pattern that tells how to traverse objects. One knowledge path usually defines many different traversals; that is, many different object paths that we call instances of the knowledge path. Some of the knowledge paths uniquely define one object path for a given object, and we call those knowledge paths **completed**. We define that an object path is the instantiation of a knowledge path if the construction edges encountered in the knowledge path match the edges encountered in the object graph. Next we informally derive the knowledge path concept from a set of requirements.

To describe the traversal of objects, we need a path concept PATH at the class level. The path concept PATH represents a set of paths and needs to have the following three properties:

1. If there is a path from A to B satisfying PATH, then there exists an A-object that contains a nested B-object.

2. The concatenation of any two paths satisfying PATH, which are from A to B and from B to C, is a path from A to C satisfying PATH.

3. We want to have the weakest path concept: if P is a path concept satisfying 1 and 2 then any path that satisfies P also satisfies PATH.

The motivation for the first condition is that we want to use paths satisfying PATH to traverse objects and to find appropriate subobjects. The second condition is needed since we are defining operations on semi-class dictionary graphs and propagation graphs that involve the concatenation of paths. Namely, we use existing object traversal descriptions to construct a bigger and more complex traversal description. The third condition is motivated by wanting to impose the least amount of restrictions.

The knowledge path concept is the weakest concept that satisfies the three properties. Suppose we give a weaker path concept that allows alternation edges to follow inheritance edges in a path. The restriction on paths in a regular expression would be $(EA \mid EI \mid EC)^*$. In other words, there is no restriction at all. Based on this weaker concept, if there is a path from vertex A to B, it is not true that there is a path in an object graph that goes from an A-object to a B-object. An example is shown in Fig. 16.21.

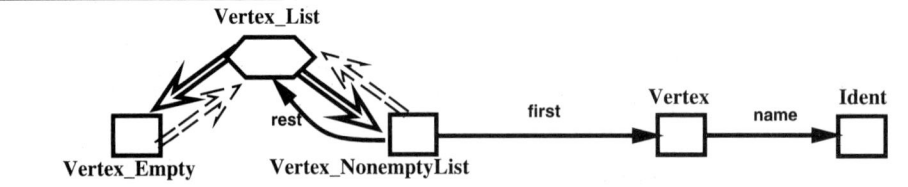

Figure 16.21: Weaker path concept

Vertex_Empty ⋯▷ Vertex_List⟹ Vertex_NonemptyList is a weaker path, but no Vertex_Empty-object can contain a Vertex_NonemptyList-object. Therefore the knowledge path concept is the weakest path concept to describe the knowledge relationships between objects; in other words, to describe possible paths between objects.

We continue with the **path instantiation** concept which shows how a knowledge path describes object traversals. The following discussions are in the context of a class dictionary graph slice, because class dictionary graph slices are the weakest concept to define objects.

To check whether an object path instantiates a knowledge path we perform two tasks recursively (see Fig. 16.22). First, we skip all consecutive alternation edges (if any) in the knowledge path. Then we check whether there is an alternation path from the target of the last alternation edge to the construction vertex of which the first object in the object path is an instance. Second, we find the first construction edge in the knowledge path, and we check that the label of the construction edge and the label of the first edge in the object path coincide. In the knowledge path we now eliminate all edges we have visited, including the first construction edge. In the object path we eliminate the first edge, and we continue with the checking recursively. More precisely:

Definition 16.28 Given a knowledge path $p = v_0\ e_1\ v_1\ ...\ v_{i-1}\ e_i\ v_i\ ...\ v_n$ in a class dictionary graph slice P and an object path $p' = w_0\ e'_1\ w_1\ ...\ w_{j-1}\ e'_j\ w_j\ ...\ w_m$ in a legal object O of P where $n \geq m \geq 0$, $v_i (0 \leq i \leq n)$ and $e_i (1 \leq i \leq n)$ are vertices and edges in P, $w_j (0 \leq j \leq m)$ and $e'_j (1 \leq j \leq m)$ are vertices and edges in O, object path p' **instantiates** knowledge path p, if the following conditions hold:

1. Find the longest path $v_0\ e_1\ v_1\ ...\ v_{r-1}\ e_r\ v_r$ of consecutive alternation edges starting at v_0. If there are no alternation edges, then $r = 0$. The following must hold:

$$v_r \stackrel{*}{\Longrightarrow} \lambda(w_0).$$

2. If $m > 0$, then there must be a construction edge in p; let e_s be the first construction edge. Assuming $e_s = v_{s-1} \stackrel{l_s}{\longrightarrow} v_s$ and $e'_1 = w_0 \stackrel{l'_1}{\longrightarrow} w_1$, we have

   (a) $l_s = l'_1$ and
   (b) object path

   $$w_1\ ...\ w_{j-1}\ e'_j\ w_j\ ...\ w_m$$

   instantiates knowledge path

   $$v_s\ ...\ v_{i-1}\ e_i\ v_i\ ...\ v_n$$

A consequence of the definition is that $\lambda(w_1) \in \mathcal{A}(v_s)$, but $\lambda(w_0) \in \mathcal{A}(v_{s-1})$ does not always hold (v_s is the target of the first construction edge e_s in Definition 16.28). For example, Fig. 16.22 illustrates an example in which the object path from w_0 to w_3 instantiates the knowledge path from v_0 to v_6. $\lambda(w_1)$ is in $\mathcal{A}(v_1)$, but $\lambda(w_2)$ is not in $\mathcal{A}(v_5)$.

A knowledge path may describe several traversals. For example, consider the class dictionary graph in Fig. 16.23 and the knowledge path Neighbors $\stackrel{a\text{-}neighbors}{\longrightarrow}$ Vertex_List. This knowledge path describes the traversal that goes from an A_Neighbors-object to a Vertex_Empty-object, or from a B_Neighbors-object to a Vertex_NonemptyList-object. If we want to have a knowledge path that describes exactly the traversal from an A_Neighbors-object to a Vertex_Empty-object, we have to use the knowledge path

Neighbors$\Longrightarrow$ A_Neighbors $\stackrel{....}{\Longrightarrow}$ Neighbors $\stackrel{a\text{-}neighbors}{\longrightarrow}$ Vertex_List$\Longrightarrow$ Vertex_Empty.

We call this knowledge path **completed**, and it is the completion of Neighbors $\stackrel{a\text{-}neighbors}{\longrightarrow}$ Vertex_List.

A completed knowledge path uniquely defines an object path.

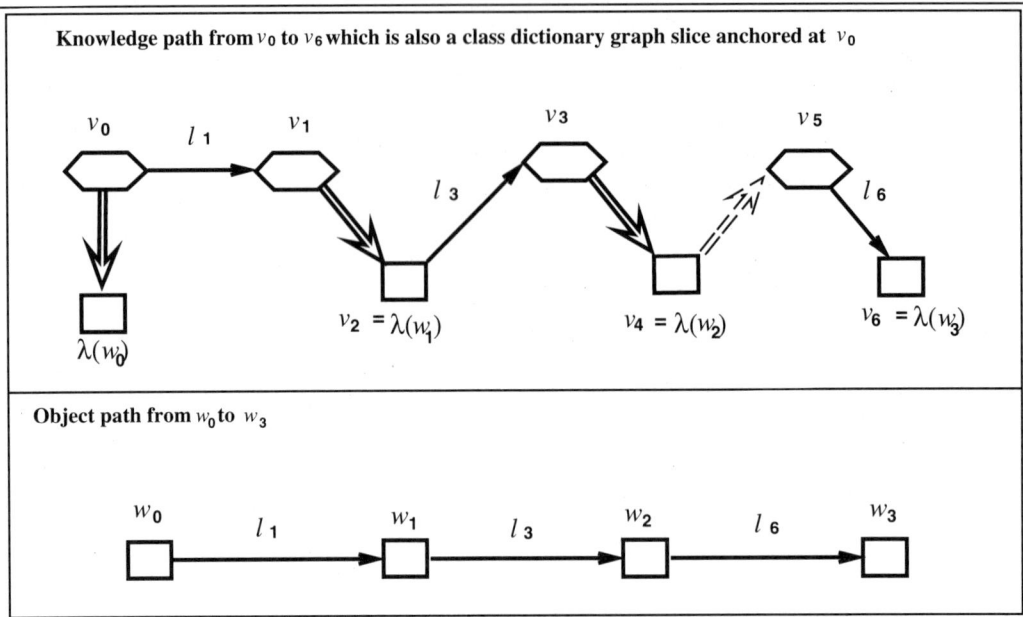

Figure 16.22: Path instantiations

Informally, a knowledge path is completed if in the knowledge path we cannot take an alternation edge to an alternation vertex and then immediately follow an outgoing construction or inheritance edge. The knowledge path must end at a construction vertex. More formally:

Definition 16.29 Let p be a knowledge path and $p = v_0 \ e_1 \ v_1 \ ... \ v_{i-1} \ e_i \ v_i \ ... \ v_n$. p is **completed**, if the following conditions hold:

1. v_n is a construction vertex and

2. If e_i is an alternation edge and v_i is an alternation vertex, then $i + 1 < n$ and e_{i+1} is also an alternation edge.

To better describe the relationship between knowledge paths and object paths, we introduce the completion of a knowledge path. A knowledge path p_1 is the completion of a knowledge path p_2, if there exists an object path that is an instantiation of both p_1 and p_2, and with the same intuition as the fourth property in Definition 16.4, every alternation vertex v on p_1 preceded by an incoming construction and alternation edge must be followed by an outgoing alternation edge. Formally,

Definition 16.30 Given two knowledge paths $p_1 = v_0^1 \ e_1^1 \ v_1^1 \ ... \ v_{i-1}^1 \ e_i^1 \ v_i^1 \ ... \ v_n^1$ and $p_2 = v_0^2 \ e_1^2 \ v_1^2 \ ... \ v_{i-1}^2 \ e_i^2 \ v_i^2 \ ... \ v_m^2$ in a class dictionary graph slice P where $m \geq 0$ and $n \geq 0$, **knowledge path p_1 is a completion of a knowledge path p_2** if the following three conditions hold:

16.7. KNOWLEDGE PATHS AND OBJECT PATHS

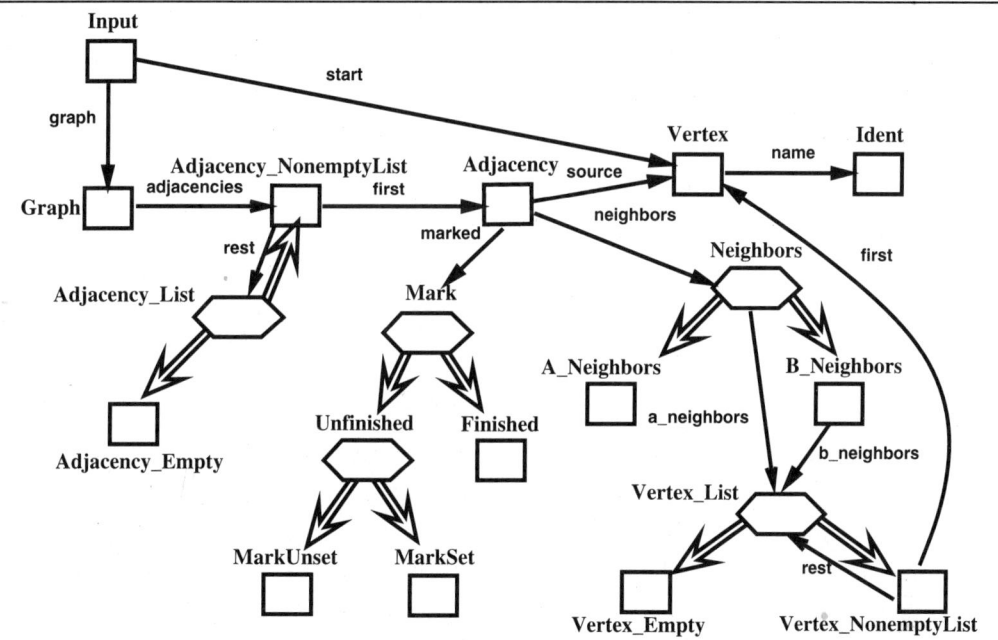

Figure 16.23: Class dictionary graph 2_graph for cycle checking on graphs with two kinds of edges

1. $v_0^1 = v_0^2$ and $v_n^2 \stackrel{*}{\Longrightarrow} v_m^1$ and

2. p_1 is completed and

3. If p_2 contains construction edges, p_1 contains exactly the same construction edges and in the same order.

The following theorems describe correspondences between knowledge paths and object paths.

Theorem 16.5 *For a class dictionary graph slice P and a legal object O of P and an object path p' in O there exists a unique completed knowledge path p in P such that p' instantiates p.*

Proof. By contradiction. If there were more than one completed knowledge path, then the Unique Label Axiom would be violated. $\square$

Theorem 16.6 *For every knowledge path p in a class dictionary graph slice P, there exists a legal object O of P and a path p' in object O such that p' instantiates p.*

Proof. By induction on the number of construction edges on the path. $\square$

Based on the property of the regular expression $(EA \mid (EI)^*EC)^*$, we have the following properties of knowledge paths:

1. Knowledge paths are closed under concatenation.

2. Splitting a knowledge path after a construction or alternation edge yields two knowledge paths.

The propagation graph calculus and the propagation directive calculus are based on the properties of knowledge paths discussed in this section.

16.8 SUMMARY

In this chapter we summarized the theory of class dictionaries.

16.9 EXERCISES

Exercise 16.1 (suggested by Walter Hürsch [Hür94])
Class dictionaries enforce the abstract superclass rule (ASR) which says that all superclasses must be abstract; that is, they cannot be instantiated. We have used this rule successfully since the first implementation of class dictionaries in 1984. One reason for the rule is that it makes important concepts of object-oriented design easier to work with. The purpose of this exercise is to give quantitative evidence to the last statement.

The strategy is to rewrite several of the formal definitions about class dictionaries assuming that ASR is violated; that is, we can have alternation edges outgoing from construction classes. Comparing the complexity (length) of the old and new formal definitions gives a quantitative measure for the simplicity promoted by ASR.

Rewrite the following definitions:

- Objects(G), where G is a class dictionary graph.

- Object-equivalence between two class dictionary graphs.

- Decomposition of object-equivalence into primitive transformations. The primitives will change. What is the new set of primitives?

- PartCluster definition.

- Instantiation of a knowledge path as an object path.

  This definition is fundamental to the semantics of propagation patterns.

16.10 BIBLIOGRAPHIC REMARKS

This chapter is based on several joint papers with Cun Xiao: [LX93a, LX93c, LX94] and Cun Xiao's thesis [Xia94].

- Parsing

  Parsing theory is covered in [HU79] and [ASU86]. The useless terminology is borrowed from [HU79]. Inductiveness is formally discussed in [LX93a]. For Post's correspondence problem, see page 200 of [HU79].

  The concepts first set and follow set are defined in a similar way in [Hec86] as we described them here.

- Class dictionaries

  [Lie88] is the first journal paper on class dictionaries. [SAK88b] describes work useful for the theory of class dictionary graphs.

- Grammatical Structures

  In his book, Erwin Engeler [Eng73] introduces the concept of a grammatical structure that satisfies two axioms: Unique readability and Induction. He then associates to a given grammar a grammatical structure. Engeler's early work has an interesting relationship to our work in object-oriented systems. The concept of an inductive class dictionary graph is a refinement of a grammatical structure and the association of a grammar to a grammatical structure is similar to the association of a class dictionary to a class dictionary graph.

Chapter 17

Selfstudy/Teacher's Guide

17.1 INTRODUCTION

The book is written with minimal reference to the Demeter Tools to keep it independent of the current implementation of adaptive software. The current implementation is, however, a very useful and well debugged companion for learning about adaptive software and using it productively. In this selfstudy guide we show one way the tools can be used to learn about adaptive software development. The guide contains an outline to follow when learning to use the tools.

This selfstudy guide has grown out of five carefully orchestrated assignments that we have developed to teach adaptive software effectively. The assignments coordinate the tasks of reading appropriate book chapters and documentation information and doing some exercises using the tools.

The Demeter System was developed with the objective of significantly improving the productiveness of software engineers with minimal training costs. We have tested the adequacy of this selfstudy guide in numerous academic and industrial courses and projects and found that we can effectively teach our method in about five weeks with three hours of lectures per week and hands-on exercises. In the five additional weeks, the students do a project of significant size which would be impossible to complete without the Demeter System in the available time. We use the same method in both a junior-level undergraduate and a graduate course, but with more emphasis on the theory in the graduate course.

17.2 EXPANDED SYLLABUS

The syllabus is outlined by the five assignments that the students solve. The first three assignments include C++ programming assignments not required by readers who have solid C++ development experience.

- Writing a simple C++ program without using virtual functions. Design rule checking a class dictionary graph.

- Writing a simple C++ program with virtual functions. Writing and debugging class dictionary graphs.

17.2. EXPANDED SYLLABUS

- Spending a few hours writing a larger C++ program. Writing and debugging class dictionaries. Implementing the C++ program with propagation patterns.

- Programming with propagation patterns without transportation patterns.

- Programming with propagation patterns with transportation patterns.

The rationale behind this assignment sequence is to give the students the confidence to write simple C++ programs. After they have learned high-level concepts such as class dictionaries and propagation patterns using the Demeter Tools/C++, they can then suddenly write much larger C++ programs (containing thousands of lines of code).

First we teach the basic concepts of object-oriented programming: classes with part-of and kind-of relationships, methods, inheritance, and delayed binding, and we show how they are expressed in C++. We teach only a small subset of C++ that is available in similar form in many other object-oriented languages, such as Smalltalk-80 and CLOS. The introduction of C++ builds on knowledge of C or Pascal. In Assignment 1, the students complete a simple C++ program without inheritance and without virtual functions, such as a program to compute the size of a tree. They write only the class definitions and they get the C++ code for constructing an object and the member function implementations.

In Assignment 2, the students complete a more complex C++ program with virtual functions, such as a simple pocket calculator. Inheritance is used only for late binding of calls to code but not to express common functionality. In the second part of the assignment, students write class dictionary graphs for several domains including C++ programs, binary trees, linked lists, and a domain of their choice (an orchestra, golf course, chess board, etc.).

In Assignments 1 and 2 the students see how tedious it is to describe objects in C++. We use this experience to motivate class dictionaries. A class dictionary is a class dictionary graph with concrete syntax added to define an application-specific language for describing objects in declarative form. The language consists of a set of sentences that can be automatically parsed into objects. In connection with class dictionaries we discuss printing, parsing, and ambiguity of class dictionaries. We now clarify the informal syntax definition for class dictionaries and object graphs by showing them a class dictionary for class dictionaries and object graphs.

In the book, class dictionaries are introduced late (Chapter 11). However, for the practical use of the tools it is very useful to read sentences to create objects. Therefore, Chapter 11 is organized so that it can be read anytime after Chapter 6.

In Assignment 3, the students work on a C++ program with over a dozen classes. They are given a time limit but are not expected to complete the program in the given time frame. A good example is to compute the total salary in a conglomerate of companies. In addition, the students learn to debug class dictionaries by writing sentences in an application-specific language and by checking whether the corresponding objects can be represented by the class dictionary. The class dictionary graph from Assignment 2 is enhanced to a class dictionary and the students write sentences for the resulting class dictionary.

Also in Assignment 3 the students implement the C++ program using propagation patterns and a class dictionary. With those new concepts, the programming task is much easier.

To debug propagation pattern code, we introduce growth plans. A growth plan consists of a sequence of larger and larger class dictionary graph slices all anchored at the same class. A class dictionary graph slice anchored at some class v contains enough classes to build at least one object of class v.

Equipped with propagation patterns, students solve several small tasks in Assignment 4. Good examples are writing a simple compiler for postfix expressions by generating code for a stack machine, computing the size of postfix expressions, and computing the size of a class dictionary graph by using a class dictionary graph that describes class dictionary graphs.

In Assignment 5, the focus is on the evolution of class structures. The same problem is solved for three related class structures. Since the solution is done with propagation patterns, the evolution is much easier to master.

After Assignment 5, students select a project from my list or they create one themselves that is related to their COOP[1] or work experience. While they work on the projects, I give lectures on a variety of object-oriented design topics that help them do their projects.

- Finding the first prototype: simplifying the data (with growth plans) and additionally simplifying the functionality, if needed.

- Parameterized classes, repetition classes, and optional parts.

- Class dictionary transformations: object-equivalence, optimization of class dictionaries (common normal form, consolidation of alternatives, tree property), flattening, weak extension, extension [LBSL91, BL91, Ber91].

- The Law of Demeter for functions (object/class and weak/strong form) [LHR88, LH89a] and its relationship to propagation patterns.

- The Law of Demeter for classes [LX93a] .

- Propagation pattern transformations: equivalence of propagation directives, adding *bypassing*, *through*, and *to-stop*.

- Testing of object-oriented programs, minimally adequate test sets.

- Adaptive programs and their evolution and reuse, splitting a project into subprojects, relationship to growth plans.

- Case studies: program evolution and modeling the design process.

The material has been divided into about eighty instructional objectives (see Chapter 14), each covering a simple learning unit. For example, the legal object objective asks students to determine whether a given object graph is legal with respect to a class dictionary graph. Many of the objectives are handled by the Demeter Tools/C++ which support the Demeter Method on UNIX platforms with C++. Therefore, the tools are also an effective learning aid, besides facilitating the programming process.

---

[1] Co-operative education is an education model where students work in industry during their study. Co-operative eduction was pioneered by Northeastern University.

17.3. ASSIGNMENT 1

The course relies on the Demeter Tools/C++ and their documentation. Each tool has a man page, and the User's Guide and Laboratory Guide contain detailed information about how to use the tools. Information about how to get the software, documentation, and course material is in Fig. A.1 (page 589). OO is pointing to the course material directory.

17.3 ASSIGNMENT 1

17.3.1 Background Tasks

- Make sure you have done the account set-up described in the User's Guide or Laboratory Guide.

- Read the preface, Chapter 1, Chapter 3, and Chapter 4 of this book.

- Learn about C++ class definition syntax from your C++ book.

17.3.2 Part 1: C++ Program Completion

Turn in the C++ program fragment you wrote, and its output.

This assignment familiarizes you with a subset of C++. You are asked to write class definitions for the following program so that it produces the output given at the end (lines starting with //). Put your entire program into one file called **tree.C** and compile with your C++ compiler, for example,

```
CC tree.C
```
or
```
gcc tree.C
```

```
#include <iostream.h>

// write here the class definitions for DemNumber and Tree

DemNumber::DemNumber() {};

Tree::Tree(DemNumber* node_in, Tree* left_in, Tree* right_in)
{
   node = node_in;
   left = left_in;
   right = right_in;
}


int max(int a, int b){
return (a>b ? a : b);}

int Tree::depth(){
 return (max (left ? left->depth() : 0, right ? right->depth() : 0) + 1);
}
```

```
int Tree::size(){
 return (left ? left->size() : 0) +
        (right ? right->size() : 0) + 1;
}.

main (){
  cout << "\nFirst Tree" << "\n";
  DemNumber *n1 = new DemNumber();
  Tree *t1 = new Tree(n1, 0, 0);
  cout<<"\ndepth of tree 1 =";
  cout<<t1->depth();
  cout<<"\nsize of tree 1 =";
  cout<<t1->size();

  cout << "\nSecond Tree" << "\n";
  Tree *t2 = new Tree(n1, t1, t1);
  cout<<"\ndepth of tree 2 =";
  cout<<t2->depth();
  cout<<"\nsize of tree 3 =";
  cout<<t2->size();

  cout << "\nThird Tree" << "\n";
  Tree *t3 = new Tree(n1, t2, t1);
  cout<<"\ndepth of tree 3 =";
  cout<<t3->depth();
  cout<<"\nsize of tree 5 =";
  cout<<t3->size();
}


// output to be produced
//First Tree
//
//depth of tree 1 =1
//size of tree 1 =1
//Second Tree
//
//depth of tree 2 =2
//size of tree 3 =3
//Third Tree
//
//depth of tree 3 =3
//size of tree 5 =5
```

17.3.3 Part 2: Laboratory Guide

After you have read the assigned chapters in this book, work through the Laboratory Guide. Run the Demeter Tools/C++ as instructed in the Laboratory Guide and turn in all files that you modified.

17.4 ASSIGNMENT 2

17.4.1 Background Tasks

- Man pages

  Read the output of:

  man sem-check

- Reading

  - User's Guide

    Read about how to check your class dictionary with sem-check.
  - This book

    Read Chapter 2 and Chapter 5.
  - C++ book

    Read about virtual functions.

17.4.2 Objectives

In this assignment you will learn the following instructional objectives and their prerequisites (see Chapter 14): Legal class dictionary graph (objective 9, page 431), and legal object graph (objective 27, page 436).

17.4.3 Part 1: Writing a Pocket Calculator in C++

This part exercises a larger subset of C++ than Assignment 1. Specifically, now you use virtual functions. Write a C++ program to evaluate prefix expressions. You have to write only the data structure part and constructor functions. Your program should behave like a pocket calculator; for example, the object corresponding to

```
Compound(
  <op> Mulsym
  <arg1> Compound (
    <op> Addsym
    <arg1> Numerical (
      <numValue> DemNumber "1")
    <arg2> Numerical (
      <numValue> DemNumber "1"))
  <arg2>  Numerical (
    <numValue> DemNumber "3"))
```

should evaluate to 6. (A simpler representation would be: (* (+ 1 1) 3).)

In the object notation above, a class name must be followed by (...) or { ... } unless it is a name of a predefined class (DemIdent, DemNumber, DemString, DemReal). Inside the parentheses (...) is a list of named parts. Each part name is surrounded by angle brackets < ... >. After the part name is an object graph. Inside the curly braces { ... } is a list of object graphs.

The prefix expressions that your program should handle are simple. They are defined by the following class dictionary graph:

```
Exp : Numerical | Compound.
Numerical = <numValue> DemNumber. // DemNumber has a part val
                                  // containing an int
Compound =
  <op> Op <arg1> Exp <arg2> Exp .
Op : Addsym | Subsym | Mulsym.
Addsym = .
Subsym = .
Mulsym = .
```

You might want to take the following program as a start. It implements most of the procedural part of your program. All you have to provide is the data structure part and constructor implementations.

```
 #include <iostream.h>
int DemNumber::eval() {
  return val;}
int Numerical::eval() {return numValue->eval();}
int Compound::eval(){ return op->apply_op(arg1->eval(), arg2->eval());  }
int Exp::eval() { return 0; }
int Addsym::apply_op(int n1,int n2) { return n1 + n2; }
int Subsym::apply_op(int n1,int n2) { return(n1 - n2); }
int Mulsym::apply_op(int n1,int n2) { return(n1 * n2); }
int Op::apply_op(int n1,int n2) { return 0; }
```

In the main program we build an object which then gets evaluated:

```
main()
{
  DemNumber* iNumber1 = new DemNumber(100);
  DemNumber* iNumber2 = new DemNumber(22);
  DemNumber* iNumber3 = new DemNumber(44);
  DemNumber* iNumber4 = new DemNumber(3);
  DemNumber* iNumber5 = new DemNumber(33);
  Numerical* iNumerical1 = new Numerical(iNumber1);
  Numerical* iNumerical2 = new Numerical(iNumber2);
  Numerical* iNumerical3 = new Numerical(iNumber3);
```

17.4. ASSIGNMENT 2

```
        Numerical* iNumerical4 = new Numerical(iNumber4);
        Numerical* iNumerical5 = new Numerical(iNumber5);
        Addsym* add = new Addsym();
        Subsym* sub = new Subsym();
        Mulsym* mul = new Mulsym();
        Compound* c1 = new Compound(add, iNumerical1, iNumerical1);
        Compound* c2 = new Compound(add, iNumerical2, iNumerical3);
        Compound* c3 = new Compound(sub, c2, iNumerical5);
        Compound* c4 = new Compound(mul, iNumerical4, c3);
        cout<< "\n\n result_1: " ;
        cout<< " = "   << c1->eval();
        cout<< "\n result_2: " ;
        cout<< " = "   << c2->eval();
        cout<< "\n result_3: " ;
        cout<< " = "   << c4->eval() << "\n\n" ;
}
```

Add the appropriate class definitions to make your prefix expression evaluator work. Your C++ compiler should compile it and when you run it you should get the right results.

17.4.4 Part 2: Checking Your Solution with Demeter

The goal of this part is to give a five-line explanation why Demeter could solve the problem with the available information.

In this part, the Demeter Tools/C++ will solve Part 1 for you. Copy the files in directory

```
$00/hw/2/expr.cl
```

to one of your own directories.

The files are (you should inspect them):

```
cd.cd
demeter-input
main.C
prog.C
user-calls.h
```

Now type

```
demeter >& sc &
```

which saves the output of the **demeter** command into file **sc**. Get up and stretch while the computer is creating the C++ classes that you did in Part 1 of this assignment. When it is done, type

```
run
```

The output of the program in Part 1 will be produced. Why could the computer solve your assignment? Find an explanation, at most five lines long. All the information available to the computer is in the above files.

17.4.5 Part 3: Learning C++

Turn in a certified class dictionary graph describing a fragment of the structure of the C++ Programming Language (certified means that the class dictionary graph has to pass the design rule test done by **sem-check -n**).

Most programs we write in this course will be written or generated in C++. Therefore, we need to learn the structure of C++ programs from our C++ textbook. For example, the following class dictionary describes some of the structure of C++ member function definitions:

```
Type = < name > DemIdent [ < attribute > Type_attribute ] .
Pointer = .
Type_attribute : Reference | Pointer .
Reference = .
Program = < program > FunctionDefinition_List .
FunctionDefinition_List ~
  FunctionDefinition_List_elements { FunctionDefinition_List_elements } .
FunctionDefinition_List_elements : FunctionDefinition .
FunctionDefinition =
  < returnType > Type < attachedToClass > ClassName
  < memberFunction > MemberFunctionName
  < formalArguments > FormalArgument_List < statements > Statement_List .
ClassName = < n > DemIdent .
MemberFunctionName = < n > DemIdent .
FormalArgument_List ~
  FormalArgument_List_elements { FormalArgument_List_elements } .
FormalArgument_List_elements : FormalArgument .
FormalArgument = .
Statement_List ~ Statement_List_elements { Statement_List_elements } .
Statement_List_elements : Assignment | FunctionMemberCall .
Assignment = < lhs > VariableName < rhs > Numeral .
VariableName = < n > DemIdent .
Numeral = < n > DemNumber .
FunctionMemberCall =
  < name > MemberFunctionName < actuals > ActualArgument_List .
ActualArgument_List ~
  ActualArgument_List_elements { ActualArgument_List_elements } .
ActualArgument_List_elements : ActualArgument .
ActualArgument = .
```

Write a class dictionary graph with at least twice as many classes (about forty) that reflects more of the structure of the C++ language. Reuse the class definitions above and modify them if you like. Make heavy use of your C++ book.

17.4.6 Part 4: Develop Your Own Class Dictionary Graph

Write your own class dictionary graph for your own favorite domain. Don't choose something too large. It should require about twenty classes.

Potential systems are: a concert, a city, a home, a kitchen, a spaceship, you name it! Be creative and imaginative.

For both Parts 3 and 4: after you have developed the class dictionary graphs, draw them in graphical form.

For the last two parts, turn in your class dictionary graphs in both textual and graphical form. Also use the **sem-check -n** command on each class dictionary and turn in a statement that your solutions passed **sem-check -n**. The **sem-check -n** command should not give any error messages; otherwise adapt your class dictionary graph.

To draw and develop the class dictionary graphs graphically, you are invited to use the

> xcddraw

command on a workstation. Alternatively, you can draw them manually.

17.5 ASSIGNMENT 3

Sample exams are in

> $OO/exams/

In $OO/exams/practice-exam-handout you find instructions on how to prepare your own exams using the instructional objectives in Chapter 14.

When you have questions about using Demeter commands, check the Demeter frequently asked question file (for the URL, see page 589). This file contains a list of frequently asked questions together with answers.

The theme of this assignment is to learn to write and debug class dictionaries and to write a complete C++ program that traverses objects to perform a simple addition task.

17.5.1 Background Tasks

- User's Guide

  Read about how to make a class dictionary LL(1).

- Reading

  - Read Chapter 6 (Class Dictionary Graphs and Objects) and Chapter 11 (Class Dictionaries) in this book.
  - In your C++ book, reread about virtual member functions and abstract classes. Also read about constructors.
  - Read the class dictionary for class dictionaries in Chapter 18, Section 18.3, page 585. It is also in

    > $OO/doc/cds/cd-class-dictionaries

    It describes the input language for **sem-check**. Keep the class dictionary handy for looking up the syntax when you write inputs.

    Also read the syntax definition for class dictionaries in the User's Guide.

17.5.2 Part 1: Trip Class Dictionary

Turn in your class dictionary checked by **sem-check**.

Prepare a file called **trip.cd** for the class dictionary given in Chapter 4 in Fig. 4.8 on page 91. It starts with

```
Trip = "TRIP" "by" <means> Means ...
```

and then call the command

```
sem-check -i trip.cd
```

If you get an error message, correct your input. Repeat until your class dictionary passes the design rule check done by **sem-check**.

The -i flag will create a file called **notmod/cds/cd-ll1-corrected**. If you get an LL(1) violation from **sem-check**, that file will tell you one way to correct it.

Turn in the class dictionary you used with the statement: it passed the design rule test.

17.5.3 Part 2: Inventing and Debugging Class Dictionaries

Turn in class dictionaries and sentences.

1. Write a class dictionary for postfix expressions. Your class dictionary should accept sentences of the form

    ```
    (2 3 +)
    (2 3 4 *)
    ((1 1 1 +) (5 5 5 *) 7 +)
    ```

2. Write a class dictionary for binary trees. Your class dictionary should accept sentences of the form

    ```
    (tree 4
      :left
        (tree 5
          :left
          :right)
      :right
        (tree 8
          :left
            (tree 9
              :left
              :right)
          :right))
    ```

3. Write a class dictionary for the class dictionary graph that you invented in Assignment 2. Add any kind of concrete syntax you like.

17.5. ASSIGNMENT 3

Use the commands sem-check, demeter and run to debug your class dictionaries. (See the quick reference page, Section 18.2, page 578 for a brief description of the Demeter commands.) sem-check should accept your class dictionaries without any errors or warnings.

For all subparts turn in the class dictionary, the set of sentences you used for debugging them, and the statement "sem-check accepted my class dictionary without warning or error and run accepted all the sentences I list."

17.5.4   Part 3: Time Consuming

Turn in your C++ program.

This part may be done in groups of three or four students to learn (by experience) about the group dynamics of object-oriented software development. Ideally, this should be the same group of students who will work together on a later project. Single-person groups are fine too, unless you want to learn about group dynamics.

In this part of the assignment you write a complete C++ program. The purpose is to give you the experience of writing a C++ program from scratch.

This part is mainly an exercise in typing and debugging C++ code and learning about software development in groups. The task the program solves is very simple and it does not require much more C++ knowledge than what you have acquired in Assignments 1 and 2.

Therefore, *spend at most three times as many hours as there are team members* on solving this part and then turn in whatever you have at that point with a description of any problems you ran into.

The reason for this time limit is that you should not waste your time debugging C++ code that can be generated with 100% precision automatically. In the last part of this assignment you will solve the task of this part in fifteen minutes, after I have told you the secret of how to do it. So don't feel intimidated if you cannot completely debug your program in the given time; it will be very easy for you to do this with an adaptive program.

Write a C++ program that computes the total of the officer salaries in a conglomerate defined by the class dictionary starting on page 55 and in graphical form in Fig. 3.1.

Write the class definitions for the above class dictionary and write a member function for class Conglomerate that adds up all the salaries in a Conglomerate-object.

Test your function with the object defined by C++ constructor calls in Chapter 3. The description starts on page 52. If you don't like this C++ code, you may replace it by better, but equivalent code.

Figure 3.4, page 59 contains another description of the same object in an English-like notation.

To implement a constructor for DemString, you might want to use:

```
DemString::DemString( char* val_in )
{
  if( val_in )
    {
      this->val = new char[strlen( val_in ) + 1];
      strcpy( this->val,val_in );
    }
  else
```

```
        this->val = NULL;
}
```

This definition is also used in the Demeter Tools/C++.
Hint: Write the member functions that you need in phases:

1. Write a member function for each of the following classes

   Conglomerate   Company
   Officer_List   Officer_Empty

2. Write a member function for each of the following classes

   Officer_NonEmpty   Officer
   Ordinary_Officer   Salary

3. Write a member function for the following class

   Shareholding_Officer

4. Write a member function for each of the following classes

   Subsidiary_List   Subsidiary_Empty

5. Write a member function for each of the following classes

   Subsidiary_NonEmpty Subsidiary

17.5.5 Part 4: Redoing the Last Part with Demeter

Copy the files in directory $OO/hw/3/congl.cl into one of your directories. Inspect them and call

```
demeter >& sc &
run
```

Enjoy a relaxation exercise while the computer does your assignment.

17.6 ASSIGNMENT 4

This assignment invites you to work with simple propagation patterns. This is much more productive than having you write C++ programs from scratch.

17.6.1 Background Tasks

- Read the following man pages:

```
man demeter
man generate
man propagate
man headers
man compile
man g_code
man g_displayAsTree
man g_draw
man run
```

Note: generate, propagate, headers, and compile are commands of the application programmer interface of the Demeter Tools. Usually those commands are called directly for you when you use "demeter".

- Read Chapter 7, Chapter 8, and Chapter 9.

  Read the quick reference page for the Demeter Tools/C++. The latest version of the reference page is always in

  $00/doc/Demeter-Tools-C++Quick-Reference

17.6.2 Part 1: Writing a Compiler

Write propagation patterns for a compiler, for a stack machine for the following programming language.

```
Example = <exps> Postfix_list.
Postfix : Numerical | Compound.
Numerical = <val> DemNumber.
Compound = "{" <arguments> Arguments <op> Op "}".
Arguments = <arg1> Postfix <arg2> Postfix .
Op : Mulsym | Addsym | Subsym.
Mulsym = "*".
Addsym = "+".
Subsym = "-".
Postfix_list ~ Postfix {Postfix }.
```

Use the following code for generating the stack machine code. The stack machine has only four instructions:

```
ADI for addition
MLI for multiplication
SBI for subtraction
```

The above three operations take the two topmost elements of the stack as arguments. The fourth operation, LOC, allows you to load a constant onto the stack. You implement only the code generator and not an interpreter for the stack machine.

```
// Implementation of member functions for the compiler.

void Addsym::code_gen() {
   cout << " ADI \n";} // adds two top-most elements
                       // and leaves result on stack

void Mulsym::code_gen() {
   cout << " MLI \n";}

void Subsym::code_gen() {
   cout << " SBI \n";}

void DemNumber::code_gen() {
   cout << " LOC %d\n",val ;} // loads constant on stack
```

Your compiler should produce the following output for the input

```
1
{2 3 *}
{3 4 +}
{{3 4 *} {2 3*} +}
```

generated stack machine code:

```
1
 LOC 1

{2 3 *}
 LOC 2
 LOC 3
 MLI

{3 4 +}
 LOC 3
 LOC 4
 ADI

{{3 4 *} {2 3 *} +}
 LOC 3
 LOC 4
 MLI
 LOC 2
 LOC 3
```

17.6. ASSIGNMENT 4

```
MLI
ADI
```

Turn in your compiler with the output produced for

`2 {1 3 *} {1000 {{3 4 +} 6 *} -}`

17.6.3 Part 2: Compute the Size of an Expression

Write a propagation pattern to compute the size of an expression. Use the class dictionary from Part 1. An operator has size 1, in general; however, the - operator has size 10. A number has size 5.

Your program should produce the following output for the input

```
1
{2 3 *}
{34 6 -}
```

Output:

```
1
size: 5

{2 3 *}
size: 11

{34 6 -}
size: 20
```

17.6.4 Part 3: Compute the Size of a Class Dictionary

For class dictionaries defined by the class dictionary in

$00/sample-class-libraries/c-nice-small/cd.cd

compute their size, according to the following definition:

Definition 17.1 Size of a class dictionary

We define the size of a class dictionary to be: number of construction edges + number of alternation edges * 1/4 + number of characters in all the strings (tokens).

Examples:

`A = . has size zero`

`A = <x> DemNumber "end".  has size 1 + 3 = 4 (3 is the size of the token)`

```
                        size
A = <x> B.              //1
```

```
Y : U | V.                //2 * (1/4)
U = <x> X "alternat".     //1 + 8
V = <x> X "alternat".     //1 + 8
```

has size 3 + 2 * (1/4) + 2 * 8

Your program should print the total size only.

Hint: For class Syntax_vertex use something like:

```
*wrapper* Syntax_vertex // interface: (float& size)
  *prefix*
    (@ size = size + strlen(*string); @)
```

- to compute the size of a token. Note that it is not possible to attach code to terminal classes such as DemString.

Turn in your propagation pattern and the output it produced for two class dictionaries:

1.

   $00/sample-class-libraries/c-nice-small/cd.cd

2. What is the size of the following class dictionary? Turn it in also.

```
Example = <exps> Prefix_list.
Prefix : Numerical | Compound.
Numerical = <val> DemNumber.
Compound = "{" <arguments> Arguments <op> Op "}".
Arguments = <arg1> Prefix <arg2> Prefix .
Op : Mulsym | Addsym .
Mulsym = "*".
Addsym = "+".
Prefix_list : Empty | NonEmpty.
Empty = .
NonEmpty = <car> Prefix <cdr> Prefix_list.
```

For each part where you write a C++ program using propagation patterns, turn in the following:

Your class dictionary, the files *.pp (i.e., your propagation patterns), the part of **main.C** where you call your propagation patterns, the propagation graph files in directory **inter-pps** with filenames of the form *.trv, generate.benefit, propagate.benefit, inputs, and outputs.

17.7 ASSIGNMENT 5

This assignment invites you to work with propagation patterns that contain transportation patterns.

17.7.1 Background Tasks

- Read the following man pages:

  ```
  man Universal
  man Repetition
  man Terminal
  ```

- Read Chapter 10 (Transportation Patterns).

17.7.2 Part 1: Write Your Own Propagation Pattern

For the class dictionary that you developed in Assignments 2 and 3, write a simple propagation pattern that uses a transportation directive. Test your program using the tools.

17.7.3 Part 2: Evolution of a Programming Tool

This part is about evolving a specific functionality through three different class structures. This assignment shows what happens during the maintenance phase of adaptive software.

The functionality is described below. The program has two inputs: a class dictionary and a class name. For the given class name print the list of all class definitions where the class is used on the right-hand side. Print each class definition at most once.

For example, let's assume that we have a class dictionary for class dictionaries in file cd.cd (for example, the class dictionary in Section 18.3.1, page 585) and the following class dictionary in file **demeter-input**:

```
Example = <exps> Expressions.
Expressions ~ { Expression }.
Expression : Variable | Numerical | Compound.
Variable = <name> DemIdent.
Numerical = <value> DemNumber.
Compound = "("
  <op> Operator
      <argument1> Expression
      <argument2> Expression ")".
Operator : MulSym | AddSym | SubSym.
MulSym = "*".
AddSym = "+".
SubSym = "-".
```

The program produces the following output: "Class **Expression** is used in the following class definitions:"

```
Expressions ~ { Expression }.
Compound = "("
  <op> Operator
      <argument1> Expression
      <argument2> Expression ")".
```

(Note that class **Compound** is printed only once.)

Write a program for *three* of the four following meta class dictionaries: DH-small, DH-nice, DH-full, DH-ancient defined below. (The word meta is used to distinguish between class dictionaries used as inputs and those used to define class dictionaries and to produce a C++ program. The meta class dictionaries are used in this assignment to produce a C++ program.) Eliminate the one for which it is hardest to write the program. Is it the largest one?

This means that you develop three applications with file **cd.cd** containing one of the four meta class dictionaries. You are allowed to add more parts to the classes defined by the meta class dictionaries. You may also add more classes. But the meta class dictionary you use in an application must accept the class dictionaries accepted by one of the three meta class dictionaries you select. In other words, you can only extend the meta class dictionaries but you cannot delete from them or change them radically.

This means that you write three closely related propagation patterns for the three applications. As inputs in file **demeter-input** you may choose any class dictionary that allows you to test your propagation pattern. For some of the four meta class dictionaries you can use the meta class dictionary itself in file **demeter-input**! Please note that the input format required by DH-small is unusual.

Why is it hard to program with one of the class dictionaries below? Give a one-paragraph description.

Your program should be called by

```
run demeter-input CLASSNAME
```

demeter-input contains the first input, namely a class dictionary. **CLASSNAME** contains the second input, namely a class name.

In **main.C** we suggest you call the propagation pattern with:

```
iCd_graph->print_references_to(argv[argc - 1]);
```

or

```
DemIdent* name=new DemIdent(argv[argc - 1]);
iCd_graph->print_references_to(name);
```

The file main.C (which is usually copied from main.C.sample) provides the connection between the Demeter generated code and the propagation patterns. It is common to process command line arguments in main.C as shown above.

The four meta class dictionaries are:

- DH-small

```
CdGraph = <adjs> List(Adjacency).
Adjacency =
  <source> Vertex
  <ns> Neighbors.
Neighbors : C | A *common* <constructNs> List(Vertex).
```

17.7. ASSIGNMENT 5

```
      A = ":" <alternatNs> List(Vertex).
      C = "=".
      Vertex = <v> DemIdent.
      List(S) ~ "(" {S} ")".
```

- DH-nice

```
   Cd_graph = <first> Adj <rest> Adj_list.
   Adj = <vertex> Vertex <ns> Neighbors ".".
   Neighbors: Construct | Alternat.
   Construct = "=" <c_ns> Any_vertex_list.
   Alternat = ":" <first> Vertex "|" <second> Vertex.
   Any_vertex : Labeled_vertex | Syntax_vertex.
   Syntax_vertex = <string> DemString.
   Labeled_vertex = "<" <label_name> DemIdent ">"
                        <class_name> Vertex.
   Adj_list: Empty_cd_graph | Cd_graph.
   Any_vertex_list: Empty | Nany_vertex_list.
   Nany_vertex_list =
      <first> Any_vertex <rest> Any_vertex_list.
   Empty = .
   Empty_cd_graph = .
   Vertex = <name> DemIdent.
```

- DH-full

```
   Cd_graph = < adjacencies > Nlist(Adjacency).
   Adjacency =
     < source > Vertex
     ["(" < parameters> Comma_list(Vertex) ")"]
     < ns > Neighbors "." .
   Neighbors :
     Neighbors_wc |
     Repetit_n
     *common*.
   Neighbors_wc :
     Construct_ns |
     Alternat_ns
     *common* < construct_ns > List(Any_vertex).
   Construct_ns = "=".
   Alternat_ns = ":"
     < alternat_ns > Bar_list(Term) [<common> Common].
   Common = "*common*".
   Repetit_n = "~" <sandwiched> Sandwich(Kernel).
   Kernel = [ <nonempty> Term ]
```

```
    "{" <repeated> Sandwich(Term) "}".
Any_vertex :
  Opt_labeled_term
  | Optional_term
  | Syntax_vertex.
Vertex = < vertex_name > DemIdent.
Syntax_vertex :
  Regular_syntax
  | Print_command.
Print_command :
  Print_indent | Print_unindent | Print_skip | Print_space *common*.
  Print_indent = "+" .
  Print_unindent = "-" .
  Print_skip = "*l" .
  Print_space = "*s" .
Regular_syntax  = < string > DemString .
Opt_labeled_term :
  Labeled
  | Regular
     *common* <vertex> Term.
Regular = .
Labeled = "<" < label_name > DemIdent ">" .
Term :
  Normal
  *common* <vertex> Vertex
  ["@" <module_name> Module_name]
  ["(" <actual_parameters> Comma_list(Term) ")" ].
Module_name = <module_name> DemIdent.
Normal = .
Optional_term = "[" <opt> Sandwich(Opt_labeled_term) "]".
// parameterized classes
List(S) ~ {S}.
Nlist(S) ~ S {S}.
Bar_list(S) ~ S {"|" S}.
Comma_list(S) ~ S {"," S}.
Sandwich(S) =
  <first> List(Syntax_vertex) <inner> S
  <second> List(Syntax_vertex).
```

- DH-ancient

```
Start = Grammar.
Grammar ~ {Rule}.
Rule = <ruleName> DemIdent Body ".".
Body : Construct | Alternat | Repetit.
```

```
Construct = "=" List(AnySymbol).
Alternat = ":" BarList(DemIdent).
SandwichedSymbol = <first> AuxList Symbol <second> AuxList.
Repetit = "~" <first> AuxList [ <nonempty> DemIdent ]
               "{" SandwichedSymbol "}" <second> AuxList.
AnySymbol : Symbol | OptSymbol | Aux.
Symbol = [ "<" <labelName> DemIdent ">" ] <symbolName> DemIdent.
OptSymbol = "[" SandwichedSymbol "]".
Aux : Syntax.
Syntax = DemString.
AuxList ~ { Aux }.

List(S) ~ {S}.
BarList(S) ~ S { "|" S}.
```

For each part where you write a C++ program using propagation patterns, turn in: your class dictionary, the files *.pp (i.e., your propagation patterns), the part of main.C where you call your propagation patterns, the propagation graph files in inter-pps (they are of the form *.trv), the transportation graph files inter-pps (they are of the form *.trn), generate.benefit, propagate.benefit, inputs, and outputs.

In this assignment you have written three C++ programs c1, c2, and c3 (those are the *-DEM.C files produced by the propagation pattern compiler) and three propagation pattern programs p1, p2, and p3 (those are your *.pp files).

Use a differential file comparator (such as diff; use man diff) to compare p1, p2 and p1, p3 and p2, p3. Do the same for the C++ programs as follows: c1, c2 and c1, c3 and c2, c3. Where are the differences bigger? Between the C++ programs or the propagation patterns? Write one paragraph of explanation and turn it in.

17.8 LEARNING C++ WITH DEMETER

The Demeter Tools/C++ can be used in a variety of different ways to learn about object-oriented design and C++.

17.8.1 Class Library Generator

This was the primary application of Demeter a few years ago. The idea is to create a class dictionary and to generate the C++ class definitions with Demeter. The functionality is implemented by manually writing the C++ member functions.

For beginning C++ programmers, the instructor can create the class dictionaries and generate an environment and create input sentences for testing. The students can first focus on the class dictionary notation and C++ statements appearing in member functions. The instructor initially should use only the basic features of class dictionaries.

17.8.2 Member Function Skeleton Generator

The next level of use of Demeter is not only to generate the class definitions in C++ but also to produce member function skeletons. The skeletons are produced by the instructor by writing propagation patterns without wrappers. It is the task of the C++ programmers to edit the C++ member functions manually to make them do the right tasks. This approach has the advantage that students learn to think in terms of traversal programs early. They also can complete interesting projects in a reasonable amount of time. The instructor has to remove the *.pp files after the generation of the skeletons. Then the regular **make** command (or **demeter** command) can be used to compile the environments with the C++ member functions completed by the student.

17.8.3 Simulating the Demeter Library

This is about reinventing the Demeter run-time library. The instructor produces a class dictionary using only construction and alternation classes. Objects are created by using the function g_code(). The member functions are very simple and don't call any generic functions starting with **g_**. The students are given all the files in /notmod/sun4 (or whatever the architecture is) and are asked to implement enough of the generic library to make the programs run. Compilation is done with make.

Chapter 18

Glossary

18.1 DEFINITIONS

1. **Law of Demeter**

   A style rule for object-oriented design and programming that suggests that a method should make only minimal assumptions about other classes. The rule essentially requires that a method attached to class A should use only the interface of the immediate part classes of A (both computed and stored), and of argument classes of the method, including A. Limits the set of clients of a class, in other words; "a method should not talk to strangers."

2. **LL(1) conditions (single inheritance class dictionary)**

   A class dictionary that satisfies the LL(1) conditions is an example of a class dictionary that is not ambiguous. Essentially, a class dictionary is LL(1) if all sentences are uniquely readable in the sense that the first sets of the alternatives of all alternation classes are pair-wise disjoint and there is no ambiguity with respect to alternatives whose first set is empty.

3. **Transportation Entry Restriction**

   A restriction about how a transportation pattern may be customized. No vertices of a transportation graph, except its source vertices, can have incoming nontransportation edges.

4. **Transportation Recursion Restriction**

   A restriction about how a transportation pattern may be customized: A source vertex of the transportation graph cannot have incoming transportation edges.

5. **abstract class**

   A class that cannot be used directly for object creation. Concrete subclasses of the abstract class are used for object creation. An object may belong to an abstract class, although it can never be an instance of that class.

6. **adaptive program**

    A program written in terms of loosely coupled contexts; for example, structure and behavior. The coupling is done through succinct subgraph specifications.

7. **adaptive programming principle**

    A program should be designed so that the interfaces of objects can be changed within certain constraints without affecting the program *at all*.

8. **at-least-one alternative rule**

    A rule for class dictionary graphs. Every alternation vertex in a class dictionary graph must have at least one outgoing alternation edge.

9. **alternation edge**

    An edge between an alternation vertex and a construction or alternation vertex. Describes an is-a relationship. Graphical representation is by a double-shafted arrow. Textual representation separates alternatives by "|".

10. **alternation vertex**

    A vertex in a class dictionary. Defines an abstract class that cannot be used to create objects. Graphical representation is by a hexagon. Textual representation includes ":" after class name. Outgoing alternation edges are given first, seperated by *common* from the outgoing construction edges.

11. **alternation-reachable**

    A vertex A is alternation-reachable from a vertex B, if A can be reached from B by following alternation edges only.

12. **ambiguous class dictionary**

    A class dictionary is ambiguous if there exist two distinct objects that map to the same sentence when they are printed.

13. **associated**

    The vertices (classes) associated with a vertex (class) v are the construction classes reachable from v by following only alternation edges.

14. **attribute**

    A part of an object is called an attribute if the type of the part is a terminal class such as DemIdent, DemNumber.

15. **bypassing clause**

    A constraint in a propagation directive that forces a set of edges to be bypassed.

16. **class-valued variable**

    A variable in an adaptive program that will be mapped to a class when the adaptive program is customized.

18.1. DEFINITIONS

17. **class dictionary**

    A graph with four kinds of vertices and five kinds of edges. The four vertex kinds are: construction, alternation, repetition, and syntax. The five kinds of edges are: construction, alternation, repetition, inheritance, and syntax.

    There are three kinds of class dictionaries: semi-class dictionary graphs, class dictionary graphs, and class dictionaries.

    The set of all semi-class dictionary graphs includes the set of all class dictionary graphs. The set of all class dictionaries includes all class dictionary graphs.

    The semi-class dictionary graphs and class dictionary graphs don't have syntax edges and vertices.

    A selector to select a program defined by propagation patterns. A collection of class definitions and simultaneously a language definition.

    A class dictionary has both a graphical and textual representation.

18. **class dictionary graph**

    A class dictionary without syntax information. A class dictionary graph consists of three kinds of classes: construction, alternation, and repetition, and four kinds of edges: construction, alternation, repetition, and inheritance.

    A group of collaborating classes and their basic relations. Serves as customizer for propagation patterns and as a specification of an application-specific set of classes.

    Satisfies unique label rule and cycle-free alternation rule. Every alternation vertex must have at least one outgoing alternation edge. Satisfies edge/vertex restrictions.

19. **class dictionary graph slice**

    A subgraph of a class dictionary that defines a subset of the objects.

20. **client of a class**

    A class or method that invokes an operation of the class.

21. **common parts**

    An alternation class has common parts if and only if it has outgoing construction edges. The common parts are common to all alternatives.

22. **compatible**

    This term is overloaded.

    A propagation directive $d = (F, c, T)$ is **compatible** with a semi-class dictionary graph S if the following conditions hold:

    - All images of source, target, and via class-valued variables are in S.
    - c is compatible with S; that is, the edge pattern of each bypassing or through clause of c matches some edge in S.

- For all images v of F in S and all images w of T in S there exists at least one knowledge path in S satisfying c.

A propagation directive expression d is **compatible** with a semi-class dictionary graph S, if each propagation directive appearing in d is compatible with d and $propagate(d_1, S)$ is not the empty subgraph for any of the subdirectives d_1 of d.

A propagation pattern p is **compatible** with a semi-class dictionary graph S, if each propagation directive expression of p is compatible with S, if all edge patterns appearing in edge wrappers are compatible with S, and if the images of all class-valued variables and relation-valued variables appearing in p are in S.

23. **component**

    A component encapsulates a group of collaborating propagation patterns. It contains sample class dictionary graphs that serve as typical customizers. It contains "meta" variable declarations for class-valued, relation-valued, and graph-valued variables. The graph-valued variables are defined by propagation directives.

24. **concrete class**

    A class that may be used by the user to create objects. It may be either a construction, repetition, or terminal class.

25. **constraint**

    A propagation directive contains a constraint that constrains the paths from the source to the target vertices.

26. **construction edge**

    An edge between a construction or alternation vertex and another vertex. Describes a has-a, knows-about, or part-of relationship. Has a label that names the part. Textual representation encloses the label between "<" and ">".

27. **construction vertex**

    A vertex in a class dictionary. Defines a concrete class that can have instances but cannot have subclasses. Has named parts and is used to *construct* objects in terms of a fixed number of part objects. Graphical representation is by a rectangle. Textual representation includes "=" after class name.

28. **contributing vertex**

    An alternation vertex is contributing if it has at least one outgoing construction or inheritance edge. (Contributing means contributing at least one part, directly or indirectly.)

29. **customizer**

    A class dictionary (or a set of equivalent objects).

18.1. DEFINITIONS

30. **cycle-free alternation rule**

    No cyclic alternation paths containing one or more edges are allowed in class dictionary graphs.

    An alternation path is a consecutive sequence of alternation edges. A path is cyclic if it starts at some vertex and returns to the same vertex.

31. **delayed binding rule (single inheritance class dictionary)**

    A restriction on the class dictionaries that may be used to customize a propagation pattern. Needed to guarantee proper traversal semantics.

    A rule for customizing class dictionaries and the corresponding propagation graphs. If a propagation graph contains an alternation vertex A and a vertex B, and B is alternation-reachable from A in the class dictionary and A is used in the propagation graph, then B has to be alternation-reachable from A in the propagation graph also. A vertex is *used* in the propagation graph if it is a source vertex of the propagation graph or has at least one incoming construction or alternation edge in the propagation graph.

    For flat class dictionaries, the rule is simpler and called subclass-invariance: Any two vertices in the propagation graph have an alternation path between them if they have one in the class dictionary.

32. **dependency metric**

    A function with two arguments that measures how dependent a propagation directive is on a semi-class dictionary graph.

33. **design pattern**

    A solution to a problem in a context.

34. **edge pattern**

    A specification of a set of edges using the wild card symbol *. For example, -> A,*,B is an edge pattern that defines the set of construction edges from A to B with any label.

35. **edge/vertex restrictions**

    Restrictions that limit the possible edges in a class dictionary, class dictionary graph or semi-class dictionary graph. For example, an alternation edge may not start from a construction vertex.

36. **edge wrapper**

    A wrapper defined for a construction, repetition, or inheritance edge. Consists of a prefix or suffix wrapper or both. Called in the source class of the edge.

37. **first set**

    The first set of a vertex of a class dictionary is the set of all tokens that may be the first token in a sentence belonging to the language of the vertex.

38. **flat class dictionary**

    A class dictionary without common parts. All parts have been flattened to construction classes.

39. **follow set**

    The follow set of a vertex V of a class dictionary with respect to a start vertex S is the set of all tokens that may follow a sentence of the language of V embedded in a sentence of S.

40. **framework**

    A class library that will be adapted to specific needs. The framework may be incomplete. The documentation of the framework explains how the framework may be completed. For a discussion of frameworks and patterns, see [GHJV95].

41. **from clause**

    A constraint in a propagation directive that specifies a set of vertices from which the knowledge paths start.

42. **graph**

    A structure with vertices and edges.

43. **incremental inheritance**

    The code in the superclass is called in addition to the code in the subclass.

44. **incremental inheritance rule**

    A restriction on the class dictionaries that may be used to customize a propagation pattern. Needed to guarantee proper traversal semantics.

    A rule for propagation graphs. If a propagation graph contains an alternation vertex A with an outgoing alternation edge from A to B, and if the alternation vertex A has outgoing construction or inheritance edges, then the propagation graph also contains the inheritance edge from B to A.

45. **inductive**

    A semi-class dictionary graph or class dictionary is inductive if every vertex in the graph is inductive. A vertex is inductive if a cycle-free class dictionary slice is anchored at the vertex.

46. **information loss (inconsistency)**

    A propagation directive has **information loss** with respect to a class dictionary graph if the propagation graph contains a completed knowledge path that does not satisfy the propagation directive. A path from a source to a target is completed if every used alternation vertex on the path has an outgoing alternation edge. A path is completed by adding alternation and inheritance edges.

    For a simpler definition for flat class dictionary graphs, see Chapter 15.

18.1. DEFINITIONS

47. **inheritance edge**

    An edge from a construction or alternation vertex to an alternation vertex. Describes from where a class inherits.

48. **instance**

    An object is an instance of a class v if it has been created by a constructor of the class. v must be an instantiable class; that is, a construction, repetition, or terminal class.

    An instance of a class satisfies all the conditions imposed by the class dictionary for that class.

49. **interface**

    A listing of the operations that an object or class provides. This includes the signatures of the operations.

50. **join**

    An operation defined for propagation graphs and propagation directives. Joins two propagation graphs together provided the targets of the first are equal to the sources of the second.

51. **knowledge path**

    A path in a class dictionary graph that satisfies the restriction that a sequence of inheritance edges is eventually followed by a construction edge and never by an alternation edge.

52. **language**

    The language of a class dictionary is the set of printed objects defined by the class dictionary.

53. **match**

    An edge pattern matches an edge in a semi-class dictionary graph if there is a mapping of the class-valued variables and relation-valued variables, and wildcard symbols to vertices and construction edge names in the semi-class dictionary graph, so that the pattern and the edge coincide.

54. **merge**

    An operation defined for propagation graphs and propagation directives. Merges two propagation graphs together provided certain conditions apply.

55. **method**

    An implementation of an operation. Code that may be executed to perform a requested service.

56. **method resolution**

    The selection of the method to perform a requested operation.

57. **multiple inheritance**

    A class dictionary has multiple inheritance if there exists a vertex that has two outgoing inheritance edges.

58. **object**

    An object with respect to a class dictionary is an object that has exactly the parts described by the class dictionary. The parts contain only objects allowed by the class dictionary. An object of a vertex (class) V is an instance of a vertex (class) associated with v. An instance of a vertex (class) v is an object created with a constructor of v. This requires that v is an instantiable class.

    A combination of state and a set of methods that explicitly embodies an abstraction characterized by the behavior of relevant requests.

59. **object creation**

    An event that causes the existence of an object that is distinct from any other objects.

60. **object destruction**

    An event that causes an object to cease to exist.

61. **object-equivalent**

    Two class dictionaries are object-equivalent if they define the same set of objects.

62. **object reference**

    A value that unambiguously identifies an object. Object references are never reused to identify another object.

63. **operation**

    A service that can be requested. An operation has an associated signature, which may restrict which actual parameters are valid.

64. **operation name**

    A name used in a request to identify an operation.

65. **optional construction edge**

    An edge that describes an optional part. Graphically represented by a dashed edge. Textual representation uses [and].

66. **optional repetition edge**

    An edge that indicates that a list may contain zero or more parts. Graphically represented by a dashed edge. Textual representation uses R ~ {S}.

67. **overriding inheritance**

    The code in the subclass overrides the code in the superclass.

18.1. DEFINITIONS

68. **parameter passing mode**

    Describes the direction of information flow for an operation parameter. The parameter passing modes are *in*, *out*, and *inout*.

69. **parameterized class**

    A parameterized class with one argument is defined by a class definition of the form

    ```
    A(S) = ...
    A(S) ~ ...
    A(S) : ...
    ```

    S is a formal parameter that is substituted by a class when the parameterized class is used. For example,

    ```
    B = <a> A(DemIdent) <b> A(DemReal).
    ```

    is a class that uses the parameterized class A twice. Class B will be expanded into

    ```
    B = <a> DemIdent_A <b> DemReal_A.
    ```

    (Several parameters may be used.)

70. **parsing a sentence**

    Scanning followed by syntax analysis and object creation. The parser consumes the sequence of tokens delivered by the scanner, checks for syntactic correctness with respect to the class dictionary, and builds the object recursively.

71. **part**

    A relationship between two classes. Implies a relationship between objects of those classes.

    A named part a is made visible to clients as a pair of operations: get_a and set_a. Read-only parts generate a get operation only. Named parts are represented by construction edges. Indexed parts are represented by repetition edges.

72. **persistent object**

    An object that can survive the process or thread that created it. A persistent object exists until it is explicitly deleted.

73. **printing an object**

    Retrieve the class definition of the object's class and recursively print the object with the tokens prescribed by the class dictionary.

74. **prefix wrapper**

    A code fragment belonging to a wrapper. Added at the beginning of the method for a vertex wrapper and after the edge traversal for an edge wrapper.

75. **propagate**

    An operator that takes a propagation directive and a semi-class dictionary graph and produces a propagation graph. The propagation graph itself is also a semi-class dictionary graph.

76. **propagation directive (= directive)**

    A succinct specification of a subgraph of a class dictionary using from, to, via, by-passing, and through clauses. The subgraph is used for purposes such as traversal or transportation.

77. **propagation directive expression (= directive expression)**

    An expression built from propagation directives of the form (F, c, T) and the operators *merge*, *join*, and *restrict*.

78. **propagation graph**

    A semi-class dictionary graph. The result of applying a propagation directive to a class dictionary. A propagation graph has a specific use as a traversal graph or as a transportation graph.

79. **propagation vertex**

    A propagation vertex of a propagation graph is either a construction vertex or a target vertex in the propagation graph. A target vertex may be an alternation vertex.

80. **propagation object**

    A propagation object of a propagation graph is an object of a propagation vertex of the propagation graph.

81. **propagation pattern**

    Specifies methods for a class dictionary. All the methods have the same name. Written in terms of class-valued and relation-valued variables. Consists of a propagation directive that specifies a traversal graph, wrappers, and transportation patterns. A propagation pattern is customized to an object-oriented program by a class dictionary.

82. **referential integrity**

    The property ensuring that an object reference that exists in the state associated with an object reliably identifies a single object.

83. **relation-valued variable**

    A variable in an adaptive program that will be mapped to a construction edge label when the adaptive program is customized.

84. **repetition edge**

    An edge between a repetition vertex and another vertex. Describes a has-a, knows-about, or part-of relationship. Textual representation encloses target vertex between "{" and "}".

18.1. DEFINITIONS

85. **repetition vertex**

    A vertex in a class dictionary. Defines a collection class, such as a list. A list is the only possibility in the current implementation. Defines a concrete class which can have instances but cannot have subclasses. Has indexed parts. Graphical representation is by an overlayed hexagon and rectangle. Textual representation includes "~" after class name.

86. **request**

    A function call in C++. Calls an operation that will use method resolution to find the appropriate method.

87. **restrict**

    An operator that takes two propagation directives and returns a new propagation directive which is the restriction of the first by the second.

    A client issues a request to cause a service to be performed. A request consists of an operation and zero or more actual parameters.

88. **satisfy**

    This term is used in several contexts, for example:

    - knowledge paths
        - A knowledge path p of a semi-class dictionary graph S satisfies a bypassing clause e if p does not contain any edge in S that matches e.
        - A knowledge path p of a semi-class dictionary graph S satisfies a through clause e if p contains at least one edge in S that matches e.
        - A knowledge path p of a semi-class dictionary graph S satisfies a constraint c if p satisfies all bypassing and through clauses in c.
    - class dictionary graphs

        A class dictionary graph satisfies the edge/vertex restrictions and the unique label, cycle-free alternation, and at-least-one alternative rules.

89. **scanning a sentence**

    Translating a sequence of characters into a sequence of terminals defined by a class dictionary. The terminals correspond to the syntax vertices (tokens) and the terminals defined by terminal vertices in the class dictionary.

90. **semi-class dictionary graph**

    A class dictionary graph where inheritance edges and alternation edges may be used independently. An alternation vertex may have zero outgoing alternation edges.

91. **sentence**

    A sequence of terminals. A sentence is a robust object description that can be used with many different class dictionaries. A parser translates a sentence into an object.

92. shortcut violation

A customizer causes a shortcut violation if the propagation graph contains more paths than allowed by the propagation directive. The propagation directive must contain the join, via, or through operator. The shortcut violation is a special kind of inconsistency.

93. signature

Defines the parameters of a given operation including their number order, data types, and passing mode, and the results if any.

94. signature extension

An implementation technique for transportation patterns.

95. single inheritance

A class dictionary is single inheritance if every vertex has at most one outgoing inheritance edge.

96. source vertex

A propagation graph has a set of source vertices. A propagation directive has a set of source vertices.

97. state

The time varying properties of an object that affect that object's behavior.

98. suffix wrapper

A code fragment belonging to a wrapper. Added at the end of the method for a vertex wrapper and after the edge traversal for an edge wrapper.

99. synchronous request

A request where the client pauses to wait for completion of the request.

100. syntax edge

An edge from a construction, alternation, or repetition vertex to a syntax vertex. Indicates the position of the syntax vertex (token).

101. syntax vertex

A vertex representing a token.

102. target vertex

A propagation graph has a set of target vertices. A propagation directive has an optional set of target vertices.

103. terminal

A sequence of characters that form a symbol belonging to the alphabet of a language. We distingiush between terminals with a value and terminals without a value. Terminals with a value represent objects of terminal classes. Terminals without a value are called tokens.

18.1. DEFINITIONS

104. **terminal vertex**

    A vertex describing a set of similar terminals. Examples are: DemIdent (for identifiers), DemNumber (for integers), DemText (for text), DemString (for strings), DemReal (for real numbers).

105. **through clause**

    A constraint in a propagation directive that forces at least one of a set of edges to be included.

106. **to clause**

    A constraint in a propagation directive that forces knowledge paths to go to a set of vertices.

107. **to-stop clause**

    A constraint in a propagation directive that forces knowledge paths to go to a set of vertices without leaving them again.

108. **token**

    A sequence of characters viewed as a "unit," such as `repeat` or `*from*`. Overloaded: in a sentence, a token is a terminal without a value and in a class dictionary, a token is a string denoting concrete syntax.

109. **transportation graph**

    A propagation graph used for transportation.

110. **transportation patterns**

    Specifies which objects are transported along which graphs. Consists of parameter declarations, a propagation directive that specifies a transportation graph, updating statements for initializing and updating parameters and wrappers that use the parameters and add to the traversal code.

111. **traversal graph**

    A propagation graph used for traversal.

112. **unique label rule**

    For all vertices V, the labels of construction edges reachable from V by following zero or more alternation edges in reverse, must be unique.

    This means that the labels of the parts of a vertex, both immediate as well as inherited parts, must be unique.

113. **use case**

    Represents interactions between a user and an object system. Used for defining user requirements.

114. **used vertex**

    A vertex on a knowledge path from a source to a target vertex is used if it has incoming construction or alternation edges or if it is a source vertex.

115. **value**

    Any entity that may be a possible actual parameter in a request. Values that serve to identify objects are called object references.

116. **vertex**

    A node in a graph.

117. **vertex wrapper**

    A wrapper defined for a construction, repetition, or alternation class.

118. **via clause**

    A constraint in a propagation directive that forces a set of vertices to be included.

119. **wrapper**

    Consists of a prefix and/or suffix wrapper. A prefix or suffix wrapper is a code fragment. Adds to the traversal code defined by a propagation directive. The wrappers add code by wrapping a prefix and/or a suffix code fragment around the traversal code. There are two kinds of wrappers: edge wrappers and vertex wrappers.

120. **zigzag violation**

    A customizer causes a zigzag violation if the propagation graph contains more paths than allowed by the propagation directive. The propagation directive must contain the merge operator. The zigzag violation is a special kind of inconsistency.

18.2 QUICK REFERENCE GUIDE WITH SYNTAX SUMMARY

In Fig. A.1, page 589, you find the URLs for the User's Guide and Laboratory Guide and the Demeter FAQ. We give a Quick Reference Guide to the Demeter Tools/C++ next.

```
*****************************************
DEMETER TOOLS/C++ Quick Reference Guide
*****************************************
In file $00/doc/Demeter-Tools-C++Quick-Reference

(version 3, Winter 1995)

A tool suite for adaptive object-oriented
application development in C++.

*** CONCEPTS

class dictionary
```

18.2. QUICK REFERENCE GUIDE WITH SYNTAX SUMMARY

Describes the inheritance and the
binary relation structure of your application. Serves as a lattice
to propagate the functionality. (should reside in file cd.cd)

propagation pattern
Describes how the functionality is distributed over the classes.
(should always reside in files with names of the form *.pp)

*** GETTING HELP

man demeter
man TOOL-NAME

As a last resort (after checking User's Guide and FAQ), send e-mail to

demeter@ccs.neu.edu

*** SIMPLEST TOOL USE

Put your class dictionary into file
cd.cd

Put your propagation patterns into files of the form
*.pp

Put your input objects into file
demeter-input

Then call the commands
demeter
cp main.C.sample main.C

Edit main.C near end where you call your propagation patterns.

Then call again
demeter

You execute your program with

run

Whenever you change something, you call again
demeter

*** DESIGN TOOLS

sem-check -n cd.cd
Checks the class dictionary graph cd.cd.

sem-check cd.cd
Checks the class dictionary cd.cd, including the LL(1) conditions.

xcddraw
To develop class dictionaries graphically.

cd-numbered-xref
To produce a class dictionary cross reference listing.

*** PROGRAMMING TOOLS

demeter

Makes Demeter act like a compiler. Put class dictionary in cd.cd, the main program in main.C and the propagation patterns in *.pp files and call demeter.
The run command allows you to run your program.

gen-imake (imake-sample is a synonym)
Creates a sample Imakefile with default settings.

gen-make (dmkmf is a synonym)
Creates a corresponding Makefile with the Demeter "knowledge".

make
The Demeter super command with one goal: to create a compiled class library.

run ...
To run the application.

*** TYPICAL TOOL USE

EDIT cd.cd
sem-check cd.cd
gen-imake
gen-make

18.2. QUICK REFERENCE GUIDE WITH SYNTAX SUMMARY

```
make
run                       - empty class library works
cp main.C.sample main.C
EDIT demeter-input
make
run demeter-input         - class library self-test works!!
EDIT demeter-input
EDIT *.pp                 - add functionality
EDIT main.C               - call functionality
make                      - spread the functions and compile
run demeter-input         - do you get the right output?

make clobber              - when software is not maintained
                            for an extended period.
```

*** REGENERATION

```
make
```

*** SAMPLE CLASS LIBRARIES

See directory $00/sample-class-libraries.
Class libraries are in subdirectories c-*/generated

*** DEMO

See directory $00/demo
File how-to-use tells you how to run the demo.

*** SYNTAX (in simplified form, reflecting typical use)

// is the comment character

Propagation directives

```
// exactly one *from*
*from* {A1, A2, ...}
    // zero or one *through*
    *through*  // one or more edge patterns, separated by ","
       -> V,m,W ,    // construction edge with label m
       => V,W   ,    // alternation edge
```

```
            :> V,W    ,     // inheritance edge
            ~> V,W          // repetition edge
    // zero or one *bypassing*
       *bypassing*  // one or more edge patterns, separated by ","
            -> V,m,W ,      // construction edge with label m
            => V,W   ,      // alternation edge
            :> V,W   ,      // inheritance edge
            ~> V,W          // repetition edge
// zero or more *via*
*via* {K1, K2, ...}
    ... // zero or one *through* and/or zero or one *bypassing*
*via* {S1, S2, ...}
    ... // zero or one *through* and/or zero or one *bypassing*
//zero or one *to*
*to* {Z1, Z2, ...}
```

Instead of V, W, or m the wildcard symbol "*" may be used.

// *merge* and *join*

```
*join* (
  *merge* (
     *from* A *via* B *to* E,   // any *from* ... *to*
     *from* A *via* C *to* E),  // any *from* ... *to*
  *from* E *to* K)              // any *from* ... *to*
```

Wrappers

Edge

```
*wrapper*
  // edge pattern
  -> *,m,*
  // zero or one
  *prefix* (@ ... @)
  // zero or one
  *suffix* (@ ... @)
```

Vertex

```
*wrapper*
  // class-valued variables, one or more
  {A,B,C}
```

18.2. QUICK REFERENCE GUIDE WITH SYNTAX SUMMARY

```
  // zero or one
  *prefix* (@ ... @)
  // zero or one
  *suffix* (@ ... @)
```

Transportation pattern

```
*carry*
  // transported variables
  // broadcasting
  *in* P* p
    = (@ ... @)  // optional, for initialization
  , // condensing
  *out* Q* q
    = (@ ... @)  // optional, for initialization
  , // broadcasting and condensing
  *inout* R* r
    = (@ ... @)  // optional, for initialization
  *along*
    // propagation directive, see above
    // defines transportation graph
  *at* A // update transported variable
      p = (@ ... @)
  *at* B // update transported variables
      q = (@ ... @), r = (@ ... @)
  // one or more wrappers, see above
    ...
// *end*
```

Propagation patterns

```
*operation*
  //signature
  void f(*in* B* b, *out* C* c)
  *traverse*
  // propagation directive, see above
    ...
  // zero or more transportation patterns, see above

  // zero or more wrappers, see above
```

Class dictionary graphs

```
// zero or more class definitions
// first class is start class
//    ordering of remaining class definitions is irrelevant
//    for single-inheritance class dictionary

// construction class
Meal =
// zero or more parts
// required part, construction edge
  <appetizer> Appetizer
// required part, construction edge
  <entree> Entree
// optional part, optional construction edge
  [<dessert> Dessert].

// alternation class
Dessert :
// alternatives, alternation edges, one or more
  ApplePie | IceCream
// separator
  *common*
// common parts, construction edges, zero or more
  <w> WhippedCream.

// repetition class
Banquet ~
// repetition edge
  Meal {Meal}.

Shrimps ~
// optional repetition edge
  {Shrimp}.

// Parameterized classes

Sandwich(S) = <first> BreadSlice <sandwiched> S <second> BreadSlice.
RecursiveList(S) : Empty(S) | NonEmpty(S).
List(S) ~ S {S}.

// Use of parameterized classes

Meat = .
Sandwiches = <s> RecursiveList(Sandwich(Meat)).
```

```
Class dictionaries
```

Syntax may optionally appear around parts.

```
A = "to-introduce" <b> B "to-separate" <c> C "to-terminate".

B : C | D
  *common*
    "to-continue" <b> B "to-separate" <c> C "to-terminate".

CommaList(S) ~
  "to-start-collection" S
  {"to-separate-collection-elements" S}
  "to-end-collection".

StatementList ~
  "begin" Statement {";" Statement} "end".

FruitList ~
  "(" {Fruit} ")".
```

18.3 SYNTAX DEFINITIONS

We provide the class dictionary which defines the syntax of class dictionaries. It is used by the Demeter Tools/C++. The User's Guide contains syntax definitions using a more standard syntax.

18.3.1 Class Dictionary Syntax

```
 1  Cd_graph =
 2    < adjacencies > Nlist(Adjacency)
 3    ["*terminal_sets*" <terminal_sets> Comma_list(Vertex) "."].
 4  Adjacency =
 5    < source > Vertex
 6    ["(" < parameters> Comma_list(Vertex) ")"]
 7    < ns > Neighbors
 8    "." .
 9  Neighbors :
10    Neighbors_wc |
11    Repetit_n
12    *common*.
13  Neighbors_wc :
14    Construct_ns |
15    Alternat_ns
16    *common* < construct_ns > List(Any_vertex).
```

```
17  Construct_ns = "=".
18  Alternat_ns = ":"
19    < alternat_ns > Bar_list(Term)
20    [<common> Common].
21  Common = "*common*".
22  Repetit_n = "~" <sandwiched> Sandwich(Kernel).
23  Kernel = [ <nonempty> Term ]
24    "{" <repeated> Sandwich(Term) "}".
25  Any_vertex :
26    Opt_labeled_term
27    | Optional_term
28    | Syntax_vertex
29    | Inherit_term.
30  Vertex = < vertex_name > DemIdent .
31  Syntax_vertex :
32    Regular_syntax
33    | Print_command
34    *common*.
35  Regular_syntax  = < string > DemString .
36  Print_command :
37    Print_indent | Print_unindent | Print_skip | Print_space.
38  Print_indent = "+" .
39  Print_unindent = "-" .
40  Print_skip = "*l" .
41  Print_space = "*s" .
42  Opt_labeled_term :
43    Labeled
44    | Regular
45      *common*  [StaticSpec] [AccessorSpec] <vertex> Term.
46
47  StaticSpec = "*static*" .
48  AccessorSpec : ReadOnlyAcc | PrivateAcc *common* .
49  ReadOnlyAcc = "*read-only*" .
50  PrivateAcc = "*private*" .
51
52  Regular = .
53  Labeled = "<" < label_name > DemIdent ">" .
54  Inherit_term = "*inherit*" <inherited> Comma_list(Term).
55
56
57  Term : Normal | CppTerm *common* <vertex> Vertex
58    <moduleRef> TermRef
59    ["(" <actual_parameters> Comma_list(Term) ")" ].
60
61  CppTerm = "$" .
```

18.3. SYNTAX DEFINITIONS

```
62
63   Normal = .
64
65   TermRef : LocalRef | ModuleRef.
66
67   ModuleRef : CompRef | LibRef *common* <moduleName> DemIdent.
68
69   LocalRef = .
70   CompRef = "@".
71   LibRef  = "@@".
72
73   Optional_term = "[" <opt> Sandwich(Opt_labeled_term) "]".
74
75   // Parameterized classes
76   List(S)  ~ {S}.
77   Nlist(S) ~ S {S}.
78   Bar_list(S)  ~ S {"|" S}.
79   Comma_list(S) ~ S {"," S}.
80   Sandwich(S) =
81     <first> List(Syntax_vertex) <inner> S
82     <second> List(Syntax_vertex)
83     .
```

```
AccessorSpec       :48    45
Adjacency          :4     2
Alternat_ns        :18    15
Any_vertex         :25    16
Bar_list           :78    19
Cd_graph           :1
Comma_list         :79    3     6    54   59
Common    :21      20
CompRef            :70    67
Construct_ns       :17    14
CppTerm            :61    57
Inherit_term       :54    29
Kernel    :23      22
Labeled            :53    43
LibRef    :71      67
List      :76      16    81    82
LocalRef           :69    65
ModuleRef          :67    65
Neighbors          :9     7
Neighbors_wc       :13    10
Nlist     :77      2
Normal    :63      57
Opt_labeled_term         :42    26    73
```

```
Optional_term    :73    27
Print_command    :36    33
Print_indent     :38    37
Print_skip       :40    37
Print_space      :41    37
Print_unindent   :39    37
PrivateAcc       :50    48
ReadOnlyAcc      :49    48
Regular          :52    44
Regular_syntax   :35    32
Repetit_n        :22    11
Sandwich         :80    22    24    73
StaticSpec       :47    45
Syntax_vertex    :31    28    81    82
Term      :57    19      23    24    45    54    59
TermRef          :65    58
Vertex    :30    3       5     6     57
```

18.4 BIBLIOGRAPHIC REMARKS

- Terminology: We adopt some of the terminology of the object model developed by the Object Management Group [Gro91]. It serves the purpose well since their model is also programming language independent.

Appendix A

Electronic Access

The Demeter software, documentation, and related course material are available on the World-Wide Web as shown by the uniform resource locators (URLs) in Fig. A.1. Readers

---

Pointers to object code for various architectures

       http://www.ccs.neu.edu/research/demeter/DemeterTools.txt

Frequently Asked Questions

       http://www.ccs.neu.edu/research/demeter/Demeter-FAQ

User's Guide

       http://www.ccs.neu.edu/research/demeter/docs/u-guide.ps

Laboratory Guide

       http://www.ccs.neu.edu/research/demeter/docs/l-guide.ps

Course material (OO points to this directory)

       http://www.ccs.neu.edu/research/demeter/course

Further information is at the Demeter Home Page

       http://www.ccs.neu.edu/research/demeter

Figure A.1: Access to software, documentation, and course material

---

who do not have access to the world-wide web can download the information by **ftp**. Directory

       ftp://ftp.ccs.neu.edu/pub/research/demeter/www-mirror

contains a mirror of DemeterTools.txt, Demeter-FAQ, u-guide.ps, l-guide.ps, and directory course. Use the protocol:

```
% ftp ftp.ccs.neu.edu
Name ( ... ): ftp
Password: your-email-address
```

and go to pub/research/demeter/www-mirror to retrieve the files. OO is a variable used in the book. It points to the course directory (see Fig. A.1).

Recent papers on adaptive software are available from URL:

ftp://ftp.ccs.neu.edu/pub/people/lieber

Published papers on adaptive software are available from URL:

ftp://ftp.ccs.neu.edu/pub/research/demeter

and its subdirectories (e.g., documents/papers).

Information about adaptive software is also available by e-mail (see Fig. A.2). You can subscribe by e-mail to a mailing list on adaptive software and you will be informed about new developments. You may also direct your individual questions to the Demeter Research Group at Northeastern University.

E-mail questions and bug reports to

```
demeter@ccs.neu.edu
```

To get regular updates on adaptive software (both regarding tool developments and theoretical advances), send the message with body

```
subscribe adaptive
```

to

```
majordomo@ccs.neu.edu
```

Figure A.2: E-mail information

Support to use the software in commercial projects is provided by Demeter International, Inc. Please contact demeter@acm.org.

Bibliography

[AB87]   M.P. Atkinson and O.P. Buneman. Types and persistence in database programming languages. *ACM Computing Surveys*, 19(2):105–190, June 1987.

[AB91]   Serge Abiteboul and Anthony Bonner. Objects and views. In James Clifford and Roger King, editors, *Proceedings of ACM SIGMOD International Conference on management of Data*, pages 238–247, Denver, Colorado, May 29-31 1991. ACM Press.

[AB92]   Mehmet Aksit and Lodewijk Bergmans. Obstacles in object-oriented software development. In *Object-Oriented Programming Systems, Languages and Applications Conference,* in *Special Issue of SIGPLAN Notices*, pages 341–358, Vancouver, Canada, 1992. ACM Press.

[Ada93] Sam Adams. Private communication. WOOD (Workshop on Object-Oriented Design, Snowbird, Utah, March 8-10), March 1993.

[AG92]   R. Allen and David Garlan. A formal approach to software architectures. In J. van Leeuwen, editor, *Proceedings of IFIP World Congress*, Madrid, Spain, 1992. Elsevier Science Publisher B.V.

[Agh86] Gul A. Agha. *Actors: a Model of Concurrent Computation in Distributed Systems*. MIT Press, Cambridge, MA, 1986.

[AH87]   S. Abiteboul and R. Hull. A formal semantic database model. *ACM Transactions on Database Systems*, 12(4):525–565, December 1987.

[ALM82] F. Allen, M. Loomis, and M. Mannino. The Integrated Dictionary/ Directory System. *ACM Computing Surveys*, 14(2), 1982.

[ASU86] Alfred V. Aho, Ravi Sethi, and Jeffrey D. Ullman. *Compilers: Principles, Techniques and Tools*. Addison-Wesley, 1986.

[Bal86] R.N. Balzer. Program enhancement. *ACM SIGSOFT Software Engineering Notes*, 11(4):66, 1986.

[BC86]   J.P. Briot and P. Cointe. The OBJVLISP project: definition of a uniform self-described and extensible object-oriented language. In *European Conference on Artificial Intelligence*, Brighton, UK, 1986.

[BDD+88]   P. Borras, D.Clement, T. Despeyroux, J. Incerpi, G. Kahn, B. Lang, and V. Pascual. Centaur: the system. In *ACM SIGSOFT Symposium on Software Development Environments*, Boston, MA, November 1988. ACM Press.

[BDG+88]   D.G. Bobrow, L.G. DeMichiel, R.P. Gabriel, S.E. Keene, G. Kiczales, and D.A. Moon. Common Lisp Object System Specification. *SIGPLAN Notices*, 23, September 1988.

[Bec87]   Kent Beck. Using a pattern language for programming. In *Object-Oriented Programming Systems, Languages and Applications Conference,* in *Special Issue of SIGPLAN Notices*, page 16. ACM Press, 1987. Addendum to OOPSLA'87 Proceedings, SIGPLAN Notices, Vol. 23, No. 5, May 1988.

[Bec94]   Kent Beck. Patterns and software development. *Dr. Dobbs Journal*, 19(2):18–22, February 1994.

[Bee87]   David Beech. Groundwork for an object-oriented database model. In Bruce Shriver and Peter Wegner, editors, *Research Directions in Object-Oriented Programming*, pages 317–354. MIT Press, 1987.

[Ber91]   Paul Bergstein. Object-preserving class transformations. In *Object-Oriented Programming Systems, Languages and Applications Conference,* in *Special Issue of SIGPLAN Notices*, pages 299–313, Phoenix, Arizona, 1991. ACM Press. SIGPLAN Notices, Vol. 26, No. 11, November.

[Ber94]   Paul Bergstein. *Managing the Evolution of Object-Oriented Systems*. PhD thesis, Northeastern University, 1994. 151 pages.

[BGV90]   Robert A. Ballance, Susan L. Graham, and Michael L. VanDeVanter. The Pan language-based editing system. In *ACM SIGSOFT Symposium on Software Development Environments*, pages 77–93, Irvine, CA, 1990. ACM Press.

[BH93]   Paul L. Bergstein and Walter L. Hürsch. Maintaining behavioral consistency during schema evolution. In S. Nishio and A. Yonezawa, editors, *International Symposium on Object Technologies for Advanced Software*, pages 176–193, Kanazawa, Japan, November 1993. JSSST, Springer Verlag, Lecture Notes in Computer Science.

[BK76]   A.W. Biermann and R. Krishnasawamy. Constructing programs from example computations. *IEEE Transactions on Software Engineering*, SE-2(3):141–153, September 1976.

[BL84]   Ronald J. Brachman and Hector J. Levesque. The tractability of subsumption in frame-based description languages. In *Proceedings AAAI-84*, pages 34–37, Austin, Texas, 1984. American Association for Artificial Intelligence.

[BL91]   Paul Bergstein and Karl Lieberherr. Incremental class dictionary learning and optimization. In *European Conference on Object-Oriented Programming*, pages 377–396, Geneva, Switzerland, 1991. Springer Verlag Lecture Notes 512.

[BLN86]   C. Batini, M. Lenzerini, and S.B. Navathe. A comparative analysis of methodologies for database schema integration. *ACM Computing Surveys*, 19(4):323–364, December 1986.

[BM84]   J.M. Boyle and M.N. Muralidharan. Program reusability through program transformation. *IEEE Transactions on Software Engineering*, SE-10(5), September 1984.

[BMG+88]   Daniel Bobrow, Linda G. De Michiel, Richard P. Gabriel, Sonya E. Keene, Gregor Kiczales, and David A. Moon. Common Lisp Object System Specification. Draft submitted to X3J13, March 1988.

[Boe88]   Barry Boehm. A spiral model of software development and enhancement. *IEEE Computer Magazine*, 21(5):61–72, May 1988.

[Boo86]   Grady Booch. Object-oriented development. *IEEE Transactions on Software Engineering*, SE-12(2), February 1986.

[Boo90]   Grady Booch. The design of the C++ Booch components. In *Object-Oriented Programming Systems, Languages and Applications Conference,* in *Special Issue of SIGPLAN Notices*, pages 1–11, Ottawa, Canada, 1990. ACM Press.

[Boo91]   Grady Booch. *Object-Oriented Design With Applications*. Benjamin/Cummings Publishing Company, Inc., 1991.

[Boo94]   Grady Booch. Design an application framework. *Dr. Dobbs Journal*, 19(2):24–32, February 1994.

[Bro86]   R. A. Brooks. A robust layered control system for a mobile robot. *IEEE Journal of Robotics and Automation*, 2(1):14–23, 1986.

[Bro87]   Frederick P. Brooks. No silver bullet, essence and accidents of software engineering. *IEEE Computer Magazine*, pages 10–19, April 1987.

[BS85]   R.J. Brachman and J.G. Schmolze. An overview of the KL-ONE knowledge representation system. *Cognitive Sciences*, 9(2):171–216, 1985.

[Car84]   Robert Cartwright. Recursive programs as definitions in first order logic. *SIAM Journal on Computing*, 13(2):374–408, May 1984.

[Cas91]   Eduardo Casais. *Managing Evolution in Object-Oriented Environments: An Algorithmic Approach*. PhD thesis, University of Geneva, 1991.

[CI84]   Robert D. Cameron and M. Robert Ito. Grammar-based definition of metaprogramming systems. *ACM Transactions on Programming Languages and Systems*, 6(1):20–54, January 1984.

[Col94]   Derek Coleman. *Object-Oriented Development—The Fusion Method*. Prentice-Hall, 1994.

[Cox86]   Brad J. Cox. *Object-Oriented Programming, An evolutionary approach.* Addison-Wesley, 1986.

[CTT93]   Stefano Ceri, Katsumi Tanaka, and Shalom Tsur. *Deductive and Object-Oriented Databases.* Springer Verlag (*LNCS* 760), 1993.

[CW85]   L. Cardelli and P. Wegner. On understanding types, data abstraction, and polymorphism. *ACM Computing Surveys*, 17(4):471, December 1985.

[CW91]   N. Coburn and G. E. Weddell. Path constraints for graph-based data models: Towards a unified theory of typing constraints, equations, and functional dependencies. In C. Delobel M. Kifer Y. Masunaga, editor, *Second International Conference, DOOD'91*, pages 313–331, Munich, Germany, 1991. Springer Verlag.

[CY90]   Peter Coad and Edward Yourdon. *Object-Oriented Analysis.* Yourdon Press, 1990. Second edition.

[Day89]   Umeshwar Dayal. Queries and views in an object-oriented data model. In Richard Hull, Ron Morrison, and David Stemple, editors, *Proceedings of the Second International Workshop on Database Programming Languages*, pages 80–102, Gleneden Beach, OR, June 4-8 1989. Morgan Kaufmann.

[DCG+89]   Peter J. Denning, Douglas E. Comer, David Gries, Michael C. Mulder, Allen B. Tucker, A. Joe Turner, and Paul R. Young. Computing as a discipline. *Communications of the ACM*, 32(1):9–23, January 1989.

[Deu89]   L. Peter Deutsch. Design reuse and frameworks in the Smalltalk-80 system. In Ted J. Biggerstaff and Alan J. Perlis, editors, *Software reusability, Applications and experience*, volume 2. ACM Press, 1989.

[DGHK+75]   Veronique Donzeau-Gouge, Gérard Huet, Gilles Kahn, Bernard Lang, and J.J. Lévy. A structure oriented program editor: A first step towards computer assisted programming. In *Proceedings of International Computing Symposium 1975*, 1975.

[DGHKL80]   Veronique Donzeau-Gouge, Gérard Huet, Gilles Kahn, and Bernard Lang. Programming environments based on structured editors: The MENTOR experience. Technical report, Res. Rep. 26 INRIA, 1980.

[DMN70]   O.J. Dahl, B. Myhrhaug, and K. Nygaard. SIMULA 67 Common Base Language. *Publication Number S-22, Norwegian Computing Center*, October 1970.

[DS89]   Stephen C. Dewhurst and Kathy T. Stark. *Programming in C++.* Prentice-Hall Software Series. Prentice-Hall, 1989.

[Eng73]   Erwin Engeler. *The Theory of Computation.* Academic Press, 1973.

[ES90]   Margaret A. Ellis and Bjarne Stroustrup. *The Annotated C++ Reference Manual*. Addison-Wesley, 1990.

[Evi94]   Mikel Evins. Objects without classes. *IEEE Computer Magazine*, 27(3):104–109, March 1994.

[FB94]   Robert W. Floyd and Richard Beigel. *The Language of Machines*. Computer Science Press, 1994.

[FHW92]   D.P. Friedman, C.T. Hayes, and M. Wand. Essentials of programming languages. MIT Press/McGraw-Hill, 1992.

[FL94]   Natalya Friedman and Karl Lieberherr. Reuse of adaptive software through opportunistic parameterization. Technical Report NU-CCS-94-17, Northeastern University, May 1994.

[Fra81]   C.W. Fraser. Syntax-directed editing of general data structures. In *Proceedings ACM SIGPLAN/SIGOA Conference on Text Manipulation*, pages 17–21, Portland, OR, 1981.

[GCN92]   David Garlan, Linxi Cai, and Robert Nord. A transformational approach to generating application-specific environments. In Herbert Weber, editor, *ACM SIGSOFT Symposium on Software Development Environments*, pages 68–77, Tyson's Corner, VA, 1992. ACM Press.

[GHJV95]   Erich Gamma, Richard Helm, Ralph Johnson, and John Vlissides. *Design Patterns: Elements of Reusable Object-Oriented Software*. Addison-Wesley, 1995.

[GJ79]   Michael R. Garey and David S. Johnson. *Computers and Intractability*. Freeman, 1979.

[GL85a]   Steven M. German and Karl J. Lieberherr. Zeus: A language for expressing algorithms in hardware. *IEEE Computer Magazine*, pages 55–65, February 1985.

[GL85b]   A.V. Goldberg and K.J. Lieberherr. GEM: A generator of environments for metaprogramming. In *SOFTFAIR II, ACM/IEEE Conference on Software Tools*, pages 86–95, San Francisco, 1985.

[Gol89]   N. M. Goldman. Code walking and recursive descent: A generic approach. In *Proceedings of the Second CLOS Users and Implementors Workshop*, 1989.

[GR83]   Adele Goldberg and David Robson. *Smalltalk-80: The Language and its Implementation*. Addison-Wesley, 1983.

[Gre89]   T.R.G. Green. Cognitive dimensions of notations. MRC Applied Psychology Unit, Rank Xerox EuroPARC, Cambridge, February 1989.

[Gro91]   Object Management Group. The common object request broker: Architecture and specification. OMG Document Number 91.12.1, Revision 1.1, 492 Old Connecticut Path, Framingham, MA 01701, December 1991.

[GS93]   David Garlan and Mary Shaw. An introduction to software architecture. In *Advances in Software Engineering and Knowledge Engineering*, volume I. World Scientific Publishing Company, 1993.

[GSOS92]   D. Garlan, M. Shaw, C. Okasaki, and R. Swonger. Experience with a course on architectures for software systems. In *Springer Verlag, Lecture Notes in Computer Science*, volume 376. Springer Verlag, 1992. Sixth SEI Conference on Software Engineering Education.

[GTC+90]   Simon Gibbs, Dennis Tsichritzis, Eduardo Casais, Oscar Nierstrasz, and Xavier Pintado. Class management for software communities. *Communications of the ACM*, 33(9):90–103, September 1990.

[Har94]   Cole Harrison. Aql: An adaptive query language. Technical Report NU-CCS-94-19, Northeastern University, October 1994. Master's Thesis.

[HB77]   Carl Hewitt and H. Baker. Laws for communicating parallel processes. In *IFIP Congress Proceedings*, pages 987–992. IFIP (International Federation for Information Processing), August 1977.

[Hec86]   Reinhold Heckmann. An efficient ELL(1)-parser generator. *Acta Informatica*, 23:127–148, 1986.

[HHG90]   Richard Helm, Ian M. Holland, and Dipayan Gangopadhyay. Contracts: Specifying behavioral compositions in object-oriented systems. In *Object-Oriented Programming Systems, Languages and Applications Conference,* in *Special Issue of SIGPLAN Notices*, pages 169–180, Ottawa, 1990. ACM Press. Joint conference ECOOP/OOPSLA.

[HK87]   Richard Hull and Roger King. Semantic database modeling: Survey, applications, and research issues. *ACM Computing Surveys*, 19(3):201–260, September 1987.

[HLM93]   Walter L. Hürsch, Karl J. Lieberherr, and Sougata Mukherjea. Object-oriented schema extension and abstraction. In *ACM Computer Science Conference, Symposium on Applied Computing*, pages 54–62, Indianapolis, Indiana, February 1993. ACM Press.

[HO87]   Daniel C. Halbert and Patrick D. O'Brien. Using types and inheritance in object-based languages. In *European Conference on Object-Oriented Programming*, pages 20–31. Springer Verlag, Lecture Notes 276, 1987.

[HO91]   William Harrison and Harold Ossher. Structure-bound messages: Separating navigation from processing. *Submitted for publication*, 1991.

[HO93] William Harrison and Harold Ossher. Subject-oriented programming (A critique of pure objects). In *Proceedings OOPSLA '93, ACM SIGPLAN Notices*, pages 411–428, October 1993. Published as Proceedings OOPSLA '93, ACM SIGPLAN Notices, volume 28, number 10.

[Hoa75] C.A.R. Hoare. Recursive data structures. *International Journal on Computer and Information Science*, pages 105–133, June 1975.

[Hol92] Ian M. Holland. Specifying reusable components using contracts. In *European Conference on Object-Oriented Programming*, pages 287–308, Utrecht, Netherlands, 1992. Springer Verlag Lecture Notes 615.

[Hol93] Ian M. Holland. *The Design and Representation of Object-Oriented Components*. PhD thesis, Northeastern University, 1993.

[HSE94] Brian Henderson-Sellers and Julian Edwards. *Booktwo of Object-Oriented Knowledge: The Working Object*. Object-oriented Series. Prentice-Hall, 1994.

[HSX91] Walter L. Hürsch, Linda M. Seiter, and Cun Xiao. In any CASE: Demeter. *The American Programmer*, 4(10):46–56, October 1991.

[HU79] John E. Hopcroft and Jeffrey D. Ullman. *Introduction to Automata Theory, Languages, and Computation*. Addison-Wesley, 1979.

[Hür94] Walter L. Hürsch. Should Superclasses be Abstract? In Remo Pareschi and Mario Tokoro, editors, *European Conference on Object-Oriented Programming*, pages 12–31, Bologna, Italy, July 1994. Springer Verlag, Lecture Notes in Computer Science.

[Hür95] Walter Hürsch. *Software Evolution*. PhD thesis, Northeastern University, 1995. In preparation.

[Jac87] Ivar Jacobson. Object-oriented development in an industrial environment. In *Object-Oriented Programming Systems, Languages and Applications Conference*, in *Special Issue of SIGPLAN Notices*, pages 183–191, Orlando, Florida, 1987.

[Jac92] Ivar Jacobson. The use case construct in object-oriented software engineering. Technical report, Objective Systems, 1992.

[JCJO92] Ivar Jacobson, Magnus Christerson, Patrick Jonsson, and Gunnar Overgaard. *Object-Oriented Software Engineering: A Use Case Driven Approach*. Addison-Wesley, 1992.

[JF88] Ralph E. Johnson and Brian Foote. Designing reusable classes. *Journal of Object-Oriented Programming*, 1(2):22–35, June/July 1988.

[Joh92] Ralph Johnson. Documenting frameworks using patterns. In *Object-Oriented Programming Systems, Languages and Applications Conference*, in *Special Issue of SIGPLAN Notices*, pages 63–76, Vancouver, Canada, 1992. ACM Press.

[Kap69]   Donald M. Kaplan. Regular expressions and the equivalence of programs. *Journal of Computer and System Sciences*, 3:361–386, 1969.

[KBR86]   Thomas S. Kaczmarek, Raymond Bates, and Gabriel Robins. Recent Developments in NIKL. In *National Conference on Artificial Intelligence*, pages 978–985. Morgan Kaufman Publishers, 1986.

[Kes93]   Linda Keszenheimer. Specifying and adapting object behavior during system evolution. In *Conference on Software Maintenance*, pages 254–261, Montreal, Canada, 1993. IEEE Press.

[Kic92]   Gregor Kiczales. Towards a new model of abstraction in software engineering. In *Proceedings of IMSA Workshop on Reflection and Meta-level Architectures*, 1992.

[Kic93]   Gregor Kiczales. Traces (a cut at the "make isn't generic" problem). In S. Nishio and A. Yonezawa, editors, *International Symposium on Object Technologies for Advanced Software*, Kanazawa, Japan, November 1993. JSSST, Springer Verlag, Lecture Notes in Computer Science.

[KKS92]   Michael Kifer, Won Kim, and Yehoshua Sagiv. Querying object-oriented databases. In Michael Stonebraker, editor, *Proceedings of ACM/SIGMOD Annual Conference on Management of Data*, pages 393–402, San Diego, CA, 1992. ACM Press.

[KL92]   Gregor Kiczales and John Lamping. Issues in the design and documentation of class libraries. In *Object-Oriented Programming Systems, Languages and Applications Conference,* in *Special Issue of SIGPLAN Notices*, pages 435–451, Vancouver, Canada, 1992. ACM.

[KMMPN85]   Bent Bruun Kristensen, Ole Lehrmann Madsen, Birger Moller-Pederson, and Kristen Nygaard. An algebra for program fragments. In *ACM SIGPLAN 85 Symposium on Programming Languages and Programming Environments*, volume 20, Seattle, WA, 1985. SIGPLAN.

[Kor86]   Henry F. Korth. Extending the scope of relational languages. *IEEE Software*, pages 19–28, January 1986.

[KRB91]   G. Kiczales, J. Des Rivière, and D.G. Bobrow. *The Art of the Metaobject Protocol*. MIT Press, 1991.

[LA94]   John Lamping and Martin Abadi. Methods as assertions. In Remo Pareschi and Mario Tokoro, editors, *European Conference on Object-Oriented Programming*, volume 821, pages 60–80, Bologna, Italy, July 1994. Springer Verlag, Lecture Notes in Computer Science.

[LaL89]   Wilf R. LaLonde. Designing families of data types using exemplars. *ACM Transactions on Programming Languages and Systems*, 11(2):212–248, April 1989.

[LBSL90]   Karl J. Lieberherr, Paul Bergstein, and Ignacio Silva-Lepe. Abstraction of object-oriented data models. In Hannu Kangassalo, editor, *Proceedings of International Conference on Entity-Relationship*, pages 81–94, Lausanne, Switzerland, 1990. Elsevier.

[LBSL91]   Karl J. Lieberherr, Paul Bergstein, and Ignacio Silva-Lepe. From objects to classes: Algorithms for object-oriented design. *Journal of Software Engineering*, 6(4):205–228, July 1991.

[LH89a]   Karl J. Lieberherr and Ian Holland. Assuring good style for object-oriented programs. *IEEE Software*, pages 38–48, September 1989.

[LH89b]   Karl J. Lieberherr and Ian Holland. Tools for preventive software maintenance. In *Conference on Software Maintenance*, pages 2–13, Miami, Florida, October 16-19, 1989. IEEE Press.

[LHLR88]   Karl J. Lieberherr, Ian Holland, Gar-Lin Lee, and Arthur J. Riel. An objective sense of style. *IEEE Computer Magazine*, June 1988. Open Channel publication.

[LHR88]   Karl J. Lieberherr, Ian Holland, and Arthur J. Riel. Object-oriented programming: An objective sense of style. In *Object-Oriented Programming Systems, Languages and Applications Conference*, in *Special Issue of SIGPLAN Notices*, number 11, pages 323–334, San Diego, CA, September 1988. A short version of this paper appears in *IEEE Computer Magazine*, June 1988, Open Channel section, pages 78-79.

[LHSLX92]   Karl J. Lieberherr, Walter Hürsch, Ignacio Silva-Lepe, and Cun Xiao. Experience with a graph-based propagation pattern programming tool. In Gene Forte et al., editor, *International Workshop on CASE*, pages 114–119, Montréal, Canada, 1992. IEEE Computer Society.

[LHX94]   Karl J. Lieberherr, Walter L. Hürsch, and Cun Xiao. Object-extending class transformations. *Formal Aspects of Computing, the International Journal of Formal Methods*, (6):391–416, 1994. Also available as Technical Report NU-CCS-91-8, Northeastern University.

[Lie85]   Karl J. Lieberherr. Toward a standard hardware description language. *IEEE Design and Test of Computers*, 2(1):55–62, February 1985.

[Lie88]   Karl J. Lieberherr. Object-oriented programming with class dictionaries. *Journal on Lisp and Symbolic Computation*, 1(2):185–212, 1988.

[Lie92]   Karl J. Lieberherr. Component enhancement: An adaptive reusability mechanism for groups of collaborating classes. In J. van Leeuwen, editor, *Information Processing '92, 12th World Computer Congress*, pages 179–185, Madrid, Spain, 1992. Elsevier.

[Lip89]   S.B. Lippman. *C++ Primer*. Addison-Wesley, 1989. Second edition.

[LR88a]   Karl J. Lieberherr and Arthur J. Riel. Demeter: A CASE study of software growth through parameterized classes. In *International Conference on Software Engineering*, pages 254–264, Raffles City, Singapore, 1988.

[LR88b]   Karl J. Lieberherr and Arthur J. Riel. Demeter: A CASE study of software growth through parameterized classes. *Journal of Object-Oriented Programming*, 1(3):8–22, August, September 1988. A shorter version of this paper was presented at the *10th International Conference on Software Engineering, Singapore, April 1988, IEEE Press*, pages 254-264.

[LR89]   Karl J. Lieberherr and Arthur J. Riel. Contributions to teaching object-oriented design and programming. In *Object-Oriented Programming Systems, Languages and Applications Conference,* in *Special Issue of SIGPLAN Notices*, pages 11–22, October 1989.

[LSLX94] Karl J. Lieberherr, Ignacio Silva-Lepe, and Cun Xiao. Adaptive object-oriented programming using graph-based customization. *Communications of the ACM*, 37(5):94–101, May 1994.

[LTP86]   Wilf R. LaLonde, Dave A. Thomas, and John R. Pugh. An exemplar based smalltalk. In *Proceedings OOPSLA '86, ACM SIGPLAN Notices*, pages 322–330, November 1986. Published as Proceedings OOPSLA '86, ACM SIGPLAN Notices, Volume 21, Number 11.

[LX93a]   Karl J. Lieberherr and Cun Xiao. Formal Foundations for Object-Oriented Data Modeling. *IEEE Transactions on Knowledge and Data Engineering*, 5(3):462–478, June 1993.

[LX93b]   Karl J. Lieberherr and Cun Xiao. Minimizing dependency on class structures with adaptive programs. In S. Nishio and A. Yonezawa, editors, *International Symposium on Object Technologies for Advanced Software*, pages 424–441, Kanazawa, Japan, November 1993. JSSST, Springer Verlag.

[LX93c]   Karl J. Lieberherr and Cun Xiao. Object-Oriented Software Evolution. *IEEE Transactions on Software Engineering*, 19(4):313–343, April 1993.

[LX94]   Karl J. Lieberherr and Cun Xiao. Customizing adaptive software to object-oriented software using grammars. *International Journal of Foundations of Computer Science, World Scientific Publishing Company*, 5(2):179–208, 1994.

[LXSL91] Karl Lieberherr, Cun Xiao, and Ignacio Silva-Lepe. Propagation patterns: Graph-based specifications of cooperative behavior. Technical Report NU-CCS-91-14, Northeastern University, September 1991.

[LZHL94] Ling Liu, Roberto Zicari, Walter Hürsch, and Karl Lieberherr. Polymorphic reuse mechanisms for object-oriented database specifications. In *International Conference on Data Engineering*, pages 180–189, Houston, February 1994. IEEE.

[Mag62]   Robert F. Mager. *Preparing Instructional Objectives*. Fearon Publishers, Inc., 1962.

[Mey88]   Bertrand Meyer. *Object-Oriented Software Construction*. Series in Computer Science. Prentice-Hall International, 1988.

[Mil71]   H.D. Mills. Top-down programming in large systems. In R. Ruskin, editor, *Debugging Techniques in Large Systems*. Prentice-Hall, 1971.

[Min75]   Marvin Minsky. A framework for representing knowledge. In P. Winston, editor, *The Psychology of Computer Vision*, pages 211–277. McGraw-Hill, 1975.

[MK88]   L. Mohan and R.L. Kashyap. An object-oriented knowledge representation for spatial information. *IEEE Transactions on Software Engineering*, 14(5):675–681, May 1988.

[MM85]   J. Martin and C. McClure. *Structured Techniques for Computing*. Prentice-Hall, 1985.

[MN88]   Ole Lehrmann Madsen and Claus Nørgaard. An object-oriented metaprogramming system. In *Proceedings of the Annual Hawaii International Conference on System Sciences*, pages 406–415, 1988.

[Moo86]   David A. Moon. Object-Oriented Programming with Flavors. In *Object-Oriented Programming Systems, Languages and Applications Conference,* in *Special Issue of SIGPLAN Notices*, pages 1–8, Portland, OR, 1986.

[Mor84]   Matthew Morgenstern. Constraint equations: a concise compilable representation for quantified constraints in semantic networks. In *National Conference on Artificial Intelligence*, pages 255–259. Morgan Kaufman Publishers, 1984.

[MS87]   David Meier and Jacob Stein. Development and implementation of an object-oriented DBMS. In Bruce Shriver and Peter Wegner, editors, *Research Directions in Object-Oriented Programming*, pages 355–392. MIT Press, 1987.

[MS89]   Victor M. Markowitz and Arie Shoshani. Abbreviated query interpretation in entity-relationship oriented databases. *Lawrence Berkeley Lab., Berkeley, CA*, 1989.

[MS93]   Victor M. Markowitz and Arie Shoshani. Object queries over relational databases: Language, implementation, and application. In *9th International Conference on Data Engineering*, pages 71–80. IEEE Press, 1993.

[NEL86]   S. Navathe, R. Elmasari, and J. Larson. Integrating user views in database design. *IEEE Computer Magazine*, 19(1):50–62, 1986.

[Osb93]   Lloyd Osborn. Information systems lessons learned. In *Educating the next generation of information specialists*, pages 40–41, Alexandria, VA, 1993. National Science Foundation.

[PB92] Carl Ponder and Bill Bush. Polymorphism considered harmful. In *SIGPLAN Notices*, pages 76–79, 1992. Also in ACM Software Engineering Notes, Vol. 19, No. 2, April 1994, pages 35-37.

[PCW86] David Lorge Parnas, Paul C. Clements, and David M. Weiss. Enhancing reusability with information hiding. In Peter Freeman, editor, *Tutorial: Software Reusability*, pages 83–90. IEEE Press, 1986.

[Poh91] Ira Pohl. *C++ for Pascal Programmers*. Addison-Wesley, 1991.

[Pol49] George Polya. *How to solve it*. Princeton University Press, 1949.

[Pre87] Roger S. Pressman. *Software Engineering: A practitioner's approach, Second edition*. McGraw-Hill, 1987.

[Pre94] Wolfgang Pree. *Design Patterns for Object-Oriented Software Development*. Addison-Wesley, 1994.

[PS83] Helmut A. Partsch and R. Steinbrueggen. Program transformation systems. *ACM Computing Surveys*, 15(3):199–236, September 1983.

[PS88] Peter F. Patel-Schneider. An approach to practical object-based knowledge representation systems. In *Proceedings of the Annual Hawaii International Conference on System Sciences*, pages 367–375, 1988.

[PS93] Jens Palsberg and Michael I. Schwartzbach. *Object-Oriented Type Systems*. John Wiley & Sons, 1993.

[PXL95] Jens Palsberg, Cun Xiao, and Karl Lieberherr. Efficient implementation of adaptive software. *ACM Transactions on Programming Languages and Systems*, 1995. Also presented at the OOPSLA 1994 poster session.

[Ral83] Anthony Ralston. *Encyclopedia of Computer Science and Engineering*. Van Nostrand Reinhold Company, Inc., 1983. Second edition.

[Rao91] Ramana Rao. Implementation Reflection in Silica. In *European Conference on Object-Oriented Programming*. Springer Verlag, 1991.

[RBP+91] James Rumbaugh, Michael Blaha, William Premerlani, Frederick Eddy, and William Lorensen. *Object-Oriented Modeling and Design*. Prentice-Hall, 1991.

[Rei87] Steven P. Reiss. On object-oriented framework for conceptual programming. In Bruce Shriver and Peter Wegner, editors, *Research Directions in Object-Oriented Programming*, pages 189–218. MIT Press, 1987.

[Rob65] J.A. Robinson. A machine-oriented logic based on the resolution principle. *Journal of the Association for Computing Machinery*, 12(1):23–41, 1965.

[RT84] T. Reps and T. Teitelbaum. The synthesizer generator. *SIGPLAN*, 19(5), 1984.

[RTD83]   Thomas Reps, Tim Teitelbaum, and Alan Demers. Incremental context-dependent analysis for language-based editors. *ACM Transactions on Programming Languages and Systems*, 5(3), July 1983.

[Rum88]   James Rumbaugh. Controlling propagation of operations using attributes on relations. In *Object-Oriented Programming Systems, Languages and Applications Conference,* in *Special Issue of SIGPLAN Notices*, pages 285–297, San Diego, CA, 1988. ACM.

[Sak88a]   Markku Sakkinen. Comments on the Law of Demeter and C++. *SIGPLAN Notices*, 23(12):38–44, December 1988.

[SAK88b]   G. Smolka and H. Ait-Kaci. Inheritance hierarchies: Semantics and unification. *Journal on Symbolic Computation*, 1988. Special issue on unification.

[Sal86]   Betty Salzberg. *An Introduction to Database Design*. Academic Press, 1986.

[San82]   David Sandberg. LITHE: A language combining a flexible syntax and classes. In *ACM Symposium on Principles of Programming Languages*, pages 142–145, Albuquerque, NM, 1982. ACM.

[SB86]   Mark Stefik and Daniel G. Bobrow. Object-oriented programming: Themes and variations. *The AI Magazine*, pages 40–62, January 1986.

[Set89]   Ravi Sethi. *Programming Languages: Concepts and Constructs*. Addison-Wesley, 1989.

[She87]   Philip Sheu. Programming object-based systems with knowledge. In *International CASE Workshop*, Index Technology, Cambridge, MA, 1987.

[SKG88]   Barbara Staudt, Charles Krüger, and David Garlan. Transformgen: Automating the maintenance of structure-oriented environments. Technical Report CMU-CS-88-186, Department of Computer Science, CMU, 11 1988.

[SL94]   Ignacio Silva-Lepe. *Techniques for Reverse-engineering and Re-engineering into the Object-Oriented Paradigm*. PhD thesis, Northeastern University, 1994. 133 pages.

[SM92]   Sally Shlaer and Stephen J. Mellor. *Object Life Cycles: Modeling the World in States*. Yourdon Press, Englewood Cliffs, 1992.

[SS77]   J.M. Smith and D.C.P. Smith. Database abstractions: Aggregation and generalization. *ACM Transactions on Database Systems*, 2(2), June 1977.

[Ste90]   Guy L. Steele. *Common Lisp: the Language*. Digital Press, second edition, 1990.

[Str86]   B. Stroustrup. *The C++ Programming Language*. Addison-Wesley, 1986.

[Str94]   Bjarne Stroustrup. *The Design and Evolution of C++*. Addison-Wesley, 1994.

[SZ87]   Andrea Skarra and Stanley Zdonik. Type evolution in an object-oriented database. In Bruce Shriver and Peter Wegner, editors, *Research Directions in Object-Oriented Programming*, pages 393–416. MIT Press, 1987.

[TYF86]   T.J. Teorey, D. Yang, and J.P. Fry. A logical design methodology for relational databases. *ACM Computing Surveys*, 18(2):197–222, June 1986.

[Ull82]   Jeffrey D. Ullman. *Principles of Database Systems*. Computer Science Press, 1982.

[US87]   David Ungar and Randall B. Smith. Self: The power of simplicity. In *Object-Oriented Programming Systems, Languages and Applications Conference*, in *Special Issue of SIGPLAN Notices*, number 12, pages 227–242. ACM, 1987.

[VdBV93]   Jan Van den Bussche and Gottfried Vossen. An extension of path expressions to simplify navigation in object-oriented queries. In *Deductive and Object-Oriented Databases*, pages 267–282. Springer Verlag (*LNCS* 760), 1993.

[Vil84]   Mark Vilain. Kl-two, a hybrid knowledge representation system. Technical Report 5694, Bolt, Beranek, and Newman, 1984.

[Wan94]   Paul S. Wang. *C++ with Object-Oriented Programming*. PWS Publishing Company, 1994.

[WB94]   David S. Wile and Robert M. Balzer. Architecture-based compilation. Sponsored by ARPA, January 1994.

[WBWW90]   Rebecca Wirfs-Brock, Brian Wilkerson, and Lauren Wiener. *Designing Object-Oriented Software*. Prentice-Hall, 1990.

[WCW90]   Jack C. Wileden, Lori A. Clarke, and Alexander L. Wolf. A comparative evaluation of object definition techniques. *ACM Transactions on Programming Languages and Systems*, 12(4):670–699, October 1990.

[Weg87]   Peter Wegner. The object-oriented classification paradigm. In Bruce Shriver and Peter Wegner, editors, *Research Directions in Object-Oriented Programming*, pages 479–560. MIT Press, 1987.

[Wer86]   Charles J. Wertz. *The Data Dictionary*. QED Information Sciences, Inc., 1986.

[WG84]   William Waite and Gerhard Goos. *Compiler Construction*. Springer Verlag, 1984.

[WG89]   Niklaus Wirth and Jürg Gutknecht. The Oberon System. *Software–Practice and Experience*, 19(9):857–893, September 1989.

[WH91]   Norman Wilde and Ross Huitt. Maintenance support for object-oriented programs. In *Conference on Software Maintenance*, pages 162–170, Sorrento, Italy, 1991. IEEE Press.

[WH92] Norman Wilde and Ross Huitt. Maintenance support for object-oriented programs. *IEEE Transactions on Software Engineering*, 18(12):1038–1044, December 1992.

[Wil83] David S. Wile. Program developments: Formal explanations of implementations. *Communications of the ACM*, 26(11):902–911, 1983.

[Wil86] David S. Wile. Organizing programming knowledge into syntax-directed experts. In *International Workshop on Advanced Programming Environments*, pages 551–565. Springer Verlag (*LNCS* 244), 1986.

[Wir71a] Niklaus Wirth. Program development by stepwise refinement. *Communications of the ACM*, 14(4):221–227, 1971.

[Wir71b] Niklaus Wirth. The Programming Language Pascal. *Acta Informatica*, 1:35–63, 1971.

[Wir74a] Niklaus Wirth. On the composition of well-structured programs. *ACM Computing Surveys*, 6(4):247–259, 1974.

[Wir74b] Niklaus Wirth. On the design of programming languages. In *IFIP, Amsterdam*, pages 386–393. North-Holland, 1974.

[Wir76] Niklaus Wirth. *Algorithms + Data Structures = Programs*. Prentice-Hall, 1976.

[Wir77] Niklaus Wirth. What can we do about the unnecessary diversity of notation for syntactic definitions? *Communications of the ACM*, 20(11):822–823, 1977.

[Wir82] Niklaus Wirth. Hades: A Notation for the Description of Hardware. Technical report, Swiss Federal Institute of Technology, August 1982.

[Wir84] Niklaus Wirth. *Programming in Modula-2*. Springer Verlag, 1984.

[Wir88] Niklaus Wirth. The programming language Oberon. *Software–Practice and Experience*, 18(7):671–690, July 1988.

[WL88] Jim Woodcock and Martin Loomes. *Software Engineering Mathematics*. Addison-Wesley, 1988.

[WMH93] Norman Wilde, Paul Matthews, and Ross Huitt. Maintaining object-oriented software. *IEEE Software*, pages 75–80, January 1993.

[Woo79] W. A. Woods. Theoretical studies in natural language understanding. Technical Report 4332, Bolt, Beranek, and Newman, 1979.

[Xia94] Cun Xiao. *Adaptive Software: Automatic Navigation Through Partially Specified Data Structures*. PhD thesis, Northeastern University, 1994. 189 pages.

Index

Λ, 144, 501
along, 311
at, 311
bypassing, 178
carry, 311
common, 122, 140, 509
from, 116, 178
in, 311
init, 115, 116, 293
inout, 311
join, 188
merge, 189
operation, 115, 208, 211
out, 311
prefix, 115, 208, 211
private, 228
suffix, 130, 208, 211
through, 130, 178
to, 116, 178
to-stop, 181
traverse, 116, 208, 211
via, 130
wrapper, 208, 211
->, 211
., 119
:, 120, 140, 142
<, 119, 137
=, 119, 137, 142
>, 119, 137
[, 139
], 139
|, 120, 140
~, 126, 140, 142
~>, 211
⟹, 120, 140
⟶, 117, 139

◇, 120, 140, 142
□, 117, 142
⬡, 123, 140, 142

abbreviated queries, 480
Abiteboul, Serge, 480
abstract class, 157, 468, 540, *565*
abstract superclass rule, 157, 469, 535, 540
abstraction, 26, 391
access independence, 279
accessor method, 32
Adams, Sam, 356
adaptive program, 454, **472**, *566*, *see* propagation pattern
    assumptions, 227, 320
    implementation, 455, **474**
        correctness, 475
adaptive programming principle, 81, *566*
adaptive software
    composition, 225, 492
    editing, 207
    further work, 590
    history, 207
    parsing, 358
    parts, 403
    reusability, 217
    usefulness, 482
aggregation, 42, *see* construction
Agha, Gul, 38
Aksit, Mehmet, 105
all-loser, 196
all-winner, 196
alternation class, 120, 140, 144, **147**, 157, **361**, 366, 509, *see* abstract

INDEX

optional part, 394
alternation edge, 120, 140, 144, **147**, 161, 566
alternation property, 272
alternation vertex, *566*, *see* alternation class
alternation-reachable, **72**, 468, **498**, *566*
ambiguous
    class dictionary, **364**, **527**, *566*
analysis, 407
Arndt, Rolf, xxxv
associated, **149**, 422, **503**
association, 26
asymptotic analysis of adaptiveness, 491
at-least-one alternative rule, *566*
atomic object, 149
attribute, *566*
avoiding conditional statement, 318, 326

Baclawski, Kenneth, xxxv
bad recursion, 382
Balzer, Robert, 107, 379, 481
Barnes, Bruce, xxxv
Beck, Kent, 253
Beigel, Robert, 199
Bergmans, Lodewijk, 105
Bobrow, Daniel, 402
Booch Method, 254
Booch, Grady, xxv, 254, 454
Boyce-Codd normal form, 397
breadth-first
    traversal, 495
broadcast, **312**
Brown, Cynthia, xxxv
Brown, George, xxxv
bypassing clause, 130, 178, *566*, *see* propagation directive

C++ code, 115
Caldarella, Jim, xxxv
Cameron, Robert, 166
Cardelli, Luca, 531
cardinality constraint, 219, 228
Cartwright, Robert, 380
Casais, Eduardo, 253, 454
castle analogy, 407

chess board, 219
Chittenden, Jeff, xxxv
circular object, 152
Clark, Clarence, xxxv
Clarke, Lori, 109
class, 24, 26, 28
    parameterized, **156**
        bounded, 531
        expanded, 156
class dictionary, 93, 117, **359**, 372, **511**, *567*
    ambiguous, **364**, 527
    debugging, 417
    design, 234, 393, 405
    design rules, 364
    edge pattern, 227
    flat, 361, **512**
    for class dictionary, 563
    grammar, 363
    inductive, 372
    left-recursive, 372
    LL(1), 372
    naming, 234
    nonambiguous, 372
    ordering of classes, 514
    parameterized
        rules, **531**
        syntax, **529**
    partial information, 227
    partitioning, 234
    self-describing, 529
    syntax, **529**
    textual representation, 359, 530
class dictionary design, 397
    buy versus inherit, 161
    dimensions, 385
class dictionary graph, 12, 135, **144**, 468, **501**, 511, *567*
    compatible
        propagation directive, 470
    concise notation, 136
    consistent
        propagation directive, 461, 475
    cycle-free, 383
    dense, 492

design, 157
extension, 410
flat, **150**
graphical notation, 136
graphical representation, 117
    summary, 142
inductive, 382, 507
    useless symbol, 523
learning, 117
minimization, 389
    tree property, 389
normalization, 396
object-equivalent, **414**
parameterization, 391
parts-centered, 157
reachable, **498**
rule, **501**
    abstract superclass, 469
    at-least-one alternative, 469
    no subclass cycle, 469
size, 386
specialization-centered, 157
textual notation, 136
textual representation, **137**, 139, 140
    summary, 142
class dictionary graph slice, 382, **500**, 501, *567*
    of class dictionary graph, 501
class graph, **468**
class graph slice, 489
class library generator, 563, *see* User's Guide
class-set, 241
class-valued variable, 88, *566*
client of a class, *567*
Clinger, William, 483
CLOS, xxviii
Coad, Peter, 428
code walker, 480
Coleman, Derek, 253
collaborating classes, 169, 202, 237, 404
common part, 122, 140, *567*
compatibility, 463
compatible, 461, *567*
    constraint, 179
    edge pattern, 179

propagation directive, 192, 193, **470**
completion of knowledge path, 273, 538
component, 225, *568*
    example, 327
    invariant, 228
composite object, 149
compositional consistency, 463
    sound, 478
concrete class, *568*
condense, **312**
conforms, **469**
consistency checking
    running time, 479
consistent, **183**, 461, **475**, *570*, 576, 578
    class dictionary graph
        propagation directive, 461, 475
    compositional, 463
constraint, 178, *568*
constraint-based programming, 25
construction class, 90, 137, 144, **147**, **361**, 365, 509, *see* concrete
construction edge, 90, 117, **139**, 144, **147**, 161, *568*
    optional, **139**
construction vertex, 117, *568*, *see* construction class
constructor, 31, 41, 533
    generated, 74
contradictory propagation directive, 196, 492
contradictory set of propagation directives, 493
convex set of paths, **468**
correctness of implementation, 475
coupling
    loose, 78
course material, 589
Cox, Brad, 38
Cunningham, Ward, 253
customizer, *568*, *see* class dictionary
customizer restriction, 255, 260
    transportation pattern, 315
cycle-free alternation rule, *569*

data abstraction, 390

INDEX

data member, 28, 533
    private, 152
database, 396
debugging, 237, 405, 417, 420
delayed binding, 97, 279
delayed binding restriction, 265, 268
delayed binding rule, 265, *569*
delayed operation selection, 24
Demeter, xxv
    FAQ, 589
    Home page, 589
    pronunciation, xxv
Demeter data model, 527
Demeter Method, 403
Demeter Tools/C++, 12, 99, 455, 544, 589
    questions, 590
    Quick Reference Guide, 578
DeMillo, Richard, xxxv
dense class dictionary graph, 492
dependency metric, **186**, **490**, *569*
depth first traversal, 212, 327
derivation tree, 514, 517
derived edge, 420
design, 407
    opportunistic planning, 397
design pattern, 425, 481, *569*
Deutsch, Peter, 106, 108
divide-and-conquer, 398
Donzeau-Gouge, Veronique, 166
download software, 589

e-mail questions, 590
EA, 144, **501**
EC, 144, **501**
edge kinds, 142
edge pattern, 130, 178, *569, see* propagation pattern
edge wrapper, 229, 245, *569, see* propagation pattern
edge/vertex restrictions, 145, 147, 176, *569*
efficiency, 344
elastic class structure, 169, 171
encapsulation, 24
Engeler, Erwin, 541

entity-relationship diagram, 135
evolution, 120, 187, 310
    unforeseen, 86
evolution history, 234
example
    area of figures, 240
    business, 400
    car, 220
    chess board, 219
    class dictionary comparison, 403
    compiler, 225
    component, 327
    cycle checking, 235
    depth first traversal, 212, 235
        with transportation, 327
    free variables, 455
    furnace, 411
    graduate school, 509
    meal, 223, 259, 359
    part clusters, 419
    patchwork, 286
    pipeline, 399
    refrigerator, 262, 265, 465
    Scheme, 455
    simulate multiple inheritance, 239
    sorting network, 399
    superclass, 418
    testing for subobjects, 326
    triples, 318
    VLSI design, 398
    work flow management, 330

FAQ, 589
finding the objects, 416
Finkelstein, Larry, xxxv
first set, **367**, **517**, *569, see* LL(1)
flat class dictionary, 362, **512**, *570*
flat class dictionary graph, 150, 171, **469**
flat Demeter Method, 173, 297, 298
Floyd, Richard, 199
follow set, **369**, **519**, *570, see* LL(1)
Foote, Brian, 106
forward path, 492
framework, 227, 454
from clause, *570, see* propagation directive

function member, 533
    public, 153
functional decomposition, 405
functional dependency, 396
Functional programming, 25
Fusion Method, 253

Gamma, Erich, 481
Garey, Michael, 402
Garlan, David, 106, 109, 110
generic operation, 26, 34
German, Steve, 402
Gibbs, Simon, 454
Gill, Helen, xxxv
Goldberg, Adele, 38
Goldberg, Andrew, xxxi, 379
Graham, Susan, 106
grammar, 363
    ambiguous, 527
    context-free, 511
grammar-based programming, 25
graph, **466**, *570*
graph algorithm, 212
graphical representation
    class dictionary graph, 120, 123, 142
growth plan, 155, 237, 405, **489**, **500**, **501**, 554

Hürsch, Walter, xxxv
Hailpern, Brent, xxxv
Harrison, William, 110, 480
Helm, Richard, 481
Henderson-Sellers, Brian, 428
Hewitt, Carl, 38
history
    Demeter Project, xxxi
    software development, 97
Hoare, Charles Anthony Richard, 167
Holland, Ian, xxxv
homework assignments, 542
hook to class dictionary, 202
Hopcroft, John, 541
hot-spot-driven approach, 110
Huet, Gérard, 166
Hull, Richard, 166

implementation, 407
implicit case analysis, 394
inconsistent
    avoid, 264, 269
    overlap with subclass invariant, 269
incremental inheritance, 245, *570*
    rule, *570*
induction, 149
inductive, 382, **489**, 507, **508**, **523**, *570*
information loss, 183, *570*, *see* consistent
    propagation directive, 262
information restriction, 204
inheritance, 25, 31, 153, **498**
    incremental, 239, 245, 279, 282
    overriding, 237, 245, 279
inheritance edge, 171, *571*
inheritance restriction, 269
instance, 33, *571*
instance variable, 28
instantiate
    knowledge path by object path, 537
intentional programming, 107
interface, *571*
Internet
    access to Demeter Tools, 589
inventor's paradox, xxv, 80, 88, 391, 475
Ito, Robert, 166

Jacobson, Ivar, xxv, 105, 428
Johnson, David, 402
Johnson, Ralph, 106, 481
join, 181, 189, *571*
    propagation directive, 192
    propagation graph, 190
judgement, 472

Keszenheimer, Linda, xxxv
key, 396
Kiczales, Gregor, 3, 108, 481
Kifer, Michael, 480
Kim, Won, 480
King, Roger, 166
Kleene's theorem for digraphs, 199
knowledge path, **176**, 177, 282, 324, **498**, 499, 535, *571*

completion, 538
instantiation, 535
traversals, 535
Knudsen, Svend, xxxi

label, 144, 147, **466**
Laboratory Guide, 589
LaLonde, Wilf, 39
Lamping, John, 481
Lang, Bernard, 166
language, 361, **362**, 514, **516**, *571*
language implementation, 225
Law of Demeter, **202**, 481, *565*
    adaptive programming, 202
    classes, 382
Law of Demeter for classes, 383, **508**
learning class dictionary graph, 120
left-recursion, **371**, *see* LL(1), inductive
legal object, **149**, 490
Lippman, Stanley, xxix
Liu, Linling, 109
LL(1) conditions, **365**, **369**, 398, 517, 527, *565*, *see* ambiguous
    implications, 521
    Rule 1, **519**
    Rule 2, **520**
loose coupling, 78, 169
Lopes, Cristina, xxxv

Madsen, Ole Lehrmann, 167
make-instance, 31
Malhotra, Ashok, xxxv
Markowitz, Victor, 480
match, *571*
McQuilken, George, xxxvii
meal, 359
meal example, 136
Meier, David, 166
Meier, Linus, xxxv
Mellor, Stephen, 428
memory leakage, 244
merge, 189, *571*
    propagation directive, 192
    propagation graph, 190
merge and inconsistency, 183

metaSize, 186
method, 24, 28, *571*
method combination, 239, 241
method resolution, *571*
metric
    class dictionary graph, 386
    Dep, 237
    dependency, 170
    structure-shyness, 490
Meyer, Bertrand, 482
minimize
    alternation edges, 388
    class dictionary graph, 389
    construction edges, 387
Minsky, Marvin, 379
Modula-2, 393
modularity, 24, 30, 395
multiple inheritance, 32, 239, 241, *572*

naming, 393
new, 31
Nierstrasz, Oscar, 454
nonambiguous, 372
nonterminal symbol, 514
normalization, 396
notation
    role expressiveness
        LL(1) conditions, 398
        viscosity, 398
NP-hard
    class dictionary minimization, 389
    propagation directive minimization, 491
Nørgaard, Claus, 167

object, **149**, 150, *572*
    building under program control, 244
    circular, 384
    creation, *572*
    destruction, *572*
    essential information, 358
    graph, **149**
    path, 536
    print, 361
    reference, *572*
    size, **152**, **490**

state, 28
transportation, 309
traversal, 256
tree, 364
object definition
    declarative, 514
    imperative, 514
object graph, **469**, **504**, *see* object
    class dictionary graph slice, 502
    syntax, **531**
    textual notation, 506
    translation, 535
Object Management Group, 34
object-equivalent, 277, **386**, 469, *572*
Objective-C, xxviii
OMT Method, 253
operation, 10, 24, *572*
    deferred, 29
operation name, *572*
operational semantics, 472
    propagation pattern, 255
    target language, **473**
optional construction edge, 90, **147**, *572*
optional repetition edge, **147**, *572*
Ossher, Harold, xxxv, 110, 480
overloading, 30
override method, 32
overriding inheritance, 245, *572*

Palsberg, Jens, xxxv, 197, 468, 492
parameter passing mode, **312**, *573*
parameterization, 88, 391
    explicit, 84
parameterized class, **156**, **529**, *573*
Parnas, David, 81
parse, **363**, 364, 521, 523, **525**
    bijection, 524
    halting property, 524
    recursive descent, **365**
    train analogy, 366
parsing a sentence, *573*
part, *573*
part variable, 28
PartCluster, 410, **504**
Parts, **503**

parts-centered design, 158
Partsch, Helmut, 166
Pascal, 394
path, 457, **467**
    constraint satisfaction, 276
    in object graph, 505
    knowledge
        completed, 273
        prematurely terminated, 459
    requirements, 536
path instantiation, 536
path set, **182**, **471**
    map to graph, **474**
Patt-Shamir, Boaz, xxxv, 494
pattern
    Adaptive Visitor, 426
    Builder, 427
    Composite, 425, 481
    Interpreter, 427
    Iterator, 427
    prototype, 244
    Visitor, 425, 481
persistent object, *573*, *see* sentence
Polya, George, 80
Pree, Wolfgang, 110
prefix expression, 33
prefix wrapper, *573*
prematurely terminated path, 273, 459
print, 361, **362**, **516**, 521
    bijection, 371, 522
printing an object, *573*
problem decomposition, 415
Prolog, 394
proof system, 472, 474, 496
    soundness, 466
propagate, *574*
propagate operator, 182, **474**
propagation directive, 57, 89, 129, **178**, *574*
    applications, 169
    cardinality constraint, 228
    compatible, 182
        class dictionary graph, 470
    consistent, **183**, 262
        class dictionary graph, 461, 475

INDEX

design tradeoff, 188
evolution, 187
expression, **192**, *574*
finding it, 185
high-level interpretation, 182, **475**
information loss, 183
join, 192
join and inconsistency, 183
low-level interpretation, 182, **475**
merge, 192
merge and inconsistency, 183
path constraint, 228
satisfaction, 272
shortcut violation, 183
subclass invariance restriction, 183
testing, 188, 492
zigzag violation, 183
propagation graph, 57, 92, 169, 178, **182**, 459, **474**, *574*
    examples, 182
propagation object, 256
propagation pattern, 88, 89, 116, **207**, 255, *574*
    design, 234, 237
    implementation, 207, 285
    operational semantics, 255
    reader, 243
    robustness, 277
    sentence, 359
    simulate multiple inheritance, 239
    with return type, 293
    with traversal directive, 255
    without traversal directive, 255
    writer, 243
propagation restriction, 261
propagation vertex, 256
prototype, 25
Pugh, John, 39

questions, 590
Quick Reference Guide, 578

reachable, 511
reducible flow graphs, 494
redundant part, 389

redundant program, 207
referential integrity, *574*
refinement of propagation directives, 486
regular
    expression, 199, 457
    set, 199
regularity, 393
Reif, John, 494
relation
    has-a, 135
    is-a, 135
relation-valued variable, 89, *574*
repetition class, 90, 123, 140, **147**, **361**, 365
    simulate, 530
repetition edge, 90, 123, 142, **147**, *574*
repetition vertex, *575*, *see* repetition class
representative class graph, 487, 493
Reps, Thomas, 106
request, 24, *575*
restrict operator, 189, 487, *575*
    propagation directive, 192
return variable, 293
return_val, 132, 293, *see* propagation pattern
reusability, 217
Riel, Arthur, xxxv, 166
robustness, 217
robustness analysis, 405
rule
    abstract superclass, 535
    class dictionary graph, 501
        no subclass cycle, 501
        unique label, 501
    class dictionary graph slice, 502
    LL(1), 517
    parameterized class dictionary, 531
    semi-class dictionary graph, 499
        no subclass cycle, 499
        unique label, 500
    terminal-buffer, 393
Rumbaugh, James, xxv, 253, 480
running time, 490

Sagiv, Yehoshua, 480

Sakkinen, Markku, 105, 253
Salasin, John, xxxv
Salzberg, Betty, 402
satisfy, *575*
    clause, 178
    constraint, 179
scanning a sentence, 366, *575*, *see* parse
Schwartzbach, Michael, 468
self-describing
    class dictionary, 529
selfstudy, 542
semantics of propagation pattern, **472**
semi-class dictionary graph, **171**, 285, **498**, *575*
    rule, **499**
sentence, 358, 359, **516**, *575*
    family of objects, 359
set of paths, **182**, 459, **471**
    traversal guidance, 458
Sethi, Ravi, 81
shared object, 152
sharing, 25, 30
Shaw, Mary, 109, 110
Sheu, Philip, 380
Shlaer, Sally, 428
shortcut violation, **183**, 464, **477**, *576*
Shoshani, Arie, 480
signature, **23**, 115, 209, 237, *576*
    extension, *576*
Silva-Lepe, Ignacio, xxxv
simplification
    behavior, 234, 415
    data, 234, 415
single inheritance, 390, *576*
size of object, **490**
Skarra, Andrea, 166
slot, 28
small methods, 206
Smalltalk, xxviii
Smith, Randall, 38
solving more general problem, 391, *see* Polya's inventor paradox
source vertex, 470, *576*
state, 28, *576*
Stefik, Mark, 402

Stein, Jacob, 166
Stroustrup, Bjarne, xxix
style rule
    class dictionary, 382
subclass edge, 457, **468**, *see* alternation edge
subclass invariance, 463, **469**
subclass invariance restriction, 183, 265
subclass relationship, 468
subject-oriented, 110
succinct subgraph specification, 169, 178, 311, 454, *see* propagation directive
suffix wrapper, *576*
syllabus, 542
synchronous request, *576*
syntax, 359
    class dictionary, **532**
    object graph, **532**
syntax chart, 365
syntax diagram, 365
syntax edge, **509**, *576*
syntax error, 366
syntax summary, *see* Quick Reference Guide
    component, 228
    propagation directives, 179
    propagation patterns, 211
syntax vertex, **509**, *576*

Tai, K.C., xxxv
target language, **473**
target vertex, 470, *576*
Teitelbaum, Tim, 106
Terminal, 533, *see* User's Guide
terminal, **365**, **511**, 576
    with a value, 365
    without a value, 365
terminal class, 365
    buffering, 393
terminal object, 149
terminal symbol, 514
terminal vertex, **511**, *577*, *see* terminal class
terminology summary, 484
testing, 188, 235, 404, 406, 492

incremental, 420
textual representation
    class dictionary graph, 142, 529
this, 32
Thomas, Dave, 39
through clause, 130, 178, *577*, *see* propagation directive
to clause, *577*, *see* propagation directive
to-stop clause, *577*, *see* propagation directive
token, 359, 365, *577*
translation to C++, 119, 120, 123, 126, 152, **532**, *see* Demeter Tools/C++
    class dictionary, 533
    object graph, **535**
    propagation pattern, 207, 285, **459**
    transportation patterns, 329
transportation directive, 311
Transportation Entry Restriction, **315**, 565
transportation graph, **311**, *577*
transportation pattern, 309, 324, *577*
    customizer restriction
        Transportation Entry Restriction, 315
        Transportation Recursion Restriction, 315
    design, 406
    packaging, 343
    syntax, **311**
    type-correct, **314**
    wrapper pushing, 330
Transportation Recursion Restriction, **315**, 565
traversal, 169, 171
    breadth-first, 495
    overriding, 282
traversal graph, 169, *577*
traversal history, **472**
traversal order, 256
traversal specification, 457, **469**, *see* propagation directive
    well-formed, 470
TRAVERSE, 255
tree object, 364, **514**
tree property, 390, *see* single inheritance

triples example, 318
Tsichritzis, Dennis, 454
type theory for adaptive software, 492
type-correct, 314

Ullman, Jeffrey, 402
Ungar, David, 38
unique label rule, *577*
Universal, 533, *see* User's Guide
unsolvable problem
    ambiguity
        class dictionary, 364
        Post's correspondence, 527
use case, 404, *577*
used vertex, 268, *578*
usefulness of adaptive software, 482
useless
    class, **523**
    symbol, **523**
User's Guide, 589

VA, 144, **501**
value, *578*
Van den Bussche, Jan, 480
variable
    class-valued, 227, 320
    relation-valued, 320
    renaming, 227
VC, 144, **501**
vertex, *578*
vertex wrapper, 229, 245, *578*
via clause, 130, *578*, *see* propagation directive
virtual, 26
virtual base class, 533
virtual function, 120
Vlissides, John, 481
Vossen, Gottfried, 480
VT, **501**

Wand, Mitchell, xxxv, 483
Wegman, Mark, xxxv
Wegner, Peter, 39, 531
well-formed traversal specification, **470**
wildcard symbol, 179
Wilde, Norman, 308, 481

Wile, David, 107, 480, 481
Wileden, Jack, 109
Wirfs-Brock, Rebbeca, xxv
Wirth, Niklaus, xxxi, 81, 104, 379
Wolf, Alexander, 109
wrapper, 89, 130, **471**, *578*
    class set, 239
    edge, 245
    ordering, 276, 283
    pushing, 291, 330
    several for same class or edge, 258
    simulate inheritance, 241
    symmetry, 281
    vertex, 245
WWW information
    on adaptive software, 589

Xiao, Cun, xxxv

Yourdon, Edward, 428

Zdonik, Stanley, 166
Zicari, Roberto, 109
zigzag violation, **183**, 464, **477**, *578*